# *Frommer's®*
# Cancún, Cozumel & the Yucatán

# My Yucatán
by David Baird

**THE YUCATAN PENINSULA, TOGETHER WITH TABASCO AND CHIAPAS,** is only a modest section of Mexico, but it offers almost all that makes this country special: beautiful beaches, mysterious ruins, thick jungles, tall mountains, and thriving Indian cultures. As with any part of Mexico, it has its own regional culture and cuisine. A trip here is not a substitute for a trip to central Mexico; rather it's a great way to get acquainted with the country.

Once I've had enough beach time (but how much is enough?), what I most like to do is rent a car and drive the back roads of the peninsula. Scattered about the area are the small villages of the Yucatek Maya, ruins, colonial convents, and many of those strange natural features known as cenotes, natural wells where water from underground rivers rises up close to the surface. If I have more time, I take a break from the lowland heat and head for the cool mountains in the central highlands of Chiapas. Here, myriad Indian villages surround the colonial city of San Cristóbal de las Casas, and each boasts a different handicrafts specialty, whether weaving, pottery, or embroidery.

In these pages, you'll see photos that show the Yucatán at its best—from the jungle ruins of Palenque to the eco-friendly water park at Xel-Ha to the beachfront megaresorts of Cancún.

**SNORKELING (left)** is my favorite water-sport, and I particularly love exploring the Yucatán coast. It has the second longest reef in the world and offers plenty of places to dive. For beginners, there are also numerous sheltered areas where swimmers are protected from the currents and the waves. Here you see a snorkeler in Chankanaab National Park.

The gorgeous, natural lagoon at **XEL-HA MARINE PARK (above)** is the park's main attraction. This ecological park was established to preserve the area's beauty and provide access to visitors. You can catch a ride on a miniature train up to the innermost part of the lagoon and then drift or paddle down with your snorkel gear to where it meets the sea. Along the way you'll see lots of fish and sea life and caves and cenotes.

It's always fun to see kids dress up on holidays in the local garb. These children are dancing around a **MAYPOLE IN MERIDA (above)**.

Mexicans have a genius for working with their hands. When given the opportunity, many artisans shine, but more often they produce the everyday goods that demand dictates. I try to seek out the less commonplace work that arises from the need for personal expression. This **MAYA VENDOR IN SAN CRISTOBAL DE LAS CASAS (right)** is selling nontraditional garments to tourists. She may have other, more interesting pieces, but the highland Maya are often difficult to engage in conversation.

I always enjoy visiting **MARKETS** when I have the chance, even when I'm not buying anything. You see a variety of produce and foodstuffs in most of them that would put a supermarket to shame. They also serve as the place where friends and neighbors meet, eat, and chat with each other about things of interest, such as local events and the latest scandals.

Chiapas is wetter than the Yucatán peninsula, and the water mostly stays above ground. There are some beautiful spots not far from Palenque where you can go for a refreshing swim in lush surroundings. This one, known as **AGUA AZUL (left)**, is one of them. I enjoy it most when 3 or 4 days have passed without rain and the water does actually get blue, as its name suggests.

Of the many cenotes I've seen, **CENOTE DZITNUP IN VALLADOLID (above)** is one of the most beautiful. It has retained its ceiling, as many do, and the roots of trees have penetrated the chamber and grown down to the water. The contrast between the bright, hot outside and the cool, dark chamber is almost otherworldly. It's no wonder that the Maya considered cenotes sacred places.

The megalithic **OLMEC HEADS (above)** are some of the most intriguing pre-Colombian artifacts. Most are in out-of-the-way places like Villahermosa and Xalapa, but this modern reproduction can be found at Chankanaab National Park on the island of Cozumel.

Like much of Chichén Itzá's art and architecture, this statue of **CHACMOOL (right)** at the Temple of the Warriors reflects a style that originated in the faraway central highlands of Mexico. That it displays little or no Maya influence has raised questions regarding the true rulers of the city.

There is no place in Mexico that fills me with more awe than Palenque, a breathtaking city of the classic Maya period. The jungle setting, the rich iconography, the elegant geometrical shape of the temple platforms—nowhere else even comes close. This building, the **TEMPLE OF THE INSCRIPTIONS** is named for the great stone hieroglyphic panels that were found inside. It also houses the tomb of the 7th-century Maya king Pacal.

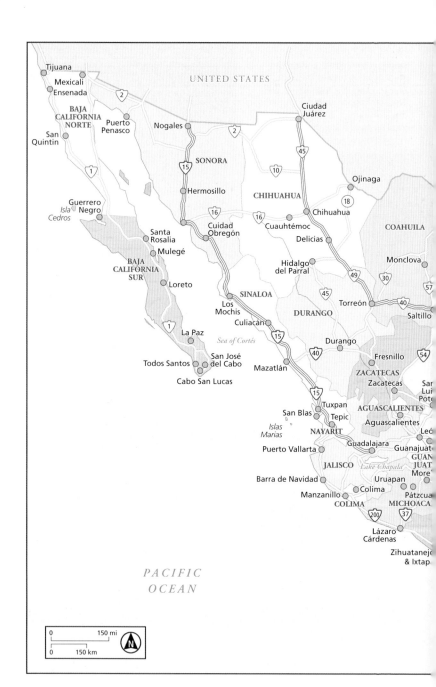

# Mexico

UNITED STATES

Piedras Negras

Nuevo Laredo

85D

Monterrey
Matamoros

NUEVO
LEÓN  85

TAMAULIPAS

Ciudad Victoria

Ciudad Mante
Tampico

SAN LUIS
POTOSÍ

an Miguel
e Allende

QUERÉTARO
Tuxpan

HIDALGO  Poza Rica
uerétaro  Papantla
Pachuca  180

Mexico City  Xalapa
oluca  TLAXCALA
uernavaca  Tlaxcala
Puebla  Veracruz

MORELOS  PUEBLA  Orizaba
axco  95  Tehuacán  Catemaco

GUERRERO  1900  175

Acapulco  Oaxaca
200  OAXACA

Puerto Escondido  Salina
Cruz  Comitan
Puerto  Huatulco
Ángel

*Gulf of
Tehuantepec*

*Gulf of Mexico*

*Bay of
Campeche*

Río Lagartos  *Isla
Mujeres*
Progreso  Valladolid
Celestún  180  Cancún
Mérida  *Cozumel*
YUCATÁN  Playa del
Carmen
Campeche  *Punta
QUINTANA  Allen*
CAMPECHE  ROO
Bacalar
261  Escárcega  *Majahual
Chetumal  Peninsula*

TABASCO
Villahermosa  186

Coatzacoalcos
Palenque  BELIZE  *Caribbean
Sea*

186  Tuxtla  San Cristóbal
Gutiérrez  de las Casas

CHIAPAS
GUATEMALA  HONDURAS
200

Tapachula  EL
SALVADOR

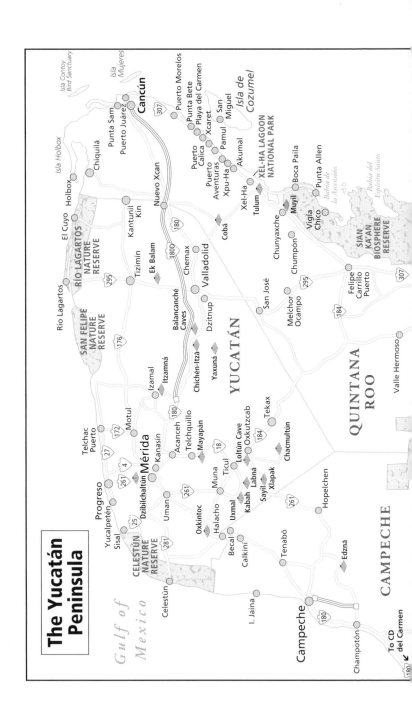

## The Yucatán Peninsula

*Gulf of Mexico*

Celestún

CELESTÚN NATURE RESERVE

Sisal
Yucalpetén
Progreso
Telchac Puerto

I. Jaina

Champotón

To CD del Carmen

Campeche

CAMPECHE

Tenabó

Calkini

Becal

Halacho

Oxkintoc

Uman

Dzibilchaltún

Mérida

Kanasín

Acanceh

Telchquillo

Mayapán

Muna

Ticul

Loltún Cave

Oxkutzcab

Labná

Sayil

Xlapak

Kabah

Uxmal

Edzná

Hopelchen

Chacmultun

Tekax

CAMPECHE

QUINTANA ROO

Valle Hermoso

Valladolid

Chichén-Itzá

Yaxuná

Dzitnup

Balancanché Caves

Izamal

Itzamná

Motul

San Felipe
Río Lagartos

SAN FELIPE NATURE RESERVE

RÍO LAGARTOS NATURE RESERVE

El Cuyo

Holbox

Isla Holbox

Tizimin

Ek Balam

Chemax

Kantunil Kin

Nuevo Xcan

Cobá

San José

Melchor Ocampo

Felipe Carrillo Puerto

Chumpón

Chunyaxche

Muyil

Vigía Chico

SIAN KA'AN BIOSPHERE RESERVE

Bahía del Espíritu Santo

Bahía de la Ascensión

Punta Allen

Boca Paila

Tulum

Xel-Ha

XEL-HA LAGOON NATIONAL PARK

Akumal

Pamul

Xpu-Ha

Puerto Aventuras

Puerto Calica

Xcaret

Playa del Carmen

Punta Bete

Puerto Morelos

Cancún

Puerto Juárez

Punta Sam

Chiquilá

Isla Mujeres

Isla Contoy Bird Sanctuary

Isla de Cozumel

San Miguel

YUCATÁN

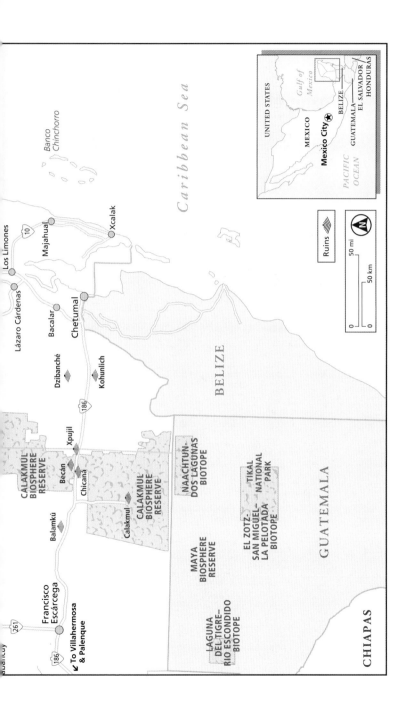

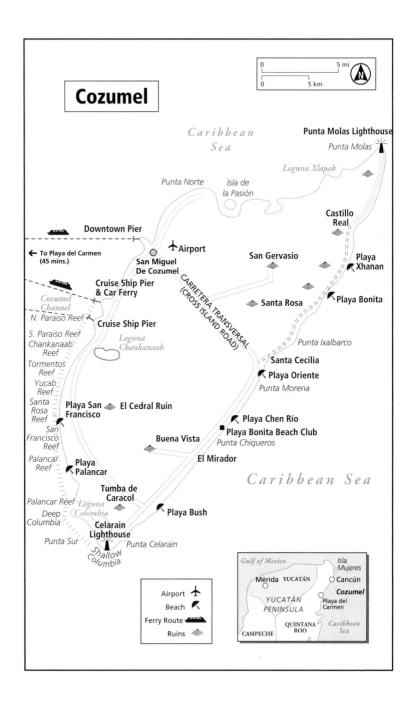

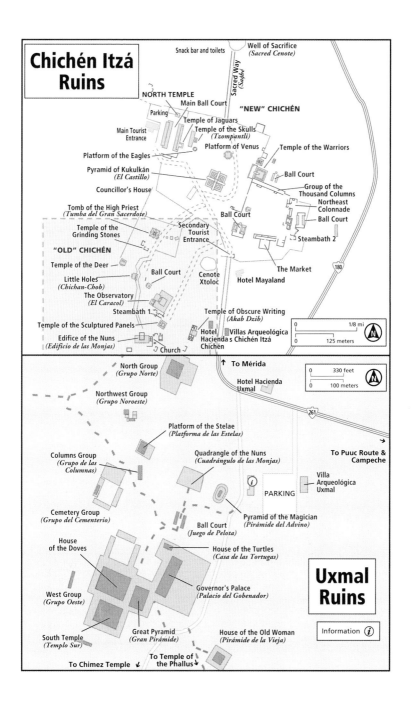

# Chichén Itzá Ruins

Snack bar and toilets

Well of Sacrifice
*(Sacred Cenote)*

Sacred Way *(Sacbé)*

NORTH TEMPLE

Main Ball Court

Parking

"NEW" CHICHÉN

Temple of Jaguars

Main Tourist Entrance

Temple of the Skulls
*(Tzompantli)*

Platform of Venus

Temple of the Warriors

Platform of the Eagles

Pyramid of Kukulkán
*(El Castillo)*

Ball Court

Councillor's House

Group of the
Thousand Columns

Northeast
Colonnade

Tomb of the High Priest
*(Tumba del Gran Sacerdote)*

Ball Court

Ball Court

Temple of the
Grinding Stones

Secondary
Tourist
Entrance

Steambath 2

"OLD" CHICHÉN

Temple of the Deer

The Market

Little Holes
*(Chichan-Chob)*

Ball Court

Cenote
Xtoloc

Hotel Mayaland

180

The Observatory
*(El Caracol)*

Steambath 1

Temple of the Sculptured Panels

Temple of Obscure Writing
*(Akab Dzib)*

Edifice of the Nuns
*(Edificio de las Monjas)*

Hotel
Hacienda
Chichén

Villas Arqueológica
Chichén Itzá

Church

0 — 1/8 mi
0 — 125 meters

N

To Mérida

North Group
*(Grupo Norte)*

Hotel Hacienda
Uxmal

0 — 330 feet
0 — 100 meters

N

Northwest Group
*(Grupo Noroeste)*

261

Platform of the Stelae
*(Plataforma de las Estelas)*

To Puuc Route &
Campeche

Columns Group
*(Grupo de las
Columnas)*

Quadrangle of the Nuns
*(Cuadrángulo de las Monjas)*

Villa
Arqueológica
Uxmal

PARKING

Cemetery Group
*(Grupo del Cementerio)*

Pyramid of the Magician
*(Pirámide del Advino)*

Ball Court
*(Juego de Pelota)*

House
of the Doves

House of the Turtles
*(Casa de las Tortugas)*

West Group
*(Grupo Oeste)*

Governor's Palace
*(Palacio del Gobernador)*

# Uxmal Ruins

South Temple
*(Templo Sur)*

Great Pyramid
*(Gran Pirámide)*

House of the Old Woman
*(Pirámide de la Vieja)*

Information ⓘ

To Chimez Temple

To Temple of
the Phallus

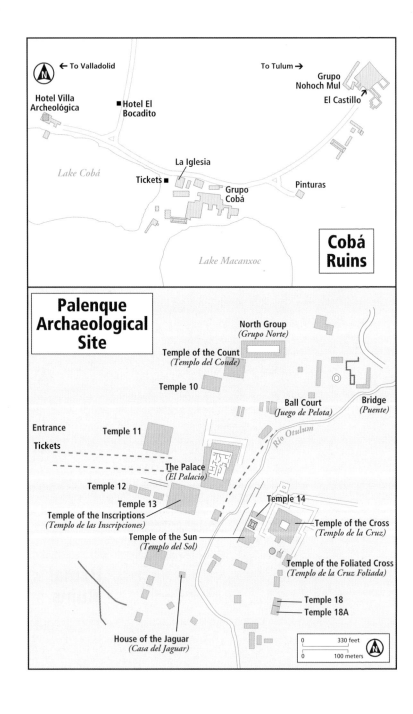

**Cobá Ruins**

← To Valladolid

To Tulum →

N

Hotel Villa Archeológica

■ Hotel El Bocadito

Grupo Nohoch Mul

El Castillo

Lake Cobá

La Iglesia

Tickets ■

Grupo Cobá

Pinturas

Lake Macanxoc

**Palenque Archaeological Site**

North Group
*(Grupo Norte)*

Temple of the Count
*(Templo del Conde)*

Temple 10

Ball Court
*(Juego de Pelota)*

Bridge
*(Puente)*

Entrance

Tickets

Temple 11

Río Otulum

The Palace
*(El Palacio)*

Temple 12

Temple 13

Temple 14

Temple of the Inscriptions
*(Templo de las Inscripciones)*

Temple of the Sun
*(Templo del Sol)*

Temple of the Cross
*(Templo de la Cruz)*

Temple of the Foliated Cross
*(Templo de la Cruz Foliada)*

Temple 18
Temple 18A

House of the Jaguar
*(Casa del Jaguar)*

0        330 feet
0        100 meters

N

# Frommer's®

# Cancún, Cozumel & the Yucatán

# 2007

## by David Baird & Lynne Bairstow

Here's what the critics say about Frommer's:

"Amazingly easy to use. Very portable, very complete."

—*Booklist*

"Detailed, accurate, and easy-to-read information for all price ranges."
—*Glamour Magazine*

"Hotel information is close to encyclopedic."

—*Des Moines Sunday Register*

"Frommer's Guides have a way of giving you a real feel for a place."
—*Knight Ridder Newspapers*

Wiley Publishing, Inc.

Published by:

## Wiley Publishing, Inc.

111 River St.
Hoboken, NJ 07030-5774

ISBN-13: 978-0-471-92236-0
ISBN-10: 0-471-92236-6

Editor: Jennifer Anmuth
Production Editor: Suzanna R. Thompson
Cartographer: Andrew Murphy
Photo Editor: Richard Fox
Anniversary Logo Design: Richard Pacifico
Production by Wiley Indianapolis Composition Services

Front cover photo: Shaded area and beach chair near ocean in Quintana Roo
Back cover photo: El Castillo, also known as Pyramid of Kukulcán, at Chichén Itzá

For information on our other products and services or to obtain technical support, please
contact our Customer Care Department within the U.S. at 800/762-2974, outside the
U.S. at 317/572-3993 or fax 317/572-4002.

Wiley also publishes its books in a variety of electronic formats. Some content that
appears in print may not be available in electronic formats.

Manufactured in the United States of America

5   4   3   2   1

# Contents

## 3 Suggested Yucatán Itineraries    70

*by David Baird*

## 4 Cancún    76

*by Lynne Bairstow*

## 5 Isla Mujeres & Cozumel    107

*by David Baird & Lynne Bairstow*

## 6 The Caribbean Coast: The Riviera Maya, Including Playa del Carmen & the Costa Maya    139

*by David Baird*

# List of Maps

## Acknowledgments

I would like to acknowledge an enormous debt to Ms. Claudia Hurtado, whose knowledge and contacts in the Riviera Maya smoothed the way for the research of that area. I would also like to extend a personal thanks to all the readers who have taken the time to write me with your suggestions.

—David Baird

I am appreciative of the invaluable contribution of my research assistant, Cecilia Mendicuti, to this book.

—Lynne Bairstow

## An Invitation to the Reader

In researching this book, we discovered many wonderful places—hotels, restaurants, shops, and more. We're sure you'll find others. Please tell us about them, so we can share the information with your fellow travelers in upcoming editions. If you were disappointed with a recommendation, we'd love to know that, too. Please write to:

*Frommer's Cancún, Cozumel & the Yucatán 2007*
Wiley Publishing, Inc. • 111 River St. • Hoboken, NJ 07030-5774

## An Additional Note

Please be advised that travel information is subject to change at any time—and this is especially true of prices. We therefore suggest that you write or call ahead for confirmation when making your travel plans. The authors, editors, and publisher cannot be held responsible for the experiences of readers while traveling. Your safety is important to us, however, so we encourage you to stay alert and be aware of your surroundings. Keep a close eye on cameras, purses, and wallets, all favorite targets of thieves and pickpockets.

## About the Authors

**David Baird** has lived in various parts of Latin America, including Mexico, Puerto Rico, Peru, and Brazil. He now makes his home in Austin, Texas, but he tries to get back to the turquoise-blue waters of the Yucatán whenever possible because he thinks he looks good in that color.

For **Lynne Bairstow,** Mexico has become more home than her native United States. For most of the past 15 years, she has lived in Puerto Vallarta, where she has developed a true appreciation and respect for the customs, culture, and natural treasures of Mexico. Her travel articles on Mexico have appeared in the *New York Times, Los Angeles Times, Private Air* magazine, *Luxury Living* magazine, and the in-flight magazines of Mexicana Airlines and Alaska Airlines. In 2000, Lynne was awarded the Pluma de Plata, a top honor granted by the Mexican government to foreign writers, for her work in the Frommer's guidebook to Puerto Vallarta.

---

# Other Great Guides for Your Trip:

*Frommer's Mexico*
*Frommer's Portable Acapulco, Ixtapa & Zihuatanejo*
*Frommer's Portable Cancún*
*Frommer's Portable Los Cabos & Baja*
*Frommer's Portable Puerto Vallarta, Manzanillo & Guadalajara*
*The Unofficial Guide to Mexico's Best Beach Resorts*

## Frommer's Star Ratings, Icons & Abbreviations

Every hotel, restaurant, and attraction listing in this guide has been ranked for quality, value, service, amenities, and special features using a **star-rating system.** In country, state, and regional guides, we also rate towns and regions to help you narrow down your choices and budget your time accordingly. Hotels and restaurants are rated on a scale of zero (recommended) to three stars (exceptional). Attractions, shopping, nightlife, towns, and regions are rated according to the following scale: zero stars (recommended), one star (highly recommended), two stars (very highly recommended), and three stars (must-see).

In addition to the star-rating system, we also use **seven feature icons** that point you to the great deals, in-the-know advice, and unique experiences that separate travelers from tourists. Throughout the book, look for:

| | |
|---|---|
| *Finds* | Special finds—those places only insiders know about |
| *Fun Fact* | Fun facts—details that make travelers more informed and their trips more fun |
| *Kids* | Best bets for kids and advice for the whole family |
| *Moments* | Special moments—those experiences that memories are made of |
| *Overrated* | Places or experiences not worth your time or money |
| *Tips* | Insider tips—great ways to save time and money |
| *Value* | Great values—where to get the best deals |

The following **abbreviations** are used for credit cards:

| | | | | | |
|---|---|---|---|---|---|
| AE | American Express | DISC | Discover | V | Visa |
| DC | Diners Club | MC | MasterCard | | |

## Frommers.com

Now that you have the guidebook to a great trip, visit our website at **www.frommers.com** for travel information on more than 3,000 destinations. With features updated regularly, we give you instant access to the most current trip-planning information available. At Frommers.com, you'll also find the best prices on airfares, accommodations, and car rentals—and you can even book travel online through our travel booking partners. At Frommers.com, you'll also find the following:

- Online updates to our most popular guidebooks
- Vacation sweepstakes and contest giveaways
- Newsletter highlighting the hottest travel trends
- Online travel message boards with featured travel discussions

# What's New in Cancún, Cozumel & the Yucatán

*by David Baird & Lynne Bairstow*

There's a lot new in Cancún and the Yucatán, mainly thanks to Mother Nature, which created the area's biggest news story of the year. On October 21, 2005, the Category 4 Hurricane Wilma came ashore Mexico's Yucatán Peninsula with winds reaching 242kmph (150 mph), and then stalled over Cancún for nearly 40 hours. It toppled trees, washed away portions of Cancún's famed white beaches, and damaged the majority of the resort's hotels, restaurants, and attractions. However, relief came quickly because Mexico's government understands the importance of Cancún as its most popular tourism destination. Cancún used the recovery as an opportunity to remake itself—renovating hotels, upgrading services, and remarketing itself as a true upscale resort destination, and not merely a spring breaker's party haven—an unwanted reputation it was gaining. Today, the results are remarkable—the beaches are back, hotels are looking better than ever, and the favorite restaurants, shops, and tours are back in business—even if the palm trees seem a little light in their branches, and the presence of construction crews remains. The areas to the south, along the Riviera Maya, suffered less damage and were largely restored.

**PLANNING YOUR TRIP TO MEXICO** The Intelligence Reform and Terrorism Prevention Act of 2004 requires that by January 1, 2008, travelers to and from the Caribbean, Bermuda, Panama, Mexico, and Canada have a passport or other secure, accepted document to enter or reenter the United States. As of December 31, 2006, this requirement will apply to all air and sea travel to or from Mexico.

As of July 1, 2006, international tourists to Mexico can make tax-free purchases while vacationing, thanks to a law recently passed by Mexico's Congress. The new law will grant international visitors a full refund of the tax added to purchases if the buyer adheres to certain criteria. The merchandise must be purchased in Mexico and verified by airport or seaport Customs, and be verified with a receipt presented at time of departure to be worth at least 1,200 Mexican pesos (approximately US$110 at current exchange rates). Reimbursement to tourists will be contingent upon any added costs a possible return may generate.

**CANCUN** For complete information, see chapter 4.

**Post–Hurricane Wilma Update** According to the government's estimates, 40% of the country's tourism income comes from the Caribbean coast. Recovering 15km (9 miles) of eroded beaches was the top priority among Cancún's renewal and restoration projects. The $21-million beach restoration project, which was funded by the private sector and the federal government, is using the same silky white sand that the area is known for, dredging it from the sea floor not far from Cancún's coastline to create miles of artificial beach along the hardest-hit areas. The project—which centered primarily on the southernmost stretch of the city's famous hotel strip, from kilometers 10 through 24—was completed in time for spring break travel in 2006, perfectly restoring Cancún's beautiful beaches.

Among other enhancements planned for Cancún are the replanting of 5,000 palm trees, as well as new gardens and sidewalks for the hotel strip's main thoroughfare, Bulevar Kukulkán. A new park has been designed to conserve 6 million hectares (2½ million acres) of land that will house a zoo and a botanical garden among other attractions, and a new bridge will be constructed, designed to alleviate traffic along Bulevar Kukulkán.

Highway 307, which services the Riviera Maya, is being expanded. Currently, the highway has two lanes south and two lanes north from downtown Cancún to just south of Playa del Carmen. The expansion project extends this configuration all the way to Tulum.

At the Cancún International Airport, construction has begun on a second runway; it's expected to be completed in the fall of 2006. A third, state-of-the-art terminal is also under construction, and it will be dedicated to servicing cargo and domestic flights. These steps should greatly improve logistics at the airport.

Additionally, the airport recently received new X-ray equipment to examine checked luggage in accordance with the request of the United States. Anticipating these enhanced security measures will require more processing time; all departing passengers using U.S. airspace should be at the airport 3 hours in advance of their flight. To enforce the 3-hour rule, the airport ticket counters will close 40 minutes in advance of flight time. If you have not been processed by that time, you will not be able to board your flight.

Despite Mexico's rapid and impressive recovery measures, many U.S. airlines delayed or discontinued service to this area following the hurricane. **Delta** (www.delta.com) was the exception; it added nonstop service to Cancún from Boston's Logan Airport and Washington's Dulles Airport starting in June 2006.

In light of Cancún's face-lift, the Mexican government is trying to make the destination more attractive to upscale travelers. New regulations—such as prohibiting more than four people sharing a room—will be put in place to restrict spring break and student tour groups. The majority of damaged hotels have taken the opportunity to upgrade their facilities and redecorate their rooms, which should ultimately lead to a new and improved Cancún.

**Accommodations**  As noted earlier, the majority of hotels in Cancún's hotel zone suffered extensive storm damage. Although renovations are equally extensive, before you make a reservation—at least through December 2006—check to ensure that the entire hotel is operational. Priority was placed on reopening rooms, but restaurants, spas, and other amenities followed on the reconstruction priority lists.

The **Presidente Inter-Continental Cancún** (© 800/327-0200; www.ic hotelsgroup.com) reopened its doors on March 10. Although many beachfront properties lost precious sand after the storm, the Presidente Inter-Continental Cancún actually *gained* more than 4.5m (15 ft.) of sand between it and the ocean. Among its other improvements are a new lobby, renovated guest rooms, and a new club floor on the fifth floor with 36 rooms that brings the total number of club rooms to 52. Additional enhancements include a new oceanfront deck bar, a larger pool with five Jacuzzis, and new beach *palapas,* including one that will be used exclusively for massages. A second phase of upgrades will add a restaurant off the lobby and a new facility for meetings. Call for details.

The **Ritz-Carlton** (Cancún; ✆ **800/ 241-3333;** www.ritzcarlton.com) expects to reopen in September 2006 after a multimillion-dollar repair and refurbishment project. New facilities and expanded services will include a culinary center offering cooking and wine classes for hotel customers, a tennis program operated by former pro and ESPN commentator Cliff Drysdale, and an upgraded and expanded fitness center.

**Events** A PGA golf tournament will be held in Cancún from February 22 to 25, 2007, with 130 players from the pro tour expected to participate. The winner will receive $650,000, and the tournament is guaranteed for the destination for the next 6 years using various golf courses in the area. By the end of 2007, the Cancún area will have a total of 16 golf courses.

**ISLA MUJERES & COZUMEL** For complete information, see Chapter 5.

**Cozumel** The island suffered extensive damage from Hurricane Wilma to all the coastal areas. The inland parts of the town did okay except for some minor flooding. The shoreline boulevard, Avenida Rafael Melgar, was completely wrecked from the storm surge, but the locals, with help from the federal government, were able to make repairs and replant trees in an amazingly short span of time. The town's shopping district is already back to normal.

All the beach hotels had to close for repairs but most have since reopened. Many have taken the opportunity to make improvements, so now is actually a great time to visit the island. Not only will you be enjoying a new mattress, but you might find that your favorite hotel

has added extra amenities. Nearly all the hotels recommended in this book are scheduled to reopen by the fall of 2006. **Hotel Sol Cabañas Caribe** will probably not reopen.

Properties on the north side of the island lost beach, but the hotels have trucked in plenty of sand, and visitors won't notice any difference. In the south, hotels gained beach.

The municipal pier, where the ferries for Playa del Carmen dock, is fine, and ferry service is close to almost normal. The three cruise-ship piers are closed and one, the **Puerta Maya,** is a total loss. Cruise ships are using tender boats to ferry passengers to and from the island. This seems to be working fine.

The **Chankanaab Park** opens this summer, along with the dolphin swim outfit inside the park.

The effect on the island's reefs is mixed. In deeper areas, the currents produced by the hurricane swept sand away from the walls, exposing more caverns. On the shallower reefs, the delicate structures, such as fan coral, were lost, and it will be a year or two before they come back. The vegetation on the island will also take about a year to come back.

**THE RIVIERA MAYA** This coast suffered two hurricanes in 2005. The first was Emily, which made landfall near the resorts of Xpu-Ha and Puerto Aventuras, then moved quickly inland and to the north. It damaged properties along a fairly narrow swath. Next came Wilma, a much more powerful storm that grazed the northern shore of the Riviera Maya, around Puerto Morelos, before hitting Cancún. It caused extensive damage to beach properties. For complete information on this region, see chapter 6.

**Puerto Morelos & Environs** Beach properties, particularly a couple of condo complexes, suffered extensive damage here. Hotels in the region were closed for many months to do repairs, but all of the spa hotels are expected to reopen by the fall of 2006.

A new adventure tour outfit, **Selvática** (© **998/849-5510;** www.selvatica.com. mx), has set up more than 2km (1¼ miles) of **zip lines** through the forest canopy at a spot inland from Puerto Morelos. They are trucking guests there from Cancún and most of the hotels along the Riviera Maya. The outfit has had success with a similar concept in Costa Rica.

The nature park **Tres Ríos** is closed, and it's not certain when it will reopen. But this was not a consequence of the hurricane; it closed before Wilma arrived.

**Tulum**   The highway to Cobá is presently under construction; expect some slowdowns.

**Playa del Carmen**   Though Playa was damaged by Wilma, you won't notice any damage now. The guys who work on *palapa* roofs can move real quickly.

Road construction is ongoing on Highway 307 between Playa and Tulum, as crews widen the road to four lanes.

There's a new hotel in Playa that was opened by the same people behind Hotel Deseo. It's called **Hotel Básico** (© **984/879-4448;** www.hotelbasico.com), and like its sister, it enjoys some novel touches. The design is industrial, with flourishes reminiscent of the 1950s.

**MERIDA, CHICHEN ITZA & THE MAYA INTERIOR**   For complete information on this region, see chapter 7.

**Mérida**   There's a new day trip from the city to a fully functional henequén hacienda, **Sotuta de Peón** (© **999/941-8639;** www.haciendatour.com). It functions much as all these haciendas did at the turn of the last century before the market crashed. The owner refurbished not only the house, but planted acres of henequén and completely refurbished the heavy machinery used to separate the fibers of the plant from the pulp. The tour is quite impressive. And don't forget your swimsuit; there's a *cenote* (a sinkhole or natural well that only exists in the Yucatán region) for swimming on the property.

**Campeche**   The city has a fancy new hotel inside the walled historic center: **Hacienda Puerta Campeche** (© **800/325-3589;** www.luxurycollection.com). It's managed by Starwood Hotels and is rather pricey, but even if you don't stay there, check out its rooftop bar. With a view of the city's land gate, it's a pleasant place to have a drink in the evening.

**Valladolid**   A bus now leaves from the main square and goes directly to the ruins of Ek Balam every morning.

**Holbox**   A few of the beach hotels still haven't recovered from the hurricane, but most are open. The beach is as broad and sandy as ever. And the last time I drove it, the highway into the area was in good shape.

# 1

# The Best of Cancún, Cozumel & the Yucatán

*by David Baird & Lynne Bairstow*

The Yucatán Peninsula welcomes more visitors than any other part of Mexico. Its tremendous variety attracts every kind of traveler with an unequaled mix of sophisticated resorts, rustic inns, ancient Maya culture, exquisite beaches, and exhilarating adventures. Between the two of us, we've logged thousands of miles crisscrossing the peninsula, and these are our personal favorites—the best places to go, the best restaurants, the best hotels, and must-see, one-of-a-kind experiences.

## 1 The Best Beach Vacations

- **Cancún:** Despite extensive damage from October 2005's Hurricane Wilma, Cancún's legendary beaches are rapidly being restored to their splendor, thanks in large part to a $19-million, government-sponsored beach renewal program. In terms of sheer beauty, Cancún has always been the site of Mexico's best beaches. The powdery, white-sand beaches boast water the color of a Technicolor dream; it's so clear you can see through to the coral reefs below. Cancún offers the widest assortment of luxury beachfront hotels, with more restaurants, nightlife, and activities than any other resort destination in the country. See chapter 4.

- **Isla Mujeres:** If laid-back is what you're after, this idyllic island offers peaceful, small-town beach life at its best. Most accommodations are smaller, inexpensive inns, with a few unique, luxurious places tossed in. Bike—or take a golf cart—around the island to explore rocky coves and sandy beaches, or focus your tanning efforts on the wide beachfront of Playa Norte. Here you'll find calm waters and *palapa* restaurants, where you can have fresh-caught fish for lunch. You're close to great diving and snorkeling just offshore, as well as Isla Contoy National Park, which features great bird life and its own dramatic, uninhabited beach. If all that tranquillity starts to get to you, you're only a ferry ride away from the action in Cancún. See chapter 5.

- **Cozumel:** It may not have lots of big, sandy beaches, but Cozumel has something the mainland doesn't: the calm, flat waters of the sheltered western shore. It's so easy that it's like swimming in an aquarium. Cozumel also has lots to see under the water. See chapter 5.

- **Playa del Carmen:** This is one of our absolute favorite Mexican beach vacations. Stylish and hip, Playa del Carmen has a beautiful beach and an eclectic assortment of small hotels, inns, and cabanas. The social scene focuses on the beach by day and the

# Mexico

UNITED STATES

Tijuana
Mexicali
Ensenada
BAJA
CALIFORNIA
NORTE    Puerto
Penasco
San
Quintin

Ciudad
Juárez

Nogales

SONORA

Hermosillo

CHIHUAHUA

Ojinaga

Chihuahua

Cuauhtémoc

Delicias

COAHUILA

Monclova

Guerrero
Negro
Isla
Cedros

Santa
Rosalia

Cuidad
Obregón

Mulegé

Hidalgo
del Parral

BAJA
CALIFORNIA
SUR    Loreto

Los Mochis

SINALOA

Torreón

Saltillo

Culiacán

DURANGO

La Paz

Durango

Fresnillo

Todos Santos
Cabo San Lucas    San José
del Cabo

Mazatlán

ZACATECAS

Zacatecas

San
Luis
Potosi

San Blas
Tuxpan
Tepic

AGUASCALIENTES

Aguascalientes

Islas
Marias

NAYARIT

León

Puerto Vallarta

Guadalajara

Guanajuat

GUAN
JUAT
More

JALISCO    Lake Chapala

Barra de Navidad

Uruapan

Manzanillo    Colima

Pátzcua

COLIMA    MICHOACA

Lázaro
Cárdenas

PACIFIC
OCEAN

Zihuatanej
& Ixtap

Gulf of California
(Sea of Cortés)

0    150 mi
0    150 km

pedestrian-only Quinta Avenida (Fifth Avenue) by night, with its fun assortment of restaurants, clubs, sidewalk cafes, and shops. You're also close to the coast's major attractions, including nature parks, ruins, and, *cenotes* (sinkholes or natural wells). Cozumel Island is just a quick ferry trip away. Enjoy it while it's still a manageable size. See chapter 6.

- **Tulum:** Fronting some of the best beaches on the entire coast, Tulum's

small *palapa* hotels offer guests a little slice of paradise far from crowds and megaresorts. The bustling town lies inland; at the coast, things are quiet and will remain so because all these hotels are small and must generate their own electricity. If you can pull yourself away from the beach, nearby are ruins to explore and a vast nature preserve. See chapter 6.

## 2 The Best Cultural Experiences

- **Exploring the Inland Yucatán Peninsula:** Travelers who venture only to the Yucatán's resorts and cities miss the rock-walled inland villages, where women wear colorful embroidered dresses and life seems to proceed as though the modern world (with the exception of highways) didn't exist. The adventure of seeing newly uncovered ruins, deep in jungle settings, is not to be missed. See chapters 6 and 7.

- **Street & Park Entertainment** (Mérida): Few cities have so vibrant a street scene as Mérida. Throughout the week you can catch music and dance performances in plazas about the city, and on Sunday, Mérida really gets going—streets are closed off, food stalls spring up everywhere, and you can enjoy a book fair, a flea market, comedy acts, band concerts, and dance groups. At night, the main plaza is the place to be: People dance to mambos and rumbas in the street in front of the town hall. See chapter 7.

- **San Cristóbal de las Casas:** The city of San Cristóbal is a living museum, with 16th-century colonial architecture and pre-Hispanic native influences. The highland Maya live in surrounding villages and arrive daily in town wearing colorful handmade clothing. The villages are a window into another world, giving visitors a glimpse of traditional Indian dress, religious customs, churches, and ceremonies. See chapter 8.

- **Regional Cuisine:** A trip to the Yucatán allows for a culinary tour of some of Mexico's finest foods. Don't miss specialties such as *pollo* or *cochinita pibil* (chicken or pork in savory *achiote* sauce), great seafood dishes, the many styles of *tamal* found throughout Chiapas and the Yucatán, and Caribbean-influenced foods such as fried bananas, black beans, and yucca root. For a glossary of popular regional dishes, see appendix B.

## 3 The Best Archaeological Sites

- **Calakmul:** Of the many elegantly built Maya cities of the Río Bec area in the lower Yucatán, Calakmul is the broadest in scope and design. It's also one of the hardest to get to—about

48km (30 miles) from the Guatemalan border and completely surrounded by jungle (actually, the Calakmul Biological Reserve). Calakmul is a walled city with the tallest pyramid in the

Yucatán—a city whose primary inhabitants are the trees that populate the plazas. Go now, while it remains infrequently visited. See "Side Trips to Maya Ruins from Chetumal" in chapter 6.

- **Tulum:** Some dismiss Tulum as less important than other ruins in the Yucatán Peninsula, but this seaside Maya fortress is still inspiring. The stark contrast of its crumbling stone walls against the clear turquoise ocean just beyond is an extraordinary sight. See "Tulum, Punta Allen & Sian Ka'an" in chapter 6.

- **Uxmal:** No matter how many times we see Uxmal, the splendor of its stone carvings remains awe-inspiring. A stone rattlesnake undulates across the facade of the Nunnery complex, and 103 masks of Chaac—the rain god— project from the Governor's Palace. See "The Ruins of Uxmal" in chapter 7.

- **Chichén Itzá:** Stand beside the giant serpent head at the foot of the El Castillo pyramid and marvel at the architects and astronomers who positioned the building so precisely that shadow and sunlight form a serpent's body slithering from peak to the earth at each equinox (Mar 21 and Sept 21). See "The Ruins of Chichén Itzá" in chapter 7.

- **Ek Balam:** In recent years, this is the site where some of Mexico's most astounding archaeological discoveries have been made. Ek Balam's main pyramid is taller than Chichén Itzá's, and it holds a sacred doorway bordered with elaborate stucco figures of priests and kings and rich iconography. See "Ek Balam: Dark Jaguar" in chapter 7.

- **Palenque:** The ancient builders of these now-ruined structures carved histories in stone that scholars have only recently deciphered. Imagine the magnificent ceremony in A.D. 683 when King Pacal was buried below ground in a secret pyramidal tomb— unspoiled until its discovery in 1952. See "Palenque" in chapter 8.

## 4 The Best Active Vacations

- **Scuba Diving in Cozumel & along the Yucatán's Caribbean Coast:** The coral reefs off the island, Mexico's premier diving destination, are among the top five dive spots in the world. The Yucatán's coastal reef, part of the second-largest reef system in the world, affords excellent diving all along the coast. Especially beautiful is the Chinchorro Reef, lying 32km (20 miles) offshore from Majahual or Xcalak. Diving from Isla Mujeres is also quite spectacular. See chapters 5 and 6.

- **Fly-Fishing off the Punta Allen & Majahual Peninsulas:** Serious anglers will enjoy the challenge of fly-fishing the saltwater flats and lagoons on the protected sides of these peninsulas. See "Tulum, Punta Allen & Sian Ka'an" and "Majahual, Xcalak & the Chinchorro Reef" in chapter 6.

- **_Cenote_ Diving on the Yucatán Mainland:** Dive into the clear depths of the Yucatán's _cenotes_ for an interesting twist on underwater exploration. The Maya considered the _cenotes_ sacred—and their vivid colors do seem otherworldly. Most are between Playa del Carmen and Tulum, and dive shops in these areas regularly run trips for experienced divers. For recommended dive shops, see "Cozumel" in chapter 5, and "Playa del Carmen" and "South of Playa del Carmen" in chapter 6.

- **An Excursion to Bonampak & Yaxchilán:** Bonampak and Yaxchilán— two remote, jungle-surrounded Maya sites along the Usumacinta River—are now accessible by car and motorboat. The experience could well be the highlight of any trip. See "Road Trips from San Cristóbal" in chapter 8.

- **Birding:** The Yucatán Peninsula, Tabasco, and Chiapas are an ornithological paradise, with hundreds of species awaiting the birder's gaze and list. One very special place is Isla Contoy, with more than 70 species of birds as well as a host of marine and animal life. See p. 115, chapter 6, and chapter 8.

## 5 The Best Places to Get Away from It All

- **Isla Mujeres:** If there's one island in Mexico that guarantees a respite from stress, it's Isla Mujeres. You'll find an ample selection of hotels and restaurants, and they're as laid-back as their patrons. Here life moves along in pure *mañana* mode. Visitors stretch out and doze beneath shady palms or languidly stroll about. For many, the best part about this getaway is that it's comfortably close to Cancún's international airport, as well as to shopping and dining, should you choose to reconnect. See "Isla Mujeres" in chapter 5.

- **The Yucatán's Riviera Maya:** Away from the busy resort of Cancún, a string of quiet getaways, including Capitán Lafitte, Paamul, Punta Bete, and a portion of Xpu-ha, offer tranquillity on beautiful beaches at low prices. See "North of Playa del Carmen" and "South of Playa del Carmen" in chapter 6.

- **Tulum:** Near the Tulum ruins, about two dozen beachside *palapa* inns offer some of the most peaceful getaways in the country. This stretch just might offer the best sandy beaches on the entire coast. Life here among the birds and coconut palms is decidedly unhurried. See "Tulum, Punta Allen & Sian Ka'an" in chapter 6.

- **Rancho Encantado Cottage Resort** (Lago Bacalar; © 800/505-6292) in the U.S., or 983/101-3358; www. encantado.com): The attractive casitas are the place to unwind at this resort, where hammocks stretch between trees. The hotel is on the shores of placid Lago (Lake) Bacalar, south of Cancún near Chetumal, and there's nothing around for miles. But if you want adventure, you can head out to the lake in a kayak, follow a birding trail, or take an excursion to Belize and the intriguing Maya ruins on the nearby Río Bec ruin route. See p. 177.

- **Hotel Eco Paraíso Xixim** (Celestún; © 988/916-2100; www.ecoparaiso. htm): In these crowded times, space is a luxury that's getting harder to come by. Space is precisely what makes this place so great: Fifteen bungalows and 5km (3 miles) of beach bordering a coconut plantation. Throw in a good restaurant, a pool, and a couple of hammocks, and you have that rare combination of comfort and isolation. See p. 210.

- **Hacienda San José Cholul:** Though only an hour outside the bustling city of Mérida, this hacienda feels like another world. The quiet, unhurried manner of both guests and staff and the beautiful tropical surroundings make it the perfect place to recoup some of the silence and slow time lost to the modern world. See "Of Haciendas & Hotels" on p. 204.

## 6 The Best Museums

- **Museo de la Cultura Maya** (Chetumal): This modern museum, one of the best in the country, explores Maya archaeology, architecture, history, and mythology. It has interactive exhibits and a glass floor that allows visitors to walk above replicas of Maya sites. See p. 178.

- **Museo Regional de Antropología** (Mérida): Housed in the Palacio Cantón, one of the most beautiful 19th-century mansions in the city, this museum showcases area archaeology and anthropological studies in handsome exhibits. See p. 197.

- **Museo Regional de Antropología Carlos Pellicer Cámara** (Villahermosa): This anthropology museum addresses Mexican history in the form of objects found at archaeological sites, with particular emphasis on the pre-Hispanic peoples of the Gulf coast region. See p. 247.

- **Parque–Museo La Venta** (Villahermosa): The Olmec, considered Mexico's mother culture, are the subject of this park/museum, which features the magnificent stone remains that were removed from the La Venta site not far away. Stroll through a jungle setting where tropical birds alight, and examine the giant carved stone heads of the mysterious Olmec. See p. 247

## 7 The Best Shopping

*Some tips on bargaining:* Although haggling over prices in markets is expected and part of the fun, don't try to browbeat the vendor or bad-mouth the goods. Vendors won't bargain with people they consider disrespectful unless they are desperate to make a sale. Be insistent but friendly.

- **Resort Wear in Cancún:** Resort clothing—especially if you can find a sale—can be a bargain here. And the selection may be wider than what's available at home. Almost every mall on the island contains trendy boutiques that specialize in locally designed and imported clothing. See "Shopping" in chapter 4.

- **Duty-Free in Cancún:** If you're looking for European perfume, fine watches, or other imported goods, you'll find the prices in Cancún's duty-free shops (at the major malls on the island and in downtown Cancún) hard to beat. See "Shopping" in chapter 4.

- **Precious Gemstones in Isla Mujeres:** Isla Mujeres, also a duty-free zone, offers an impressive selection of both precious stones and superb craftsmen who can make jewelry designs to order. See "Isla Mujeres" in chapter 5.

- **Quinta Avenida, Playa del Carmen:** This pedestrian-only street offers leisurely shopping at its best. No cars, no hassle, simply stroll down the street and let your eye pick out objects of interest. Expect a good bit of merchandise popular with counterculture types, such as batik clothing and fabric, Guatemalan textiles, and inventive jewelry and artwork. But you'll also find quality Mexican handicrafts, premium tequilas, and Cuban cigars. See "Playa del Carmen" in chapter 6.

- **Mérida:** This is *the* marketplace for the Yucatán—the best place to buy hammocks, *guayaberas,* Panama hats, and Yucatecan *huipiles.* See "Exploring Mérida" in chapter 7.

- **San Cristóbal de las Casas:** Deep in the heart of the Maya highlands, San Cristóbal has shops, open plazas, and markets that feature the distinctive waist-loomed wool and cotton textiles of the region, as well as leather shoes, handsome pottery, and Guatemalan textiles. Highland Maya Indians sell direct to tourists from their armloads of textiles, dolls, and attractive miniature likenesses of Subcomandante Marcos—complete with ski masks. See "San Cristóbal de las Casas" in chapter 8.

## 8 The Hottest Nightlife

Although, as expected, Cancún is the source of much of the Yucatán's nightlife, that resort city isn't the only place to have a good time after dark. Along the Caribbean coast, beachside dance floors with live bands and extended happy hours in seaside bars dominate the nightlife. Here are some favorite hot spots, from live music in hotel lobby bars to hip techno dance clubs.

- **Carlos 'n' Charlie's & Dady'O:** These Cancún bars all offer good drinks, hot music, and great dance floors. **Mango Tango** is a top spot for live Cuban and Caribbean rhythms in Cancún, while **Glazz**, in the La Isla Shopping Village, is making its mark as a hip lounge and martini bar. See chapter 4.

- **Forum by the Sea:** Here's one place that has it all: The newest of the seaside entertainment centers in Cancún has a dazzling array of dance clubs, sports bars, fast food, and fine dining, with shops open late as well. You'll find plenty of familiar names here, including the Hard Rock Cafe and Rainforest Cafe. It's also the home of Cancún's hottest club, **Coco Bongo,** which can pack in up to 3,000 revelers—and does so regularly. See p. 105.

- **The City:** Currently Cancún's newest and hottest offering, **The City** (www.thecitycancun.com) is a day-and-night club, offering a Beach Club with a wave machine for simulated surfing, a water slide and beach cabanas, a Terrace bar serving food and drinks, and the sizzling Club, at which the world's top DJs have spun through the night until the sun once again rises over the turquoise waters. This is truly a City that never sleeps. See p. 105.

- **Lobby Lounge:** Located in Cancún's luxurious Ritz-Carlton, this is the most elegant evening spot on the island. Romantic live music, a selection of fine cigars, and more than 120 premium tequilas (plus tastings) allow you to savor the spirit of Mexico. See p. 105.

- **San Cristóbal de las Casas:** This city, small though it may be, has a live-music scene that can't be beat for fun and atmosphere. The bars and clubs are all within walking distance, and they're a real bargain. See "San Cristóbal de las Casas" in chapter 8.

- **Quinta Avenida, Playa del Carmen:** Stroll along lively, pedestrian-only Fifth Avenue to find the bar that's right for you. With live-music venues, tequila bars, sports bars, and cafes, you're sure to find something to fit your mood. See p. 153.

## 9 The Most Luxurious Hotels

- **Aqua** (Cancún; ✆ **800/343-7821** in the U.S.; www.fiestamericana.com): This resort, part of the Fiesta Americana chain, was designed with a water theme in mind. The spa is a 1,500 sq.-m (over 16,146-sq.-ft.) facility that blends Eastern, pre-Hispanic, and Western treatment philosophies. Tai Chi, yoga, and Pilates classes are offered, and you can indulge in a full array of massages and treatments.

After you've rejuvenated, you can partake of the exceptional cuisine offered at the resorts' three restaurants under the direction of celebrity chefs, or chill in the Lounge to cool tunes and tempting drinks. See p. 84.

- **Le Méridien Cancún Resort & Spa** (Cancún; ✆ **800/543-4300** in the U.S., or 998/881-2200; www.meridien cancun.com.mx): This is the most intimate of the luxury hotels in Cancún, with an understated sense of highly personalized service. Most notable is its 4,570-sq.-m (49,191-sq.-ft.) Spa del Mar. See p. 86.

- **Ritz-Carlton** (Cancún; ✆ **800/241-3333** in the U.S., or 998/881-0808; www.ritzcarlton.com): For years, thick carpets, sparkling glass and brass, and rich mahogany have surrounded guests at this hotel, the standard-bearer of luxury in Cancún. The service is impeccable, leaving guests with an overall sense of pampered relaxation. And now, thanks to a multimillion-dollar repair and refurbishment project that's scheduled to be completed in September 2006, the best is getting even better. See p. 87.

- **Presidente      Inter-Continental Cozumel** (Cozumel; ✆ **800/327-0200** in the U.S., or 987/872-9500; www.cozumel.intercontinental.com): Surrounded by shady palms, this hotel also has the best beach on the island, right in front of Paraíso Reef. Favorite rooms are the deluxe beachside units with spacious patios and direct access to the beach—you can even order romantic in-room dining on the patios, complete with a trio to serenade you. See p. 134.

- **Ikal del Mar** (north of Playa del Carmen; ✆ **888/230-7330** in the U.S.; www.ikaldelmar.com): Small, secluded, and private, Ikal del Mar offers extraordinary personal service

and spa treatments. Rooms are spread out through the jungle, and there's a beautiful seaside pool and restaurant. See p. 158.

- **Maroma** (north of Playa del Carmen; ✆ **866/454-9351** in the U.S.; www.maromahotel.com): You can't ask for a better setting for a resort than this beautiful stretch of Caribbean coast with palm trees and manicured gardens. You'll start to relax before you even take the first sip of your welcome cocktail. Service is very attentive, and the rooms are large and luxurious. See p. 158.

- **Paraíso de la Bonita** (north of Playa del Carmen; ✆ **866/751-9175** in the U.S.; www.paraisodelabonita.com): Operated by Inter-Continental Hotels, this resort has a super-equipped spa based on the elaborate system of thalassotherapy. The guest rooms are elaborate, and the hotel provides all kinds of services. It has three pools and an immaculately kept beach. See p. 158.

- **Hacienda Xcanatún** (outskirts of Mérida; ✆ **888/883-3633** in the U.S.; www.xcanatun.com): Large, boldly designed suites built with extravagance in mind, extensive grounds, private spa, excellent restaurant, and ample staff—this hotel does the difficult trick of being small in size but large in offerings. See "Of Haciendas & Hotels" on p. 204.

## 10 The Best Inexpensive Inns

- **Rey del Caribe Hotel** (Cancún; ✆ **998/884-2028;** www.reycaribe.com): A unique oasis in downtown Cancún, this hotel has considered every detail in its quest for an organic and environmentally friendly lifestyle. Set in a tropical garden, the Rey del Caribe provides sunny rooms, warm service, yoga and meditation classes,

and healthful dining—all a welcome respite from party-hearty Cancún. See p. 90.

- **Casa San Juan** (Mérida; ✆ **999/986-2937;** www.casasanjuan.com): This B&B, in a colonial house in Mérida's historic district, is the perfect combination of comfort and character at a great price. The guest rooms in the original building evoke an earlier time, while the modern rooms in back are quite large and border a lovely patio. See p. 203.

- **Hotel Ojo de Agua** (Puerto Morelos; ℂ 998/871-0027; www.ojo-de-agua. com): If you're seeking an inexpensive beach vacation with plenty of activities, there's no better place than this. It's a rarity—a bargain beach hotel with the watersports choices of a large resort. See p. 156.

- **Hotel Colonial** (Campeche; ℂ 981/ 816-2222): Okay, so it's not the most comfortable hotel in town. But it is by far the most endearing. It exudes character and a sense of timelessness that relaxes the spirit and conjures up images of an uncomplicated era. And for $25, it's a steal. See p. 229.

- **Hotel Real del Valle** (San Cristóbal; ℂ 967/678-0680): In a city of inexpensive lodging, this beats all the other bargain hotels for its combination of location, room size, and service. See p. 270.

## 11 The Best Unique Inns

- **Casa de los Sueños Resort & Spa Zenter** (Isla Mujeres; ℂ 998/877-0651; www.casadelossuenosresort. com): This luxury B&B is steeped in vibrant colors. Its small but well-appointed spa and "Zenter," which is also accessible to nonguests, offers yoga classes, massages, and holistic spa treatments, which take place either outdoors or in a tranquil indoor space. See p. 116.

- **Hotel Villa Rolandi Gourmet & Beach Club** (Isla Mujeres; ℂ 998/ 877-0700; www.villarolandi.com): In addition to being steps away from an exquisite private cove, a tranquil infinity pool, and Isla's finest dining, this intimate inn also pampers guests with every conceivable in-room amenity. Each unit even has a private Jacuzzi on the balcony and a shower that converts into a steam room. See p. 117.

- **Deseo Hotel + Lounge** (Playa del Carmen; ℂ 984/879-3620; www. hoteldeseo.com): Perhaps it should be Hotel = Lounge. That might be an overstatement, but the lounge is at the center of everything, making Deseo the perfect fit for outgoing types who are into an alternative lodging experience. Enjoy a cocktail at the bar or on one of the large daybeds and chill to the modern lounge music. See p. 147.

- **Casa Mexilio Guest House** (Mérida; ℂ 877/639-4546 in the U.S. and Canada, or 999/928-2505; www.casa mexilio.com): An imaginative arrangement of rooms around a courtyard features a pool surrounded by a riot of tropical vegetation. The rooms are divided among different levels for privacy and are connected by stairs and catwalks. Breakfast here provides an extra incentive for getting out of bed. See p. 202.

- **Casa Na-Bolom** (San Cristóbal de las Casas; ℂ 967/678-1418): This unique house-museum is terrific for anthropology buffs. Built as a seminary in 1891, it was transformed into the headquarters of two anthropologists. The 12 guest rooms, named for surrounding villages, are decorated with local objects and textiles; all rooms have fireplaces and private bathrooms, and the room rate includes breakfast. See p. 263.

## 12 The Best Restaurants

Best doesn't necessarily mean most luxurious. Although some of the restaurants listed here are fancy affairs, others are simple places to get fine, authentic Yucatecan cuisine.

- **Aioli** (Cancún; ℂ **998/881-2200**): Simply exquisite French and Mediterranean gourmet specialties served in a warm and cozy country French setting, at the hotel Le Méridien. For quality and exceptional service, it's Cancún's best value in fine dining. See p. 92.

- **Labná** (Ciudad Cancún; ℂ **998/892-3056**): Steep yourself in Yucatecan cuisine and music at this downtown eatery, which showcases Maya culture and cuisine. The Labná Special is a sample of the most traditional of this region's cuisine. See p. 96.

- **La Dolce Vita** (Cancún; ℂ **998/885-0150**): A longtime favorite, La Dolce Vita remains untouched by newer arrivals. It continues to draw diners with such blissful dishes as green tagliolini with lobster medallions, veal with morels, and fresh salmon with cream sauce, all served (at night) to the sound of live jazz music. See p. 93.

- **100% Natural, for** *Licuados: Licuados,* drinks made from fresh fruit mixed with water or milk, are much more popular than soft drinks. This restaurant chain offers the widest selection, including innovative mixtures like the Cozumel (spinach, pineapple, and orange) and the Caligula (orange, pineapple, beet, celery, parsley, carrot, and lime juices)—a healthy indulgence. Cancún has several branches. See p. 96.

- **Zazil Ha** (Isla Mujeres; ℂ **998/877-0279**): It doesn't get more relaxed and casual than Zazil Ha, with its sandy floor beneath thatched *palapas* and palms. This is the place for island atmosphere and well-prepared food. Along with its signature seafood and Caribbean cuisine, this restaurant continues to prove that vegetarian cuisine can be both artfully and tastefully prepared. It also offers special menus for those participating in yoga retreats on the island. See p. 121.

- **Cabaña del Pescador** (Cozumel; no phone): If you want an ideally seasoned, succulent lobster dinner, Cabaña del Pescador (Lobster House) is the place. If you want anything else, you're out of luck—lobster dinner, expertly prepared, is all it serves. When you've achieved perfection, why bother with anything else? See p. 135.

- **Prima** (Cozumel; ℂ **987/872-4242**): The Italian food here is fresh, fresh, fresh—from the hydroponically grown vegetables to the pasta and garlic bread. And it's all prepared after you walk in, most of it by owner Albert Domínguez, who concocts unforgettable shrimp fettuccine with pesto, crab ravioli with cream sauce, and crisp house salad in a chilled bowl. See p. 136.

- **Media Luna** (Playa del Carmen; ℂ **984/873-0526**): The inviting atmosphere of this sidewalk cafe on Avenida 5 is enough to lure you in. The expertly executed and innovative menu, together with great prices, makes it one of the top choices on the Caribbean coast. See p. 152.

- **La Pigua** (Campeche; ℂ **981/811-3365**): Campeche's regional specialty is seafood, and nowhere else will you find seafood like this. Mexican caviar, coconut-battered shrimp, and chiles stuffed with shark are just a few of the unique specialties. Thinking about La Pigua's pompano in a fine green herb sauce makes me want to start checking flight schedules. See p. 230.

- **Yaxché** (Playa del Carmen; © **984/ 873-2502**): No restaurant in the Yucatán explores the region's culinary traditions and use of local ingredients more than this one. Its menu presents several pleasant surprises and is a welcome relief from the standard offerings of most Yucatecan restaurants. See p. 151.

# 2

# Planning Your Trip to the Yucatán

*by Lynne Bairstow*

**A**little planning can make the difference between a good trip and a great trip. When should you go? What's the best way to get there? How much should you plan on spending? What festivals or special events will occur during your visit? What safety or health precautions should you take? We'll answer these and other questions in this chapter. In addition to these basics, I highly recommend taking a little time to learn about the culture and traditions of Mexico and the Yucatán. It can make the difference between simply getting away for a few days and truly adding cultural understanding to your trip. See appendix A for more details.

## 1 The Regions in Brief

Travelers to the peninsula have an opportunity to see pre-Hispanic ruins—such as **Chichén Itzá, Uxmal,** and **Tulum**—and the living descendants of the cultures that built them, as well as the ultimate in resort Mexico: **Cancún.** The peninsula borders the dull aquamarine Gulf of Mexico on the west and north, and the clear blue Caribbean Sea on the east. It covers almost 197,600 sq. km (76,294 sq. miles), with nearly 1,600km (1,000 miles) of shoreline. Underground rivers and natural wells called *cenotes* are a peculiar feature of this region.

Lovely rock-walled Maya villages and crumbling henequén haciendas dot the interior of the peninsula. The placid interior contrasts with the hubbub of the Caribbean coast. From Cancún south to **Chetumal,** the jungle coastline is spotted with all kinds of development, from posh to budget. It also boasts an enormous array of wildlife, including hundreds of species of birds. The Gulf Coast beaches, while good enough, don't compare to those on the Caribbean. National parks near **Celestún** and **Río Lagartos** on the Gulf Coast are home to amazing flocks of flamingos.

To present the Maya world in its entirety, this book also covers the states of **Tabasco** and **Chiapas.** The Gulf Coast state of Tabasco was once home to the Olmec, the mother culture of Mesoamerica. At Villahermosa's Parque–Museo La Venta, you can see the impressive 40-ton carved rock heads that the Olmec left behind.

**San Cristóbal de las Casas,** in Chiapas, inhabits cooler, greener mountains, and is more in the mold of a provincial colonial town. Approaching San Cristóbal from any direction, you see small plots of corn tended by colorfully clad Maya. The surrounding villages are home to many craftspeople, from woodcarvers to potters to weavers. In the eastern lowland jungles of Chiapas lie the classic Maya ruins of **Palenque.** Deeper into the interior, for those willing to make the trek, are **Yaxchilán** and **Bonampak.**

# The Yucatán Peninsula

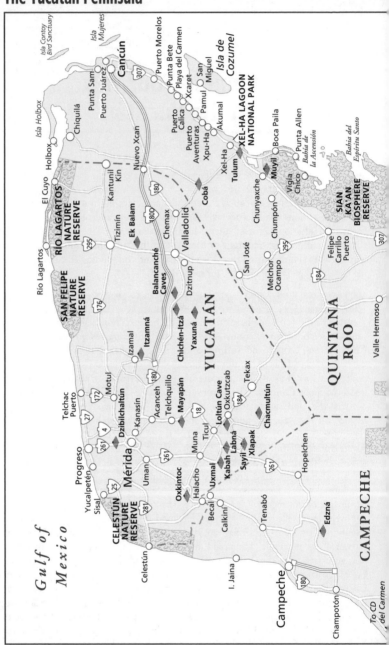

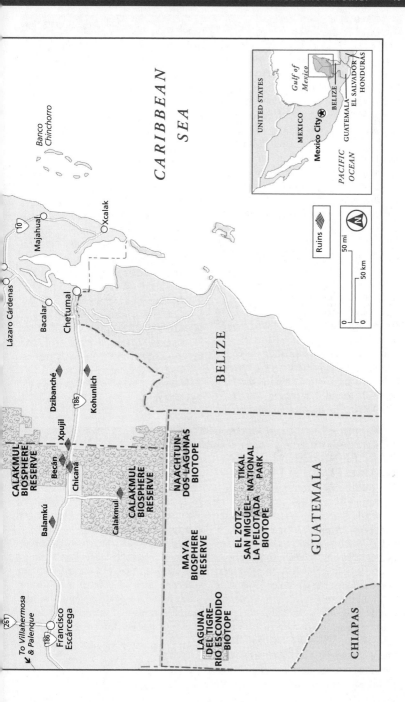

CARIBBEAN

SEA

Banco
Chinchorro

Xcalak

Majahual

Bacalar

Chetumal

Lázaro Cárdenas

BELIZE

Dzibanché

Kohunlich

185

Xpujil

CALAKMUL
BIOSPHERE
RESERVE

Becán

Chicaná

Calakmul

CALAKMUL
BIOSPHERE
RESERVE

Balamkú

NAACHTUN–
DOS LAGUNAS
BIOTOPE

TIKAL
NATIONAL
PARK

EL ZOTZ–
SAN MIGUEL–
LA PELOTADA
BIOTOPE

MAYA
BIOSPHERE
RESERVE

GUATEMALA

LAGUNA
DEL TIGRE–
RÍO ESCONDIDO
BIOTOPE

Francisco
Escárcega

261

185

To Villahermosa
& Palenque

CHIAPAS

UNITED STATES

Gulf of
Mexico

MEXICO

México City

BELIZE

GUATEMALA

EL SALVADOR

HONDURAS

PACIFIC
OCEAN

Ruins

50 mi

50 km

0

0

## 2 Visitor Information

The **Mexico Hot Line** (℃ **800/44-MEXICO**) is an excellent source for general information; you can request brochures on the country and get answers to the most common questions from the exceptionally well-trained, knowledgeable staff.

More information about Mexico is available on the official site of Mexico's Tourism Promotion Board, **www.visit mexico.com**. The **U.S. State Department** (℃ **202/501-4444;** www.travel.state.gov) offers a **Consular Information Sheet** on Mexico, with safety, medical, driving, and general travel information gleaned from reports by its offices in Mexico, and it's consistently updated. You can also request the Consular Information Sheet by fax at **202/647-1488.**

The **Centers for Disease Control and Prevention Hot Line** (℃ **800/311-3435** or 404/639-3534; www.cdc.gov) is a source of medical information for travelers to Mexico and elsewhere. For travelers to Mexico and Central America, the number with recorded messages is ℃ **877/ FYI-TRIP.** The toll-free fax number for

requesting information is 888/407-4747. Information available by fax is also available at **www.cdc.gov/travel**.

**MEXICAN GOVERNMENT TOURIST BOARD** The board has offices in major North American cities, in addition to the main office in Mexico City (℃ **55/ 5278-4200**).

**United States:** Chicago (℃ **312/228-0517**); Houston (℃ **713/772-2581,** ext. 105, or 713/772-3819); Los Angeles (℃ **310/282-9112**); and New York (℃ **212/308-2110**). The Mexican Embassy is at 1911 Pennsylvania Ave. NW, Washington, DC 20005 (℃ **202/ 728-1750** or 202/728-1600).

**Canada:** 2055 Rue Peel, Suite 1000, Montreal, QC H3A 1V4 (℃ **514/288-2502**); Commerce Court West, 199 Bay St., Suite 4440, Toronto, ON M5L 1E9 (℃ **416/925-0704**); 710 West Hastings St., Suite 1177, Vancouver, BC V6E 2K3 (℃ **604/684-1859**); Embassy office: 1500-45 O'Connor St., Ottawa, ON K1P 1A4 (℃ **613/233-8988;** fax 613/ 235-9123).

## 3 Entry Requirements & Customs

### ENTRY REQUIREMENTS
### PASSPORTS

The Intelligence Reform and Terrorism Prevention Act of 2004 requires that by January 1, 2008, travelers to and from the Caribbean, Bermuda, Panama, Mexico, and Canada have a passport or other secure, accepted document to enter or re-enter the United States. As of press time, this requirement is scheduled to apply to all air and sea travel to or from Mexico, effective December 31, 2006.

For information on how to get a passport, go to "Passports" in "Fast Facts: Mexico," later in this chapter—the websites listed provide downloadable passport applications as well as the current fees for

processing passport applications. For an up-to-date, country-by-country listing of passport requirements around the world, go to the "Foreign Entry Requirement" Web page of the U.S. State Department at **http://travel.state.gov**.

Safeguard your passport in an inconspicuous, inaccessible place like a money belt, and keep a copy of the critical pages with your passport number in a separate place. If you lose your passport, visit the nearest consulate of your native country as soon as possible for a replacement.

### ONCE YOU'RE IN MEXICO

You must carry a **Mexican Tourist Permit (FMT),** the equivalent of a tourist

# Tabasco & Chiapas

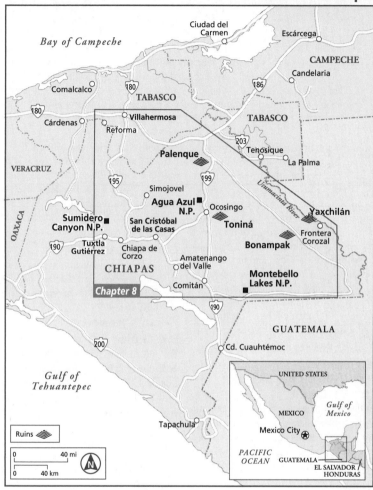

visa, which Mexican border officials issue, free of charge, after proof of citizenship (via your passport) is accepted. Airlines generally provide the necessary forms aboard your flight to Mexico. The FMT is more important than a passport in Mexico, so guard it carefully. If you lose it, you may not be permitted to leave the country until you can replace it—a bureaucratic hassle that can take anywhere from a few hours to a week.

The FMT can be issued for up to 180 days. Sometimes officials don't ask but just stamp a time limit, so be sure to say "6 months," or at least twice as long as you intend to stay. If you decide to extend your stay, you may request that additional time be added to your FMT from an official immigration office in Mexico.

***Note:*** Children under age 18 who are traveling without parents or with only one parent must have a notarized letter

> **⟨Tips⟩  Passport Savvy**
>
> Allow plenty of time before your trip to apply for a passport; processing normally takes 3 weeks but can take longer during busy periods (especially spring). And keep in mind that if you need a passport in a hurry, you'll pay a higher processing fee. When traveling, safeguard your passport in an inconspicuous, inaccessible place like a money belt and keep a copy of the critical pages with your passport number in a separate place. If you lose your passport, visit the nearest consulate or embassy of your native country as soon as possible for a replacement.

from the absent parent(s) authorizing the travel. Mexican law requires that any non-Mexican under the age of 18 departing Mexico must carry notarized written permission from any parent or guardian not traveling with the child. This permission must include the name of the parent, the name of the child, the name of anyone traveling with the child, and the notarized signature(s) of the absent parent(s). The child must carry the original letter—not a copy—as well as proof of the parent/child relationship (usually a birth certificate or court document)—and an original custody decree, if applicable.

## CUSTOMS
### WHAT YOU CAN BRING INTO MEXICO
When you enter Mexico, Customs officials will be tolerant as long as you have no illegal drugs or firearms. You're allowed to bring in two cartons of cigarettes or 50 cigars, plus 1 kilogram (2.2 lb.) of smoking tobacco; two 1-liter bottles of wine or hard liquor, and 12 rolls of film. A laptop computer, camera equipment, and sports equipment that could feasibly be used during your stay are also allowed. The underlying guideline is: Don't bring anything that looks as if it's meant to be resold in Mexico.

### WHAT YOU CAN TAKE HOME
#### U.S. Citizens
For specifics on what you can bring back and the corresponding fees, download the invaluable free pamphlet *Know Before You*

*Go* online at **www.cbp.gov.** (Click on "Travel," and then click on "Know Before You Go! Online Brochure.") Or contact the **U.S. Customs & Border Protection (CBP),** 1300 Pennsylvania Ave. NW, Washington, DC 20229 (**℃ 877/287-8667**), and request the pamphlet.

#### Canadian Citizens
For a clear summary of Canadian rules, write for the booklet *I Declare,* issued by the **Canada Border Services Agency** (**℃ 800/461-9999** in Canada, or 204/983-3500; **www.cbsa-asfc.gc.ca**).

#### U.K. Citizens
For information, contact **HM Customs & Excise** at ℃ **0845/010-9000** (from outside the U.K., 020/8929-0152), or consult their website at **www.hmce.gov.uk**.

#### Australian Citizens
A helpful brochure available from Australian consulates or Customs offices is *Know Before You Go.* For more information, call the **Australian Customs Service** at ℃ **1300/363-263,** or log on to **www.customs.gov.au**.

#### New Zealand Citizens
Most questions are answered in a free pamphlet available at New Zealand consulates and Customs offices: *New Zealand Customs Guide for Travellers, Notice no. 4.* For more information, contact **New Zealand Customs,** The Customhouse, 17–21 Whitmore St., Box 2218, Wellington (℃ **04/473-6099** or 0800/428-786; **www.customs.govt.nz**).

## GOING THROUGH CUSTOMS

Mexican Customs inspection has been streamlined. At most points of entry, tourists are requested to press a button in front of what looks like a traffic signal, which alternates on touch between red and green. Green light and you go through without inspection; red light and your luggage or car may be inspected. If you have an unusual amount of luggage or an oversize piece, you may be subject to inspection anyway.

## 4 Money

### CURRENCY

The currency in Mexico is the Mexican **peso.** Paper currency comes in denominations of 20, 50, 100, 200, 500, and 1,000 pesos. Coins come in denominations of 1, 2, 5, 10, and 20 pesos, and 20 and 50 **centavos** (100 centavos = 1 peso). The current exchange rate for the U.S. dollar, and the one used in this book, is around 11 pesos; at that rate, an item that costs 11 pesos would be equivalent to US$1.

Getting **change** is a problem. Small-denomination bills and coins are hard to come by, so start collecting them early in your trip. Shopkeepers everywhere always seem to be out of change and small bills; that's doubly true in markets.

Many establishments that deal with tourists, especially in coastal resort areas, quote prices in dollars. To avoid confusion, they use the abbreviations "Dlls." for dollars and "M.N." (*moneda nacional,* or national currency) for pesos.

Don't forget to have enough pesos to carry you over a weekend or Mexican holiday, when banks are closed. In general, avoid carrying the U.S. $100 bill, the bill most commonly counterfeited in Mexico and therefore the most difficult to exchange, especially in smaller towns. Because small bills and coins in pesos are hard to come by in Mexico, the $1 bill is very useful for tipping. A tip of U.S. coins

cannot be exchanged into Mexican currency and is of no value to the service provider.

The bottom line on exchanging money: Ask first, and shop around. Banks generally pay the top rates.

Exchange houses *(casas de cambio)* are generally more convenient than banks because they have more locations and longer hours; the rate of exchange may be the same as at a bank or slightly lower. Before leaving a bank or exchange-house window, count your change in front of the teller.

Large airports have currency-exchange counters that often stay open whenever flights are operating. Though convenient, they generally do not offer the most favorable rates.

A hotel's exchange desk commonly pays less favorable rates than banks; however, when the currency is in a state of flux, higher-priced hotels are known to pay higher rates than banks, in an effort to attract dollars. ***Note:*** In almost all cases, you receive a better rate by changing money first, then paying.

### BANKS & ATMs

Banks in Mexico are rapidly expanding and improving services. They tend to be open weekdays from 9am until 5pm, and often for at least a half-day on Saturday. In larger resorts and cities, they can generally

---

### Money Matters

The **universal currency sign ($)** is used to indicate pesos in Mexico. The use of the symbol in this book, however, denotes U.S. currency.

## *Tips*  A Few Words about Prices

The peso's value continues to fluctuate—at press time, it was roughly 11 pesos to the dollar. Prices in this book (which are always given in U.S. dollars) have been converted to U.S. dollars at 11 pesos to the dollar. Most hotels in Mexico—with the exception of places that receive little foreign tourism—quote prices in U.S. dollars. Thus, currency fluctuations are unlikely to affect the prices most hotels charge.

Mexico has a **value-added tax** of 15% (*Impuesto de Valor Agregado,* or IVA; pronounced "ee-vah") on most everything, including restaurant meals, bus tickets, and souvenirs. (Exceptions are Cancún, Cozumel, and Los Cabos, where the IVA is 10%; as ports of entry, they receive a break on taxes.) Hotels charge the usual 15% IVA, plus a locally administered bed tax of 2% (in most areas), for a total of 17%. In Cancún, Los Cabos, and Cozumel, hotels charge the 10% IVA plus 2% room tax. The prices quoted by hotels and restaurants do not necessarily include IVA. You may find that upper-end properties (three or more stars) quote prices without IVA included, while lower-priced hotels include IVA. Always ask to see a printed price sheet and always ask if the tax is included.

accommodate the exchange of dollars (which used to stop at noon) anytime during business hours. During times when the currency is in flux, a particular bank may not exchange dollars, so check before standing in line. Some, but not all, banks charge a service fee of about 1% to exchange traveler's checks. However, you can pay for most purchases directly with traveler's checks at the establishment's stated exchange rate. Don't even bother with personal checks drawn on a U.S. bank—the bank will wait for your check to clear, which can take weeks, before giving you your money.

Travelers to Mexico can easily withdraw money from **ATMs** in most major cities and resort areas. The U.S. State Department has an advisory against using ATMs in Mexico for safety reasons, stating that they should only be used during business hours, but this pertains primarily to Mexico City, where crime remains a significant problem. In most resorts in Mexico, the use of ATMs is perfectly safe—just use the same precautions you would at any ATM. Universal bankcards (such as the Cirrus and PLUS systems) can be used. This is a convenient way to withdraw money and avoid carrying too much with you at any time. The exchange rate is generally more favorable than that at a currency house. Most machines offer Spanish/English menus and dispense pesos, but some offer the option of withdrawing dollars. Be sure to check the daily withdrawal limit before you depart.

For **Cirrus** locations abroad, check ✆ 800/424-7787 or **www.mastercard. com**. For **PLUS** outlets abroad, check ✆ 800/843-7587 or **www.visa.com**. Before you leave home, check your daily withdrawal limit, and make sure that your personal identification number (PIN) works in international destinations. Also keep in mind that many banks impose a fee every time a card is used at a different bank's ATM, and that fee can be higher for international transactions (up to $5 or more) than for domestic ones. To compare banks' ATM fees within the U.S., use **www.bankrate.com**. For international withdrawal fees, ask your bank.

You can also get cash advances on your credit card at an ATM. Keep in mind that credit card companies try to protect themselves from theft by limiting the funds someone can withdraw outside their home country, so call your credit card company before you leave home. And keep in mind that you'll pay interest from the moment of your withdrawal, even if you pay your monthly bills on time.

## TRAVELER'S CHECKS

Traveler's checks are something of an anachronism from the days before the ATM made cash accessible at any time. Given the fees you'll pay for ATM use at banks other than your own, however, you might be better off with traveler's checks if you're withdrawing money often.

You can get traveler's checks at almost any bank. **American Express** offers denominations of $20, $50, $100, $500, and (for cardholders only) $1,000. You'll pay a service charge ranging from 1% to 4%. You can also get American Express traveler's checks over the phone by calling ⓒ **800/221-7282;** Amex gold and platinum cardholders who use this number are exempt from the 1% fee.

**Visa** offers traveler's checks at Citibank locations nationwide, as well as at several other banks. The service charge ranges between 1.5% and 2%; checks come in denominations of $20, $50, $100, $500, and $1,000. Call ⓒ **800/227-6811** for information. **MasterCard** also offers traveler's checks. Call ⓒ **800/223-7373** for a location near you.

If you do choose to carry traveler's checks, keep a record of their serial numbers separate from your checks in the event that they are stolen or lost. You'll get a refund faster if you know the numbers.

## CREDIT CARDS

Credit cards are a safe way to carry money. They provide a convenient record of all your expenses, and they generally offer relatively good exchange rates. You can also withdraw cash advances from your credit cards at banks or ATMs, provided you know your PIN. If you've forgotten yours, or didn't even know you had one, call the number on the back of your credit card and ask the bank to send it to you. It usually takes 5 to 7 business days, though some banks will provide the number over the phone if you tell them your mother's maiden name or some other personal information.

Keep in mind that when you use your credit card abroad, most banks assess a 2% fee above the 1% fee charged by Visa or MasterCard or American Express for currency conversion on credit charges. But credit cards still may be the smart way to go when you factor in things like exorbitant ATM fees and higher traveler's check exchange rates (and service fees).

In Mexico Visa, MasterCard, and American Express are the most accepted cards. You'll be able to charge most hotel, restaurant, and store purchases, as well as almost all airline tickets, on your credit card. Pemex gas stations have begun to accept credit card purchases for gasoline, starting in January 2006, though this option may not be available everywhere—check before you pump. You can get cash advances of several hundred dollars on your card, but there may be a wait of 20 minutes to 2 hours.

Charges will be made in pesos, then converted into dollars by the bank issuing the credit card. Generally you receive the favorable bank rate when paying by credit card. However, be aware that some establishments in Mexico add a 5% to 7% surcharge when you pay with a credit card. This is especially true when using American Express. Many times, advertised discounts will not apply if you pay with a credit card.

For tips and telephone numbers to call if your wallet is stolen or lost, go to "Lost & Found" in the "Fast Facts: Mexico," later in this chapter.

---

**Tips    Dear Visa: I'm Off to Cancún!**

Some credit card companies recommend that you notify them of any impending trip abroad so that they don't become suspicious and block your charges when the card is used numerous times in a foreign destination. Even if you don't call your credit card company in advance, you can call always the toll-free emergency number (see "Fast Facts: Mexico," later in this chapter) if a charge is refused—a good reason to carry the phone number with you. But perhaps the most important lesson is to carry more than one card on your trip; if one card doesn't work for any number of reasons, you'll have a backup.

---

## 5 When to Go

### SEASONS

**High season** in the Yucatán begins around December 20 and continues to Easter. This is the best time for calm, warm weather; snorkeling, diving, and fishing (the calmer weather means clearer and more predictable seas); and for visiting the ruins that dot the interior of the peninsula. Book well in advance if you plan to be in Cancún around the holidays.

**Low season** begins the day after Easter and continues to mid-December; during low season, prices may drop 20% to 50%. In Cancún and along the Riviera Maya, demand by European visitors is creating a summer high season, with hotel rates approaching those charged in the winter months.

Generally speaking, Mexico's **dry season** runs from November to April, with the **rainy season** stretching from May to October. It isn't a problem if you're staying close to the beaches, but for those bent on road-tripping to Chichén Itzá, Uxmal, or other sites, temperatures and humidity in the interior can be downright stifling from May to July. Later in the rainy season, the frequency of **tropical storms** and **hurricanes** increases; such storms, of course, can put a crimp in your vacation. But they can lower temperatures, making climbing ruins a real joy, accompanied by cool air and a slight wind. November is especially ideal for Yucatán travels. Cancún, Cozumel, and Isla Mujeres also have a rainy season from November to January, when northern storms hit. This usually means diving visibility is diminished—and conditions may prevent boats from even going out.

Villahermosa is sultry and humid all the time. San Cristóbal de las Casas, at an elevation of 2,152m (7,059 ft.), is much cooler than the lowlands and is downright cold in winter.

## YUCATAN CALENDAR OF EVENTS

During national holidays, Mexican banks and governmental offices—including Immigration—are closed.

### January

**New Year's Day (Año Nuevo).** National holiday. Perhaps the quietest day in all of Mexico; most people stay home or visit a church. All businesses close. In traditional indigenous communities, new tribal leaders are inaugurated with colorful ceremonies rooted in the pre-Hispanic past. January 1.

**Three Kings Day (Día de Reyes).** Nationwide. Commemorates the Three Kings bringing gifts to the Christ Child. On this day, children receive presents, much like the traditional gift-giving that accompanies Christmas in the United States. Friends and families gather to share the Rosca de Reyes, a special cake. Inside the cake is a small doll representing the Christ Child; whoever receives the doll in his or her piece must host a tamales-and-*atole* party on February 2. January 6.

## February

**Candlemas (Día de la Candelaria).** Nationwide. Music, dances, processions, food, and other festivities lead up to a blessing of seed and candles in a ceremony that mixes pre-Hispanic and European traditions marking the end of winter. Those who attended the Three Kings Day celebration reunite to share *atole* and tamales at a party hosted by the recipient of the doll found in the Rosca. February 2.

**Constitution Day (Día de la Constitución).** National holiday. Celebration in honor of the signing of the constitution that currently governs Mexico, signed in 1917 as a result of the revolutionary war of 1910. This holiday is celebrated with small parades. February 5.

**Carnaval.** This celebration takes place over the 3 days preceding Ash Wednesday and the beginning of Lent. It is celebrated with special gusto in Cozumel, where it resembles Mardi Gras in New Orleans, with a festive atmosphere and parades. Transportation and hotels are packed, so it's best to make reservations well in advance and arrive a couple of days before the celebrations begin.

**Ash Wednesday.** The start of Lent and a time of abstinence, this is a day of reverence nationwide, but some towns honor it with folk dancing and fairs.

## March

**Benito Juárez's Birthday.** National holiday. Small hometown celebrations crop up countrywide. March 21.

**Spring Equinox,** Chichén Itzá. On the first day of spring, the Temple of Kukulkán—Chichén Itzá's main pyramid—aligns with the sun, and the shadow of the plumed serpent moves slowly from the top of the building down. When the shadow reaches the bottom, the body joins the carved stone snake's head at the base of the pyramid. According to ancient legend, at the moment that the serpent is whole, the earth is fertilized to ensure a bountiful growing season. Visitors come from around the world to marvel at this sight, so advance arrangements are advisable. The serpent view is at its peak on March 21, but the shadow can be seen from March 19 to 23. Elsewhere, the equinox is celebrated with festivals and celebrations to welcome spring in the custom of the ancient Mexicans, with dances and prayers to the elements and the four cardinal points, to renew their energy for the year. It's customary to wear white with a red ribbon.

## April

**Holy Week (Semana Santa).** This celebrates the last week in the life of Christ from Palm Sunday to Easter Sunday with somber religious processions almost nightly, spoofing of Judas, and reenactments of specific biblical events, plus food and craft fairs. Businesses close during this traditional week of Mexican national vacations.

If you plan on traveling to or around Mexico during Holy Week, make your reservations early. Airline seats on flights into and out of the country will be reserved months in advance. Buses to almost anywhere in Mexico will be full, so try arriving on the Wednesday or Thursday before Good Friday. The week following Easter is also a traditional vacation period.

## May

**Labor Day.** National holiday. Workers' parades take place countrywide, and everything closes. May 1.

**Holy Cross Day (Día de la Santa Cruz).** Workers place a cross on top of unfinished buildings and celebrate with food, bands, folk dancing, and fireworks around the work site. May 3.

**Cinco de Mayo.** National holiday. This holiday celebrates the defeat of the French at the Battle of Puebla. May 5.

**Feast of San Isidro.** The patron saint of farmers is honored with a blessing of seeds and work animals. May 15.

**Cancún Jazz Festival.** For dates and schedule information, check ℭ **800/ 44-MEXICO** or www.cancun.info.

### June

**Navy Day (Día de la Marina).** All coastal towns celebrate with naval parades and fireworks. June 1.

**Corpus Christi.** Nationwide. The day honors the Body of Christ (the Eucharist) with religious processions, Masses, and food. Dates vary.

**Día de San Pedro (St. Peter and St. Paul's Day).** Nationwide. Celebrated wherever St. Peter is the patron saint, this holiday honors anyone named Pedro or Peter. June 26.

### August

**Assumption of the Virgin Mary.** This is celebrated throughout the country with special Masses and in some places with processions. August 15 to 17.

### September

**Independence Day.** This day of parades, picnics, and family reunions throughout the country celebrates Mexico's independence from Spain. At 11pm on September 15, the president of Mexico gives the famous independence *grito* (shout) from the National Palace in Mexico City, and local mayors do the same in every town and municipality all over Mexico. On September 16, every city and town conducts a parade in which both government and civilians display their pride in being Mexican. For these celebrations, all important government buildings are draped in the national colors—red, green, and white—and the towns blaze with lights. September 15 and 16; September 16 is a national holiday.

**Fall Equinox,** Chichén Itzá. The same shadow play that occurs during the spring equinox repeats at the fall equinox. September 21 to 22.

### October

**"Ethnicity Day" or Columbus Day (Día de la Raza).** This commemorates the fusion of the Spanish and Mexican peoples. October 12.

### November

**Day of the Dead (Día de los Muertos).** What's commonly called the Day of the Dead is actually 2 days: All Saints' Day, honoring saints and deceased children, and All Souls' Day, honoring deceased adults. Relatives gather at cemeteries countrywide, carrying candles and food, and often spend the night beside the graves of loved ones. Weeks before, bakers begin producing bread formed in the shape of mummies or round loaves decorated with bread "bones." Decorated sugar skulls emblazoned with glittery names are sold everywhere. Many days ahead, homes and churches erect special altars laden with Day of the Dead bread, fruit, flowers, candles, favorite foods, and photographs of saints and of the deceased. On the 2 nights, children dress in costumes and masks, often carrying through the streets mock coffins and pumpkin lanterns, into which they expect money will be dropped. November 1 and 2; November 1 is a national holiday.

**Revolution Day.** National holiday. This commemorates the start of the Mexican Revolution in 1910 with parades, speeches, rodeos, and patriotic events. November 20.

**Sixth Annual Yucatán Bird Festival,** Mérida, Yucatán. Bird-watching sessions, workshops, and exhibits are the highlights of this festival, designed to illustrate the special role birds play in our environment and in the Yucatán territory. Call ✆ **800/44-MEXICO** or check out www.yucatanbirds.org.mx for details. Mid-November.

## December

**Feast of the Virgin of Guadalupe.** Throughout the country, religious processions, street fairs, dancing, fireworks, and Masses honor the patroness of Mexico. This is one of Mexico's most moving and beautiful displays of traditional culture. The Virgin of Guadalupe appeared to a young man, Juan Diego, in December 1531, on a hill near Mexico City. He convinced the bishop that he had seen the apparition by revealing his cloak, upon which the Virgin was emblazoned. It's customary for children to dress up as Juan Diego, wearing mustaches and red bandannas. One of the most famous and elaborate celebrations takes place at the Basílica of Guadalupe, north of Mexico City, where the Virgin appeared. Every village celebrates this day, though, often with processions of children carrying banners of the Virgin and with *charreadas* (rodeos), bicycle races, dancing, and fireworks. December 12.

**Christmas Posadas.** On each of the 9 nights before Christmas, it's customary to reenact the Holy Family's search for an inn, with door-to-door candlelit processions in cities and villages nationwide. These are also hosted by most businesses and community organizations, taking the place of the northern tradition of a Christmas party. December 15 to 24.

**Christmas.** Mexicans extend this celebration and often leave their jobs beginning 2 weeks before Christmas all the way through New Year's Day. Many businesses close, and resorts and hotels fill up. Significant celebrations take place on December 24.

**New Year's Eve.** As in the rest of the world, New Year's Eve in Mexico is celebrated with parties, fireworks, and plenty of noise. December 31.

## 6 Travel Insurance

Check your existing insurance policies and credit card coverage before you buy travel insurance. You may already be covered for lost luggage, canceled tickets, or medical expenses. The cost of travel insurance varies widely, depending on the cost and length of your trip, your age and health, and the type of trip you're taking, but expect to pay between 5% and 8% of the vacation itself. You can get estimates from various providers through **InsureMyTrip.com.** Enter your trip cost and dates, your age, and other information, for prices from more than a dozen companies.

If you'll be driving in Mexico, see "Getting There: By Car" and "Getting Around Mexico: By Car," later in this chapter, for information on **collision** and **damage** and **personal accident insurance.**

### TRIP-CANCELLATION INSURANCE

Trip-cancellation insurance will help retrieve your money if you have to back out of a trip or depart early, or if your travel supplier goes bankrupt. Permissible reasons for trip cancellation can range from sickness to natural disasters to the State Department declaring a destination unsafe for travel.

For more information, contact one of the following recommended insurers: **Access America** (✆ 866/807-3982; www.accessamerica.com); **Travel Guard International** (✆ 800/826-4919; www.travelguard.com); **Travel Insured International**

(© 800/243-3174; www.travelinsured.com); and **Travelex Insurance Services** (© 888/457-4602; www.travelex-insurance.com).

**MEDICAL INSURANCE** For travel overseas, most health plans (including Medicare and Medicaid) do not provide coverage, and the ones that do often require you to pay for services upfront and reimburse you only after you return home. Even if your plan does cover overseas treatment, most out-of-country hospitals make you pay your bills upfront, and send you a refund only after you've returned home and filed the necessary paperwork with your insurance company. As a safety net, you may want to buy travel medical insurance, particularly if you're traveling to a remote or high-risk area where emergency evacuation is a possible scenario. If you require additional medical insurance, try **MEDEX Assistance** (© 410/453-6300; www.medexassist.com) or **Travel Assistance International** (© 800/821-2828; www.travelassistance.com; for general information on services,

call the company's Worldwide Assistance Services, Inc., at © **800/777-8710,** or go to www.worldwideassitance.com).

**LOST-LUGGAGE INSURANCE** On flights within the U.S., checked baggage is covered up to $2,500 per ticketed passenger. On international flights (including U.S. portions of international trips), baggage coverage is limited to approximately $9.07 per pound, up to approximately $635 per checked bag. If you plan to check items more valuable than what's covered by the standard liability, see if your homeowner's policy covers your valuables, get baggage insurance as part of your comprehensive travel-insurance package, or buy Travel Guard's "BagTrak" product.

If your luggage is lost, immediately file a lost-luggage claim at the airport, detailing the luggage contents. Most airlines require that you report delayed, damaged, or lost baggage within 4 hours of arrival. The airlines are required to deliver luggage, once found, directly to your house or destination free of charge.

## 7 Health & Safety

### STAYING HEALTHY
### GENERAL AVAILABILITY OF HEALTHCARE

In most of the Yucatán's resort destinations, healthcare meeting U.S. standards is now available. Mexico's major cities are also known for their excellent healthcare, although the facilities available may be sparser, and equipment older than what is available at home. Prescription medicine is broadly available at Mexico pharmacies; however be aware that you may need a copy of your prescription, or to obtain a prescription from a local doctor.

Contact the **International Association for Medical Assistance to Travelers** (**IAMAT;** © **716/754-4883,** or 416/652-0137 in Canada; www.iamat.org) for tips on travel and health concerns in the

countries you're visiting, and lists of local, English-speaking doctors. The U.S. **Centers for Disease Control and Prevention** (© **800/311-3435;** www.cdc.gov) provides up-to-date information on health hazards by region or country and offers tips on food safety. The website **www.trip prep.com**, sponsored by a consortium of travel medicine practitioners, may also offer helpful advice on traveling abroad. You can find listings of reliable clinics overseas at the **International Society of Travel Medicine** (www.istm.org).

### COMMON AILMENTS

**HIGH-ALTITUDE HAZARDS** Travelers to certain regions of Mexico occasionally experience **elevation sickness,** which results from the relative lack of oxygen and

---

**Tips** **Over-the-Counter Drugs in Mexico**

Antibiotics and other drugs that you'd need a prescription to buy in the States are available over-the-counter in Mexican pharmacies. Mexican pharmacies also carry a limited selection of common over-the-counter cold, sinus, and allergy remedies.

---

the decrease in barometric pressure that characterizes high elevations (more than 1,515m/4,969 ft.). Symptoms include shortness of breath, fatigue, headache, insomnia, and even nausea. Mexico City is at 2,121m (6,957 ft.) above sea level, as are a number of other central and southern cities, such as San Cristóbal de las Casas (even higher than Mexico City). At high elevations, it takes about 10 days to acquire the extra red blood corpuscles you need to adjust to the scarcity of oxygen. To help your body acclimate, drink plenty of fluids, avoid alcoholic beverages, and don't overexert yourself during the first few days. If you have heart or lung problems, talk to your doctor before going above 2,424m (7,951 ft.).

**BUGS, BITES & OTHER WILDLIFE CONCERNS** **Mosquitoes** and **gnats** are prevalent along the coast and in the Yucatán lowlands. Insect repellent *(repelente contra insectos)* is a must, and it's not always available in Mexico. If you'll be in these areas and are prone to bites, bring along a repellent that contains the active ingredient DEET. Avon's Skin So Soft also works extremely well. Another good remedy to keep the mosquitoes away is to mix citronella essential oil with basil, clove, and lavender essential oils. If you're sensitive to bites, pick up some antihistamine cream from a drugstore at home.

Most readers won't ever see a scorpion *(alacrán).* But if one stings you, go immediately to a doctor. In Mexico you can buy scorpion toxin antidote at any drugstore. It is an injection and it costs around $25. This is a good idea if you plan to

camp in a remote area where medical assistance can be several hours away.

**MORE SERIOUS DISEASES** You shouldn't be overly concerned about tropical diseases if you stay on the normal tourist routes and don't eat street food. However, both dengue fever and cholera have appeared in Mexico in recent years. Talk to your doctor or to a medical specialist in tropical diseases about precautions you should take. You can also get medical bulletins from the U.S. State Department and the Centers for Disease Control and Prevention (see "Visitor Information," earlier in this chapter). You can protect yourself by taking some simple precautions: Watch what you eat and drink; don't swim in stagnant water (ponds, slow-moving rivers, or wells); and avoid mosquito bites by covering up, using repellent, and sleeping under netting. The most dangerous areas seem to be on Mexico's west coast, away from the big resorts.

**WHAT TO DO IF YOU GET SICK AWAY FROM HOME**

Any foreign consulate can provide a list of area doctors who speak English. If you get sick, consider asking your hotel concierge to recommend a local doctor—even his or her own. You can also try the emergency room at a local hospital. Many hospitals also have walk-in clinics for emergency cases that are not life-threatening; you may not get immediate attention, but you won't pay the high price of an emergency room visit. We list hospitals and emergency numbers under "Fast Facts" in each destination's chapter.

If you suffer from a chronic illness, consult your doctor before you depart. For conditions like epilepsy, diabetes, or heart problems, wear a **MedicAlert Identification Tag** (© **888/633-4298;** www.medicalert.org), which will immediately alert doctors to your condition and give them access to your records through MedicAlert's 24-hour hot line.

Pack **prescription medications** in your carry-on luggage, and carry them in their original containers, with pharmacy labels—otherwise they won't make it through airport security. Also bring along copies of your prescriptions in case you lose your pills or run out. Don't forget an extra pair of contact lenses or prescription glasses. Carry the generic name of prescription medicines, in case a local pharmacist is unfamiliar with the brand name.

Contact the **International Association for Medical Assistance to Travelers** (© **716/754-4883** or 416/652-0137; www.iamat.org) for tips on travel and health concerns in Mexico and lists of local English-speaking doctors. The U.S. **Centers for Disease Control and Prevention** (© **800/311-3435;** www.cdc.gov) provides up-to-date information on necessary vaccines and health hazards by region or country.

**EMERGENCY EVACUATION** In extreme medical emergencies, a service from the United States will fly people to American hospitals. **Global Lifeline** (© **888/554-9729,** or 01-800/305-9400 in Mexico; www.globallifeflight.com) is a 24-hour air ambulance. Other companies also offer air evacuation service; for a list, refer to the U.S. State Department website, http://travel.state.gov.

## STAYING SAFE
### CRIME
I have lived and traveled in Mexico for more than a dozen years, have never had any serious trouble, and rarely feel suspicious of anyone or any situation. You will probably feel physically safer in most Mexican cities and villages than in any comparable place at home. However, crime in Mexico has received attention in the North American press over the past several years. Many feel this unfairly exaggerates the real dangers, but it should be noted that crime, including taxi robberies, kidnappings, and highway carjackings, is on the rise. The most severe problems have been concentrated in Mexico City, where even longtime foreign residents will attest to the overall lack of security. Isolated incidents have also occurred in Cancún, Ixtapa, Baja, and even traditionally tranquil Puerto Escondido. Check the U.S. State Department advisory before you travel for any notable "hot spots." See "Visitor Information," earlier in this chapter, for information on the latest **U.S. State Department advisories.**

Precautions are necessary, but travelers should be realistic. Common sense is essential. You can generally trust people whom you approach for help or directions—but be wary of anyone who approaches you offering the same. The more insistent the person is, the more cautious you should be. The crime rate is, on the whole, much lower in Mexico than in most parts of the United States, and the nature of crimes in general is less violent—most crime is motivated by robbery or jealousy. Random, violent, or serial crime is essentially unheard of in Mexico. You are much more likely to meet kind and helpful Mexicans than you are to encounter those set on thievery and deceit. (See also "Emergencies" under "Fast Facts: Mexico," later in this chapter.)

### BRIBES & SCAMS
As is the case around the world, there are the occasional bribes and scams in Mexico, targeted at people believed to be naive—such as the telltale tourist. For years, Mexico was known as a place where

bribes—called *mordidas* (bites)—were expected; however, the country is rapidly changing. Frequently, offering a bribe today, especially to a police officer, is considered an insult, and it can land you in deeper trouble.

If you believe a **bribe** is being requested, here are a few tips on dealing with the situation. Even if you speak Spanish, don't utter a word of it to Mexican officials. That way you'll appear innocent, all the while understanding every word.

When you are crossing the border, should the person who inspects your car ask for a tip, you can ignore this request—but understand that the official may suddenly decide that a complete search of your belongings is in order. If faced with a situation where you feel you're being asked for a *propina* (literally, "tip"; colloquially, "bribe"), how much should you offer? Usually $3 to $5 or the equivalent in pesos will do the trick. Many tourists have the impression that everything works better in Mexico if you "tip," however, in reality, this only perpetuates the *mordida* attitude. If you are pleased with a service, feel free to tip, but you shouldn't tip simply to attempt to get away with something illegal or inappropriate, whether it is crossing the border without having your car inspected or not getting a ticket that's deserved.

Whatever you do, **avoid impoliteness;** under no circumstances should you insult a Latin American official. Extreme politeness, even in the face of adversity, rules Mexico. In Mexico, *gringos* have a reputation for being loud and demanding. By adopting the local custom of excessive courtesy, you'll have greater success in negotiations of any kind. Stand your ground, but do it politely.

As you travel in Mexico, you may encounter several types of **scams,** which are typical throughout the world. One involves some kind of a **distraction** or feigned commotion. While your attention is diverted, a pickpocket makes a grab for your wallet. In another common scam, an **unaccompanied child** pretends to be lost and frightened and takes your hand for safety. Meanwhile the child or an accomplice plunders your pockets. A third involves **confusing currency.** A shoeshine boy, street musician, guide, or other individual might offer you a service for a price that seems reasonable—in pesos. When it comes time to pay, he or she tells you the price is in dollars, not pesos. Be very clear on the price and currency when services are involved.

## ECOTOURISM

The **International Ecotourism Society (TIES)** defines ecotourism as "responsible travel to natural areas that conserves the environment and improves the well-being of local people." You can find ecofriendly travel tips, statistics, and touring companies and associations—listed by destination under "Travel Choice"—at the TIES website, www.ecotourism.org. **Ecotravel.com** is part online magazine and part ecodirectory that lets you search for touring companies in several categories (water-based, land-based, spiritually oriented, and so on). Also check out **Conservation International** (www. conservation.org)—which, with *National Geographic Traveler,* annually presents **World Legacy Awards** (www.wlaward.org) to those travel tour operators, businesses, organizations, and places that have made a significant contribution to sustainable tourism.

For information about the ethics of swimming with dolphins and other outdoor activities, visit the **Whale and Dolphin Conservation Society** (www.wdcs.org) and **Tread Lightly** (www.treadlightly.org).

For companies that specialize in ecotourism in Mexico, see "The Active Traveler," later in this chapter.

## *Tips* Treating & Avoiding Digestive Trouble

It's called "travelers' diarrhea" or *turista,* the Spanish word for "tourist": persistent diarrhea, often accompanied by fever, nausea, and vomiting, that used to attack many travelers to Mexico. (Some in the U.S. call this "Montezuma's revenge," but you won't hear it called that in Mexico.) Widespread improvements in infrastructure, sanitation, and education have practically eliminated this ailment, especially in well-developed resort areas. Most travelers make a habit of drinking only bottled water, which also helps to protect against unfamiliar bacteria. In resort areas, and generally throughout Mexico, only purified ice is used. If you do come down with this ailment, nothing beats Pepto Bismol, readily available in Mexico. Imodium is also available in Mexico and is used by many travelers for a quick fix. A good high-potency (or "therapeutic") vitamin supplement and even extra vitamin C can help; yogurt is good for healthy digestion.

Since dehydration can quickly become life-threatening, the Public Health Service advises that you be careful to replace fluids and electrolytes (potassium, sodium, and the like) during a bout of diarrhea. Drink Pedialyte, a rehydration solution available at most Mexican pharmacies, or natural fruit juice, such as guava or apple (stay away from orange juice, which has laxative properties), with a pinch of salt added.

*How to prevent it:* The U.S. Public Health Service recommends the following measures for preventing travelers' diarrhea: **Drink only purified water** (boiled water, canned or bottled beverages, beer, or wine). **Choose food carefully.** In general, avoid salads (except in first-class restaurants), uncooked vegetables, undercooked protein, and unpasteurized milk or milk products, including cheese. Choose food that is freshly cooked and still hot. In addition, something as simple as **clean hands** can go a long way toward preventing *turista.*

## 8 Specialized Travel Resources

### FAMILY TRAVEL

Children are considered the national treasure of Mexico, and Mexicans will warmly welcome and cater to your children. Many parents were reluctant to bring young children into Mexico in the past, primarily due to health concerns, but I can't think of a better place to introduce children to the exciting adventure of exploring a different culture. Cancún is one of the best destinations. Hotels can often arrange for a babysitter.

Before leaving, ask your doctor which medications to take along. Disposable diapers cost about the same in Mexico but are of poorer quality. You can get Huggies Supreme and Pampers identical to the ones sold in the United States, but at a higher price. Many stores sell Gerber's baby foods. Dry cereals, powdered formulas, baby bottles, and purified water are easily available in midsize and large cities or resorts.

Cribs may present a problem; only the largest and most luxurious hotels provide them. However, rollaway beds are often available. Child seats or highchairs at restaurants are common.

Consider bringing your own car seat; they are not readily available for rent in Mexico.

Every country's regulations differ, but in general children traveling abroad should have plenty of documentation on hand, particularly if they're traveling with someone other than their own parents (in which case a notarized form letter from a parent is often required). For details on entry requirements for children traveling abroad, go to the U.S. State Department website (www.travel.state.gov); click on "International Travel," "Travel Brochures," and "Foreign Entry Requirements."

Throughout this book, the "Kids" icon distinguishes attractions, hotels, restaurants, and other destinations that are particularly attractive and accommodating to children and families.

**Familyhostel** (© **800/733-9753;** www.learn.unh.edu/familyhostel) takes the whole family, including kids ages 8 to 15, on moderately priced domestic and international learning vacations. Lectures, fields trips, and sightseeing are guided by a team of academics.

Recommended family travel Internet sites include **Family Travel Forum** (www.familytravelforum.com), a comprehensive site that offers customized trip planning; **Family Travel Network** (www.familytravelnetwork.com), an award-winning site that offers travel features, deals, and tips; **Traveling Internationally with Your Kids** (www.travelwithyourkids.com), a comprehensive site offering sound advice for long-distance and international travel with children; and **Family Travel Files** (www.thefamilytravelfiles.com), which offers an online magazine and a directory of off-the-beaten-path tours and tour operators for families.

## TRAVELERS WITH DISABILITIES

Mexico may seem like one giant obstacle course to travelers in wheelchairs or on crutches. At airports, you may encounter steep stairs before finding a well-hidden elevator or escalator—if one exists. Airlines will often arrange wheelchair assistance to the baggage area. Porters are generally available to help with luggage at airports and large bus stations, once you've cleared baggage claim.

Mexican airports are upgrading their services, but it is not uncommon to board from a remote position, meaning you either descend stairs to a bus that ferries you to the plane, which you board by climbing stairs, or you walk across the tarmac to your plane and ascend the stairs. Deplaning presents the same problem in reverse.

Escalators (and there aren't many in the country) are often out of order. Stairs without handrails abound. Few restrooms are equipped for travelers with disabilities; when one is available, access to it may be through a narrow passage that won't accommodate a wheelchair or a person on crutches. Many deluxe hotels (the most expensive) now have rooms with bathrooms for people with disabilities. Those traveling on a budget should stick with one-story hotels or hotels with elevators. Even so, there will probably still be obstacles somewhere. Generally speaking, no matter where you are, someone will lend a hand, although you may have to ask for it.

Most disabilities shouldn't stop anyone from traveling. There are more options and resources out there than ever before.

Many travel agencies offer customized tours and itineraries for travelers with disabilities. **Flying Wheels Travel** (© **507/451-5005;** www.flyingwheelstravel.com) offers escorted tours and cruises that emphasize sports and private tours in minivans with lifts. **Access-Able Travel Source** (© **303/232-2979;** www.accessable.com) offers extensive access information and advice for traveling around the world with disabilities. **Accessible**

Journeys (© 800/846-4537 or 610/521-0339; www.disabilitytravel.com) caters specifically to slow walkers and wheelchair travelers and their families and friends.

Organizations that offer assistance to disabled travelers include **MossRehab** (© **1-800-CALLMOSS** or 215/456-9900; www.mossresourcenet.org), which provides a library of accessible-travel resources online; the **American Foundation for the Blind (AFB)** (© **800/232-5463;** www.afb.org), a referral resource for the blind or visually impaired that includes information on traveling with Seeing Eye dogs; and **SATH** (Society for Accessible Travel & Hospitality) (© **212/447-7284;** www.sath.org; annual membership fees: $45 adults, $30 seniors and students), which offers a wealth of travel resources for all types of disabilities and informed recommendations on destinations, access guides, travel agents, tour operators, vehicle rentals, and companion services. **AirAmbulanceCard.com** is now partnered with SATH and allows you to preselect top-notch hospitals in case of an emergency for $195 a year ($295 per family), among other benefits.

For more information, check out the quarterly magazine *Emerging Horizons* (www.emerginghorizons.com; $15 per year, $20 outside the U.S.); and *Open World* magazine, published by SATH (see above; subscription: $13 per year, $21 outside the U.S.).

## SENIOR TRAVEL

Mexico is a popular country for retirees. For decades, North Americans have been living indefinitely in Mexico by returning to the border and recrossing with a new tourist permit every 6 months. Mexican immigration officials have caught on, and now limit the maximum time in the country to 6 months within any year. This is to encourage even partial residents to acquire proper documentation.

Some of the most popular places for long-term stays are Guadalajara, Lake Chapala, Ajijic, and Puerto Vallarta, all in the state of Jalisco; San Miguel de Allende and Guanajuato in Guanajuato state; Cuernavaca in Morelos; and Alamos in Sinaloa.

*AIM,* Apdo. Postal 31–70, 45050 Guadalajara, Jal., is a well-written, informative newsletter for prospective retirees. Issues have evaluated retirement in Aguascalientes, Puebla, San Cristóbal de las Casas, Puerto Angel, Puerto Escondido and Huatulco, Oaxaca, Taxco, Tepic, Manzanillo, Melaque, and Barra de Navidad. Subscriptions are $18 to the United States and $25 to Canada. Back issues are three for $5.

**Sanborn Tours,** 2015 S. 10th St., Post Office Drawer 519, McAllen, TX 78505-0519 (© **800/395-8482;** www.sanborns.com) offers a "Retire in Mexico" orientation tour.

Mention the fact that you're a senior when you make your travel reservations. Although all of the major U.S. airlines except America West have canceled their senior discount and coupon book programs, many hotels still offer discounts for seniors.

Members of **AARP** (formerly known as the American Association of Retired Persons), 601 E St. NW, Washington, DC 20049 (© **888/687-2277;** www.aarp.org), get discounts on hotels, airfares, and car rentals. AARP offers members a wide range of benefits, including *AARP: The Magazine* and a monthly newsletter. Anyone over 50 can join.

Many reliable agencies and organizations target the 50-plus market. **Elderhostel** (© **877/426-8056;** www.elderhostel.org) arranges study programs for those aged 55 and over (and a spouse or companion of any age) in the U.S. and in more than 80 countries around the world. Most courses last 5 to 7 days in the U.S.

(2–4 weeks abroad), and many include airfare, accommodations in university dormitories or modest inns, meals, and tuition. **ElderTreks** (✆ **800/741-7956;** www.eldertreks.com) offers small-group tours to off-the-beaten-path or adventure-travel locations, restricted to travelers 50 and older. Recommended publications offering travel resources and discounts for seniors include the quarterly magazine *Travel 50 & Beyond* (www.travel50 andbeyond.com); *Travel Unlimited: Uncommon Adventures for the Mature Traveler* (Avalon); *101 Tips for Mature Travelers,* available from Grand Circle Travel (✆ **800/221-2610** or 617/ 350-7500; www.gct.com); and *Unbelievably Good Deals and Great Adventures That You Absolutely Can't Get Unless You're Over 50* (McGraw-Hill), by Joann Rattner Heilman.

## GAY & LESBIAN TRAVELERS

Mexico is a conservative country, with deeply rooted Catholic religious traditions. Public displays of same-sex affection are rare and still considered shocking for men, especially outside of urban or resort areas. Women in Mexico frequently walk hand in hand, but anything more would cross the boundary of acceptability. However, gay and lesbian travelers are generally treated with respect and should not experience any harassment, assuming they give the appropriate regard to local culture and customs.

The **International Gay and Lesbian Travel Association (IGLTA;** ✆ **800/448-8550** or 954/776-2626; www.iglta.org) is the trade association for the gay and lesbian travel industry, and offers an online directory of gay- and lesbian-friendly travel businesses; go to their website and click on "Members."

Many agencies offer tours and travel itineraries specifically for gay and lesbian travelers. **Above and Beyond Tours** (✆ **800/397-2681;** www.abovebeyond tours.com) is the exclusive gay and lesbian tour operator for United Airlines. **Now, Voyager** (✆ **800/255-6951;** www. nowvoyager.com) is a well-known San Francisco–based, gay-owned and -operated travel service. **Olivia Cruises & Resorts** (✆ **800/631-6277;** www.olivia.com) charters entire resorts and ships for exclusive lesbian vacations and offers smaller group experiences for both gay and lesbian travelers. (In 2005, tennis great Martina Navratilova was named Olivia's official spokesperson.)

**Gay.com Travel** (✆ **800/929-2268** or 415/644-8044; www.gay.com/travel or www.outandabout.com), is an excellent online successor to the popular *Out & About* print magazine. It provides regularly updated information about gay-owned, gay-oriented, and gay-friendly lodging, dining, sightseeing, nightlife, and shopping establishments in every important destination worldwide. It also offers trip-planning information for gay and lesbian travelers for more than 50 destinations, along various themes, ranging from "Sex & Travel" to "Vacations for Couples."

The following travel guides are available at many bookstores, or you can order them from any online bookseller: *Frommer's Gay & Lesbian Europe* (www.frommers. com), an excellent travel resource to the top European cities and resorts; *Spartacus International Gay Guide* (Bruno Gmünder Verlag; www.spartacusworld. com/gayguide) and *Odysseus: The International Gay Travel Planner* (Odysscus Enterprises Ltd.), both good, annual, English-language guidebooks focused on gay men; and the *Damron* guides (www. damron.com), with separate, annual books for gay men and lesbians.

## STUDENT TRAVEL

Because Mexicans consider higher education more a luxury than a birthright,

---

**Tips  Advice for Female Travelers**

As a female traveling alone, I feel safer traveling in Mexico than in the United States. But I use the same common-sense precautions I use anywhere else in the world and am alert to what's going on around me. Mexicans in general, and men in particular, are nosy about single travelers, especially women. If a taxi driver or anyone else with whom you don't want to become friendly asks about your marital status, family, and so forth, my advice is to make up a set of answers (regardless of the truth): "I'm married, traveling with friends, and I have three children." Saying you're single and traveling alone may send the wrong message. U.S. television—widely viewed now in Mexico—has given many Mexican men the image of American single women as being sexually promiscuous. Check out the award-winning website **Journeywoman** (www. journeywoman.com), a "real-life" women's travel information network; or the travel guide *Safety and Security for Women Who Travel* by Sheila Swan and Peter Laufer (Travelers' Tales, Inc.), offering common-sense tips on safe travel.

---

there is no formal network of student discounts and programs. Most Mexican students travel with their families rather than with other students, so student discount cards are not commonly recognized.

However, more hostels have entered the student travel scene. The **Mexican Youth Hostel Network,** or Red Mexicana de Albergues Juveniles (www.hostelling mexico.com), offers a list of hostels that meet international standards in Mexico City, Cuernavaca and surrounding areas, Oaxaca, and Veracruz. The **Mexican Youth Hostel Association,** or Asociación Mexicana de Albergues Juveniles (www. hostels.com./en/mx.html), offers a list of hostels in Mexico City, Zacatecas, Guanajuato, Puerto Escondido, Uxmal, Palenque, Tulum, Cancún, and Playa del Carmen.

If you're a student planning to travel outside the U.S., you'd be wise to arm yourself with an **International Student Identity Card (ISIC),** which offers substantial savings on rail passes, plane tickets, and entrance fees. It also provides you with basic health and life insurance and a 24-hour help line. The card is available for $22 from **STA Travel** (© 800/781-4040 in North America; www.sta.com or www.statravel.com), the biggest student travel agency in the world. If you're no longer a student but are still under 26, you can get a **International Youth Travel Card (IYTC)** for the same price from the same people, which entitles you to some discounts (but not on museum admissions). **Travel CUTS** (© 800/667-2887 or 416/614-2887; www.travelcuts.com) offers similar services for both Canadians and U.S. residents. Irish students may prefer to turn to **USIT** (© 01/602-1600; www.usitnow.ie), an Ireland-based specialist in student, youth, and independent travel.

## 9 Planning Your Trip Online

### SURFING FOR AIRFARES

The "big three" online travel agencies, **Expedia.com, Travelocity,** and **Orbitz** sell most of the air tickets bought on the Internet. (Canadian travelers should try expedia.ca and travelocity.ca; U.K. residents can go for expedia.co.uk and opodo.co.uk.) **Kayak.com** is also gaining popularity and uses a sophisticated search engine (developed at MIT). Each has different business deals with the airlines and may offer different fares on the same flights, so it's wise to shop around. Expedia, Kayak, and Travelocity will also send you **e-mail notification** when a cheap fare becomes available to your favorite destination. Of the smaller travel-agency websites, **SideStep** (www.side step.com) has gotten the best reviews from Frommer's authors. The website (with optional browser add-on) purports to "search 140 sites at once," but in reality only beats competitors' fares as often as other sites do.

Also remember to check **airline websites,** especially those for low-fare carriers such as Southwest, whose fares are often misreported or simply missing from travel agency websites. Even with major airlines, you can often shave a few bucks from a fare by booking directly through the airline and avoiding a travel agency's transaction fee. But you'll get these discounts only by **booking online:** Most airlines now offer online-only fares that even their phone agents know nothing about. For the websites of airlines that fly to and from your destination, go to "Getting There," later in this chapter.

Great **last-minute deals** are available through free weekly e-mail services provided directly by the airlines. Most of these are announced on Tuesday or Wednesday and must be purchased online. Most are only valid for travel that weekend, but some (such as Southwest's) can be booked weeks or months in advance. Sign up for weekly e-mail alerts at airline websites or check megasites that compile comprehensive lists of last-minute specials, such as **SmarterTravel** (www.smartertravel.com). For last-minute trips, **Site59** (www.site59.com) and **Last MinuteTravel.com** in the U.S. and **lastminute.com** in Europe often have better air-and-hotel package deals than the major-label sites.

If you're willing to give up some control over your flight details, use what is called an "**opaque" fare service** like **Priceline** (www.priceline.com; www.price line.co.uk for Europeans) or its smaller competitor **Hotwire** (www.hotwire.com). Both offer rock-bottom prices in exchange for travel on a "mystery airline" at a mysterious time of day, often with a mysterious change of planes en route. The mystery airlines are all major, well-known

---

*Tips*  **Frommers.com: The Complete Travel Resource**

For an excellent travel-planning resource, we highly recommend **Frommers.com** (www.frommers.com), voted Best Travel Site by *PC Magazine.* We're a little biased, of course, but we guarantee that you'll find the travel tips, reviews, monthly vacation giveaways, bookstore, and online-booking capabilities thoroughly indispensable. Among the special features, you'll find our popular **Destinations** section, where you'll get expert travel tips, hotel and dining recommendations, and advice on the sights to see in more than 3,500 destinations around the globe; the **Frommers.com Newsletter,** with the latest deals, travel trends, and money-saving secrets; and our **Travel Talk** area featuring **Message Boards,** where Frommer's readers post queries and share advice (sometimes even our authors show up to answer questions). When your research is finished, the **Book a Trip** area takes you to Frommer's preferred online partners for booking your vacation at affordable prices.

carriers—and the possibility of being sent from Philadelphia to Chicago via Tampa is remote; the airlines' routing computers have gotten a lot better than they used to be. Your chances of getting a 6am or 11pm flight, however, are still pretty high. Hotwire tells you flight prices before you buy; Priceline usually has better deals than Hotwire, but you have to play their "name our price" game. If you're new at this, the helpful folks at **BiddingForTravel** (www.biddingfortravel.com) do a good job of demystifying Priceline's prices and strategies. Priceline and Hotwire are great for flights within North America and between the U.S. and Europe. But for flights to other parts of the world, consolidators will almost always beat their fares. *Note:* In 2004, Priceline added nonopaque service to its roster. You now have the option to pick exact flights, times, and airlines from a list of offers—or opt to bid on opaque fares as before.

## SURFING FOR HOTELS

Shopping online for hotels is generally done one of two ways: by booking through the hotel's own website or through an independent booking agency (or a fare-service agency like Priceline; see below). These Internet hotel agencies have multiplied in mind-boggling numbers of late. This competitiveness can be a boon to consumers who have the patience and time to shop and compare the online sites for good deals—but shop they must, for prices can vary considerably from site to site. And keep in mind that hotels at the top of a site's listing may be there for no other reason than that they paid money to get the placement.

**Expedia.com** offers a long list of special deals and "virtual tours" or photos of available rooms so you can see what you're paying for (a feature that helps counter the claims that the best rooms are often held back from bargain-booking websites). **Travelocity** posts unvarnished customer reviews and ranks its properties according to the AAA rating system. **Trip Advisor** (www.tripadvisor.com) is another excellent source of unbiased user reviews of hotels around the world. While even the finest hotels can inspire a misleadingly poor review from a picky or crabby traveler, the body of user opinions, when take as a whole, is usually a reliable indicator.

Also reliable are **Hotels.com** and **Quikbook** (www.quikbook.com). An excellent free program, **TravelAxe** (www.travelaxe.net), can help you search multiple hotel sites at once, even ones you may never have heard of—and conveniently lists the total price of the room, including the taxes and service charges. Another booking site, **Travelweb** (www.travelweb.com), is partly owned by the hotels it represents (including the Hilton, Hyatt, and Starwood chains) and is therefore plugged directly into the hotels' reservations systems—unlike independent online agencies, which have to fax or e-mail reservation requests to the hotel, a good portion of which get misplaced in the shuffle. More than once, travelers have arrived at the hotel, only to be told that they have no reservation. To be fair, many of the major sites are undergoing improvements in service and ease of use, and Expedia.com will soon be able to plug directly into the reservations systems of many hotel chains—none of which can be bad news for consumers. In the meantime, it's a good idea to **get a confirmation number** and **make a printout** of any online booking transaction.

In the opaque website category, **Priceline** and **Hotwire** are even better for hotels than for airfares; through both, you're allowed to pick the neighborhood and quality level of your hotel before paying. Priceline's hotel product even covers Europe and Asia, though it's much better at getting five-star lodging for three-star prices than at finding anything at the bottom of the scale. On the down side, many hotels stick Priceline guests in their least desirable rooms. Be sure to go to the BiddingForTravel website (see above) before bidding on a hotel room on Priceline; it features a fairly up-to-date list of hotels that Priceline uses in major cities. For both Priceline and Hotwire, you pay upfront, and the fee is nonrefundable. *Note:* Some hotels do not provide loyalty program credits or points or other frequent-stay amenities when you book a room through opaque online services.

## SURFING FOR RENTAL CARS

For booking rental cars online, the best deals are usually at rental-car company websites, although all the major online travel agencies also offer rental-car reservations services. Priceline and Hotwire work well for rental cars, too; the only "mystery" is which major rental company you get, and for most travelers the difference between Hertz, Avis, and Budget is negligible.

## TRAVEL BLOGS & TRAVELOGUES

More and more travelers are using travel web logs, or **blogs,** to chronicle their journeys online. You can search for blogs about Mexico at **www.travelblog.com** or post your own travelogue at **www.travel blog.org**. For blogs that cover general travel news and highlight various destinations, try **Written Road** (www.written road.com) or Gawker Media's snarky **Gridskipper** (www.gridskipper.com). For more literary travel essays, try **Salon.com** for its travel section (www.salon.com/ wanderlust) and its literary guide (www. salon.com/books/literary_guide), and **World Hum** (www.worldhum.com), which also has an extensive list of other travel-related journals, blogs, online communities, newspaper coverage, and bookstores.

## 10  The 21st-Century Traveler

### INTERNET ACCESS AWAY FROM HOME

Travelers have any number of ways to check their e-mail and tap into the Internet on the road. Of course, using your own laptop—or even a PDA or electronic organizer with a modem—gives you the most flexibility, though dialing long-distance to the United States or Canada from Mexico can be costly. A better option is to gain access to your e-mail and even your office computer from cybercafes.

#### WITHOUT YOUR OWN COMPUTER

It's hard nowadays to find a city or town in Mexico that *doesn't* have a few cybercafes. The "Fast Facts" sections in this book list cybercafes in major destinations. Although there's no definitive directory of cybercafes—these are independent businesses, after all—three places to start looking are

www.cybercaptive.com, www.netcafe guide.com, and www.cybercafe.com.

Aside from formal cybercafes, most **youth hostels** and **public libraries** have Internet access. Avoid **hotel business centers** unless you're willing to pay exorbitant rates.

Most major airports now have **Internet kiosks** scattered throughout their gates. These give you basic Web access for a per-minute fee that's usually higher than cybercafe prices.

#### WITH YOUR OWN COMPUTER

More and more hotels, cafes, and retailers are signing on as Wi-Fi (wireless fidelity) "hotspots." Mac owners have their own networking technology: Apple AirPort. **T-Mobile Hotspot** (www.t-mobile.com/ hotspot) serves up wireless connections at more than 1,000 Starbucks coffee shops nationwide. **Boingo** (www.boingo.com)

and **Wayport** (www.wayport.com) have set up networks in airports and high-class hotel lobbies. IPass providers (see below) also give you access to a few hundred wireless hotel lobby setups. To locate other hotspots that provide **free wireless networks** in cities around the world, go to **www.personaltelco.net/index.cgi/ WirelessCommunities**.

For dial-up access, most business-class hotels throughout the world offer dataports for laptop modems, and a few thousand hotels in the U.S. and Europe now offer free high-speed Internet access. In addition, major Internet Service Providers (ISPs) have **local access numbers** around the world, allowing you to go online by placing a local call. The **iPass** network also has dial-up numbers around the world. You'll have to sign up with an iPass provider, who will then tell you how to set up your computer for your destination(s). For a list of iPass providers, go to www.ipass.com and click on "Individuals Buy Now." One solid provider is **i2roam** (*©* **866/811-6209** or 920/235-0475; www.i2roam.com).

Wherever you go, bring a **connection kit** of the right power and phone adapters, a spare phone cord, and a spare Ethernet network cable—or find out whether your hotel supplies them to guests.

## USING A CELLPHONE

The three letters that define much of the world's **wireless capabilities** are GSM (Global System for Mobiles), a big, seamless network that makes for easy cross-border cellphone use throughout Europe and dozens of other countries worldwide, including Mexico. In the U.S., T-Mobile, AT&T Wireless, and Cingular use this quasi-universal system; in Canada, Microcell and some Rogers customers are GSM, and all Europeans and most Australians use GSM.

If your cellphone is on a GSM system, and you have a world-capable multiband phone such as many Sony Ericsson, Motorola, or Samsung models, you can make and receive calls across civilized areas on much of the globe, from Andorra to Uganda. Just call your wireless operator and ask for international roaming to be activated on your account. Unfortunately, per-minute charges can be high—usually $1 to $1.50 in western Europe and up to $5 in places like Russia and Indonesia.

That's why it's important to buy an "unlocked" world phone from the get-go. Many cellphone operators sell locked phones that restrict you from using any other removable computer memory phone chip (called a **SIM card**) other than the ones they supply. Having an unlocked phone allows you to install a cheap, prepaid SIM card (found at a local retailer) in your destination country. (Show your phone to the salesperson; not all phones work on all networks.) You'll get a local phone number—and much, much lower calling rates. Getting an already locked phone unlocked can be a complicated process, but it can be done; just call your cellular operator and say you'll be going abroad for several months and want to use the phone with a local provider.

For many, **renting** a phone is a good idea. (Even world-phone owners will have to rent new phones if they're traveling to non-GSM regions, such as Japan or Korea.) While you can rent a phone from any number of overseas sites, including kiosks at airports and at car-rental agencies, we suggest renting the phone before you leave home. That way you can give loved ones and business associates your new number, make sure the phone works, and take the phone wherever you go— especially helpful for overseas trips through several countries, where local phone-rental agencies often bill in local currency and may not let you take the phone to another country.

Phone rental isn't cheap. You'll usually pay $40 to $50 per week, plus airtime fees of at least a dollar a minute. If you're traveling to Europe, though, local rental companies often offer free incoming calls within their home country, which can save you big bucks. The bottom line: Shop around.

Two good wireless rental companies are **InTouch USA** (© **800/872-7626;** www.intouchglobal.com) and **RoadPost** (© **888/290-1606** or 905/272-5665; www.roadpost.com). Give them your itinerary, and they'll tell you what wireless products you need. InTouch will also, for free, advise you on whether your existing phone will work overseas; simply call © **703/222-7161** between 9am and 4pm EST, or go to http://intouchglobal.com/travel.htm.

For trips of more than a few weeks spent in one country, **buying a phone** becomes economically attractive, as many nations have cheap, no-questions-asked prepaid phone systems. Once you arrive at your destination, stop by a local cellphone shop and get the cheapest package; you'll probably pay less than $100 for a phone and a starter calling card. Local calls may be as low as 10¢ per minute, and in many countries incoming calls are free.

Wilderness adventurers, or those heading to less-developed countries, might consider renting a **satellite phone ("sat-phone"),** which is different from a cellphone in that it connects to satellites and

## Online Traveler's Toolbox

Veteran travelers usually carry some essential items to make their trips easier. Following is a selection of handy online tools to bookmark and use.

- **Airplane Seating & Food.** Find out which seats to reserve and which to avoid (and more) on major airlines at www.seatguru.com. Check out the type of meal (with photos) you'll likely be served on airlines at www.airlinemeals.com.
- **Foreign Languages for Travelers** (www.travlang.com). Learn basic terms in more than 70 languages.
- **Intellicast** (www.intellicast.com) and **Weather.com** (www.weather.com). Weather forecasts for all 50 states and cities around the world.
- **Mapquest** (www.mapquest.com). Choose a specific address or destination and, in seconds, this site returns a map and detailed directions.
- **Time and Date** (www.timeanddate.com). See what time (and day) it is anywhere in the world.
- **Travel Warnings** (http://travel.state.gov, www.fco.gov.uk/travel, www.voyage.gc.ca, www.dfat.gov.au/consular/advice). These sites report on places where health concerns or unrest might threaten American, British, Canadian, and Australian travelers. Generally, U.S. warnings are the most paranoid; Australian warnings are the most relaxed.
- **Universal Currency Converter** (www.xe.com/ucc). See what your dollar or pound is worth in more than 100 other countries.
- **Visa ATM Locator** (www.visa.com), for locations of PLUS ATMs worldwide, or **MasterCard ATM Locator** (www.mastercard.com), for locations of Cirrus ATMs worldwide.

works where there's no cellular signal or ground-based tower. You can rent satellite phones from **RoadPost** (© 888/290-1606 or 905/272-5665; www.roadpost.com). InTouch USA (see above) offers a wider range of satphones but at higher rates. Per-minute call charges can be even cheaper than roaming charges with a regular cellphone, but the phone itself is more expensive (up to $150 a week), and depending on the service you choose, people calling you may incur high long-distance charges. As of this writing, satphones were outrageously expensive to buy, so don't even think about it.

## 11 Getting There

### BY PLANE

The airline situation in Mexico is rapidly improving, with many new regional carriers offering scheduled service to areas previously not served. In addition to regularly scheduled service, charter service direct from U.S. cities to resorts is making Mexico more accessible. For information about saving money on airfares using the Internet, see "Planning Your Trip Online," earlier in this chapter. Note that in 2006, several new low-cost national carriers were set to debut, resulting from an opening up of Mexico's airline industry, and this should certainly set the stage for more competitive fares in the future.

**THE MAJOR INTERNATIONAL AIRLINES** The main airlines operating direct or nonstop flights from the United States to Mexico include **Aero California** (© 800/237-6225), **Aeromexico** (© 800/237-6639; www.aeromexico.com), **Air France** (© 800/237-2747; www.airfrance.com), **Alaska Airlines** (© 800/252-7522; www.alaskaair.com), **America West** (© 800/327-7810; www.americawest.com), **American Airlines** (© 800/223-5436; www.aa.com), **Continental** (© 800/537-9222; www.continental.com), **Frontier Airlines** (© 800/432-1359; www.frontierairlines.com), **Mexicana** (© 800/531-7921; www.mexicana.com), **Northwest/KLM** (© 800/225-2525; www.nwa.com), **Taca** (© 800/400-8222; www.taca.com), **United** (© 800/538-2929; www.united.com), and **US Airways** (© 800/428-4322; www.usairways.com). **Southwest Airlines** (© 800/435-9792; www.southwest.com) serves the U.S. border.

The main departure points in North America for international airlines are Atlanta, Chicago, Dallas/Fort Worth, Denver, Houston, Los Angeles, Las Vegas, Miami, New York, Orlando, Philadelphia, Phoenix, Raleigh/Durham, San Antonio, San Francisco, Seattle, Toronto, and Washington, D.C.

### FLYING FOR LESS: TIPS FOR GETTING THE BEST AIRFARE

- Passengers who can book their ticket either **long in advance or at the last minute,** or who **fly midweek** or **at less-trafficked hours** may pay a fraction of the full fare. If your schedule is flexible, say so, and ask if you can secure a cheaper fare by changing your flight plans.
- Search **the Internet** for cheap fares (see "Planning Your Trip Online," earlier in this chapter).
- Keep an eye on local newspapers for **promotional specials** or **fare wars,** when airlines lower prices on their most popular routes. You rarely see fare wars offered for peak travel times, but if you can travel in the off-months, you may snag a bargain.
- **Consolidators,** also known as bucket shops, are great sources for international tickets, although they usually can't beat Internet fares within North America. Start by looking in Sunday newspaper travel sections;

> **Tips** | **Getting through the Airport**
>
> • Arrive at the airport 1 hour before a domestic flight and 2 hours before an international flight; if you show up late, tell an airline employee and he or she will probably whisk you to the front of the line.
>
> • Beat the ticket-counter lines by using airport electronic kiosks or even online check-in from your home computer, from which you can print out boarding passes in advance. Curbside check-in is also a good way to avoid lines.
>
> • Bring a current, government-issued photo ID such as a driver's license or passport. Children under 18 do not need government-issued photo IDs for flights within the U.S., but they do for international flights to most countries.
>
> • Speed up security by removing your jacket and shoes before you're screened. In addition, remove metal objects such as big belt buckles. If you've got metallic body parts, a note from your doctor can prevent a long chat with the security screeners.
>
> • Use a TSA-approved lock for your checked luggage. Look for Travel Sentry certified locks at luggage or travel shops and Brookstone stores (or online at www.brookstone.com).

U.S. travelers should focus on the *New York Times, Los Angeles Times,* and *Miami Herald.* For less-developed destinations, small travel agents who cater to immigrant communities in large cities often have the best deals. *Beware:* Bucket shop tickets are usually nonrefundable or rigged with stiff cancellation penalties, often as high as 50% to 75% of the ticket price, and some put you on charter airlines, which may leave at inconvenient times and experience delays. Several reliable consolidators are worldwide and available online. **STA Travel** has been the world's leading consolidator for students since purchasing Council Travel, but their fares are competitive for travelers of all ages. **ELTExpress (Flights.com)** (© 800/TRAV-800; www.eltexpress. com) has excellent fares worldwide, particularly to Europe. They also have "local" websites in 12 countries.

**FlyCheap** (© 800/FLY-CHEAP; www.1800flycheap.com) is owned by package-holiday megalith MyTravel and has especially good fares to sunny destinations. **Air Tickets Direct** (© 800/778-3447; www.airtickets direct.com) is based in Montreal and leverages the currently weak Canadian dollar for low fares; they also book trips to places that U.S. travel agents won't touch, such as Cuba.

• Join **frequent-flier clubs.** Frequent-flier membership doesn't cost a cent, but it does entitle you to better seats, faster response to phone inquiries, and prompter service if your luggage is stolen or your flight is canceled or delayed, or if you want to change your seat. And you don't have to fly to earn points; **frequent-flier credit cards** can earn you thousands of miles for doing your everyday shopping. To play the frequent-flier game to your best advantage, consult

Randy Petersen's **Inside Flyer** (www. insideflyer.com). Petersen and friends review all the programs in detail and post regular updates on changes in policies and trends. Petersen will also field direct questions (via e-mail) if a partner airline refuses to redeem points, for instance, or if you're still not sure after researching the various programs which one is right for you. It's well worth the $12 online subscription fee, good for 1 year.

## LONG-HAUL FLIGHTS: HOW TO STAY COMFORTABLE

Long flights can be trying; stuffy air and cramped seats can make you feel as if you're being sent parcel post in a small box. But with a little advance planning, you can make an otherwise unpleasant experience almost bearable.

- Go to **www.seatguru.com**, which has extensive details about almost every seat on six major U.S. airlines. For international airlines, research firm Skytrax has posted a list of average seat pitches at **www.airlinequality.com**.
- Emergency exit seats and bulkhead seats typically have the most legroom. Emergency exit seats are usually left unassigned until the day of a flight (to ensure that someone able-bodied fills the seats); it's worth getting to the ticket counter early to snag one of these spots for a long flight. Many passengers find that bulkhead seating (the row facing the wall at the front of the cabin) offers more legroom, but keep in mind that bulkheads are where airlines often put baby bassinets, so you may be sitting next to an infant.
- To have two seats for yourself in a three-seat row, try for an aisle seat in a center section toward the back of coach. If you're traveling with a companion, book an aisle and a window seat. Middle seats are usually booked last, so chances are good you'll end up

with three seats to yourselves. And in the event that a third passenger is assigned the middle seat, he or she will probably be more than happy to trade for a window or an aisle.

- Ask about entertainment options. Many airlines offer seatback video systems where you get to choose your movies or play video games—but only on some of their planes. (Boeing 777s are your best bet.)
- To sleep, avoid the last row of any section or the row in front of an emergency exit, as these seats are the least likely to recline. Avoid seats near highly trafficked toilet areas. Avoid seats in the back of many jets—these can be narrower than those in the rest of coach. You also may want to reserve a window seat so you can rest your head and avoid being bumped in the aisle.
- Get up, walk around, and stretch every 60 to 90 minutes to keep your blood flowing. This helps avoid **deep vein thrombosis,** or "economy-class syndrome," a potentially deadly condition caused by sitting in cramped conditions for too long. Other preventive measures include drinking lots of water and avoiding alcohol (see next bullet).
- Drink water before, during, and after your flight to combat the lack of humidity in airplane cabins—which can be drier than the Sahara. Bring a bottle of water on board. Avoid alcohol, which will dehydrate you.
- If you're flying with kids, don't forget to carry on toys, books, pacifiers, and chewing gum to help them relieve ear pressure buildup during ascent and descent. Let each child pack his or her own backpack with favorite toys.

## BY CAR

Driving is not the cheapest way to get to Mexico, but it is the best way to see the country. Even so, you may think twice about taking your own car south of the border once you've pondered the bureaucracy involved. One option is to rent a car once you arrive and tour around a specific region. Rental cars in Mexico are generally new, clean, and well maintained. Although they're pricier than in the United States, discounts are often available for rentals of a week or longer, especially when you make arrangements in advance from the United States. (See "Car Rentals," in the "Getting Around Mexico" section later in this chapter, for more details.)

If, after reading the section that follows, you have additional questions or you want to confirm the current rules, call your nearest Mexican consulate or the Mexican Government Tourist Office. Although travel insurance companies are generally helpful, they may not have the most accurate information. To check on road conditions or to get help with any travel emergency while in Mexico, call ✆ **01-800/482-9832,** or 55/5089-7500 in Mexico City. English-speaking operators staff both numbers.

In addition, check with the **U.S. State Department** (see "Visitor Information," earlier in this chapter) for warnings about dangerous driving areas.

## CAR DOCUMENTS

To drive your car into Mexico, you'll need a **temporary car-importation permit,** which is granted after you provide a required list of documents (see below). The permit can be obtained through Banco del Ejército (Banjercito) officials, who have a desk, booth, or office at the Mexican Customs *(aduana)* building after you cross the border into Mexico.

The following strict requirements for border crossing were accurate at press time:

- **A valid driver's license,** issued outside of Mexico.
- **Current, original car registration and a copy of the original car title.** If the registration or title is in more than one name and not all the named people are traveling with you, a notarized letter from the absent person(s) authorizing use of the vehicle for the trip is required; have it ready. The registration and your credit card (see below) must be in the same name.
- **A valid international major credit card.** With a credit card, you are required to pay only a $23 car-importation fee. The credit card must be in the same name as the car registration. If you do not have a major credit card (American Express, Diners

---

*Tips*  **Carrying Car Documents**

You must carry your temporary car-importation permit, tourist permit (see "Entry Requirements," earlier in this chapter), and, if you purchased it, your proof of Mexican car insurance (see below) in the car at all times. The temporary car-importation permit papers are valid for 6 months to a year, while the tourist permit is usually issued for 30 days. It's a good idea to overestimate the time you'll spend in Mexico, so that if you have to (or want to) stay longer, you'll avoid the hassle of getting your papers extended. Whatever you do, don't overstay either permit. Doing so invites heavy fines, confiscation of your vehicle (which will not be returned), or both. Also remember that 6 months does not necessarily equal 180 days—be sure that you return before the earlier expiration date.

Club, MasterCard, or Visa), you must post a bond or make a deposit equal to the value of the vehicle. Check cards are not accepted.

- **Original immigration documentation.** This is either your tourist permit (FMT) or the original immigration booklet, FM2 or FM3, if you hold more permanent status.
- **A signed declaration promising to return to your country of origin with the vehicle.** Obtain this form (Carta Promesa de Retorno) from AAA or Sanborn's before you go, or from Banjercito officials at the border. There's no charge. The form does not stipulate that you must return by the same border entry through which you entered.
- **Temporary Importation Application.** By signing this form, you state that you are only temporarily importing the car for your personal use and will not be selling it. This is to help regulate the entry and restrict the resale of unauthorized cars and trucks. Make sure the permit is canceled when you return to the U.S.

If you receive your documentation at the border, Mexican officials will make two copies of everything and charge you for the copies. For up-to-the-minute information, a great source is the Customs office in Nuevo Laredo, or Módulo de Importación Temporal de Automóviles, Aduana Nuevo Laredo (Module for the Temporary Importation of Automobiles, Nuevo Laredo Customs) (© **867/712-2071**).

*Important reminder:* Someone else may drive, but the person (or relative of the person) whose name appears on the car-importation permit must *always* be in the car. (If stopped by police, a nonregistered family member driving without the registered driver must be prepared to prove familial relationship to the registered driver—no joke.) Violation of this rule subjects the car to impoundment and the driver to imprisonment, a fine, or both. You can drive a car with foreign license plates only if you have a foreign (non-Mexican) driver's license.

## MEXICAN AUTO INSURANCE

Liability auto insurance is legally required in Mexico. U.S. insurance is invalid; to be insured in Mexico, you must purchase Mexican insurance. Any party involved in an accident who has no insurance may be sent to jail and have his or her car impounded until all claims are settled. This is true even if you just drive across the border to spend the day. U.S. companies that broker Mexican insurance are commonly found at the border crossing, and several quote daily rates.

You can also buy car insurance through **Sanborn's Mexico Insurance,** P.O. Box 52840, 2009 S. 10th, McAllen, TX (© **956/686-3601;** fax 800/222-0158 or 956/686-0732; www.sanbornsinsurance.com). The company has offices at all U.S. border crossings. Its policies cost the same as the competition's do, but you get legal coverage (attorney and bail bonds if needed) and a detailed mile-by-mile guide for your proposed route. Most of the Sanborn's border offices are open Monday through Friday, and a few are staffed on Saturday and Sunday. **AAA** auto club (www.aaa.com) also sells insurance.

## RETURNING TO THE UNITED STATES WITH YOUR CAR

You *must* return the car documents you obtained when you entered Mexico when you cross back with your car, or at some point within 180 days. (You can cross as many times as you wish within the 180 days.) If the documents aren't returned, heavy fines are imposed ($250 for each 15 days late), your car may be impounded and confiscated, or you may be jailed if you return to Mexico. You can only return the car documents to a Banjercito official on duty at the Mexican Customs building *before* you cross back into the United States. Some border cities have Banjercito officials on duty 24 hours a day, but others do not; some do not have Sunday hours.

## BY SHIP

Numerous cruise lines serve Mexico. Some (including whale-watching trips) cruise from California to the Baja Peninsula and ports of call on the Pacific coast, or from Houston or Miami to the Caribbean (which often includes stops in Cancún, Playa del Carmen, and Cozumel). Several cruise-tour specialists offer substantial discounts on unsold cabins if you're willing to take off at the last minute. One such company is **The Cruise Line,** 150 NW 168 St., North Miami Beach, FL 33169 (© **800/777-0707** or 305/521-2200).

## BY BUS

Greyhound-Trailways (or its affiliates) offers service from around the United States to the Mexican border, where passengers disembark, cross the border, and buy a ticket for travel into Mexico. Many border crossings have scheduled buses from the U.S. bus station to the Mexican bus station.

## 12 Packages for the Independent Traveler

Before you start your search for the lowest airfare, you may want to consider booking your flight as part of a travel package. Package tours are not the same thing as escorted tours. Package tours are simply a way to buy the airfare, accommodations, and other elements of your trip (such as car rentals, airport transfers, and sometimes even activities) at the same time and often at discounted prices.

You can buy a package at any time of the year, but the best deals usually coincide with high season—from mid-December to April—when demand is at its peak, and companies are more confident about filling planes. You might think that package rates would be better during low season, when room rates and airfares plunge. But the key is air access, which is much easier during the winter.

### WHERE TO BROWSE

- One specialist in Mexico vacation packages is **www.mexicotravelnet. com**, an agency that offers most of the well-known travel packages to Mexico beach resorts, plus offers last-minute specials.
- Check out **www.2travel.com** and find a page with links to a number of the big-name Mexico packagers, including several of those listed here.
- For last-minute air-only or package bargains, check out **Vacation Hot Line** (www.vacationhotline.net). Once you find your deal, you'll need to call to make booking arrangements. This service offers packages from the popular Apple and Funjet vacation wholesalers.
- Several big **online travel agencies**—Expedia.com, Travelocity, Orbitz, Site59, and Lastminute.com—also do a brisk business in packages. If you're unsure about the pedigree of a smaller packager, check with the Better Business Bureau in the city where the company is based, or go online at www.bbb.org. If a packager won't tell you where they're based, don't fly with them.
- Travel packages are also listed in the travel section of your local Sunday newspaper. Or check ads in the national travel magazines such as *Arthur Frommer's Budget Travel Magazine, Travel + Leisure, National Geographic Traveler,* and *Condé Nast Traveler.*

Package tours can vary by leaps and bounds. Some offer a better class of hotels than others. Some offer the same hotels for lower prices. Some offer flights on scheduled airlines, while others book charters. Some limit your choice of accommodations and travel days. You are often required to make a large payment upfront. On the plus side, packages can save you money, offering group prices but allowing for independent travel. Some even let you add on a few guided excursions or escorted day trips (also at prices lower than if you booked them yourself) without booking an entirely escorted tour.

Before you invest in a package tour, get some answers. Ask about the **accommodations choices** and prices for each. Then look up the hotels' reviews in a Frommer's guide and check their rates online for your specific dates of travel. You'll also want to find out what **type of room** you get. If you need a certain type of room, ask for it; don't take whatever is thrown your way. Request a nonsmoking room, a quiet room, a room with a view, or whatever you fancy.

Finally, look for **hidden expenses.** Ask whether airport departure fees and taxes, for example, are included in the total cost.

## RECOMMENDED PACKAGERS

- **Aeromexico Vacations** (✆ 800/245-8585; www.aeromexico.com) offers year-round packages to almost every destination it serves, including Acapulco, Cancún, Cozumel, Ixtapa/Zihuatanejo, Los Cabos, and Puerto Vallarta. Aeromexico has a large (more than 100) selection of resorts in these destinations and more, in a variety of price ranges. The best deals are from Houston, Dallas, San Diego, Los Angeles, Miami, and New York, in that order.
- **Alaska Airlines Vacations** (✆ 800/468-2248; www.alaskaair.com) sells packages to Ixtapa/Zihuatanejo, Los Cabos, Manzanillo/Costa Alegre, Mazatlán, and Puerto Vallarta. Alaska flies direct from Los Angeles, San Diego, San Jose, San Francisco, Seattle, Vancouver, Anchorage, and Fairbanks. The website offers unpublished discounts that are not available through the phone operators.
- **American Airlines Vacations** (✆ 800/321-2121; www.aavacations.com) has year-round deals to Acapulco, Cancún, the Riviera Maya, Guadalajara, Los Cabos, Mexico City, and Puerto Vallarta. You don't have to fly with American if you can get a better deal on another airline; land-only packages include hotel, hotel tax, and airport transfers. American's hubs to Mexico are Dallas/Fort Worth, Chicago, and Miami. The website offers unpublished discounts that are not available through the operators.
- **America West Vacations** (✆ 800/2-FLY-AWV; www.americawestvacations.com) has deals to Acapulco, Guadalajara, Ixtapa, Mazatlán, Manzanillo, Mexico City, Los Cabos, and Puerto Vallarta, mostly from its Phoenix gateway. Many packages to Los Cabos include car rentals. The website offers discounted featured specials that are not available through the operators. You can also book hotels without air by calling the toll-free number.
- **Apple Vacations** (✆ 800/365-2775; www.applevacations.com) offers inclusive packages to all the beach resorts, and has the largest choice of hotels in Acapulco, Cancún, Cozumel, Huatulco, Ixtapa, Loreto, Los Cabos, Manzanillo, Mazatlán, Puerto Vallarta, and the Riviera Maya. Scheduled carriers for the air portion include American, United, Mexicana, Delta, US Airways, Reno Air, Alaska Airlines, Aero California,

and Aeromexico. Perks include baggage handling and the services of a company representative at major hotels.

- **Classic Custom Vacations** (© 800/635-1333;    www.classiccustom vacations.com) specializes in package vacations to Mexico's finest luxury resorts. It combines discounted first-class and economy airfare on American, Continental, Mexicana, Alaska, America West, and Delta with stays at the most exclusive hotels in Cancún, the Riviera Maya, Mérida, Oaxaca, Guadalajara, Mexico City, Puerto Vallarta, Mazatlán, Costa Alegre, Manzanillo, Ixtapa/Zihuatanejo, Acapulco, Huatulco, and Los Cabos. In many cases, packages also include meals, airport transfers, and upgrades. The prices are not for bargain hunters but for those who seek luxury, nicely packaged.

- **Continental Vacations** (© 800/301-3800; www.covacations.com) has year-round packages to Cancún, Cozumel, Puerto Vallarta, Cabo San Lucas, Acapulco, Ixtapa, Mazatlán, Mexico City, and Guadalajara. The best deals are from Houston; Newark, N.J.; and Cleveland. You must fly Continental. The Internet deals offer savings not available elsewhere.

- **Delta Vacations** (© 800/221-6666; www.deltavacations.com) has year-round packages to Acapulco, Los Cabos, Cozumel, and Cancún. Atlanta is the hub, so expect the best prices from there.

- **Funjet Vacations** (book through any travel agent; www.funjet.com for general information) is one of the largest vacation packagers in the United States. Funjet has packages to Acapulco, Cancún, Cozumel, the Riviera Maya, Huatulco, Los Cabos, Mazatlán, Ixtapa, and Puerto Vallarta. You can choose a charter or fly on American, Continental, Delta, Aeromexico, US Airways, Alaska Air, or United.

- **GOGO Worldwide Vacations** (© 888/636-3942; www.gogowwv. com) has trips to all the major beach destinations, including Acapulco, Cancún, Mazatlán, Puerto Vallarta, and Los Cabos. It offers several exclusive deals from higher-end hotels. Book through any travel agent.

- **Mexicana Vacations,** or MexSeaSun Vacations (© 800/531-7921; www. mexicana.com), offers getaways to all the resorts. Mexicana operates daily direct flights from Los Angeles to Los Cabos, Mazatlán, Cancún, Puerto Vallarta, Manzanillo, and Ixtapa/Zihuatanejo.

- **Pleasant Mexico Holidays** (© 800/742-9244; www.pleasantholidays. com) is one of the largest vacation packagers in the United States, with hotels in Acapulco, Cancún, Cozumel, Ixtapa/Zihuatanejo, Los Cabos, Mazatlán, and Puerto Vallarta.

### REGIONAL PACKAGERS

**From the East Coast: Liberty Travel** (© 888/271-1584; www.libertytravel. com), one of the biggest packagers in the Northeast, often runs a full-page ad in the Sunday papers, with frequent Mexico specials. You won't get much in the way of service, but you will get a good deal.

**From the West: Suntrips** (© 800/SUNTRIPS, or 800/786-8747 for departures within 14 days; www.suntrips.com) is one of the largest West Coast packagers for Mexico, with departures from San Francisco and Denver; regular charters to Cancún, Cozumel, Los Cabos, and Puerto Vallarta; and a large selection of hotels.

**From the Southwest:** Town and Country (book through travel agents) packages regular deals to Los Cabos, Mazatlán, Puerto Vallarta, Ixtapa, Manzanillo, Cancún, Cozumel, and Acapulco

## *Finds*  Out-of-the-Ordinary Places to Stay

**Mexico Boutique Hotels** (www.mexicoboutiquehotels.com) specializes in smaller places to stay with a high level of personal attention and service. Most options have fewer than 50 rooms, and the accommodations consist of entire villas, *casitas,* bungalows, or a combination. The Yucatán is especially noted for luxury haciendas throughout the peninsula.

with America West from the airline's Phoenix and Las Vegas gateways.

**Resort Packages:** The biggest hotel chains and resorts also sell packages. To take advantage of these offers, contact your travel agent or call the hotels directly.

## 13 The Active Traveler

**Golf** courses are plentiful in Mexico, concentrated in the resort areas. Cancún and Playa del Carmen boast excellent options. Visitors can also enjoy **tennis, waterskiing, surfing, bicycling,** and **horseback riding. Scuba diving** is excellent off the Yucatán's Caribbean coast; Cozumel is considered one of the top five dive spots in the world.

**PARKS**   Most of the national parks and nature reserves are understaffed or unstaffed. Reliable Mexican companies (such as **AMTAVE** members; see below) and many U.S.-based companies offer adventure trips.

**OUTDOORS ORGANIZATIONS & TOUR OPERATORS   AMTAVE** (Asociación Mexicana de Turismo de Aventura y Ecoturismo, A.C.) is an active association of eco- and adventure-tour operators. It publishes an annual catalog of participating firms and their offerings, all of which must meet certain criteria for security, quality, and training of the guides, as well as for sustainability of natural and cultural environments. For more information, contact AMTAVE (*©* **55/ 5688-3883;** www.amtave.org).

**The Archaeological Conservancy,** 5301 Central Ave. NE, Suite 402, Albuquerque, NM 87108 (*©* **505/266-1540;** www.americanarchaeology.com/tour.html),

presents one trip to Mexico per year led by an expert, usually an archaeologist. The trips change from year to year and space is limited; make reservations early.

**ATC Tours and Travel,** Calle 16 de Septiembre 16, 29200 San Cristóbal de las Casas, Chi. (*©* **967/678-2550** or 967/ 678-2557; fax 967/678-3145; www.atc tours.com.), a Mexico-based tour operator with an excellent reputation, offers specialist-led trips primarily in southern Mexico. In addition to trips to the ruins of Palenque and Yaxchilán (extending into Belize and Guatemala by river, plane, and bus, if desired), ATC offers horseback tours to Chamula or Zinacantán, and day trips to the ruins of Toniná around San Cristóbal de las Casas; birding in the rainforests of Chiapas and Guatemala (including in the El Triunfo Reserve of Chiapas, where you can see the rare quetzal bird and orchids); hikes to the shops and homes of native textile artists of the Chiapas highlands; and walks from the Lagos de Montebello in the Montes Azules Biosphere Reserve, with camping and canoeing. The company can also prepare custom itineraries.

**Culinary Adventures,** 6023 Reid Dr. NW, Gig Harbor, WA 98335 (*©* **253/ 851-7676;** fax 253/851-9532; www. marilyntausend.com) specializes in a short but select list of cooking tours in Mexico.

They feature well-known cooks and travel to regions known for excellent cuisine. The owner, Marilyn Tausend, is the coauthor of *Mexico the Beautiful Cookbook* and *Cocinas de la Familia* (Family Kitchens). Most trips take place in central Mexico, but ask about itineraries in the Yucatán.

**Mexico Travel Link Ltd.,** 300-3665 Kingsway, Vancouver, BC V5R 5W2 Canada (© **604/454-9044;** fax 604/454-9088; www.mexicotravel.net), offers cultural, sports, and adventure tours to the Maya Route, and other destinations off the beaten path.

**Trek America,** P.O. Box 189, Rockaway, NJ 07866 (© **800/221-0596** or 973/983-1144; fax 973/983-8551; www.trekamerica.com), organizes lengthy, active trips that combine trekking, hiking, van transportation, and camping in the Yucatán and Chiapas.

## 14  Tips on Accommodations

### MEXICO'S HOTEL RATING SYSTEM

The hotel rating system in Mexico is called "Stars and Diamonds." Hotels may qualify to earn one to five stars, or five diamonds. Many hotels that have excellent standards are not certified, but all rated hotels adhere to strict standards. The guidelines relate to service, facilities, and hygiene more than to prices.

Five-diamond hotels meet the highest requirements for rating: The beds are comfortable, bathrooms are in excellent working order, all facilities are renovated regularly, infrastructure is top-tier, and services and hygiene meet the highest international standards.

Five-star hotels usually offer similar quality, but with lower levels of service and detail in the rooms. For example, a five-star hotel may have less luxurious linens, or perhaps room service for less than 24 hours.

Four-star hotels are less expensive and more basic, but they still guarantee cleanliness and basic services such as hot water and purified drinking water. Three-, two-, and one-star hotels are at least working to adhere to certain standards: Bathrooms are cleaned and linens are washed daily, and you can expect a minimum standard of service. Two- and one-star hotels generally provide bottled water rather than purified water.

The nonprofit organization Calidad Mexicana Certificada, A.C., known as **Calmecac** (**www.calmecac.com.mx**), is responsible for hotel ratings. For additional details about the rating system, visit Calmecac's website or www.starsanddiamonds.com.

### HOTEL CHAINS

In addition to the major international chains, you'll run across a number of less-familiar brands as you plan your trip to Mexico. They include:

- **Brisas Hotels & Resorts** (www.brisas.com.mx). These were the hotels that originally attracted jet-set travelers to Mexico. Spectacular in a retro way, these properties offer the laid-back luxury that makes a Mexican vacation so unique.
- **Fiesta Americana** and **Fiesta Inn** (www.posadas.com). Part of the Mexican-owned Grupo Posadas company, these hotels set the country's midrange standard for facilities and services. They generally offer comfortable, spacious rooms and traditional Mexican hospitality. Fiesta Americana hotels offer excellent beach-resort packages. Fiesta Inn hotels are usually more business oriented. Grupo Posadas also owns the more luxurious Aqua and Caesar Park hotels and the eco-oriented Explorean hotels.

- **Hoteles Camino Real** (www.camino real.com). Once known as the premier Mexican hotel chain, Camino Real still maintains a high standard of service at its properties, although the company was sold in 2005, and many of the hotels that once formed a part of it have been sold off, or have become independent. Its beach hotels are traditionally located on the best beaches in the area. This chain also focuses on the business market. The hotels are famous for their vivid and contrasting colors.
- **Hoteles NH Krystal** (www.nh-krystal.mexico-hoteles.com). Grupo Chartwell recently acquired this family-owned chain. The hotels are noted for their family-friendly facilities and five-star standards. The beach properties' signature feature is a pool, framed by columns, overlooking the sea.
- **Quinta Real Grand Class Hotels and Resorts** (www.quintareal.com). These hotels, owned by Summit Hotels and Resorts, are noted for architectural and cultural details that reflect their individual regions. At these luxury properties, attention to detail and excellent service are the rule.

## HOUSE RENTALS & SWAPS
House and villa rentals and swaps are becoming more common in Mexico, but no single recognized agency or business provides this service exclusively for Mexico. In the chapters that follow, we have provided information on independent services that we have found to be reputable.

With regard to general online services, the most extensive inventory of homes is found at **VRBO** (Vacation Rentals by Owner; www.vrbo.com). They have over 33,000 homes and condominiums worldwide, including a large selection in Mexico. Another good option is **VacationSpot** (© **888/903-7768;** www.vacationspot. com) owned by Expedia.com, and a part

of its sister company, Hotels.com. It has fewer choices, but the company's criteria for adding inventory are much more selective, and often include on-site inspections. They also offer toll-free phone support.

You might also consider trying **Home-Link International** (www.homelink.org), the largest and oldest home-swapping organization, founded in 1952, with over 11,000 listings worldwide ($75 for a yearly membership). **HomeExchange.org** ($50 for 6,000 listings) and **InterVac.com** ($69 for over 10,000 listings) are also reliable.

## SAVING ON YOUR HOTEL ROOM
The **rack rate** is the maximum rate that a hotel charges for a room. Hardly anybody pays this price, however. To lower the cost of your room:

- Ask about special rates or other discounts.
- Dial direct.
- Book online.
- Remember the law of supply and demand.
- Look into group or long-stay discounts.
- Avoid excess charges and hidden costs.
- Consider the pros and cons of all-inclusive resorts and hotels.
- Carefully consider your hotel's meal plan.
- Book an efficiency.
- Consider enrolling in hotel "frequent-stay" programs, which are upping the ante lately to win the loyalty of repeat customers.

## LANDING THE BEST ROOM
Somebody has to get the best room in the house, and it might as well be you. You can start by joining the hotel's frequent-guest program, which may make you eligible for upgrades. Always ask about a corner room. They're often larger and quieter, with more windows and light, and they often cost the same as standard

rooms. When you make your reservation, ask if the hotel is renovating; if it is, request a room away from the construction. Ask about nonsmoking rooms, rooms with views, rooms with twin, queen-, or king-size beds. If you're a light sleeper, request a quiet room away from vending machines, elevators, restaurants, bars, and dance clubs. Ask for a room that has been most recently renovated or redecorated.

In resort areas, ask the following questions before you book a room:

- What's the view like?
- Does the room have air-conditioning or ceiling fans? Do the windows open? If they do, and the nighttime entertainment takes place alfresco, you may want to find out when showtime is over.
- What's included in the price?
- How far is the room from the beach and other amenities? If it's far, is there transportation and is it free?

## 15 Getting Around Mexico

*An important note:* If your travel schedule depends on a vital connection—say, a plane trip or a ferry or bus connection— call to find out if the connection is still available.

### BY PLANE

Mexico has two large private national carriers: **Mexicana** (© **01-800/509-8960** toll-free in Mexico), and **Aeromexico** (© **01-800/021-4000** toll-free in Mexico), in addition to several up-and-coming regional carriers. Mexicana and Aeromexico offer extensive connections to the United States as well as within Mexico.

Several new regional carriers are operated by or can be booked through Mexicana or Aeromexico. Regional carriers are Mexicana's **Clic** and **Aero Mar,** and Aeromexico's **Aerolitoral.** For points inside the state of Oaxaca only—Oaxaca City, Puerto Escondido, and Huatulco— contact **Zapotec Tours** (© **800/44-OAXACA,** or 773/506-2444 in Illinois). The regional carriers are expensive, but they go to difficult-to-reach places. In each applicable section of this book, we've mentioned regional carriers with all pertinent telephone numbers.

Because major airlines can book some regional carriers, read your ticket carefully to see if your connecting flight is on one of these smaller carriers—they may use a different airport or a different counter.

**AIRPORT TAXES**   Mexico charges an airport tax on all departures. Passengers leaving the country on international flights pay $24—in dollars or the peso equivalent. It has become a common practice to include this departure tax in your ticket price, but double-check to make sure so you're not caught by surprise at the airport. Taxes on each domestic departure within Mexico are around $17, unless you're on a connecting flight and have already paid at the start of the flight.

Mexico also charges an $18 "tourism tax," the proceeds of which go into a tourism promotional fund. Your ticket price may not include it, so be sure to have enough money to pay it at the airport upon departure.

**RECONFIRMING        FLIGHTS** Although Mexican airlines say it's not necessary to reconfirm a flight, it's still a good idea. To avoid getting bumped on popular, possibly overbooked flights, check in for an international flight 1½ hours in advance of travel.

### BY CAR

Most Mexican roads are not up to U.S. standards. Driving at night is dangerous—the roads are rarely lit; trucks, carts, pedestrians, and bicycles usually have no lights; and you can hit potholes, animals, rocks, dead ends, or uncrossable bridges without warning.

The spirited style of Mexican driving sometimes requires super vision and reflexes. Be prepared for new customs, as when a truck driver flips on his left turn signal when there's not a crossroad for miles. He's probably telling you the road's clear ahead for you to pass. Another custom that's very important to respect is turning left. Never turn left by stopping in the middle of a highway with your left signal on. Instead, pull onto the right shoulder, wait for traffic to clear, then proceed across the road.

**GASOLINE**    There's one government-owned brand of gas and one gasoline station name throughout the country—**Pemex** (Petroleras Mexicanas). There are two types of gas in Mexico: *magna*, 87-octane unleaded gas, and premium 93 octane. In Mexico, fuel and oil are sold by the liter, which is slightly more than a quart (40 liters equals about 11 gal.). Many franchise Pemex stations have bathroom facilities and convenience stores.

*Important note:* Beginning in January 2006, gas stations began the practice of accepting both credit and debit cards for gas purchases, marking an important change from prior years.

**TOLL ROADS**    Mexico charges some of the highest tolls in the world for its network of new toll roads; as a result, they are rarely used. Generally speaking, though, using toll roads cuts travel time. Older toll-free roads are generally in good condition, but travel times tend to be longer.

**BREAKDOWNS**    If your car breaks down on the road, help might already be on the way. Radio-equipped green repair trucks operated by uniformed English-speaking officers patrol major highways during daylight hours. These **"Green Angels"** perform minor repairs and adjustments free, but you pay for parts and materials.

Your best guide to repair shops is the Yellow Pages. For repairs, look under "Automóviles y Camiones: Talleres de Reparación y Servicio"; auto-parts stores are under "Refacciones y Accesorios para Automóviles." To find a mechanic on the road, look for a sign that says TALLER MECANICO.

Places called *vulcanizadora* or *llantera* repair flat tires, and it is common to find them open 24 hours a day on the most traveled highways.

**MINOR ACCIDENTS**    When possible, many Mexicans drive away from minor accidents, or try to make an immediate settlement, to avoid involving the police. If the police arrive while the involved persons are still at the scene, everyone may be locked in jail until blame is assessed. In any case, you have to settle up immediately, which may take days. Foreigners who don't speak fluent Spanish are at a distinct disadvantage when trying to explain their version of the event. Three steps may help the foreigner who doesn't wish to do as the Mexicans do: If you were in your own car, notify your Mexican insurance company, whose job it is to intervene on your behalf. If you were in a rental car, notify the rental company immediately and ask how to contact the nearest adjuster. (You did buy insurance with the rental, right?) Finally, if all else fails, ask for the nearest Green Angel, who may be able to explain to officials that you are covered by insurance. See also "Mexican Auto Insurance" in "Getting There," earlier in this chapter.

**CAR RENTALS**    You'll get the best price if you reserve a car at least a week in advance in the United States. U.S. car-rental firms include **Advantage** (© 800/777-5500 in the U.S. and Canada;

www.arac.com), **Avis** (✆ 800/331-1212 in the U.S., 800/TRY-AVIS in Canada; www.avis.com), **Budget** (✆ 800/527-0700 in the U.S. and Canada; www.budget.com), **Hertz** (✆ 800/654-3131 in the U.S. and Canada; www.hertz.com), **National** (✆ 800/CAR-RENT in the U.S. and Canada; www.nationalcar.com), and **Thrifty** (✆ 800/847-4389 in the U.S. and Canada; www.thrifty.com), which often offers discounts for rentals in Mexico. For European travelers, **Kemwel Holiday Auto** (✆ 800/678-0678; www.kemwel.com) and **Auto Europe** (✆ 800/223-5555; www.autoeurope.com) can arrange Mexican rentals, sometimes through other agencies. These and some local firms have offices in Mexico City and most other large Mexican cities. You'll find rental desks at airports, all major hotels, and many travel agencies.

Cars are easy to rent if you are 25 or over and have a major credit card, valid driver's license, and passport with you. Without a credit card, you must leave a cash deposit, usually a big one. One-way rentals are usually simple to arrange but more costly.

Car-rental costs are high in Mexico because cars are more expensive. The condition of rental cars has improved greatly over the years, and clean new cars are the norm. The basic cost of the 1-day rental of a Volkswagen Beetle at press time, with unlimited mileage (but before 15% tax and $15 daily insurance), was $48 in Cancún, $52 in Mexico City, $44 in Puerto Vallarta, $48 in Oaxaca, and $38 in Mérida. Renting by the week gives you a lower daily rate. Avis was offering a basic 7-day rate for a VW Beetle (before tax or insurance) of $220 in Cancún and Puerto Vallarta, $180 in Mérida, and $250 in Mexico City. Prices may be considerably higher if you rent around a major holiday.

Also double-check charges for insurance—some companies will increase the insurance rate after several days. Always ask for detailed information about all charges you will be responsible for.

Car-rental companies usually write credit card charges in U.S. dollars.

**Deductibles** Be careful—these vary greatly; some are as high as $2,500, which comes out of your pocket immediately in case of damage. On a VW Beetle, Hertz's deductible is $1,000 and Avis's is $500.

**Insurance** Insurance is offered in two parts: **Collision and damage** insurance covers your car and others if the accident is your fault, and **personal accident** insurance covers you and anyone in your car. Read the fine print on the back of your rental agreement and note that insurance may be invalid if you have an accident while driving on an unpaved road.

**Damage** Always inspect your car carefully and note every damaged or missing item, no matter how minute, on your rental agreement, or you may be charged.

## BY TAXI

Taxis are the preferred way to get around almost all of Mexico's resort areas, and around Mexico City. Fares for short trips within towns are generally preset by zone, and are quite reasonable compared with U.S. rates. For longer trips or excursions to nearby cities, taxis can generally be hired for around $10 to $15 per hour, or for a negotiated daily rate. A negotiated one-way price is usually much less than the cost of a rental car for a day, and a taxi travels much faster than a bus. For anyone who is uncomfortable driving in Mexico, this is a convenient, comfortable alternative. A bonus is that you have a Spanish-speaking person with you in case you run into trouble. Many taxi drivers speak at least some English. Your hotel can assist you with the arrangements.

## Bus Hijackings

The U.S. State Department notes that bandits target long-distance buses traveling at night, but there have been daylight robberies as well. Buses are more common targets than individual cars—they offer thieves more bucks for the bang.

## BY BUS

Except for the Baja peninsula, where bus service is not well developed, Mexican buses run frequently, are readily accessible, and can get you almost anywhere you want to go. They're often the only way to get from large cities to other nearby cities and small villages. Don't hesitate to ask questions if you're confused about anything, but note that little English is spoken in bus stations.

Dozens of Mexican companies operate large, air-conditioned, Greyhound-type buses between most cities. Classes are second *(segunda)*, first *(primera)*, and deluxe *(ejecutiva)*, which goes by a variety of names. Deluxe buses often have fewer seats than regular buses, show video movies, are air-conditioned, and make few stops. Many run express from point to point. They are well worth the few dollars more. In rural areas, buses are often of the school-bus variety, with lots of local color.

Whenever possible, it's best to buy your reserved-seat ticket, often using a computerized system, a day in advance on long-distance routes and especially before holidays. See appendix B for a list of helpful bus terms in Spanish.

## 16 Food & Drink

Authentic Mexican food differs dramatically from what is frequently served in the United States under that name. For many travelers, Mexico will be new and exciting culinary territory. Even grizzled veterans will be pleasantly surprised by the wide variation in specialties and traditions offered from region to region.

Despite regional differences, some generalizations can be made. Mexican food usually isn't pepper-hot when it arrives at the table (though many dishes must have a certain amount of piquancy, and some home cooking can be very spicy, depending on a family's or chef's tastes). Chiles and sauces add piquant flavor after the food is served; you'll never see a table in Mexico without one or both of these condiments. Mexicans don't drown their cooking in cheese and sour cream, a la Tex-Mex, and they use a great variety of ingredients. But the basis of Mexican food is simple—tortillas, beans, chiles, squash, and tomatoes—the same as it was centuries ago, before the Europeans arrived.

## THE BASICS

**TORTILLAS**   Traditional tortillas are made from corn that's boiled in water and lime, and then ground into *masa* (a grainy dough), patted and pressed into thin cakes, and cooked on a hot griddle known as a *comal*. In many households, the tortilla takes the place of fork and spoon; Mexicans merely tear them into wedge-shaped pieces, which they use to scoop up their food. Restaurants often serve bread rather than tortillas because it's easier, but you can always ask for tortillas. A more recent invention from northern Mexico is the flour tortilla, which is seen less frequently in the rest of Mexico.

**ENCHILADAS**   The tortilla is the basis of several Mexican dishes, but the most famous of these is the enchilada. The original name for this dish would have been *tortilla enchilada,* which simply means a tortilla dipped in a chile sauce. In like manner, there's the *entomatada* (tortilla dipped in a tomato sauce) and the *enfrijolada* (a bean sauce). The enchilada began as a very simple dish: A tortilla is dipped in chile sauce (usually with ancho chile) and then into very hot oil, and then is quickly folded or rolled on a plate and sprinkled with chopped onions and a little *queso cotija* (crumbly white cheese) and served with a few fried potatoes and carrots. You can get this basic enchilada in food stands across the country. I love them, and if you come across them in your travels, give them a try. In restaurants you get the more elaborate enchilada, with different fillings of cheese, chicken, pork, or even seafood, and sometimes in a casserole.

**TACOS**    A taco is anything folded or rolled into a tortilla, and sometimes a double tortilla. The tortilla can be served either soft or fried. Flautas and quesadillas are species of tacos. For Mexicans, the taco is the quintessential fast food, and the taco stand *(taquería)*—a ubiquitous sight—is a great place to get a filling meal. See the section "Eating Out: Restaurants, *Taquerías* & Tipping," below, for information on taquerías.

**FRIJOLES**    An invisible "bean line" divides Mexico: It starts at the Gulf Coast in the southern part of the state of Tamaulipas and moves inland through the eastern quarter of San Luis Potosí and most of the state of Hidalgo, then goes straight through Mexico City and Morelos and into Guerrero, where it curves slightly westward to the Pacific. To the north and west of this line, the pink bean known as the *flor de mayo* is the staple food; to the south and east, including all of the Yucatán, the standard is the black bean.

In private households, beans are served at least once a day and, among the working class and peasantry, with every meal, if the family can afford it. Mexicans almost always prepare beans with a minimum of condiments—usually just a little onion and garlic and perhaps a pinch of herbs. Beans are meant to be a contrast to the heavily spiced dishes. Sometimes they are served at the end of a meal with a little Mexican-style sour cream.

Mexicans often fry leftover beans and serve them on the side as *frijoles refritos.* "Refritos" is usually translated as refried, but this is a misnomer—the beans are fried only once. The prefix "re" actually means "well" (as in thoroughly).

**TAMALES**    You make a tamal by mixing corn masa with a little lard, adding one of several fillings—meats flavored with chiles (or no filling at all)—then wrapping it in a corn husk or in the leaf of a banana or other plant, and finally steaming it. Every region in Mexico has its own traditional way of making tamales. In some places, a single tamal can be big enough to feed a family, while in others they are barely 3 inches long and an inch thick.

**CHILES**    Many kinds of chile peppers exist, and Mexicans call each of them by one name when they're fresh and another when they're dried. Some are blazing hot with only a mild flavor; some are mild but have a rich, complex flavor. They can be pickled, smoked, stuffed, stewed, chopped, and used in an endless variety of dishes.

## MEALTIME

**MORNING**    The morning meal, known as *el desayuno,* can be something light, such as coffee and sweet bread, or something more substantial: eggs, beans, tortillas, bread, fruit, and juice. It can be eaten early or late and is always a sure bet in Mexico. The variety and sweetness of the fruits is remarkable, and you can't go wrong with Mexican egg dishes.

**MIDAFTERNOON**   The main meal of the day, known as *la comida* (or *el almuerzo*), is eaten between 2 and 4pm. Stores and businesses close, and most people go home to eat and perhaps take a short afternoon siesta before going about their business. The first course is the *sopa,* which can be either soup *(caldo)* or rice *(sopa de arroz)* or both; then comes the main course, which ideally is a meat or fish dish prepared in some kind of sauce and served with beans, followed by dessert.

**EVENING**   Between 8 and 10pm, most Mexicans have a light meal called *la cena.* If eaten at home, it is something like a sandwich, bread and jam, or perhaps a couple of tacos made from some of the day's leftovers. At restaurants, the most common thing to eat is *antojitos* (literally, "little cravings"), a general label for light fare. Antojitos include tostadas, tamales, tacos, and simple enchiladas, and are big hits with travelers. Large restaurants offer complete meals as well.

## EATING OUT: RESTAURANTS, *TAQUERIAS* & TIPPING

Avoid eating at those inviting sidewalk restaurants that you see beneath the stone archways that border the main plazas. These places usually cater to tourists and don't need to count on getting any return business. But they are great for getting a coffee or beer.

Most nonresort towns have one or two restaurants (sometimes one is a coffee shop) that are social centers for a large group of established patrons. These establishments over time become virtual institutions, and change comes very slowly. The food is usually good standard fare, cooked as it was 20 years ago; the decor is simple. The patrons have known each other and the staff for years, and the *charla* (banter), gestures, and greetings are

friendly, open, and unaffected. If you're curious about Mexican culture, eating and observing the goings-on is fun.

During your trip, you're going to see many *taquerías* (taco joints). These are generally small places with a counter or a few tables set around the cooking area; you get to see exactly how the cooks make their tacos before deciding whether to order. Most tacos come with a little chopped onion and cilantro, but not tomato and lettuce. Find one that seems popular with the locals and where the cook performs with brio (a good sign of pride in the product). Sometimes there will be a woman making the tortillas right there (or working the masa into *gorditas, sopes,* or *panuchos* if these are also served). You will never see men doing this—this is perhaps the strictest gender division in Mexican society. Men may do all other cooking and kitchen tasks, and work with prepared tortillas, but they will never be found working masa.

For the main meal of the day many restaurants offer a multicourse blue-plate special called *comida corrida* or *menú del día.* This is the least expensive way to get a full dinner. In Mexico, you need to ask for your check; it is generally considered inhospitable to present a check to someone who hasn't requested it. If you're in a hurry to get somewhere, ask for the check when your food arrives.

**Tips** are about the same as in the United States. You'll sometimes find a 15% **value-added tax** on restaurant meals, which shows up on the bill as "IVA." This is a boon to arithmetically challenged tippers, saving them from undue exertion.

To summon the waiter, wave or raise your hand, but don't motion with your index finger, which is a demeaning gesture that may even cause the waiter to ignore you. Or if it's the check you want, you can motion to the waiter from across the room using the universal pretend-you're-writing gesture.

Most restaurants do not have **non-smoking sections;** when they do, we mention it in the reviews. But Mexico's wonderful climate allows for many open-air restaurants, usually set inside a courtyard of a colonial house, or in rooms with tall ceilings and plenty of open windows.

## DRINKS

All over Mexico you'll find shops selling *jugos* (juices) and *licuados* (smoothies) made from several kinds of tropical fruit. They're excellent and refreshing; while traveling, I take full advantage of them. You'll also come across *aguas frescas*—water flavored with hibiscus, melon, tamarind, or lime. Soft drinks come in more flavors than in any other country I know. Pepsi and Coca-Cola taste the way they did in the United States years ago, before the makers started adding corn syrup. The coffee is generally good, and **hot chocolate** is a traditional drink, as is *atole*—a hot, corn-based beverage that can be sweet or bitter.

Of course, Mexico has a proud and lucrative **beer**-brewing tradition. A lesser-known brewed beverage is *pulque,* a pre-Hispanic drink: the fermented juice of a few species of maguey or agave. Mostly you find it for sale in *pulquerías* in central Mexico. It is an acquired taste, and not every gringo acquires it. **Mezcal** and **tequila** also come from the agave. Tequila is a variety of mezcal produced from the *A. tequilana* species of agave in and around the area of Tequila, in the state of Jalisco. Mezcal comes from various parts of Mexico and from different varieties of agave. The distilling process is usually much less sophisticated than that of tequila, and, with its stronger smell and taste, mezcal is much more easily detected on the drinker's breath. In some places such as Oaxaca, it comes with a worm in the bottle; you are supposed to eat the worm after polishing off the mezcal. But for those teetotalers out there who are interested in just the worm, I have good news—you can find these worms for sale in Mexican markets when in season. *¡Salud!*

## 17  Recommended Books & Films

Studying up on Mexico can be one of the most fun bits of "research" you'll ever do. If you'd like to learn more about this fascinating country before you go—which I encourage—these books and movies are an enjoyable way to do it.

### BOOKS

**HISTORY & CULTURE** For an overview of pre-Hispanic cultures, pick up a copy of Michael D. Coe's *Mexico: From the Olmecs to the Aztecs* or Nigel Davies's *Ancient Kingdoms of Mexico.* Richard Townsend's *The Aztecs* is a thorough, well-researched examination of the Aztec and the Spanish conquest. For the Maya, Michael Coe's *The Maya* is probably the best general account. For a survey of Mexican history through modern times, *A Short History of Mexico* by J. Patrick McHenry (Doubleday) provides a complete, yet concise account.

John L. Stephens's *Incidents of Travel in the Yucatán, Vol. I and II* (Dover Publications) are considered among the great books of archaeological discovery, as well as being travel classics. The two volumes chart the course of Stephens's discoveries of the Yucatán, beginning in 1841. Before his expeditions, little was known of the region, and the Maya culture had not been discovered. During his travels, Stephens found and described 44 Maya sites, and his account of these remains the most authoritative in existence.

For a more modern explorations of the archaeology of the region, Peter Tompkins *Mysteries of the Mexican Pyramids* is a visually rich book, which explores not only the ruins of the Maya in the Yucatán, but the whole of Mexico's archaeological treasures.

For contemporary culture, start with Octavio Paz's classic, *The Labyrinth of Solitude,* which still generates controversy among Mexicans because of some of the generalizations Paz makes about them. For a recent collection of writings by Subcomandante Marcos, leader of the Zapatista movement, try *Our Word Is Our Weapon.* Another source is *Basta! Land and the Zapatista Rebellion* by George Collier, et al. For those already familiar with Mexico and its culture, Guillermo Bonfil's *Mexico Profundo: Reclaiming a Civilization* is a rare bottom-up view of Mexico today.

Lesley Byrd Simpson's *Many Mexicos* (University of California Press) provides comprehensive account of Mexican history with a cultural context. A classic on understanding the culture of this country is *Distant Neighbors,* by Alan Riding (Vintage).

**ART & ARCHITECTURE** *Art and Time in Mexico: From the Conquest to the Revolution,* by Elizabeth Wilder Weismann, covers religious, public, and private architecture. *Casa Mexicana,* by Tim Street-Porter, takes readers through the interiors of some of Mexico's finest homes-turned-museums, public buildings, and private homes.

*Maya Art and Architecture,* by Mary Ellen Miller (Thames and Hudson) showcases the best of the artistic expression of this culture, with interpretations into its meanings.

For a wonderful read on the food of the Yucatán and Mexico, pick up *Mexico, One Plate at a Time,* by celebrity chef and Mexico aficionado Rick Bayless (Scribner).

**NATURE** *A Naturalist's Mexico,* by Roland H. Wauer, is a fabulous guide to birding. *A Hiker's Guide to Mexico's Natural History,* by Jim Conrad, covers flora and fauna and tells how to find the easy-to-reach as well as out-of-the-way spots he describes. *Peterson Field Guides: Mexican Birds,* by Roger Tory Peterson and Edward L. Chalif, is an excellent guide.

## MOVIES

Mexico has served as a backdrop for countless movies. Here are just a few of my favorites, all available on DVD.

The 2003 blockbuster *Frida,* starring Selma Hayak and Alfred Molina, is not only an entertaining way to learn about two of Mexico's most famous personalities, but also of its history. The exquisite cinematography perfectly captures Mexico's inherent spirit of Magic Realism.

*Que Viva México* is a little-known masterpiece by Russian filmmaker Sergei Eisenstein, who created a documentary of Mexican history, politics and culture, out of a series of short *novellas,* which ultimately tie together. Although Eisenstein's budget ran out before he could complete the project, in 1979 this film was completed by Grigory Alexandrov, the film's original producer. It's an absolute must for anyone interested in Mexico or Mexican cinema.

Mexico's contemporary filmmakers are creating a sensation lately, and none more so than director Alfonso Cuarón. One of his early and highly acclaimed movies is the 2001 classic *Y Tu Mamá También (And Your Mother Too),* featuring current heartthrobs Gael Garcia Bernal and Diego Luna. This sexy, yet compelling, coming-of-age movie not only showcases both the grit and beauty of Mexico, but the universality of love and life lessons.

*Like Water for Chocolate* is the 1993 film based on the book of the same name by Laura Esquivel, filmed by the author's husband, acclaimed contemporary Mexican director Alfonso Arau. Expect to be very hungry after watching this lushly visual film, which tells the story of a young woman who suppresses her passions under the watchful eye of a stern mother, and channels them into her cooking. In the process, we learn of the traditional norms of Mexican culture, and a great deal of the country's culinary treasures.

## *FAST FACTS:* Mexico

*Abbreviations*  Dept. (apartments); Apdo. (post office box); Av. (*avenida;* avenue); c/ (*calle;* street); Calz. (*calzada;* boulevard). "C" on faucets stands for *caliente* (hot), "F" for *fría* (cold). "PB" *(planta baja)* means ground floor; in most buildings the next floor up is the first floor (1).

*ATMs*  See "Banks & ATMs," p. 23.

*Business Hours*  In general, businesses in larger cities are open between 9am and 7pm; in smaller towns many close between 2 and 4pm. Most close on Sunday. In resort areas it is common to find stores open at least in the mornings on Sunday, and for shops to stay open late, often until 8pm or even 10pm. Bank hours are Monday through Friday from 9 or 9:30am to anywhere between 3 and 7pm. Increasingly, banks open on Saturday for at least a half-day.

*Cameras & Film*  Film costs about the same as in the United States. Tourists wishing to use a video or still camera at any archaeological site in Mexico or at many museums operated by the Instituto de Antropología e Historia (INAH; www.inah. gob.mx) must pay $4 per camera at each site visited. (Listings for specific sites and museums note this fee.) Also, use of a tripod at any archaeological site requires a permit from INAH. It's courteous to ask permission before photographing anyone. It is never considered polite to take photos inside a church in Mexico.

*Car Rentals*  See "Getting Around Mexico," p. 55.

*Driving Rules*  See "Getting Around Mexico," p. 55.

*Drug Laws*  It may sound obvious, but don't use or possess illegal drugs in Mexico. Mexican officials have no tolerance for drug users, and jail is their solution, with very little hope of getting out until the sentence (usually a long one) is completed or heavy fines or bribes are paid. Remember, in Mexico the legal system assumes you are guilty until proven innocent. *Note:* It isn't uncommon to be befriended by a fellow user, only to be turned in by that "friend," who collects a bounty. Bring prescription drugs in their original containers. If possible, pack a copy of the original prescription with the generic name of the drug.

U.S. Customs officials are on the lookout for diet drugs that are sold in Mexico but illegal in the U.S. Possession could land you in a U.S. jail. If you buy antibiotics over-the-counter (which you can do in Mexico) and still have some left, U.S. Customs probably won't hassle you.

*Electricity*  The electrical system in Mexico is 110 volts AC (60 cycles), as in the United States and Canada. In reality, however, it may cycle more slowly and overheat your appliances. To compensate, select a medium or low speed on hair dryers. Many older hotels still have electrical outlets for flat two-prong plugs; you'll need an adapter for any plug with an enlarged end on one prong or with three prongs. Many better hotels have three-hole outlets (*trifásicos* in Spanish). Those that don't may have loan adapters, but to be sure, it's always better to carry your own.

*Embassies & Consulates*  The Embassy of the **United States** in Mexico City is at Paseo de la Reforma 305, next to the Hotel María Isabel Sheraton at the corner of Río Danubio (© **55/5080-2000** or 55/5511-9980); hours are Monday through

Friday from 8:30am to 5:30pm. Visit www.usembassy-mexico.gov for addresses of the U.S. consulates inside Mexico. There are U.S. Consulates General at López Mateos 924-N, Ciudad Juárez (© 656/611-3000); Progreso 175, Guadalajara (© 333/268-2100); Av. Constitución 411 Pte., Monterrey (© 818/345-2120); and Tapachula 96, Tijuana (© 664/622-7400). In addition, there are consular agencies in Acapulco (© 744/469-0556); Cabo San Lucas (© 624/143-3566); Cancún (© 998/883-0272); Cozumel (© 987/872-4574); Hermosillo (© 662/289-3500); Ixtapa/Zihuatanejo (© 755/553-2100); Matamoros (© 868/812-4402); Mazatlán (© 669/916-5889); Mérida (© 999/925-5011); Nogales (© 631/313-4820); Nuevo Laredo (© 867/714-0512); Oaxaca (© 951/514-3054); Puerto Vallarta (© 322/222-0069); San Luis Potosí (© 444/811-7802); and San Miguel de Allende (© 415/152-2357).

The Embassy of **Australia** in Mexico City is at Rubén Darío 55, Col. Polanco (© 55/51101-2200). It's open Monday through Friday from 9am to 1pm.

The Embassy of **Canada** in Mexico City is at Schiller 529, Col. Polanco (© 55/5724-7900); it's open Monday through Friday from 9am to 1pm. At other times, the name of a duty officer is posted on the door. Visit www.dfait-maeci.gc.ca for addresses of consular agencies in Mexico. There are Canadian consulates in Acapulco (© 744/484-1305); Cancún (© 998/883-3360); Guadalajara (© 333/615-6215); Mazatlán (© 669/913-7320); Monterrey (© 818/344-2753); Oaxaca (© 951/513-3777); Puerto Vallarta (© 322/293-0098); San José del Cabo (© 624/142-4333); and Tijuana (© 664/684-0461).

The Embassy of **New Zealand** in Mexico City is at Jaime Balmes 8, 4th Floor, Col. Los Morales, Polanco (© 55/5283-9460; kiwimexico@compuserve.com.mx). It's open Monday through Friday from 8am to 3pm.

The Embassy of the **United Kingdom** in Mexico City is at Río Lerma 71, Col. Cuauhtémoc (© 55/5242-8500; www.embajadabritanica.com.mx). It's open Monday through Friday from 8:30am to 3:30pm.

The Embassy of **Ireland** in Mexico City is at Bulevar Cerrada, Avila Camacho 76, 3rd floor, Col. Lomas de Chapultepec (© 55/5520-5803). It's open Monday through Friday from 9am to 5pm.

The **South African** Embassy in Mexico City is at Andrés Bello 10, 9th floor, Col. Polanco (© 55/5282-9260). It's open Monday through Friday from 8am to 3:30pm.

*Emergencies* In case of emergency, dial © 065 from any phone within Mexico. For police emergency numbers, turn to "Fast Facts" in the chapters that follow. The 24-hour **Tourist Help Line** in Mexico City is © 01-800/987-8224 or 55/5089-7500, or you can now simply dial **078**. The operators don't always speak English, but they are always willing to help. The tourist legal assistance office (Procuraduría del Turista) in Mexico City (© 55/5625-8153 or 55/5625-8154) always has an English speaker available. Though the phones are frequently busy, they operate 24 hours.

*Holidays* See "Yucatán Calendar of Events," p. 26.

*Internet Access* In large cities and resort areas, a growing number of top hotels offer business centers with Internet access. You'll also find cybercafes in destinations that are popular with ex-pats and business travelers. Even in remote spots, Internet access is common.

*Language* Spanish is the official language in Mexico. English is spoken and understood to some degree in most tourist areas. Mexicans are very accommodating with foreigners who try to speak Spanish, even in broken sentences. For basic vocabulary, refer to appendix B.

*Legal Aid* International Legal Defense Counsel, 111 S. 15th St., 24th Floor, Packard Building, Philadelphia, PA 19102 (℃ **215/977-9982**), is a law firm specializing in legal difficulties of Americans abroad. See also "Embassies & Consulates" and "Emergencies," above.

*Liquor Laws* The legal drinking age in Mexico is 18; however, asking for ID or denying purchase is extremely rare. Grocery stores sell everything from beer and wine to national and imported liquors. You can buy liquor 24 hours a day, but during major elections, dry laws often are enacted for as much as 72 hours in advance of the election—and they apply to tourists as well as local residents. Mexico does not have laws that apply to transporting liquor in cars, but authorities are beginning to target drunk drivers more aggressively. It's a good idea to drive defensively.

It is not legal to drink in the street; however, many tourists do so. Use your judgment—if you are getting drunk, you shouldn't drink in the street, because you are more likely to get stopped by the police.

*Lost & Found* To replace a **lost passport,** contact your embassy or nearest consular agent. You must establish a record of your citizenship and fill out a form requesting another FMT (tourist permit) if it, too, was lost. If your documents are stolen, get a police report from local authorities; having one *might* lessen the hassle of exiting the country without all your identification. Without the FMT, you can't leave the country, and without an affidavit affirming your passport request and citizenship, you may have problems at U.S. Customs when you get home. It's important to clear everything up *before* trying to leave. Mexican Customs may, however, accept the police report of the loss of the FMT and allow you to leave.

If your wallet is stolen, the police probably won't be able to recover it. Be sure to notify all of your credit card companies right away, and file a report at the nearest police precinct. Your credit card company or insurer may require a police report number or record of the loss. Most credit card companies have an emergency toll-free number to call if your card is lost or stolen; these numbers are not toll-free within Mexico (see "Telephone & Fax," below, for instructions on calling U.S. toll-free numbers). The company may be able to wire you a cash advance off your credit card immediately, and, in many places, can deliver an emergency credit card in a day or two. **Visa**'s U.S. emergency number is ℃ **800/847-2911** or 410/581-9994. American Express cardholders and traveler's check holders should call ℃ **800/221-7282.** MasterCard holders should call ℃ **800/307-7309** or 636/722-7111. For other credit cards, call the toll-free number directory at ℃ **800/555-1212.**

If you need emergency cash over the weekend when all banks and American Express offices are closed, you can have money wired to you via **Western Union** (℃ **800/325-6000;** www.westernunion.com).

Identity theft or fraud are potential complications of losing your wallet, especially if you've lost your driver's license along with your cash and credit cards. Notify the major credit-reporting bureaus immediately; placing a fraud alert on your records may protect you against liability for criminal activity. The three major U.S. credit-reporting agencies are **Equifax** (② 800/766-0008; www.equifax.com), **Experian** (② 888/397-3742; www.experian.com), and **TransUnion** (② 800/680-7289; www.transunion.com). Finally, if you've lost all forms of photo ID call your airline and explain the situation; they might allow you to board the plane if you have a copy of your passport or birth certificate and a copy of the police report you've filed.

*Mail*  Postage for a postcard or letter is 1 peso; it may arrive anywhere from 1 to 6 weeks later. A registered letter costs $1.90 pesos. Sending a package can be quite expensive—the Mexican postal service charges $8 pesos per kilo (2.2 lb.)—and unreliable; it takes 2 to 6 weeks, if it arrives at all. The recommended way to send a package or important mail is through FedEx, DHL, UPS, or another reputable international mail service.

*Newspapers & Magazines*  There currently is no national English-language newspaper. Newspaper kiosks in larger cities carry a selection of English-language magazines.

*Passports*  **For Residents of the United States:** Whether you're applying in person or by mail, you can download passport applications from the U.S. State Department website at **http://travel.state.gov**. To find your regional passport office, either check the U.S. State Department website or call the **National Passport Information Center** toll-free number (② 877/487-2778) for automated information.

**For Residents of Canada:** Passport applications are available at travel agencies throughout Canada or from the central **Passport Office,** Department of Foreign Affairs and International Trade, Ottawa, ON K1A 0G3 (② 800/567-6868; www.ppt.gc.ca).

**For Residents of the United Kingdom:** To pick up an application for a standard 10-year passport (5-year passport for children under 16), visit your nearest passport office, major post office, or travel agency or contact the **United Kingdom Passport Service** at ② 0870/521-0410 or search its website at www.ukpa.gov.uk.

**For Residents of Ireland:** You can apply for a 10-year passport at the **Passport Office,** Setanta Centre, Molesworth Street, Dublin 2 (② 01/671-1633; www.irl gov.ie/iveagh). Those under age 18 and over 65 must apply for a €12 3-year passport. You can also apply at 1A South Mall, Cork (② 021/272-525) or at most main post offices.

**For Residents of Australia:** You can pick up an application from your local post office or any branch of Passports Australia, but you must schedule an interview at the passport office to present your application materials. Call the **Australian Passport Information Service** at ② 131-232, or visit the government website at www.passports.gov.au.

**For Residents of New Zealand:** You can pick up a passport application at any New Zealand Passports Office or download it from their website. Contact the

**Passports Office** at © **0800/225-050** in New Zealand or 04/474-8100, or log on to www.passports.govt.nz.

*Pets* Taking a pet into Mexico is easy but requires a little planning. Animals coming from the United States and Canada need to be checked for health within 30 days before arrival in Mexico. Most veterinarians in major cities have the appropriate paperwork—an official health certificate, to be presented to Mexican Customs officials, that ensures the pet's vaccinations are up-to-date. When you and your pet return from Mexico, U.S. Customs officials will require the same type of paperwork. If your stay extends beyond the 30-day time frame of your U.S.-issued certificate, you'll need an updated Certificate of Health issued by a veterinarian in Mexico. To check last-minute changes in requirements, consult the Mexican Government Tourist Office nearest you (see "Visitor Information," earlier in this chapter).

*Police* In Mexico City, police are to be suspected as frequently as they are to be trusted; however, you'll find many who are quite honest and helpful. In the rest of the country, especially in the tourist areas, most are very protective of international visitors. Several cities, including Puerto Vallarta, Mazatlán, Cancún, and Acapulco, have a special corps of English-speaking Tourist Police to assist with directions, guidance, and more.

*Safety* See "Health & Safety," p. 30.

*Smoking* Smoking is permitted and generally accepted in most public places, including restaurants, bars, and hotel lobbies. Nonsmoking areas and hotel rooms for nonsmokers are becoming more common in higher-end establishments, but they tend to be the exception rather than the rule.

*Taxes* The 15% IVA (value-added) tax applies on goods and services in most of Mexico, and it's supposed to be included in the posted price. This tax is 10% in Cancún, Cozumel, and Los Cabos. There is a 5% tax on food and drinks consumed in restaurants that sell alcoholic beverages with an alcohol content of more than 10%; this tax applies whether you drink alcohol or not. Tequila is subject to a 25% tax. Mexico imposes an exit tax of around $24 on every foreigner leaving the country, as well as a tourism tax of $18 (see "Airport Taxes" under "Getting Around Mexico: By Plane," earlier in this chapter).

*Telephone & Fax* Mexico's telephone system is slowly but surely catching up with modern times. All telephone numbers have 10 digits. Every city and town that has telephone access has a two-digit (Mexico City, Monterrey, and Guadalajara) or three-digit (everywhere else) area code. In Mexico City, Monterrey, and Guadalajara, local numbers have eight digits; elsewhere, local numbers have seven digits. To place a local call, you do not need to dial the area code. Many fax numbers are also regular telephone numbers; ask whoever answers for the fax tone *("me da tono de fax, por favor")*. Cellular phones are very popular for small businesses in resort areas and smaller communities. To call a cellular number inside the same area code, dial 044 and then the number. To dial the cellular phone from anywhere else in Mexico, first dial 01, and then the three-digit area code and the seven-digit number. To dial it from the U.S., dial 011-52, plus the three-digit area code and the seven-digit number.

The **country code** for Mexico is **52.**

**To call Mexico:** If you're calling Mexico from the United States:

1. Dial the international access code: 011.
2. Dial the country code: 52.
3. Dial the two- or three-digit area code, then the eight- or seven-digit number. For example, if you wanted to call the U.S. consulate in Acapulco, the whole number would be 011-52-744-469-0556. If you wanted to dial the U.S. Embassy in Mexico City, the whole number would be 011-52-55-5209-9100.

**To make international calls:** To make international calls from Mexico, first dial 00, then the country code (U.S. or Canada 1, U.K. 44, Ireland 353, Australia 61, New Zealand 64). Next, dial the area code and number. For example, to call the British Embassy in Washington, you would dial 00-1-202-588-7800.

**For directory assistance:** Dial ⓒ **040** if you're looking for a number inside Mexico. *Note:* Listings usually appear under the owner's name, not the name of the business, and your chances to find an English-speaking operator are slim to none.

**For operator assistance:** If you need operator assistance in making a call, dial **090** to make an international call, and **020** to call a number in Mexico.

**Toll-free numbers:** Numbers beginning with 800 within Mexico are toll-free, but calling a U.S. toll-free number from Mexico costs the same as an overseas call. To call an 800 number in the U.S., dial 001-880 and the last seven digits of the toll-free number. To call an 888 number in the U.S., dial 001-881 and the last seven digits of the toll-free number. For a number with an 887 prefix, dial 882; for 866, dial 883.

*Time Zone* Central time prevails throughout most of Mexico. The states of Sonora, Sinaloa, and parts of Nayarit are on Mountain Standard Time. The state of Baja California Norte is on Pacific Standard Time, but Baja California Sur is on MST. All of Mexico observes **daylight saving time.**

*Tipping* Most service employees in Mexico count on tips for the majority of their income, and this is especially true for bellboys and waiters. Bellboys should receive the equivalent of 50¢ to $1 per bag; waiters generally receive 10% to 20%, depending on the level of service. It is not customary to tip taxi drivers, unless they are hired by the hour or provide touring or other special services.

*Toilets* Public toilets are not common in Mexico, but an increasing number are available, especially at fast-food restaurants and Pemex gas stations. These facilities and restaurant and club restrooms commonly have attendants, who expect a small tip (about 50¢).

*Useful Phone Numbers* **Tourist Help Line,** available 24 hours (ⓒ 01-800/987-8224 toll-free inside Mexico, or dial 078). **Mexico Hot Line** (ⓒ 800/44-MEXICO). **U.S. Dept. of State Travel Advisory,** staffed 24 hours (ⓒ 202/647-5225). **U.S. Passport Agency** (ⓒ 877/487-2777). **U.S. Centers for Disease Control and Prevention International Traveler's Hot Line** (ⓒ 877/394-8747).

**Water** Most hotels have decanters or bottles of purified water in the rooms, and the better hotels have either purified water from regular taps or special taps marked *agua purificada*. Some hotels charge for in-room bottled water. Virtually any hotel, restaurant, or bar will bring you purified water if you specifically request it but will usually charge you for it. Drugstores and grocery stores sell bottled purified water. Some popular brands are Santa María, Ciel, and Bonafont. Evian and other imported brands are also widely available.

# 3

# Suggested Yucatán Itineraries

*by David Baird*

The following itineraries assume you're flying in and out of Cancún, by far the most common point of entry for the Yucatán. The airport is south of town in the direction of the Riviera Maya, so if you rent a car to drive down the coast, you won't have to deal with city traffic. For traveling around the Yucatán, rental cars work well. The roads are all easy to figure out, and there's not much traffic when you move inland. Finding your way around Mérida is a little tricky, but

Cancún and the other cities of the peninsula are easy.

These itineraries are merely suggestions; you should tweak them to your specific tastes and interests. However, I recommend against being too ambitious with your vacation time. The heat and humidity bring about a lethargy that can be enjoyable if you're not preoccupied with a timetable. Keep in mind as well that it gets dark early here and it's not a good idea to do much night driving.

## 1 Northern Yucatán in a Week

You could extend this itinerary to 10 days, even 2 weeks—it all depends on how much time you want to spend on the beach. Once you've spent a little time in that clear blue water, it's hard to pull yourself away to move inland. But you'll probably find something in this trip to entice you.

### Days ❶ & ❷: Somewhere on the Caribbean Coast

Spend a few days relaxing on the beach. See chapter 6 for more details.

### Day ❸: Chichén Itzá ✧✧✧

Have a morning swim before driving to the ruins of **Ek Balam** (p. 240), which lie north of the colonial city of Valladolid. If you're coming from Cancún or the northern Riviera Maya, you can take the modern toll highway and save a lot of travel time, though the toll of $22 is a bit pricey. If you're in Playa del Carmen or farther south, you're better off driving south to Tulum and taking the highway to Cobá. You can stop and see the ruins of **Cobá** (p. 171) if you allow enough

time. When you get to Valladolid, head north on Highway 295 to the turnoff for Ek Balam. After climbing the main pyramid and inspecting the beautifully worked sacred doorway, head back to Valladolid for a late lunch. Drive to Chichén Itzá via the old highway. Shortly after leaving town, stop to enjoy **Cenote Dzitnup** (p. 240). Continue on to **Chichén Itzá** (p. 230) and check into a hotel in the area. In the evening, see the sound-and-light show, and then visit the ruins the next morning.

### Days ❹ & ❺: Mérida & Environs ✧✧

Drive to **Mérida** (p. 188) and enjoy an evening in this bustling tropical city. The next day, you can explore the city, or

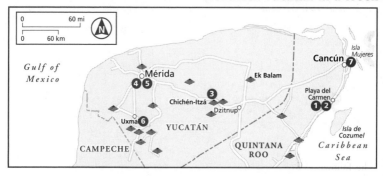

perhaps do some shopping. Or, as a third option, enjoy Mérida in the evening when there's always something going on and take side trips during the day. Choices include the **Celestún National Wildlife Refuge** (p. 209), where you can take a boat ride and see some pink flamingos, or **Dzibilchaltún** (p. 210), to see the ruins and site museum. You might also consider visiting **Progreso** and **Xcambó** (p. 211), for another good chance of seeing flamingos.

### Day ❻: The Ruins of Uxmal ★★★

No matter whether you take the short way or the long way (for details on both routes, see p. 212), try to get to **Uxmal** by

late afternoon, so that you can rest and cool off before seeing the sound-and-light show. Uxmal's **Pyramid of the Magician** is one of the most dramatic structures in the Maya world and it becomes even more intriguing when lit at night. The next morning, you can explore the ruins in more detail. See p. 215.

### Day ❼: Cancún

This last day will necessarily include a good bit of driving. Take the short route back via Uman, then use the loop or *periférico* to avoid entering Mérida. After about 45 minutes, you'll see signs for the highway to Cancún. See chapter 4.

## 2 An Ecoadventure for the Whole Family

If you've got your own mask and snorkel (and fins, too) bring them for this trip; you can always get rentals, but you're better off with gear that fits you comfortably.

### Day ❶: Arrive at Cancún Airport

For this itinerary, it's best to stay in the lower Riviera Maya, at a hotel or condo in the **Xpu-Ha–Akumal–Tulum** area. That puts you close to most of the places you'll be going. The drive from the airport to this part of the coast is at most 2 hours. See p. 161, p. 162, and p. 168.

### Day ❷: Xel-Ha & the Ruins of Tulum ★★★

Start by enjoying a nice swim at **Xel-Ha's** lovely lagoon (p. 163), go snorkeling, or

simply enjoy the parklands encircling the water. You can stay here the whole day or combine this with a trip to see the ruins in **Tulum** (which you should do in the morning, when the air is cooler). See p. 166.

### Day ❸: Hidden Worlds ★★★ & Aktun Chen ★

Between Akumal and Tulum are two attractions, each interesting in its own way. At **Hidden Worlds** (p. 164), you can snorkel in a couple of different *cenotes* (sinkholes or wellsprings) and subterranean

# An Ecoadventure for the Whole Family

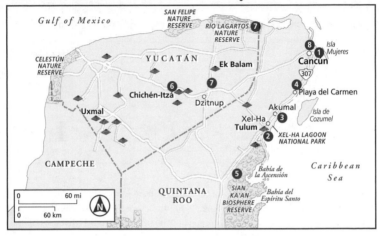

rivers for which the Yucatán is famous. The water is cold, but this outfit provides wet suits and snorkel gear if you don't bring your own. **Aktun Chen** (p. 163) is a cavern that you can hike through and see lots of rock formations. There's also a small zoo with local species such as spider monkeys and tropical birds, including a toucan.

## Day ❹: Alltournative

Consider spending today with **Alltournative,** an adventure tour agency based in Playa del Carmen. Its day trips combine adventure with nature and interactions with contemporary Maya in one of their own villages. The tour company will pick you up at almost any hotel in the Riviera Maya. You can fly out over the jungle on a zip line, try your hand at rappelling, and have a Maya-style meal all in the same day. See p. 146.

## Day ❺: Sian Ka'an Biosphere Reserve ᚛

Explore the largest wildlife preserve in the Yucatán; snorkel down canals built by the Maya, visit the large, pristine lagoon at the center of the park, and observe various forms of wildlife as you get an up-close-and-personal view of the peninsula's

natural habitat. Tour agencies do full-day tours. See p. 170.

## Day ❻: Chichén Itzá ᚛᚛᚛

Go for a morning snorkel trip with one of the local dive shops, and then drive to **Chichén Itzá** in the afternoon. Check into a hotel, and in the evening you can enjoy the sound-and-light show at the ruins. Return the next morning to get a closer look in daylight. See p. 230.

## Day ❼: Cenote Dzitnup ᚛, Ek Balam ᚛᚛᚛ & Río Lagartos Nature Reserve ᚛

After seeing the ruins, head east on the old federal highway until you get to **Cenote Dzitnup,** shortly before the town of Valladolid. You'll find a dark *cenote* with a beautiful pool of water illuminated by a column of sunlight that penetrates the roof. Nearby is a second *cenote*. After a quick dip, continue into **Valladolid** (p. 237) for lunch. After you're nourished, head north on Highway 295 to the turnoff for the recently excavated ruins of **Ek Balam** (p. 240), noted for a beautifully sculpted sacred doorway on the tallest pyramid in northern Yucatán. Continue north, past the town of Tizimín, until you get to the coastal village of **Río Lagartos.** Here you can get a room at one of the economical hotels fronting the water and arrange for an early-morning boat tour of the wildlife sanctuary. Not only will you see those eye-catching natural wonders—pink flamingos—but you'll see a host of other species as well, and enjoy a boat ride through mangrove and saltwater estuaries. See p. 241.

### Day ❽: Cancún
After your visit with pink flamingos, it's time to get back to Cancún and civilization. See chapter 4.

## 3 La Ruta Maya

This route, which connects the major Maya sites in Mexico, could be done quickly in 2 weeks, or more slowly in a month or perhaps broken up into two trips. I've kept the trip to the minimum by avoiding the city of Mérida, but you may want to visit it. There's a risk of overdosing on ruins by seeing too many in too short a time. I give you the fast-track approach here, but that doesn't mean that I'm encouraging you to move through this area that quickly. The best mode of travel would be a rental car: The highways have little traffic and are, for the most part, in good shape.

### Day ❶: Arrive in Cancún
After you arrive, enjoy the remainder of the day with a swim in the Caribbean or a relaxing afternoon poolside. See chapter 4.

### Day ❷: Ek Balam 𝕮𝕮𝕮 & Chichén Itzá 𝕮𝕮𝕮
Get on the modern toll highway that heads toward Mérida and take the exit for Valladolid. Head north, away from the town, to visit the ruins of **Ek Balam** (p. 240). Highlights include a sacred doorway richly decorated with vivid figures of gods and men. Then head back to the town of Valladolid for lunch before driving the short distance to **Chichén Itzá** (p. 230) on the old federal highway. Just outside of town, stop to see the *cenotes* of **Dzitnup** (p. 240) and **Sammulá** (p. 240). Farther on is the **Balankanché Cave** (p. 237). When you get to Chichén, check into your hotel, and then go to the ruins later in the evening for the sound-and-light show. See p. 232.

### Day ❸: Continuing to Uxmal 𝕮𝕮𝕮
Spend more time at the ruins of **Chichén Itzá** in the morning, then continue west on the toll highway toward Mérida, and turn off at Ticopó. Head south toward the town of **Acanceh** (p. 213) and Highway 18. Stop to see the small but interesting ruins in the middle of town, then proceed down Highway 18 to the ruins of **Mayapán** (p. 213). Afterward, continue through Ticul to Santa Elena and Uxmal. Experience the sound-and-light show. See p. 215.

### Day ❹: Edzná
Visit **Uxmal** (p. 214) in the morning, then drive back toward Santa Elena and take Highway 261 south to Hopelchén and on to the impressive ruins of **Edzná** (p. 223). Nearby is a fancy hacienda-turned-hotel called **Uayamón** (p. 205; reservations can be made through Starwood hotels) or drive into the town of **Campeche** and stay at more modest digs.

### Days ❺ & ❻: Palenque 𝕮𝕮, Bonampak & Yaxchilán
Stay on Highway 261 to Escárcega, then head west on Highway 186 toward Villahermosa then south on Highway 199 to the town of **Palenque** (p. 250) with its magnificent ruins. The next day go to the ruins of **Bonampak** and **Yaxchilán** (p. 257), using one of the local tour operators.

# La Ruta Maya

## Days ❼ & ❽: San Cristóbal de las Casas ✿✿

Keep south on Highway 199 toward **San Cristóbal** (p. 258). On the way, take a swimming break at **Misol-Ha** (p. 257), and visit the ruins of **Toniná** outside of the town of Ocosingo. From San Cristóbal, go with one of the local guides to see the present-day Maya communities of **Chamula** and **Zinacantan** (p. 266). Spend some time enjoying the town.

## Day ❾: Calakmul ✿✿✿

Retrace your steps to Escárcega and continue east on Highway 186. If you have time, visit the fascinating sculptures of **Balamkú** (p. 185). Spend the night at one of the hotels in the vicinity of the

turnoff for **Calakmul,** one of the prime city-states of the Classic age of the Maya, and not often visited.

## Day ❿: Calakmul & Becán ✿✿✿

Get to **Calakmul** (p. 184) early. Keep your eyes open for wildlife as you drive along a narrow jungle road. All the area surrounding the city is a **wildlife preserve.** For most of the city's history, Calakmul was the main rival to the city of Tikal, which is in present-day Guatemala. It eventually defeated Tikal and subjugated it for 100 years. Calakmul's **Structure 2** is the highest Maya pyramid in Mexico. Afterward, continue east on Highway 186 to see the ruins of **Becán,** a large ceremonial center with tall temples.

Also in the vicinity are **Xpujil** and **Chi-canná.** Spend the night on the shores of **Lake Bacalar,** where you can cool off in its blue waters. See p. 176.

### Days ⓫ & ⓬: Tulum

Drive north on Highway 307 to **Tulum** and settle into one of the small beach hotels there. In the morning, walk through the ruins and enjoy the lovely view of the coast. See p. 165.

### Day ⓭: Back to Cancún

Drive back to Cancún. Depending on your schedule, you can enjoy some more beach time, or head straight to the airport (25 min. south of Cancún) and depart. See chapter 4.

# 4

# Cancún

*by Lynne Bairstow*

On October 21, 2005, Hurricane Wilma roared ashore with winds reaching 242kmph (150 mph), and then stalled over Cancún for nearly 40 hours. It toppled trees, demolished homes, and damaged the resort's hotels, restaurants, attractions—and Cancún's reputation as the favored playground in Mexico, at least for a while. However, relief came quickly because Mexico's government understands the importance of Cancún as its most popular tourism destination.

The majority of damaged hotels took the opportunity to upgrade their facilities and redecorate their rooms, which should ultimately lead to a new and improved Cancún. However, at press time, many of these were still undergoing renovations, so personal reviews of all accommodations were not possible, and complete details of the upgrades were often unavailable. There have been some reports of selected rooms retaining a strong smell of mildew, so please, let us know of your experiences or any comments you may have. Also, the noise of construction and piles of debris were omnipresent at press time, but this should be the memory by the fall of 2006.

Cancún remains Mexico's calling card to the world, perfectly showcasing both the country's breathtaking natural beauty and the depth of its 1,000-year history. Simply stated, Cancún is the reason most people travel to Mexico. The sheer number of travelers underscores Cancún's magnetic appeal, with almost three million people visiting this enticing beach resort annually—most of them on their first trip to the country. The reasons for this are both numerous and obvious.

Cancún offers an unrivaled combination of high-quality accommodations, dreamy beaches, easy air access, and a wide diversity of shopping, dining, nightlife, and nearby activities—most of them exceptional values. There is also the lure of ancient cultures evident in all directions and a number of ecologically oriented theme parks.

No doubt about it—Cancún embodies Caribbean splendor, with translucent turquoise waters and powdery white-sand beaches, coupled with coastal areas of great natural beauty. But Cancún is also a modern megaresort. Even a traveler feeling apprehensive about visiting foreign soil will feel completely at ease here. English is spoken, dollars are accepted, roads are well paved, and lawns are manicured. Malls are the mode for shopping and dining, and you could swear that some hotels are larger than a small town. Travelers feel comfortable in Cancún. You do not need to spend a day getting your bearings, because you immediately see familiar names for dining, shopping, nightclubbing, and sleeping.

In 1974, a team of Mexican government computer analysts picked Cancún for tourism development due to its ideal mix of elements to attract travelers—and they were right on. It's actually an island, a 24km (15-mile) sliver of land connected to the mainland by two bridges and separated from it by the expansive Nichupté lagoon. (*Cancún* means "golden snake" in Mayan.)

In addition to attractions of its own, Cancún is a convenient distance from the more traditional resorts of Isla Mujeres and from the coastal zone now known as the Riviera Maya—extending down from Cancún, through Playa del Carmen, to the Maya ruins at Tulum, Cozumel, Chichén Itzá, and Cobá. All are within day-trip distance.

You will run out of vacation days before you run out of things to do in Cancún. Snorkeling, jet-skiing, jungle tours, and visits to ancient Maya ruins and modern ecological theme parks are among the most popular diversions. There are a dozen malls with name-brand and duty-free shops (with European goods at prices better than in the U.S.), and more than 350 restaurants and nightclubs. The 28,000-plus hotel rooms in the area offer something for every taste and every budget.

Cancún's luxury hotels have pools so spectacular that you may find it tempting to remain poolside, but don't. Set aside some time to simply gaze into the ocean and wriggle your toes in the fine, brilliantly white sand. It is, after all, what put Cancún on the map—and not even a tempest of nature has been able to take that away.

## 1 Orientation

### GETTING THERE

**BY PLANE** If this is not your first trip to Cancún, you'll notice that the airport's facilities and services continue to expand. **Aeromexico** (© **800/237-6639** in the U.S., or 01/800-021-4000 in Mexico; www.aeromexico.com) offers direct service from Atlanta, Houston, Miami, and New York, plus connecting service via Mexico City from Dallas, Los Angeles, and San Diego. **Mexicana** (© **800/531-7921** in the U.S., 01/800-502-2000 in Mexico, or 998/881-9090; www.mexicana.com.mx) flies from Chicago, Denver, Los Angeles, Oakland, San Antonio, San Francisco, and San Jose via Mexico City, with nonstop service from Miami and New York. In addition to these carriers, many **charter** companies—such as Apple Vacations, Funjet, and Friendly Holidays—travel to Cancún; these package tours make up as much as 60% of arrivals by U.S. visitors (see "Packages for the Independent Traveler," in chapter 2).

Regional carrier **Click Mexicana,** a Mexicana affiliate (© **998/884-2000**) flies from Cozumel, Havana, Mexico City, Mérida, Chetumal, and other points within Mexico. You'll want to confirm departure times for flights to the U.S. Here are the Cancún airport numbers of major international carriers: **American** (© **01-800/904-6000** in Mexico; www.aa.com), **Continental** (© **998/886-0006;** www.continental.com), and **Northwest** (© **998/886-0044** or -0046; www.nwa.com).

Most major car-rental firms have outlets at the airport, so if you're renting a car, consider picking it up and dropping it off at the airport to save on airport-transportation costs. Another way to save money is to arrange for the rental before you leave home. If you wait until you arrive, the daily cost will be around $50 to $75 for a Chevrolet Atos. Major agencies include **Avis** (© **800/331-1212** in the U.S., or 998/886-0221; www.avis.com); **Budget** (© **800/527-0700** in the U.S., or 998/886-0417; fax 998/884-4812; www.budget.com); **Dollar** (© **800/800-3665** in the U.S., or 998/886-2300; www.dollar.com); **National** (© **800/227-7368** in the U.S., or 998/886-0153; www.nationalcar.com); and **Hertz** (© **800/654-3131** in the U.S. and Canada, or 998/884-1326; www.hertz.com). The Zona Hotelera (Hotel Zone) is 10km (6¼ miles)—a 20-minute drive—from the airport along wide, well-paved roads.

Rates for a private taxi from the airport are around $25 to downtown Cancún, or $28 to $40 to the Hotel Zone, depending on your destination. *Colectivos* (vans) run from the airport into town. Buy tickets, which cost about $9, from the booth to the far right as you exit the airport terminal. There's minibus transportation ($9.50) from the airport to the Puerto Juárez passenger ferry to Isla Mujeres, or you can hire a private taxi for about $40. There is no *colectivo* service returning to the airport from Ciudad Cancún or the Hotel Zone, so you'll have to take a taxi, but the rate will be much less than for the trip from the airport. (Only federally chartered taxis may take fares *from* the airport, but any taxi may bring passengers *to* the airport.) Ask at your hotel what the fare should be, but expect to pay about half what you paid from the airport to your hotel.

**BY CAR**    From Mérida or Campeche, take Highway 180 east to Cancún. This is mostly a winding, two-lane road that branches off into the express toll road 180D between Izamal and Nuevo Xcan. Nuevo Xcan is approximately 40km (25 miles) from Cancún. Mérida is about 80km (50 miles) away.

**BY BUS**    Cancún's **ADO bus terminal** (© **998/884-4352** or -4804) is in downtown Ciudad Cancún at the intersection of avenidas Tulum and Uxmal. All out-of-town buses arrive here. Buses run to Playa del Carmen, Tulum, Chichén Itzá, other nearby beach and archaeological zones, and other points within Mexico.

---

*Tips*   **The Best Websites for Cancún**

- **All About Cancún: www.cancunmx.com**   This site is a good place to start planning. There's a database of answers to the most common questions, called "The Online Experts." It's slow, but it has input from lots of recent travelers to the region.

- **Cancún Convention & Visitors Bureau: www.cancun.info**   The official site of the Cancún Convention & Visitors Bureau lists excellent information on events and attractions. Its hotel guide is one of the most complete available, and it has an active message board of recent visitors to Cancún.

- **Cancún Online: www.cancun.com**   This comprehensive guide has lots of information about things to do and see in Cancún, with most details provided by paying advertisers. You can even reserve a tee time or conduct wedding planning online.

- **Cancún Travel Guide: www.go2cancun.com**   This group specializing in online information about Mexico has put together an excellent resource for Cancún rentals, hotels, and attractions. Note that it lists only paying advertisers, but you'll find most of the major players.

- **Mexico Web Cancún Chat: www.mexicoweb.com/chats/cancun**   This is one of the more active chats online specifically about Cancún. The users share inside information on everything from the cheapest beer to the quality of food at various all-inclusive resorts.

# Downtown Cancún

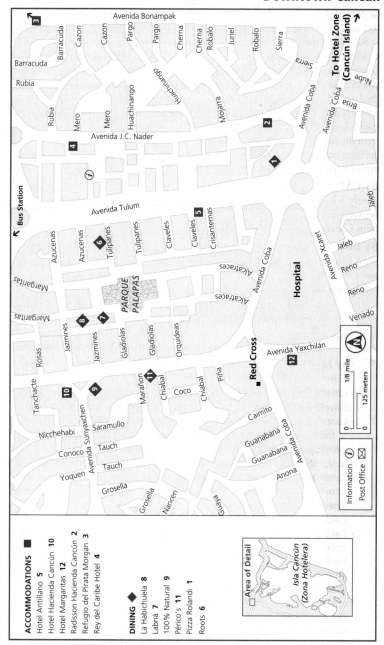

## VISITOR INFORMATION

The **State Tourism Office,** Cancún Center, Bulevar Kukulkán Km 9, 1st floor, Zona Hotelera (© **998/881-9000** or 884-8073; www.qroo.gob.mx), is open Monday to Friday from 9am to 5pm. The **Convention & Visitors Bureau** tourist information office is also in the Cancún Center, first floor (© **866/891-7773** in the U.S., or 998/881-2745; fax 998/881-0402). The **Cancún Municipal Tourism Office** is found downtown, Avenida Cobá at Avenida Tulum (© **998/884-6531** or -3438). It's open Monday through Friday from 9am to 7pm. Each office lists hotels and their rates, and ferry schedules. For information prior to your arrival in Cancún, visit the Convention Bureau's website, **www.cancun.info**.

Pick up copies of the free monthly *Cancún Tips* (www.cancuntips.com.mx) booklet and a seasonal tabloid of the same name.

## CITY LAYOUT

There are really two Cancúns: **Isla Cancún (Cancún Island)** and **Ciudad Cancún (Cancún City)**. The latter, on the mainland, has restaurants, shops, and less expensive hotels, as well as pharmacies, dentists, automotive shops, banks, travel and airline agencies, and car-rental firms—all within an area about 9 blocks square. The city's main thoroughfare is **Avenida Tulum.** Heading south, Avenida Tulum becomes the highway to the airport and to Tulum and Chetumal; heading north, it intersects the highway to Mérida and the road to Puerto Juárez and the Isla Mujeres ferries.

The famed **Zona Hotelera,** or Hotel Zone (also called the Zona Turística, or Tourist Zone), stretches out along Isla Cancún, which is a sandy strip 22km (14 miles) long, shaped like a "7." It connects to the mainland by the Playa Linda Bridge at the north end and the Punta Nizuc Bridge at the southern end. Between the two areas lies Laguna Nichupté. Avenida Cobá from Cancún City becomes Bulevar Kukulkán, the island's main traffic artery. Cancún's international airport is just inland from the south end of the island.

**FINDING AN ADDRESS**    Cancún's street-numbering system is a holdover from its early days. Addresses are still given by the number of the building lot and by the *manzana* (block) or *supermanzana* (group of blocks). The city is relatively compact, and the downtown commercial section is easy to cover on foot.

On the island, addresses are given by kilometer number on Bulevar Kukulkán or by reference to some well-known location. In Cancún, streets are named after famous Maya cities. Chichén Itzá, Tulum, and Uxmal are the names of the boulevards in Cancún, as well as nearby archaeological sites.

## GETTING AROUND

**BY TAXI**    Taxi prices in Cancún are clearly set by zone, although keeping track of what's in which zone can take some doing. The minimum fare within the Hotel Zone is $6 per ride, making it one of the most expensive taxi areas in Mexico. In addition, taxis operating in the Hotel Zone feel perfectly justified in having a discriminatory pricing structure: Local residents pay about half of what tourists pay, and prices for guests at higher-priced hotels are about double those for budget hotel guests—these are all established by the taxi union. Rates should be posted outside your hotel; if you have a question, all drivers are required to have an official rate card in their taxis, though it's generally in Spanish.

Within the downtown area, the cost is about $1.50 per cab ride (not per person); within any other zone, it's $6. Traveling between two zones will also cost $6, and if you cross two zones, that'll cost $8. Settle on a price in advance, or check at your hotel. Trips to the airport from most zones cost $15. Taxis can also be rented for $18 per hour for travel around the city and Hotel Zone, but this rate can generally be negotiated down to about $15. If you want to hire a taxi to take you to Chichén Itzá or along the Riviera Maya, expect to pay about $30 per hour—many taxi drivers feel that they are also providing guide services.

**BY BUS**    Bus travel within Cancún continues to improve and is increasingly popular. In town, almost everything is within walking distance. Ruta 1 and Ruta 2 (HOTELES) city buses travel frequently from the mainland to the beaches along Avenida Tulum (the main street) and all the way to Punta Nizuc at the far end of the Hotel Zone on Isla Cancún. Ruta 8 buses go to Puerto Juárez/Punta Sam for ferries to Isla Mujeres. They stop on the east side of Avenida Tulum. All these city buses operate between 6am and 10pm daily. Beware of private buses along the same route; they charge far more than the public ones. Public buses have the fare painted on the front; at press time, the fare was 65¢.

**BY MOPED**    Mopeds are a convenient but dangerous way to cruise around through the very congested traffic. Rentals start at $25 for a day, and a credit card voucher is required as security. You should receive a crash helmet (it's the law) and instructions on how to lock the wheels when you park. Read the fine print on the back of the rental agreement regarding liability for repairs or replacement in case of accident, theft, or vandalism.

---

## FAST FACTS: Cancún

*American Express*    The local office is at Av. Tulum 208 and Agua (© **998/881-4000** or -4055; www.americanexpress.com/mexico), 1 block past the Plaza México. It's open Monday through Friday from 9am to 6pm, Saturday from 9am to 1pm. Another branch of American Express is located in the hotel zone, in the La Isla Shopping Center (© **998/885-3905**).

*Area Code*    The telephone area code is **998.**

*Climate*    It's hot but not overwhelmingly humid. The rainy season is May through October. August through October is hurricane season, which brings erratic weather. November through February is generally sunny but can also be cloudy, windy, somewhat rainy, and even cool.

*Consulates*    The **U.S. Consular Agent** is in the Plaza Caracol 2, Bulevar Kukulkán Km 8.5, 3rd level, 320–323 (© **998/883-0272**). The office is open Monday through Friday from 9am to 2pm. The **Canadian Consulate** is in the Plaza Caracol, 3rd level, local 330 (© **998/883-3360**). The office is open Monday through Friday from 9am to 5pm. The **United Kingdom** has a consular office in Cancún (© **998/881-0100,** ext. 65898; fax 998/848-8662; information@britishconsulate cancun.com). Irish, Australian, and New Zealand citizens should contact their embassies in Mexico City.

*Crime* Car break-ins are just about the only crime here. They happen frequently, especially around the shopping centers in the Hotel Zone. VW Beetles and Golfs are frequent targets.

*Currency Exchange* Most banks are downtown along Avenida Tulum and are usually open Monday through Friday from 9:30am to 4pm. Many have automated teller machines for after-hours cash withdrawals. In the Hotel Zone, you'll find banks in the Kukulcan Plaza and next to the convention center. There are also many *casas de cambio* (exchange houses). Downtown merchants are eager to change cash dollars, but island stores don't offer very good exchange rates. Avoid changing money at the airport as you arrive, especially at the first exchange booth you see—its rates are less favorable than those of any in town or others farther inside the airport concourse.

*Drugstores* With locations in both Flamingo Plaza (© **998/885-1351**) and Kukulcan Plaza (© **998/885-0860**), **Farmacia Roxanna** offers delivery service within the Hotel Zone. Plenty of drugstores are in the major shopping malls in the Hotel Zone, and are open until 10pm. In downtown Cancún, **Farmacia Cancún** is located at Av. Tulum 17 (© **998/884-1283**). You can stock up on Retin-A, Viagra, and many other prescription drugs without a prescription.

*Emergencies* To report an emergency, dial © **060,** which is supposed to be similar to 911 emergency service in the United States. For first aid, the **Cruz Roja,** or Red Cross (© **065** or 998/884-1616; fax 998/883-9218), is open 24 hours on Avenida Yaxchilán between avenidas Xcaret and Labná, next to the Telmex building. **Total Assist,** Claveles 5, SM 22, at Avenida Tulum (© **998/884-1058** or -1092; totalassist@prodigy.net.mx), is a small (nine-room) emergency hospital with English-speaking doctors. It's open 24 hours and accepts American Express, MasterCard, and Visa. Desk staff may have limited command of English. Another facility that caters to English-speaking visitors is **Ameri-Med,** Plaza Las Américas, in downtown Cancún (© **998/881-3434**) with 24-hour emergency service. **Air Ambulance** service is available by calling © **01-800/305-9400** in Mexico.

*Internet Access* **C@ncunet,** in a kiosk on the second floor of Kukulcan Plaza, Bulevar Kukulkán Km 13 (© **998/885-0055** or 840-6099), offers Internet access at $4 for 15 minutes, or $7 per hour. It's open daily from 10am to 10pm.

*Luggage Storage & Lockers* Hotels will generally tag and store luggage while you travel elsewhere.

*Newspapers & Magazines* Most hotel gift shops and newsstands carry English-language magazines and English-language Mexican newspapers.

*Police* Cancún has a fleet of English-speaking tourist police to help travelers. Dial © **998/884-1913** or -2342. The **Procuraduría Federal del Consumidor (consumer protection agency),** Av. Cobá 9–11 (© **998/884-2634** or -2701), is opposite the Social Security Hospital and upstairs from the Fenix drugstore. It's open Monday through Saturday from 9am to 3pm.

*Post Office* The main *correo* is at the intersection of avenidas Sunyaxchen and Xel-Ha (© **998/884-1418**). It's open Monday through Friday from 9am to 4pm, and Saturday from 9am to noon just for the purchase of stamps.

*Safety* Aside from car break-ins, there is very little crime in Cancún. People are generally safe late at night in tourist areas; just use ordinary common sense. As at any other beach resort, don't take money or valuables to the beach. See "Crime," above.

Swimming on the Caribbean side presents a danger because of the undertow. See the information on beaches in "Beaches, Watersports & Boat Tours," later in this chapter, for information about flag warnings

*Seasons* Technically, high season is from December 15 to April; low season is from May to December 15, when prices drop 10% to 30%. Some hotels are starting to charge high-season rates during June and July, when Mexican, European, and school-holiday visitors often travel, although rates may still be lower than in winter months.

*Special Events* The annual **Mexico-Caribbean Food Festival,** featuring special menus of culinary creations throughout town, is held each year between September and November. Additional information is available through the Convention and Visitors Bureau.

## 2 Where to Stay

Island hotels—almost all of them offering clean, modern facilities—line the beach like dominoes. Extravagance is the byword in the newer hotels. Some hotels, while exclusive, affect a more relaxed attitude. The water on the upper end of the island facing Bahía de Mujeres is placid, while beaches lining the long side of the island facing the Caribbean are subject to choppier water and crashing waves on windy days. (For more information on swimming safety, see "Beaches, Watersports & Boat Tours," later in this chapter.) Be aware that the farther south you go on the island, the longer it takes (20–30 min. in traffic) to get back to the "action spots," which are primarily between the Plaza Flamingo and Punta Cancún on the island and along Avenida Tulum on the mainland.

Following Hurricane Wilma's devastation, the news item that received the most coverage was the destruction of Cancún's famed white-sand beaches, certainly key to selecting a hotel location for many. Immediately following the storm, literally all of the sand was washed away from the northern border of Isla Cancún, and Punta Cancún. However, thanks in part to Mother Nature, and in part to a more than $20-million effort by Mexico's government to pump the dislocated sand back to the beach, by spring of 2006 this was no longer an issue. At press time, a large beach had already developed along Punta Cancún, in front of the Forum Plaza, with sufficient sand in place along the north shore. The southern beaches of Isla Cancún actually benefited from the storm, and those areas enjoyed especially wide beachfronts.

Almost all major hotel chains are represented on Cancún Island, so this list can be viewed as a representative summary, with a select number of notable places. The reality is that Cancún is so popular as a package destination from the U.S. that prices and special deals are often the deciding factor for those traveling here (see "Packages for the Independent Traveler," in chapter 2). Ciudad Cancún offers independently owned, smaller, less expensive lodging; prices are lower here off season (May to early

Dec). For condo, home, and villa rentals, check with **Cancún Hideaways** (© 817/ **468-0564;** fax 817/557-3483; www.cancun-hideaways.com), a company specializing in luxury properties, downtown apartments, and condos—many at prices much lower than comparable hotel stays. Owner Maggie Rodriguez, a former resident of Cancún, has made this niche market her specialty.

The hotel listings in this chapter begin on Cancún Island and finish in Cancún City, where bargain lodgings are available. Parking is free at all island hotels.

## CANCUN ISLAND
### VERY EXPENSIVE

**Aqua** ✿✿✿    Stunning, stylish, and sensual, Aqua quickly emerged as Cancún's most coveted place to stay following its 2005 opening—only to be severely damaged by Hurricane Wilma. Extensive repairs rebuilt this mainly glass structure, slated to open by late fall 2006. A member of the Fiesta Americana chain, the entire hotel seems to mirror the predominant colors of Cancún—turquoise and white—in a sublimely chic manner. This hotel was built for sophisticated travelers who appreciate hip style and look for the cutting edge in places to stay. Aqua aims to stimulate your five senses, and upon arrival—under a crystal cube fountain—you're offered a fusion tea, and a blend of relaxing and stimulating aromatherapy. The oasis of eight oceanfront pools is surrounded by chaises, queen-size recliners, and private cabanas. All rooms and common areas emphasize the views to the pool and ocean beyond. Rooms are generous in size, and all face the ocean and have balconies. Very large bathrooms feature a soaking tub and organic bath products. Guests can tailor their turndown service by selecting from a pillow menu and choice of aromatherapy oils and candles. Miniature Zen gardens or a fishbowl add unique touches to room decor. Suites offer extras like Bose surround-sound systems. Twenty-nine rooms are "Grand Club," which include continental breakfast and a club room with butler service, snacks, bar service, and private check-in. The 1,500-sq.-m (16,145-sq.-ft.) spa is among the hotel's most notable attractions, with 12 treatment rooms offering a blend of Eastern, pre-Hispanic, and Western treatments. Outdoor Pilates, Tai Chi, and yoga classes are offered daily, and massage cabanas are also available on the beach. Another hallmark of this hotel is certain to be its collection of restaurants, chief among them **SIETE,** under the direction of premier Mexican chef and cookbook author Patricia Quintana, featuring her sophisticated take on traditional Mexican cuisine. Chef Michelle Bernstein, formerly a rising culinary star in Miami, presides over **MB,** serving healthy comfort food. There's also an Italian restaurant, deli, lounge, and 24-hour room service. After dark, the hotel shifts moods, with fire pits, torch lights, and ambient music.

Bulevar Kukulkán Km 12.5, 77500 Cancún, Q. Roo. © **800/343-7821** in the U.S., or 998/881-7600. Fax 998/881-7601. www.fiestaamericana.com. 371 units. $254–$379 double; $435 Grand Club double; $580–$1,110 suite. Ask about Fiesta Break packages. AE, DC, MC, V. Small pets allowed with prior reservation. **Amenities:** 4 restaurants; poolside snack bar; lounge and bar; 8 outdoor pools; tennis court; fitness center; spa w/12 treatment rooms; watersports on the beach; concierge; travel agency; business center; salon; room service; babysitting; laundry service; club floors w/special amenities and complimentary cocktails. *In room:* A/C, flatscreen TV/DVD, CD player, high-speed Internet access, minibar, hair dryer, iron, safe.

**Fiesta Americana Grand Coral Beach** ✿    This is an ideal choice for any type of traveler looking to be at the heart of all that Cancún has to offer. The spectacular hotel, which opened in 1991, has one of the best locations in Cancún, with 300m (984 ft.) of prime beachfront and proximity to the main shopping and entertainment

# Isla Cancún (Zona Hotelera)

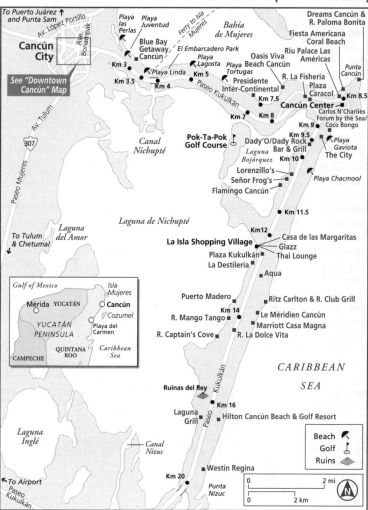

**ACCOMMODATIONS**
Aqua **Km 12.5**
Blue Bay Getaway Cancún **Km 3.5**
Dreams Cancún Resort & Spa **Km 9.5**
Fiesta Americana Grand Coral Beach **Km 9.5**
Flamingo Cancún **Km 11.5**
Hilton Cancún Beach & Golf Resort **Km 17**
Le Méridien Cancún Resort & Spa **Km 14**
Marriott Casa Magna **Km 14.5**
Oasis Viva Beach Cancún **Km 8.5**
Presidente Inter-Continental Cancún **Km 7.5**

Ritz-Carlton Hotel **Km 13.5**
Riu Palace Las Americas **Km 8.5**
Westin Regina Cancún **Km 20**

**DINING**
Aioli **Km 14**
Captain's Cove **Km 15**
Casa de las Margaritas **Km 12.5**
Club Grill **Km 13.5**
Glazz **Km 12.5**
La Destilería **Km 12.6**

La Dolce Vita **Km 14.6**
La Fisheria
  (in Plaza Caracol) **Km 8.5**
Laguna Grill **Km 16.5**
Lorenzillo's **Km 10.5**
Mango Tango **Km 14.2**
Paloma Bonita (at Punta
  Cancún) **Km 9.5**
Puerto Madero **Km 8.5**
Thai Lounge **Km 12.5**

85

centers. The key word here is *big*—everything at the Fiesta Americana seems oversize, from the lobby to the suites. Service is gracious, if cool: The hotel aims for a sophisticated ambience. It's embellished with elegant dark-green granite and an abundance of marble. The large guest rooms are also decorated with marble, and all have balconies facing the ocean, most of which were remodeled in 2004. The hotel's great Punta Cancún location (opposite the Cancún Center) has the advantage of facing the beach to the north, meaning that the surf is calm and perfect for swimming.

Bulevar Kukulkán Km 9.5, 77500 Cancún, Q. Roo. © **800/343-7821** in the U.S., or 998/881-3200. Fax 998/881-3273. www.fiestaamericana.com. 602 units. High season $442–$465 double; $570–$838 club-floor double; low season $279–$301 double, $407–$674 club-floor double. AE, MC, V. **Amenities:** 3 restaurants including the gourmet Basilique; poolside snack bar; 5 bars; outdoor pool w/swim-up bars; 3 indoor tennis courts w/stadium seating; fitness center w/weights; sauna; watersports rentals on the beach; concierge; travel agency; car-rental desk; business center; salon; room service; massage; babysitting; laundry service; 2 concierge floors w/complimentary cocktails; rooms for those w/limited mobility. *In room:* A/C, TV, minibar, hair dryer, iron, safe.

**Hilton Cancún Beach & Golf Resort** *(R)* *(Kids)*   Grand, expansive, and fully equipped, this is a true resort in every sense of the word and is especially perfect for anyone whose motto is "the bigger the better." The Hilton Cancún sits on 100 hectares (247 acres) of prime beachside property, a location that gives every room a sea view (some have both sea and lagoon views), with an 18-hole par-72 golf course across the street. Like the sprawling resort, rooms are grandly spacious and immaculately decorated in minimalist style, and following Hurricane Wilma, all received an update, with common areas renovated as well. It's a very kid-friendly hotel, with one of the island's best children's activity programs, special children's pool, and babysitting available. The hotel is especially appealing to golfers because it's one of only two in Cancún with an on-site course (the other is the Meliá). Greens fees for guests are $77 for 9 holes, $99 for 18 holes, and include the use of a cart. It recently added the Wellness Spa, highlights of which are oceanfront massage cabanas, yoga, and aromatherapy.

Bulevar Kukulkán Km 17, Retorno Lacandones, 77500 Cancún, Q. Roo. © **800/228-3000** in the U.S., or 998/881-8000. Fax 998/881-8080. www.hiltoncancun.com. 426 units. High season $269–$415 double, $440–$585 Beach Club double, $555–$779 suite; low season $119–$300 double, $350–$550 Beach Club double, $395–$500 suite. AE, DC, MC, V. **Amenities:** 2 restaurants; 7 interconnected outdoor pools w/swim-up bar; 2 whirlpools; golf course across the street; golf clinic; 2 lighted tennis courts; Wellness Spa w/spa services and fully equipped gym; watersports center; Kids' Club; concierge; tour desk; car-rental desk; salon; room service; babysitting; laundry service. *In room:* A/C, TV, minibar, coffeemaker, hair dryer, iron, safe, bathrobes, house shoes.

**Le Méridien Cancún Resort & Spa** *(R)(R)(R)*   Of all the luxury properties in Cancún, Le Méridien is the most inviting, with a refined yet welcoming sense of personal

---

**(Tips) Important Note on Hotel Prices**

Cancún's hotels, in all price categories, generally set their rates in dollars, so they are immune to swings in the peso. Travel agents and wholesalers always have air/hotel packages available, and Sunday papers often advertise inventory-clearing packages at prices much lower than the rates listed here. Cancún also has numerous all-inclusive properties, which allow you to take a fixed-cost vacation. Note that the price quoted when you call a hotel's reservation number from the United States may not include Cancún's 12% tax. Prices can vary considerably throughout the year, so it pays to consult a travel agent or shop around.

service. From the intimate lobby and reception area to the best concierge service in Cancún, guests feel immediately pampered. The relatively small establishment is more elegant boutique hotel than immense resort—a welcome relief. The decor throughout the rooms and common areas is classy and comforting, not overdone. Rooms are generous in size, and most have small balconies overlooking the pool, with a view to the ocean. Each has a very large marble bathroom with a separate tub and glassed-in shower. The hotel attracts many Europeans as well as younger, sophisticated travelers, and is ideal for a second honeymoon or romantic break.

A highlight of—or even a reason for—staying here is the **Spa del Mar,** one of Mexico's most complete European spa facilities, with more than 4,570 sq. m (49,190 sq. ft.) of services dedicated to your body and soul. A complete fitness center with extensive cardio and weight machines is on the upper level. The spa consists of a health snack bar, a full-service salon, and 14 treatment rooms, as well as men's and women's steam rooms, saunas, whirlpools, cold plunge pool, inhalation rooms, tranquillity rooms, lockers, and changing areas.

**Aioli** is a splendid fine-dining value (see "Where to Dine," later in this chapter).

Retorno del Rey Km 14, Zona Hotelera, 77500, Cancún, Q. Roo. © 800/543-4300 in the U.S., or 998/881-2200. Fax 998/881-2201. www.meridiencancun.com.mx. 213 units. High season $560 double, $780 suite; low season $280 double, $420 suite. Ask about special spa packages. Additional $10 per day resort fee enables access to Spa de Mar, kids' club, and other extra services. AE, DC, MC, V. Small pets accepted with prior reservation. **Amenities:** 2 restaurants; lobby bar; 3 cascading outdoor pools; 2 lighted championship tennis courts; whirlpool; watersports equipment; supervised children's program w/clubhouse, play equipment, wading pool; concierge; tour desk; car rental; business center w/Internet access; small shopping arcade; 24-hr. room service; massage *palapa* on the beach; babysitting; laundry service. *In room:* A/C, TV, dataport, minibar, hair dryer, iron, safe.

**Ritz-Carlton** &&&    For those who want to feel indulged, this is the place to stay. On 3 hectares (7½ acres), the nine-story Ritz-Carlton sets the standard for elegance in Cancún. The hotel fronts a 370m (1,214-ft.) white-sand beach, and all rooms overlook the ocean, pool, and tropical gardens. The style—in both public areas and guest rooms—is sumptuous and formal, with thick carpets, elaborate chandeliers, and fresh flowers throughout. In all rooms, marble bathrooms have telephones, separate tubs and showers, and lighted makeup mirrors. The luxury Kayantá Spa offers an excellent selection of Maya and Mexican-inspired treatments and massages. The hotel has won countless accolades for service. The **Club Grill** is one of the best restaurants in the city; see "Where to Dine," later in this chapter. Although the hotel was closed for renovations due to hurricane damage, it should be open by the time you arrive; as we went to press, the official reopening was scheduled for early September 2006.

Retorno del Rey 36, off Bulevar Kukulkán Km 13.5, 77500 Cancún, Q. Roo. © 800/241-3333 in the U.S. and Canada, or 998/881-0808. Fax 998/881-0815. www.ritzcarlton.com. 365 units. $299–$439 double; $439–$569 club floor and suites. Ask about golf, spa, and weekend packages. AE, MC, V. **Amenities:** 5 restaurants; lounge; 2 connecting outdoor pools (heated in winter); 3 lighted tennis courts; fully equipped fitness center and Kayantá Spa; Ritz Kids' program w/supervised activities; concierge; travel agency; business center; shopping arcade; salon; 24-hr. room service; babysitting; laundry service; dry cleaning; club floors. *In room:* A/C, TV, dataport, minibar, hair dryer, iron, safe, bathrobes.

**Riu Palace Las Américas** &&    The all-inclusive Riu Palace is part of a family of Riu resorts in Cancún known for their grand, opulent style. This one is the smallest of the three in Cancún, and the most elegant, steeped in pearl-white Greco style, and my choice for a high-end all-inclusive vacation in Cancún. The location is prime—near the central shopping, dining, and nightlife centers, just 5 minutes walking to the Convention Center. All rooms are spacious junior suites with ocean or lagoon views, a separate seating area, and a balcony or terrace. Eight also feature a Jacuzzi. Two central pools overlook the ocean and a wide stretch of beach, with one heated during winter months. The hotel offers guests virtually 24 hours of all-inclusive snacks, meals, and beverages. And, if that's not enough, guests have exchange privileges at the Riu Cancún, next door.

Bulevar Kukulkán, Lote 4, 77500 Cancún, Q. Roo. © 888/666-8816 in the U.S., or 998/891-4300. www.riu.com. 372 units. High season $480–$750 double; low season $337–$530 double. Rates are all-inclusive. AE, MC, V. **Amenities:** 6 restaurants; 5 bars; 2 outdoor pools; tennis; fitness center; spa (extra charges apply); solarium; room service; sports program; windsurfing. In room: A/C, TV, hair dryer, iron, safe, bathrobes.

## EXPENSIVE

**Dreams Cancún Resort & Spa** 🎿🎿 *Kids*   Formerly the Camino Real Cancún, the all-inclusive Dreams Resort is among the island's most appealing places to stay, located on 1.5 hectares (3¾ acres) at the tip of Punta Cancún. The setting is sophisticated, but the hotel is very welcoming to children. The architecture of the hotel is contemporary and sleek, with bright colors and strategic angles. Rooms in the newer 18-story club section have extra services and amenities; rates here include full breakfast. The lower-priced rooms have lagoon views. The all-inclusive concept is more oriented to quality experiences than unlimited buffets—your room price here includes gourmet meals, 24-hour room service, and premium brand drinks, as well as the use of all resort amenities, watersports, evening entertainment, airport transfers, and tips. The fitness center and spa are the focal points of the resort's amenities.

Bulevar Kukulkán, 77500 Punta Cancún (Apdo. Postal 14), Cancún, Q. Roo. © 866/237-3267 in the U.S., or 998/848-7000. Fax 998/848-7001. www.dreamscancun.com. 379 units. High season $500 double, $560 club double; low season $370 double, $430 club double. AE, DC, MC, V. **Amenities:** 3 restaurants; nightclub; outdoor pool; private saltwater lagoon w/sea turtles and tropical fish; 3 lighted tennis courts; fitness center w/steam bath; watersports; sailing pier; jet skis; travel agency; car rental; 24-hour business center w/Internet access; salon; 24-hr. room service; massage; babysitting (w/advance notice); beach volleyball. In room: A/C, TV, minibar, hair dryer, iron, safe.

**Marriott Casa Magna** 🎿🎿 *Kids*   This is quintessential Marriott—those who are familiar with the chain's standards will feel at home here and appreciate the hotel's attention to detailed service. Entering through a half-circle of Roman columns, you pass through a domed foyer to a wide, lavishly marbled 14m-high (46-ft.) lobby filled with plants and shallow pools. Guest rooms hold contemporary furnishings, tiled floors, and ceiling fans; most have balconies. The hotel caters to family travelers with specially priced packages (up to two children stay free with parent) and the Club Amigos supervised children's program. In 2001 Marriott opened the 450-room luxury **JW Marriott Cancún**, Bulevar Kukulkán Km 14.5, 77500 Cancún, Q. Roo (© **998/848-9600;** www.marriott.com), on the beach next to the Casa Magna. Its hallmark is a 1,860-sq.-m (20,020-sq.-ft.) spa and fitness center.

Bulevar Kukulkán Km 14.5, 77500 Cancún, Q. Roo © 800/228-9290 in the U.S., or 998/881-2000. Fax 998/881-2085. www.marriott.com. 452 units. $149–$219 double; $319–$339 suite. Ask about packages. AE, MC, V. **Amenities:** 5 restaurants; lobby bar w/live music; outdoor pool; 2 lighted tennis courts; health club w/saunas, whirlpool, aerobics, and juice bar; concierge; travel agency; car rental; salon w/massage and facials; room service; babysitting; laundry service. In room: A/C, TV, dataport, minibar, coffeemaker, hair dryer, iron, safe.

**Presidente Inter-Continental Cancún** 🎿   On the island's best beach, facing the placid Bahía de Mujeres, the Presidente's location is reason enough to stay here, and it's just a 2-minute walk to Cancún's public Pok-Ta-Pok Golf Club (Club de Golf Cancún). For its ambience, I consider it an ideal choice for a romantic getaway or for couples who enjoy indulging in the sports of golf and tennis, or even shopping. Cool and spacious, the Presidente boasts a postmodern design with lavish marble and wicker accents and a strong use of color. All rooms have tastefully simple unfinished pine furniture, and guests have a choice of two double beds or one king-size. Sixteen units on the first floor have patios with outdoor whirlpool tubs. The expansive pool has a pyramid-shaped waterfall. Coming from Cancún City, you'll reach the Presidente on the left side of the street before you get to Punta Cancún. Extensive renovations and room upgrades occurred post-Hurricane Wilma.

Bulevar Kukulkán Km 7.5, 77500 Cancún, Q. Roo. © 800/327-0200 in the U.S., or 998/848-8700. Fax 998/883-2602. www.ichotelsgroup.com. 299 units. High season $240–$300 double; low season $150–$350 double. Rates include unlimited golf at Pok-Ta-Pok. AE, MC, V. Ask about special packages. **Amenities:** 3 restaurants; 2 outdoor pools; lighted tennis courts; fitness center; whirlpool; watersports equipment rental; marina; travel agency; car-rental desk; shopping arcade; 24-hr. room service; babysitting; laundry service; nonsmoking floors; club floors; rooms for those w/limited mobility. *In room:* A/C, TV, dataport, minibar, hair dryer, safe.

**The Westin Resort & Spa Cancún** ⟨⟨  The strikingly austere architecture of The Westin Resort, impressive with its elegant use of stone and marble, is the stamp of leading Latin American architect Ricardo Legorreta. The hotel consists of two sections, the main building and the more exclusive six-story hot-pink tower. Standard rooms are unusually large and beautifully furnished with cool, contemporary furniture. Those on the sixth floor have balconies, and first-floor rooms have terraces. Rooms in the tower all have ocean or lagoon views, furniture with Olinalá lacquer accents, Berber area rugs, oak tables and chairs, and terraces with lounge chairs. It's important to note that this hotel is a 15- to 20-minute ride from the lively strip that lies between the Plaza Flamingo and Punta Cancún, so it's a good choice for those who want a little more seclusion than Cancún typically offers. However, it is easy to join the action—buses stop in front, and taxis are readily available. The hotel took the opportunity of Hurricane Wilma damage for a complete renovation, and reopened in July 2006.

Bulevar Kukulkán Km 20, 77500 Cancún, Q. Roo. © 800/228-3000 in the U.S., 01-800/215-7000 in Mexico, or 998/848-7400. Fax 998/885-0666. www.starwoodhotels.com/westin. 293 units. High season $319–$499 double; low season $139–$299 double. AE, DC, MC, V. **Amenities:** 2 restaurants; 2 bars; 5 outdoor pools; 2 lighted tennis courts; gym w/Stairmaster, bicycle, weights, aerobics, steam; sauna; *temazcal* (sweat lodge); 3 whirlpools; concierge; travel agency; car rental; pharmacy/gift shop; salon; room service; massage; babysitting; laundry service. *In room:* A/C, TV, dataport, minibar, coffeemaker, hair dryer, iron, safe.

## MODERATE

**Blue Bay Getaway Cancún** ⟨  The adults-only Blue Bay Getaway Cancún is a spirited yet relaxing all-inclusive resort favored by young adults. Surrounded by acres of tropical gardens, it's ideally located at the northern end of the Hotel Zone, close to the major shopping plazas, restaurants, and nightlife. Its beach boasts calm waters for swimming. The comfortable, modern rooms are in two sections. The central building features 72 rooms decorated in rustic wood, the main lobby, administrative offices, restaurants, and Las Margaritas bar. The remaining nine buildings feature colorful Mexican decor; rooms have lagoon, garden, and ocean views. Safes are available for an extra charge. During the evenings, guests may enjoy a variety of theme-night dinners, nightly shows, and live entertainment in an outdoor theater. Note that clothing is optional on the beaches of this Blue Bay resort.

Bulevar Kukulkán Km 3.5, 77500 Cancún, Q. Roo. © 800/211-1000 in the U.S., or 998/848-7900. Fax 998/848-7994. www.bluebaycancun.com. 385 units. High season $325 double; low season $225 double. Rates include food, beverages, and activities. AE, MC, V. **Amenities:** 4 restaurants; 4 bars; 3 outdoor pools; 4 whirlpools; tennis court; exercise room w/daily aerobics classes; watersports equipment; snorkeling and scuba lessons; marina; bicycles; game room w/pool and Ping-Pong tables; rooms for those w/limited mobility. *In room:* A/C, TV, dataport, hair dryer.

**Flamingo Cancún**    The Flamingo seems to have been inspired by the dramatic, slope-sided architecture of the Dreams Cancún, but the Flamingo is considerably smaller and less expensive. And with two pools, it's a friendly, accommodating choice for families. The clean, comfortable, and modern guest rooms—all with balconies—border a courtyard facing the interior swimming pool and *palapa* pool-bar. You can choose an all-inclusive plan, which includes meals. The Flamingo is in the heart of the island hotel district, opposite the Flamingo Shopping Center and close to other hotels, shopping centers, and restaurants.

Bulevar Kukulkán Km 11.5, 77500 Cancún, Q. Roo. ℂ **998/848-8870.** Fax 998/883-1029. www.flamingocancun.com. 221 units. Free, unguarded parking across the street in the Plaza Flamingo. High season $170 double, low season $120 double; all-inclusive plan high season $260 double, low season $220 double. AE, MC, V. **Amenities:** 2 restaurants; 2 bars; 2 pools; fitness center; kids' club, travel agency; room service; safe. *In room:* A/C, TV, dataport, hair dryer, minibar.

**Oasis Viva Beach Cancún**    From the street, this hotel may not be much to look at, but on the ocean side you'll find a small but pretty patio garden and Cancún's best beach for safe swimming. The location is ideal, close to all the shops and restaurants near Punta Cancún and the Cancún Center. Rooms overlook the lagoon or the ocean, and all were remodeled post–Hurricane Wilma. They are large, with pleasing, comfortable decor, marble floors, and either two double beds or a king-size bed. Several studios have kitchenettes. There is wheelchair access within the hotel's public areas.

Bulevar Kukulkán Km 8.5, 77500 Cancún, Q. Roo. ℂ **800/221-2222** in the U.S., or 998/883-0800. Fax 998/883-2087. 216 units. High season $155–$210 double; low season $155–$185 double. Rates include buffet breakfast. Children under 12 stay free in parent's room. AE, MC, V. **Amenities:** Restaurant; 2 snack bars; 3 bars; 2 outdoor pools (1 for adults, 1 for children); 2 lighted tennis courts; watersports equipment rental; marina; nonsmoking areas; wheelchair access. *In room:* A/C, TV.

## CANCUN CITY
### MODERATE

**Radisson Hacienda Cancún** ★★ *(Value*    This is the nicest hotel in downtown Cancún, and one of the best values in the area. The Radisson offers all the expected comforts of a chain, yet in an atmosphere of Mexican hospitality. Resembling a hacienda, the hotel has rooms that are set off from a large rotunda-style lobby, lush gardens, and a pleasant pool area. All have brightly colored fabric accents; views of the garden, the pool, or the street; and a small sitting area and balcony. Bathrooms have a combination tub/shower. Guests have access to shuttle service to Isla Cancún's beaches, or to the Pok-Ta-Pok Golf course. The hotel is behind the state government building, within walking distance of downtown Cancún dining and shopping.

Av. Náder 1, SM2, Centro, 77500 Cancún, Q. Roo. ℂ **800/333-3333** in the U.S., or 998/881-6500. Fax 998/884-7954. www.radissoncancun.com. 248 units. $140 double; $168 junior suite. Ask about special all-inclusive rates. AE, MC, V. **Amenities:** 2 restaurants; lively lobby bar; outdoor pool w/adjoining bar and separate wading area for children; tennis courts; small gym; sauna; travel agency; car rental; salon. *In room:* A/C, TV, coffeemaker, hair dryer, iron, safe.

**Rey del Caribe Hotel** ★★ *(Value*    This hotel in the center of downtown is a unique oasis—a 100% ecological hotel, where every detail has been thought out to achieve the goal of living in an organic and environmentally friendly manner. The whole atmosphere of the place is one of warmth, which derives from the on-site owners, who, caring as much as they do for Mother Earth, extend this sentiment to guests as well. You easily forget you're in the midst of downtown Cancún in the tropical jungle setting, with blooming orchids and other flowering plants. Surrounding gardens are populated with statues of Maya deities—it's a lovely, tranquil setting. There's a daily-changing schedule of yoga, Tai Chi, and meditation sessions, as well as special classes on astrology, tarot, and other subjects. The on-site spa offers facial and body treatments. Rooms are large and sunny, with your choice of one king-size or two full-size beds, a kitchenette, and terrace. The detail of ecological sensitivity is truly impressive, ranging from the use of collected rainwater to waste composting. Recycling is encouraged and solar power used wherever possible.

Av. Uxmal SM 2A (corner of Nader), 77500 Cancún, Q. Roo. ℂ 998/884-2028. Fax 988/884-9857. www.reycaribe.com. 25 units. High season $74 double; low season $53 double. Rates include breakfast. MC, V. **Amenities:** Restaurant; outdoor pool; hot tub; classes. *In room:* A/C, kitchenette.

## INEXPENSIVE

**Hotel Antillano**    A quiet and very clean choice, the Antillano is close to the Ciudad Cancún bus terminal. Rooms overlook Avenida Tulum, the side streets, or the interior lawn and pool. Pool-view rooms are most desirable because they are quietest. Rooms feature coordinated furnishings, one or two double beds, a sink area separate from the bathroom, and red-tile floors. Guests have the use of the hotel's beach club on the island.

Av. Claveles 1 (corner of Av. Tulum, opposite Restaurant Rosa Mexicana), 77500 Cancún, Q. Roo. ℂ 998/884-1532. Fax 998/884-1878. www.hotelantillano.com. 48 units. High season $75 double; low season $65 double. Rates include breakfast. AE, MC, V. Street parking. **Amenities:** Restaurant; small bar; outdoor pool; travel agency; babysitting. *In room:* A/C, TV.

**Hotel Hacienda Cancún**  *Value*    This extremely pleasing little hotel is a great value. The facade has been remodeled to look like a hacienda. The guest rooms are very comfortable; all have rustic Mexican furnishings and two double beds, but no views. There's a nice small pool and cafe under a shaded *palapa* in the back.

Sunyaxchen 39–40, 77500 Cancún, Q. Roo. ℂ 998/884-3672. Fax 998/884-1208. hhda@Cancun.com.mx. 35 units. High season $60 double; low season $48 double. MC, V. Street parking. From Av. Yaxchilán, turn west on Sunyaxchen; it's on the right next to the Hotel Caribe International, opposite 100% Natural. **Amenities:** Restaurant; outdoor pool. *In room:* A/C, TV, safe.

**Hotel Margaritas**  *☆ Value*    Located in downtown Cancún, this four-story hotel (with elevator) is comfortable and unpretentious, offering one of the best values in Cancún. The pleasantly decorated rooms, with white-tile floors and small balconies, are exceptionally clean and bright. Lounge chairs surround the attractive pool, which has a wading section for children. The hotel offers complimentary safes at the front desk.

Av. Yaxchilán 41, SM22, Centro, 77500 Cancún, Q. Roo. ℂ 01-800/640-7473 in Mexico, or 998/884-9333. Fax 998/884-1324. www.margaritascancun.com. 100 units. High season $90 double; low season $78 double. AE, MC, V. **Amenities:** Restaurant; outdoor pool; travel agency; room service; babysitting; medical service; money exchange. *In room:* A/C, TV.

**Refugio del Pirata Morgan**    Although not actually in the town of Cancún, but on the highway leading north from Cancún to Punta Sam, this is the place for those who want a true encounter with nature. On a wide, virgin stretch of beach (which expanded even more post-Wilma), away from the crowd of hotels and nightlife, this "refuge" is exactly that: no phones, no television, just blissful peace and quiet. There are 10 simple cabanas, with both beds and hammocks, each named for the predominate color of the decor. A small restaurant offers a basic selection of dining choices featuring fresh fish—otherwise, the nearest restaurant is 2km (1¼ miles) away.

Carretera Punta Sam, Isla Blanca, Km 9, 77500 Cancún, Q. Roo. © **998/860-3386** (within Mexico dial 044 first, as this is a cellphone). 10 units. $40 room; $5 hammock. Camping available $6 adult, $3 children. No credit cards. **Amenities:** Restaurant. *In room:* Fan.

## 3 Where to Dine

U.S.-based franchise chains, which really need no introduction, dominate the Cancún restaurant scene. These include Hard Rock Cafe, Rainforest Cafe, Tony Roma's, TGI Friday's, Ruth's Chris Steak House, and the gamut of fast-food burger places. The establishments listed here are locally owned, one-of-a-kind restaurants or exceptional selections at area hotels. Many schedule live music. Unless otherwise indicated, parking is free.

One unique way to combine dinner with sightseeing is aboard the **Lobster Dinner Cruise** (© **998/849-4748**). Cruising around the tranquil, turquoise waters of the lagoon, passengers feast on lobster dinners accompanied by wine. Cost is $79 per person. There are two daily departures from the Royal Mayan Marina. A sunset cruise leaves at 4:30pm during the winter and 5:30pm during the summer; a moonlight cruise leaves at 7:30pm winter, 8:30pm summer. Another—albeit livelier—option is the **Captain Hook Lobster Dinner Cruise** (© **998/849-4451**), which is similar, but with the added attraction of a pirate show, making this the choice for families. It costs $80 and departs at 7pm from El Embarcadero.

The restaurants of the new Aqua Fiesta Americana (not yet reopened from hurricane damage at press time) promise to be exceptional, including "7," under the direction of renowned Mexican Chef Patricia Quintana.

### CANCUN ISLAND
#### VERY EXPENSIVE

**Aioli** 𝒢𝒢𝒢 FRENCH    For the quality and originality of the cuisine, coupled with excellent service, this is my top pick for the best fine-dining value in Cancún. The Provençal—but definitely not provincial—Aioli offers exquisite French and Mediterranean gourmet specialties in a warm and cozy country French setting. Though it serves perhaps the best breakfast buffet in Cancún (for $20), most diners from outside the hotel come here in the evening, when low lighting and superb service make it a top choice for a romantic dinner. Starters include traditional pâtés and a delightful escargot served in the shell with white wine–and–herbed butter sauce. A specialty is duck breast, or the equally scrumptious rack of lamb, prepared in Moroccan style and served with couscous. Desserts are decadent; the signature "Fifth Element" is a sinfully delicious temptation rich with chocolate.

In Le Méridien Cancún Resort & Spa, Retorno del Rey Km 14. © **998/881-2200**. Reservations required. Main courses $15–$40. AE, MC, V. Daily 6:30am–11pm.

**Club Grill** 𝒢𝒢𝒢 INTERNATIONAL    This is the place for that special night out. Cancún's most elegant and stylish restaurant is also among its most delicious. Even rival restaurateurs give it an envious thumbs up. The gracious service starts as you enter the anteroom, with its comfortable seating and selection of fine tequilas and Cuban cigars. It continues in a candlelit dining room with shimmering silver and crystal. Elegant plates of peppered scallops, truffles, and potatoes in tequila sauce; grilled lamb; or mixed grill arrive at a leisurely pace. The restaurant has smoking and nonsmoking sections. A band plays romantic music for dancing from 8pm on. *Note:* The Ritz-Carlton hotel was undergoing repairs at press time, but was expected to reopen in September 2006.

In the Ritz-Carlton hotel, Retorno del Rey, 36 Bulevar Kukulkán Km 13.5. $\mathcal{C}$ **998/881-0808**. Reservations required. No sandals or tennis shoes; men must wear long pants. Main courses $11–$40. AE, DC, MC, V. Tues–Sun 7–11pm.

## EXPENSIVE

**Casa de las Margaritas** $\mathcal{F}$ MEXICAN    La Casa de las Margaritas is a celebration of the flavors and *¡fiesta!* spirit of Mexico. With a decor as vibrant as a *piñata,* and a soundtrack of background music that ranges from mariachi to *marimba,* the experience here is a crash course in the festive spirit of this colorful country. On the menu, best bets include the Margarita shrimp, sautéed in a garlic, crème, and chipotle chile sauce; chicken breast served with three flavorful mole sauces; or the platter of chicken enchiladas topped with a tomato-and-sun-dried-pepper sauce. They also serve a spectacular Sunday brunch.

Paseo Kukulkán Km 12.5, La Isla Shopping Mall Local E-17. $\mathcal{C}$ **998/883-3222** or -3054. www.lacasadelas margaritas.com. Reservations recommended. Main courses $6–$23. AE, MC, V. Valet parking. Mon–Sat 11am–midnight; Sun brunch noon–5pm.

**La Dolce Vita** $\mathcal{FFF}$ ITALIAN/SEAFOOD    Casually elegant La Dolce Vita is Cancún's favorite Italian restaurant. Appetizers include pâté of quail liver and carpaccio in vinaigrette, and mushrooms Provençal. The chef specializes in homemade pastas combined with fresh seafood. You can order green tagliolini with lobster medallions, linguine with clams or seafood, or rigatoni Mexican-style (with *chorizo,* mushrooms, and jalapeños) as a main course, or as an appetizer for half price. Other main courses include veal with morels, fresh salmon with cream sauce, and fresh fish in a variety of sauces. Recently added choices include vegetarian lasagna and grilled whole lobster. You have a choice of dining in air-conditioned comfort or on an open-air terrace with a view of the lagoon. Live jazz plays Monday through Saturday from 7 to 11pm. They also have a location downtown on Av. Cobá 83, SM3 at Av. Nader ($\mathcal{C}$ **998/884-3393**).

Bulevar Kukulkán Km 14.6, on the lagoon, opposite the Marriott Casa Magna. $\mathcal{C}$ **998/885-0150** or -0161. Fax 998/885-0590. www.dolcevitacancun.com. Reservations required for dinner. Main courses $9–$37. AE, MC, V. Daily noon–midnight.

**Laguna Grill** $\mathcal{FF}$ FUSION    Laguna Grill offers diners a contemporary culinary experience in a lush, tropical setting overlooking the lagoon. A tropical garden welcomes you at the entrance, while a small creek traverses through the restaurant set with tables made from the trunks of regional, tropical trees. As magical as the decor is, the real star here is the kitchen, with its offering of Pacific-rim cuisine fused with regional flavors. Starters include martini *gyoza* (steamed dumplings) and shrimp tempura served on a mango mint salad, or ahi tuna and shrimp ceviche in a spicy Oriental sauce. Fish and seafood dominate the menu of entrees, in a variety of preparations that combine Asian and Mexican flavors such as ginger, cilantro, garlic, and hoisin sauce. Grilled shrimp are served over a cilantro and *guajillo* chile risotto. For beef-lovers, the rib-eye served over a garlic, spinach, and sweet-potato mash is sublime. Desserts are as creative as the main dishes; the pineapple-papaya strudel in Malibu rum sauce is a standout. If you're an early diner, request a table on the outside deck for a spectacular sunset view. An impressive selection of wines is available.

Bulevar Kukulkán Km 16.5. $\mathcal{C}$ **998/885-0267**. www.lagunagrill.com.mx. Reservations recommended. Main courses $15–$45. AE, MC, V. Daily 2pm–midnight.

**Lorenzillo's** ☆☆☆ *(Kids)* SEAFOOD   Live lobster is the overwhelming favorite, and part of the appeal is selecting your dinner out of the giant lobster tank. Lorenzillo's sits on the lagoon under a giant *palapa* roof. A dock leads down to the main dining area, and when that's packed (which is often), a wharf-side bar handles the overflow. In addition to lobster—which comes grilled, steamed, or stuffed—good bets are shrimp stuffed with cheese and wrapped in bacon, the Admiral's filet coated in toasted almonds and light mustard sauce, and seafood-stuffed squid. Desserts include the tempting "Martinique": Belgian chocolate with hazelnuts, almonds, and pecans, served with vanilla ice cream. The sunset pier offers a lighter menu of cold seafood, sandwiches, and salads. There's a festive, friendly atmosphere, and children are very welcome—after all, most of the patrons are wearing bibs! The restaurant was located in a temporary building while rebuilding the original *palapa*-topped location, damaged in Hurricane Wilma, but it's set to be ready in October 2006.

Bulevar Kukulkán Km 10.5. © **998/883-1254.** www.lorenzillos.com.mx. Reservations recommended. Main courses $8–$50. AE, MC, V. Daily noon–midnight. Valet parking available.

**Mango Tango** ☆☆ INTERNATIONAL   The beauty of dining here is that you can stay and enjoy a hot nightspot—Mango Tango has made a name for itself with sizzling floor shows (featuring salsa, tango, and other Latin dancing) and live reggae music (see "Cancún After Dark," later in this chapter)—but its kitchen deserves attention as well. Try the peel-your-own shrimp, Argentine-style grilled meat with *chimichurri* sauce, and other grilled specialties. Mango Tango salad is shrimp, chicken, avocado, red onion, tomato, and mushrooms served on mango slices. Entrees include rice with seafood and fried bananas. Creole gumbo comes with lobster, shrimp, and squid, and coconut-and-mango cake is a suitable finish to the meal.

Bulevar Kukulkán Km 14.2, opposite the Ritz-Carlton hotel. © **998/885-0303.** Reservations recommended. Main courses $12–$57; 3-course dinner show $40. AE, MC, V. Daily 2pm–2am.

**Paloma Bonita** ☆ *(Kids)* REGIONAL/MEXICAN/NOUVELLE MEXICAN   In a stylish setting overlooking the water, Paloma Bonita captures the essence of the country through its music and food. Being that Paloma Bonita is in a hotel (the Dreams Cancún), prices are higher and the flavors more institutionalized than at traditional Mexican restaurants in Ciudad Cancún, but this is a good choice for the Hotel Zone. There are three sections: La Cantina Jalisco, with an open kitchen and tequila bar; the Salón Michoacán, which features that state's cuisine; and the Patio Oaxaca. The menu encompasses the best of Mexico's other cuisines, with a few international dishes. Prix-fixe dinners include appetizer, main course, and dessert. Jazz trios, *marimba* and *Jarocho* music, and mariachis serenade you while you dine. A nice starter is Mitla salad, with slices of the renowned Oaxaca cheese dribbled with olive oil and coriander dressing. Wonderful stuffed chile La Doña—a mildly hot poblano pepper filled with lobster and *huitlacoche* (a type of mushroom that grows on corn) in a cream sauce—comes as an appetizer or a main course.

In the Hotel Dreams, Punta Cancún (enter from the street). © **998/848-7000,** ext. 8060 or 8061. Reservations recommended. Prix-fixe dinner $30–$45; main courses $25–$31. AE, DC, MC, V. Daily 6:30–11:30pm.

**Puerto Madero** ☆☆ ARGENTINE/STEAKS/SEAFOOD   As a tribute to the famed Puerto Madero of Buenos Aires, this restaurant has quickly earned a reputation for its authentic Argentine cuisine and ambience. Overlooking the Nichupté Lagoon, the decor re-creates a 20th-century dock warehouse, with elegant touches of modern architecture. Puerto Madero offers an extensive selection of prime quality beef cuts, whole wheat pastas, fish, and shellfish, meticulously prepared with Buenos Aires gusto. In addition to the classic *carpaccio,* the tuna tartar and halibut steak are favorites, but the real standout here is the grilled steaks, served in ample portions. It's also a top choice for a splurge on lobster. Enjoy a glass of wine, from their extensive selection, or a cocktail, while viewing the sunset from their lagoon-side deck. Service is excellent.

Marina Barracuda, Bulevar Kukulkán Km 14. (C) **998/883-2829** or -2830. www.puertomaderocancun.com. Valet parking. Reservations recommended. Main courses $12–$60. AE, MC, V. Daily 1pm–1am.

## MODERATE

**Glazz** ✿✿✿ ASIAN/FUSION    Glazz combines a sexy lounge and sophisticated dining, right in the heart of Cancún's hotel zone. For dinner, Glazz features a menu of sophisticated and artfully presented Asian entrees and sushi. Specialties include Thai lettuce wraps or green papaya salad for starters. Entrees include wok-cooked Glazz spicy chicken; Mandarin salmon, wrapped in bok-choy and served with mango and asparagus; Panang curry; and the vegetarian Buddah's Feast of seasonal vegetables stir-fried in oyster-flavored sauce with tofu tempura. Libations include specialty sakes, martinis, and creative "sakitinis."

Paseo Kukulkán Km 12.5, La Isla Shopping Mall. (C) **998/883-1881.** www.glazz.com.mx. Main courses $9–$14. AE, MC, V. Daily 6pm–12:30am; sushi served until 1:30am; lounge stays open until 2:30am.

**La Destilería** MEXICAN    If you want to experience tequila in its native habitat, you won't want to miss this place—even though it's across the country from the region that produces the beverage. La Destilería is more than a tequila-inspired restaurant; it's a mini-museum honoring the "spirit" of Mexico. It serves over 150 brands of tequila, including some treasures that never find their way across the country's northern border, so be adventurous! The margaritas are among the best on the island. When you decide to have some food with your tequila, the menu is refined Mexican, with everything from quesadillas with squash blossom flowers, to shrimp in a delicate tequila-lime sauce. They even serve *escamoles* (crisp-fried ant eggs) as an appetizer for the adventurous—or for those whose squeamishness has been diminished by the tequila!

Bulevar Kukulkán Km 12.65, across from Kukulcan Plaza. (C) **998/885-1086** or -1087. www.orraca.com. Main courses $8–$30. AE, MC, V. Daily 1pm–midnight.

**La Fisheria** ✿ (Kids) SEAFOOD    If you're at the mall shopping, this is your best bet. Patrons find a lot to choose from at this restaurant overlooking Bulevar Kukulkán and the lagoon. The expansive menu includes shark fingers with jalapeño dip, grouper filet stuffed with seafood in lobster sauce, Acapulco-style ceviche in tomato sauce, New England clam chowder, steamed mussels, grilled red snapper with pasta—you get the idea. The menu changes daily, but there's always *tikin xik,* that great Yucatecan grilled fish marinated in *achiote* (a spice) sauce. For those not inclined toward seafood, a pizza from the wood-burning oven, or perhaps a grilled chicken or beef dish, might do. La Fisheria has a nonsmoking section.

Plaza Caracol shopping center, Bulevar Kukulkán Km 8.5, 2nd floor. (C) **998/883-1395.** Main courses $7–$21. AE, MC, V. Daily 11am–11pm.

**Thai Lounge** ✿✿ THAI    With a backdrop that includes three dolphins cavorting in an enormous aquarium, the Thai Lounge offers a unique and calming setting with individual pagodas for cozy dining, low lights, and soft, chill music. Classic Thai specialties such as spicy chicken soup, Thai salad, chicken satay, and chicken and shrimp curries are served in an ultrachic atmosphere.

La Isla Shopping Center, Local B-4. © **998/883-1401**. Reservations recommended during high season. Main courses $6–$18. AE, MC, V. Daily 6pm–1am.

## CANCÚN CITY
### EXPENSIVE

**La Habichuela** ✦ GOURMET SEAFOOD/CARIBBEAN/MEXICAN  In a garden setting with soft music playing in the background, this restaurant is ideal for a romantic evening. For an all-out culinary adventure, try *habichuela* (string bean) soup; shrimp in any number of sauces, including Jamaican tamarind, tequila, or ginger and mushroom; and Maya coffee with *xtabentun* (a strong, sweet, anise-based liqueur). Grilled seafood and steaks are excellent, but this is a good place to try a Mexican specialty such as chicken mole or *tampiqueña*-style beef (thinly sliced, marinated, and grilled). For something totally divine, try *cocobichuela,* which is lobster and shrimp in curry sauce served in a coconut shell and topped with fruit.

Margaritas 25. © **998/884-3158**. www.lahabichuela.com. Reservations recommended in high season. Main courses $15–$39. AE, MC, V. Daily noon–midnight.

**Périco's** ✦✦✦ MEXICAN/SEAFOOD/STEAKS  Périco's has colorful murals that almost dance off the walls, a bar area with saddles for barstools, colorful leather tables and chairs, and accommodating waiters; it's always booming and festive. The extensive menu offers well-prepared steak, seafood, and traditional Mexican dishes for reasonable rates (except for lobster). This is a place not only to eat and drink, but also to let loose and join in the fun, so don't be surprised if everybody drops their forks and dons huge sombreros to shimmy and shake in a conga dance around the dining room. It's fun whether or not you join in, but it's definitely not the place for a romantic evening alone. There's *marimba* music from 7:30 to 9:30pm, and mariachis from 9:30pm to midnight.

Yaxchilán 61. © **998/884-3152**. www.pericos.com.mx. Reservations recommended. Main courses $14–$39. AE, MC, V. Daily 1pm–1am.

### MODERATE

**Labná** ✦ YUCATECAN  To steep yourself in Yucatecan cuisine and music, head directly to this showcase of Maya moods and regional foods. Specialties served here include a sublime lime soup, *poc chuc* (marinated, barbecue-style pork), chicken or pork *pibil* (sweet and spicy barbecue sauce served over shredded meat), and appetizers such as *papadzules* (tortillas stuffed with boiled eggs in a green pumpkin sauce). The Labná Special is a sampler of four typically Yucatecan main courses, including *poc chuc,* while another specialty of the house is baked suckling pig, served with guacamole. The refreshing Yucatecan beverage, *agua de chaya*—a blend of sweetened water and the leaf of the *chaya* plant, abundant in the area, to which D'aristi liquor can be added for an extra kick—is also served here. The large, informal dining room is decorated with fascinating black-and-white photographs of the region, dating from the 1900s.

Margaritas 29, next to City Hall and the Habichuela restaurant. © **998/892-3056**. Main courses $5–$25. AE, MC, V. Daily noon–10pm.

### INEXPENSIVE

**100% Natural** ✦✦ VEGETARIAN/MEXICAN  If you want a healthy reprieve from an overindulgent night—or just like your meals as fresh and natural as possible—this is your oasis. No matter what your dining preference, you owe it to yourself to try a Mexican tradition, the fresh-fruit *licuado.* The blended drink combines fresh fruit, ice, and either water or milk. More creative combinations may mix in yogurt, granola, or other goodies. And 100% Natural serves more than just meal-quality drinks—there's a bountiful selection of basic Mexican fare and terrific sandwiches served on whole-grain bread, both with options for vegetarians. Breakfast is a delight as well as a good value. The space abounds with plants and cheery colors. There are several locations in town, including branches at Playa Chac-Mool, across from Sr. Frogs, and downtown.

Av. Sunyaxchen 63. (© **998/884-0102.** Main courses $2.80–$13. MC, V. Daily 8am–11pm.

**Pizza Rolandi** *Kids* ITALIAN    This is an institution in Cancún, and the Rolandi name is synonymous with dining in both Cancún and neighboring Isla Mujeres. Pizza Rolandi and its branch in Isla Mujeres (see chapter 5) have become standards for dependably good casual fare. At this shaded outdoor patio restaurant, you can choose from almost two dozen wood-oven pizzas and a full selection of spaghetti, calzones, Italian-style chicken and beef, and desserts. There's a full bar as well.

Cobá 12. (© **998/884-4047.** Fax 998/884-3994. www.rolandi.com. Pasta $5–$8; pizza and main courses $8–$18. AE, MC, V. Daily noon–11pm.

**Roots** *𝒻* INTERNATIONAL    This popular hangout for local residents is also a great spot for visitors to Cancún. Located in the heart of downtown, this restaurant and jazz club offers a unique cosmopolitan ambience. The Caribbean-themed menu offers a range of casual dining choices, including salads, pastas, and even fresh squid. It's all accompanied by the best of Cancún musicians, performing live on their intimate stage. Decking the walls are original works of art by local painters.

Tulipanes 26, SM 22. (© **998/884-2437.** roots@Cancun.com. Main courses $6–$17. MC, V. Daily 6pm–1am.

## 4 Beaches, Watersports & Boat Tours

**THE BEACHES**    Big hotels dominate the best stretches of beach. All of Mexico's beaches are public property, so you can use the beach of any hotel by walking through the lobby or directly onto the sand. Be especially careful on beaches fronting the open Caribbean, where the undertow can be quite strong. By contrast, the waters of Bahía de Mujeres (Mujeres Bay), at the north end of the island, are usually calm and ideal for swimming. Get to know Cancún's water-safety pennant system, and make sure to check the flag at any beach or hotel before entering the water. Here's how it goes:

| | |
|---|---|
| **White** | Excellent |
| **Green** | Normal conditions (safe) |
| **Yellow** | Changeable, uncertain (use caution) |
| **Black** or **red** | Unsafe—use the swimming pool instead! |

In the Caribbean, storms can arrive and conditions can change from safe to unsafe in a matter of minutes, so be alert: If you see dark clouds heading your way, make for the shore and wait until the storm passes.

Playa Tortuga (Turtle Beach), Playa Langosta (Lobster Beach), Playa Linda (Pretty Beach), and Playa Las Perlas (Beach of the Pearls) are some of the public beaches. At most beaches, you can rent a sailboard and take lessons, ride a parasail, or partake in a variety of watersports. There's a small but beautiful portion of public beach on **Playa Caracol,** by the Xcaret Terminal. It faces the calm waters of Bahía de Mujeres and, for that reason, is preferable to those facing the Caribbean.

**WATERSPORTS**   Many beachside hotels offer watersports concessions that rent rubber rafts, kayaks, and snorkeling equipment. On the calm Nichupté lagoon are outlets for renting **sailboats, jet skis, windsurfers,** and **water skis.** Prices vary and are often negotiable, so check around.

**DEEP-SEA FISHING**   You can arrange a day of **deep-sea fishing** at one of the numerous piers or travel agencies for $220 to $360 for 4 hours, $420 for 6 hours, and $520 for 8 hours for up to four people; for up to 8 people, the prices are $420 for 4 hours, $550 for 6 hours, or $680 for 8 hours. Marinas will sometimes assist in putting together a group. Charters include a captain, a first mate, bait, gear, and beverages. Rates are lower if you depart from Isla Mujeres or from Cozumel—and frankly, the fishing is better closer to those departure points.

**SCUBA & SNORKELING**   Known for its shallow reefs, dazzling color, and diversity of life, Cancún is one of the best places in the world for beginning scuba diving. Punta Nizuc is the northern tip of the **Gran Arrecife Maya (Great Mesoamerican Reef),** the largest reef in the Western Hemisphere and one of the largest in the world. In addition to the sea life along this reef system, several sunken boats add a variety of dive options. Inland, a series of caverns and *cenotes* (wellsprings) are fascinating venues for the more experienced diver. Drift diving is the norm here, with popular dives going to the reefs at **El Garrafón** and the **Cave of the Sleeping Sharks**—although be aware that the famed "sleeping sharks" have departed, driven off by too many people watching them snooze. Note that immediately following Hurricane Wilma, snorkeling and shore dives were less than impressive; however, deeper dives found many underwater caves that had opened up.

A variety of hotels offer resort courses that teach the basics of diving—enough to make shallow dives and slowly ease your way into this underwater world of unimaginable beauty. Scuba trips run around $64 for two-tank dives at nearby reefs, and $100 and up for locations farther out. One preferred dive operator is **Scuba Cancún,** Bulevar Kukulkán Km 5 (© **998/849-7508** or -4736; www.scubacancun.com.mx), on the lagoon side. Phone reservations (© **998/849-4736**) are available from 7:30 to 10:30pm. Full certification takes 3½ days and costs $410. Scuba Cancún is open daily from 9am to 6pm, and accepts major credit cards. The largest operator is **Aquaworld,** across from the Meliá Cancún at Bulevar Kukulkán Km 15.2 (© **998/848-8300** or -8327; www. aquaworld.com.mx). It offers resort courses and diving from a man-made anchored dive platform, Paradise Island. Aquaworld has the **Sub See Explorer,** a boat with picture windows that hang beneath the surface. The boat doesn't submerge—it's an updated version of a glass-bottom boat—but it does provide nondivers with a look at life beneath the sea. This outfit is open 24 hours a day and accepts all major credit cards.

Scuba Cancún also offers diving trips, in good weather only, to 20 nearby reefs, including Cenotes Caverns (9m/30 ft.) and the open ocean (9–18m/30–60 ft.). The average dive is around 11m (36 ft.). Two-tank dives cost $140. Discounts apply if you bring your own equipment. Dives usually start around 10am and return by 2:15pm. Snorkeling trips cost $27 and leave every afternoon at 2pm and 4:30pm for shallow reefs about a 20-minute boat ride away.

Besides snorkeling at **El Garrafón Natural Park** (see "Boating Excursions," below), travel agencies offer an all-day excursion to the natural wildlife habitat of **Isla Contoy,** which usually includes time for snorkeling. The island, 90 minutes past Isla Mujeres, is a major nesting area for birds and a treat for nature lovers. You can call any travel agent or see any hotel tour desk to get a selection of boat tours to Isla Contoy. Prices range from $44 to $65, depending on the length of the trip, and generally include drinks and snorkeling equipment.

The Great Mesoamerican Reef also offers exceptional snorkeling opportunities. In Puerto Morelos, 37km (23 miles) south of Cancún, the reef hugs the coastline for 15km (9⅓ miles). The reef is so close to the shore (about 460m/1,509 ft.) that it forms a natural barrier for the village and keeps the waters calm on the inside of the reef. The water here is shallow, from 1.5 to 9m (5–30 ft.), resulting in ideal conditions for snorkeling. Stringent environmental regulations implemented by the local community have kept the reef here unspoiled. Only a select few companies are allowed to offer snorkel trips, and they must adhere to guidelines that will ensure the reef's preservation. **Cancún Mermaid** (© **998/843-6517;** www.cancunmermaid.com) is considered the best—it's a family-run ecotour company that has operated in the area since the 1970s. It's known for highly personalized service. The tour typically takes snorkelers to two sections of the reef, spending about an hour in each area. When conditions allow, the boat drops off snorkelers and then follows them along with the current—an activity known as "drift snorkeling," which enables snorkelers to see as much of the reef as possible. The trip costs $50 for adults, $35 for children, and includes boat, snorkeling gear, life jackets, a light lunch, bottled water, sodas, and beer, plus round-trip transportation to and from Puerto Morelos from Cancún hotels. Departures are Monday through Saturday at 9am or noon. A minimum of four snorkelers is required for a trip, and reservations are required.

**JET-SKI TOURS**    Several companies offer the popular **Jungle Cruise,** which takes you by jet ski or WaveRunner (you drive your own watercraft) through Cancún's lagoon and mangrove estuaries out into the Caribbean Sea and a shallow reef. The excursion runs about 2½ hours and costs $35 to $55, including snorkeling and beverages. Some of the motorized miniboats seat one person behind the other—meaning that the person in back gets a great view of the driver's head; others seat you side by side.

The operators and names of boats offering excursions change often. To find out what's available, check with a local travel agent or hotel tour desk. The popular **Aquaworld,** Bulevar Kukulkán Km 15.2 (© **998/848-8300** or -8327), calls its trip the Jungle Tour and charges $50 for the 2½-hour excursion, which includes 45 minutes of snorkeling time. It even gives you a free snorkel, but has the less desirable one-behind-the-other seating configuration. Departures are daily every hour between 8am and 3pm.

## BOATING EXCURSIONS
**ISLA MUJERES**    The island of **Isla Mujeres,** just 13km (8 miles) offshore, is one of the most pleasant day trips from Cancún. At one end is **El Garrafón Natural Park,** which is good for snorkeling. At the other end is a captivating village with small shops, restaurants, and hotels, and **Playa Norte,** the island's best beach. If you're looking for relaxation and can spare the time, it's worth several days. For complete information about the island, see chapter 5.

There are four ways to get there: **public ferry** from Puerto Juárez, which takes between 15 and 45 minutes; **shuttle boat** from Playa Linda or Playa Tortuga—an hour-long ride, with irregular service; **watertaxi** (more expensive, but faster), next to the Xcaret Terminal; and daylong **pleasure-boat trips,** most of which leave from the Playa Linda pier.

The inexpensive Puerto Juárez **public ferries** *ß* are just a few kilometers from downtown Cancún. From Cancún City, take the Ruta 8 bus on Avenida Tulum to Puerto Juárez. The air-conditioned *Caribbean Express* (20 min.) costs $4 per person. Departures are every half-hour from 6 to 8:30am and then every 15 minutes until 8:30pm. The slower *Caribbean Savage* (45–60 min.) costs about $3.50. It departs every 2 hours, or less frequently depending on demand. Upon arrival, the ferry docks in downtown Isla Mujeres near all the shops, restaurants, hotels, and Norte beach. You'll need a taxi to get to El Garrafón park, at the other end of the island. You can stay as long as you like on the island (even overnight) and return by ferry, but be sure to double-check the time of the last returning ferry.

**Pleasure-boat cruises** to Isla Mujeres are a favorite pastime. Modern motor yachts, catamarans, trimarans, and even old-time sloops—more than 25 boats a day—take swimmers, sun lovers, snorkelers, and shoppers out on the translucent waters. Some tours include a snorkeling stop at El Garrafón, lunch on the beach, and a short time for shopping in downtown Isla Mujeres. Most leave at 9:30 or 10am, last about 5 or 6 hours, and include continental breakfast, lunch, and rental of snorkel gear. Others, particularly sunset and night cruises, go to beaches away from town for pseudo-pirate shows and include a lobster dinner or Mexican buffet. If you want to actually see Isla Mujeres, go on a morning cruise, or travel on your own using the public ferry from Puerto Juárez. Prices for the day cruises run around $45 per person.

**El Garrafón Natural Park** *ßß* is under the same management as Xcaret (© **998/884-9422** or 877-1101; www.garrafon.com). The basic entrance fee of $29 includes access to the reef and a museum, as well as use of kayaks, inner tubes, life vests, the pool, hammocks, and public facilities and showers. Snorkel gear and lockers can be rented for an extra charge. There are also nature trails as well as several restaurants on-site. An all-inclusive option is available for $59, which includes dining on whatever you choose at any of the restaurants, plus unlimited domestic drinks and use of snorkel gear, locker, and towel. El Garrafón also has full dive facilities and gear rentals, plus a gift shop.

Other excursions go to the **reefs** in glass-bottom boats, so you can have a near-scuba-diving experience and see many colorful fish. However, the reefs are some distance from the shore and are impossible to reach on windy days with choppy seas. They've also suffered from overvisitation, and their condition is far from pristine. Nautibus's **Atlantis Submarine** (© **987/872-5671**) takes you close to the aquatic action. Departures vary, depending on weather conditions. Prices are $79 for adults, $45 for children ages 4 to 12. The submarine descends to a depth of 30m (98 ft.). Atlantis Submarine departs Monday to Saturday every hour from 8am until 2pm; the

---

### *Tips* An All-Terrain Tour

**Cancún Mermaid** (© **998/843-6517**; www.cancunmermaid.com) offers all-terrain-vehicle (ATV) jungle tours for $49 per person and $66 double. The ATV tours travel through the jungles of Cancún and emerge on the beaches of the Riviera Maya. The 2½-hour tour includes equipment, instruction, the services of a tour guide, and bottled water; it departs daily at 8am and 1:30pm. The company picks you up at your hotel. Another ATV option is Rancho Loma Bonita; see "Horseback Riding," below.

tour lasts about an hour. The submarine departs from Cozumel, so you either need to take a ferry to get there or purchase the package that includes round-trip ground and water transportation from your hotel in Cancún ($103 adults, $76 children 4–12). Reservations are recommended.

## 5 Outdoor Activities & Attractions

### OUTDOOR ACTIVITIES

**DOLPHIN SWIMS**    On Isla Mujeres, you have the opportunity to swim with dolphins at **Dolphin Discovery** ✴ (✆ 998/849-4757; fax 998/849-4758; www.dolphin discovery.com). There are several options for dolphin interaction, but my choice is the Royal Swim, which includes an educational introduction followed by 30 minutes of swim time. The price is $129 (MasterCard and Visa are accepted), with transportation to Isla Mujeres an additional $15 for program participants. Advance reservations are required. Assigned swimming times are 10am, noon, 2, or 3:30pm, and you must arrive 1½ hour before your scheduled swim time. In Cancún, **Wet 'n Wild** (✆ 998/193-2000) marine park offers guests a chance to swim with dolphins and view them in their aquarium. The price of the dolphin swim ($115) includes admission to the park. It's a fun place for a family to spend the day, with its numerous pools, water slides, and rides. Visitors can also snorkel with manta rays, tropical fish, and tame sharks. It's at the southern end of Cancún, between the airport and the Hotel Zone. Admission is $25 for adults, $19 for children 3 to 11 (American Express, MasterCard, and Visa are accepted). It is open daily from 10am to 5:30pm.

La Isla Shopping Center, Bulevar Kukulkán Km 12.5, has an impressive **Interactive Aquarium** (✆ 998/883-0411, -0436, or -0413; www.aquariumcancun.com.mx), with dolphin swims and the chance to feed a shark while immersed in the water in an acrylic cage. Guides inside the main tank use underwater microphones to point out the sea life, and even answer your questions. Open exhibition tanks enable visitors to touch a variety of marine life, including sea stars and manta rays. The educational dolphin program is $60, while the dolphin swim is $115. The entrance fee to the aquarium is $6 for adults, $4 for children, and it's open daily from 9am to 7pm.

**GOLF & TENNIS**    The 18-hole **Pok-Ta-Pok Club,** or Club de Golf Cancún (✆ 998/883-0871), is a Robert Trent Jones, Sr., design on the northern leg of the island. Greens fees run $140 per 18 holes, with clubs renting for $40 and shoes for $18. A caddy costs $35. The club is open daily, accepts American Express, MasterCard, and Visa, and has tennis courts.

The **Hilton Cancún Golf & Spa Resort** (✆ 998-881-8000; fax 998/881-8084) has a championship 18-hole, par-72 course designed around the Ruinas Del Rey. Greens fees for the public are typically $175 for 18 holes and $125 for 9 holes; Hilton Cancún guests pay discounted rates of $125 for 18 holes, or $90 for 9 holes, which includes a golf cart. Golf clubs and shoes are available for rent. The club is open daily from 6am to 6pm and accepts American Express, MasterCard, and Visa. *Note:* The golf club is currently undergoing a multimillion dollar renovation, but expects to reopen in December 2006. For details, call ✆ 1-800-HILTONS or go to www.hilton.com.

The **Gran Meliá Cancún** (✆ 998/881-1100, ext. 193) has a 9-hole executive course; the fee is $43. The club is open daily from 7am to 4:30pm and accepts American Express, MasterCard, and Visa.

The first Jack Nicklaus Signature Golf Course in the Cancún area has opened at the **Moon Palace Golf Resort,** along the Riviera Maya (www.palaceresorts.com). Two additional PGA courses are planned for the area just north of Cancún, Puerto Cancún, in 2007 and 2008.

**HORSEBACK RIDING   Rancho Loma Bonita** (© 998/887-5465 or -5423), about 30 minutes south of town, is Cancún's most popular option for horseback riding. Five-hour packages include 2 hours of riding through the mangrove swamp to the beach, where you have time to swim and relax. The tour costs $54 for both adults and children. The ranch also offers a four-wheel ATV ride on the same route as the horseback tour. It costs $72 per person if you want to ride on your own, $55 if you double up. Prices for both tours include transportation to the ranch, riding, soft drinks, and lunch, plus a guide and insurance. Visa is accepted, but cash is preferred.

## ATTRACTIONS

**A MUSEUM**   To the right side of the entrance to the Cancún Convention Center is the **Museo Arqueológico de Cancún** (© 998/883-0305), a small but interesting museum with relics from archaeological sites around the state. Admission is $3; free on Sunday and holidays. It's open Tuesday through Friday from 9am to 8pm, Saturday and Sunday from 10am to 7pm.

Another cultural enclave is the **Museo de Arte Popular Mexicano** (© 998/849-7777), on the second floor of the El Embarcadero Marina, Bulevar Kukulkán Km 4. It displays a representative collection of masks, regional folkloric costumes, nativity scenes, religious artifacts, musical instruments, Mexican toys, and gourd art, spread over 1,370 sq. m (14,747 sq. ft.) of exhibition space. Admission is $10, with kids under 12 paying half price. The museum is open daily from 11am to 11pm.

**BULLFIGHTS**   Cancún has a small bullring, **Plaza de Toros** (© 998/884-8372; bull@prodigy.net.mx), near the northern (town) end of Bulevar Kukulkán. Bullfights take place every Wednesday at 3:30pm during the winter tourist season. A sport introduced to Mexico by the Spanish viceroys, bullfighting is now as much a part of Mexican culture as tequila. The bullfights usually include four bulls, and the spectacle begins with a folkloric dance exhibition, followed by a performance by the *charros* (Mexico's sombrero-wearing cowboys). You're not likely to see Mexico's best bullfights in Cancún—the real stars are in Mexico City. Keep in mind that if you go to a bullfight, *you're going to see a bullfight,* so stay away if you're an animal lover or you can't bear the sight of blood. Travel agencies in Cancún sell tickets, which cost $35 for adults, free for children under 6; seating is by general admission. American Express, MasterCard, and Visa are accepted

**SIGHTSEEING**   **La Torre Cancún,** a rotating tower at the El Embarcadero park and entertainment complex, once offered the best possible view of Cancún and should do so again soon, although its reopening date was uncertain at press time. It's located at Paseo Kukulkán Km 4 (© 998/849-7777). Former prices were $9 for one ride, and $14 for a day and night pass.

## 6 Shopping

Despite the surrounding natural splendor, shopping has become a favorite activity. Cancún is known throughout Mexico for its diverse shops and festive malls catering to a large number of international tourists. Visitors from the United States may find apparel more expensive in Cancún, but the selection is much broader than at other Mexican resorts. Numerous duty-free shops offer excellent value on European goods. The largest is **UltraFemme,** Avenida Tulum, Supermanzana 25 (© **998/884-1402** or 887-4559), specializing in imported cosmetics, perfumes, and fine jewelry and watches. The downtown Cancún location offers slightly lower prices than branches in Plaza Caracol, Kukulcan Plaza, Maya Fair Plaza, Flamingo Plaza, and the international airport.

Handicrafts are more limited and more expensive in Cancún than in other regions of Mexico because they are not produced here. They are available, though; several **open-air crafts markets** are on Avenida Tulum in Cancún City and near the convention center in the Hotel Zone. One of the biggest is **Coral Negro,** Bulevar Kukulkán Km 9.5 (©/fax **998/883-0758**), open daily from 7am to 11pm. A small restaurant inside, Xtabentun, serves Yucatecan food and pizza slices, and metamorphoses into a dance club around 9 to 11pm.

Cancún's main venues are the **malls**—not quite as grand as their U.S. counterparts, but close. All are air-conditioned, sleek, and sophisticated. Most are on Bulevar Kukulkán between Km 7 and Km 12. They offer everything from fine crystal and silver to designer clothing and decorative objects, along with numerous restaurants and clubs. Stores are generally open daily from 10am to 10pm.

The **Kukulcan Plaza** (© **998/885-2200;** www.kukulcanplaza.com) offers a large selection—more than 300—of shops, restaurants, and entertainment. There's a branch of Banco Serfin; OK Maguey Cantina Grill; a theater with U.S. movies; an Internet access kiosk; Tikal, which sells Guatemalan textile clothing; several crafts stores; a liquor store; several bathing-suit specialty stores; record and tape outlets; a leather goods store (including shoes and sandals); and a store specializing in silver from Taxco. The Fashion Gallery features designer clothing. In the food court are a number of U.S. franchise restaurants, including Ruth's Chris Steak House, plus one featuring specialty coffee. There's also a large indoor parking garage. The mall is open daily from 10am to 10pm, until 11pm during high season. Assistance for those with disabilities is available upon request, and wheelchairs, strollers, and lockers are available at the information desk.

Planet Hollywood anchors the **Plaza Flamingo** (© **998/883-2945**), which has branches of Bancrecer, Subway, and La Casa del Habano (Cuban cigars).

The long-standing **Plaza Caracol** (© **998/883-1038;** www.caracolplaza.com) holds Cartier jewelry, Guess, Waterford Crystal, Señor Frog clothing, Samsonite luggage, and La Fisheria restaurant. It's just before you reach the convention center as you come from downtown Cancún.

**Maya Fair Plaza/Centro Comercial Maya Fair,** frequently called "Mayfair" (© **998/883-2801**), is the oldest mall. The lively center holds open-air restaurants and bars, including the Outback Steakhouse and Sanborn's Café, and several stores sell silver, leather, and crafts.

Because the entertainment-oriented **Forum by the Sea,** Bulevar Kukulkán Km 9 (© **998/883-4425**), suffered extensive hurricane damage, it received a complete face-lift. Most people come here for the food and fun, choosing from Hard Rock Cafe, Coco Bongo, and Rainforest Cafe, plus an extensive food court. Shops include Tommy Hilfiger, Levi's, Diesel, Swatch, and Harley Davidson. The mall is open daily from 10am to midnight (bars remain open later).

The most intriguing mall is the **La Isla Shopping Village,** Bulevar Kukulkán Km 12.5 (© **998/883-5025;** www.laislacancun.com.mx), an open-air festival mall that looks like a small village. Walkways lined with shops and restaurants cross little canals. It also has a "riverwalk" alongside the Nichupté lagoon, and an interactive aquarium and dolphin swim facility, as well as the Spacerocker and River Ride Tour—great for kid-friendly fun. It suffered extensive hurricane damage, but was fully reopened in March 2006. Shops include Guess, Diesel, DKNY, Bulgari, and UltraFemme. Dining choices include Johnny Rockets, Come and Eat, Häagen-Dazs, and the beautiful Mexican restaurant La Casa de las Margaritas. You also can find a movie theater, a video arcade, and several nightclubs, including Glazz. It's across from the Sheraton, on the lagoon side of the street.

## 7 Cancún After Dark

One of Cancún's main draws is its active nightlife. The hottest centers of action are the **Centro Comercial Maya Fair, Forum by the Sea,** and **La Isla Shopping Village.** Hotels also compete, with happy-hour entertainment and special drink prices to entice visitors and guests from other resorts. Lobby bar hopping at sunset is one great way to plan next year's vacation.

### THE CLUB & MUSIC SCENE

Clubbing in Cancún is a favorite part of the vacation experience and can go on each night until the sun rises over that incredibly blue sea. Several big hotels have nightclubs or schedule live music in their lobby bars. At the clubs, expect to stand in long lines on weekends, pay a cover charge of $15 to $25 per person, and pay $5 to $8 for a drink. Some of the higher-priced clubs include an open bar or live entertainment. The places listed in this section are air-conditioned and accept American Express, MasterCard, and Visa.

A great idea to get you started is the **Bar Hopper Tour** *✶✶* (© **998/883-5402**). For $60, it takes you by bus bar to club to bar to club—generally a range of four to five top choices—where you bypass any lines and spend about an hour at each establishment. The price includes entry to the clubs, one welcome drink at each, and transportation by air-conditioned bus, allowing you to get a great sampling of the best of Cancún's nightlife. The tour runs from 8pm to 3:30am, with the meeting point at Come and Eat restaurant in the La Isla Hopping Village. American Express, Visa, and MasterCard are accepted.

Numerous restaurants, such as **Carlos 'n' Charlie's, Hard Rock Cafe, Señor Frog's, TGI Friday's,** and **Iguana Wana,** double as nighttime party spots, offering wildish fun at a fraction of the price of more costly clubs.

Most of Cancún's most popular clubs were located at the exact point on the island where the most damage was done, so they've just received a makeover. Most reopened in time for spring break in 2006—but it's still up in the air which will assume the top hot spot, and, as any good clubber knows, popularity can shift like the sands on the beach. So take this list as a starting point—extensive research showed me that these were the current hot spots at press time.

**Carlos 'n' Charlie's**    This is a reliable place to find both good food and packed-frat-house entertainment in the evening. There's a dance floor, and live music starts nightly around 8:30pm. A cover charge kicks in if you're not planning to eat. It's open daily from 11am to 2am. Bulevar Kukulkán Km 4.5. © **998/883-1862.**

**Carlos O'Brian's**  With recorded music, this is only slightly tamer than other Carlos Anderson restaurants and nightspots in town (Señor Frog and Carlos 'n' Charlie's). It's open daily from 9am to midnight. Tulum 107, SM22. © 998/883-1092.

**The City** 🎵🎵🎵  This was Cancún's hottest club pre-Wilma, and promises to be once again, after reopening in March 2006. It features progressive electronic music spun by some of the world's top DJs. With visiting DJs from New York, L.A., and Mexico City—Moby even played here—the music is sizzling. You actually need never leave, as The City is a day-and-night club. The City Beach Club opens at 8am, and features a pool with a wave machine for surfing and boogie-boarding, a tower-high waterslide, food and bar service, plus beach cabanas. The Terrace Bar, overlooking the action on Bulevar Kukulkán, serves food and drinks all day long. For a relaxing evening vibe, the Lounge features comfy couches, chill music, and an extensive menu of martinis, snacks, and desserts. Open at 10pm, the 72,500-sq.-m (26,910-sq.-ft.) nightclub has nine bars, stunning light shows, and several VIP areas. Located in front of Coco Bongo, The City also has a second location in Playa del Carmen. Bulevar Kukulkán, Km 9.5. © 998/848-8380. www.thecitycancun.com.

**Coco Bongo** 🎵🎵  Continuing its reputation as one of the hottest spots in town, its main appeal is that it has no formal dance floor, so you can dance anywhere—and that includes on the tables, on the bar, or even on the stage with the live band! This place can—and regularly does—pack in up to 3,000 people. You have to experience it to believe it. Despite its capacity, lines are long on weekends and in high season. The music alternates between Caribbean, salsa, house, hip-hop, techno, and classics from the 1970s and 1980s. It draws a mixed crowd, but the young and hip dominate. Forum by the Sea, Bulevar Kukulkán Km 9.5. © 998/883-5061. www.cocobongo.com.mx. Cover $15, or $25 with open bar.

**Dady'O**  A highly favored rave with frequent long lines. It opens nightly at 10pm. Bulevar Kukulkán Km 9.5. © 998/883-3333. www.dadyo.net. Cover $15.

**Dady Rock Bar and Grill**  The offspring of Dady'O, it opens at 7pm and goes as long as any other nightspot, offering a combination of live bands and DJs spinning music, along with an open bar, full meals, a buffet, and dancing. Bulevar Kukulkán Km 9.5. © 998/883-1626.

**Glazz**  Among Cancún's newest nocturnal offerings, Glazz combines a restaurant with a sleek lounge and sophisticated nightclub for a complete evening of entertainment. Geared for those over 30, music is mostly lounge and house, and there are live entertainment acts (anything from drummers to sultry dancers) periodically through the evening. The staff is known as being among the top in town. The China Bistro is already earning rave reviews, while the Lounge's vast selection of martinis and tequilitinis is dangerously tempting. The Club is pure Miami-style, with plenty of neon and a very hot DJ. It's open nightly from 7pm to 5am. A dress code prohibits sandals or shorts. La Isla Shopping Village, Bulevar Kukulkán Km 12.5, Local B-7. © 998/883-1881. www.glazz.com.mx. Cover $10.

**Lobby Lounge** 🎵  The most refined and upscale of Cancún's nightly gathering spots, with live dance music and a list of more than 120 premium tequilas for tasting or sipping. Ritz-Carlton hotel, Retorno del Rey 36, off Bulevar Kukulkán Km 13.5. © 998/885-0808, ext. 5310.

## THE PERFORMING ARTS
Several hotels host **Mexican fiesta nights,** including a buffet dinner and a folkloric dance show; admission, including dinner, ranges from $35 to $50.

You can also get in the party mood at **Mango Tango** ⊛, Bulevar Kukulkán Km 14.2 (© **998/885-0303**), a lagoon-side restaurant and dinner-show establishment opposite the Ritz-Carlton hotel. Diners can choose from two levels, one nearer the music and the other overlooking it all. Music is loud and varied but mainly features reggae or salsa. A 45-minute floor show starts nightly at 8:30pm. A variety of packages are available—starting at $49 per person—depending on whether you want dinner and the show, open bar and the show, or the show alone. For dancing, which starts at 9:30pm, there's a $10 cover charge. See "Where to Dine," earlier in this chapter, for a restaurant review.

Tourists mingle with locals at the downtown **Parque de las Palapas** (the main park) for Noches Caribeñas, which involves free live tropical music for anyone who wants to listen and dance. Performances begin at 7:30pm on Sunday, and sometimes there are performances on Friday and Saturday.

# 5

# Isla Mujeres & Cozumel

*by David Baird & Lynne Bairstow*

Mexico's two main Caribbean islands are idyllic places to get away from the hustle and bustle of Cancún and the Riviera Maya. Neither Isla Mujeres nor Cozumel is particularly large, and they have that island feel—small roads that don't go very far, lots of mopeds, few (or no) buses and trucks, and a sense of being set apart from the rest of the world. Yet they're just a short ferry ride from the mainland. Both offer a variety of lodging choices, ample outdoor activities, and a laid-back atmosphere that makes a delightful contrast with the mainland experience.

## EXPLORING MEXICO'S CARIBBEAN ISLANDS

**ISLA MUJERES**   A day trip to Isla Mujeres on a party boat is one of the most popular excursions from Cancún. This fish-shaped island is just 13km (8 miles) northeast of Cancún, a quick boat ride away, allowing ample time to get a taste of the peaceful pace of life. To fully explore the village and its shops and cafes, relax at the broad, tranquil Playa Norte, or snorkel or dive El Garrafón Reef (an underwater park), you'll need more time. Overnight accommodations range from rustic to offbeat chic.

Passenger ferries go to Isla Mujeres from Puerto Juárez, and car ferries leave from Punta Sam, both near Cancún. More expensive passenger ferries, with less frequent departures, leave from the Playa Linda pier on Cancún Island.

**COZUMEL**   Cozumel is larger than Isla Mujeres and farther from the mainland (19km/12 miles off the coast from Playa del Carmen). It has its own international airport. Life here turns around two major activities: scuba diving and being a port of call for cruise ships. It is far and away the most popular destination along this coast for both. Despite the cruise-ship traffic and all the stores that it has spawned, life on the island moves at a relaxed and comfortable pace. There is just one town, San Miguel de Cozumel. North and south of town are resorts; the rest of the shore is deserted and predominantly rocky, with a scattering of small sandy coves that you can have practically all to yourself.

## 1 Isla Mujeres ★★★

13km (8 miles) N of Cancún

**Isla Mujeres (Island of Women)** is a casual, laid-back refuge from the conspicuously commercialized action of Cancún, visible across a narrow channel. It's known as the best value in the Caribbean, assuming that you favor an easygoing vacation pace and prefer simplicity to pretense. This is an island of white-sand beaches and turquoise waters, complemented by a town filled with Caribbean-colored clapboard houses and rustic, open-air restaurants. Hotels are clean and comfortable, but if you're looking for

> ## ⟨*Tips*⟩ The Best Websites for Isla Mujeres & Cozumel
>
> - **Isla Mujeres Tourist Information: www.isla-mujeres.net** The official site of the Isla Mujeres Tourism Board provides complete information on Isla, from getting there to where to stay.
> - **My Isla Mujeres: www.myislamujeres.com** Get a local's view of the island; especially notable are the active chat room and message boards on this site.
> - **Cozumel.net: www.cozumel.net** This site is a cut above the typical dining/lodging/activities sites. Click on "About Cozumel" to find schedules for ferries and island-hop flights, and to check the latest news. There's also a comprehensive listing of B&Bs and vacation home rentals, plus great info on diving, maps, and a chat room.
> - **Cozumel Travel Planner: www.go2cozumel.com** This is a well-done guide to area businesses and attractions, by an online Mexico specialist.
> - **Travel Notes: www.travelnotes.cc** This site boasts more than 1,000 pages of information on and photos of Cozumel island—with an emphasis on diving, deep sea fishing, and other ocean activities.
> - **Cozumel Hotel Association: www.islacozumel.com.mx** Operated by the tourism-promotion arm of the hotel association, this site gives more than just listings of the member hotels. There's info on packages and specials, plus brief descriptions of most of the island's attractions, restaurants, and recreational activities.

lots of action or opulence, you'll be happier in Cancún. A few recent additions provide more luxurious lodging, but they still maintain a decidedly casual atmosphere.

Francisco Hernández de Córdoba, seeing figurines of partially clad females along the shore, gave the island its name when he landed in 1517. These are now believed to have been offerings to the Maya goddess of fertility and the moon, Ixchel. Their presence indicates that the island was probably sacred to the Maya.

At midday, suntanned visitors hang out in open-air cafes and stroll streets lined with frantic souvenir vendors. Calling attention to their bargain-priced wares, they give a carnival atmosphere to the hours when tour-boat traffic is at its peak. Befitting the size of the island, most of the traffic consists of golf carts, *motos* (mopeds), and bicycles. Once the tour boats leave, however, Isla Mujeres reverts to its more typical, tranquil way of life.

Days in "Isla"—as the locals call it—can alternate between adventurous activity and absolute repose. Trips to the Isla Contoy bird sanctuary are popular, as are the excellent diving, fishing, and snorkeling—in 1998, the island's coral coast became part of Mexico's Marine National Park system. Note, however, that the reef suffered substantial hurricane damage in 2005, so is not up to offering the stellar underwater vistas it once did. The upside of Hurricane Wilma's impact is that Playa Norte received an infusion of white sand, and is now broader and more beautiful than ever, despite the "haircuts" suffered by many of the palm trees. The island and several of its traditional hotels attract regular gatherings of yoga practitioners. In the evening, most people find

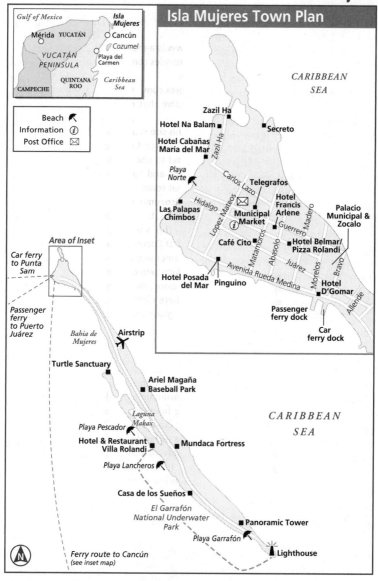

## Isla Mujeres Town Plan

Gulf of Mexico
Isla Mujeres

Mérida  YUCATÁN          O Cancún

YUCATÁN                  Cozumel
PENINSULA          Playa del
                   Carmen

                              Caribbean
CAMPECHE    QUINTANA          Sea
            ROO

Beach
Information (i)
Post Office

CARIBBEAN SEA

Zazil Ha
Hotel Na Balam                    Secreto

Hotel Cabañas
María del Mar

Playa
Norte
              Carlos Lazo   Telegrafos
                                          Hotel
                                          Francis
Las Palapas   Hidalgo   Municipal  Arlene   Palacio
Chimbos                 Market              Municipal &
                                    Guerrero  Zocalo

              Café Cito                Hotel Belmar/
                                       Pizza Rolandi

Area of Inset

Car ferry              Hotel Posada   Avenida Rueda Medina   Hotel
to Punta               del Mar   Pinguino                    D'Gomar
Sam

Passenger                                     Passenger
ferry                                         ferry dock
to Puerto
Juárez      Bahía de     Airstrip               Car
            Mujeres                             ferry dock

Turtle Sanctuary

              Ariel Magaña
              Baseball Park

            Laguna          CARIBBEAN
            Makax           SEA
Playa Pescador

Hotel & Restaurant  Mundaca Fortress
Villa Rolandi

Playa Lancheros

    Casa de los Sueños

    El Garrafón
    National Underwater
    Park                Panoramic Tower
              Playa Garrafón
                              Lighthouse

Ferry route to Cancún
(see inset map)

the slow, casual pace one of the island's biggest draws. The cool night breeze is a perfect accompaniment to casual open-air dining and drinking in small street-side restaurants. Many people pack it in as early as 9 or 10pm, when most of the businesses close. Those in search of a party, however, will find kindred souls at the bars on Playa Norte that stay open late.

## ESSENTIALS

**GETTING THERE & DEPARTING**   Puerto Juárez, just north of Cancún, is the **dock** (© 998/877-0618) for passenger ferries to Isla Mujeres, the least expensive way to travel to Isla. The air-conditioned *Caribbean Express* leaves every half-hour, makes the trip in 20 minutes, has storage space for luggage, and costs about $4. These boats operate daily, starting at 6:30am and ending at 8:30pm. They might leave early if they're full, so arrive ahead of schedule. Pay at the ticket office—or, if the ferry is about to leave, aboard.

*Note:* Upon arrival by taxi or bus in Puerto Juárez, be wary of pirate "guides" who tell you either that the ferry is canceled or that it's several hours until the next ferry. They'll offer the services of a private *lancha* (small boat) for about $40—and it's nothing but a scam. Small boats are available and, on a co-op basis, charge $15 to $25 one-way, based on the number of passengers. They take about 50 minutes and are not recommended on days with rough seas. Check with the clearly visible ticket office—the only accurate source for information.

Taxi fares are posted by the street where the taxis park, so be sure to check the rate before agreeing to a taxi for the ride back to Cancún. Rates generally run $12 to $15, depending upon your destination. Moped and bicycle rentals are also readily available as you depart the ferry. This small complex also has public bathrooms, luggage storage, a snack bar, and souvenir shops.

Isla Mujeres is so small that a vehicle isn't necessary, but if you're taking one, you'll use the **Punta Sam** port a little beyond Puerto Juárez. The ferry (40 min.) runs five or six times daily between 8am and 8pm, year-round except in bad weather. Times are generally as follows: Cancún to Isla 8am, 11am, 2:45pm, 5:30pm, and 8:15pm; Isla to Cancún 6:30am, 9:30am, 12:45pm, 4:15pm, and 7:15pm. Always check with the tourist office in Cancún to verify this schedule. Cars should arrive an hour before the ferry departure to register for a place in line and pay the posted fee, which varies depending on the weight and type of vehicle. The sole gas pump in Isla is at the intersection of Avenida Rueda Medina and Calle Abasolo, just northwest of the ferry docks.

There are also ferries to Isla Mujeres from the **Playa Linda,** known as the Embarcadero pier in Cancún, but they're less frequent and more expensive than those from Puerto Juárez. A **Water Taxi** (© 998/886-4270 or -4847; asterix@cablered.net.mx) to Isla Mujeres operates from **Playa Caracol,** between the Fiesta Americana Coral Beach Hotel and the Xcaret terminal on the island, with prices about the same as those from Playa Linda and about four times the cost of the public ferries from Puerto Juárez. Scheduled departures are at 9am, 11am, and 1pm, with returns from Isla Mujeres at noon and 5pm. Adult round-trip fares are $15; kids 3 to 12 pay $7.50; free for children under 3.

To get to Puerto Juárez or Punta Sam from **Cancún,** take any Ruta 8 city bus from Avenida Tulum. If you're coming from **Mérida,** you can fly to Cancún and proceed to Puerto Juárez or take a bus directly to Puerto Juárez. From **Cozumel,** you can fly to Cancún (there are daily flights) or take a ferry to Playa del Carmen (see "Cozumel," later in this chapter), then travel to Puerto Juárez.

**Arriving**   Ferries arrive at the docks (© 998/877-0065) in the center of town. The main road that passes in front is Avenida Rueda Medina. Most hotels are close by. Tricycle taxis are the least expensive and most fun way to get to your hotel; you and your luggage pile in the open carriage compartment, and the driver pedals through the streets. Regular taxis are always lined up in a parking lot to the right of the pier, with their rates posted. If someone on the ferry offers to arrange a taxi for you, politely decline, unless you'd like some help with your luggage down the short pier—it just means an extra, unnecessary tip for your helper.

**VISITOR INFORMATION** The **City Tourist Office** (𝕮/fax **998/877-0767** or -0307) is at Av. Rueda Medina 130, on your left as you reach the end of the pier. It's open Monday through Friday from 9am to 4pm, closed on Saturdays and Sundays. Also look for *Islander,* a free publication with local information, advertisements, and event listings.

**ISLAND LAYOUT** Isla Mujeres is about 8km (5 miles) long and 4km (2½ miles) wide, with the town at the northern tip. "Downtown" is a compact 4 blocks by 6 blocks, so it's very easy to get around. The **ferry docks** are at the center of town, within walking distance of most hotels, restaurants, and shops. The street running along the waterfront is **Avenida Rueda Medina,** commonly called the *malecón* **(boardwalk).** The **Mercado Municipal (town market)** is by the post office on **Calle Guerrero,** an inland street at the north edge of town, which, like most streets in the town, is unmarked.

**GETTING AROUND** A popular form of transportation on Isla Mujeres is the electric **golf cart,** available for rent at many hotels for $15 per hour or $45 per day. **El Sol Golf Cart Rental,** Av. Francisco I. Madero 5 (𝕮 **998/877-0791** or -0068), will deliver, or you can pick one up. The golf carts don't go more than 30kmph (20 mph), but they're fun. Anyway, you aren't on Isla Mujeres to hurry. Many people enjoy touring the island by *moto* **(motorized bike or scooter).** Fully automatic versions are available for around $25 per day or $7 per hour. They come with seats for one person, but some are large enough for two. There's only one main road with a couple of offshoots, so you won't get lost. Be aware that the rental price does not include insurance, and any injury to yourself or the vehicle will come out of your pocket. **Bicycles** are also available for rent at some hotels for $3 per hour or $7 per day, including a basket and a lock.

If you prefer to use a taxi, rates are about $2.50 for trips within the downtown area, or $4.50 for a trip to the southern end of Isla. You can also hire them for about $10 per hour. The number to call for taxis is 𝕮 **998/877-0066.**

---

### *FAST FACTS:* Isla Mujeres

*Area Code* The telephone area code is **998.**

*Consumer Protection* You can reach the local branch of **Profeco** consumer protection agency at 𝕮 **998/887-2877.**

*Currency Exchange* Isla Mujeres has numerous *casas de cambio,* or money exchanges, that you can easily spot along the main streets. Most of the hotels listed here change money for their guests, although often at less favorable rates than the commercial enterprises. There is only one bank in Isla, HSBC Bank, across from the ferry docks (𝕮 **998/877-0104**). It's open Monday through Friday from 8:30am to 6pm, and Saturdays from 9am to 2pm.

*Hospital* The **Hospital de la Armada** is on Avenida Rueda Medina at Ojón P. Blanco (𝕮 **998/877-0001**). It's less than a kilometer (½ mile) south of the town center. It will only treat you in an emergency. Otherwise, you're referred to the **Centro de Salud** on Avenida Guerrero, a block before the beginning of the *malecón* (© **998/877-0117**).

*Internet Access* Owned by a lifelong resident of Isla, **Cyber Isla Mujres.com,** Av. Francisco y Madero 17, between Hidalgo and Juaréz streets (© **998/877-0272**), offers Internet access for $1.50 per hour daily 8am to 10pm, and serves complimentary coffee from Veracruz all day.

*Pharmacy* **Isla Mujeres Farmacia** (© **998/877-0178**) has the best selection of prescription and over-the-counter medicines. It's on Calle Benito Juárez, between Morelos and Bravo, across from Rachet & Rome jewelry store.

*Post & Telegraph Office* The *correo* is at Calle Guerrero 12 (© **998/877-0085**), at the corner of López Mateos, near the market. It's open Monday through Friday from 9am to 4pm.

*Taxis* To call for a taxi, dial © **998/877-0066**.

*Telephone* Ladatel phones accepting coins and prepaid phone cards are at the plaza and throughout town.

*Tourist Seasons* Isla Mujeres's tourist season (when hotel rates are higher) is a bit different from that of other places in Mexico. High season runs December through May, a month longer than in Cancún. Some hotels raise their rates in August, and some raise their rates beginning in mid-November. Low season is from June to mid-November.

## BEACHES & OUTDOOR ACTIVITIES

**THE BEACHES**    The most popular beach in town is alternately referred to as **Playa Cocoteros** ("Cocos," for short), or **Playa Norte** ⩪. The long stretch of beach extends around the northern tip of the island, to your left as you get off the boat. This is a truly splendid beach—a wide swath of fine white sand and calm, translucent, turquoise-blue water. Topless sunbathing is permitted. The beach is easily reached on foot from the ferry and from all downtown hotels. Watersports equipment, beach umbrellas, and lounge chairs are available for rent. Those in front of restaurants usually cost nothing if you use the restaurant as your headquarters for drinks and food.

El Garrafón Natural Park ⩪⩪ (see "Snorkeling," below) is best known as a snorkeling area, but there is a nice stretch of beach on either side of the park. **Playa Lancheros** is on the Caribbean side of Laguna Makax. Local buses go to Lancheros, then turn inland and return downtown. The beach at Playa Lancheros is nice, but the few restaurants there are expensive.

**SWIMMING**    Wide Playa Norte is the best swimming beach, with Playa Lancheros second. There are no lifeguards on duty on Isla Mujeres, which does not use the system of water-safety flags employed in Cancún and Cozumel.

**SNORKELING**    By far the most popular place to snorkel is **El Garrafón Natural Park** ⩪⩪. It is at the southern end of the island, where you'll see numerous schools of colorful fish. The pricy but well-equipped park has two restaurant-bars, beach chairs, a swimming pool, kayaks, changing rooms, rental lockers, showers, a gift shop, and snack bars. Once a public national underwater park, Garrafón, since late 1999, has been operated by the same people who manage Xcaret, south of Cancún. Public facilities have been vastly improved, with new attractions and facilities added each year. Activities at the park include snorkeling and "Snuba" (a tankless version of scuba diving, when you descend while breathing through a long air tube), crystal-clear canoes for viewing underwater life, and a zip-line that takes you over the water. The underwater minisub **Sea Trek** provides a great view of the submarine landscape, and you can keep dry, if that's your preference. On land, they have tanning decks, shaded hammocks, a 12m (40-ft.) climbing tower, and—of course!—a souvenir superstore. Several restaurants and snack bars are available. Admission (covering park entry and use of the facilities, but not most rental equipment) is $29 for adults, $15 for children (American Express, MasterCard, and Visa are accepted). You can also choose a package ($59) that includes food, beverages, locker rental, and snorkeling gear rental. Day-trip packages from Cancún (© **998/884-9422** or 984/875-6000) are also available. Prices start at $22 and include round-trip transportation from the pier on Km 4 outside Cancún. The park is open daily from 9am to 5pm.

Also good for snorkeling is the **Manchones Reef,** off the southeastern coast. The reef is just offshore and accessible by boat.

Another excellent location is around *el faro* (the lighthouse) in the **Bahía de Mujeres** at the southern tip of the island, where the water is about 2m (6½ ft.) deep. Boatmen will take you for around $25 per person if you have your own snorkeling equipment or $30 if you use theirs.

**DIVING**    Most of the dive shops on the island offer the same trips for the same prices: one-tank dives cost $55, two-tank dives $70. **Bahía Dive Shop,** Rueda Medina 166, across from the car-ferry dock (© **998/877-0340**), is a full-service shop that offers resort and certification classes as well as dive equipment for sale or rent. The shop is open daily from 10am to 7pm, and accepts MasterCard and Visa. Another respected dive shop is **Coral Scuba Center,** at Matamoros 13A and Rueda Medina (© **998/877-0061** or -0763). It's open daily from 8am to 12:30pm and 4 to 10pm.

PADI-certified dive guides and dive instruction are available at **El Garrafón** (© **984/875-6000**). Discover Scuba classes are available for $65, with one-tank dives to the Garrafón reef priced at $45, or two-tank dives for $60. Open Water, Advanced, and Rescue PADI certification are also available.

**Cuevas de los Tiburones (Caves of the Sleeping Sharks)** is Isla's most renowned dive site—but the name is slightly misleading, as shark sightings are rare these days. Two sites where you could traditionally see the sleeping shark are the Cuevas de Tiburones and **La Punta,** but the sharks have mostly been driven off, and a storm collapsed the arch featured in a Jacques Cousteau film showing them, but the caves survive. Other dive sites include a **wreck** 15km (9⅓ miles) offshore; **Banderas** reef, between Isla Mujeres and Cancún, where there's always a strong current; **Tabos** reef on the eastern shore; and **Manchones** reef, 1km (½ mile) off the southeastern tip of the island, where the water is 4.5 to 11m (15–36 ft.) deep. **The Cross of the Bay** is close to Manchones reef. A bronze cross, weighing 1 ton and standing 12m (40 ft.) high, was placed in the water between Manchones and Isla in 1994, as a memorial to those who have lost their lives at sea.

**FISHING**    To arrange a day of fishing, ask at the **Sociedad Cooperativa Turística** (the boatmen's cooperative), on Avenida Rueda Medina (no phone), next to Mexico Divers and Las Brisas restaurant, or the travel agency mentioned in "A Visit to Isla

Contoy," below. Four to six others can share the cost, which includes lunch and drinks. Captain Tony Martínez (© **998/877-0274**) also arranges fishing trips aboard the *Marinonis,* with advanced reservations recommended. Year-round you'll find bonito, mackerel, kingfish, and amberjack. Sailfish and sharks (hammerhead, bull, nurse, lemon, and tiger) are in good supply in April and May. In winter, larger grouper and jewfish are prevalent. Four hours of fishing close to shore costs around $110; 8 hours farther out goes for $250. The cooperative is open Monday through Saturday from 8am to 1pm and 5 to 8pm, and Sunday from 7:30 to 10am and 6 to 8pm.

**YOGA** Increasingly, Isla is becoming known as a great place to combine a relaxing beach vacation with yoga practice and instruction. The trend began at **Hotel Na Balam** ⏒⏒ (© **998/877-0279** or -0058; www.nabalam.com), which offers yoga classes under its large poolside *palapa,* complete with yoga mats and props. The classes, which begin at 9am Monday through Friday, are free to guests, $10 per class to visitors. Na Balam is also the site of frequent yoga instruction vacations featuring respected teachers and a more extensive practice schedule; the current schedule of yoga retreats is posted on their website. Local yoga culture extends down the island to Casa de los Sueños Resort and Zenter (© **998/877-0651;** www.casadelossuenosresort.com), where yoga classes, as well as chi gong and Pilates, are regularly held.

## MORE ATTRACTIONS
**DOLPHIN DISCOVERY** ⏒⏒ You can swim with live dolphins (© **998/877-0207** or 849-4757; fax 998/849-4751; www.dolphindiscovery.com) in an enclosure at Treasure Island, on the side of Isla Mujeres that faces Cancún. Groups of six people swim with two dolphins and one trainer. Swimmers view an educational video and spend time in the water with the trainer and the dolphins before enjoying 15 minutes of free swimming time with them. Reservations are recommended, and you must arrive an hour before your assigned swimming time, at 9am, 11am, 1pm, or 3pm. The cost is $129 per person, plus $10 if you need round-trip transportation from Cancún.

**A TURTLE SANCTUARY** ⏒⏒ As recently as 20 years ago, fishermen converged on the island nightly from May to September, waiting for the monster-size turtles to lumber ashore to deposit their Ping-Pong-ball-shaped eggs. Totally vulnerable once they begin laying their eggs, and exhausted when they have finished, the turtles were easily captured and slaughtered for their highly prized meat, shell, and eggs. Then a concerned fisherman, Gonzalez Cahle Maldonado, began convincing others to spare at least the eggs, which he protected. It was a start. Following his lead, the fishing secretariat founded the **Centro de Investigaciones** 11 years ago; although the local government provided assistance in the past, now the center relies solely on private donations. Since opening, at least 28,000 turtles have been released, and every year local schoolchildren participate in the event, thus planting the notion of protecting the turtles for a new generation of islanders.

Six species of sea turtles nest on Isla Mujeres. An adult green turtle, the most abundant species, measures 1 to 1.5m (3¼–5 ft.) in length and can weigh as much as 450 pounds. At the center, visitors walk through the indoor and outdoor turtle pool areas, where the creatures paddle around. The turtles are separated by age, from newly hatched up to 1 year. People who come here usually end up staying at least an hour, especially if they opt for the guided tour, which I recommend. They also have a small gift shop and snack bar. The sanctuary is on a piece of land separated from the island by Bahía de Mujeres and Laguna Makax, at Carr. Sac Bajo #5; you'll need a taxi to get

there. Admission is $3; the shelter is open daily from 9am to 5pm. For more informa-
tion, call © **998/877-0595.**

**SIGHTS OF PUNTA SUR** 🐾🐾   At Punta Sur (the southern point of the island, just
inland from **Garrafón National Park;** call © **998/877-1100** or go to www.garrafon.
com) and part of the park, is Isla's newest attraction, the **Panoramic Tower.** At 50m
(164-ft.) high, the tower offers visitors a bird's-eye view of the entire island. The tower
holds 20 visitors at a time, and rotates for 10 minutes while you can snap photos or
simply enjoy the scenery. Entry fee is $5, a professional photo of you at the tower
(touch-ups are included!) is $10, and package prices are available. Entrance to the
tower is included if you purchase Garrafón's all-inclusive admission.

Next to the tower you'll find **Sculptured Spaces,** an impressive and extensive garden of large sculptures donated to Isla Mujeres by internationally renowned sculptors
as part of the 2001 First International Sculpture Exhibition. Among Mexican sculptors represented by works are José Luis Cuevas and Vlaadimir Cora.

Nearby is the **Caribbean Village,** with narrow lanes of colorful clapboard buildings
that house cafes and shops displaying folkloric art. Plan to have lunch or a snack here
at the kiosk and stroll around, before heading on to the lighthouse and Maya ruins.

Also at this southern point of the island, and part of the ruins, is **Cliff of the Dawn,**
the southeasternmost point of Mexico. Services are available from 7am to 8pm, but
you can enter at any time; if you make it there early enough to see the sun rise, you
can claim you were the first person in Mexico that day to be touched by the sun!

**A MAYA RUIN** 🐾🐾   Just beyond the lighthouse, at the southern end of the island,
are the strikingly beautiful remains of a small Maya temple, believed to have been built
to pay homage to the moon and fertility goddess Ixchel. The location, on a lofty bluff
overlooking the sea, is worth seeing and makes a great place for photos. It is believed
that Maya women traveled here on annual pilgrimages to seek Ixchel's blessings of fertility. If you're at El Garrafón park and want to walk, it's not too far. Turn right from
El Garrafón. When you see the lighthouse, turn toward it down the rocky path.

**A PIRATE'S FORTRESS**   The Fortress of Mundaca is about 4km (2½ miles) in the
same direction as El Garrafón, less than a kilometer (about ½ mile) to the left. A slave
trader who claimed to have been the pirate Mundaca Marecheaga built the fortress. In
the early 19th century, he arrived at Isla Mujeres and set up a blissful paradise, while
making money selling slaves to Cuba and Belize. According to island lore, he decided
to settle down and build this hacienda after being captivated by the charms of an
island girl. However, she reputedly spurned his affections and married another
islander, leaving him heartbroken and alone on Isla Mujeres. Admission is $2; the
fortress is open daily from 10am to 6pm.

**A VISIT TO ISLA CONTOY** 🐾   If possible, plan to visit this pristine uninhabited
island, 30km (20 miles) by boat from Isla Mujeres, that became a national wildlife
reserve in 1981. Lush vegetation covers the oddly shaped island, which is 6km (3¾
miles) long and harbors 70 species of birds as well as a host of marine and animal life.
Bird species that nest on the island include pelicans, brown boobies, frigates, egrets,
terns, and cormorants. Flocks of flamingos arrive in April. June, July, and August are
good months to spot turtles burying their eggs in the sand at night. Most excursions
troll for fish (which will be your lunch), anchor en route for a snorkeling expedition,
skirt the island at a leisurely pace for close viewing of the birds without disturbing the
habitat, and then pull ashore. While the captain prepares lunch, visitors can swim,

sun, follow the nature trails, and visit the fine nature museum, which has bathroom facilities. The trip from Isla Mujeres takes about 45 minutes each way and can be longer if the waves are choppy. Because of the tight-knit boatmen's cooperative, prices for this excursion are the same everywhere: $40. You can buy a ticket at the **Sociedad Cooperativa Turística** on Avenida Rueda Medina, next to Mexico Divers and Las Brisas restaurant (no phone), or at one of several **travel agencies,** such as **La Isleña,** on Morelos between Medina and Juárez (© **998/877-0578;** www.isla-mujeres.net/islenatours). La Isleña is open daily from 7:30am to 9:30pm and is a good source for tourist information. Isla Contoy trips leave at 8:30am and return around 4pm. The price (cash only) is $42 for adults, $21 for children. Boat captains should respect the cooperative's regulations regarding ecological sensitivity and boat safety, including the availability of life jackets for everyone on board. If you're not given a life jacket, ask for one. Snorkeling equipment is usually included in the price, but double-check that before heading out. On the island, there is a small government museum with bathroom facilities.

## SHOPPING

Shopping is a casual activity here. There are only a few shops of any sophistication. Shop owners will bombard you, especially on Avenida Hidalgo, selling Saltillo rugs, onyx, silver, Guatemalan clothing, blown glassware, masks, folk art, beach paraphernalia, and T-shirts in abundance. Prices are lower than in Cancún or Cozumel, but with such overeager sellers, bargaining is necessary.

The one treasure you're likely to take back is a piece of fine jewelry—Isla is known for its excellent, duty-free prices on gemstones and handcrafted work made to order. Diamonds, emeralds, sapphires, and rubies can be purchased as loose stones and then mounted while you're off exploring. The superbly crafted gold, silver, and gems are available at very competitive prices in the workshops near the central plaza. The stones are also available in the rough. **Rachat & Rome** (© **998/877-0331**) located at the corner of Morelos and Juárez streets, is the grandest store, with a broad selection of jewelry at competitive prices. It's open daily from 9:30am to 5pm and accepts all major credit cards.

## WHERE TO STAY

You'll find plenty of hotels in all price ranges on Isla Mujeres. Rates peak during high season, which is the most expensive and most crowded time to go. Elizabeth Wenger of **Four Seasons Travel** in Montello, Wisconsin (© **800/552-4550** in the U.S.), specializes in Mexico travel and books a lot of hotels in Isla Mujeres. Her service is invaluable in the high season. Those interested in private home rentals or longer-term stays can contact **Mundaca Travel and Real Estate** in Isla Mujeres (© **998/877-0025;** fax 998/877-0076; www.mundaca.com.mx), or book online with **Isla Beckons** property rental service (www.islabeckons.com).

### VERY EXPENSIVE

**Casa de los Sueños Resort & Spa Zenter** ✿✿✿    This "house of dreams" is easily Isla Mujeres's most intimate, sophisticated, and relaxing property. Though it was originally built as a private residence, luckily it became an upscale, adults-only B&B in early 1998 (it has since changed ownership), and now caters to guests looking for a rejuvenating experience, with the adjoining Zenter offering spa services and yoga classes. Its location on the southern end of the island, adjacent to El Garrafón National

Park, also makes it ideal for snorkeling and diving enthusiasts. The captivating design features vivid sherbet-colored walls—think watermelon, mango, and blueberry—and a sculpted architecture. There's a large, open interior courtyard; tropical gardens; a sunken living area (with wireless Internet access); and an infinity pool that melts into the cool Caribbean waters. All rooms have balconies or terraces and face west, offering stunning views of the sunset over the sea, as well as the night lights of Cancún. In addition, the rooms—which have names such as Serenity, Passion, and Love—also have large marble bathrooms, Egyptian cotton bedding, and luxury bath amenities, and are decorated in a serene style that blends Asian simplicity with Mexican details. One master suite ideal for honeymooners has an exceptionally spacious bathroom area, complete with whirlpool and steam room/shower, plus other deluxe amenities. Complimentary continental breakfast is served in your room, and a restaurant adjacent to their private pier serves healthful fusion cuisine—it's open to nonguests as well. The Zenter offers a very complete menu of massages and holistic spa treatments, as well as yoga classes, held either outdoors or in a serene indoor space.

Carretera Garrafón s/n, 77400 Isla Mujeres, Q. Roo. © **998/877-0651** or -0369. Fax 998/877-0708. www.casadelos suenosresort.com. 7 units. High season $350–$450 double; low season $300–$400 double. Rates include continental breakfast. MC, V. No children under 15. **Amenities:** Restaurant; infinity pool; spa; open-air massage area; 24-hr. room service; breakfast delivery; yoga center. *In room:* TV/VCR, hair dryer, iron, safe.

### Hotel Villa Rolandi Gourmet & Beach Club ꞏ꞊꞊ This hotel has become a great addition to Isla's options for guests who enjoy its tranquillity—but also like being pampered. Villa Rolandi is a great value for a luxury stay, with Mediterranean-style rooms that offer every conceivable amenity, as well as its own small, private beach in a sheltered cove. Each of the oversize suites has an ocean view and a large terrace or balcony with a full-size private whirlpool. TVs offer satellite music and movies, and rooms all have a sophisticated in-room sound system. A recessed seating area extends out to the balcony or terrace. Bathrooms are large and tastefully decorated in deep-hued Tikal marble. The stained-glass shower has dual showerheads, stereo speakers, and jet options, and converts into a steam room.

Dining is an integral part of a stay at Villa Rolandi. Its owner is a Swiss-born restaurateur who made a name for himself with his restaurants on Isla Mujeres and in Cancún (see Casa Rolandi and Pizza Rolandi under "Where to Dine," below). This intimate hideaway with personalized service is ideal for honeymooners, who receive a complimentary bottle of domestic champagne upon arrival (when the hotel is notified in advance).

Fracc. Lagunamar, SM 7, Mza. 75, Locals 15 and 16, 77400 Isla Mujeres, Q. Roo. © **998/877-0700.** Fax 998/877-0100. www.villarolandi.com. 20 units. High season $380–$450 double; low season $290–$350 double. Rates include round-trip transportation from Playa Linda in Cancún aboard private catamaran yacht, continental breakfast, and a la carte lunch or dinner in the on-site restaurant. AE, MC, V. Children under 14 not accepted. **Amenities:** Restaurant (see "Where to Dine," below); infinity pool w/waterfall; small fitness room w/basic equipment and open-air massage area; concierge; tour desk; 24-hr. room service; breakfast delivery. *In room:* TV/VCR, dataport, minibar, hair dryer, iron, safe.

## EXPENSIVE

### Hotel Na Balam ꞏ꞊ (Finds Na Balam is known as a haven for yoga students and those interested in an introspective vacation. This popular, two-story hotel near the end of Playa Norte has comfortable rooms on a quiet, ideally located portion of the beach. Rooms are in three sections; some face the beach, and others are across the street in a garden setting with a swimming pool. All rooms have a terrace or balcony with

hammocks. Each spacious suite contains a king-size or two double beds, a seating area, and folk-art decorations. Two were redecorated in 2004 in a more sophisticated style, and with small pools with hydromassage situated under coconut trees—ask if these are available for the best of Na Balam. Though other rooms are newer, the older section is well kept, with a bottom-floor patio facing the peaceful, palm-filled, sandy inner yard and Playa Norte. Yoga classes (free for guests; $10 per class for nonguests) start at 9am Monday through Friday. The restaurant, **Zazil Ha,** is one of the island's most popular (see "Where to Dine," below). A beachside bar serves a selection of natural juices and is one of the most popular spots for sunset watching.

Zazil Ha 118, 77400 Isla Mujeres, Q. Roo. ✆ 998/877-0279. Fax 998/877-0446. www.nabalam.com. 31 units. High season $202–$332 suite; low season $150–$280 suite. Ask about weekly and monthly rates. AE, MC, V. **Amenities:** Restaurant; 2 bars; outdoor swimming pool; mopeds, golf carts, and bikes for rent; game room w/TV and VCR; diving and snorkeling trips available; Internet access; salon; in-room massage; babysitting; laundry service; library; yoga classes. *In room:* A/C, fan.

**Secreto** 🐟🐟 *(Finds)*    This new boutique hotel looks like a Hamptons beach house, but it is one of the best B&B values in the Caribbean. What sets Secreto apart—aside from the stunning setting and outstanding value—is the exemplary service. The sophisticated, romantic property has nine suites that overlook a central pool area to the private beach beyond. Located on the northern end of the island, Secreto is within walking distance of town, yet feels removed enough to make for an idyllic, peaceful retreat. The captivating contemporary design features clean, white spaces and sculpted architecture in a Mediterranean style. Tropical gardens surround the pool area, and an outdoor living area offers comfy couches and places to dine. All rooms have private verandas with comfortable seating, ideal for ocean-gazing beyond Halfmoon Beach, and are accented with original artwork. Three suites have king-size beds draped in mosquito netting, while the remaining six have two double beds; all rooms are non-smoking. Transportation from Cancún airport can be arranged on request, for an additional $50 per van (not per person).

Sección Rocas, Lote 1, 77400 Isla Mujeres, Q. Roo. ✆ 998/877-1039. Fax 998/877-1048. www.hotelsecreto.com. 9 units. $185–$225 double. Extra person $15. 1 child under 5 stays free in parent's room. Rates include continental breakfast. MC, V. **Amenities:** Outdoor pool; private cove beach; tours, diving, and snorkeling available; dinner delivery from Rolandi's restaurant available. *In room:* A/C, TV, CD player, fridge, safe, bathrobes.

## MODERATE

**Hotel Cabañas María del Mar** 🐟    A good choice for simple beach accommodations, the Cabañas María del Mar is on the popular Playa Norte. The older two-story section behind the reception area and beyond the garden offers nicely outfitted rooms facing the beach. All have two single or double beds, refrigerators, and oceanview balconies strung with hammocks. Eleven single-story cabanas closer to the reception area are decorated in a rustic Mexican style. The third section, **El Castillo,** is located across the street, over and beside Buho's restaurant. It contains all "deluxe" rooms, but some are larger than others; the five rooms on the ground floor have large patios. Upstairs rooms have small balconies. All have ocean views, and a predominately white decor. Rooms were remodeled in 2004. There's a small pool in the garden.

Av. Arq. Carlos Lazo 1 (on Playa Norte, ½ block from the Hotel Na Balam), 77400 Isla Mujeres, Q. Roo. ✆ 800/223-5695 in the U.S., or 998/877-0179. Fax 998/877-0213. 73 units. High season $110–$121 double; low season $66–$99 double. MC, V. **Amenities:** Outdoor pool; bus for tours and boat for rent; golf cart and *moto* rentals. *In room:* Fridge (in cabanas).

## INEXPENSIVE

**Hotel Belmar** 𝒜𝒜    Situated in the center of Isla's small-town activity, this hotel sits above Pizza Rolandi (be sure to consider the restaurant noise) and is run by the same people. Each of the simple but stylish tile-accented rooms comes with two twin or double beds. Prices are high considering the lack of views, but the rooms are pleasant. This is one of the few island hotels that has televisions (with U.S. channels) in rooms. It has one large colonial-decorated suite with a whirlpool and a patio.

Av. Hidalgo 110 (between Madero and Abasolo, 3½ blocks from the passenger-ferry pier), 77400 Isla Mujeres, Q. Roo. ℂ **998/877-0430.** Fax 998/877-0429. www.rolandi.com. 11 units. High season $56–$95 double; low season $32–$95 double. AE, MC, V. **Amenities:** Restaurant/bar (see "Where to Dine," below); room service until 11:30pm; laundry service. *In room:* A/C, TV, fan.

**Hotel D'Gomar** *Value*    This hotel is known for comfort at reasonable prices. You can hardly beat the value for basic accommodations, which are regularly updated. Rooms have two double beds and a wall of windows offering great breezes and views. The higher prices are for air-conditioning, which is hardly needed with the breezes and ceiling fans. The only drawback is that there are five stories and no elevator. But it's conveniently located cater-cornered (look right) from the ferry pier, with exceptional rooftop views. The name of the hotel is the most visible sign on the "skyline."

Rueda Medina 150, 77400 Isla Mujeres, Q. Roo. ℂ **998/877-0541.** 16 units. High season $35–$40 double; low season $30–$35 double. No credit cards. *In room:* Fan.

**Hotel Francis Arlene** 𝒜    The Magaña family operates this neat little two-story inn built around a small, shady courtyard. This hotel is very popular with families and seniors, and it welcomes many repeat guests. You'll notice the tidy cream-and-white facade from the street. Some rooms have ocean views, and all are remodeled or updated each year. They are comfortable, with tile floors, tiled bathrooms, and a very homey feel. Each downstairs room has a coffeemaker, refrigerator, and stove; each upstairs room comes with a refrigerator and toaster. Some have either a balcony or a patio. Higher prices are for the 14 rooms with air-conditioning; other units have fans. Rates are substantially better if quoted in pesos; in dollars, they are 15% to 20% higher.

Guerrero 7 (5½ blocks inland from the ferry pier, between Abasolo and Matamoros), 77400 Isla Mujeres, Q. Roo. ℂ/fax **998/877-0310** or -0861. www.francisarlene.com. 26 units. High season $55–$80 double; low season $35–$65 double. No credit cards. **Amenities:** In-room massage; safe; money exchange. *In room:* A/C (in some), kitchenettes (in some), fridge, no phone.

**Hotel Posada del Mar** *Kids*    Simply furnished, quiet, and comfortable, this long-established hotel faces the water and a wide beach 3 blocks north of the ferry pier. This is probably the best choice in Isla for families. The ample rooms are in a three-story building or one-story bungalow units. For the spaciousness of the rooms and the location, this is among the best values on the island and is very popular with readers, though I consistently find the staff to be the least gracious on the island. A wide, seldom-used but appealing stretch of Playa Norte is across the street, where watersports equipment is available for rent. A great, casual *palapa*-style bar and a lovely pool are on the back lawn along with hammocks, and the restaurant **Pinguino** (see "Where to Dine," below) is by the sidewalk at the front of the property, and also provides room service to hotel guests.

Av. Rueda Medina 15 A, 77400 Isla Mujeres, Q. Roo. ℂ **800/544-3005** in the U.S., or 998/877-0044. Fax 998/877-0266. www.posadadelmar.com. 61 units. High season $80–$100 double; low season $52–$72 double. Children under 12 stay free in parent's room. AE, MC, V. **Amenities:** Restaurant/bar; outdoor pool. *In room:* A/C, TV, fan.

## WHERE TO DINE

At the **Municipal Market,** next to the telegraph office and post office on Avenida Guerrero, obliging, hardworking women operate several little food stands. At the **Panadería La Reyna** (no phone), at Madero and Juárez, you can pick up inexpensive sweet bread, muffins, cookies, and yogurt. It's open Monday through Saturday from 7am to 9:30pm.

*Cocina económica* (literally, "economical cuisine") restaurants usually aim at the local population. These are great places to find good food at rock-bottom prices, and especially so on Isla Mujeres, where you'll find several, most of which feature delicious regional specialties. But be aware that the hygiene is not what you'll find at more established restaurants, so you're dining at your own risk.

### EXPENSIVE

**Casa Rolandi** ✈ ITALIAN/SEAFOOD   The gourmet Casa Rolandi restaurant and bar has become Isla's favored fine-dining experience. It boasts a view of the Caribbean and the most sophisticated menu in the area. There's a colorful main dining area as well as more casual, open-air terrace seating for drinks or light snacks. The food is the most notable on the island, but the overall ambience lacks the sophistication of the menu. Along with seafood and northern Italian specialties, the famed wood-burning-oven pizzas are a good bet. Careful—the wood-oven-baked bread, which arrives looking like a puffer fish, is so divine that you're likely to fill up on it. This is a great place to enjoy the sunset, and it offers a selection of more than 80 premium tequilas.

On the pier of Villa Rolandi, Lagunamar SM 7. ⓒ **998/877-0700.** Main courses $8–$35. AE, MC, V. Daily 11am–11pm.

### MODERATE

**Las Palapas Chimbo's** ✈ SEAFOOD   If you're looking for a beachside *palapa*-covered restaurant where you can wiggle your toes in the sand while relishing fresh seafood, this is the best of them. It's the locals' favorite on Playa Norte. Try the delicious fried whole fish, which comes with rice, beans, and tortillas. You'll notice a bandstand and dance floor in the middle of the restaurant, and sex-hunk posters all over the ceiling—that is, when you aren't gazing at the beach and the Caribbean. Chimbo's becomes a lively bar and dance club at night, drawing a crowd of drinkers and dancers (see "Isla Mujeres After Dark," below).

Playa Norte. No phone. Sandwiches and fruit $2.50–$4.50; seafood $6–$9. No credit cards. Daily 8am–midnight. From the pier, walk left to the end of the *malecón,* then right onto the Playa Norte; it's about ½ block on the right.

**Pinguino** MEXICAN/SEAFOOD   The best seats on the waterfront are on the deck of this restaurant and bar, especially in late evening, when islanders and tourists arrive to dance and party. This is the place to feast on sublimely fresh lobster—you'll get a large, beautifully presented lobster tail with a choice of butter, garlic, and secret sauces. The grilled seafood platter is spectacular, and fajitas and barbecued ribs are also popular. Breakfasts include fresh fruit, yogurt, and granola, or sizable platters of eggs, served with homemade wheat bread. Pinguino also has nonsmoking areas.

In front of the Hotel Posada del Mar (3 blocks west of the ferry pier), Av. Rueda Medina 15. ⓒ **998/877-0044,** ext. 157. Breakfast $1.50–$6; main courses $4–$10; daily special $7. AE, MC, V. Daily 7am–11pm; bar closes at midnight.

**Pizza Rolandi** ✈✈ ITALIAN/SEAFOOD   You're bound to dine at least once at Rolandi's, which is practically an Isla institution. The plate-size pizzas and calzones feature exotic ingredients—including lobster, black mushrooms, pineapple, and Roquefort cheese—as well as more traditional tomatoes, olives, basil, and salami. A wood-burning oven provides the signature flavor of the pizzas, as well as baked

# THE TRAVELOCITY GUARANTEE

## ...THAT SAYS EVERYTHING YOU BOOK WILL BE RIGHT, OR WE'LL WORK WITH OUR TRAVEL PARTNERS TO MAKE IT RIGHT, RIGHT AWAY.

*To drive home the point,*
*we're going to use the word "right" in every single sentence.*

Let's get right to it. Right to the meat! Only Travelocity guarantees everything about your booking will be right, or we'll work with our travel partners to make it right, right away. Right on!

*Here's a picture taken smack dab right in the middle of Antigua, where the Guarantee also covers you.*

*The Guarantee covers all but one of the items pictured to the right.*

Now, you may be thinking, "Yeah, right, I'm so sure." That's OK; you have the right to remain skeptical. That is until we mention help is always right around the corner. Call us right off the bat, knowing our customer service reps are there for you 24/7. Righting wrongs. Left and right.

For example, what if the ocean view you booked actually looks out at a downright ugly parking lot? You'd be right to call – we're there for you. And no one in their right mind would be pleased to learn the rental car place has closed and left them stranded. Call Travelocity and we'll help get you back on the right track.

Now if you're guessing there are some things we can't control, like the weather, well you're right. But we can help you with most things – to get all the details in righting,* visit travelocity.com/guarantee.

*Sorry, spelling things right is one of the few things not covered under the Guarantee.*

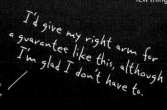

*I'd give my right arm for a guarantee like this, although I'm glad I don't have to.*

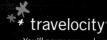
travelocity
*You'll never roam alone.*

chicken, roast beef, and mixed seafood casserole with lobster. The extensive menu also offers a selection of salads and light appetizers, as well as an ample array of pasta dishes, steaks, fish, and scrumptious desserts. The setting is the open courtyard of the Hotel Belmar, with a porch overlooking the action on Avenida Hidalgo.

Av. Hidalgo 10 (3½ blocks inland from the pier, between Madero and Abasolo). ℭ **998/877-0430,** ext. 18. Main courses $3.70–$13. AE, MC, V. Daily 11am–11:30pm.

**Zazil Ha** 🦐🦐 CARIBBEAN/INTERNATIONAL   Here you can enjoy some of the island's best food while sitting at tables on the sand among palms and gardens. The food—terrific pasta with garlic, shrimp in tequila sauce, fajitas, seafood pasta, and delicious mole enchiladas—enhances the serene environment. Caribbean specialties include cracked conch, coconut sailfish, jerk chicken, and stuffed squid. A selection of fresh juices complements the vegetarian menu, and there's even a special menu for those participating in yoga retreats. Between the set meal times, you can order all sorts of enticing food, such as vegetable and fruit drinks, tacos and sandwiches, ceviche, and terrific nachos. It's likely you'll stake this place out for several meals.

At the Hotel Na Balam (at the end of Playa Norte, almost at the end of Calle Zazil Ha). ℭ **998/877-0279.** Fax 998/877-0446. Breakfast $2–$9; main courses $8.50–$16. AE, MC, V. Daily 7:30–10:30am, 12:30–3:30pm, and 6:30–11pm.

### INEXPENSIVE

**Café Cito** 🍃 CREPES/ICE CREAM/COFFEE/FRUIT DRINKS   Sabina and Luis Rivera own this cute, Caribbean-blue corner restaurant where you can begin the day with flavorful coffee and a croissant and cream cheese, or end it with a hot-fudge sundae. Terrific crepes come with yogurt, ice cream, fresh fruit, or chocolate sauce, as well as ham and cheese. The two-page ice cream menu satisfies almost any craving, even one for waffles with ice cream and fruit. The three-course fixed-price dinner includes soup, a main course (such as fish or curried shrimp with rice and salad), and dessert.

Calle Matamoros 42, at Juárez (4 blocks from the pier). ℭ **998/877-1470.** Crepes $2–$4.50; breakfast $3–$5; sandwiches $3–$4. No credit cards. Daily 8am–2pm; high season Fri–Wed 5:30–10:30 or 11:30pm.

## ISLA MUJERES AFTER DARK

Those in a party mood by day's end may want to start out at the beach bar of the **Na Balam** hotel on Playa Norte, which hosts a crowd until around midnight. On Saturday and Sunday, live music plays between 4 and 7pm. **Las Palapas Chimbo's** restaurant on the beach becomes a jammin' dance joint with a live band from 9pm until whenever. Farther along the same stretch of beach, **Buho's,** the restaurant/beach bar of the Cabañas María del Mar, has its moments as a popular, low-key hangout, complete with swinging seats! **Pinguino** in the Hotel Posada del Mar offers a convivial late-night hangout, where a band plays nightly during high season from 9pm to midnight. Near Matéos and Hidalgo, **KoKo Nuts** caters to a younger crowd, with alternative music for late-night dancing. The **Om Bar and Chill Lounge,** on Calle Matamoros, serves beer on tap at each table, in a jazzy atmosphere. For a late night dance club, **Club Nitrox,** on Avenida Guererro, is open Wednesday to Sunday from 9pm to 3am.

## 2 Cozumel 🌴🌴🌴

70km (43 miles) S of Cancún; 19km (12 miles) SE of Playa del Carmen

Cozumel has ranked for years among the top five dive destinations in the world. Tall reefs line the southwest coast, creating towering walls that offer divers a fairy-tale landscape to explore. For nondivers, it has the beautiful water of the Caribbean with all the accompanying watersports and seaside activities. The island gets a lot more visitors from North America than Europe for reasons that probably have to do with the limited flights. It is in many ways more "cozy and mellow" than the mainland—no big highways, no big construction projects. It's dependable. And one of my favorite things about this island is that the water on the protected side (western shore) is as calm as an aquarium, unless a front is blowing through. The island is 45km (28 miles) long and 18km (11 miles) wide, and lies 19km (12 miles) from the mainland. Most of the terrain is flat and clothed in a low tropical forest.

The only town on the island is San Miguel, which, despite the growth of the last 20 years, can't be called anything more than a small town. It's not a stunningly beautiful town, but it and its inhabitants are agreeable—life moves along at a slow pace, and every Sunday evening, residents congregate around the plaza to enjoy live music and see their friends. Staying in town can be fun and convenient. You get a choice of a number of restaurants and nightspots.

Because Cozumel enjoys such popularity with the cruise ships, the waterfront section of town holds wall-to-wall jewelry stores, duty-free, and souvenir shops. When Hurricane Wilma hit the island in October 2005, this section, including the attractive shoreline boulevard, Avenida Rafael Melgar, were severely damaged. But such was the effort of the town's merchants and the local and federal government that by early 2006 all signs of the destruction were gone, and a casual visitor would never have guessed how serious the devastation from the hurricane was. This and the area around the town's main square are about as far as most cruise-ship passengers venture into town.

Should you come down with a case of island fever, **Playa del Carmen** and the mainland are a 40-minute ferry ride away. Some travel agencies on the island can set you up with a tour of the major ruins on the mainland, such as **Tulum** or **Chichén Itzá,** or a visit to a nature park such as **Xel-Ha** or **Xcaret** (see "Trips to the Mainland," later in this chapter).

The island has its own ruins, but they cannot compare with the major sites of the mainland. During pre-Hispanic times, Maya women would cross over to the island to make offerings to the goddess of fertility, Ixchel. More than 40 sites containing shrines remain around the island, and archaeologists still uncover the small dolls that were customarily part of those offerings.

## ESSENTIALS
### GETTING THERE & DEPARTING
**BY PLANE**   There are fewer international commercial flights in and out of Cozumel than charter flights. You might inquire about buying a ticket on one of these charters. Some packagers, such as **Funjet** (www.funjet.com), will sell you just a ticket. But look into packages, too. Several of the island's independent hotels work with packagers. Flight availability changes between high season and low season. **Continental** (© **800/231-0856** in the U.S., or 987/872-0596) flies to and from Houston and Newark. **US Airways** (© **800/428-4322** in the U.S., or 01-800/007-8800 in Mexico) flies to and from Charlotte. **American Airlines** (© **800/433-7300** in the U.S., or 01-800/904-6000 in Mexico) offers nonstop service to/from Dallas. **Mexicana** (© **800/531-7921** in the U.S., or 987/872-0157) and **Aeromexico** (© **800/237-6639** in the U.S., or 01-800/021-4000 in Mexico) fly from Mexico City.

**BY FERRY**   Passenger ferries run to and from Playa del Carmen. **Barcos México** (© **987/872-1508** or -1588) and **Ultramar** (© **987/869-2775**) offer departures

## An All-Inclusive Vacation in Cozumel

Booking a room at an all-inclusive should be done through a vacation package. Booking only lodging, even with frequent-flier mileage to burn, doesn't make economic sense—the discounts offered by most packagers are so deep. I include websites for you to find out more info about the properties, but don't expect to find clear info on rates. The game of setting rates with these hotels is complicated and always in flux. Hurricane Wilma damaged all these properties. All were closed and some won't open until summer of 2006. All have taken the opportunity to make upgrades to the rooms, so expect things like new mattresses and extra amenities.

Two all-inclusives are north of town: **El Cozumeleño** (www.elcozumeleno.com) and the **Meliá Cozumel** (www.meliacozumel.com). Both occupy multistory modern buildings. Both have attractive rooms. El Cozumeleño is the larger of the two resorts and has the nicest hotel pool on the island. It's best suited for active types. The Meliá is quieter and offers golf discounts for the nearby golf course. The Cozumeleño has a small beach that was lost with Wilma, but the hotel is bringing in sand to replace what was lost and should be back to normal by the time this book goes to press. The Meliá's beach is long and narrow and pretty, but occasionally seaweed washes up, which doesn't happen on the rest of the island's coast. The advantages of staying in these two are the proximity to town, with its restaurants, clubs, movie theaters, and so on, and the fact that most rooms at these hotels come with lovely views of the ocean.

Of the all-inclusives to the south, my favorites are the two **Occidental** properties (**Allegro Cozumel** and **Grand Cozumel;** www.occidentalhotels.com) and the **Iberostar Cozumel** (www.iberostar.com). These are "village" style resorts with two- and three-story buildings, often with thatched roofs, spread over a large area at the center of which is the pool and activities area. The Allegro is older than the other two and has the plainest rooms, but these were completely remodeled after the hurricane. Before the hurricane this hotel had the broadest beach, and all three of these properties gained beach from Wilma. The Grand Cozumel, next door to the Allegro, is the newest property. Its rooms are larger and more attractive than the Allegro, and staying here gives you access to both Occidental resorts. Like the Occidental chain, Iberostar has several properties in the Mexican Caribbean. This one is the smallest. I like its food and service and the beauty of the grounds. The rooms are attractive and well maintained. The added sand from Wilma improved the resort a lot. The advantage to staying in these places is that you're close to a lot of dive sites; the disadvantage is that you're somewhat isolated from town, and you don't have the lovely views that the taller buildings in the north give you.

Of the other all-inclusives, I've heard several complaints about the service at the **Reef Club** (unless you stay in the VIP section), and I think the rooms are too closely set together. The **Costa Club** is on the inland side of the road in a crowded section of the island.

almost every hour on the hour between 5am and midnight. It is rather curious that the two companies have arranged their service to coincide instead of spacing them so as to offer the consumer more choices. The trip takes 30 to 45 minutes, depending on conditions, and costs $11 one-way. The boats are air-conditioned. In Playa del Carmen, the ferry dock is 1½ blocks from the main square. In Cozumel, the ferries use Muelle Fiscal, the town pier, a block from the main square. Luggage storage at the Cozumel dock costs $2 per day.

The car ferry that used to operate from Puerto Morelos now uses the Calica pier just south of Playa del Carmen. The fare for a standard car is $80. **Marítima Chancanaab** (© **987/872-0950**) has four departures daily from Calica at 7am, 1, 5, and 9pm. Arrive 1 hour before departure. The schedule is subject to change, so double-check it. The ferry docks in Cozumel at the **Muelle Internacional** (the **International Pier,** which is south of town near La Ceiba Hotel).

**BY BUS** If you plan to travel on the mainland by bus, there is a ticket office for **ADO buses** called **Ticket Bus** where you can purchase tickets in advance. One is located on the municipal pier and is open while the ferries are running. Another is on Calle 2 Norte and Avenida 10 (© **987/872-1706**). Hours are from 8am to 9pm daily.

## ORIENTATION

**ARRIVING** Cozumel's **airport** is inland from downtown. **Transportes Terrestres** provides hotel transportation in air-conditioned Suburbans. Buy your ticket as you exit the terminal. To hotels downtown, the fare is $5 per person; to hotels along the north shore, $7, and to hotels along the south shore, $8 to $15. Passenger ferries arrive at the Muelle Fiscal, the municipal pier, by the town's main square. Cruise ships dock at the **Punta Langosta** pier, a few blocks south of the Muelle Fiscal; at the **International Pier,** near La Ceiba hotel; and at the **Puerta Maya** pier, farther south. These three piers took heavy damage from the hurricane. The Puerta Maya was completely destroyed, the other two are nonoperational and won't be fully repaired for some time. Cruise-ship companies are anchoring their ships just offshore and ferrying passengers and crew to land in large tender boats. It seems to be working smoothly—I heard no complaints from passengers.

**VISITOR INFORMATION** The **Municipal Tourism Office** (©/fax **987/ 869-0212**) has placed information booths at the municipal ferry pier, on the main square. They're open Monday to Friday 9am to 7pm and Saturday 10am to 3pm. There are other information booths at each of the ferry piers and at the airport.

**CITY LAYOUT** San Miguel's main waterfront street is **Avenida Rafael Melgar.** Running parallel to Rafael Melgar are other *avenidas* numbered in multiples of five—5, 10, 15. **Avenida Juárez** runs perpendicular to these, heading inland from the ferry dock. Avenida Juárez divides the town into northern and southern halves. The *calles* (streets) that parallel Juárez to the north have even numbers. The ones to the south have odd numbers, with the exception of Calle Rosado Salas, which runs between calles 1 and 3.

---

*Tips* **Be Streetwise**

North-south streets—the *avenidas*—have the right of way, and traffic doesn't slow down or stop.

**ISLAND LAYOUT**   One road runs along the western coast of the island, which faces the Yucatán mainland. It has different names. North of town it's **Santa Pilar** or **San Juan;** in the city it is **Avenida Rafael Melgar;** south of town it's **Costera Sur.** Hotels stretch along this road north and south of town. The road runs to the southern tip of the island (Punta Sur), passing **Chankanaab National Park. Avenida Juárez** (and its extension, the **Carretera Transversal**) runs east from the town across the island. It passes the airport and the turnoff to the ruins of San Gervasio before reaching the undeveloped ocean side of the island. It then turns south and follows the coast to the southern tip of the island, where it meets the Costera Sur.

**GETTING AROUND**   You can walk to most destinations in town. Getting to outlying hotels and beaches requires a taxi or rental car or a moped.

**Car rentals** are roughly the same price as on the mainland, depending on demand. **Avis** (© 987/872-0099) and **Executive** (© 987/872-1308) have counters in the airport. Other major rental companies have offices in town. Rentals are easy to arrange through your hotel or at any of the many local rental offices.

**Moped rentals** are readily available and cost $20 to $40 for 24 hours, depending upon the season. If you rent a moped, be careful. Riding a moped made a lot more sense when Cozumel had less traffic; now it involves a certain amount of risk as taxi drivers and other motorists have become more numerous and pushier. Moped accidents easily rank as the greatest cause of injury in Cozumel. Before renting one, inspect it carefully to see that all the gizmos—horn, light, starter, seat, mirror—are in good shape. I've been offered mopeds with unbalanced wheels, which made them unsteady at higher speeds, but the renter quickly exchanged them upon my request. You are required to stay on paved roads. It's illegal to ride a moped without a helmet outside of town (subject to a $25 fine).

Cozumel has lots of **taxis** and a strong drivers' union. Fares have been standardized—there's no bargaining. Here are a few sample fares for two people (there is an additional charge for extra passengers to most destinations): island tour, $60; town to southern hotel zone, $6 to $18; town to northern hotels, $5 to $7; town to Chankanaab, $9 (for up to four people); in and around town, $3 to $4.

---

*FAST FACTS:* **Cozumel**

*Area Code* The telephone area code is **987**.

*Climate* From October to December there can be strong winds all over the Yucatán, as well as some rain. June through October is the rainy season.

*Diving* Bring proof of your diver's certification and your log. Underwater currents can be strong, and many of the reef drops are quite steep, so dive operators want to make sure divers are experienced.

*Internet Access* Several cybercafes are in and about the main square. If you go just a bit off Avenida Rafael Melgar and the main square, prices drop. **Modutel,** Av. Juárez 15 (at Av. 10), offers good rates. Hours are Monday through Saturday from 10am to 8pm.

*Money Exchange* The island has several banks and *casas de cambio,* as well as ATMs. Most places accept dollars, but you usually get a better deal paying in pesos.

*Post Office* The *correo* is on Avenida Rafael Melgar at Calle 7 Sur (© **987/872-0106**), at the southern edge of town. It's open Monday through Friday from 9am to 3pm, Saturday from 9am to noon.

*Recompression Chamber* There are four *cámaras de recompresión*. The best are **Buceo Médico Mexicano,** staffed 24 hours, at Calle 5 Sur 21-B, between Avenida Rafael Melgar and Avenida 5 Sur (© **987/872-2387** or -1430); and the **Hyperbaric Center of Cozumel** (© **987/872-3070**) at Calle 4 Norte, between avenidas 5 and 10.

*Seasons* High season is August and from Christmas to Easter.

## EXPLORING THE ISLAND

For **diving** and **snorkeling,** there are plenty of dive shops to choose from, including those recommended below. For **island tours, ruins tours** on and off the island, **evening cruises,** and other activities, go to a travel agency. I recommend **InterMar Cozumel Viajes,** Calle 2 Norte 101-B, between avenidas 5 and 10 (© **987/872-1535** or -2022; fax 987/872-0895; cozumel@travel2mexico.com). Office hours are Monday through Saturday from 8am to 8pm, Sunday from 9am to 5pm.

### WATERSPORTS

**SCUBA DIVING**    Cozumel is the number-one dive destination in the Western Hemisphere. Don't forget your dive card and dive log. Dive shops will rent you scuba gear, but won't take you out on a boat until you show some documentation. If you have a medical condition, bring a letter signed by a doctor stating that you've been cleared to dive. A two-tank morning dive costs around $60; some shops offer an additional afternoon one-tank dive for $15 for those who took the morning dives. A lot of divers save some money by buying a dive package with a hotel. These usually include two dives a day.

Diving in Cozumel is drift diving, which can be a little disconcerting for novices. The current that sweeps along Cozumel's reefs, pulling nutrients into them and making them as large as they are, also dictates how you dive here. The problem is that it pulls at different speeds at different depths and in different places. When it's pulling strong, it can quickly scatter a dive group. The role of the dive master becomes more important, especially with choosing the dive location. Cozumel has a lot of dive locations. To mention but a few: the famous **Palancar Reef,** with its caves and canyons, plentiful fish, and a wide variety of sea coral; the monstrous **Santa Rosa Wall,** famous for its depth, sea life, coral, and sponges; the **San Francisco Reef,** which has a shallower drop-off wall and fascinating sea life; and the **Yucab Reef,** with its beautiful coral.

I've seen a number of news reports about reef damage caused by Hurricane Wilma. Almost all of it occurred in the shallower parts, above 15m (50 ft.). In deeper areas, the currents produced by Wilma actually improved matters by clearing sand away from parts of the reef, and in some cases exposing new caverns. Wildlife is plentiful. In the shallow parts, it will take a year or two for things such as fan coral to grow back. The greatest impact here is to the snorkeling.

# San Miguel de Cozumel

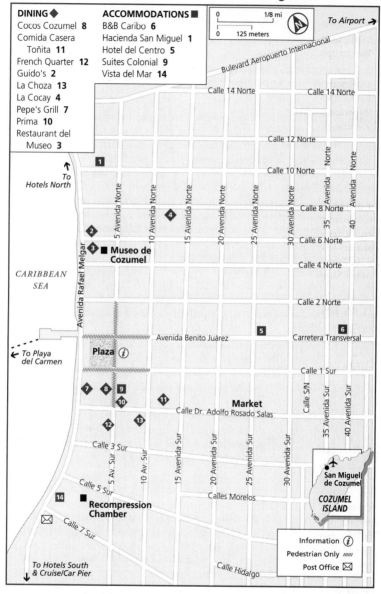

**DINING ◆**
Cocos Cozumel **8**
Comida Casera
  Toñita **11**
French Quarter **12**
Guido's **2**
La Choza **13**
La Cocay **4**
Pepe's Grill **7**
Prima **10**
Restaurant del
  Museo **3**

**ACCOMMODATIONS ■**
B&B Caribo **6**
Hacienda San Miguel **1**
Hotel del Centro **5**
Suites Colonial **9**
Vista del Mar **14**

To Airport →

Bulevard Aeropuerto Internacional

Calle 14 Norte          Calle 14 Norte

Calle 12 Norte

↑
To
Hotels North

Calle 10 Norte

Calle 8 Norte

5 Avenida Norte
10 Avenida Norte
15 Avenida Norte
20 Avenida Norte
25 Avenida Norte
30 Avenida Norte
35 Avenida Norte
40 Avenida Norte

Calle 6 Norte

Avenida Rafael Melgar

■ **Museo de Cozumel**

Calle 4 Norte

*CARIBBEAN SEA*

Calle 2 Norte

Avenida Benito Juárez          Carretera Transversal

**Plaza** (i)

← To Playa del Carmen

Calle 1 Sur

Calle S/N
35 Avenida Sur
40 Avenida Sur

**Market**
Calle Dr. Adolfo Rosado Salas

5 Av. Sur
10 Av. Sur
15 Avenida Sur
20 Avenida Sur
25 Avenida Sur
30 Avenida Sur

Calle 3 Sur

Calle 5 Sur

■ **Recompression Chamber**

Calles Morelos

San Miguel de Cozumel

*COZUMEL ISLAND*

☒ Calle 7 Sur

Information (i)
Pedestrian Only ////
Post Office ☒

To Hotels South
& Cruise/Car Pier
↓

Calle Hidalgo

Finding a dive shop in town is even easier than finding a jewelry store. Cozumel has more than 50 dive operators. I know and can recommend Bill Horn's **Aqua Safari,** which has a location on Avenida Rafael Melgar at Calle 5 (© **987/872-0101;** fax 987/872-0661; www.aquasafari.com). I also know Roberto Castillo at **Liquid Blue**

---

*Moments*  **Carnaval**

*Carnaval* (similar to Mardi Gras) is Cozumel's most colorful fiesta. It begins the Thursday before Ash Wednesday, with daytime street dancing and nighttime parades on Thursday, Saturday, and Monday (the best).

---

**Divers** (© 987/869-2812; www.liquidbluedivers.com), on Avenida 5 between Rosado Salas and Calle 3 Sur. He does a good tour, has a fast boat, and keeps the number of divers to 12 or fewer. His wife, Michelle, handles the Internet inquiries and reservations and is quick to respond to questions.

A popular activity in the Yucatán is *cenote* diving. The peninsula's underground *cenotes* (seh-*noh*-tehs)—sinkholes or wellsprings—lead to a vast system of underground caverns. The gently flowing water is so clear that divers seem to float on air through caves complete with stalactites and stalagmites. If you want to try this but didn't plan a trip to the mainland, contact **Yucatech Expeditions,** Avenida 5, on the corner of Calle 3 Sur (©/fax **987/872-5659;** www.yucatech.net), which offers a trip five times a week. *Cenotes* are 30 to 45 minutes from Playa del Carmen, and a dive in each *cenote* lasts around 45 minutes. Dives are within the daylight zone, about 40m (131 ft.) into the caverns, and no more than 18m (59 ft.) deep. Company owner Germán Yañez Mendoza inspects diving credentials carefully, and divers must meet his list of requirements before cave diving is permitted. For information and prices, call or drop by the office.

**SNORKELING**    Anyone who can swim can snorkel. When contracting for a snorkel tour, stay away from the companies that cater to the cruise ships. Those tours are crowded and not very much fun. For a good snorkeling tour, contact **Victor Casanova** (© **987/872-1028;** wildcatcozumel@hotmail.com). He speaks English, owns a couple of boats, and does a good 5-hour tour. He takes his time and doesn't rush through the trip. You can also try the **Kuzamil Snorkeling Center,** 50 Av. bis 565 Int. 1, between 5 Sur and Hidalgo, Colonia Adolfo López Mateos (© **987/872-4637** or -0539). Even though you won't see a lot of the more delicate structures, such as fan coral, you will still see plenty of sea creatures and enjoy the clear, calm water of Cozumel's protected west side.

**BOAT TRIPS**    Travel agencies and hotels can arrange boat trips, a popular pastime on Cozumel. There are evening cruises, cocktail cruises, glass-bottom boat cruises, and other options. One novel boat ride is offered by **Atlantis Submarines** (© **987/872-5671**). The sub can hold 48 people. It operates almost 3km (2 miles) south of town in front of the Casa del Mar hotel and costs $81 per adult, $47 for kids 4 to 12. This is a superior experience to the **Sub See Explorer** offered by **Aqua World,** which is really just a glorified glass-bottom boat.

**FISHING**    The best months for fishing are March through June, when the catch includes blue and white marlin, sailfish, tarpon, and swordfish. The least expensive option would be to contact a boat owner directly. Try Victor Casanova, listed above under snorkeling. Or try an agency such as **Aquarius Travel Fishing,** Calle 3 Sur 2 between Avenida Rafael Melgar and Avenida 5 (© **987/872-1092;** gabdiaz@yahoo.com).

## CHANKANAAB NATIONAL PARK & PUNTA SUR ECOLOGICAL RESERVE

**Chankanaab National Park** ⸙⸙ is the pride of many islanders. *Note:* The park did close for a period after the hurricane, but at press time it was partially open to the public. The beach was open, with new facilities and newly planted palm trees. The dolphin area was also open, but the archaeological and botanical areas remained closed. For more information, call the tourism office at ⓒ **987/869-0212.**

In Mayan, Chankanaab means "little sea," which refers to a beautiful landlocked pool connected to the sea through an underground tunnel—a sort of miniature ocean. I understand that there was some damage to this natural pool, but it was mostly surface wear. Snorkeling in this natural aquarium is not permitted, but the park has a lovely ocean beach for sunbathing and snorkeling. Arrive early to stake out a chair and *palapa* before the cruise-ship crowd arrives. Likewise, the snorkeling is best before noon. There are bathrooms, lockers, a gift shop, several snack huts, a restaurant, and a *palapa* for renting snorkeling gear.

You can also swim with dolphins. **Dolphin Discovery** (ⓒ **800/293-9698;** www. dolphindiscovery.com) has several programs for experiencing these sea creatures. These are popular, so plan ahead—you should make reservations well in advance. The surest way is through the website—make sure to pick the Cozumel location, as there are a couple of others on this coast. There are three different programs for swimming with dolphins. The one of longest duration costs $125 and features close interaction with the beautiful swimmers. There are also swim and snorkel programs for $75 and $99 that get you in the water with these creatures. Dolphin Discovery also offers a program only in Cozumel where you can swim with sea lions ($59); make reservations for this. There is also a sea lion show, which doesn't require reservations. The show includes some scarlet macaws, which, like the sea lions, were rescued from illegal captivity. It costs $5 per adult, $3.50 per child. Tickets are available through any travel agency in town (and remember that you also have to pay for admission to the park).

Surrounding the landlocked pool is a botanical garden with shady paths and 351 species of tropical and subtropical plants from 22 countries, as well as 451 species from Cozumel. Several Maya structures have been re-created within the gardens to give visitors an idea of Maya life in a jungle setting. There's a small natural history museum as well. Admission to the park costs $10; it's open daily from 8am to 5pm. The park is south of town, just past the Fiesta Americana Hotel. Taxis run constantly between the park, the hotels, and town ($10 from town for up to four people).

**Punta Sur Ecological Reserve** (admission $10) is a large area that encompasses the southern tip of the island, including the Columbia Lagoon. The only practical way of going there is to rent a car or scooter; there is no taxi stand, and, usually, few people. This is an ecological reserve, not a park, so don't expect much infrastructure. The reserve has an information center, several observation towers, and a snack bar. The observation towers were destroyed in the hurricane, and I'm not certain that they will be rebuilt anytime soon. The information center was struck hard, too. And many of the trees on this side of the island came down, while others completely lost their leaves. These, I am told, will make a comeback, but before you go all the way out to the park and pay admission, ask around about the condition of the vegetation—it adds a good bit to a visit here. Punta Sur has some interesting snorkeling (bring your own gear), and lovely beaches kept as natural as possible. Regular hours are daily 9am to 5pm.

## THE BEACHES

Along both the west and east sides of the island you'll see signs advertising beach clubs. A "beach club" in Cozumel can mean just a *palapa* hut that's open to the public and serves soft drinks, beer, and fried fish. It can also mean a recreational beach with the full gamut of offerings from banana boats to parasailing. They also usually have locker rooms, a pool, and food. The two biggest of these are **Mr. Sancho's** (© 987/879-0021; www.mrsanchos.com) and **Playa Mía** (© 987/872-9030; www.playamia.com). They get a lot of business from the cruise ships. Mr. Sancho's is free, while Playa Mía charges between $12 for simple admission to $42 for the full all-inclusive package. Quieter versions of beach clubs are **Nachi Cocom** (closed until the summer of 2006), **Playa San Francisco** (no phone), **Paradise Beach** (no phone, next to Playa San Francisco), and **Playa Palancar** (no phone). All of these beaches are south of Chankanaab Park, and easily visible from the road. Several have swimming pools with beach furniture, a restaurant, and snorkel rental. Nachi Cocom costs $10; the others cost around $5.

Once you get to the end of the island the beach clubs become simple places where you can eat and drink and lay out on the beach for free. **Paradise Cafe** is on the southern tip of the island across from Punta Sur nature park, and as you go up the eastern side of the island you pass **Playa Bonita, Chen Río,** and **Punta Morena.** Except on Sundays, when the locals head for the beaches, these places are practically deserted. Most of the east coast is unsafe for swimming because of the surf. The beaches tend to be small and occupy gaps in the rocky coast.

## TOURS OF THE ISLAND

Travel agencies can arrange a variety of tours, including horseback, jeep, and ATV tours. Taxi drivers charge $60 for a 4-hour tour of the island, which most people would consider only mildly amusing, depending on the driver's personality. The best horseback tours are offered at **Rancho Palmitas** (no phone) on the Costera Sur highway, across from the Occidental Cozumel resort. Unless you're staying in one of the resorts on the south end, the easiest way to arrange a tour is probably to talk to the owners of Cocos Cozumel restaurant (see the listing later in this chapter, making sure to note the limited hours). Rides can be from 1 to 2½ hours long and cost $20 to $30.

## OTHER ATTRACTIONS

**MAYA RUINS**    One of the most popular island excursions is to **San Gervasio** (100 B.C.–A.D. 1600). Follow the paved transversal road. You'll see the well-marked turnoff about halfway between town and the eastern coast. Stop at the entrance gate and pay the $1 road-use fee. About 3km (2 miles) farther, pay the $5 fee to enter; still and video camera permits cost $5 each. A small tourist center at the entrance sells cold drinks and snacks.

When it comes to Cozumel's Maya ruins, getting there is most of the fun—do it for the mystique and for the trip, not for the size or scale of the ruins. The buildings, though preserved, are crudely made and would not be much of a tourist attraction if they were not the island's principal ruins. More significant than beautiful, this site was once an important ceremonial center where the Maya gathered, coming even from the mainland. The important deity was Ixchel, the goddess of weaving, women, childbirth, pilgrims, the moon, and medicine. Although you won't see any representations of Ixchel at San Gervasio today, Bruce Hunter, in his *Guide to Ancient Maya Ruins,* writes that priests hid behind a large pottery statue of her and became the voice of the goddess, speaking to pilgrims and answering their petitions. Ixchel was the wife of Itzamná, the sun god.

Guides charge $20 for a tour for one to six people. A better option is to find a copy of the green booklet *San Gervasio,* sold at local checkout counters and bookstores, and tour the site on your own. Seeing it takes 30 minutes. Taxi drivers offer a tour to the ruins for about $30; the driver will wait for you outside the ruins.

**A HISTORY MUSEUM**   The **Museo de la Isla de Cozumel** 𝕗, Avenida Rafael Melgar between calles 4 and 6 Norte (𝓒 **987/872-1475**), is more than just a nice place to spend a rainy hour. On the first floor an exhibit illustrates endangered species, the origin of the island, and its present-day topography and plant and animal life, including an explanation of coral formation. The second-floor galleries feature the history of the town, artifacts from the island's pre-Hispanic sites, and colonial-era cannons, swords, and ship paraphernalia. It's open daily from 9am to 5pm. Admission is $3. A good rooftop restaurant serves breakfast and lunch.

**GOLF**   Cozumel has a new 18-hole course designed by Jack Nicklaus. It's at the **Cozumel Country Club** (𝓒 **987/872-9570**), just north of San Miguel. Greens fees are $165 for a morning tee time, including cart rental and tax. Afternoon tee times cost $99. Tee times can be reserved 3 days in advance. A few hotels have special memberships with discounts for guests and advance tee times; guests at Playa Azul Golf and Beach Club pay no greens fees, just the cart cost ($25).

## TRIPS TO THE MAINLAND

**PLAYA DEL CARMEN & XCARET**   Going on your own to the nearby seaside village of **Playa del Carmen** and the **Xcaret** nature park is as easy as a quick ferry ride from Cozumel (for ferry information, see "Getting There & Departing" on p. 110). For information on Playa and Xcaret, see chapter 6. Cozumel travel agencies offer an Xcaret tour that includes the ferry ride, transportation to the park, and the admission fee. The price is $90 for adults, $48 for kids. The tour is available Monday through Saturday.

**CHICHEN ITZA, TULUM & COBA**   Travel agencies can arrange day trips to the ruins of **Chichén Itzá** 𝕗𝕗𝕗 by air or bus. The ruins of **Tulum** 𝕗, overlooking the Caribbean, and **Cobá** 𝕗, in a dense jungle setting, are closer and cost less to visit. These cities are quite a contrast to Chichén Itzá. Cobá is a large, mostly unrestored city beside a lake in a remote jungle setting, while Tulum is smaller, more compact, and right on the beach. It's more intact than Cobá. A trip to both Cobá and Tulum begins at 8am and returns around 6pm. A shorter, more relaxing excursion goes to Tulum and the nearby nature park of Xel-Ha.

## SHOPPING

If you like shopping for silver jewelry, you can spend a great deal of time examining the wares of all the jewelers along Avenida Rafael Melgar. Some duty-free stores sell items such as perfumes and designer wares. If you're interested in Mexican folk art, there are three stores on Avenida Rafael Melgar that have merchandise better than what most stores offer: **Los Cinco Soles** (𝓒 **987/872-2040**), **Indigo** (𝓒 **987/872-1076**), and **Viva México** (𝓒 **987/872-5466**). There are also some import/export stores in the Punta Langosta Shopping Center in the southern part of town in front of the Punta Langosta Pier. Prices for serapes, T-shirts, and the like are lower on the side streets off Avenida Melgar.

## WHERE TO STAY

I've grouped Cozumel's hotels by location—**north** of town, **in town,** and **south** of town—and I describe them in that order. The prices I've quoted are rack rates and include the 12% tax. High season is from December to Easter. Expect rates from Christmas to New Year's to be still higher than the regular high-season rates quoted here. Low season is the rest of the year, though a few hotels raise their rates in August when Mexican families go on vacations.

All of the beach hotels in Cozumel, even the small ones, have deals with vacation packagers. Keep in mind that some packagers will offer last-minute deals to Cozumel with hefty discounts; if you're the flexible sort, keep an eye open for these.

Most hotels have an arrangement with a dive shop and offer dive packages. These can be good deals, but if you don't buy a dive package, it's quite okay to stay at one hotel and dive with a third-party operator—any dive boat can pull up to any hotel pier to pick up customers. Most dive shops won't pick up from the hotels north of town.

All the beach hotels suffered damage from the two hurricanes that passed through here. All were closed, and a few are still closed as of the time of this writing. A couple may not reopen. But the rest of the properties took advantage of the closure to make upgrades to amenities and rooms. This is good news for those who come now. Some of the hotels in town are also remodeling, but nothing major. Flooding was the main problem, and it has brought a lot of peeling paint.

As an alternative to a hotel, you can try **Cozumel Vacation Villas and Condos,** Av. Rafael Melgar 685 (between calles 3 and 5 Sur; ✆ **800/224-5551** in the U.S., or 987/872-0729; www.cvvmexico.com), which offers accommodations by the week.

### NORTH OF TOWN

**Carretera Santa Pilar,** or San Juan, is the name of Avenida Rafael Melgar's northern extension. All the hotels lie close to each other on the beach side of the road a short distance from town and the airport.

#### Expensive

**Playa Azul Golf and Beach Hotel** 🏨🏨🏨    This quiet hotel is perhaps the most relaxing of the island's beachside properties. It's smaller, and service is personal. It's an excellent choice for golfers; guests pay no greens fees, only cart rental. The hotel's small, sandy beach has been restored to its pre-hurricane condition, with new shade *palapas* and the return of the beach bar. Almost all the rooms have balconies and ocean views. The units in the original section are all suites—very large, with oversize bathrooms with showers. The new wing has mostly standard rooms that are comfortable and large, decorated with light tropical colors and rattan furniture. The corner rooms are master suites and have large balconies with Jacuzzis overlooking the sea. If you prefer lots of space over having a Jacuzzi, opt for a suite in the original building. Rooms contain a king-size bed or two double beds; suites offer two convertible single sofas in the separate living room. The hotel also offers deep sea– and fly-fishing trips. For a family or group, the hotel rents a garden house with lovely rooms.

Carretera San Juan Km 4, 77600 Cozumel, Q. Roo. ✆ **987/872-0199** or -0043. Fax 987/872-0110. www.playa azul.com. 50 units. High season $230 double, $275–$325 suite; low season $157–$170 double, $196–$290 suite. Discounts and packages sometimes available. AE, MC, V. **Amenities:** Restaurant; 2 bars; medium-size outdoor pool; unlimited golf privileges at Cozumel Country Club; spa; watersports equipment rental; game room; tour info; room service until 11pm; in-room massage; babysitting; laundry service. *In room:* A/C, TV, coffeemaker, hair dryer, safe.

## Moderate
### Condumel Condobeach Apartments
If you want some distance from the crowds, consider lodging here. It's not a full-service hotel, but in some ways it's more convenient. The one-bedroom apartments are designed and furnished in practical fashion—large and airy, with glass sliding doors that face the sea and allow for good cross-ventilation (especially in the upper units). They also have ceiling fans, air-conditioning, and two twin beds or one king-size. Each apartment has a separate living room and a full kitchen with a partially stocked fridge, so you don't have to run to the store on the first day. There's a small, well-tended beach area (with shade *palapas* and a grill for guests' use) that leads to a low, rocky fall-off into the sea.

Carretera Hotelera Norte s/n, 77600 Cozumel, Q. Roo. 🕾 **987/872-0892.** Fax 987/872-0661. www.condumel.com. 10 units. High season $140 double; low season $120 double. No credit cards. *In room:* A/C, kitchen, no phone.

## IN TOWN
Staying in town is not like staying in Playa del Carmen, where you can walk to the beach. The oceanfront in town is too busy for swimming, and there's no beach, only the *malecón*. Consequently, there's no real premium for staying close to the water. You'll have to drive or take a cab to the beach; it's pretty easy. English is spoken in almost all of the hotels.

## Expensive
### Hacienda San Miguel 🕾
This is a peaceful hotel built in Mexican colonial style around a large garden courtyard. The property is well maintained and the service is good. It's located a half-block from the shoreline on the town's north side. Rooms are large and attractive and come with equipped kitchens, including full-size refrigerators. Most of the studios have a queen-size bed or two doubles. The junior suites have more living area and come with a queen-size and a twin bed. The two-bedroom suite comes with four double beds.

Calle 10 Norte 500 (between Rafael Melgar and Av. 5), 77600 Cozumel, Q. Roo. 🕾 **866/712-6387** in the U.S., or 987/872-1986. Fax 987/872-7036. www.haciendasanmiguel.com. 11 units. $101 studio; $114 junior suite; $165 2-bedroom suite. Rates include continental breakfast. MC, V. Guarded parking on street. **Amenities:** Tour info; car rental. *In room:* A/C, TV, kitchen, hair dryer, safe, no phone.

## Moderate
### Suites Colonial
Around the corner from the main square, on a pedestrian-only street, you'll find this pleasant four-story hotel. Standard rooms, called "studios," have large bathrooms and attractive red-tile floors, but they could be better lit. These units have one double and one twin bed and are trimmed in yellow pine, which seems oddly out of place here. The suites hold two double beds, a kitchenette, and a sitting and dining area. There's free coffee and sweet bread in the morning. When making a reservation, specify the Suites Colonial.

Av. 5 Sur 9 (Apdo. Postal 286), 77600 Cozumel, Q. Roo. 🕾 **987/872-9080.** Fax 987/872-9073. www.suitescolonial.com. 28 units. $60–$69 studio; $81 suite. Rates include continental breakfast. Extra person $20. AE, MC, V. From the plaza, walk ½ block south on Av. 5 Sur; the hotel is on the left. *In room:* A/C, TV, fridge.

### Vista del Mar 🕾
This hotel is located on the town's shoreline boulevard. All the rooms in front have ocean views. The balconies are large enough to be enjoyable and are furnished with a couple of chairs. Rooms are a little larger than your standard room, with better lighting than you find in most of the hotels in town. They are simply furnished and decorated, but come with several amenities. Bathrooms are

medium-size or a little smaller and have showers. The rooms in back go for $10 less than the oceanview rooms and look out over a small pool and large Jacuzzi.

Av. Rafael Melgar 45 (between calles 5 and 7 Sur), 77600 Cozumel, Q. Roo. © 888/309-9988 in the U.S., or 987/872-0545. Fax 987/872-7036. www.hotelvistadelmar.com. 20 units. $87–$97 double. Discounts sometimes available. AE, MC, V. No parking. **Amenities:** Bar; outdoor pool; Jacuzzi; tour info; car rental; in-room massage; laundry service. *In room:* A/C, TV, wireless high-speed Internet, fridge, hair dryer, safe.

### Inexpensive

**B&B Caribo** 🖈 *Value*    The Americans who manage this B&B make guests feel at home. The rates are a good deal and include air-conditioning, a good breakfast, and several little extras. Six neatly decorated rooms come with cool tile floors, white furniture, and big bottles of purified drinking water; these units share a guest kitchen. The six apartments have small kitchens. Rooms have a double bed and a twin bed. There are a number of common rooms and a rooftop terrace.

Av. Juárez 799, 77600 Cozumel, Q. Roo. © 987/872-3195. www.bandbcaribo.com. 12 units. High season $50 double, $60 apt; low season $35 double, $40 apt. Rates include breakfast. Long-term discounts available. Ask about yoga vacations. AE, MC, V. From the plaza, walk 6½ blocks inland on Juárez; Caribo is on the left. **Amenities:** Massage. *In room:* A/C.

**Hotel del Centro**    Five blocks from the waterfront, this two-story hotel is a bargain for those wanting a hotel with a pool. The rooms are small to medium in size but modern and attractive. The hotel underwent a complete remodeling after the hurricanes. Rooms come with two double beds or one king-size (costing $10 less). Bathrooms are medium-size. A courtyard with an oval pool is on the west side of the building. Next door is a club that's reopened after a hiatus of a couple of years. It may not survive, but if it does, ask for a room on the opposite side of the hotel.

Av. Juárez 501, 77600 Cozumel, Q. Roo. © 987/872-5471. 14 units. $45–$65 double. Discounts sometimes available in low season. No credit cards. **Amenities:** Medium-size outdoor pool. *In room:* A/C, TV, no phone.

### SOUTH OF TOWN

The hotels in this area tend to be more spread out and farther from town than hotels to the north. Some are on the inland side of the road; some are on the beach side, which means a difference in price. Those farthest from town are all-inclusive properties. The beaches tend to be slightly better than those to the north, but all the hotels have swimming pools and piers from which you can snorkel, and all of them accommodate divers. Head south on Avenida Rafael Melgar, which becomes the coastal road **Costera Sur** (also called Carretera a Chankanaab).

### Very Expensive

**Presidente Inter-Continental Cozumel** 🖈🖈🖈    This is Cozumel's finest hotel in terms of location, on-site amenities, and service. Palatial in scale and modern in style, the Presidente spreads out across a long stretch of coast with only distant hotels for neighbors. This resort has been closed for many months, undergoing a serious makeover after the hurricanes, but it's scheduled to reopen in September 2006. The rooms have all been redesigned (some enlarged) and the amenities have been updated. Standard rooms come in three categories: pool view, ocean view, and beachfront. In addition to location, the pool-view rooms are smaller than the other two, which for the most part are in a long two-story building facing the water. Downstairs rooms are beachfront, upstairs are ocean view, with the main difference being a patio or balcony. They are oversize and have large, well-lit bathrooms. Most rooms come with a choice of one king-size or two double beds. The suites and reef rooms are extremely large and well furnished. A long stretch of sandy beach area dotted with *palapas* and palm trees fronts the entire hotel.

Costera Sur Km 6.5, 77600 Cozumel, Q. Roo. ℂ **800/327-0200** in the U.S., or 987/872-9500. Fax 987/872-9528. www.cozumel.intercontinental.com. 220 units. High season $390 pool view, $440–$525 ocean view/beachfront, $535 ocean suites, from $750 reef rooms and other suites; low season $325 pool view, $380–$450 ocean view/beachfront, $460 ocean suite, from $650 reef rooms and other suites. Discounts and packages available. AE, MC, V. **Amenities:** 2 restaurants (international, Mexican); snack bar; 2 bars; large outdoor pool; wading pool; access to golf club; 2 lighted tennis courts; fully equipped gym; whirlpool; watersports equipment rental; dive shop; children's activities center; concierge; tour desk; car rental; business center; shopping arcade; 24-hr. room service; in-room massage; babysitting; laundry service; dry cleaning; nonsmoking rooms. *In room:* A/C, TV w/pay movies, dataport, minibar, hair dryer.

## Expensive

**El Cid La Ceiba** 🐟🐟   On the beach side of the road, La Ceiba is a fun place to stay. It has snorkeling and shore diving to a submerged airplane (the hotel provides unlimited tanks) in front of the hotel. Lots of divers come here. Much of the hotel is now a time-share property, but it still has 30 hotel rooms. All rooms have ocean views, balconies, and two doubles or one king-size bed. Bathrooms are roomy and well lit, with granite countertops and strong water pressure. Superior rooms are larger than standard and have more furniture. The emphasis here is on watersports, particularly scuba diving, but non-divers can enjoy the large pool area, tennis court, and seaside restaurant. This hotel is undergoing an extensive refurbishing with several upgrades. Higher prices are for suites.

Costera Sur Km 4.5 (Apdo. Postal 284), 77600 Cozumel, Q. Roo. ℂ **800/435-3240** in the U.S., or 987/872-0844. Fax 987/872-0065. www.elcid.com. 98 units. High season $250–$462 double; low season $135–$245 double. AE, MC, V. **Amenities:** 2 restaurants; 2 bars; 2 large outdoor pools; access to golf club; lighted tennis court; small exercise room w/sauna; whirlpool; watersports equipment rental; dive shop; tour desk; car rental, room service until 10:30pm; in-room massage; babysitting; laundry service. *In room:* A/C, TV, fridge, coffeemaker.

## WHERE TO DINE

The island offers a number of good restaurants. Taxi drivers will often steer you toward restaurants that pay them commissions; don't heed their advice.

**Zermatt** (ℂ **987/872-1384**), a nice little bakery, is on Avenida 5 at Calle 4 Norte. For inexpensive local fare during the day, I like **Comida Casera Toñita,** listed below, and a small hole in the wall on Calle 6 Norte between Rafael Melgar and Avenida 5 called **El Morrito III** (no phone). In the evenings, my favorite place to eat tacos is at the corner of Avenida 30 and Calle Morelos. It's called **Los Seras** (no phone). It's next to a car wash of the same name.

### VERY EXPENSIVE

**Cabaña del Pescador (Lobster House)** 🐟🐟🐟 LOBSTER   The thought I often have when I eat a prepared lobster dish is that the cook could have simply boiled the lobster to better effect. The owner of this restaurant seems to agree. The only item on the menu is lobster boiled with a hint of spices and served with melted butter, accompanied by sides of rice, vegetables, and bread. The weight of the lobster you select determines the price, with side dishes included. Candles and soft lights illuminate the inviting dining rooms set amid gardens, fountains, and a small duck pond—*muy romántico.* The owner, Fernando, welcomes you warmly and will even send you next door to his brother's excellent Mexican seafood restaurant, El Guacamayo, if you must have something other than lobster.

Carretera Santa Pilar Km 4 (across from Playa Azul Hotel). No phone. Lobster (by weight) $19–$30. No credit cards. Daily 6–10:30pm.

**Pepe's Grill** 🍴🍴 STEAKS/SEAFOOD   The chefs at Pepe's seem fascinated with fire; what they don't grill in the kitchen, they flambé at your table. The most popular grilled items are the good-quality beef (prime rib or filet mignon) and the lobster. For something out of the ordinary, try shrimp Bahamas, flambéed with a little banana and pineapple in a curry sauce. Pepe's is a second-story restaurant with one large air-conditioned dining room under a massive beamed ceiling. The lighting is soft, and a guitar trio plays background music. Large windows look out over the harbor. The children's menu offers breaded shrimp and broiled chicken. For dessert there are more incendiary specialties: bananas Foster, crêpes suzette, and café Maya (coffee, vanilla ice cream, and three liqueurs).

Av. Rafael Melgar (at Salas). ℂ **987/872-0213.** Reservations recommended. Main courses $18–$35; children's menu $7. AE, MC, V. Daily 5–11:30pm.

## EXPENSIVE

**French Quarter** 🍴🍴🍴 LOUISIANA/SOUTHERN   In a pleasant upstairs open-air setting, French Quarter serves Southern and Creole classics. I found the jambalaya and étouffée delicious. You also have the choice of dining indoors or having a cocktail in the downstairs bar. The menu lists blackened fish (very good) and fresh lump crabmeat. Filet mignon with red-onion marmalade is a specialty of the house.

Av. 5 Sur 18. ℂ **987/872-6321.** Reservations recommended during Carnaval. Main courses $10–$27. AE, MC, V. Wed–Mon 5–10:30pm.

**La Cocay** 🍴🍴🍴 SEAFOOD/MEDITERRANEAN   In its new, more convenient location, this restaurant offers sophisticated cooking in comfortable surroundings, either inside or out. The dining room is furnished in modern style with soft light and music. The garden in back is lovely. I tried a few tapas for appetizers, and they were beautifully seasoned concoctions of garbanzos, chorizo, bell peppers, panela cheese, and sun-dried tomatoes on small slices of bread. A couple of the main courses also showed a sure touch: pork in a Moroccan sauce and scallops with a cognac glaze. The chocolate torte that the restaurant is known for takes a little extra time to prepare—order it early.

Calle 8 Norte 208 (between avs. 10 and 15). ℂ **987/872-5533.** Reservations recommended. Main courses $9–$30. AE, MC, V. Mon–Sat 1:30–11pm.

**Prima** 🍴🍴🍴 NORTHERN ITALIAN   Everything at this ever-popular hangout is fresh—pastas, vegetables, and seafood. Owner Albert Domínguez grows most of the vegetables in his local hydroponic garden. The menu changes daily and concentrates on seafood. It might include shrimp scampi, fettuccine with pesto, and lobster and crab ravioli with cream sauce. The fettuccine Alfredo is wonderful, the salads crisp, and the steaks USDA choice. Pizzas are cooked in a wood-burning oven. Desserts include Key lime pie and tiramisu. Dining is upstairs on the breezy terrace.

Calle Rosado Salas 109A (corner of Av. 5) ℂ **987/872-4242.** Reservations recommended during high season. Pizzas and pastas $6–$14; seafood $10–$20; steaks $15–$20. AE, MC, V. Daily 5–11pm.

## MODERATE

**El Moro** 🍴 _Value_ REGIONAL   El Moro is an out-of-the-way place that has been around for a long time and has always been popular with the locals, who come for the food, the service, and the prices—but not the decor, which is orange, orange, orange, and Formica. Get there by taxi, which will cost a couple of bucks. Portions are generous. Any of the shrimp dishes use the real jumbo variety when available. For something different, try the *Pollo Ticuleño,* a specialty from the town of Ticul, a layered dish of tomato sauce, mashed potatoes, crispy baked corn tortilla, and fried chicken breast, topped with shredded cheese and green peas. Other specialties include enchiladas and seafood prepared many ways, plus grilled steaks and sandwiches.

75 bis Norte 124 (between calles 2 and 4 Norte). © **987/872-3029.** Reservations not accepted. Main courses $5–$15. MC, V. Fri–Wed 1–11pm.

**Guido's** ✔✔MEDITERRANEAN     The inviting interior, with sling chairs and rustic wood tables, makes this a restful place in daytime and a romantic spot at night. The specialty is oven-baked pizzas. Also keep an eye out for the daily specials, which may include an appetizer of sea bass carpaccio, a couple of meat dishes, and usually a fish dish. The other thing that people love here is *pan de ajo*—a house creation of bread made with olive oil, garlic, and rosemary. There's a good, well-priced wine list.

Av. Rafael Melgar, between calles 6 and 8 Norte. © **987/872-0946.** Main courses $8–$13; daily specials $10–$14. AE. Mon–Sat 11am–11pm.

**La Choza** ✔YUCATECAN/MEXICAN     For Mexican food I like this place, and so do a lot of locals. Platters of poblano chiles stuffed with shrimp, *arrachera* (skirt steak), and *pollo en relleno negro* (chicken in a sauce of blackened chiles) are among the specialties. The table sauces and guacamole are great, and the daily specials can be good, too. This is an open-air restaurant with well-spaced tables under a tall thatched roof. Breakfasts are good as well.

Rosado Salas 198 (at Av. 10 Sur). © **987/872-0958.** Reservations accepted for groups of 6 or more. Breakfast $4; main courses $9–$15. AE, MC, V. Daily 7am–10pm.

**INEXPENSIVE**

**Cocos Cozumel** MEXICAN/AMERICAN     Cocos offers the largest breakfast menu on the island, including all the American and Mexican classics, from *huevos divorciados* (fried eggs on corn tortillas) to ham and eggs. Indulge in stateside favorites like hash browns, corn flakes and bananas, gigantic blueberry muffins, cinnamon rolls, and bagels, or go for something with tropical ingredients, like a blended fruit drink. The service and the food are excellent. The American and Mexican owners, Terri and Daniel Ocejo, are good folk and can set you up with a horseback ride or a fishing or snorkeling trip.

Av. 5 Sur 180 (1 block south of the main plaza). © **987/872-0241.** Breakfast $4–$6. No credit cards. Tues–Sun 6am–noon. Closed Sept–Oct.

**Comida Casera Toñita** HOME-STYLE YUCATECAN     The owners have made the living room of their home into a comfortable dining room, complete with filled bookshelves and classical music playing in the background. Whole fried fish, fish filet, and fried chicken are on the regular menu. Daily specials give you a chance to taste authentic regional food, including *pollo a la naranja* (chicken in bitter-orange sauce), chicken mole (in a vinegar-based sauce), *pollo en escabeche* (chicken stewed in a lightly pickled sauce), and pork chops with *achiote* seasoning.

Calle Rosado Salas 265 (between avs. 10 and 15). © **987/872-0401.** Breakfast $3–$5; main courses $5–$7; daily specials $3; fruit drinks $2. No credit cards. Mon–Sat 8am–6pm.

**Restaurant del Museo** BREAKFAST/MEXICAN     The most pleasant place in San Miguel to have breakfast or lunch (weather permitting) is at this rooftop cafe above the island's museum. It offers a serene view of the water, removed from the traffic noise below and sheltered from the sun above. The tables and chairs are comfortable and the food reliable. Choices are limited to the mainstays of American and Mexican breakfasts, and lunch dishes such as enchiladas and guacamole.

Av. Rafael Melgar (corner of Calle 6 Norte). © 987/872-0838. Reservations not accepted. Breakfast $4–$5; lunch main courses $5–$9. No credit cards. Daily 7am–2pm.

## COZUMEL AFTER DARK

On my last visit, most of the music and dance venues along Avenida Rafael Melgar had still not reopened. **Carlos 'n' Charlie's** (© **987/869-1646**), which is in the Punta Langosta shopping center, was the only one. In town, there are a few Latin music clubs; one is at the corner of Rosado Salas and Avenida 5 Sur (across from Prima) called **La Pura Vida** (© **987/878-7831**). On Sunday evenings, the place to be is the main square, which usually has a free concert and lots of people strolling about and visiting with friends. People sit in outdoor cafes enjoying the cool night breezes until the restaurants close.

The town of San Miguel has three **movie theaters.** Your best option is **Cinépolis,** the modern multicinema in the Chedraui Plaza Shopping Center at the south end of town. It mainly shows Hollywood movies. Most of these are in English with Spanish subtitles *(película subtitulada),* but before buying your tickets, make sure the movie hasn't been dubbed *(doblada).*

# The Caribbean Coast:
# The Riviera Maya, Including Playa del Carmen & the Costa Maya

*by David Baird*

Perhaps I should go on about how the Riviera Maya has "endless stretches of pristine beaches of soft white sand gently caressed by the turquoise-blue waters of the Caribbean," yadda, yadda, yadda . . . but my bet is that you've already heard it. You've seen the ads, the brochures, and the articles in the Sunday travel section. So I'll spare you the purple prose and get right to the things you'll need to know.

The Yucatán's Caribbean coast is 380km (236 miles) long, stretching from Cancún all the way to Chetumal, at the border with Belize. The northern half of the coast has been dubbed the "Riviera Maya"; the southern half, the "Costa Maya." In between is the large Sian Ka'an Biopreserve.

A long reef system, the second longest in the world, protects most of the shore. Where there are gaps in the reef—Playa del Carmen, Xpu-Ha, and Tulum—you find good beaches. The action of the surf washes away silt and seagrass and erodes rocks, leaving a sandy bottom. Where the reef is prominent, you get good snorkeling and diving with lots of fish and other sea creatures. Here mangrove often occupies the shoreline; the beaches are usually sandy up to the water's edge, but shallow, with a silty or rocky floor.

Inland you'll find jungle, caverns, the famous *cenotes* (natural wells leading to underwater rivers), and the even more famous ruins of the Maya. Activities abound.

So do lodging options. On this coast you can stay in a variety of communities or distance yourself from all of them. There's just about every choice you can think of: rustic cabins, secluded spa resorts, boutique hotels, B&Bs, all-inclusive mega-resorts, whatever you want. With so many options, you need to make some decisions. I hope that what follows will help.

In 2005, two hurricanes came through the area. The first, Emily, made landfall near Xpu-Ha and damaged many hotels and lodgings south of Playa. But it didn't pack the destructive force of Wilma, which swept through Cozumel and Cancún, wreaking a good bit of damage to Playa and points north. The locals, with help from the Mexican government, were quick to begin cleanup and rebuilding. After just a few months, very little of the damage could be seen in Playa and the southern part of the coast, while most of the hotels in the north were up and running. Perhaps they had lost a few cabanas or so, but life returned to normal surprisingly quickly.

> ## _Tips_  The Best Websites for Playa del Carmen & the Caribbean Coast
>
> • **Tourism Board: www.rivieramaya.com**  Good general info that's kept up-to-date. You'll find a comprehensive list of accommodations and service providers for this coast as well as special deals that some hotels occasionally offer through this website.
>
> • **Ecotravels in Mexico: www.planeta.com/mexico.html**  This site covers the whole country and has a nice section on the Yucatán (about halfway down the page).
>
> • **Playa information: www.playa.info**  This site offers good information about Playa del Carmen. It's run by real estate interests, so there's a slant toward Playacar and property sales.
>
> • **South of Playa: www.locogringo.com**  This is a good resource for travel information for the southern Riviera Maya—Akumal and Tulum.
>
> • **The Net Traveler: www.thenettraveler.com**  This site specializes in information about the Yucatán, Quintana Roo (home state of Cancún), and Chiapas, as well as other areas in the old Maya empire. Its information on archaeological sites, as well as on diving in the region's caves and _cenotes,_ is especially good.

## EXPLORING MEXICO'S CARIBBEAN COAST

A single road, Highway 307, runs down the coast from Cancún to Chetumal. The section between Cancún's airport and Playa del Carmen (51km/32 miles) is a four-lane divided highway with speed limits up to 110kmph (68 mph). There are a couple of traffic lights and several reduced-speed zones around the major turnoffs. From Playa to Tulum (80km/50 miles), the road is a smooth two-lane highway with wide shoulders. In 2006 construction will widen the road to four lanes. Speed limits are lower, with more places requiring you to slow down. It takes 1½ hours to drive from the Cancún airport to Tulum.

From Tulum, the highway turns inland to skirt the edges of Sian Ka'an. The roadway is narrower, without shoulders, and in some areas the forest crowds in on both sides. The speed limit is mostly 80kmph (50 mph), but you'll need to slow down where the road passes through villages, and keep an eye out for _topes_ (speed bumps). After the town of Limones, new road construction has widened and smoothed the highway. To drive from Tulum to Chetumal takes 3 hours.

**PLAYA DEL CARMEN**    Playa, as it is called, is the most happening place on the coast—a delightful beach (especially when the wind and currents are flowing in the right direction), hotels for every budget, a good choice of restaurants, and an active nightlife, most of which is on or around Quinta Avenida (Fifth Ave.), Playa's well-known promenade. In the last few years the town has grown quickly, and local residents and the tourism board are working to keep it from becoming a smaller version of Cancún.

**PUERTO MORELOS**    This town between Playa and Cancún remains a little village affectionately known by the locals as "Muerto Morelos" (_muerto_ means "dead")

for its phenomenally quiet low season. It has a few small hotels and rental houses, and nearby are a few secluded spa resorts. The coast is sandy and well protected by an off-shore reef, which means good snorkeling and diving nearby, but the lack of surf means seagrass and shallow water. If you're looking for good swimming, head farther down the coast. If you're looking for a relaxing seaside retreat with a clean beach in an easy-going community, this will work for you.

**PUERTO AVENTURAS**   The first major town south of Playa is a modern condo-marina development with a 9-hole golf course, several restaurants, and a few hotels. I don't think it's a fun place to stay, but you might come here to go deep-sea fishing or swim with dolphins.

**AKUMAL**   A bit farther south is Akumal and Half Moon Bay. The community is relatively old for this shore, which means that it's already built up and doesn't have the boomtown feel of Playa and Tulum. Akumal has a strong ecological orientation and is a prominent scuba and snorkeling center. The locals are a mix of Americans and Mex-icans, who enjoy the unhurried lifestyle of the Tropics, making this a good place to relax and work on your hammock technique. There are a few hotels; most of the lodg-ing is rental houses and condos. Consequently, the town is a favorite with families who enjoy the calmness of the place and can save money by buying groceries and cooking for themselves.

**TULUM**   The town of Tulum (near the ruins of the same name) has a hotel district of about 30 *palapa* (palm-leaf roofed) hotels, which stretch down the coast of the Punta Allen peninsula. A few years ago it was mainly a destination for backpacker types, but with some of the most beautiful beaches on this coast and many improve-ments in hotel amenities, it now attracts people with big budgets. Construction is booming, both in the town and along the coast. Here you can enjoy the beach in rel-ative solitude and quiet (unless your hotel is busy building additional rooms). The downside of this is that Tulum doesn't have the variety of restaurants that Playa and Cancún do, but you can still eat well.

**COSTA MAYA**   South of Tulum lies the large Sian Ka'an Biosphere Preserve and, beyond that, what is known as the Costa Maya, which designates the rest of the coast all the way down to Belize. The Costa Maya is a relaxing getaway. Most of the coast is along the Majahual Peninsula, which has a lot of sandy beaches with silt bottoms. It's attractive to scuba divers, snorkelers, fly-fishermen, and people who want to get away from the crowds. Farther south is Lake Bacalar, a large, clear freshwater lake fed by *cenotes.* Inland from here are the impressive Maya ruins of the Río Bec area.

## 1 Playa del Carmen ★★★

32km (20 miles) S of Puerto Morelos; 70km (43 miles) S of Cancún; 10km (6½ miles) N of Xcaret; 13km (8 miles) N of Puerto Calica

Though it no longer has the feel of a village, Playa still provides that rare combina-tion of simplicity (a small town that can be traversed on foot) and variety (many unique hotels, restaurants, and stores). There is a comfortable feel to the town. The local architecture has adopted elements of native building—rustic clapboard walls, stucco, thatched roofs, rough-hewn wood, and a ramshackle, unplanned look to many structures—that reflect the town's taste for Third World chic. Slicker architecture has appeared, with chain restaurants and stores, detracting from Playa's individuality, but Playa still retains the feel of a cosmopolitan getaway with a counterculture ethos.

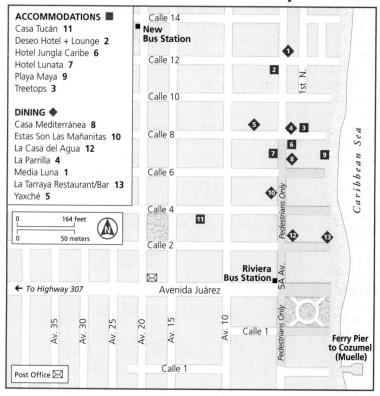

**ACCOMMODATIONS** ■
Casa Tucán **11**
Deseo Hotel + Lounge **2**
Hotel Jungla Caribe **6**
Hotel Lunata **7**
Playa Maya **9**
Treetops **3**

**DINING** ◆
Casa Mediterránea **8**
Estas Son Las Mañanitas **10**
La Casa del Agua **12**
La Parrilla **4**
Media Luna **1**
La Tarraya Restaurant/Bar **13**
Yaxché **5**

Calle 14
New Bus Station
Calle 12
Calle 10
Calle 8
Calle 6
Calle 4
Calle 2
1st N.
Caribbean Sea
Pedestrians Only

0    164 feet
0    50 meters

Riviera Bus Station
← To Highway 307
Avenida Juárez
5A Av.
Av. 35
Av. 30
Av. 25
Av. 20
Av. 15
Av. 10
Calle 1
Pedestrians Only
Ferry Pier to Cozumel (Muelle)
Post Office ⊠
Calle 1

Playa is perfect for enjoying the simple (and perhaps the best) pleasures of a seaside vacation—taking in the sun and the sea air while working your toes into the sand; cooling down with a swim in clear water; and strolling aimlessly down the beach, listening to the wash of waves, and feeling the light touch of tropical breezes. A strong European influence has made topless sunbathing (nominally against the law in Mexico) a nonchalantly accepted practice anywhere there's a beach. The beach grows and shrinks, from broad and sandy to narrower with rocks, depending on the currents and wind. When this happens, head to the beaches in north Playa.

From Playa it's easy to shoot out to Cozumel on the ferry, drive south to the nature parks and the ruins at Tulum and Cobá, or drive north to Cancún. Directly south of town is the Playacar development, which has a golf course, several large all-inclusive resorts, and a residential section.

## ESSENTIALS

**GETTING THERE & DEPARTING    By Air**    You can fly into Cancún and take a bus directly from the airport (see "By Bus," below), or fly into Cozumel and take the passenger ferry.

**By Car    Highway 307** is the only highway that passes through Playa. As you approach Playa from Cancún, the highway divides. Keep to the inside lanes to permit

---

## Tips **Driving the Riviera Maya**

Driving along this coast isn't difficult. There's only one highway, so you can't get lost. Speed limits are clearly posted, but lots of cars ignore them, *except around Playa*, where police are known to ticket drivers. Watch your speed when you're passing through town. Maximum speed for the center lanes is 60kmph (40 mph), and for the outside lanes 40kmph (25 mph).

South of Playa, the highway is a two-lane undivided highway with wide shoulders, but that might be changing with new road construction. If you find that it's still undivided, you should know that you're not allowed to stop on the highway to make a left turn. You're supposed to pull over to the right and wait for traffic in both directions to clear before crossing the road. Another tip: It's customary for drivers here to pretend that there's a center passing lane. Oncoming traffic moves to the right to make room for the passing vehicle. You do the same, but when you do so look out for cyclists and cars on the shoulder. This is why I recommend that you not drive at night. As far as gas availability goes, there are several more gas stations in the Riviera Maya now, so you shouldn't have a problem getting gas. But pay attention and make sure that the gasoline-station attendant gives you back the right amount of money—I've had people try to shortchange me.

---

turning left at any of the traffic lights. The two main arteries into Playa are Avenida Constituyentes, which works well for destinations in northern Playa, and Avenida Juárez, which leads to the town's main square. If you stay in the outside lanes, you will need to continue past Playa until you get to the turnaround, then double back, staying to your right.

**By Ferry**  Air-conditioned passenger ferries to Cozumel leave from the town's pier 1 block from the main square. There is also a car ferry to Cozumel from the Calica pier just south of the Playacar development. The schedule for the passenger ferries has been in flux since the hurricanes. As of the latest information, ferries have been departing every hour in the mornings, and every 2 hours in the afternoons. For more information about both ferries, see "Getting There & Departing" in the Cozumel section of chapter 5.

**By Taxi**  Taxi fares from the Cancún airport are about $50 to $60 one-way.

**By Bus**  **Autobuses Riviera** offers service from the Cancún airport about 12 times a day. Cost is $8 one-way. You'll see a ticket counter in the corridor leading out of the airport. From the Cancún bus station there are frequent departures—almost every 30 minutes.

### ORIENTATION

**ARRIVING**  Playa has two **bus stations.** Buses coming from Cancún and places along the coast, such as Tulum, arrive at the Riviera bus station, at the corner of Juárez and Quinta Avenida, by the town square. Buses coming from destinations in the interior of the peninsula arrive at the new ADO station, on Avenida 20 between calles 12 and 14.

*A word of caution:* Approach any timeshare salesperson as you would a wounded rhino. And remember that whatever free trinket is offered for simply viewing apartments, it either won't materialize or won't be worth the time you invest in your dealings with these people. You have been warned.

**CITY LAYOUT**    The main street, **Avenida Juárez**, leads to the town square from Highway 307. As it does so, it crosses several numbered avenues that run parallel to the beach, all of which are multiples of 5. **Quinta Avenida (Fifth Avenue)** is closest to the beach; it's closed to traffic from the *zócalo* to Calle 6 (and some blocks beyond, in the evening). On this avenue are many hotels, restaurants, and shops. Almost all of the town is north and west of the square. To the south is "Playacar," a golf-course development of private residences and a dozen resort hotels.

---

## FAST FACTS: Playa del Carmen

*Area Code* The telephone area code is **984**.

*Doctor* For serious medical attention, go to Hospitén in Cancún (© **998/881-3700**). In Playa, Dr. G. Ambriz speaks English and was trained in the U.S. and Europe. His office is at the corner of Avenida 30 and Calle 14 (© **984/109-1245**).

*Internet Access* Internet cafes are all over town; most have fast connection speeds.

*Money Exchange* Playa has several banks and ATMs. Many currency-exchange houses are close to the pier or along Quinta Avenida at Calle 8.

*Parking* Most parking in Playa is on the street. Spots can be hard to come by. The most accessible parking lot is the Estacionamiento México, at avenidas Juárez and 10 (where the entrance is located). It's open daily 24 hours and charges $1.25 per hour, $10 per day. There's also a 24-hour lot a block from the pier, where you can leave your car while you visit Cozumel.

*Pharmacy* The **Farmacia del Carmen,** Avenida Juárez between avenidas 5 and 10 (© **984/873-2330**), is open 24 hours.

*Post Office* The *correo,* on Avenida Juárez, 3 blocks from the plaza, is on the right past the Hotel Playa del Carmen and the launderette.

*Seasons* The main high season is from mid-December to Easter. There is a mini high season in August. Low season is all other months.

---

## EXPLORING PLAYA & THE RIVIERA MAYA

The main activity in Playa is hanging out on the beach and enjoying Quinta Avenida. But there are actually plenty of activities to do up and down this coast. The following is a brief list to help you consider your options.

**GOLF & TENNIS**    If golf is your bag, the Playacar Golf Club (© **984/873-4990;** www.palace-resorts.com/playacar-golf-club) has an 18-hole **golf course** designed by Robert Von Hagge. It's operated by the Palace Resorts hotel chain, which offers golf packages. Greens fees are $180 in the morning (including tax and cart) and $120 after 2pm; club rental costs $30. The club also has two **tennis** courts, which cost $10 per hour.

**HORSEBACK RIDING**    There are a few places along the highway that offer horseback rides. The best of these, **Rancho Punta Venado,** is just south of Playa past the Calica Pier. This ranch is less touristy than the others, and the owner takes good care of his horses. It has a nice stretch of coast with a sheltered bay and offers kayaking and snorkeling outings. It's best to make arrangements ahead of time and tell them you're a Frommer's reader, so that they can schedule you on a day when they have fewer customers. You can contact them through e-mail (gabriela@puntavenado.com) or by calling directly to the ranch's cellphone (© **044-984/116-3213**); there is a charge for the call. Talk to Gabriela or Francisco; both speak English. You might also try dropping by. The turnoff for the ranch is 2km (1¼ miles) south of the Calica overpass near Km 279.

**DAY SPA**    To relax after all that exertion, try **Spa Itzá** (used to be called Itzá Spa, but they must have gotten tired of all the jokes). It's in downtown Playa between calles 12 and 14 in a retail area called Calle Corazón. The phone is © **984/803-2588.**

**VISITING THE RUINED CITIES OF THE MAYA**    There are four cities within easy reach of Playa and most of the coast. The easiest to reach is **Tulum** (see the section on Tulum later in this chapter where my coauthor and I air our different views of the city). A half-hour inland from Tulum on a pock-marked road is **Cobá,** rising up from a jungle setting. This city has not been reconstructed to the same degree as the other three and doesn't have the rich imagery or clearly delineated architecture. Its description is also in the Tulum section. The other two cites, **Chichén Itzá** and **Ek Balam,** are 2½ hours distant in the interior of the peninsula. My favorite way of seeing them is to rent a car and drive to Chichén in the afternoon, check into a hotel (perhaps one with a pool), see the sound-and-light show that evening, and then tour the ruins in the cool of the morning before the big bus tours arrive. Then drive back via Valladolid and Ek Balam. See chapter 7 for a description of these places.

**TOURS**    From Playa and the rest of the coast there are tours to these ruins. The tour buses usually stop at a few places along the way for refreshments and souvenirs, which is why I prefer the small tours. Some combine the ruins of Tulum with a visit to a nature park. There is a tour agency in Playa called **Alltournative** (© **984/873-2036;** www.alltournative.com), which offers small tours that combine a little of everything: culture (visit a contemporary Maya village); adventure (kayaking, rappelling, snorkeling, *cenote* diving); natural history; and ruins. It offers these tours daily using vans for transportation. The tours are fun. You can call the agency directly or arrange a tour through your hotel; they pick up at most of the large resorts along the coast. A new outfit called **Selvática** (© **998/849-5510;** www.selvatica.com.mx), operating out of offices in Cancún, offers guests a little adventure tourism in the jungle, with 2.5km (1½ miles) of zip lines strung up in the forest canopy. There is also mountain biking and swimming in *cenotes.* They pick up from hotels in the Riviera Maya on Tuesdays and Thursdays. The $75 cost includes transportation, activities, a light lunch, locker, and all equipment. Buy tickets and get more information at any travel agency in Playa. Another interesting option is an ecological tour of the **Sian Ka'an Biopreserve.** To do this, however, you have to get to Tulum. See the Tulum section, later in this chapter.

**DEEP-SEA FISHING**    The largest marina on the coast is at **Puerto Aventuras,** not far south of Playa. Here's where you'll find most of your options for boating and fishing. See p. 160.

**SCUBA/SNORKELING**    In Playa, **Cyan-Ha Dive Center** (© **984/803-2517;** www.cyanha.com) arranges reef and cavern diving. The owner, Carlos Quintanar, has been in Playa for over 20 years. His shop is in the Shangri-la Caribe Resort, and he and his staff speak English. Snorkeling trips cost around $20 and include soft drinks and equipment. Two-tank dive trips are $60; resort courses with SSI and PADI instructors cost $80. The area around Akumal has a number of underwater caverns and *cenotes* that have become popular scuba and snorkeling destinations. The **Akumal Dive Shop** specializes in cavern diving and offers a variety of dives. But the easiest way to try cavern diving or snorkeling is through **Hidden Worlds Cenotes,** which is right on the highway 15km (9 miles) south of Akumal. They provide everything, including wet suit. See "South of Playa del Carmen," later in this chapter.

**SWIMMING WITH DOLPHINS**   In the two nature parks south of Playa, Xcaret and Xel-Ha, you can have the opportunity of interacting with these intelligent creatures. Also, there's an outfit in Puerto Aventuras called **Dolphin Discovery** that is quite good. See "South of Playa del Carmen," later in this chapter.

**THE NATURE PARKS: XCARET & XEL-HA**   These parks make full-day excursions, offering opportunities for swimming, snorkeling, and other seaside activities, and educational tours about the region's natural history and local Maya culture and entertainment. They are completely self-contained and offer food, drink, watersports equipment, and various kinds of merchandise. Xcaret is just south of Playa, while Xel-Ha is farther south, almost to Tulum. (See section 3, later in this chapter.)

**Cozumel** is a half-hour away by ferry; in my opinion, it makes for a poor day trip unless you simply want to shop. You'll see exactly what the cruise-ship passengers see—lots of duty-free, souvenir, and jewelry stores. To enjoy Cozumel best, you have to spend at least a couple of nights there to explore the island. See chapter 5.

## WHERE TO STAY

Playa has a lot of small hotels with affordable prices that give you a better feel for the town than staying in one of the resorts in Playacar. Don't hesitate to book a place that's not on the beach. Town life here is much of the fun, and staying on the beach in Playa has its disadvantages—in particular, the noise from a couple of beach bars. Beaches are public property in Mexico, and you can lay out your towel anywhere you like. There are some beach clubs in north Playa where for a small sum you can have the use of lounge chairs, towels, and food and drink.

High season is from mid-December to Easter. August is also high season for some hotels but not others. During other times of the year you can come to Playa and look for walk-in offers. The rates listed below include the 12% hotel tax. I don't include the rates for Christmas to New Year's, which are still higher than the standard high-season rates.

### EXPENSIVE

**Deseo Hotel + Lounge** ୧୧୧   In a town where being hip is a raison d'être, there is no hotel hipper than this one. Its creators, the owners of **Habita** in Mexico City, seek to redefine our notions of a hotel by designing an environment that fosters social interaction. The lounge plays the central role, appropriating all the functions of lobby, restaurant, bar, and pool area. It's a raised open-air platform with bar, pool, and self-serve kitchen furnished with large daybeds for sunning or for enjoying an evening drink when the bar is in full swing. The rooms face two sides of the lounge. The clientele is predominantly 25- to 45-year-olds, and the music seems by design to provide an artsy background that's sufficiently monotonous not to compete with the setting.

The guest rooms play their part. They are comfortable, original, and visually striking, but, unlike the usual plush hotel room, they don't tempt one to isolation amid an array of amenities—no TV, no cushy armchair. There is a simplicity that gives them an almost Asian feel, heightened by nice touches such as sliding doors of wood and frosted glass. The mattresses, however, are thick and luxurious. All rooms have king-size beds. From the bottom of each bed, a little drawer slides out with a night kit containing three things: incense, earplugs, and condoms.

And if Deseo doesn't work for you, the owners have opened another archly styled hotel 2 blocks down called **Hotel Básico** (© **984/879-4448;** www.hotelbasico.com). It's a fun mix of industrial and '50s styles, built with materials that have found a lot of favor with architects these days: concrete, plywood, and plastics. Along with all this you get a cushy bed and a forceful shower. As with Deseo, the common areas are not wasted space.

Av. 5 (at Calle 12), 77710 Playa del Carmen, Q. Roo. © **984/879-3620.** Fax 984/879-3621. www.hoteldeseo.com. 15 units. $180 lounge view; $199 balcony; $244 suite. Rates include continental breakfast. AE, MC, V. No parking. Children under 18 not accepted. **Amenities:** Bar; small rooftop pool; Jacuzzi; tour info; ground transfer; room service until 11pm; in-room massage; laundry service. *In room:* A/C, minibar, hair dryer (on request), safe.

**Hotel Lunata** ⭐⭐    In the middle of Playa there isn't a more comfortable or more attractive place to stay than this small hotel on Quinta Avenida. The rooms offer character, good looks, and polish. There are a few standard rooms, which are midsize and come with a queen-size or a double bed. Deluxe rooms are large and come with a king-size bed and small fridge. Junior suites come with two doubles. Bathrooms are well designed and have good showers. Light sleepers should opt for a room facing the garden. On my last stay, I took a room facing the street with double-glazed glass doors that opened to a balcony. I enjoyed looking out over Quinta Avenida, and, with the doors shut, the noise was not bothersome.

Av. 5 (between calles 6 and 8), 77710 Playa del Carmen, Q. Roo. © **984/873-0884.** Fax 984/873-1240. www.lunata.com. 10 units. High season $110 standard, $140–$155 deluxe and junior suite; low season $95 standard, $115–$135 deluxe and junior suite. Rates include continental breakfast. Promotional rates available. AE, MC, V. Secure parking $5. No children under 13 allowed. **Amenities:** Free use of bike and watersports equipment; tour desk; in-room massage; laundry service; nonsmoking rooms. *In room:* A/C, TV, fridge (in some), hair dryer (on request), safe, no phone.

**Hotel Quinto Sol** ⭐    This three-story hotel in north Playa wraps around an ancient tree laden with orchids. The building's design has an Italian touch, with a lot of curves and rounded corners in the stuccowork. Highlights include a rooftop Jacuzzi and proximity to the beaches on Playa's north side. The rooms are large and attractive, with good air-conditioning; bathrooms come with showers and could use a little more light. "Studios" are comparable to "standards" but come with kitchenettes. Minisuites are larger than either, and have a few extra details plus balconies. This part of Quinta Avenida is usually quiet.

Av. 5 Norte 330 (at Calle 28), 77710 Playa del Carmen, Q. Roo. © **984/873-3292** or -3293. Fax 984/873-3294. www.hotelquintosol.com. 20 units. High season $105–$125 standard or studio, $140–$165 suite; low season $85–$105 standard or studio, $110–$130 suite. Rates include continental breakfast. MC, V. Street parking. **Amenities:** Restaurant; bar; discount at Playa Mamita's beach club; Jacuzzi; tour info; room service until 11pm; laundry service; nonsmoking rooms. *In room:* A/C, TV, kitchenette (in some), minibar, coffeemaker (on request), hair dryer, safe.

**Playa Maya** ⭐ *Value*    Of the beach hotels in downtown Playa, this one would be my first choice. There are a lot of reasons to like it (good location, good price, comfortable rooms, and friendly and helpful management), but one thing that really strikes my fancy is that you enter this hotel from the beach. This little, seemingly inconsequential detail shouldn't be any reason for picking a hotel, but it just sets the mood of the place and creates a little separation from the busy street scene. To get back to more practical matters, the design and location make it a quiet hotel, too, as it is a couple of blocks away from the nearest beach bar and it's sheltered by the neighboring hotels. The pool and sunning terrace are attractive and nicely set apart. Rooms are large with midsize bathrooms. A couple come with private garden terraces with Jacuzzis; others have balconies facing the beach.

Zona FMT (between calles 6 and 8 Norte), 77710 Playa del Carmen, Q. Roo. ✆ 984/803-2022. www.playa-maya.com. 20 units. High season $125–$165 double; low season $100–$130 double. Rates include continental breakfast. MC, V. **Amenities:** Restaurant; bar; outdoor pool; Jacuzzi; room service until 6pm; massage, laundry service. *In room:* A/C, TV, high-speed wireless Internet, fridge, hair dryer, safe.

**Shangri-La Caribe** ✿✿✿   This hotel—a loose grouping of cabanas on one of the best beaches in Playa—is hard to beat for sheer fun and leisure. And it's far enough from the center of town to be quiet. The older, south side of the hotel (the "Caribe" section) consists of one- and two-story cabanas. The north side ("Playa" section) has a few larger buildings, holding four to six rooms. A preference for one or the other section is a matter of taste; the units in both are similar in amenities, privacy, and price. All rooms have a patio or porch complete with hammock. Most come with two double beds, but a few have a king-size bed. Windows are screened, and ceiling fans circulate the breeze. The real difference in price depends on the proximity to the water—oceanfront, ocean view, or garden view. Garden view is the best bargain, being only a few steps farther from the water. Many garden-view rooms (mostly in a third section called "Pueblo") have air-conditioning, which adds $6 to the price. Book well in advance during high season.

Calle 38 (Apdo. Postal 253), 77710 Playa del Carmen, Q. Roo. ✆ 800/538-6802 in the U.S. and Canada, or 984/873-0611. Fax 984/873-0500. www.shangrilacaribe.net. 107 units. High season $190–$225 garden view, $245 ocean view, $295 oceanfront; low season $150–$190 garden view, $200–$220 ocean view, $250–$270 oceanfront. Rates include breakfast and dinner. AE, MC, V. Free guarded parking. From Hwy. 307 from Cancún, U-turn at the light for Av. Constituyentes, making sure to get into the far right lane; backtrack to the Volkswagen dealership, turn right, and head for the beach—this will be Calle 38. **Amenities:** 2 restaurants; poolside grill; 3 bars; 2 large outdoor pools; whirlpool; watersports equipment; dive shop; game room; tour desk; ground transfer; car rental; in-room massage; babysitting; laundry service. *In room:* Hair dryer, no phone.

## MODERATE

**Jungla Caribe** ✿   Located right in the heart of the action, "La Jungla" is an imaginative piece of work—a colorful execution of neoclassical *a la tropical*. It's the right place for those who enjoy original lodging and seek out the commotion that comes with the location, which quiets down around 11pm. All but the eight *sencilla* (standard) rooms are large, with gray-and-black marble floors, air-conditioning, large bathrooms, and the occasional Roman column. Doubles and junior suites face Quinta Avenida and come with two double beds. Catwalks lead from the main building to the "tower" section of suites in back (the quietest). The *sencilla* rooms face Calle 8, are small with ample bathrooms, and have no air-conditioning. They come with one double bed and a balcony. It is best for people who go to bed late because of the mariachis who play across the street. There's an attractive pool in the courtyard surrounded by vegetation and shaded by a giant *ramón* tree.

Av. 5 Norte (at Calle 8), 77710 Playa del Carmen, Q. Roo. ✆/fax 984/873-0650. www.jungla-caribe.com. 25 units. High season $70 *sencilla*, $90 double, $120–$130 suite; low season $50 *sencilla*, $65 double, $90–$100 suite. AE, MC, V. **Amenities:** Restaurant; 2 bars; outdoor pool; tour info; room service until 11pm. *In room:* A/C, TV, no phone.

**Treetops** 🌴 🅥𝑎𝑙𝑢𝑒    The rooms at Treetops encircle a patch of preserved jungle (and a small *cenote*) that shades the hotel and lends it the proper tropical feel. Rooms are large and have balconies or patios that overlook the "jungle." Some of the upper rooms have the feel of a treehouse, especially the "treehouse" suite. The two other suites are large, with fully loaded kitchenettes—good for groups of four. The location is excellent: a half-block from the beach, a half-block from Quinta Avenida. The American owners are helpful, attentive hosts.

Calle 8 s/n, 77710 Playa del Carmen, Q. Roo. ℭ/fax **984/873-0351**. www.treetopshotel.com. 22 units. High season $94 double, $105 kitchen studio, $147–$176 suite; low season $85 double, $94 kitchen studio, $116–$145 suite. MC, V. **Amenities:** Restaurant; bar; small outdoor pool. *In room:* A/C, kitchenette (in some), fridge, no phone.

## INEXPENSIVE

**Casa Tucán**    This small hotel in the middle of Playa has simple rooms for a low price. You have a choice of standard room or a cabana. Both come with ceiling fans; the cabanas get a little more air circulation. For $10 more you can get a room with a kitchenette. The hotel is welcoming and the staff is very helpful with travel and tour advice.

Calle 4 (between avs. 10 and 15), 77710 Playa del Carmen, Q. Roo. ℭ/fax **984/873-0283**. www.casatucan.de. 22 units. $45 double; $55 kitchenette studio. MC, V. **Amenities:** Restaurant; small outdoor pool; tour info; laundry service. *In room:* Kitchenette (in some), no phone.

## WHERE TO DINE

Aside from the restaurants listed below, I would point you in the direction of a few that don't need a full review. For fish tacos and inexpensive seafood, try **El Oasis,** on Calle 12, between avenidas 5 and 10 (no phone). For *arrachera* (fajita) tacos, the place to go is **Super Carnes H C de Monterrey** (ℭ **984/803-0488**) on 1 Sur between avenidas 20 and 25. For something Mexican farther off the beaten path, you might try **Pozolería Mi Abuelita** (no phone) on Avenida 30, between calles 20 and 22. This is a restaurant of the people and should be considered only by adventurous diners. It's open in the evenings and serves good *pozole rojo* and *enchiladas verdes.*

### EXPENSIVE

**La Casa del Agua** 🌴🌴 EUROPEAN/MEXICAN    Excellent food in inviting surroundings. Instead of obtrusive background music, you hear the sound of falling water. The Swiss owners work at presenting what they like best about the Old and New worlds. They do a good job with seafood—try the grilled seafood for two. For a mild dish, try chicken in a wonderfully scented sauce of fine herbs accompanied by fettuccine; for something heartier, there's the tortilla soup listed as "Mexican soup." The restaurant offers a number of cool and light dishes that would be appetizing for lunch or an afternoon meal, for example, an avocado stuffed with shrimp and flavored with a subtle horseradish sauce on a bed of alfalfa sprouts and julienne carrots—a good mix of tastes and textures. For dessert, try the chocolate mousse. This is an upstairs restaurant under a large and airy *palapa* roof.

Av. 5 (at Calle 2). ℭ **984/803-0232**. Main courses $12–$25. AE, MC, V. Daily noon–midnight.

**La Parrilla** MEXICAN/GRILL    Still a fun place, but it's having problems handling its success. Prices have gone up, and service is slower. But the fajitas remain good as well as many of the Mexican standards such as tortilla soup, enchiladas, and quesadillas. Mariachis show up around 8pm; plan accordingly.

Av. 5 (at Calle 8). ℭ **984/873-0687**. Reservations recommended in high season. Main courses $10–$22. AE, MC, V. Daily noon–1am.

**Yaxché** ✿✿✿ REGIONAL   The menu here makes use of many native foods and spices to present a more elaborate regional cooking than the usual offerings at Yucatecan restaurants—and it was about time for someone to show a little creativity with such an interesting palette of tastes. Excellent examples are a cream of *chaya* (a native leafy vegetable), and an *xcatic* chile stuffed with *cochinita pibil*. I also like the classic Mexican-style fruit salad with lime juice and dried powdered chile. There are several seafood dishes; the ones I had were fresh and well prepared.

Calle 8 (between avs. 5 and 10). ℂ **984/873-2502.** Reservations recommended in high season. Main courses $10–$25. AE, MC, V. Daily noon–midnight.

## MODERATE

**Casa Mediterránea** ✿✿✿ ITALIAN   Tucked away on a quiet little patio off Quinta Avenida, this small, homey restaurant serves excellent food. Maurizio Gabrielli and Mary Michelon are usually there to greet customers and make recommendations. Maurizio came to Mexico to enjoy the simple life, and this inclination shows in the restaurant's welcoming, unhurried atmosphere. The menu is mostly northern Italian, with several dishes from other parts of Italy. There are daily specials, too. Pastas (except penne and spaghetti) are made in-house, and none is precooked. Try fish and shrimp ravioli or penne alla Veneta. There are several wines, mostly Italian, to choose from. The salads are good and carefully prepared—dig in without hesitation.

Av. 5 (between calles 6 and 8; look for a sign for Hotel Marietta). ℂ **984/876-3926.** Reservations recommended in high season. Main courses $8–$15. No credit cards. Daily 1–11pm.

**Estas Son Las Mañanitas** MEXICAN/ITALIAN   For dependable food in an advantageous spot for people-watching, try this restaurant. It's simple outdoor dining on "la Quinta"—comfortable chairs and tables under *palapa* umbrellas. The Italian owner is vigilant about maintaining quality and consistency. He offers an excellent *sopa de lima,* a large seafood pasta, grilled shrimp with herbs, and Tex-Mex specialties such as chili and fajitas. The hot sauces are good.

Av. 5 (between calles 4 and 6). ℂ **984/873-0114.** Main courses $8–$15. AE, MC, V. Daily 7am–11:30pm.

**La Cueva del Chango** ✿ HIPPIE MEXICAN   Good food in original surroundings with a relaxed "mañana" attitude. True to its name ("The Monkey's Cave"), the place suggests a cave and has little waterways meandering through it, and there are two spider monkeys that hang about in the back of the place. But take away the water and the monkeys, and, oddly enough, it brings to mind the Flintstones. You'll enjoy great juices, blended fruit drinks, salads, soups, Mexican specialties with a natural twist, and handmade tortillas. The fish is fresh and delicious. Mosquitoes can sometimes be a problem, but the management has bug spray for the guests.

Calle 38 (between Av. 5 and the beach, near the Shangri-la Caribe). ℂ **984/116-3179.** Main courses $4–$12. No credit cards. Daily 8am–11pm.

**La Vagabunda** ITALIAN/MEXICAN   This place is old-style Playa in its simplicity and charm. A large *palapa* shelters several simple wood tables sitting on a gravel floor. It's low-key and quiet—a good place for breakfast, with many options, including delicious blended fruit drinks, waffles, and omelets. The specials are a good value. In the afternoon and evening, you can order light fare such as panini, pastas, and ceviche.

Av. 5 (between calles 24 and 26). ℂ **984/873-3753.** Breakfast $4–$6; main courses $7–$12. MC, V. High season daily 7am–11:30pm; low season daily 7am–3:30pm.

## Choosing an All-Inclusive in the Riviera Maya

There are more than 40 all-inclusive resorts on this coast. Most people are familiar with the concept—large hotels that work with economies of scale to offer lodging, food, and drink all for a single, low rate. All-inclusives offer convenience and economy, especially for families with many mouths to feed. And, because they are enclosed areas, they make it easy for parents to keep an eye on their children.

There is a certain sameness about these hotels. They're usually built around a large pool with activities and an activities organizer. There's often a quiet pool, too. One large buffet restaurant and a snack bar serve the needs of most guests, but there are usually a few specialty restaurants as well (at no extra charge)—the guest just has to make reservations at those places. Colored bracelets serve to identify guests. In the evenings, a show is presented at the hotel's theater.

These resorts work best for those who are looking for a relaxing beach vacation and to get away from the cold weather. They don't work for those who aim to get away from crowds—these hotels are large and operate with a high occupancy rate. Yes, staying at these all-inclusives is convenient, and hassle-free. They make everything easy, including taking tours and day trips—all the organizing is done for you. On the downside, you don't often get the spontaneity or the sense of adventure that comes with other styles of travel. The question you have to ask yourself is, *what kind of vacation are you looking for?*

The best way to get a room at an all-inclusive is through a vacation packager or one of its travel agents. You get a better deal than by contacting the hotel directly. Even if you have frequent-flier miles to burn, you will still find

**Media Luna** ★★★ FUSION   This restaurant has an inventive menu that favors grilled seafood, sautés, and pasta dishes. Everything is fresh and prepared beautifully. Try the very tasty pan-fried fish cakes with mango and honeyed *hoisin* sauce. Another choice is the black pepper–crusted fish. Be sure to eye the daily specials. For lunch you can get sandwiches and salads, as well as black-bean quesadillas and crepes. The decor is primitive-tropical chic.

Av. 5 (between calles 12 and 14). ✆ 984/873-0526. Breakfast $4–$6; sandwich with salad $5–$7; main courses $8–$15. No credit cards. Daily 8am–11:30pm.

**Sol Food** ★★★ ECLECTIC   In keeping with the name of this restaurant, the owners will put just about anything under the sun on their menu. I quite enjoyed myself trying a sampling of dishes, including the spinach salad (conventionally made except for the Asian vinagrette) and pad Thai (just how I like it, with a marked tamarind flavor). A most memorable dish was the rice with calamari and shrimp. It had a little bite to it *(chile de árbol),* a little sweetness (roasted red pepper), and a little saltiness (Parmesan cheese), making for a wonderful combination. Another dish indicative of it difficult to match the rates of a full package offered by one of the biggies like Funjet.

Of the many all-inclusives in the Riviera Maya, there are a few that are my favorites and might bear looking into:

**Iberostar Quetzal** or **Tucan** (two names for different halves of the same hotel; www.iberostar.com). Of the several all-inclusives that are in Playa del Carmen/Playacar, I like this one. The food is better than at most, and the central part of the hotel is made of raised walkways and terraces over the natural mangrove habitat.

The **Copacabana** resort in Xpu-Ha (www.hotelcopacabana.com). Also has raised walkways, preserving much of the flora and making it visually interesting. And Xpu-Ha is blessed with a stunning beach.

Also in Xpu-Ha is the **Xpu-Ha Palace** (www.palaceresorts.com), built on the grounds of a failed nature park. It has some keen features, including lagoons and jungle and offers several facilities for kids, including a small crocodile hatchery. The hotel is spread out over a large area and necessarily involves a good bit of walking, but this also makes it feel like more of a getaway.

**Aventura Spa Palace** (www.palaceresorts.com). Another hotel in the Palace chain—this one just for grown-ups. It has a large spa and gym and attractive common areas and guest rooms. There is a large pool but no beach; guests can take a shuttle to the Xpu-Ha property if they want.

**Freedom Paradise** (www.freedomparadise.com) is billed as the first size-friendly vacation resort. The management has worked hard to create an environment that large people will find comfortable. I like it because it doesn't have all the froufrou of so many other resorts—it's friendly and unpretentious.

their menu is the sautéed shrimp in a maple-Dijon-chipotle glaze. There's indoor/outdoor dining and comfortable furniture.

Av. 5 (between calles 20 and 22). No phone. Main courses $9–$18. No credit cards. Daily 7:30am–11:30pm.

## INEXPENSIVE

**La Tarraya Restaurant/Bar** *Value* SEAFOOD THE RESTAURANT THAT WAS BORN WITH THE TOWN, proclaims the sign. It's right on the beach, with the water practically lapping at the foundations. Because the owners are fishermen, the fish is so fresh it's practically still wiggling. The wood hut doesn't look like much, but you can have your fish prepared in several ways. If you haven't tried the Yucatecan specialty *tik-n-xic*—fish with *achiote* and bitter-orange sauce, cooked in a banana leaf—this is a good place to do so.

Calle 2 Norte. © 984/873-2040. Main courses $4–$7; whole fish $8 per kilo. No credit cards. Daily 7am–9pm.

## PLAYA DEL CARMEN AFTER DARK

It seems as if everyone in town is out strolling along "la Quinta" until midnight; there's pleasant browsing, dining, and drinking available at the many establishments on the street. Here's a quick rundown of the bars that you won't find on Quinta Avenida. The beach bar that is an institution in Playa is the **Blue Parrot** (© 984/873-0083). It gets live acts, mostly rock, and attracts a mixed crowd. It's between calles 12 and 14. Just to the south is **Om** (no phone), which gets a younger crowd with louder musical acts. For salsa, go to **Mambo Café** (© 984/803/2656) on Calle 6 between avenidas 5 and 10.

**Alux** (© 984/110-5050; www.aluxplaya.com) is a one-of-a-kind club occupying a large cave with two dramatically lit chambers and several nooks and sitting areas. It's worth going to, if only for the novelty. The local conservancy group approved all the work, and great care was taken not to contaminate the water, which is part of a larger underground river system. The club books a variety of music acts, usually with no cover. Often there's belly dancing, which is quite in keeping with the surroundings, and I couldn't help but think that I had stepped into a scene from a James Bond film. The bar is cash only and is open Tuesday to Sunday from 7pm to 2am. Take Avenida Juárez across to the other side of the highway—2 blocks down on your left.

For movie going, **Cine Hollywood,** Avenida 10 and Calle 8, in the Plaza Pelícanos shopping center, shows a lot of films in English with Spanish subtitles. Before you buy your ticket, make sure the film is subtitled *(subtitulada)* and not dubbed *(doblada)*.

## 2 North of Playa del Carmen

### EN ROUTE TO PUERTO MORELOS

As you drive north from Playa del Carmen, you'll pass a number of roadside attractions, all-inclusive hotels, small cabana hotels, and secluded resorts, and the nature park called Tres Ríos. The turnoff for Puerto Morelos is only about 30km (20 miles) from Playa.

**Tres Ríos** is halfway between Playa and Puerto Morelos. It's the simplest of the nature parks and, indeed, might better be thought of as an elaborate beach club with organized activities such as beach volleyball and soccer, snorkel and scuba tours, watersports equipment rental, horseback riding, and food service. The park has been closed since before Hurricane Wilma, but the website says that it will reopen sometime in 2006. For more information try © 998/887-8077, or go to www.tres-rios.com.

Just before you get to the Puerto Morelos turnoff, you'll pass **Rancho Loma Bonita,** which has all the markings of a tourist trap and offers horseback riding and ATV tours. You'll also come across **Jardín Botánico Dr. Alfredo Barrera** (no phone). Opened in 1990 and named after a biologist who studied tropical forests, the botanical garden is open Monday to Saturday from 9am to 5pm. Admission is $7. This place is disappointing because it's not being maintained well. It will be of most interest to gardeners and plant enthusiasts, but I'm afraid it will bore children. They are much more likely to enjoy the interactive zoo at CrocoCun (see "Exploring in & around Puerto Morelos," below).

**BEACH CABANAS**    Five kilometers (3 miles) north of Playa are some economical lodgings on a mostly rocky beach. A sign that says PUNTA BETE marks the access road to Xcalacoco; in a short time you arrive at the water. Before you do, the road forks off in a few places, and you'll see signs for different cabanas. The word conjures up visions of idyllic native-style dwellings with thatched roofs, but as often as not on the Yucatecan coast, it means simple lodging. This is mostly the case here, with rates running $45 to $60 a night for two people. Of the four groupings of cabanas in Xcalacoco, the one I like best is **Coco's Cabañas** (for reservations © 998/874-7056; for info see www.travel-center.com). It's a grouping of a handful of rooms with electricity and ceiling fans; a good, inexpensive little restaurant; and a small pool. Two of the rooms have air-conditioning. Next door is Ikal del Mar, a spa resort (see "Spa Resorts Near Puerto Morelos," below).

A few minutes after passing Xcalacoco/Punta Bete, you'll see a large sign on the right side of the road marking the entrance to La Posada del Capitán Lafitte.

**La Posada del Capitán Lafitte** ✦✦   Two kilometers (1¼ miles) from the highway, down an unpaved road, this lovely seaside retreat sits on a solitary stretch of sandy beach. I like this hotel for its simplicity and seclusion. You can enjoy relative isolation while still having all the amenities of a relaxing vacation. The beach is powdery white sand with a rocky bottom below the water. The two-story white-stucco bungalows hold four rooms each. Rooms are medium-size and comfortable, with tile floors and bathrooms, either two double beds or one king-size bed, and an oceanfront porch. Service is personal and attentive. Twenty-nine bungalows have air-conditioning; the rest have fans.

Carretera Cancún–Tulum Km 62, 77710 Playa del Carmen, Q. Roo. ✆ **800/538-6802** in the U.S. and Canada, or 984/873-0214. Fax 984/873-0212. www.mexicoholiday.com. 57 units. High season $220–$270 double; low season $140–$170 double. Christmas and New Year's rates are higher. Minimum 2–4 nights. Rates include breakfast and dinner. MC, V. Free guarded parking. **Amenities:** Restaurant; poolside grill; bar; midsize outdoor pool; watersports equipment; dive shop; activities desk; car rental; limited room service; laundry service. *In room:* A/C (in some), minibar.

## PUERTO MORELOS

Puerto Morelos remains a quiet place—perfect for a relaxed vacation of lying on the white-sand beach and reading, with perhaps the occasional foray into watersports, especially snorkeling, diving, kitesurfing, windsurfing, and kayaking. Offshore lies a prominent reef, which has been declared a national park for its protection. It's shallow and makes for easy snorkeling, and it protects the coast from storm surges. The beaches are great and are maintained by the local government. The water is shallow, calm, and clear, with seagrass growing on the bottom. The town has a good bit of community spirit and a relaxed feel. There is a large English-language new and used bookstore that stocks 20,000 titles that you might want to check out if you forgot to bring your reading material. The ferry that used to depart from here for Cozumel has moved down the coast to the Calica pier just south of Playa del Carmen.

### ESSENTIALS

**GETTING THERE   By Car**   At Km 31 there's a traffic light at the intersection, and a large sign pointing to Puerto Morelos.

**By Bus**   Buses from Cancún to Tulum and Playa del Carmen usually stop here, but be sure to ask in Cancún if your bus makes the Puerto Morelos stop.

### EXPLORING IN & AROUND PUERTO MORELOS

Puerto Morelos attracts visitors who seek seaside relaxation without crowds and high prices. The town has several hotels and a few restaurants. For outdoor recreation, there are two dive shops and plenty of recreational boats for fishing or snorkeling. On the main square, you'll find the bookstore, **Alma Libre** (✆ **998/871-0713;** www.alma librebooks.com). It has more English-language books than any other in the Yucatán, and not just whodunits, sci-fi, and spy novels. The owners, a couple of Canadians named Joanne and Rob Birce, stock everything from volumes on Maya culture to English classics to maps of the region. The store is open October through the first week in June, Tuesday to Sunday 10am to 3pm and 6 to 9pm.

On the ocean side of the main square is **Mystic Divers** (©/fax **998/871-0634;** www.mysticdiving.com). It's well recommended, not only for diving but for fishing trips, too. The owner, Victor Reyes, speaks English and takes small groups. He is a PADI and NAUI instructor and gives his customers a lot of personal attention. The shop is open all year. The reef directly offshore is very shallow and is protected by law. Snorkelers are required to wear a life vest to prevent them from diving down to the reef. I'm unaccustomed to snorkeling in a vest and found it a bit bothersome, but it didn't prevent me from getting a close look at the reef, which is quite shallow—3m (10 ft.) at its deepest, rising to within a foot of the surface. In a short time, I spotted four different eels and sea snakes, lots of fish, and a ray.

Just north of Puerto Morelos is **CrococCun** (© **998/850-3719**), a zoological park that raises crocodiles. It's a lot more than just your average roadside attraction. There's an interactive zoo with crocodiles in all stages of development, as well as animals of nearly all the species that once roamed the Yucatán Peninsula. A visit to the new reptile house is fascinating, though it may make you think twice about venturing into the jungle. The rattlesnakes and boa constrictors are particularly intimidating, and the tarantulas are downright enormous. The guided tour lasts 1½ hours. Children enjoy the guides' enthusiasm and are entranced by the spider monkeys and wild pigs. Wear plenty of bug repellent. The restaurant sells refreshments. CrococCun is open daily from 8:30am to 5:30pm. As with other attractions along this coast, entrance fees are high: $18 adults, $12 children 6 to 12, free for children under 6. The park is at Km 30 on Highway 307.

## WHERE TO STAY

Hurricane Wilma did a good bit of damage to Puerto Morelos and the surrounding area. Some beachfront condos were destroyed and several hotels were damaged. For vacation rentals, check out the website of Alma Libre books (www.almalibrebooks.com).

**Amar Inn** Simple, rustic rooms on the beach, in a home-style setting, make this small inn a good place for those wanting a quiet seaside retreat. The cordial hostess, Ana Luisa Aguilar, is the daughter of Luis Aguilar, a Mexican singer and movie star of the 1940s and 1950s. She keeps busy promoting environmental and equitable-development causes. She can line up snorkeling and fishing trips and jungle tours for guests with local operators. There are three cabanas in back, opposite the main house, and six upstairs rooms with views of the beach. The best is a third-story room with a great view of the ocean. The cabanas get less of a cross-breeze than the rooms in the main house but still have plenty of ventilation. They are large and come with kitchenettes. Rooms in the main building are medium to large. Bedding choices include one or two doubles, one king-size, or five twin beds. Most of the mattresses were replaced after the hurricane with newer, cushier ones. A full Mexican breakfast is served in the garden.

Av. Javier Rojo Gómez (at Lázaro Cárdenas), 77580 Puerto Morelos, Q. Roo. © **998/871-0026.** amar_inn@hotmail.com. 9 units. High season $60–$75 double; low season $50–$60 double. Rates include full breakfast. No credit cards. From the plaza, turn left; it's 1km (½ mile) down, past the Hotel Ojo de Agua. **Amenities:** Tour and rental info. *In room:* Fridge, fan, no phone.

**Hotel Ojo de Agua** ⚓ *Value* What I like best about this hotel is that it offers the convenience and service of a higher-priced hotel, including a good dive shop and watersports instruction and equipment rental. Two three-story buildings stand on the beach at a right angle to each other. The simply furnished rooms have balconies or terraces;

most have a view of the ocean. Standard rooms have one queen-size bed (again, new mattresses). Deluxe rooms are large and have two doubles. Studios have a double and two twins and a small kitchenette but no air-conditioning (the rest of the rooms do have air-conditioning). Some rooms come with TV and phone. If you've wanted to try windsurfing or kitesurfing, this is a good place: The American who rents the boards takes his time with customers and is quite helpful.

Av. Javier Rojo Gómez, Supermanzana 2, Lote 16. 77580 Puerto Morelos, Q. Roo. (C) 998/871-0027 or -0507. Fax 998/871-0202. www.ojo-de-agua.com. 36 units. High season $60 double, $65–$75 studio or deluxe; low season $50 double, $55–$60 studio or deluxe. Weekly and monthly rates available. AE, MC, V. **Amenities:** Restaurant; bar; outdoor pool; watersports equipment; scuba shop; tour info; room service until 10pm. *In room:* A/C (in some), TV (in some), kitchenette (in some), no phone (in some).

## WHERE TO DINE

Puerto Morelos has a few restaurants. Most are on or around the main square and include **Los Pelícanos** for seafood; **Hola Asia** for Asian food; and **Le Café d'Amancia** for coffee and pastries. A couple of blocks away is a German and seafood place called **Bodo's.** It has a good lunch special and a good menu. The most expensive restaurant in town is **John Grey's,** which is a couple of blocks north of the plaza and about 3 blocks inland. It's open for dinner except on Sundays. The owner is a former chef for the Ritz-Carlton, and I've enjoyed his cooking.

## SPA RESORTS NEAR PUERTO MORELOS ★★★

In the area around Puerto Morelos, four spa resorts offer different versions of the hedonistic resort experience. Only 20 to 30 minutes from the Cancún airport, they are well situated for a quick weekend escape from the daily grind. You can jet down to Cancún, get whisked away by the hotel car, and be on the beach with a cocktail in hand before you can figure out whether you crossed a time zone. All four resorts pride themselves on their service, amenities, and spa and salon treatments. Being in the Yucatán, they like to add the healing practices of the Maya, especially the use of the native steam bath called *temazcal.* Rates quoted below include taxes but not the 5%-to-10% service charge. All of these hotels were affected to a greater or lesser degree by Hurricane Wilma. From what I've seen the buildings have been repaired and remodeled, but the vegetation was also affected. Fortunately, things grow back fast in the Tropics.

**Ceiba del Mar**    This resort, the largest of the four, was still closed when I was on the coast. It's scheduled to reopen in August. The Ceiba del Mar is made up of several three-story buildings, each with a rooftop terrace with Jacuzzi. Rooms will be completely remodeled. They are large and have a terrace or balcony. The bathtub area can be opened up to the entire room. Service, when I was there, was attentive and unobtrusive, as exemplified by the delivery of coffee and juice each morning, accomplished without disturbing the guests through the use of a blind pass-through. Check the website for updates.

Av. Niños Héroes s/n, 77580 Puerto Morelos, Q. Roo. (C) 877/545-6221 in the U.S., or 998/872-8060. Fax 998/872-8061. www.ceibadelmar.com. 90 units. High season $450–$550 deluxe and junior suite, from $850 suite; low season $415–$470 deluxe and junior suite, from $800 suite. Rates include continental breakfast. Spa packages available. AE, MC, V. Free parking. **Amenities:** 2 restaurants; 2 bars; 2 outdoor pools; lighted tennis court; complete state-of-the-art gym w/sauna, steam room, whirlpool, and Swiss showers; spa offering a wide variety of treatments; 8 rooftop Jacuzzis; dive shop w/watersports equipment; bikes for guests' use; concierge; tour info; car rental; salon; 24-hr. room service; babysitting; laundry service; nonsmoking rooms. *In room:* A/C, TV/VCR, CD player, high-speed wireless Internet, minibar, hair dryer, safe.

**Ikal del Mar**   The smallest and most private of the four resorts in this section, Ikal has 30 well-separated bungalows, each with its own piece of jungle, a little pool, and an outdoor shower. The bungalows are large, filled with amenities, and decorated in a modern, simple style. The bathrooms have only a shower. Service here is the most personal of the four—the numerous staff will do just about anything for you. A bar and restaurant (with excellent food) overlooking an inviting pool make for an attractive common area. If there's a drawback, it's the beach, which is rockier than the beaches of the other three. The same company now manages a small hotel-spa in Xpu-Ha called **Esencia** (✆ **984/873-4830;** www.hotelesencia.com). It's a more conventional property with a variety of room categories, which start at $625/night for high season.

Playa Xcalacoco, Carretera Cancún–Tulum, 77710 Q. Roo. ✆ **888/230-7330** in the U.S. and Canada, or 984/877-3000. Fax 713/528-3697. www.ikaldelmar.com. 30 units. High season $700–$800 double; low season $650 double. Rates include full breakfast. AE, MC, V. Free secure parking. Children under 18 not accepted. **Amenities:** Restaurant; 2 bars; large outdoor pool; spa; 2 Jacuzzis; steam bath; watersports equipment; concierge; tour info; car rental; courtesy shuttle to Playa; salon; 24-hr. room service; in-room massage; laundry service. *In room:* A/C, TV/DVD, fridge, hair dryer, safe.

**Maroma**   My personal favorite, this resort has been around the longest, owns a large parcel of land inland that it protects from development, and has a gorgeous beach and beautifully manicured grounds. Two- and three-story buildings contain the large guest rooms; most have king-size beds. While it is not the retreat into the jungle that Ikal is, my two most vivid memories of the place are the sound of the sea breeze rustling the lush palm trees, and the sight of a pair of toucans—most uncommon on this coast. I also have a fond memory of the beach bar, which was washed away by the hurricane, but I've been told they've rebuilt it. I could do without the staff dressing in native peasant garb, but it seems okay with them. As at Ikal, the smaller size makes for more personal service and a deeper sense of escape.

Carretera 307 Km 51, 77710 Q. Roo. ✆ **866/454-9351** in the U.S., or 998/872-8200. Fax 998/872-8220. www.maromahotel.com. 61 units. $480 garden-view double; $540–$740 premium or deluxe double; $770–$850 oceanfront double; from $940 suite. Rates include ground transfer, full breakfast, snorkeling tour. AE, MC, V. Free valet parking. No children under 16 allowed. **Amenities:** Restaurant; 3 bars; 3 outdoor spring-fed pools; fitness center; spa; Jacuzzi; steam bath; watersports equipment rental; game room; concierge; tours; car rental; salon; room service until 11pm; in-room massage; laundry service; dry cleaning. *In room:* A/C, hair dryer.

**Paraíso de la Bonita**   This resort has the most elaborate spa of all. I'm not a spa-goer and cannot discuss the relative merits of different treatments, but my work takes me to plenty of spas, and this one, which operates under the French system of thalasso-therapy, is beyond anything I've seen. It uses seawater, sea salts, and sea algae in its treatments. I was impressed just in viewing the different apparatuses. The beach is lovely and open. The pool area and the common areas of the spa are uncommonly attractive. The rooms occupy some unremarkable three-story buildings. They are, in decor and furnishings, more impressive than the rooms of the others. The ground-floor rooms have a plunge pool; upstairs rooms come with a balcony. This resort was still closed for remodeling when I was last on the coast.

Carretera Cancún–Chetumal Km 328, Bahía Petenpich, 77710 Q. Roo. ✆ **866/751-9175** in the U.S., or 998/872-8300. Fax 998/872-8301. www.paraisodelabonita.com. 90 units. High season from $785 suite, from $1,338 2-bedroom suite; low season from $670 suite, from $1,225 2-bedroom suite. Rates include ground transfer. AE, MC, V. Free valet parking. No children under 12 allowed. **Amenities:** 2 restaurants; 2 bars; 4 outdoor pools; 1 lighted tennis court; spa; 2 Jacuzzis; watersports equipment rental; concierge; tour info; rental cars; salon; 24-hr. room service; in-room massage; laundry service; dry cleaning; nonsmoking rooms. *In room:* A/C, TV/DVD, dataport, minibar, hair dryer, safe.

## 3 South of Playa del Carmen

South of Playa del Carmen you'll find a succession of small communities and resorts and two nature parks. From north to south, this section covers them in the following order: Xcaret, Paamul, Puerto Aventuras, Xpu-Ha, Akumal, Xel-Ha, Punta Solimán, and Tankah. This section spans about 56km (35 miles).

**HEADING SOUTH FROM PLAYA DEL CARMEN**    Renting a car is the best way to move around down here. Southbound buses depart regularly from Playa, but the best they might do is get you close to your destination. And from the highway it can be a hot walk to the coast. Another option is to hire a car and driver.

Beyond Paamul, you'll see signs for this or that *cenote* or cave. There are thousands of *cenotes* in the Yucatán, and each is slightly different. These turnoffs are less visited than the major attractions and can make for a pleasant visit. Two major attractions bear specific mention: **Hidden Worlds,** offering remarkable snorkeling and diving tours of a couple of *cenotes,* and **Aktun Chen** cavern with a small nature park. Both are south of Akumal and described later in this chapter.

### XCARET: A PARK CELEBRATING THE YUCATAN

A billboard in the airport of faraway Guadalajara reads in Spanish "And when visiting Xcaret, don't forget to enjoy the pleasures of the Riviera Maya, too." An exaggeration, but its point is well taken: Xcaret (pronounced "Eesh-ca-*ret*") is the biggest attraction in these parts and is practically a destination unto itself. It even has its own resort (not recommended). If you're coming to these shores to avoid crowds, avoid this place. If you're here for entertainment and activities, you should consider visiting Xcaret. What Xcaret does, it does very well, and that is to present in one package a little bit of everything that the Yucatán (and the rest of Mexico for that matter) has to offer.

Think of the activities that people come to the Yucatán for: hanging out on the beach, scuba and snorkeling, cavern diving, visiting ruins, taking a siesta in a hammock under a grove of palm trees, hiking through tropical forest, meeting native Maya peoples—Xcaret has all that plus handicraft exhibitions, a bat cave, a butterfly pavilion, mushroom and orchid nurseries, and lots of wildlife on display (the park has several conservation programs for endangered species), native jaguars, manatees, sea turtles, monkeys, macaws, flamingos, and a petting aquarium. Children love it. What probably receives most of the comments is the underground river (a natural feature of the park and common in much of the Yucatán) that's been opened in places to allow snorkelers to paddle along with the current. What else? A number of tours and shows, including *charros* (Mexican cowboys) from the state of Jalisco, and the Totonac Indian *voladores* ("flyers" who do a daring pole dance high above the ground) from the state of Veracruz.

The park is famous for its evening spectacle that is a celebration of the Mexican nation. I've seen it and have to say that it is some show, with a large cast and lots of props. It starts with the Maya and an interpretation of how they may have played the pre-Hispanic game/ritual known as *pok-ta-pok,* and then to another version of a ball-game still practiced in the western state of Michoacán. From there it moves on to the arrival of the Spanish and eventually to the forging of the new nation, its customs, its dress, and its music and dance.

Xcaret is 10km (6½ miles) south of Playa del Carmen (you'll know when you get to the turnoff). It's open daily from 8:30am to 9pm. Admission prices are $59 for adults,

$41 for children 5 to 12. Certain activities cost extra: horseback ride $30, snuba/ sea trek/snorkel tour $45, scuba $50 to $75, swimming with dolphins $115. Other costs: lockers $2 per day, snorkel equipment $10 per day, food and drink variable. The park is an all-day affair; it's best to arrive early and register for tours and activities as soon as you can. For more info call © 998/883-3143 or visit www.xcaret.net.

Four kilometers (2½ miles) south of the entrance to Xcaret is the turnoff for **Puerto Calica,** the cruise-ship pier. Passengers disembark here for tours of Playa, Xcaret, the ruins, and other attractions on the coast.

Here's a tip: Fewer ships arrive on weekends than on weekdays, which makes the weekend a good time for visiting the major attractions on this coast.

## PAAMUL: SEASIDE GETAWAY
About 15km (10 miles) beyond Xcaret and 25km (15 miles) from Playa del Carmen is Paamul, which in Mayan means "a destroyed ruin." The exit is clearly marked. At Paamul (also written Pamul), you can enjoy the Caribbean with relative quiet; the water at the out-of-the-way beach is wonderful, but the shoreline is rocky. There are six rooms for rent, a restaurant, and many trailer and RV lots with hookups.

There's also a dive shop. **Scubamex** (© 984/873-0667; fax 984/874-1729; www. scubamex.com) is a fully equipped PADI-, NAUI-, and SSI-certified dive shop next to the cabanas. Using two boats, the staff takes guests on dives 8km (5 miles) in either direction. If it's too choppy, the reefs in front of the hotel are also good. The cost for a two-tank dive is $45, plus $25 to rent gear. Snorkeling is also excellent in this protected bay and the one next to it. The shop offers a great 3-hour snorkeling trip ($25).

### WHERE TO STAY & DINE
**Cabañas Paamul** ✿ Hurricane Emily destroyed the cabanas that used to be here, and the owner, instead of replacing them, decided to go upscale. When I visited, he was building four to six units in a two-story building right on the water's edge. The units should be completed by November 2006. From what I could see, they will be large and have air-conditioning and a kitchenette. They'll also have balconies with a view of the bay. I was told that they will go for $120 per night double occupancy. The trailer park survived, but I could still see the remains of a few trailers. Trailer guests have access to 12 showers and separate bathrooms for men and women. Laundry service is available nearby. The large, breezy *palapa* restaurant is a Brazilian-style grill under the management of Kalú da Silva, a retired Brazilian soccer player, who closed his restaurant in León, Guanajuato, to live on the coast. Restaurant customers are welcome to use the beach.

Carretera Cancún–Tulum Km 85. © 984/875-1053. paamulmx@yahoo.com. 4 units; 190 trailer spaces (all with full hookups). $120 double. Ask about discount for stays longer than 1 week. RV space with hookups $25 per day, $500 per month. No credit cards. **Amenities:** Restaurant; bar. *In room:* A/C, kitchenette.

## PUERTO AVENTURAS: A RESORT COMMUNITY
Five kilometers (3 miles) south of Paamul and 104km (65 miles) from Cancún is the glitzy development of Puerto Aventuras, on Chakalal Bay. It's a condo-marina community with a 9-hole golf course. At the center of the development is a collection of restaurants bordering a dolphin pool. They offer a variety of food—Mexican, Italian, steaks, even a popular pub. The major attraction is the dolphins. To swim with them in a highly interactive program, you must make reservations by contacting **Dolphin Discovery** (© 998/849-4757; www.dolphindiscovery.com). Make reservations well

---

**Tips   In Case of Emergency**

The Riviera Maya south of Puerto Aventuras is susceptible to power failures that can last for hours. Gas pumps and cash machines shut down when this happens, and once the power returns, they attract long lines. It's a good idea to keep a reserve of gas and cash.

---

in advance—the surest way is by e-mail to salesinternet@dolphindiscovery.com.mx or through the link on the website. A 1-hour session costs $125. There are shorter programs for less.

This is also the place to come for boating and deep-sea fishing. I recommend **Captain Rick's Sportfishing Center** (© **984/873-5195** or -5387; www.fishyucatan. com). The best fishing on this coast is from March to August. The captain will be happy to combine a fishing trip with some snorkeling, which makes for a leisurely day.

I don't find Puerto Aventuras to be an interesting place for lodging and prefer to stay elsewhere on the coast. It's like a mini Cancún, but lacking Cancún's vibrancy. There are a couple of fancy hotels. The main one is the **Omni Puerto Aventuras** (© **800/843-6664** in the U.S., or 984/873-5101). It looks larger than its 30 rooms would indicate and was probably intended to be bigger but didn't get the expected traffic.

## XPU-HA: BEAUTIFUL BEACH

Three kilometers (2 miles) beyond Puerto Aventuras is **Xpu-Ha** (Eesh-poo-*hah*) ✹✹✹, a wide bay lined by a broad, beautiful sandy beach. Much of the bay is taken up by private houses and condos. There are a few all-inclusive resorts. One is **Xpu-Ha Palace** and another is the **Copacabana.** These suffered great damage with Hurricane Emily, but they will have remodeled and reopened by the time this book goes on sale. The beach is big enough to accommodate the hotel guests, residents and day-trippers without feeling crowded.

Also on the beach are a few small hotels. Two of these are expensive: **Al Cielo** (© **984/ 840-9012;** www.alcielohotel.com) and **Esencia** (© **984/873-4830;** www.hotelesencia. com). They are lovely places that offer personal service and attractive rooms away from the crowds. Both are close to Xpu-Ha Palace. And there are a few simple hotels offering basic lodging—a couple of beds, a cement floor, small private bathroom, and minimum decoration. These are rented on a first-come, first-served basis. Rates vary from $40 to $70 a night, depending upon how busy they are. Lodging options are better in nearby Akumal, and, if you're renting a car, you can come for the day to enjoy the beach.

## AKUMAL: BEAUTIFUL BAYS & CAVERN DIVING

Continuing south on Highway 307 for 2km (1¼ miles), you'll come to the turnoff for Akumal, marked by a traffic light. This is a small, ecologically oriented community built on the shores of two beautiful bays. Akumal has been around long enough that it feels more relaxed than booming places such as Playa and Tulum, and lodging tends to go for less here. Akumal draws a lot of families, who can save money by renting a unit with a kitchen to fix meals. Less than 1km (½ mile) down the road is a white arch. Just before it are a couple of grocery stores (the one named Super Chomak has an ATM) and a laundry service. Just after it (to the right) is the Club Akumal Caribe/Hotel Villas Maya. If you follow the road to the left and keep to the left, you'll come to Half Moon Bay, lined with two- and three-story condos, and eventually to Yal-ku Lagoon, which is a snorkeling park. For renting a condo, contact **Info-Akumal** (✆ 800/381-7048 in the U.S.; www.info-akumal.com), (**Akumal Vacations** (✆ 800/448-7137 in the U.S.; www. akumalvacations.com), or **Loco Gringo** (www.locogringo.com).

Both bays have sandy beaches with rocky or silt bottoms. If you want a real sandy beach, you can drive to Tulum or Xpu-Ha. But if you want to dive, this is the place. There are three dive shops in town and at least 30 dive sites offshore. The **Akumal Dive Shop** (✆ 984/875-9032; www.akumal.com), one of the oldest and best dive shops on the coast, offers courses in technical diving and cavern diving trips. It and **Akumal Dive Adventures** (✆ 984/875-9157), at the Vista del Mar hotel on Half Moon Bay, offer resort courses as well as complete certification. The operator of Akumal Dive Adventures is an American who is competent and personable. He took me to one of his favorite dive sites, where we had some close encounters with a couple of nursing sharks, a ray, and a turtle.

**Yal-ku Lagoon** is a park that is like a miniature and more primitive Xel-Ha. It's open daily from 8am to 5:30pm. Admission is $7 for adults, $4 for children 3 to 14. The lagoon is about 700m (2,296 ft.) long and about 200m (656 ft.) at its widest. You can paddle around comfortably in sheltered water with little current and see fish and a few other creatures. It makes for a relaxing outing, but for sheer variety, I prefer snorkeling along the reefs.

## WHERE TO STAY

Rates below are for two people and include taxes. Most hotels and condo rentals charge higher rates for the holidays than those listed here.

### Club Akumal Caribe/Hotel Villas Maya Club 🖈🖈 *Kids*    The hotel rooms and garden bungalows of this hotel sit along Akumal Bay. Both are large and comfortable, with tile floors and good-size bathrooms. The 40 **Villas Maya Bungalows** are simply and comfortably furnished and have kitchenettes. The 21 rooms in the three-story beachside **hotel** are more elaborately furnished and come with refrigerators. They have a king-size bed or two queen-size beds, tile floors, and Mexican accents. There is a large pool on the grounds. Other rooms belonging to the hotel are condos and the lovely **Villas Flamingo** on Half Moon Bay. The villas have two or three bedrooms and large living, dining, and kitchen areas, as well as lovely furnished patios just steps from the beach. The four villas share a pool.

Carretera Cancún–Tulum (Hwy. 307) Km 104. ✆ 984/875-9010. www.hotelakumalcaribe.com. (Reservations: P.O. Box 13326, El Paso, TX 79913. ✆ 800/351-1622 in the U.S., 800/343-1440 in Canada, or 915/584-3552.) 70 units. High season $110 bungalow, $140 hotel room, $200–$500 villa or condo; low season $66 bungalow, $84 hotel room, $130–$245 villa or condo. Reservations with prepayment by check only. Low-season packages available. AE, MC, V. Free parking. **Amenities:** 2 restaurants; bar; large outdoor pool; tour desk; children's activities (seasonal); in-room massage; babysitting; dive shop. *In room:* A/C, kitchenette (in some), fridge, coffeemaker, no phone.

### Vista del Mar Hotel and Condos 🖈 *Value*    This beachside property is a great place to stay for several reasons. It offers hotel rooms at good prices, and large, fully equipped condos that you don't have to rent by the week. The lovely, well-tended beach in front of the hotel has chairs and umbrellas. There's an on-site dive shop, which eliminates the hassle of organizing dive trips. Hotel rooms are small and contain either a queen-size bed or a double and a twin bed. They consist of a well-equipped kitchen, a living area, two or three bedrooms, and one or two bathrooms.

All have balconies or terraces facing the sea and are furnished with hammocks. Several rooms come with whirlpool tubs.

Half Moon Bay, 77760 Akumal, Q Roo. (*C*) 877/425-8625 in the U.S. Fax 505/988-3882. www.akumalinfo.com. 27 units. High season $90 double, $196–$280 condo; low season $73 double, $112–$162 condo. MC, V. **Amenities:** Restaurant; bar; small outdoor pool; watersports equipment rental; dive shop. *In room:* A/C, TV, CD player, kitchenette, fridge, coffeemaker, no phone.

## WHERE TO DINE

There are about 10 places to eat in Akumal, and a convenient grocery store, **Super Chomak,** by the archway. The **Turtle Bay Café and Bakery** is good (not open for supper in low season), as is **La Buena Vida,** on Half Moon Bay.

## XEL-HA: SNORKELING & SWIMMING ⋒⋒

Before you get to Xel-Ha (Shell-*hah*) nature park you'll pass the turnoff for **Aktun Chen** ⋒ cavern (a bit beyond Akumal). Of the several caverns that I've toured in the Yucatán, this is one of the best—it has lots of geological features, good lighting, several underground pools, and large chambers, all carefully preserved. The tour takes about an hour and requires a good amount of walking, but the footing is good. You exit not far from where you enter. There is also a zoo with specimens of the local fauna. Some of the critters are allowed to run about freely. In my opinion, the cost of admission is high—$17 for adults, $9 for children—but this is true of several attractions on this coast. The cavern is open 9am to 5pm daily. The turnoff is to the right, and the cave is about 4km (2½ miles) from the road.

Thirteen kilometers (8 miles) south of Akumal is **Xel-Ha** ((*C*) **998/884-9422** in Cancún, 984/873-3588 in Playa, or 984/875-6000 at the park; www.xelha.com.mx). The centerpiece of Xel-Ha is a large, beautiful lagoon where freshwater and saltwater meet. You can swim, float, and snorkel in beautifully clear water surrounded by jungle. A small train takes guests upriver to a drop-off point. There, you can store all your clothes and gear in a locked sack that is taken down to the locker rooms in the main part of the building. The water moves calmly toward the sea, and you can float along with it. Snorkeling here offers a higher comfort level than the open sea—there are no waves and currents to pull you about, but there are a lot of fish of several species, including rays.

Inside the park, you can rent snorkeling equipment and an underwater camera. Platforms allow nonsnorkelers to view the fish. Another way to view fish is to use the park's "snuba" gear—a contraption that allows you to breathe air through 6m (20-ft.) tubes connected to scuba tanks floating on the surface. It frees you of the cumbersome tank while allowing you to stay down without having to hold your breath. Rental costs $45 for approximately an hour. Like snuba but more involved is "sea-trek," a device consisting of an elaborate plastic helmet with air hoses. It allows you to walk around on the bottom breathing normally and perhaps participate in feeding the park's stingrays.

In the last year the park has completely remodeled and enlarged the dolphin area. This has improved experience of swimming with these intelligent, powerful creatures. A 1-hour swim costs $115 plus park admission. You can also participate in a program that includes transportation from most hotels in the Riviera Maya and takes you to the dolphin area. It includes locker and equipment, too, all for $139. Make reservations ((*C*) **998/887-6840**) at least 24 hours in advance.

Other attractions include a plant nursery, an apiary for the local, stingless Maya bees, and a lovely path through the tropical forest bordering the lagoon. Xel-Ha is open daily from 8:30am to 5pm. Parking is free. Admission is $33 adults, and $23 children ages 5 to 11; children under 5 enter free. Admission includes use of inner tubes, life vest, and shuttle train to the river, and the use of changing rooms and showers. (Though not listed on the Web page, the park often has discount admission during the weekend.) An all-inclusive option includes snorkeling equipment rental, locker rental, towels, food, and beverages. Adults can visit all week long for $59, and children visit for $41. These prices are not discounted on the weekend. The park has five restaurants, two ice-cream shops, and a store. It accepts American Express, MasterCard, and Visa, and has an ATM.

Signs clearly mark the turnoff to Xel-Ha. Xel-Ha is close to the ruins of Tulum. A popular day tour from Cancún or Playa combines the two. If you're traveling on your own, the best time to enjoy Xel-Ha without the crowds is during the weekend from 9am to 2pm.

About 2km (1 mile) south of Xel-Ha is the **Hidden Worlds Cenotes** ✦✦✦ (© 984/877-8535; www.hiddenworlds.com.mx), which offers an excellent opportunity to snorkel or dive in a couple of nearby caverns. The caverns are part of a vast network that makes up a single underground river system. The water is crystalline (and cold) and the rock formations impressive. These caverns were filmed for the IMAX production *Journey into Amazing Caves*. The people running the show are resourceful. The snorkel tour costs $40 and takes you to two different caverns (a half tour costs $25). The main form of transportation is "jungle mobile," with a guide who throws in tidbits of information and lore about the jungle plant life that you see. There is some walking involved, so take shoes or sandals. I've toured several caverns, but floating through one gave me an entirely different perspective. For divers, a one-tank dive is $50, a two-tank experience is $90. The owners have installed on the property a 180m (590-ft.) zip line. I haven't tried it, but it looks fast.

## PUNTA SOLIMAN & TANKAH BAYS

The next couple of turnoffs lead to Punta Solimán and Tankah bays. On Punta Solimán Bay is a beach restaurant called **Oscar y Lalo's.** Here you can rent kayaks and snorkel equipment and paddle out to the reefs for some snorkeling. Three kilometers (2 miles) farther is the turnoff for Tankah, where there are a handful of lodgings. The most interesting is **Casa Cenote** (© 998/874-5170; www.casacenote.com). It has an underground river that surfaces at a *cenote* in the back of the property then goes underground and bubbles up into the sea just a few feet offshore. Casa Cenote has seven rooms, all on the beach. The double rate is around $150. The American owner provides kayaks and snorkeling gear and can arrange dives, fishing trips, and sailing charters.

A beach road connects the two bays. I found the snorkeling in Tankah better than in Punta Solimán. Snorkeling in the latter was both interesting and frustrating. I've never before experienced so many thermoclines, which are produced by fresh water seeping from the floors of the bay and coming in contact with the warmer salt water. Light passing through the water is refracted in funny ways. At first I found the effect interesting—it lent an ethereal shininess to everything I was seeing—but then it just got annoying as it cut down sharply on visibility. At one point I was floating through some of the worst of it, trying not to stir up the water, when a giant silvery barracuda came ghostlike through the shimmering water and crossed my field of vision about 2m (6 ft.) away. As he passed slowly by me I was astonished at how beautiful and luminescent he looked. Still, I will take clear water over shimmering water every time.

## 4 Tulum ★★★, Punta Allen & Sian Ka'an

Tulum *pueblo* (130km/80 miles from Cancún) is a small town on Highway 307 where it intersects the road to Cobá. Nearby is an incredible beach, which has become the Tulum hotel zone—a collection of about 30 *palapa* hotels stretching from the Tulum ruins southward, along the Punta Allen Peninsula, all the way to the entrance to the Sian Ka'an Biopreserve. The Tulum ruins are a walled Maya city of the post-Classic age perched on a rocky cliff overlooking the Caribbean. Tulum beach used to be a destination for backpackers, but the *palapa* hotels have gone upscale, and the beach now attracts a well-heeled crowd that seeks to get away from the bustle of the big hotels and resorts. The town of Tulum has several modest hotels, more than a dozen restaurants, several stores and pharmacies, three cybercafes, a few dive shops, a bank, two cash machines, and a new bus station.

For those who really want to leave the modern world behind, there's the Punta Allen Peninsula. Getting to the end of the peninsula from Tulum can take 1½ to 3 hours, depending on the condition of the road. It's a quiet, out-of-the-way place; the generator (if there is one) shuts down at 10pm. For most people, Tulum will be far enough away from the crowds. But in Punta Allen you'll find great fishing and snorkeling, the natural riches of the Sian Ka'an Biosphere Reserve, and a chance to rest up at what truly feels like the end of the road. A few beach cabanas offer reliable power, telephones, and hot showers.

**ORIENTATION**    To visit the Tulum area, get a rental car; it will make everything much easier. Coming from the north you'll pass the entrance to the ruins before arriving at the town. You'll come to a highway intersection with a traffic light. To the right is the highway leading to the ruins of Cobá (see "Cobá Ruins," later in this chapter); to the left is the Tulum hotel zone, which begins about 2km (1½ miles) away. The road sign reads BOCA PAILA, which is a place halfway down the **Punta Allen Peninsula.** This road eventually goes all the way to the tip of the peninsula and the town of Punta Allen, a lobstering and fishing village. It is a rough road that is slow going for most of the way. A few kilometers down the road, you will enter the **Sian Ka'an Biosphere Reserve.**

The town of Tulum is growing quickly. It now extends for 3 or more blocks in either direction from the highway. The highway widens here and is called Avenida Tulum. It is lined with stores, restaurants, and the offices of service providers. One place that I find handy to visit is a travel agency/communications/package center

---

### *Tips* Getting to the Beach

If you're staying elsewhere but want some beach time in Tulum, the easiest thing to do is drive to El Paraiso Beach Club. It's about 1km (½ mile) south of the ruins. This is a great place—there's a long, broad beach that is pure sand, and access is free. The owners make money selling food and drink (there's a nice little beach bar) so they ask you not to bring your own. There are also some inexpensive cabanas for rent (to make reservations: elparaiso_tulum@hotmail.com). If you want a beach all to yourself, you can drive down the dirt road toward Punta Allen. After you pass the last of the beach hotels there are a couple of places where the beach comes into view. You can pull over and spread out your beach towel.

called **Savana** (© 984/871-2081) on the east side of Avenida Tulum between *calles* Orion and Beta. The staff speaks English for the most part and can answer questions about tours and calling home.

## EXPLORING THE TULUM ARCHAEOLOGICAL SITE

Thirteen kilometers (8 miles) south of Xel-Ha are the ruins of Tulum, a Maya fortress-city on a cliff above the sea. The ruins are open to visitors daily from 7am to 5pm in the winter, 8am to 6pm in the summer. It's always best to go early, before the crowds start showing up (around 9:30am). The entrance to the ruins is about a 5-minute walk from the archaeological site. There are artisans' stands, a bookstore, a museum, a restaurant, several large bathrooms, and a ticket booth. Admission fee to the ruins is $4. If you want to ride the shuttle from the visitor center to the ruins, it's another $1.50. Parking is $3. A video camera permit costs $4. Licensed guides have a stand next to the path to the ruins and charge $20 for a 45-minute tour in English, French, or Spanish for up to four persons. In some ways, they are like performers and will tailor their presentation to the responses they receive from you. Some will try to draw connections between the Maya and Western theology, and they will point out architectural details that you might otherwise miss.

By A.D. 900, the end of the Classic period, Maya civilization had begun its decline, and the large cities to the south were abandoned. Tulum is one of the small city-states that rose to fill the void. It came to prominence in the 13th century as a seaport, controlling maritime commerce along this section of the coast, and remained inhabited

---

*Fun Fact* **Tulum: A Friendly Difference of Opinion**

Two of us cover the entirety of Mexico for Frommer's, and almost without exception we agree on the country's top destinations. However, we have an ongoing dialogue regarding the relative merits and beauty of the ruins at Tulum. Herewith we present our respective cases, and leave it for you to decide with whom you agree.

**Lynne says:** Ancient Tulum is my favorite of all the ruins, poised as it is on a rocky hill overlooking the transparent, turquoise Caribbean. It's not the largest or most important of the Maya ruins in this area, but it's the only one by the sea, which makes it the most visually impressive. Intriguing carvings and reliefs decorate the well-preserved structures, which date from the 12th to 16th centuries A.D., in the post-Classic period.

**David says:** Aside from the spectacular setting, Tulum is not as impressive a city as Chichén Itzá, Uxmal, or Ek Balam (see chapter 7). The stonework is cruder than that at these other sites, as if construction of the platforms and temples had been hurried. The city's builders were concerned foremost with security and defense. They chose the most rugged section on this coast and then built stout walls on the other three sides. This must have absorbed a tremendous amount of energy that might otherwise have been used to build the large ceremonial centers and more varied architecture that we see in other sites in the Yucatán.

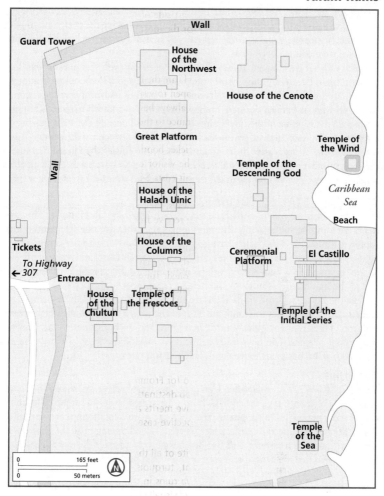

well after the arrival of the Spanish. The primary god here was the diving god, depicted on several buildings as an upside-down figure above doorways. Seen at the Palace at Sayil and Cobá, this curious, almost comical figure is also known as the bee god.

The most imposing building in Tulum is a large stone structure above the cliff called the **Castillo** (castle). Actually a temple as well as a fortress, it was once covered with stucco and painted. In front of the Castillo are several unrestored palacelike buildings partially covered with stucco. On the **beach** below, where the Maya once came ashore, tourists swim and sunbathe, combining a visit to the ruins with a dip in the Caribbean.

The **Temple of the Frescoes,** directly in front of the Castillo, contains interesting 13th-century wall paintings, though entrance is no longer permitted. Distinctly Maya, they represent the rain god Chaac and Ixchel, the goddess of weaving, women, the moon, and medicine. On the cornice of this temple is a relief of the head of the rain god. If you pause a slight distance from the building, you'll see the eyes, nose, mouth, and chin. Notice the remains of the red-painted stucco—at one time all the buildings at Tulum were painted bright red.

Much of what we know of Tulum at the time of the Spanish Conquest comes from the writings of Diego de Landa, third bishop of the Yucatán. He wrote that Tulum was a small city inhabited by about 600 people who lived in platform dwellings along a street and who supervised the trade traffic from Honduras to the Yucatán. Though it was a walled city, most of the inhabitants probably lived outside the walls, leaving the interior for the residences of governors and priests and ceremonial structures. Tulum survived about 70 years after the conquest, when it was finally abandoned. Because of the great number of visitors this site receives, it is no longer possible to climb all of the ruins. In many cases, visitors are asked to remain behind roped-off areas to view them.

## WHERE TO STAY IN TULUM

If you can afford staying at one of the small beach hotels in Tulum, do so. The experience is enjoyable and relaxing. But most are on the expensive side. Demand is high, supply is limited, and the hotels have to generate their own electricity (bring a flashlight). Most of the inexpensive hotels are not that comfortable, and some aren't even secure. If you're on a budget, you will be more comfortable staying in Akumal or in one of the modest hotels in town and being a day-tripper to the beach.

Take the Boca Paila road from Highway 307. Three kilometers (2 miles) ahead, you come to a T-junction. To the south are most of the *palapa* hotels; to the north are several, too. The pavement quickly turns into sand, and on both sides of the road you start seeing cabanas. The rates listed below don't include the week of Christmas and New Year, when prices go above regular high season rates.

### Expensive

**Ana y José** 🏖🏖   This *palapa* hotel has gone "boutique" with a spa, suites, and serious remodeling of rooms. It's a far cry now from what it used to be—a simple collection of cabins and a restaurant on the beach. Now there are marble countertops and marble tile floors. Rooms are large and comfortable. There's air-conditioning in all the lower rooms that don't catch the sea breeze. The two beachfront rock cabins at the front of the property have remained unchanged and are a little lower in price than the oceanview rooms. And this beach is excellent. Ana y José is 6.5km (4 miles) south of the Tulum ruins.

Carretera Punta Allen Km 7 (Apdo. Postal 15), 77780 Tulum, Q. Roo. ✆ **998/887-5470.** Fax 998/887-5469. www.anayjose.com. 22 units. $165–$200 garden and pool view; $230–$260 beachfront and oceanview; $245–$325 suite. AE, MC, V. Free parking. **Amenities:** Restaurant; outdoor pool; spa; tour info; car rental. *In room:* No phone.

**Azulik** 🏖🏖   Azulik is all about slowing down, leaving civilization behind (except for niceties like indoor plumbing and room service), and enjoying the simple life (with or without clothes). I enjoyed the simple life during an all-too-brief stay here, and what I liked most about Azulik was the design and positioning of the individual cabanas. All but three of them sit on a stone ledge next to, and a little above, the sea. The ledge is just high enough to provide privacy while you sit out on the semi-shaded wood deck in front of your cabana enjoying either the sun or the stars. For that purpose they come with chairs, hammocks, and a wooden tub for soaking. (There is a larger wooden tub indoors for bathing.) Each cabana is constructed entirely of wood, glass, and thatch. There is no electricity, only candles. Each has a king-size bed with mosquito netting, and a queen-size bed suspended on ropes for lounging during the day. This property shares a good restaurant and a good spa with a sister hotel.

Carretera Boca Paila Km 5.5, 77780 Tulum, Q. Roo. ℂ 877/532-6737 in the U.S. and Canada. www.azulik.com. 15 units. High season $240–$260 double; low season $190–$210 double. MC, V. Limited parking. Children under 18 not accepted. **Amenities:** Restaurant; bar; spa; limited room service. *In room:* Safe, no phone.

**Sueños Tulum** ℱ   Fronting a pure white-sand beach are five buildings of two and three stories. The rooms are a departure from the usual square floor plan; they have interesting angles and architectural layouts with stone, stucco, and wood surfaces. They are large and comfortable and, except for the two ground-floor beach suites, they each come with a small balcony. The hotel has a small restaurant for guests only, serving Mexican home cooking.

Carretera Tulum-Boca Paila Km 9.5, 77780 Tulum, Q. Roo. ℂ 984/877-2152. wwwsuenostulum.com. 12 units. High season $157–$202 beach and junior suite, $250 master suite; low season $112–$157 beach and junior suite, $202 master suite. 3-night minimum stay. Continental breakfast included. No credit cards. **Amenities:** Restaurant; outdoor pool. *In room:* Safe, no phone.

## Moderate
**Dos Ceibas** ℱ   Of all the places along this coast, this one reminds me the most of the way hotels in Tulum used to be. Simple, quiet, and ecological without being pretentious. This is a good choice for a no-fuss beach vacation. The one- and two-story cottages are spread out through the vegetation. Rooms are simply furnished and come with ceiling fans, and almost all have private patios or porches. Price varies according to the size of the rooms. The grounds are well tended. The electricity is solar generated and comes on at 6pm. There is a pure sand beach.

Carretera Tulum-Boca Paila Km 10, 77780 Tulum, Q. Roo. ℂ 984/877-6024. www.dosceibas.com. 8 units. High season $70–$150 double; low season $60–$135 double. MC, V. **Amenities:** Restaurant; massage; yoga classes. *In room:* No phone.

**Zamas** ℱℱ   The owners of these cabanas, a couple from San Francisco, have made their rustic getaway most enjoyable by concentrating on the essentials: comfort, privacy, and good food. The cabanas are simple, attractive, well situated for catching the breeze, and not too close together. Most rooms are in individual structures; the suites and oversize rooms are in modest two-story buildings. For the money, I like the individual garden *palapas,* which are attractive, spacious, and comfortable, and come with a queen-size bed and a twin or a king-size and a queen-size. Two small beachfront cabanas with one queen-size bed go for a little less. The most expensive rooms are the upstairs oceanview units, which enjoy a large terrace and lots of sea breezes. They come with a king-size and a queen-size bed or two queen-size beds. The restaurant serves the freshest seafood—I've seen the owner actually flag down passing fishermen to buy their catch. A white-sand beach stretches between large rocky areas.

Carretera Punta Allen Km 5, 77780 Tulum, Q. Roo. ℂ 415/387-9806 in the U.S. www.zamas.com. 20 units. High season $105–$150 beachfront double, $110–$135 garden double, $180 oceanview double; low season $85–$95 beachfront double, $80–$115 garden double, $135 oceanview double. No credit cards. **Amenities:** Restaurant. *In room:* No phone.

## Inexpensive
**Cabañas Tulum**   Next to Ana y José is a row of cinder block facing the same beautiful ocean and beach. Rooms are simple and poorly lit, with basic bathrooms. All rooms have two double beds (most with new mattresses), screens on the windows, a

table, one electric light, and a porch facing the beach. Electricity is available from 7 to 11am and 5 to 11pm.

Carretera Punta Allen Km 7 (Apdo. Postal 63), 77780 Tulum, Q. Roo. © **984/879-7395.** Fax 984/871-2092. www.hotel stulum.com. 32 units. $50–$70 double. No credit cards. **Amenities:** Restaurant; game room. *In room:* No phone.

## WHERE TO DINE

There are several restaurants in the town of Tulum. They are reasonably priced and do an okay job. On the main street are **Charlie's** (© **984/871-2136**), my favorite for Mexican food, and **Don Cafeto's** (© **984/871-2207**). A good Italian-owned Italian restaurant, **Il Giardino** (© **984/804-1316;** closed Wed), is a block off the highway on the town's northernmost cross street, Satelite. Also in town are a couple of roadside places that grill chicken and serve it with rice and beans. And there's a local people's restaurant at the southern end of town called **Doña Tina.** Meals on the coast are going to be more expensive but more varied. Many of the hotels have restaurants—I've eaten well at **Copal** and **Mezzanine,** which are both north of the T-junction, and **Zamas,** which is south.

---

### The Sian Ka'an Biosphere Reserve

Down the peninsula a few miles south of the Tulum ruins, you'll pass the guardhouse of the Sian Ka'an Biosphere Reserve. The reserve is a tract of 500,000 hectares (1.3 million acres) set aside in 1986 to preserve tropical forests, savannas, mangroves, coastal and marine habitats, and 110km (70 miles) of coastal reefs. The area is home to jaguars, pumas, ocelots, margays, jaguarundis, spider and howler monkeys, tapirs, white-lipped and collared peccaries, manatees, brocket and white-tailed deer, crocodiles, and green, loggerhead, hawksbill, and leatherback sea turtles. It also protects 366 species of birds—you might catch a glimpse of an ocellated turkey, a great curassow, a brilliantly colored parrot, a toucan or trogon, a white ibis, a roseate spoonbill, a jabiru (or wood stork), a flamingo, or one of 15 species of herons, egrets, and bitterns.

The park has three parts: a "core zone" restricted to research; a "buffer zone," to which visitors and families already living there have restricted use; and a "cooperation zone," which is outside the reserve but vital to its preservation. There are two principal entrances to the biopreserve: one is from the community of Muyil, which is off Highway 307, south of Tulum (you take a boat down canals built by the Maya that connect to the Boca Paila lagoon); or from the community of Punta Allen (by jeep down the peninsula which separates the Boca Paila Lagoon from the sea).

Visitors can arrange day trips in Tulum from a few different outfits, whose offices are just a couple of blocks apart and even have similar names. **Sian Ka'an Tours** (© **984/871-2363;** siankaan_tours@hotmail.com) is on the west side of Avenida Tulum, next to El Basilico Restaurant, at the corner of Calle Beta. **Community Sian Ka'an Tours** is on the same side of the road, 2 blocks north between Orion and Centauro streets (© **984/114-0750;** www.siankaan tours.org). The latter is a community organization of Muyil and Punta Allen. Both will pick up customers from any of the area hotels.

## EXPLORING THE PUNTA ALLEN PENINSULA

If you've been captured by an adventurous spirit and an excessively sanguine opinion of your rental car's off-road capabilities, you might want to take a trip down the Punta Allen Peninsula, especially if your interests lie in fly-fishing, birding, or simply exploring new country. The far end of the peninsula is only 50km (30 miles) away, but it can be a very slow trip (up to 3 hr., depending on the condition of the road). Not far from the last cabana hotel is the entrance to the 500,000-hectare (1.3-million-acre) **Sian Ka'an Biosphere Reserve** (see below).

Halfway down the peninsula, at a small bridge, is the **Boca Paila Fishing Lodge** (www.bocapaila.com). Not for the general traveler, it specializes in hosting fly-fishers, with weeklong all-inclusive fishing packages. At this point the peninsula is quite narrow. You can see the Boca Paila lagoon on one side and the sea on the other. Another 25km (15 miles) gets you to the village of Punta Allen. Just before the town is a little hotel called **Rancho Sol Caribe** (www.cancun.net/links/small_properties/rancho_sol_caribe). It has only four rooms and a lovely beach all to itself. Punta Allen is a lobstering and fishing village on a palm-studded beach. Isolated and rustic, it's very much the laid-back end of the line. It has a lobster cooperative, a few streets with modest homes, and a lighthouse. The **Cuzan Guest House** (www.flyfishmx.com) is a collection of 12 cabins and one restaurant on a nice sandy beach. Its main clientele is fly-fishers, and it offers all-inclusive fishing packages. But co-owner Sonia Litvak, a Californian, will rent to anyone curious enough to want to go down there. She also offers snorkeling trips and boat tours.

## 5 Cobá Ruins

168km (104 miles) SW of Cancún

Older than most of Chichén Itzá and much larger than Tulum, Cobá was the dominant city of the eastern Yucatán before A.D. 1000. The site is large and spread out, with thick forest growing between the temple groups. Rising high above the forest canopy are tall and steep pyramids of the Classic Maya style. Of the major sites, this one is the least reconstructed and so disappoints those who expect another Chichén Itzá. The stone sculpture here has worn off and has become difficult to make out. But the structures themselves and the surrounding jungle and twin lakes make the experience enjoyable. This is not a *cenote* area, and the water has nowhere to go but stay on the surface. The forest canopy is also higher than in the northern part of the peninsula.

### ESSENTIALS

**GETTING THERE & DEPARTING    By Car**    The road to Cobá begins in Tulum and continues for 65km (40 miles). Watch out for both *topes* (speed bumps) and potholes. The road is going to be repaved and widened this year. Close to the village of Cobá you will come to a triangle offering you three choices: Nuevo Xcan, Valladolid, and Cobá. Make sure not to get on the other two roads. The entrance to the ruins is a short distance down the road past some small restaurants and the large lake.

**By Bus**    Several buses a day leave Tulum and Playa del Carmen for Cobá. Several companies offer bus tours.

### EXPLORING THE COBA RUINS

The Maya built many intriguing cities in the Yucatán, but few grander than Cobá ("water stirred by wind"). Much of the 67-sq.-km (26-sq.-mile) site remains unexcavated. A 100km (62-mile) *sacbé* (a pre-Hispanic raised road or causeway) through the jungle

---

### For Your Comfort at Cobá

Visit Cobá in the morning or after the heat of the day has passed. Mosquito repellent, drinking water, and comfortable shoes are imperative.

---

linked Cobá to Yaxuná, once an important Maya center 50km (30 miles) south of Chichén Itzá. It's the Maya's longest known *sacbé,* and at least 50 shorter ones lead from here. An important city-state, Cobá flourished from A.D. 632 (the oldest carved date found here) until after the rise of Chichén Itzá, around 800. Then Cobá slowly faded in importance and population until it was finally abandoned. Scholars believe Cobá was an important trade link between the Yucatán Caribbean coast and inland cities.

Once at the site, keep your bearings—you can get turned around in the maze of dirt roads in the jungle. And bring bug spray. As spread out as this city is, renting a bike (which you can do at the entrance for $2.50) is a good option. Branching off from every labeled path, you'll notice unofficial narrow paths into the jungle, used by locals as shortcuts through the ruins. These are good for birding, but be careful to remember the way back.

The **Grupo Cobá** holds an impressive pyramid, **La Iglesia (the Temple of the Church),** which you'll find if you take the path bearing right after the entrance. Though the urge to climb the temple is great, the view is better from El Castillo in the Nohoch Mul group farther back.

From here, return to the main path and turn right. You'll pass a sign pointing right to the ruined *juego de pelota* **(ball court),** but the path is obscure.

Continuing straight ahead on this path for 5 to 10 minutes, you'll come to a fork in the road. To the left and right you'll notice jungle-covered, unexcavated pyramids, and at one point, you'll see a raised portion crossing the pathway—this is the visible remains of the *sacbé* to Yaxuná. Throughout the area, carved stelae stand by pathways or lie forlornly in the jungle underbrush. Although protected by crude thatched roofs, most are weatherworn enough that they're indiscernible.

The left fork leads to the **Nohoch Mul Group,** which contains **El Castillo.** With the exception of Structure 2 in Calakmul, this is the tallest pyramid in the Yucatán (rising even higher than the great El Castillo at Chichén Itzá and the Pyramid of the Magician at Uxmal). Visitors are permitted to climb to the top. From this lofty perch, you can see unexcavated jungle-covered pyramidal structures poking up through the forest canopy all around.

The right fork (more or less straight on) goes to the **Conjunto Las Pinturas.** Here, the main attraction is the **Pyramid of the Painted Lintel,** a small structure with traces of its original bright colors above the door. You can climb up to get a close look. Though maps of Cobá show ruins around two lakes, there are really only two excavated groups.

Admission is $4, free for children under age 12. Parking is $1. A video camera permit costs $4. The site is open daily from 8am to 5pm, sometimes longer.

### WHERE TO STAY & DINE

If nightfall catches you in Cobá, you have limited lodging choices. There is one tourist hotel called **Villas Arqueológicas Cobá,** which fronts the lake and is operated by Club Med. Though smaller than its sister hotels in Uxmal and Chichén Itzá, it's the same in style—modern rooms that are attractive and functional so long as you're not too tall. It has a restaurant that serves all three meals. It could be empty or full since most of its business comes from bus tours. To make reservations, call © **800/258-2633** in the U.S., or 55/5203-3086 in Mexico. It has a swimming pool. There's also a cheap hotel in town called **El Bocadito** (no phone) with simple rooms for $25 per night. It has a small restaurant, and there are a couple more in the town as well.

## EN ROUTE TO THE LOWER CARIBBEAN COAST: FELIPE CARRILLO PUERTO

Mexico's lower Caribbean coast is officially called the Costa Maya. This area attracts fishermen, divers, archaeology enthusiasts, birders, and travelers looking to get away from the crowds. For divers there is some great diving along the coastal reefs and at the Chinchorro Reef, which lies about 30km (20 miles) offshore (see below). You'll find sandy beaches good for sunbathing, but not for swimming because of the prominent coastal reef. But if you want to snorkel or dive among less-visited reefs, kayak in calm turquoise water, or perhaps do some fly-fishing away from the crowds, this area is a great option. And there's fine swimming in Lake Bacalar.

You also might enjoy the astounding Maya ruins in the Río Bec area, west of Bacalar. Here, too, you'll find a richer ecosystem than the northern part of the peninsula. The forest canopy is higher, and the wildlife is more abundant. If you're interested in exploring this territory, see "Side Trips to Maya Ruins from Chetumal," later in this chapter.

Continue south on Highway 307 from Tulum. The road narrows, the speed limit drops, and you begin to see *topes.* Down the road some 25km (15 miles), a sign points to the small but interesting ruins of **Muyil.** Take bug spray. The principal ruins are a small group of buildings and a plaza dominated by the Castillo, a pyramid of medium height but unusual construction. From here, a canal dug by the Maya enters what is now the Sian Ka'an preserve and empties into a lake, with other canals going from there to the saltwater estuary of Boca Paila. The local community offers a boat ride through these canals and lakes. The 3½-hour tour includes snorkeling the canal and letting the current carry you along. Soft drinks are also included. This is much the same Sian Ka'an tour offered by travel agencies in Tulum, but without some of the infrastructure. The agencies charge more but provide transportation, better interpretation, and lunches.

**Felipe Carrillo Puerto** (pop. 60,000) is the first large town you pass on the road to Ciudad Chetumal. It has two gas stations, a market, a bus terminal, and a few modest hotels and restaurants. Next to the gas station in the center of town is a bank with an ATM. Highway 184 goes from here into the interior of the peninsula, leading eventually to Mérida, which makes Carrillo Puerto a turning point for those making the "short circuit" of the Yucatán Peninsula.

The town is of interest for having been a rebel stronghold during the War of the Castes and the center of the intriguing millenarian cult of the "Talking Cross." The town is still home to a strong community of believers in the cult who practice their own brand of religion and are respected by the whole town. Every month a synod of sorts is held here for the church leaders in 12 neighboring towns.

---

**⌐Tips Last Gas**

It's a good idea to fill up in Felipe Carrillo Puerto, the last gas station before Bacalar.

## 6 Majahual, Xcalak & the Chinchorro Reef

South of Felipe Carrillo Puerto, the speed bumps begin in earnest. In 45 minutes you reach the turnoff for Majahual and Xcalak, which is after the town of Limones. From here the highway has been widened and repaved. The roadwork was done to facilitate bus tours from the cruise-ship pier in **Majahual** (mah-hah-*wahl*) to some of the Maya ruins close by. Many passengers elect to enjoy some beach time in Majahual instead. The best option is to keep your distance from the pier and stay either in the lower Majahual area or at the bottom of the peninsula near Xcalak. You'll come to the turnoff for Xcalak before you get to Majahual. Xcalak has a decent dive shop. From Mahajual to Xcalak takes a little less than an hour.

**Xcalak** (eesh-kah-*lahk*) is a depopulated, weather-beaten fishing village with a few comfortable places to stay and a couple of restaurants. It once had a population as large as 1,200 before the 1958 hurricane washed most of the town away; now it has only 300 permanent residents. It's charming in a run-down way, and you'll certainly feel miles away from the crush of the crowds. From here you work your way back up the coast to get to one of the several small inns just beyond the town.

### ORIENTATION
**ARRIVING   By Car**   Driving south from Felipe Carrillo Puerto, you'll come to the clearly marked turnoff onto Highway 10, 2.5km (1½ miles) after Limones, at a place called Cafetal. From there it's a 50km (30-mile) drive to the coast, and Majahual. The pier is north of the road; Hotel Balamkú, which I like, is to the south. If you're going to Xcalak, the turnoff will be 2km (1¼ miles) before Mahajual, at a military checkpoint. The road is paved, but usually with some potholes. It's 55km (34 miles) long.

### DIVING THE CHINCHORRO REEF
The **Chinchorro Reef Underwater National Park** is 38km (24 miles) long and 13km (8 miles) wide. The oval reef is as shallow as 1m (3¼ ft.) on its interior and as deep as 900m (2,952 ft.) on its exterior. It lies some 30km (19 miles) offshore. Locals claim it's the last virgin reef system in the Caribbean. It's invisible from the ocean side; hence, one of its diving attractions is the **shipwrecks**—at least 30—that decorate the underwater landscape. One is on top of the reef. Divers have counted 40 cannons at one wreck site. On the west side are walls and coral gardens.

**Aventuras XTC** (© 983/831-0461; www.xtcdivecenter.com) is a fully equipped dive shop in Xcalak (technical diving, Nitrox, snorkel and fishing trips). You can arrange dives to the local reefs, San Pedro in Belize, and to the Chinchorro Reef, weather permitting.

### WHERE TO STAY & DINE
**Balamkú Inn on the Beach** *finds*   This is a comfortable and friendly place to stay in south Majahual. Rooms are in one- and two-story thatched bungalows distributed across 110m (360 ft.) of beautiful white beach. They are large and breezy with large attractive bathrooms and comfortable mattresses. All have terraces facing the beach. This hotel is very ecological. All the energy is produced by wind and sun. The toilets use very little water, and waste is all composted. To run this kind of operation takes a rare combination of skills and talents, which these owners have in ample supply.

Carretera Costera Km 5.7, Majahual, Q. Roo. © 983/839-5332. www.balamku.com. 10 units. $70–$85 double. Rates include full breakfast. AE, MC, V for deposits only; no credit cards at hotel. Free guarded parking. **Amenities:** Watersports equipment; activities arranged; airport transportation arranged; in-room massage; nonsmoking rooms. *In room:* No phone.

# The Yucatán's Lower Caribbean Coast

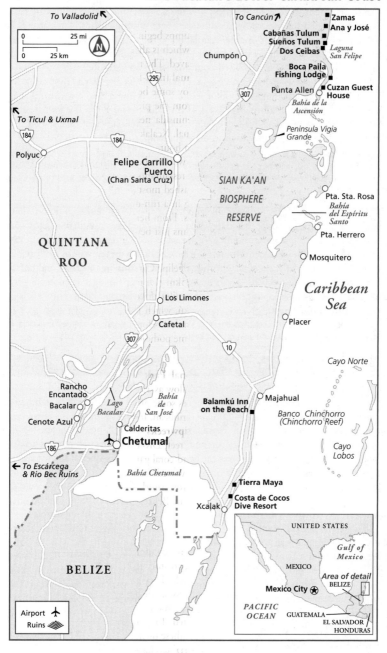

To Valladolid

To Cancún

Zamas
Ana y José
Cabañas Tulum
Sueños Tulum
Dos Ceibas
Laguna
San Felipe

Chumpón

Boca Paila
Fishing Lodge

Punta Allen
Cuzan Guest
House

Bahía de la
Ascensión

To Ticul & Uxmal

Peninsula Vigia
Grande

Polyuc

Felipe Carrillo
Puerto
(Chan Santa Cruz)

SIAN KA'AN

BIOSPHERE

RESERVE

Pta. Sta. Rosa

Bahía
del Espíritu
Santo

QUINTANA
ROO

Pta. Herrero

Mosquitero

Caribbean
Sea

Los Limones

Cafetal

Placer

Cayo Norte

Rancho
Encantado

Bacalar

Cenote Azul

Bahía
de
San José

Lago
Bacalar

Balamkú Inn
on the Beach

Majahual

Banco Chinchorro
(Chinchorro Reef)

Calderitas

Chetumal

Cayo
Lobos

To Escárcega
& Rio Bec Ruins

Bahía Chetumal

Tierra Maya

Costa de Cocos
Dive Resort

Xcalak

BELIZE

UNITED STATES

Gulf of
Mexico

MEXICO

Area of detail

Mexico City

BELIZE

PACIFIC
OCEAN

GUATEMALA

EL SALVADOR

HONDURAS

Airport

Ruins

295

307

184

184

307

10

186

**Costa de Cocos Dive & Fly-Fishing Resort** 🐟🐟    Several free-standing cabanas sit around a large, attractive sandy beach graced with coconut palms. The cabanas are comfortable and have a lot of cross-ventilation, ceiling fans, hot water, and comfortable beds. They also come with 24-hour electricity using wind and solar power and purified tap water. One is a two-bedroom unit with two bathrooms.

Activities for guests include kayaking, snorkeling, scuba diving, and fly-fishing. The resort has experienced English-speaking fishing guides and a dive instructor. It has a large dive boat capable of taking divers to the Chinchorro Reef. The casual restaurant/bar offers good home-style cooking, usually with a choice of one or two main courses at dinner and sandwiches and pizza at lunch.

Carretera Majahual–Xcalak Km 52, Q. Roo. www.costadecocos.com. 16 cabanas. High season $90 double; low season $75 double. Dive and fly-fishing packages available by e-mail request. Rates include breakfast buffet. AE, MC, V. Free parking (through Paypal). **Amenities:** Restaurant; bar; watersports equipment; dive shop; airport transportation. *In room:* No phone.

**Tierra Maya** 🐟    This is a comfortable, modern-style hotel on the beach. Rooms in the two-story building are spacious and designed to have good cross ventilation. They come with ceiling fans, and some rooms have the option of air-conditioning for an extra charge. All have private balconies or terraces looking out to the sea, hammocks, and bottled purified water. Solar generators provide electricity. Bathrooms are large, and beds are either twins or queen-size beds. The owners arrange diving, fishing, and snorkeling trips for guests. Guests have Internet access and the use of kayaks and bikes.

Carretera Majahual–Xcalak Km 54, Q. Roo. www.tierramaya.net. 7 units. High season $90–$110 double; low season $80–$100 double. Rates include continental breakfast. MC, V for advance payments. **Amenities:** Restaurant; bar; watersports equipment; bikes; ground transportation; Internet access. *In room:* A/C (in some), no phone.

## 7 Lago Bacalar 🌟🌟🌟

104km (65 miles) SW of Felipe Carrillo Puerto; 37km (23 miles) NW of Chetumal

Bacalar Lake is an elaborate trick played upon the senses. I remember once standing on a pier on the lake and gazing down into perfectly clear water. As I lifted my eyes I could see the blue tint of the Caribbean. Beyond lay a dense tropical forest. A breeze blowing in from the sea smelled of the salt air, and though I knew it to be untrue, I couldn't help but believe that the water I was gazing on was, in fact, an inlet of the sea and not a lake at all—perhaps a well-sheltered lagoon like Xel-Ha. Lakes in tropical lowlands, especially those surrounded by tropical jungle, are turbid and muddy. How could this one be so clear? The answer is that Bacalar is not fed by surface runoff, but by several *cenotes* that lie beneath its surface. Only in the Yucatán is such a thing possible.

This is the perfect spot for being bone idle. But there's plenty to do, too. You can explore the jungle, visit some particularly elegant Maya ruins in the nearby Río Bec area, or take in a wonderful museum about the Maya in Chetumal. The town of Bacalar is quiet and quaint. There are a few stores and a couple of restaurants. An 18th-century fort with a moat and stout bastions is by the lake. Inside the fort is a small museum (admission is 50¢) that has several artifacts on display. All text is in Spanish.

**ORIENTATION**    Driving south on Highway 307, the town of Bacalar is 1½ hours beyond Felipe Carrillo Puerto, clearly marked by signs. If you're driving north from Chetumal, it takes about a half-hour. Buses going south from Cancún and Playa del Carmen stop here, and there are frequent buses from Chetumal.

## WHERE TO STAY

**Hotel Laguna** The Laguna overlooks the lake from a lovely vantage point. All the rooms share the view and have little terraces that make enjoyable sitting areas. The mid-size rooms have ceiling fans, and most come with two double beds. The mattresses in the bungalows aren't good. The bathrooms are simple but have no problem delivering hot water. A restaurant that shares the same view is open from 7am to 9pm. The bar makes a credible margarita. The highest occupancy rates are from July to August and December to January, when you should make a reservation. The hotel is hard to spot from the road; look for the sign about 1km (½ mile) after you pass through the town of Bacalar.

Bulevar Costera de Bacalar 479, 77010 Lago Bacalar, Q. Roo. ② **983/834-2206.** Fax 983/834-2205. 34 units. $50 double; $80–$95 bungalow for 5–8 persons. No credit cards. **Amenities:** Restaurant; bar; small outdoor pool. *In room:* No phone.

**Rancho Encantado Cottage Resort** ⟨⟨ This beautiful, serene lakeside retreat consists of 13 white-stucco cottages scattered over a shady lawn beside the smooth Lago Bacalar. Each is large and has mahogany louvered windows, a red-tile floor, a dining table and chairs, a living room or sitting area, a porch with chairs, and hammocks strung between trees. Some rooms have cedar ceilings and red-tiled roofs, and others have thatched roofs. All are decorated with folk art and murals inspired by Maya ruins. There are four waterfront cottages (nos. 9–12). Beds come in different combinations of doubles and twins. There is also a new "laguna suite," a one-bedroom town house with study, air-conditioning, and private dock; it rents by the week. Orange, lime, mango, sapote, ceiba, banana, palm, and oak trees; wild orchids; and bromeliads on the grounds make great bird shelters, attracting flocks of chattering parrots, turquoise-browed motmots, toucans, and many more species.

The hotel offers almost a dozen excursions. Among them are day trips to the **Río Bec** ruin route, an extended visit to **Calakmul,** outings to the **Majahual Peninsula,** and a riverboat trip to the Maya ruins of **Lamanai,** deep in a Belizian forest. Excursions cost $55 to $115 per person, depending on the length and difficulty of the trip, and several have a three-person minimum. To find the Rancho, look for the hotel's sign on the left about 3km (2 miles) before Bacalar.

Carretera Bacalar–Felipe Carrillo Puerto Km 3, 77930 Chetumal, Q. Roo. ②/fax **983/101-3358.** www.encantado.com. (Reservations: P.O. Box 1256, Taos, NM 87571. ② **800/505-6292** in the U.S., or ②/fax 505/894-7074.) 13 units. High season $150–$200 double; low season $100–$135 double. Rates include continental breakfast and dinner. MC, V. **Amenities:** Restaurant; bar; large outdoor whirlpool; spa; watersports equipment; tour desk; massage service. *In room:* Fridge, coffeemaker.

## WHERE TO DINE

Besides the restaurants at the hotels discussed above, you may enjoy the **Restaurante Cenote Azul,** a comfortable open-air thatched-roof restaurant on the edge of the beautiful Cenote Azul. Main courses cost $5 to $12. To get to Restaurant Cenote Azul, follow the highway to the south edge of town and turn left at the restaurant's sign; follow the road around to the restaurant. At the restaurant you can take a dip in placid Cenote Azul as long as you don't have creams or lotions on your skin.

## 8 Chetumal

251km (156 miles) S of Tulum; 37km (23 miles) S of Lago Bacalar

Capital of the state, and the second-largest city (after Cancún), Chetumal (pop. 210,000) is not a tourist destination. The old part of town, down by the river (Río

Hondo), has a Caribbean feel, but the rest is unremarkable. Chetumal is the gateway to Belize, to Tikal, and to the Río Bec ruins. If you're going to spend the night here, visit the **Museo de la Cultura Maya** (© **983/832-6838**), especially if you plan to follow the Río Bec ruin route (see "Side Trips to Maya Ruins from Chetumal," below).

## ESSENTIALS
### GETTING THERE & DEPARTING
**BY PLANE** **Aviacsa** (© **983/872-7698**) has a direct flight to and from Mexico City. The airport is west of town, just north of the entrance from the highway.

**BY CAR** It's a little more than 3 hours from Tulum. If you're heading to Belize, you won't be able to take your rental car because the rental companies won't allow it. To get to the ruins of Tikal in Guatemala, you must go through Belize to the border crossing at Ciudad Melchor de Mencos.

**BY BUS** The main bus station (© **983/832-5110**) is 20 blocks from the town center on Insurgentes at Niños Héroes. Buses go to Cancún, Tulum, Playa del Carmen, Puerto Morelos, Mérida, Campeche, Villahermosa, and Tikal, Guatemala.

**To Belize:** Buses depart from the Lázaro Cárdenas market (most often called *el mercado nuevo*). Ask for Autobuses Novelo. The company has local service every 45 minutes ($12) and four express buses per day ($16).

### VISITOR INFORMATION
The **State Tourism Office** (© **983/835-0860,** ext. 1811) is at Calzada del Centenario 622, between Comonfort and Ciricote. Office hours are Monday to Friday from 9am to 6pm.

### ORIENTATION
The telephone **area code** is **983.**

All traffic enters the city from the west and feeds onto Avenida Obregón into town. Avenida Héroes is the main north-south street.

## A MUSEUM NOT TO MISS
**Museo de la Cultura Maya** ✷✷✷   This modern museum unlocks the complex world of the Maya through interactive exhibits and genuine artifacts. Push a button, and an illustrated description appears, explaining the medicinal and domestic uses of plants with their Mayan and scientific names; another exhibit describes the social classes of the Maya by their manners of dress. One of the most fascinating exhibits describes the Maya's ideal of personal beauty and the subsequent need to deform craniums, scar the face and body, and induce cross-eyed vision. An enormous screen flashes images taken from an airplane flying over more than a dozen Maya sites from Mexico to Honduras. Another large television shows the architectural variety of Maya pyramids and how they were probably built. Then a walk on a glass floor takes you over representative ruins in the Maya world. In the center of the museum is the three-story, stylized, sacred ceiba tree, which the Maya believed connected Xibalba (the underworld), earth, and the heavens. If you can arrange it, see the museum before you tour the Río Bec ruins.

Av. Héroes s/n. © **983/832-6838.** Admission $6. Tues–Thurs 9am–7pm; Fri–Sat 9am–8pm. Between Colón and Gandhi, 8 blocks from Av. Obregón, just past the Holiday Inn.

## WHERE TO STAY

**Hotel Holiday Inn Puerta Maya**   This modern hotel (formerly the Hotel Continental) has the best air-conditioning in town and is only a block from the Museo de la Cultura Maya. Most rooms are midsize and come with two double beds or one king-size bed. Bathrooms are roomy and well lit.

Av. Héroes 171, 77000 Chetumal, Q. Roo. ℭ 800/465-4329 in the U.S., or 983/835-0400. Fax 983/832-1676. 85 units. $125 double. AE, MC, V. Free secure parking. From Av. Obregón, turn left on Av. Héroes, go 6 blocks, and look for the hotel on the right. **Amenities:** Restaurant; bar; midsize outdoor pool; room service; laundry service. *In room:* A/C, TV.

**Hotel Nachancán**   One block from *el mercado nuevo* (the new market) and buses to Belize, this hotel offers plain rooms, with one or two double beds. Bathrooms are small, with no counter space, but they offer plenty of hot water. A cab to the Museo de la Cultura Maya costs $1.

Calzada Veracruz 379, 77000 Chetumal, Q. Roo. ℭ 983/832-3232. 20 units. $33 double; $45 suite. No credit cards. Drive the length of Av. Obregón to where it stops at Calzada Veracruz, turn left, and drive 2km (1¼ miles); the hotel will be on the right. **Amenities:** Restaurant; bar. *In room:* A/C, TV, no phone.

## WHERE TO DINE

If you want to eat in air-conditioned surroundings in a modern, comfortable setting, try **Espress Café & Restaurant,** Calle 22 de Enero 141, corner of Bulevar Bahía (ℭ **983/833-3013**). It serves well-prepared Mexican food, light fare such as sandwiches, and good breakfasts. It's open daily from 8am to midnight. For an economical meal with some local atmosphere, try **Restaurante Pantoja,** on the corner of calles Ghandi and 16 de Septiembre (no phone), 2 blocks east of the Museum of Maya Culture. It offers a cheap daily special, good green enchiladas, and such local specialties as *poc chuc.* It's open Monday to Saturday from 7am to 9pm. To sample excellent *antojitos,* the local supper food, go to **El Buen Gusto,** on Calzada Veracruz across from the market (no phone). A Chetumal institution, it serves excellent *salbutes* and *panuchos* (both dishes are similar to *gorditas*), tacos, and sandwiches. Doors open around 7pm and close around midnight every night. If for some reason it's closed, go next door **La Ideal,** which many locals hold to be the better of the two supper joints. It has delicious *tacos de pierna* and *agua de horchata.*

## ONWARD FROM CHETUMAL

From Chetumal you have several choices. The Maya ruins of Lamanai, in Belize, are an easy day trip if you have transportation (not a rental car). You can explore the Río Bec ruin route directly west of the city (see below) by taking Highway 186.

### 9  Side Trips to Maya Ruins from Chetumal

A few miles west of Bacalar and Chetumal begins an area of Maya settlement known to archaeologists as the Río Bec region. A number of ruins stretch from close to Bacalar well into the state of Campeche. These ruins are numerous, intriguing, and dramatic. Their architecture is heavily stylized, with lots of decoration. In recent years, excavation has led to many discoveries. With excavation has come restoration, but the ruins here have not been rebuilt to the same degree as those at Uxmal and Chichén Itzá. But often the buildings were in such great shape that no reconstruction was necessary.

Nor have these sites been cleared of jungle growth in the same manner as the marquee ruins mentioned above. Trees and vines grow in profusion around the buildings, giving the sites the feel of lost cities. In visiting them, you can imagine what John Lloyd Stephens and Frederick Catherwood must have felt when they traipsed through the Yucatán in the 19th century. And watch for wildlife; on my last visit I saw several denizens of the tropical forest. The fauna along the entire route is especially rich. You might see a toucan, a grand curassow, or a macaw hanging about the ruins, and orioles, egrets, and several birds of prey are extremely common. Gray fox, wild turkey, tesquintle (a bushy-tailed, plant-eating rodent), the raccoon relative coatimundi (with its long tapered snout and tail), and armadillos inhabit the area in abundance. At Calakmul, and in the surrounding jungle, circulate two groups of spider monkeys and four groups of howler monkeys.

**THE ROUTE'S STARTING POINT**    Halfway between Bacalar and Chetumal is the turnoff for Highway 186 to Escárcega (about 20km/12 miles from either town). It's a major highway and is well marked. This is the same road that leads to Campeche, Palenque, and Villahermosa. There are a couple of gas stations on the route; one is at the town of Xpujil. Keep plenty of cash with you, as credit cards are little used in the area. The Río Bec sites are at varying distances off this highway. You pass through a guard station at the border with Campeche state. The guards might ask you to present your travel papers, or they might just wave you on. You can divide your sightseeing into several day trips from Bacalar or Chetumal, or you can spend the night in this area and see more the next day. If you get an early start, you can easily visit a few of the sites mentioned here in a day.

Evidence shows that these ruins, especially Becán, were part of the **trade route** linking the Caribbean coast at Cobá to Edzná and the Gulf coast, and to Lamanai in Belize and beyond. At one time, a great number of cities thrived in this region, and much of the land was dedicated to the intensive cultivation of maize. Today everything lies hidden under a dense jungle, which blankets the land from horizon to horizon.

I've listed the following sites in east-to-west order, the way you would see them driving from the Caribbean coast. If you decide to tour these ruins, take the time to visit the Museo de la Cultura Maya (p. 178) in Chetumal first. It will lend context to what you see. If you want a guide to show you the area, contact **Luis Téllez** (© **983/832-3496;** www.sacbetravel.com), who lives in Chetumal. The best way to reach him is through the e-mail link on his website. Luis is the best guide for this region; he's knowledgeable, speaks English, and is a good driver. He's acquainted with most of the archaeologists excavating these ruins and stays current with their discoveries. He also knows and can identify the local wildlife and guides many tours for birders. Entry to each site is $2 to $4. Informational signs at each building are in Mayan, Spanish, and English. There are few if any refreshments at the ruins, so bring your own water and food. All the principal sites have toilets.

**Food & Lodging**    Your lodging choices are growing. On the upscale side are the Explorean hotel (see below) near Kohunlich and the ecovillage in Chicanná. Food and lodging of the no-frills sort can be found in the town of Xpujil and near Calakmul.

The **Explorean** (© **888/679-3748** in the U.S.; www.theexplorean.com) is an ecolodge for adventure travelers who like their comfort. It sits all alone on the crest of a small hill not far from the ruins of Kohunlich. It has a small pool and spa and lovely rooms, and offers guide services and adventure tours (mountain biking, rappelling, kayaking) all as part of an all-inclusive package. The cost is over $500 for two people and, in addition to the tours, includes food and drink. The hotel is a member of the Fiesta Americana chain.

**Tips  Recommended Reading**

For a bit of background reading to help you make the most of your visit, I recommend *A Forest of Kings: The Untold Story of the Ancient Maya,* by Linda Schele and David Freidel (William Morrow, 1990); *The Blood of Kings: Dynasty and Ritual in Maya Art,* by Linda Schele and Mary Ellen Miller (George Braziller, 1968); and *The Maya Cosmos,* by David Freidel and Linda Schele (William Morrow, 1993). *Arqueología Mexicana* magazine devoted its July/August 1995 issue to the Quintana Roo portion of the Río Bec ruin route. Last, though it lacks historical and cultural information and many sites have expanded since it was written, Joyce Kelly's *An Archaeological Guide to Mexico's Yucatán Peninsula* (University of Oklahoma, 1993), is the best companion book to have.

The **Chicanná Eco Village,** Carretera Escárcega Km 296 (© **981/816-2233** for reservations), is just beyond the town of Xpujil. It offers 28 nicely furnished rooms distributed among several two-story thatched bungalows. The comfortable rooms have two doubles or a king-size bed, ceiling fans, a large bathroom, and screened windows. The manicured lawns and flower beds are lovely, with pathways linking the bungalows to each other and to the restaurant and swimming pool. Double rooms go for $113.

In the village of Xpujil (just before the ruins of Xpujil) are three modest hotels and a couple of restaurants. The best food and lodging are at **Restaurant y Hotel Calakmul** (© **983/871-6029**), run by Doña María Cabrera. The hotel has 12 rooms that go for $40. They have tile floors, private bathrooms with hot water, and good beds. The restaurant is open daily from 6am to midnight. Main courses cost $4 to $8. The chicken cooked in herbs is worth ordering. Between Xpujil and Calakmul are three hotels. Two are simple, comfortable, and attractive; one is large and was made with bus tours in mind. **Rio Bec Dreams** (© **983/871-6057;** www.riobecdreams.com) is a good choice because the owners live on the premises and keep maintenance and service sharp. It's 11km (7 miles) west of Xpujil. You can choose between a private or shared bathroom. The rooms are attractive and well spaced across a nice tract of tropical forest. Each has a little terrace for enjoying the surroundings, plenty of windows with screening, and lots of cross-ventilation. The hotel's restaurant is better than anything else in the area. Another choice is **Puerta Calakmul** (www.puertacalakmul.com.mx), at the turnoff for the ruins of Calakmul. It was recently purchased by the owners of the Chicanná Eco Village, listed above. When I last passed through, the hotel was closed for remodeling.

## DZIBANCHE & KINICHNA

The turnoff for this site is 37km (23 miles) from the highway intersection and is well marked. From the turnoff it's another 23km (14 miles) to the ruins. You should ask about the condition of the road before going. These unpaved roads can go from good to bad pretty quickly. But this is such an important site that road repair is generally kept up. Dzibanché (or Tzibanché) means "place where they write on wood"—obviously not the original name, which remains unknown. Exploration began here in 1993, and the site opened to the public in late 1994. Scattered over 42 sq. km (16 sq. miles) are several groupings of buildings and plazas; only a small portion is excavated. It dates from the Classic period (A.D. 300–900) and was occupied for around 700 years.

**TEMPLES & PLAZAS** Two large adjoining plazas have been cleared. The most important structure yet excavated is called the Temple of the Owl, which is in the main plaza, Plaza Xibalba. Archaeologists found a stairway that descends from the top of the structure deep into the pyramid, ending in a burial chamber. It's closed to visitors. But there they uncovered a number of beautiful polychromatic lidded vessels, one of which has an owl painted on the top handle with its wings spreading onto the lid. White owls were messengers of the gods of the underworld in the Maya religion. Also found here were the remains of a sacrificial victim and what appear to be the remains of a Maya queen, which is unique in the archaeology of the Maya.

Opposite the Temple of the Owl is the **Temple of the Cormorant,** named after a polychromed drinking vessel found here depicting the bird. Here, too, archaeologists have found evidence of an interior tomb similar to the one in the Temple of the Owl, but excavations of it have not yet begun. Other magnificently preserved pottery pieces found during excavations include an incense burner with an almost three-dimensional figure of the diving god attached to the outside, and another incense burner with an elaborately dressed representation of the god Itzamná attached.

Situated all by itself is **Structure 6,** a miniature rendition of Teotihuacán's style of *tablero* and *talud* architecture. Each step of the pyramid is made of a *talud* (sloping surface) crowned by a *tablero* (vertical stone facing). Teotihuacán was near present-day Mexico City, but its influence stretched as far as Guatemala. At the top of the pyramid is a doorway, its wooden lintel still intact after centuries of weathering. This detail gave the site its name. Carved into the wood are date glyphs for the year A.D. 733.

Near the site is another city, **Kinichná** (kee-neech-*nah*). About 2.5km (1½ miles) north, it is reachable by a road that becomes questionable during the rainy season. An Olmec-style jade figure was found there. It has a large acropolis with five buildings on three levels, which have been restored and are in good condition, with fragments of the remaining stucco still visible.

## KOHUNLICH ✦

Kohunlich (Koh-*hoon*-leech), 42km (26 miles) from the turnoff for Highway 186, dates from around A.D. 100 to 900. Turn left off the road, and the entrance is 9km (5½ miles) ahead. From the parking area, you enter the grand, parklike site, crossing a large and shady ceremonial area flanked by four large, conserved pyramidal edifices. Continue walking, and just beyond this grouping you'll come to Kohunlich's famous **Pyramid of the Masks** under a thatched covering. The masks, actually enormous plaster faces, date from around A.D. 500 and are on the facade of the building. Each mask has an elongated face and wears a headdress with a mask on its crest and a mask on the chin piece, essentially masks within masks. The top one is thought to represent the astral world, while the lower one represents the underworld, suggesting that the wearer of this headdress is among the living and not in either of the other worlds. Note the carving on the pupils, which suggests a solar connection, possibly with the night sun that illuminated the underworld. This may mean that the person had shamanic vision.

It's speculated that masks covered much of the facade of this building, which is built in the Río Bec style, with rounded corners, a false stairway, and a false temple on the top. At least one theory holds that the masks are a composite of several rulers at Kohunlich. Recent excavations of buildings immediately to the left after you enter uncovered two intact pre-Hispanic skeletons and five decapitated heads that were probably used in a ceremonial ritual. To the right after you enter (follow a shady path through the jungle) is another recently excavated plaza. It's thought to have housed priests or rulers, due to the high quality of pottery found there and the fine architecture of the rooms. Scholars believe that Kohunlich became overpopulated, leading to its decline.

## XPUJIL

Xpujil (eesh-poo-*heel;* also spelled Xpuhil), meaning either "cattail" or "forest of kapok trees," flourished between A.D. 400 and 900. This is a small site that's easy to get to. Look for a blue sign on the highway pointing to the right. The entrance is just off the highway. After buying a ticket ($3), you have to walk 180m (590 ft.) to the main structure. Along the path are some *chechén* trees. Don't touch; they are poisonous and will provoke blisters. You can recognize them by their blotchy bark. On the right, you'll see a platform supporting a restored two-story building with a central staircase on the eastern side. Decorating the first floor are the remnants of a decorative molding and two galleries connected by a doorway. About 90m (295 ft.) farther you come to the site's main structure—a rectangular ceremonial platform 2m (6½ ft.) high and 50m (164 ft.) long supporting the palace, decorated with three tall towers shaped like miniature versions of the pyramids in Tikal, Guatemala. These towers are purely decorative, with false stairways and temples, too small to serve as such. The effect is beautiful. The main body of the building holds 12 rooms, which are now in ruins.

## BECAN  ⭑⭑⭑

Becán (beh-*kahn*) is about 7km (4½ miles) beyond Xpujil and is visible on the right side of the highway. Becán means "moat filled by water," and, in fact, it was protected by a moat spanned by seven bridges. The extensive site dates from the early Classic to the late post-Classic (600 B.C.–A.D. 1200) period. Although it was abandoned by A.D. 850, ceramic remains indicate that there may have been a population resurgence between 900 and 1000, and it was still used as a ceremonial site as late as 1200. Becán was an administrative and ceremonial center with political sway over at least seven other cities in the area, including Chicanná, Hormiguero, and Payán.

The first plaza group you see after you enter was the center for grand ceremonies. From the highway, you can see the back of a pyramid (Structure 1) with two temples on top. Beyond and in between the two temples you can see the Temple atop Structure 4, which is opposite Temple 1. When the high priest appeared exiting the mouth of the earth monster in the center of this temple (which he reached by way of a hidden side stairway that's now partially exposed), he would have been visible from well beyond the immediate plaza. It's thought that commoners had to watch ceremonies from outside the plaza—thus the site's position was for good viewing purposes. The back of Structure 4 is believed to have been a civic plaza where rulers sat on stone benches while pronouncing judgments. The second plaza group dates from around A.D. 850 and has perfect twin towers on top, where there's a big platform. Under the platform are 10 rooms that are thought to be related to Xibalba (shee-*bahl*-bah), the underworld. Hurricane Isidore damaged them, and they are closed until they can be repaired. Earth monster faces probably covered this building (and appeared on other buildings as well). Remains of at least one ball court have been unearthed. Next to the ball court is a well-preserved figure in an elaborate headdress behind glass. He was excavated not far from where he is now displayed. The markings are well defined, displaying a host of details.

## CHICANNA

Slightly over 1.5km (1 mile) beyond Becán, on the left side of the highway, is Chicanná, which means "house of the mouth of snakes." Trees loaded with bromeliads shade the central square surrounded by five buildings. The most outstanding edifice features a monster-mouth doorway and an ornate stone facade with more superimposed masks. As you enter the mouth of the earth monster, note that you are walking on a platform configured as the open jaw of the monster with stone teeth on both sides. Again you find a lovely example of an elongated building with ornamental miniature pyramids on each end.

## CALAKMUL 𝒦𝒦𝒦

This area is both a massive Maya archaeological zone, with at least 60 sites, as well as a 70,000-hectare (172,900-acre) rainforest designated in 1989 as the Calakmul Biosphere Reserve, including territory in both Mexico and Guatemala. The best way to see Calakmul is to spend the night at Xpujil or Chicanná and leave early in the morning for Calakmul. If you're the first one to drive down the narrow access road to the ruins (1½ hr. from the highway), you'll probably see plenty of wildlife. On my last trip to the ruins, I saw two groups of spider monkeys swinging through the trees on the outskirts of the city and a group of howler monkeys sleeping in the trees in front of Structure 2. I also saw a couple of animals that I couldn't identify, and heard the growl of a jungle cat that I wasn't able to see.

**THE ARCHAEOLOGICAL ZONE**    Since 1982, archaeologists have been excavating the ruins of Calakmul, which dates from 100 B.C. to A.D. 900. It's the largest of the area's 60 known sites. Nearly 7,000 buildings have been discovered and mapped. At its zenith, at least 60,000 people may have lived around the site, but by the time of the Spanish Conquest in 1519, there were fewer than 1,000 inhabitants. Visitors arrive at a large plaza filled with a forest of trees. You immediately see several stelae; Calakmul contains more of these than any other site, but they are much more weathered and indistinguishable than the stelae of Palenque or Copán in Honduras. On one of them you can see the work of looters who carefully used some sort of stone-cutting saw to slice off the face of the monument. By Structure 13 is a stele of a woman dating from A.D. 652. She is thought to have been a ruler.

Several structures here are worth checking out; some are built in the Petén style, some in the Río Bec style. Structure 3 must have been the residence of a noble family. Its design is unique and quite lovely; it managed to retain its original form and was never remodeled. Offerings of shells, beads, and polychromed tripod pottery were found inside. Structure 2 is the tallest pyramid in the Yucatán, at 54m (177 ft.). From the top of it you can see the outline of the ruins of El Mirador, 50km (31 miles) across the forest in Guatemala. Notice the two stairways that ascend along the sides of the principal face of the pyramid in the upper levels, and when appreciated in conjunction with how the masks break up the space of the front face, you can see just how complex the design was.

Temple 4 charts the line of the sun from June 21, when it falls on the left (north) corner; to September 21 and March 21, when it lines up in the east behind the middle temple on the top of the building; to December 21, when it falls on the right (south) corner. Numerous jade pieces, including spectacular masks, were uncovered here, most of which are on display in the Museo Regional in Campeche. Temple 7 is largely unexcavated except for the top, where in 1984 the most outstanding jade mask yet to be found at Calakmul was uncovered. In *A Forest of Kings,* Linda Schele and David Freidel tell of wars between the Calakmul, Tikal, and Naranjo (the latter two in Guatemala), and how Ah-Cacaw, king of Tikal (120km/74 miles south of Calakmul), captured King Jaguar-Paw in A.D. 695 and later Lord Ox-Ha-Te Ixil Ahau, both of Calakmul. The site is open Tuesday to Sunday from 7am to 5pm, but it gets so wet during the rainy season from June to October that it's best not to go.

**CALAKMUL BIOSPHERE RESERVE**   Set aside in 1989, this is the peninsula's only high-forest selva, a rainforest that annually records as much as 5m (16 ft.) of rain. Notice that the canopy of the trees is higher here than in the forest of Quintana Roo. It lies very close to the border with Guatemala, but, of course, there is no way to get there. Among the plants are cactus, epiphytes, and orchids. Endangered animals include the white-lipped peccary, jaguar, and puma. So far, more than 250 species of birds have been recorded. At present, no overnight stay

> ### A Driving Caution
> Numerous curves in the road make seeing oncoming traffic (what little there is) difficult.

or camping is permitted. If you want a tour of a small part of the forest and you speak Spanish, you can inquire for a guide at one of the two nearby *ejidos* (cooperatives). Some old *chicleros* (the men who tap sapodilla trees for their gum) living there have expert knowledge of flora and fauna and can take you on a couple of trails.

The turnoff on the left for Calakmul is located 53km (33 miles) from Xpujil, just before the village of Conhuas. There's a guard station there where you pay $4 per car and $2 per person toll. From the turnoff, it's an hour drive on a paved one-lane-road. Admission to the site is $3.50.

## BALAMKU 🐾🐾

Balamkú (bah-lahm-*koo*) is easy to get to and worth the visit. A couple of buildings in it were so well preserved that they required almost no reconstruction. Inside one you will find three impressive figures of men sitting in the gaping maws of crocodiles and toads as they descend into the underworld. The whole concept of this building, with its molded stucco facade, is life and death. On the head of each stucco figure are the eyes, nose, and mouth of a jaguar figure, followed by the full face of the human figure, then a neck formed by the eyes and nose of another jaguar, and an Olmec-like face on the stomach, with its neck decorated by a necklace. These figures were saved from looters who managed to get away with a fourth one. Now they're under the protection of a caretaker, who keeps the room under lock and key. If you speak Spanish, you can get the caretaker to explain something of the figures and their complex symbolism. There's also a beautiful courtyard and another set of buildings adjacent to the main group.

# 7

# Mérida, Chichén Itzá & the Maya Interior

*by David Baird*

Ask most people about the Yucatán, and they think of Cancún, the Caribbean coast, and Chichén Itzá. But there's much more to visit than just those places. With a little exploring, you'll find a variety of things to do. You might spend a morning scrambling over Maya ruins and in the afternoon take a dip in the cool, clear water of a *cenote* (natural well). The next day may find you strolling along a lonely beach or riding in a skiff through mangroves to visit a colony of pink flamingos, and by the evening you might be dancing in the streets of **Mérida.** This chapter covers the interior of the Yucatán Peninsula, including the famous Maya ruins at **Chichén Itzá** and **Uxmal,** the flamingo sanctuaries at **Celestún** and **Río Lagartos,** as well as many other spots that might find special favor with you.

## EXPLORING THE YUCATAN'S MAYA HEARTLAND

The best way to see the Yucatán is by car. The terrain is flat, there is little traffic once you get away from the cities, and the main highways are in good shape. If you drive at all around this area, you will add at least one new word to your Spanish vocabulary— *topes* (*toh*-pehs), meaning speed bumps. And along with *topes* you might learn a few new curse words. *Topes* come in varying shapes and sizes and with varying degrees of warning. Don't let them surprise you.

Off the main highways, the roads are narrow and rough, but hey—you'll be driving a rental car. Rentals are, in fact, a little pricey compared with those in the U.S. (due perhaps to wear and tear?), but some promotional deals are available, especially in low season. For more on renting a car, see "By Car," in "Mérida: Gateway to the Maya Heartland," below.

Plenty of buses ply the roads between the major towns and ruins. And plenty of tour buses circulate, too. But buses to the smaller towns and ruins and the haciendas are infrequent or nonexistent. One bus company, Autobuses del Oriente (ADO), controls most of the first-class bus service and does a good job with the major destinations. Second-class buses go to some out-of-the-way places, but they can be slow, stop a lot, and usually aren't air-conditioned. I will take them when going short distances. If you don't want to rent a car, a few tour operators take small groups to more remote attractions such as ruins, *cenotes,* and villages.

The Yucatán is *tierra caliente* **(the hotlands).** Don't travel in this region without a hat, sunblock, mosquito repellent, and water. The coolest weather is from November to February; the hottest is from April to June. From July to October, thundershowers moderate temperatures. More tourists come to the interior during the winter months, but not to the same extent as on the Caribbean coast. The high-season/low-season distinction is less pronounced here.

Should you decide to travel into this part of the world, don't miss **Mérida.** It is, and has been for centuries, the cultural and commercial center of the Yucatán. You won't find a more vibrant tropical city anywhere. Every time I visit, there is some festival or celebration to attend, on top of the nightly performances that the city offers its citizens and visitors. It's also the Yucatán's shopping center, where you can buy the area's specialty items, such as hammocks, Panama hats, and the embroidered native blouses known as *huipiles.* Aside from Mérida, here are some other places to consider:

---

**Tips**  **Mapping the Region**

To check out the region surrounding Mérida, see "The Yucatán Peninsula" map on p. 18.

---

**CHICHEN ITZA & VALLADOLID**    These destinations are almost midway between Mérida and Cancún. From Mérida it's 2½ hours by car to Chichén on the new *autopista* (toll road). You can spend a day at the ruins and then stay at one of the nearby hotels—or drive 40km (25 miles) to Valladolid, a quiet, charming colonial town with a pleasant central square. Valladolid features two eerie *cenotes.* The spectacular ruins at Ek Balam are only 40km (25 miles) to the north. Also in the area is the Río Lagartos Nature Reserve, teeming with flamingos and other native birds.

**CELESTUN NATIONAL WILDLIFE REFUGE**    These flamingo-sanctuary wetlands along the Gulf coast contain a unique shallow-water estuary where fresh water from *cenotes* mixes with salt water, creating the perfect feeding ground for flamingos. Touring this area by launch is relaxing and rewarding. Only 1½ hours from Mérida, Celestún makes for an easy day trip.

**DZIBILCHALTUN**    This Maya site, now a national park, is 14km (8⅔ miles) north of Mérida along the road to Progreso. Here you'll find pre-Hispanic ruins, nature trails, a *cenote,* and the Museum of the Maya. You can make this the first stop in a day trip to Progreso and other attractions north of Mérida.

**PROGRESO**    A modern city and Gulf coast beach escape 34km (21 miles) north of Mérida, Progreso has a wide beach and oceanfront drive that's popular on the weekends and during the summer. The recent arrival of cruise ships might make Progreso even more popular, but with so much beach, you'll easily have a place to yourself. From Progreso you can drive down the coast to **Uaymitún** to see some flamingos and visit the recently excavated ruins of **Xcambó.**

**UXMAL**    Smaller than Chichén, but architecturally more striking and mysterious, Uxmal is about 80km (50 miles) south of Mérida. You can see it in a day, though it's a good idea to extend that somewhat to see the sound-and-light show and spend the night at one of the hotels by the ruins. Several other nearby sites make up the Puuc route and can be explored the following day. It's also possible, though a bit rushed, to see Uxmal and the other ruins on a 1-day trip by special excursion bus from Mérida.

**CAMPECHE**    This beautiful, walled colonial city has been so meticulously restored that it's a delight just to stroll down the streets. Campeche is about 3 hours southwest of Mérida in the direction of Palenque. A full day should give you enough time to see its highlights and museums, but there is something about Campeche that makes you want to linger there.

*Tips* **The Best Websites for Mérida, Chichén Itzá & the Maya Interior**

- **Maya: Portraits of a People: www.nationalgeographic.com/explorer/ maya/more.html** A fascinating collection of articles from *National Geographic* and other sources.
- **Yucatán Travel Guide: www.mayayucatan.com** Yucatán's Ministry of Tourism maintains this site. It has an update section and good general info on different destinations in the state.
- **Mexico's Yucatán Directory: www.mexonline.com/yucatan.htm** A nice roundup of vacation rentals, tour operators, and information on the Maya sites. For more information on Mexico's indigenous history, see the links on the pre-Columbian page (www.mexonline.com/precolum.htm).

## 1 Mérida: Gateway to the Maya Heartland ★★

1,440km (893 miles) E of Mexico City; 320km (198 miles) W of Cancún

Mérida is the capital of the state of Yucatán and has been the dominant city in the region since the Spanish Conquest. It is a busy city and suffers from the same problems that plague other colonial cities in Mexico—traffic and noise. Still, it is a fun city and has many admirers. I get comments from people all the time about how much they enjoyed Mérida. People here know how to have a good time, and they seem driven to organize concerts, theater productions, art exhibits, and such. In recent years the city has been in the midst of a cultural explosion.

### ESSENTIALS

**GETTING THERE & DEPARTING  By Plane  Aeromexico** (✆ **01-800/ 021-4000** in Mexico, or 999/927-9277; www.aeromexico.com) flies nonstop to/from Miami and Mexico City. **Mexicana** (✆ **01-800/502-2000** in Mexico, or 999/ 924-6633; www.mexicana.com.mx) has nonstop service to and from Mexico City. **Continental** (✆ **999/946-1888** or -1900; www.continental.com) has nonstop service to and from Houston. **Click** (✆ **01-800/122-5425** in Mexico), a Mexican budget airline, provides nonstop service to and from Mexico City and Veracruz. **Aviacsa** (✆ **01-800/006-2000** in Mexico) provides nonstop service to and from Villahermosa and Mexico City. Taxis from the airport to the city run $11.

**By Car  Highway 180** is the old *carretera federal* (federal highway) between Mérida and Cancún. The trip takes 6 hours, and the road is in good shape; you will pass through many Maya villages. A four-lane divided *cuota,* or *autopista* (toll road) parallels Highway 180 and begins at the town of Kantunil, 56km (35 miles) east of Mérida. By avoiding the tiny villages and their not-so-tiny speed bumps, the *autopista* cuts 2 hours from the journey between Mérida and Cancún; one-way tolls cost $30. Coming from the direction of Cancún, Highway 180 enters Mérida by feeding into Calle 65, which passes 1 block south of the main square.

Coming from the south (Campeche or Uxmal), you will enter the city on Avenida Itzáes. To get to the town center, turn right on Calle 59 (the first street after the zoo).

A *periférico* (loop road) encircles Mérida, making it possible to skirt the city. Directional signs into the city are generally good, but going around the city on the loop requires vigilance.

**By Bus**   There are five bus stations in Mérida, two of which offer first-class buses; the other three provide local service to nearby destinations. The larger of the first-class stations, **CAME,** is on Calle 70, between calles 69 and 71 (see "City Layout," below). The ADO bus line and its affiliates operate the station. When you get there, you'll see a row of ticket windows; all but the last couple to the right sell first-class tickets. The last two windows sell tickets for ADO's deluxe services, ADO-GL and UNO. The former is only slightly better than first class; the latter has superwide roomy seats. Unless it's a long trip, I generally choose the bus that has the most convenient departure time. Tickets can be purchased in advance; just ask the ticket agent for the different options and departure times for the route you need.

The other first-class station is the small **Maya K'iin** used by the bus company **Elite.** It's at Calle 65 no. 548, between calles 68 and 70.

**To and from Cancún:** You can pick up a bus at the CAME (almost every hour) or through Elite (five per day). Both bus lines also pick up passengers at the Fiesta Americana Hotel, across from the Hyatt (12 buses per day). You can buy a ticket in the hotel's shopping arcade at the **Ticket Bus** agency or at the Elite ticket agency. Cancún is 4 hours away; a few buses stop in **Valladolid.** If you're downtown, you can purchase tickets from the agency in Pasaje Picheta, on the main square a couple of doors down from the Palacio de Gobierno.

**To and from Chichén Itzá:** Three buses per day (2½-hr. trip) depart from the CAME. Also, check out tours operating from the hotels in Mérida if you want to visit for the day.

**To and from Playa del Carmen, Tulum, and Chetumal:** From the CAME, there are 10 departures per day for Playa del Carmen (5-hr. trip), six for Tulum (6-hr. trip), and eight for Chetumal (7-hr. trip). From Maya K'iin there are three per day to Playa, which stop at the Fiesta Americana.

**To and from Campeche:** From the CAME station, there are 36 departures per day. Elite has four departures per day. It's a 2½-hour trip.

**To and from Palenque and San Cristóbal de las Casas:** There is service to San Cristóbal twice daily from the CAME, and once daily on Elite. To Palenque there are three and one, respectively. There have been reports of minor theft on buses to Palenque. You should do three things: Don't take second-class buses to this destination; check your luggage so that it's stowed in the cargo bay; and put your carry-on in the overhead rack, not on the floor.

The main **second-class bus station** is around the corner from the CAME on Calle 69, between calles 68 and 70.

**To and from Uxmal:** There are four buses per day. (You can also hook up with a tour to Uxmal through most hotels or any travel agent or tour operator in town.) One bus per day combines Uxmal with the other sites to the south (Kabah, Sayil, Labná, and Xlapak—known as the Puuc route) and does the whole round-trip in a day. It stops for 2 hours at Uxmal and 30 minutes at each of the other sites.

**To and from Progreso and Dzibilchaltún:** The bus station that serves these destinations is the **Estación Progreso,** Calle 62 no. 524, between calles 65 and 67. The trip to Progreso takes an hour by second-class bus.

**To and from Celestún:** The Celestún station is at Calle 50 between calles 65 and 67. The trip takes 1½ to 2 hours, depending on how often the bus stops. There are 10 buses per day.

**To and from Izamal:** The bus station is at the corner of Calle 65 and Calle 48. Departures are every half-hour. The trip takes 1½ hours.

**ORIENTATION  Arriving by Plane**  Mérida's airport is 13km (8 miles) from the city center on the southwestern outskirts of town, near the entrance to Highway 180. The airport has desks for renting a car, reserving a hotel room, and getting tourist information. Taxi tickets to town ($11) are sold outside the airport doors, under the covered walkway.

**VISITOR INFORMATION**  There are city tourism offices and state tourism offices, which have different resources; if you can't get the information you're looking for at one, go to the other. I have better luck with the city's **visitor information office** (© **999/942-0000,** ext. 80119), which is on the ground floor of the Ayuntamiento building facing the main square on Calle 62. Look for a glass door under the arcade. Hours are Monday to Saturday from 8am to 8pm and Sunday from 8am to 2pm. Monday through Saturday, at 9:30am, the staff offers visitors a free tour of the area around the main square. The state operates two downtown tourism offices: One is in the **Teatro Peón Contreras,** facing Parque de la Madre (© **999/924-9290**); and the other is on the main plaza, in the **Palacio de Gobierno,** immediately to the left as you enter. These offices are open daily from 8am to 9pm. There are also information booths at the airport and the CAME bus station.

Also keep your eye out for the free monthly magazine *Yucatán Today;* it's a good source of information for Mérida and the rest of the region.

**CITY LAYOUT**  Downtown Mérida has the standard layout of towns in the Yucatán: Streets running north-south are even numbers; those running east-west are odd numbers. The numbering begins on the north and the east sides of town, so if you're walking on an odd-numbered street and the even numbers of the cross streets are increasing, then you are heading west; likewise, if you are on an even-numbered street and the odd numbers of the cross streets are increasing, you are going south.

Address numbers don't tell you anything about what cross street to look for. This is why addresses almost always list cross streets, usually like this: "Calle 60 no. 549 × 71 y 73." The "×" is a multiplication sign—shorthand for the word *por* (meaning "by")—and *y* means "and." So this place would be on Calle 60 between calles 71 and 73. Outside of the downtown area, the numbering of streets gets a little crazy, so it's important to know the name of the neighborhood where you're going. This is the first thing taxi drivers will ask you.

The town's main square is the busy **Plaza Mayor,** referred to simply as **El Centro.** It's bordered by calles 60, 62, 61, and 63. Calle 60, which runs in front of the cathedral, is an important street to remember; it connects the main square with several smaller plazas, some theaters and churches, and the University of Yucatán, just to the north. Here, too, you'll find a concentration of handicraft shops, restaurants, and hotels. Around Plaza Mayor are the cathedral, the Palacio de Gobierno (state government building), the Ayuntamiento (town hall), and the Palacio Montejo. The plaza always has a crowd, and it's full on Sunday, when it holds a large street fair. (See "Festivals & Special Events in Mérida," below.) Within a few blocks are several smaller plazas and the bustling market district.

## (Moments) Festivals & Special Events in Mérida

Many Mexican cities offer weekend concerts in the park and such, but Mérida surpasses them all by offering performances every day of the week. Unless otherwise indicated, admission to the following is free.

**Sunday**   Each Sunday from 9am to 9pm, there's a fair called Mérida en Domingo (Mérida on Sunday). The main plaza and a section of Calle 60 from El Centro to Parque Santa Lucía close to traffic. Parents come with their children to stroll around and take in the scene. There are booths selling food and drink, along with a lively little flea market and used-book fair, children's art classes, and educational booths. At 11am in front of the Palacio del Gobierno, musicians play everything from jazz to classical and folk music. Also at 11am, the police orchestra performs Yucatecan tunes at the Santa Lucía park. At 11:30am, you'll find bawdy comedy acts at the Parque Hidalgo, on Calle 60 at Calle 59. There's a lull in the midafternoon, and then the plaza fills up again as people walk around and visit with friends. Around 7pm in front of the Ayuntamiento, a large band starts playing mambos, rumbas, and cha-cha-chas with great enthusiasm; you may see 1,000 people dancing in the street. Afterward, folk ballet dancers reenact a typical Yucatecan wedding inside.

**Monday**   *Vaquería regional,* traditional music and dancing to celebrate the Vaquerías feast, was associated originally with the branding of cattle on Yucatecan haciendas. Among the featured performers are dancers with trays of bottles or filled glasses on their heads—a sight to see.

**Tuesday**   At 9pm in Parque Santiago, Calle 59 at Calle 72, the Municipal Orchestra plays Latin and American big-band music from the 1940s.

**Wednesday**   At 9pm in the Teatro Peón Contreras, Calle 60 at Calle 57, the University of Yucatán Ballet Folklórico presents "Yucatán and Its Roots." Admission is $5.

**Thursday**   Yucatecan *trova* music (boleros, baladas) and dance are presented at the Serenata in Parque Santa Lucía at 9pm.

**Friday**   At 9pm in the courtyard of the University of Yucatán, Calle 60 at Calle 57, the University of Yucatán Ballet Folklórico performs typical regional dances from the Yucatán.

**Saturday**   Noche Mexicana at the park at the beginning of Paseo de Montejo begins at 9pm. It features several performances of traditional Mexican music and dance. Some of the performers are amateurs who acquit themselves reasonably well; others are professional musicians and dancers who thoroughly know their craft. Food stands sell very good *antojitos* (finger foods), as well as drinks and ice cream.

Mérida's most fashionable district is the broad, tree-lined boulevard **Paseo de Montejo** and its surrounding neighborhood. The Paseo de Montejo parallels Calle 60 and begins 7 blocks north and a little east of the main square. There are a number of trendy restaurants, modern hotels, offices of various banks and airlines, and a few clubs here, but the boulevard is mostly known for its stately mansions built during the boom times of the henequén industry. Near where the Paseo intersects Avenida Colón, you'll find the two fanciest hotels in town: the Hyatt and the Fiesta Americana.

**GETTING AROUND  By Car**  In general, reserve your car in advance from the U.S. to get the best weekly rates during high season (Nov–Feb); in low season, I usually do better renting a car once I get to Mérida. The local rental companies are competitive and have promotional deals that you can get only if you are there. When comparing, make sure that it's apples to apples; ask if the price quote includes the IVA tax and insurance coverage. Practically everybody offers free mileage. For tips on saving money on car rentals, see "Getting Around," in chapter 2. Rental cars are generally a little more expensive (unless you find a promotional rate) than in the U.S. By renting for only a day or two, you can avoid the high cost of parking lots in Mérida. These *estacionamentos* charge one price for the night and double that if you leave your car for the following day. Many hotels offer free parking, but make sure they include daytime parking in the price.

**By Taxi**  Taxis are easy to come by and much cheaper than in Cancún.

**By Bus**  City buses are a little tricky to figure out but aren't needed very often because almost everything of interest is within walking distance of the main plaza. Still, it's a bit of a walk from the plaza to the Paseo de Montejo, and you can save yourself some work by taking a bus, minibus, or *colectivo* (Volkswagen minivan) that is heading north on Calle 60. Most of these will take you within a couple of blocks of the Paseo de Montejo. The *colectivos* or *combis* (usually painted white) run out in several directions from the main plaza along simple routes. They usually line up along the side streets next to the plaza.

---

## FAST FACTS: Mérida

*American Express*  The office is at Paseo de Montejo 492 (© **999/942-8200**). It's open for travelers' services weekdays from 9am to 2pm and 4 to 6pm.

*Area Code*  The telephone area code is **999**.

*Bookstore*  The Librería Dante, Calle 59 between calles 60 and 62 (© **999/928-3674**), has a small selection of English-language cultural-history books on Mexico. It's open Monday to Saturday from 8am to 9:30pm, Sunday from 10am to 6pm. There is another Librería Dante on the main plaza in the Nuevo Olimpo.

*Business Hours*  Generally, businesses are open Monday to Saturday from 10am to 2pm and 4 to 8pm.

*Climate*  From November to February, the weather can be pleasantly cool and windy. In other months, it's just hot, especially during the day. Rain can occur any time of year, especially during the rainy season (July–Oct), and usually comes in the form of afternoon tropical showers.

*Consulates*  The **American Consulate** is at Paseo de Montejo 453, at Avenida Colón (© **999/925-6219** or -5011). Office hours are Monday to Friday from 9am to 1pm.

*Currency Exchange*  I prefer *casas de cambio* (currency exchange offices) over banks. There are many of these; one called **Cambios Portales**, Calle 61 no. 500

(© **999/923-8709**), is on the north side of the main plaza in the middle of the block. It's open daily from 8:30am to 8:30pm. There are also many ATMs; one is on the south side of the same plaza.

*Hospitals* The best hospital is **Centro Médico de las Américas,** Calle 54 no. 365 between 33-A and Avenida Pérez Ponce. The main phone number is © **999/ 926-2619**; for emergencies, call © **999/927-3199**. You can also call the Cruz Roja (Red Cross) at © **999/924-9813**.

*Internet Access* There are so many Internet access providers in town that you hardly have to walk more than a couple of blocks to find one.

*Pharmacy* **Farmacia Yza,** Calle 63 no. 502, between calles 60 and 62 (© **999/924- 9510**), on the south side of the plaza, is open 24 hours.

*Police* Mérida has a special body of police to assist tourists. They patrol the downtown area and the Paseo de Montejo. They wear white shirts bearing the words POLICIA TURISTICA. Their phone number is © **999/925-2555**.

*Post Office* The *correo* is near the market at the corner of calles 65 and 56. A branch office is at the airport. Both are open Monday to Friday from 8am to 7pm, Saturday from 9am to noon.

*Seasons* There are two high seasons for tourism, but they aren't as pronounced as on the coast. One is in July and August, when Mexicans take their vacations, and the other is between November 15 and Easter Sunday, when Canadians and Americans flock to the Yucatán to escape winter weather.

*Spanish Classes* Maya scholars, Spanish teachers, and archaeologists from the United States are among the students at the **Centro de Idiomas del Sureste,** Calle 14 no. 106 at Calle 25, Col. México, 97000 Mérida, Yuc. (© **999/926-1155**; fax 999/926-9020). The school has two locations: in the Colonia México, a northern residential district, and on Calle 66 at Calle 57, downtown. Students live with local families or in hotels; sessions running 2 weeks or longer are available for all levels of proficiency and areas of interest. For brochures and applications, contact the director, Chloe Conaway de Pacheco.

*Telephones* There are long-distance phone service centers at the airport and the bus station. In the downtown area is **TelWorld,** Calle 59 no. 495-4 between calles 56 and 58. To use the public phones, buy a **Ladatel** card from just about any newsstand or store. The cards come in a variety of denominations and work for long distance within Mexico and even abroad.

## EXPLORING MERIDA

Most of Mérida's attractions are within walking distance from the downtown area. To see a larger area of the city, take a popular **bus tour** by **Transportadora Carnaval.** The owner bought a few buses, painted them bright colors, pulled out the windows, raised the roof several inches, and installed wooden benches so that the buses remind you of the folksy buses of coastal Latin America, known as *chivas* in Colombia and Venezuela or as *guaguas* in other places. You can find these buses on the corner of calles 60 and 55 (next to the church of Santa Lucía) at 10am, 1pm, 4pm, and 7pm. The tour costs $7 per person and lasts 2 hours. Another option for seeing the city is a **horse-drawn**

**carriage.** A 45-minute ride around central Mérida costs $25. You can usually find the carriages beside the cathedral on Calle 61.

**EXPLORING PLAZA MAYOR** Downtown Mérida is a great example of a lowland colonial city. The town has a casual, relaxed feel. Buildings lack the severe baroque and neoclassical features that characterize central Mexico; most are finished in stucco and painted light colors. Mérida's gardens add to this relaxed, tropical atmosphere. Gardeners do not strive for control over nature. Here, natural exuberance is the ideal, with plants growing in a wild profusion that disguises human intervention. Mérida's plazas are a slightly different version of this aesthetic: Unlike the highland plazas, with their carefully sculpted trees, Mérida's squares are typically built around large trees that are left to grow as tall as possible. Hurricane Isidore blew down several of these in 2002, and has changed the appearance of these plazas as well as the Paseo de Montejo.

**Plaza Mayor** has this sort of informality. Even when there's no orchestrated event in progress, the park is full of people sitting on the benches, talking with friends, or taking a casual stroll. A plaza like this is a great advantage for a big city such as Mérida, giving it a personal feel and a sense of community. Notice the beautiful scale and composition of the major buildings surrounding it. The most prominent of these is the cathedral.

The oldest **cathedral** on the continent, it was built between 1561 and 1598. Much of the stone in the cathedral's walls came from the ruined buildings of Tihó, the former Maya city. The original finish was stucco, and you can see some remnants still clinging to the bare rock. However, people like the way the unfinished walls show the cathedral's age. Notice how the two top levels of the bell towers are built off-center from their bases—an uncommon feature. Inside, decoration is sparse, with altars draped in fabric colorfully embroidered like a Maya woman's shift. The most notable item is a picture of Ah Kukum Tutul Xiú, chief of the Xiú people, visiting the Montejo camp to make peace; it's hanging over the side door on the right.

To the left of the main altar is a small shrine with a curious figure of Christ that is a replica of one recovered from a burned-out church in the town of Ichmul. In the 1500s a local artist carved the original figure from a miraculous tree that was hit by lightning and burst into flames—but did not char. The statue later became blistered in the church fire at Ichmul, but it survived. In 1645 it was moved to the cathedral in Mérida, where the locals attached great powers to the figure, naming it *Cristo de las Ampollas* (Christ of the Blisters). It did not, however, survive the sacking of the cathedral in 1915 by revolutionary forces, so another figure, modeled after the original, was made. Take a look in the side chapel (daily 8–11am and 4:30–7pm), which contains a life-size diorama of the Last Supper. The Mexican Jesus is covered with prayer crosses brought by supplicants asking for intercession.

Next door to the cathedral is the old bishop's palace, now converted into the city's contemporary art museum, **Museo de Arte Contemporáneo Ateneo de Yucatán** (© **999/928-3236**). The palace was confiscated and rebuilt during the Mexican Revolution in 1915. The museum's entrance faces the cathedral from the recently constructed walkway between the two buildings called the Pasaje de la Revolución. The 17 exhibition rooms display work by contemporary artists, mostly from the Yucatán. (The best known are Fernando García Ponce and Fernando Castro Pacheco, whose works also hang in the government palace described below.) Nine of the rooms hold the museum's permanent collection; the rest are for temporary exhibits. It's open Wednesday to Monday from 10am to 6pm. Admission is free.

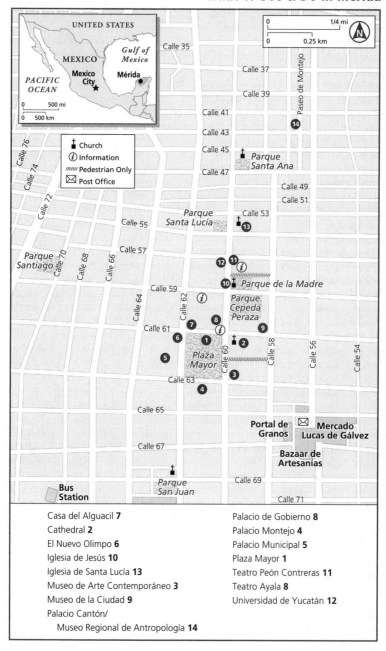

UNITED STATES

Gulf of Mexico

MEXICO

PACIFIC OCEAN

Mexico City

Mérida

0   500 mi
0   500 km

✝ Church
ⓘ Information
///// Pedestrian Only
✉ Post Office

Casa del Alguacil **7**
Cathedral **2**
El Nuevo Olimpo **6**
Iglesia de Jesús **10**
Iglesia de Santa Lucía **13**
Museo de Arte Contemporáneo **3**
Museo de la Ciudad **9**
Palacio Cantón/
   Museo Regional de Antropología **14**

Palacio de Gobierno **8**
Palacio Montejo **4**
Palacio Municipal **5**
Plaza Mayor **1**
Teatro Peón Contreras **11**
Teatro Ayala **8**
Universidad de Yucatán **12**

Moving clockwise around the plaza, on the south side is the **Palacio Montejo.** Its facade, with heavy decoration around the doorway and windows, is a good example of the Spanish architectural style known as plateresque. But the content of the decoration is very much a New World creation. Conquering the Yucatán was the Montejo family business, begun by the original Francisco Montejo and continued by his son and nephew, both named Francisco Montejo. Construction of the house started in 1542 under the son, Francisco Montejo El Mozo ("The Younger"). Bordering the entrance are politically incorrect figures of conquistadors standing on the heads of vanquished Indians—borrowed, perhaps, from the pre-Hispanic custom of portraying victorious Maya kings treading on their defeated foes. The posture of the conquistadors and their facial expression of wide-eyed dismay make them less imposing than the Montejos might have wished. A bank now occupies the building, but you can enter the courtyard, view the garden, and see for yourself what a charming residence it must have been for the descendants of the Montejos, who lived here as recently as the 1970s. (Curiously enough, not only does Mérida society keep track of who is descended from the Montejos, but it also keeps track of who is descended from the last Maya king, Tutul Xiú.)

In stark contrast to the severity of the cathedral and Casa Montejo is the light, unimposing **Ayuntamiento** or **Palacio Municipal (town hall).** The exterior dates from the mid–19th century, an era when a tropicalist aesthetic tinged with romanticism began asserting itself across coastal Latin America. On the second floor, you can see the meeting hall of the city council and enjoy a view of the plaza from the balcony. Next door to the Ayuntamiento is a recently completed building called **El Nuevo Olimpo (The New Olympus).** It took the place of the old Olimpo, which a misguided town council demolished in the 1970s, to the regret of many older Meridanos. The new building tries to incorporate elements of the original while presenting something new. It holds concert and gallery space, a bookstore, and a lovely courtyard. There is a comfortable cafe under the arches, and a bulletin board at the entrance to the courtyard with postings of upcoming performances.

Cater-cornered from the Nuevo Olimpo is the old **Casa del Alguacil (Magistrate's House).** Under its arcades is something of an institution in Mérida: the **Dulcería y Sorbetería Colón,** an ice-cream and sweet shop that will appeal to those who prefer less-rich ice creams. A spectacular side doorway on Calle 62 bears viewing, and across the street is the new **Cine Mérida,** with two movie screens showing art films and one stage for live performances. Returning to the main plaza, down a bit from the ice-cream store, is a **shopping center** of boutiques and convenience food vendors called **Pasaje Picheta.** At the end of the arcade is the **Palacio de Gobierno (state government building),** dating from 1892. Large murals by the Yucatecan artist Fernando Castro Pacheco, executed between 1971 and 1973, decorate the walls of the courtyard. Scenes from Maya and Mexican history abound, and the painting over the stairway depicts the Maya spirit with ears of sacred corn, the "sunbeams of the gods." Nearby is a painting of mustachioed Lázaro Cárdenas, who as president in 1938 expropriated 17 foreign oil companies and was hailed as a Mexican liberator. Upstairs is a long, wide gallery with more of Pacheco's paintings, which achieve their effect by localizing color and imitating the photographic technique of double exposure. The palace is open Monday to Saturday from 8am to 8pm, Sunday from 9am to 5pm. There is a small tourism office to the left as you enter.

Farther down Calle 61 is the **Museo de la Ciudad (City Museum).** It faces the side of the cathedral and occupies the former church of San Juan de Dios. An exhibit outlining the history of Mérida will be of interest to those curious about the city; there is explanatory text in English. Hours are Monday to Friday from 10am to 2pm and 4 to 8pm, Saturday and Sunday from 10am to 2pm. Admission is free.

**EXPLORING CALLE 60**    Heading north from Plaza Mayor up Calle 60, you'll see many of Mérida's old churches and squares. Several stores along Calle 60 sell gold-filigree jewelry, pottery, clothing, and folk art. A stroll along this street leads to the Parque Santa Ana and continues to the fashionable boulevard Paseo de Montejo and its **Museo Regional de Antropología (Anthropology Museum).**

The first place of interest is the **Teatro Daniel de Ayala,** only because it sometimes schedules interesting performances. On the right side of Calle 60 will be a small park called **Parque Cepeda Peraza** (or Parque Hidalgo). Named for 19th-century General Manuel Cepeda Peraza, the *parque* was part of Montejo's original city plan. Small outdoor restaurants front hotels on the park, making it a popular stopping place at any time of day. Across Calle 59 is the **Iglesia de Jesús,** or El Tercer Orden (the Third Order). Built by the Jesuit order in 1618, it has the richest interior of any church in Mérida, making it a favorite spot for weddings. The entire block on which the church stands belonged to the Jesuits, who are known as great educators. The school they left behind after their expulsion became the Universidad de Yucatán.

On the other side of the church is the **Parque de la Madre.** The park contains a modern statue of the Madonna and Child, a copy of the work by Renoir. Beyond the Parque de la Madre and across the pedestrian-only street is the **Teatro Peón Contreras,** an opulent theater designed by Italian architect Enrico Deserti a century ago. The theater is noted for its Carrara marble staircase and frescoed dome. Try to get a peek at it, and look at the performance schedule to see if anything of interest will take place during your stay. National and international performers appear here frequently. In the southwest corner of the theater, facing the Parque de la Madre, is a **tourist information office.** Across Calle 60 is the main building of the **Universidad de Yucatán.** Inside is a flagstone courtyard where the *ballet folklórico* performs on Friday nights.

A block farther north is **Parque Santa Lucía.** Bordered by an arcade on the north and west sides, this park was where visitors first alighted from the stagecoach. On Sunday, Parque Santa Lucía holds a used-book market, and several evenings a week it hosts popular entertainment. On Thursday nights, performers present Yucatecan songs and poems. Facing the park is the **Iglesia de Santa Lucía** (1575).

Four blocks farther up Calle 60 is **Parque Santa Ana;** if you turn right, you'll come to the beginning of the Paseo de Montejo in 2 blocks.

**EXPLORING THE PASEO DE MONTEJO**    The Paseo de Montejo is a broad, tree-lined boulevard that runs north-south starting at Calle 47, 7 blocks north and 2 blocks east of the main square. In the late 19th century, stalwarts of Mérida's upper crust (mostly plantation owners) decided that the city needed something grander than its traditional narrow streets lined by wall-to-wall town houses. They built this monumentally proportioned boulevard and lined it with mansions. Things went sour with the henequén bust, but several of these mansions survive—some in private hands, others as offices, restaurants, or consulates. Today, this is the fashionable part of town, with many restaurants, trendy dance clubs, and expensive hotels.

Of the mansions that survived, the most notable is the Palacio Cantón, which houses the **Museo Regional de Antropología (Anthropology Museum)** 𝕰𝕰 (𝐶 999/923-0557). Designed and built by Enrico Deserti, the architect of the Teatro Peón

Contreras, it was constructed between 1909 and 1911, during the last years of the Porfiriato. It was the residence of General Francisco Cantón Rosado, who enjoyed his palace for only 6 years before dying in 1917. For a time the mansion served as the official residence of the state's governor.

Viewing the museum also affords you an opportunity to see some of the surviving interior architecture. The museum's main focus is the pre-Columbian cultures of the peninsula, especially the Maya. Topics include cosmology, history, and culture. Captions for the permanent displays are mostly in Spanish. Starting with fossil mastodon teeth, the exhibits take you through the Yucatán's history, paying special attention to the daily life of its inhabitants.

Exhibits illustrate such strange Maya customs as tying boards to babies' heads to create the oblong shape that they considered beautiful, and filing teeth or perforating them to inset jewels. There are enlarged photos of several archaeological sites and drawings that illustrate the various styles of Maya dwellings. Even if you know only a little Spanish, this is a worthwhile stop, and it provides good background for explorations of Maya sites. The museum is open Tuesday to Saturday from 8am to 8pm, Sunday from 8am to 2pm. Admission is $3.50.

## SHOPPING

Mérida is known for hammocks, *guayaberas* (lightweight men's shirts worn untucked), and Panama hats. Baskets and pottery made in the Yucatán are for sale in the **central market.** Mérida is also the place to pick up prepared *adobo,* a pastelike mixture of ground *achiote* seeds (annatto), oregano, garlic, *masa,* and other spices used as a marinade for making dishes such as *cochinita pibil* (pit-baked pork). Simply mix the paste with sour orange to a soupy consistency before applying to the meat. Try it on chicken for *pollo pibil.* It can be purchased in a bottle, too.

**EXPLORING THE MARKET** Mérida's bustling **market district** is a few blocks southeast of the Plaza Mayor. The market and surrounding few blocks make up the commercial center of the city. Hordes of people come here to shop and work. It is by far the most crowded part of town, and the city government is refurbishing the whole area to relieve the traffic congestion. Behind the post office (at calles 65 and 56) is the oldest part of the market, the **Portal de Granos (Grains Arcade),** a row of maroon arches where the grain merchants used to sell their goods. Just east, between calles 56 and 54, is the market building, Mercado Lucas de Gálvez. The city has built a new municipal market building on the south side of this building, but it was having difficulty persuading the market venders to move. When this happens the city's plan is to tear down the Lucas de Gálvez and replace it with a plaza. Inside, chaos seems to reign, but after a short while a certain order emerges. Here you can find anything from fresh fish to flowers to leather goods. In and around the market you can find more locally manufactured goods; a secondary market is on calle 56, labeled **Bazaar de Artesanías (crafts market)** in big letters. Another crafts market, **Bazaar García Rejón,** lies a block west of the market on Calle 65 between calles 58 and 60.

## CRAFTS

**Casa de las Artesanías**     This store occupies the front rooms of a restored monastery. Here you can find a wide selection of crafts, 90% of which come from the Yucatán. For the most part, the quality of work is higher than elsewhere, but so are the prices. The monastery's back courtyard is used as a gallery, with rotating exhibits on folk and fine arts. It's open Monday to Saturday from 9am to 8pm, Sunday from 9am to 1pm. Calle 63 no. 513 (between calles 64 and 66). ℂ 999/928-6676.

**Miniaturas**    This fun little store is packed to the rafters with miniatures, a traditional Mexican folk art form that has been evolving in a number of directions, including social and political satire, pop art, and bawdy humor. Alicia Rivero, the owner, collects them from several parts of Mexico and offers plenty of variety, from traditional miniatures, such as dollhouse furniture, to popular cartoon characters and celebrities. The store also sells other forms of folk art such as masks, games, and traditional crafts. Hours are Monday to Saturday from 10am to 8pm. Calle 59 no. 507A-4 (between calles 60 and 62). ℂ 999/928-6503.

### GUAYABERAS

Business suits are hot and uncomfortable in Mérida's tropical climate, so businessmen, bankers, and bus drivers alike wear the *guayabera*, a loose-fitting shirt decorated with narrow tucks, pockets, and sometimes embroidery, worn over the pants rather than tucked in. Mérida is famous as the best place to buy *guayaberas,* which can go for less than $15 at the market or for more than $50 custom-made. A *guayabera* made of linen can cost about $80. Most are made of cotton, although other materials are available. The traditional color is white.

Most shops display ready-to-wear shirts in several price ranges. *Guayabera* makers pride themselves on being innovators. I have yet to enter a shirt-maker's shop in Mérida that did not present its own version of the *guayabera.* When looking at *guayaberas,* here are a few things to keep in mind: When Yucatecans say *seda,* they mean polyester; *lino* is linen or a linen/polyester combination. Take a close look at the stitching and such details as the way the tucks line up over the pockets; with *guayaberas,* the details are everything.

**Guayaberas Jack**    The craftsmanship here is good, the place has a reputation to maintain, and some of the salespeople speak English. Prices are as marked. This will give you a good basis of comparison if you want to hunt for a bargain elsewhere. If the staff does not have the style and color of shirt you want, they will make it for you in about 3 hours. This shop also sells regular shirts and women's blouses. Hours are Monday to Saturday from 10am to 8pm, Sunday from 10am to 2pm. Calle 59 no. 507A (between calles 60 and 62). ℂ 999/928-6002.

### HAMMOCKS

Natives across tropical America used hammocks long before the Europeans arrived in the New World. The word comes from the Spanish *hamaca,* which is a borrowing from Taino, a Caribbean Indian language. Hammocks are still in use throughout Latin America and come in a wide variety of forms, but none is so comfortable as the Yucatecan hammock, which is woven with cotton string in a fine mesh. For most of us, of course, the hammock is lawn furniture, something to relax in for an hour or so on a lazy afternoon. But for the vast majority of Yucatecans, hammocks are the equivalent of beds, and they greatly prefer hammocks to mattresses. I know a hotel owner who has 150 beds in his establishment but won't sleep on any of them. When he does, he complains of waking up unrested and sore. Many well-to-do Meridanos keep a bed just for show. In hotels that cater to Yucatecans, you will always find hammock hooks in the walls because many Yucatecans travel with their own hammock.

My advice to the hammock buyer: The woven part should be cotton, it should be made with fine string, and the strings should be so numerous that when you get in it and stretch out diagonally (the way you're supposed to sleep in these hammocks), the gaps between the strings remain small. Don't pay attention to the words used to describe the size of a hammock; they have become practically meaningless. Good hammocks don't cost a lot of money ($20–$35). If you want a superior hammock, ask for one made with fine crochet thread *hilo de crochet* (the word *crochet* is also sometimes bandied about, but you can readily see the difference). This should run about $100.

Nothing beats a tryout; the shops mentioned here will gladly hang a hammock for you to test-drive. When it's up, look to see that there are no untied strings. You can also see what street vendors are offering, but you have to know what to look for, or they are likely to take advantage of you.

**Hamacas El Aguacate**   El Aguacate sells hammocks wholesale and retail. It has the greatest variety and is the place to go for a really fancy or extra-large hammock. A good hammock is the no. 6 in cotton; it runs around $35. The store is open Monday to Friday from 8:30am to 7:30pm, Saturday from 8am to 5pm. It's 6 blocks south of the main square. Calle 58 no. 604 (at Calle 73). ℭ **999/928-6429.**

**Tejidos y Cordeles Nacionales**   This place near the municipal market sells only cotton hammocks, priced by weight—a pretty good practice because hammock lengths are fairly standardized. The prices are better than at El Aguacate, but quality control isn't as good. My idea of a good hammock weighs about 1½ kilograms (3½ lb.) and runs about $30. Calle 56 no. 516-B (between calles 63 and 65). ℭ **999/928-5561.**

## PANAMA HATS

Another useful and popular item is this soft, pliable hat made from the fibers of the *jipijapa* palm in several towns south of Mérida along Highway 180, especially Becal, in the neighboring state of Campeche. The hat makers in these towns work inside caves so that the moist air keeps the palm fibers pliant.

*Jipi* hats come in various grades determined by the quality (pliability, softness, and fineness) of the fibers and closeness of the weave. The difference in weave is easy to see, as a fine weave improves the shape of a hat. It has more body and retains its shape better. You'll find Panama hats for sale in several places, but often without much selection. There is a hat store in one of the market buildings: Walk south down Calle 56 past the post office; right before the street ends in the market place, turn left into a passage with hardware stores at the entrance. The fourth or fifth shop is the **Casa de los Jipis.**

## WHERE TO STAY

Mérida is easier on the budget than the resort cities. The stream of visitors is steadier than on the coast, so most hotels no longer use a high-season/low-season rate structure. Still, you are more likely to find promotional rates during low season. Mérida has a convention center, which attracts large trade shows that can fill the city's hotels, so it's a good idea to make reservations. The rates quoted here include the 17% tax. When inquiring about prices, always ask if the price quoted includes tax. Most hotels in Mérida offer at least a few air-conditioned rooms, and some also have pools. But many inexpensive hotels haven't figured out how to provide a comfortable bed. Either the mattresses are poor quality, or the bottom sheet is too small to tuck in properly. Some hotels here would offer a really good deal if only they would improve their beds. One last thing to note: In Mérida, free parking is a relative concept—for many hotels, free parking means only at night; during the day there may be a charge.

# Where to Stay & Dine in Mérida

UNITED STATES

MEXICO

Gulf of Mexico

PACIFIC OCEAN

Mexico City

Mérida

0  500 mi
0  500 km

0  0.25 mi
0  0.25 km

N

† Church
ⓘ Information
///// Pedestrian Only
✉ Post Office

Av. Colon

Av. Perez

Paseo de Montejo

Calle 35

Calle 37

Calle 39

Calle 41

Calle 43

Calle 45

Calle 47

Calle 49

Calle 51

Calle 53

Calle 55

Calle 57

Calle 59

Calle 61

Calle 63

Calle 65

Calle 67

Calle 69

Calle 72

Calle 70

Calle 68

Calle 66

Calle 64

Calle 62

Calle 60

Calle 58

Calle 56

Calle 54

Parque Santa Ana

Parque Santa Lucía

Parque Santiago

Parque de la Madre

Parque Cepeda Peraza

Plaza Mayor

Portal de Granos

Mercado Lucas de Gálvez

Bazaar de Artesanías

Bus Station

Parque San Juan

## ACCOMMODATIONS ■
Casa Mexilio Guest House **6**
Casa San Juan **17**
Fiesta Americana Mérida **1**
Hotel Caribe **13**
Hotel Dolores Alba **16**
Hotel Maison Lafitte **8**
Hotel Medio Mundo **4**
Hotel Mucuy **10**
Hyatt Regency Mérida **2**

## DINING ◆
Alberto's Continental **7**
Café Alameda **9**
Eladio's **15**
La Flor de Santiago **5**
Restaurante Amaro **11**
Restaurante Kantún **3**
Restaurant Los Almendros **14**
Vito Corleone **12**

## VERY EXPENSIVE

**Fiesta Americana Mérida** ⓡⓡ   This six-story hotel on the Paseo de Montejo is built in the grand *fin de siècle* style of the old mansions along the Paseo. Guest rooms are off the cavernous lobby, so all face outward and have views of one or another of the avenues. The rooms are comfortable and large, with furnishings and decorations striving for, and achieving, innocuousness in light, tropical colors. The floors are tile and the bathrooms large and well equipped. Service is very attentive, better than at the Hyatt. There is a shopping center on the ground floor, below the lobby.

Av. Colón 451, corner of Paseo Montejo, 92127 Mérida, Yuc. ⓒ 800/343-7821 in the U.S. and Canada, or 999/942-1111. Fax 999/942-1112. www.fiestaamericana.com.mx. 350 units. $210 double; $240 executive level; $260 junior suite. AE, DC, MC, V. Free secure parking. **Amenities:** 2 restaurants; bar; midsize outdoor pool; tennis court; health club w/saunas, men's steam room, unisex whirlpool, and massage; children's programs; concierge; tour desk; small business center; shopping arcade; 24-hr. room service; babysitting; laundry service; dry cleaning; executive-level rooms. *In room:* A/C, TV w/pay movies, Internet connection, minibar, coffeemaker, hair dryer, safe.

**Hyatt Regency Mérida** ⓡⓡ   This Hyatt is much like Hyatts elsewhere, wherein lies this hotel's chief asset. The rooms are dependably comfortable and quiet, the quietest in a noisy city. They're carpeted and well furnished, with great bathrooms. In decoration and comfort, I find them superior to those of the Fiesta Americana, but they certainly don't have any local flavor. The Hyatt's facilities, especially its tennis courts and health club, also rank above the Fiesta Americana's. The pool is more attractive and larger, but its location keeps it in the shade for most of the day, and the water never gets a chance to heat up. Rising 17 stories, the Hyatt is not hard to find in Mérida's skyline; it's near the Paseo de Montejo and across Avenida Colón from the Fiesta Americana.

Calle 60 no. 344 (at Av. Colón), 97000 Mérida, Yuc. ⓒ 800/223-1234 in the U.S. and Canada, or 999/942-1234. Fax 999/925-7002. www.merida.regency.hyatt.com. 299 units. $175 standard double; $200 Regency Club double. Ask about promotional rates. AE, DC, MC, V. Free guarded parking. **Amenities:** 2 restaurants; 2 bars (1 swim-up, open seasonally); large outdoor pool; 2 lighted tennis courts; state-of-the-art health club w/men's and women's steam rooms, whirlpool, sauna, and massage; children's activities (seasonal); concierge; tour desk; car rental; business center; shopping arcade; 24-hr. room service; babysitting; laundry service; dry cleaning; nonsmoking rooms; executive-level rooms. *In room:* A/C, TV, dataport, minibar, hair dryer.

## MODERATE

**Casa Mexilio Guest House** ⓡ *Moments*   This bed-and-breakfast is unlike any other I know. The owners are geniuses at playing with space in an unexpected and delightful manner. Rooms are at different levels, creating private spaces joined to each other and to rooftop terraces by stairs and catwalks. Most are spacious and airy, furnished and decorated in an engaging mix of new and old, polished and primitive. Five come with air-conditioning. A small pool with a whirlpool and profuse tropical vegetation take up most of the central patio. Breakfasts are great. It's 4 blocks west of the plaza. A small bar serves drinks during happy hour, and, weather permitting, you can have your cocktail on one of the rooftop terraces.

Calle 68 no. 495 (between calles 57 and 59), 97000 Mérida, Yuc. ⓒ 877/639-4546 in the U.S. and Canada, or 999/928-2505. www.casamexilio.com. 9 units. $50–$85 double; $120 penthouse. Rates include full breakfast. MC, V. **Amenities:** Bar; small outdoor pool; whirlpool; nonsmoking rooms. *In room:* A/C (in some), no phone.

**Hotel Caribe**   This three-story colonial-style hotel (no elevator) is great for a couple of reasons: Its location at the back of Plaza Hidalgo is both central and quiet, and it has a nice little pool and sun deck on the rooftop with a view of the cathedral. The rooms are moderately comfortable, though they aren't well lit, and have only small windows facing the central courtyard. Thirteen *clase económica* rooms don't have air-conditioning, but standard rooms do; and superior rooms (on the top floor) have been remodeled and have safes, hair dryers, larger windows, and quieter air-conditioning. Avoid the rooms on the ground floor. The hotel offers a lot of variety in bedding arrangements, mostly combinations of twins and doubles. Mattresses are often softer than standard. The TVs add little value to the rooms. Nearby parking is free at night but costs extra during the day beginning at 7am. The restaurant serves good Mexican food.

Calle 59 no. 500 (at Calle 60), 97000 Mérida, Yuc. © 888/822-6431 in the U.S. and Canada, or 999/924-9022. Fax 999/924-8733. www.hotelcaribe.com.mx. 53 units. $48 *clase económica* double; $54–$60 standard or superior double. AE, MC, V. **Amenities:** Restaurant; bar; small outdoor pool; tour desk; room service until 10pm; laundry service. *In room:* A/C (in some), TV, hair dryer (in some), safe (in some).

**Hotel Maison Lafitte** 🔮   This new three-story hotel offers modern, attractive rooms with good air-conditioning as well as tropical touches such as wooden louvers over the windows, and light furniture with caned backs and seats. Rooms are medium to large, with midsize bathrooms that have great showers and good lighting. Most rooms come with either two doubles or a king-size bed. Rooms are quiet and look out over a pretty little garden with a fountain. A couple of rooms don't have windows. The location is excellent.

Calle 60 no. 472 (between calles 53 and 55), 97000 Mérida, Yuc. © 800/538-6802 in the U.S. and Canada, or 999/928-1243. Fax 999/923-9159. www.maisonlafitte.com.mx. 30 units. $80 double. Rates include full breakfast. AE, MC, V. Free limited secure parking for compact cars. **Amenities:** Restaurant; bar; small outdoor pool; tour desk; car rental; limited room service; in-room massage; laundry service; dry cleaning. *In room:* A/C, TV, minibar, hair dryer, safe.

**Hotel Medio Mundo** 🔮 *Finds*   This is a quiet courtyard hotel with beautiful rooms and a good location 3 blocks north of the main plaza. The English-speaking owners have invested their money in the right places, going for high-quality mattresses, good lighting, quiet air-conditioning units, lots of space, and good bathrooms with strong showers. What they didn't invest in were TVs, which adds to the serenity. Higher prices are for the eight rooms with air-conditioning, but all units have windows with good screens and get ample ventilation. Breakfast is served in one of the two attractive courtyards.

Calle 55 no. 533 (between calles 64 and 66), 97000 Mérida, Yuc. ©/fax **999/924-5472**. www.hotelmediomundo.com. 12 units. $55–$75 double. MC, V. **Amenities:** Small outdoor pool; tour info; in-room massage; laundry service; non-smoking rooms. *In room:* A/C (in some), no phone.

## INEXPENSIVE

**Casa San Juan** 🔮 *Value*   This B&B, in a colonial house, is loaded with character and provides a good glimpse of the old Mérida that lies behind the colonial facades in the historic district. Guest rooms are beautifully decorated, large, and comfortable. Those in the original house have been modernized but maintain a colonial feel, with 7m (23-ft.) ceilings and 45-centimeter-thick (18-in.) walls. The modern rooms in back look out over the rear patio. The lower rate is for the three rooms without air-conditioning (they have ceiling and floor fans). Choice of beds includes one queen-size, one double, or two twins, all with good mattresses and sheets. Breakfast includes fruit or juice, coffee, bread, and homemade preserves. Casa San Juan is 4 blocks south of the main square.

Calle 62 no. 545a (between calles 69 and 71), 97000 Mérida, Yuc. ©/fax **999/986-2937**. www.casasanjuan.com. 8 units (7 with private bathroom). $30–$60 double. No credit cards. Rates include continental breakfast. Parking nearby $2. *In room:* A/C (in some), no phone.

**Hotel Dolores Alba** *Value*   The Dolores Alba offers attractive, comfortable rooms, an inviting swimming pool, good air-conditioning, and free parking, all for a great price. The three-story section (with elevator) surrounding the back courtyard offers

## Of Haciendas & Hotels

**Haciendas** in the Yucatán have had a bumpy history. During the colonial period they were isolated, self-sufficient fiefdoms—not terribly efficient, but they didn't have to be. Mostly they produced foodstuffs—enough for the needs of the owners and peasants plus a little extra that the owners could sell for a small sum in the city. The owners, though politically powerful, especially within the confines of their large estates, were never rich.

This changed in the 19th century, when the expanding world market created high demand for henequén, the natural fiber of the sisal plant, which was used to bale hay. In a few years, all of the haciendas shifted to mass production of this commodity. Prices and profits kept climbing through the end of the century and into the 20th. Hacienda owners now had lots of cash to spend on their estates and on heavy machinery to process the henequén fiber more efficiently. Then came the bust. Throughout the 1920s, prices and demand fell, and there was no other commodity that could replace sisal. The haciendas entered a long decline, but by then, the cultivation and processing of the sisal plant had become part of local culture.

To see and understand what things were like during the golden age, you can visit a couple of haciendas. One, by the name of **Sotuta de Peón,** has recently been thoroughly refurbished and operates much like in the old days—a living museum involving an entire community (see "Side Trips from Mérida," later in this chapter). At the other one, **Yaxcopoil** (see "En Route to Uxmal," later in this chapter), you can stroll through the shell of a once bustling estate and look for remnants of faded splendor.

Now another boom of sorts has brought haciendas back; this time as retreats, country residences, and hotels. The hotels convey an air of the past—elegant gateways, thick walls, open arches, and high ceilings—you get the feel of an era gone by. Indeed, there are a few features that make a guest feel like lord and master, especially the extravagant suites and personal service. But what strikes me the most when I visit these haciendas is the contrast between them and the world outside. They are like little islands of order and tranquillity in the sea of chaos that is the Yucatán.

large rooms with good-size bathrooms. Beds (either two doubles or one double and one twin) have supportive foam-core mattresses, usually in a combination of one medium-firm and one medium-soft. All rooms have windows or balconies looking out over the pool. An old mango tree shades the front courtyard. The older rooms in this section are decorated with local crafts and have small bathrooms. The family that owns the Hotel Dolores Alba outside Chichén Itzá manages this hotel; you can make reservations at one hotel for the other. This hotel is 3½ blocks from the main square.

Calle 63 no. 464 (between calles 52 and 54), 97000 Mérida, Yuc. ✆ **999/928-5650.** Fax 999/928-3163. www.dolores alba.com. 100 units. $40–$45 double. MC, V (with 8% surcharge). Internet specials available. Free guarded sheltered parking. **Amenities:** Restaurant; outdoor pool; tour desk; room service until 9pm; laundry service; laundromat. *In room:* A/C, TV, safe.

There are five luxury hacienda hotels. The most opulent of these is **Xcanatún** (𝄫 888/883-3633 in the U.S.; www.xcanatun.com). It's on the outskirts of Mérida, off the highway to Progreso. The suites are large and have extravagant bathrooms. The decor is in muted colors with rich materials and modern pieces that evoke the simplicity of an earlier age. It has the best restaurant in the Mérida area and a complete spa. The owners personally manage their hotel and keep the service sharp.

The other four luxury hotels are all owned by Roberto Hernández, one of the richest men in Mexico. The hospitality and reservation system are handled by **Starwood Hotels** (𝄫 800/325-3589 in the U.S. and Canada; www.luxurycollection.com). The owner has taken great pains to restore all four haciendas to original condition, and all are beautiful. **Temozón,** off the highway to Uxmal, is the most magnificent. **Uayamón,** located between the ruins of Edzná and the colonial city of Campeche, is perhaps the most romantic. **San José Cholul,** located east of Mérida toward Izamal, is my personal favorite, and picturesque **Santa Rosa** lies southwest of Mérida, near the town of Maxcanú. Packages are available for staying at two or more of these haciendas. All offer personal service, activities, and spas.

Two haciendas offer economical lodging. On the western outskirts of Mérida by the highway to Chichén Itzá and Cancún is **San Pedro Nohpat** (𝄫 999/988-0542; www.haciendaholidays.com). It retains only the land that immediately surrounds the residence, but it offers a great bargain in lodging—large, comfortable rooms and an attractive garden area and pool. The other is **Blanca Flor** (𝄫 999/925-8042; www.mexonline.com/blancaflor.htm), which lies between Mérida and Campeche just off the highway. It's the only hacienda hotel that actually operates like one, producing most of the food served there. The owners work with bus tours but also welcome couples and individuals. Rooms are in a modern building and are large and simply furnished.

Two other haciendas can be leased by small groups for retreats and group vacations: **Hacienda Petac** (𝄫 800/225-4255 in the U.S.; www.hacienda petac.com) and **San Antonio Millet** (𝄫 999/910-6144; www.haciendasan antonio.com.mx). Both have beautiful rooms, common areas, and grounds.

**Hotel Mucuy** 𝘝𝘢𝘭𝘶𝘦    The Mucuy is a simple, quiet, pleasant hotel in a great location. The gracious owners strive to make guests feel welcome, with conveniences such as a communal refrigerator in the lobby and, for a small extra charge, the use of a washer and dryer. Guest rooms are basic; most contain two twin beds or a queen-size (with comfortable mattresses) and some simple furniture. A neat garden patio with comfortable chairs is the perfect place for sitting and reading. The Mucuy is named for a small dove said to bring good luck to places where it alights. The hotel has a few rooms with air-conditioning, which cost $5 more.

Calle 57 no. 481 (between calles 56 and 58), 97000 Mérida, Yuc. 𝄫 999/928-5193. Fax 999/923-7801. cofelia@ yahoo.com.mx. 24 units. $22 double. No credit cards. **Amenities:** Small outdoor pool; laundromat. *In room:* A/C (in some), no phone.

## WHERE TO DINE

The people of Mérida have strong ideas and traditions about food. Certain dishes are always associated with a particular day of the week. In households across the city, Sunday would feel incomplete without *puchero* (a kind of stew). On Monday, at any restaurant that caters to locals, you are sure to find *frijol con puerco* (pork and beans). Likewise, you'll find *potaje* (potage) on Thursday; fish, of course, on Friday; and *chocolomo* (a beef dish) on Saturday. These dishes are heavy and slow to digest; they are for the midday meal, and not suitable for supper. What's more, Meridanos don't believe that seafood is a healthy supper food. All seafood restaurants in Mérida close by 6pm unless they cater to tourists. The preferred supper food is turkey (which, by the way, is said to be high in tryptophan, a soporific), and it's best served in the traditional *antojitos—salbutes* (small thin rounds of *masa* fried and topped with turkey, pork, or chicken, and onions, tomatoes, and lettuce) and *panuchos* (sliced open and lightly stuffed with bean paste, before having toppings added) and turkey soup.

Another thing you may notice about Mérida is the surprising number of Middle Eastern restaurants. The city received a large influx of Lebanese immigrants around 1900. This population has had a strong influence on local society, to the point where Meridanos think of *kibbe* the way Americans think of pizza. Speaking of pizza, if you want to get some to take back to your hotel room, try **Vito Corleone,** on Calle 59 between calles 60 and 62. Its pizzas have a thin crust with a slightly smoky taste from the wood-burning oven.

It's becoming more difficult to recommend good restaurants for fine dining in the downtown area. Most of the best places are in the outlying districts, near the upper-class neighborhoods and shopping plazas. They are a little difficult to get to. If you want something special, I would recommend dining at the Hacienda Xcanatún on the outskirts of town, off the Progreso road. (See "Of Haciendas & Hotels," above.)

### EXPENSIVE

**Alberto's Continental** ✦ LEBANESE/YUCATECAN/ITALIAN   There's nothing quite like dining here at night in a softly lit room or on the wonderful old patio framed in Moorish arches. Nothing glitzy—just elegant *mudejar*-patterned tile floors, simple furniture, decoration that's just so, and the gurgling of a fountain creating a romantic mood. I find the prices on the expensive side. For supper, you can choose a sampler plate of four Lebanese favorites, or traditional Yucatecan specialties, such as *pollo pibil* or fish Celestún (bass stuffed with shrimp). You can finish with Turkish coffee.

Calle 64 no. 482 (at Calle 57). ℂ **999/928-5367.** Reservations recommended. Main courses $8–$20. AE, MC, V. Daily 1–11pm.

### MODERATE

**El Príncipe Tutul Xiu** ✦ (Finds) REGIONAL   This is a new restaurant that serves Yucatecan specialties from a limited menu. The original is in the town of Maní—the owner opened this restaurant because he got tired of hearing Meridanos asking him why he didn't open one in the capital. It's a short taxi ride from downtown, and to return you can pick up a local bus that passes by the restaurant. This is a great place to try the famous *sopa de lima,* and one of the six typical main courses. These are served with great handmade tortillas. And you can order, with confidence, one of the flavored waters such as an *horchata* or *tamarindo.*

Calle 123 no. 216 (between calles 46 and 46b), Colonia Serapio Rendón. ℂ **999/929-7721.** Reservations not accepted. Main courses $6. MC, V. Daily 11am–6pm.

**Restaurante Amaro** REGIONAL/VEGETARIAN   The menu in this courtyard restaurant offers some interesting vegetarian dishes, such as *crema de calabacitas* (cream of squash soup), apple salad, and avocado pizza. There is also a limited menu of fish and chicken dishes; you might want to try the Yucatecan chicken. The *agua de chaya* (chaya is a leafy vegetable prominent in the Maya diet) is refreshing on a hot afternoon. All desserts are made in-house. The restaurant is a little north of Plaza Mayor.

Calle 59 no. 507 interior 6 (between calles 60 and 62). (✆ **999/928-2451**. Main courses $5–$9. MC, V. Mon–Sat 11am–2am.

**Restaurante Kantún** (✦ (Value) SEAFOOD   This modest little restaurant serves up the freshest seafood for a good price. The owner-chef, a son of a cook, is always on the premises taking care of details. He tells me that he will stay open late by special arrangement for parties as small as four people. The menu includes excellent ceviches and seafood cocktails, and fish cooked in a number of ways. I had the *especial Kantún,* which was lightly battered and stuffed with lobster, crab, and shrimp. The dining room is air-conditioned, the furniture comfortable, and the service attentive.

Calle 45 no. 525-G (between calles 64 and 66). (✆ **999/923-4493**. Reservations recommended on Good Friday. Main courses $6–$12. MC, V. Daily noon–6pm.

**Restaurant Los Almendros** (Overrated) YUCATECAN   Ask where to eat Yucatecan food, and locals will inevitably suggest this place because of its reputation. After all, this was the first place to offer tourists such Yucatecan specialties as *salbutes, panuchos* and *papadzules* (both similar to *gorditas*), *cochinita pibil,* and *poc chuc.* The menu even comes with color photographs to facilitate acquaintance with these strange-sounding dishes. The food is okay and not much of a risk, but you can find better elsewhere. Still, it's a safe place to try Yucatecan food for the first time, and it's such a fixture that the idea of a guidebook that doesn't mention this restaurant is unthinkable. It's 5 blocks east of Calle 60, facing the Parque de la Mejorada.

Calle 50A no. 493. (✆ **999/928-5459**. Main courses $4–$9; daily special $5–$9. AE, MC, V. Daily 10am–11pm.

## INEXPENSIVE

**Café Alameda** (✦ MIDDLE EASTERN/VEGETARIAN   The trappings here are simple and informal (metal tables, plastic chairs), and it's a good place for catching a light meal. The trick is figuring out the Spanish names for popular Middle Eastern dishes. Kibbe is *quebbe bola* (not *quebbe cruda*), hummus is *garbanza,* and shish kabob is *alambre.* I leave it to you to figure out what a spinach pie is called (and it's excellent). Café Alameda is a treat for vegetarians, and the umbrella-shaded tables on the patio are perfect for morning coffee and *mamules* (walnut-filled pastries).

Calle 58 no. 474 (between calles 55 and 57). (✆ **999/928-3635**. Main courses $2–$5. No credit cards. Daily 7:30am–5:30pm.

**Eladio's** (✦ YUCATECAN   This is where locals come to relax in their off hours, drink very cold beer, and snack or dine on Yucatecan specialties. You have two choices: order a beer and enjoy *una botana* (a small portion that accompanies a drink, in this case usually a Yucatecan dish), or order from the menu. *Cochinita, poc chuc,* and *longaniza asada* (a local variety of sausage) are all good. Or try a *panucho* or *salbute* if you're there in the evening. Often there is live music in this open-air restaurant, which is around the corner from Los Almendros, by Parque la Mejorada.

Calle 59 (at Calle 44). (✆ **999/923-1087**. Main courses $4–$5. MC, V. Daily noon–8pm.

**La Flor de Santiago** REGIONAL    I enjoy the food here as much as anywhere else in the downtown area, but often it can be annoying because the cooks run out of food. The restaurant has its own bakery with a wood-fired stove for baking sweet breads for breakfast and supper. On the menu are several of the regional dishes that you see elsewhere, like *panuchos* and *salbutes,* and some things that aren't so commonly on the menu, like *pibito,* also called *mucbil pollo;* a traditional food for Day of the Dead, it's much like a tamal on the outside, with chicken and a soft center on the inside. There are also several sandwiches, *comida corrida,* and a large choice of beverages. The dining area is classic, with its high ceiling, plain furniture, and local clientele.

Calle 70 no. 478 (between calles 57 and 59). ℂ 999/928-5591. *Comida corrida* $3.50; main courses $3–$6. No credit cards. Daily 7am–11pm.

## MERIDA AFTER DARK

For nighttime entertainment, see the box, "Festivals & Special Events in Mérida," earlier in this chapter, or check out the theaters noted here.

**Teatro Peón Contreras,** Calle 60 at Calle 57, and **Teatro Ayala,** Calle 60 at Calle 61, feature a wide range of performing artists from Mexico and around the world. **El Nuevo Olimpo,** on the main square, schedules frequent concerts; and **Cine Mérida,** a half-block north of the Nuevo Olimpo, has two screens for showing classic and art films, and one live stage.

Mérida's club scene offers everything from ubiquitous rock/dance to some one-of-a-kind spots that are nothing like what you find back home. Most of the dance clubs are in the big hotels or on Paseo de Montejo. For dancing, a small cluster of clubs on Calle 60, around the corner from Santa Lucía, offer live rock and Latin music. For salsa, go to **Mambo Café** in the Plaza las Américas shopping center.

**La Trova** *Moments*    It's hard to overstate the importance of *música de trío* or *trova* in Mexican popular culture. This music, mainly in the form of songs called boleros, may have been at its most popular in the 1940s and 1950s, but every new Mexican pop music heartthrob feels compelled to release a new version of the classics. I like the originals best, and so do most Mexicans. And if you understand colloquial Spanish, all the better; the language of boleros is vivid, passionate, and quite Mexican. The Yucatán is especially well known for its *trova*—so much so, that Mérida has built a museum to popular song (Museo de la Canción Yucateca). But I prefer listening to it live. The best place by far to do this is La Trova, a cozy and comfortable bar in the old Mérida Misión Hotel at the corner of calles 60 and 57. The musical director for the bar is a local legend, and he lines up some of the best trios I've ever heard. It's open daily from 9pm to 2am. Calle 60 no. 491. ℂ 999/923-9500. Cover $9.

## ECOTOURS & ADVENTURE TRIPS

The Yucatán Peninsula has seen a recent explosion of companies that organize nature and adventure tours. One well-established outfit with a great track record is **Ecoturismo Yucatán,** Calle 3 no. 235, Col. Pensiones, 97219 Mérida (ℂ **999/920-2772;** fax 999/925-9047; www.ecoyuc.com). Alfonso and Roberta Escobedo create itineraries to meet just about any special or general interest you may have for going to the Yucatán or southern Mexico. Alfonso has been creating adventure and nature tours for more than a dozen years. Specialties include archaeology, birding, natural history, and kayaking. The company also offers day trips that explore contemporary Maya culture and life in villages in the Yucatán. Package and customized tours are available.

# SIDE TRIPS FROM MERIDA
## SOTUTA DE PEON

What started out as one man's hobby—to restore an old hacienda for a weekend get-away and perhaps see what it takes to plant a couple of acres of henequén—spiraled out of control until it grew into one of the best living museums you'll see anywhere, and has engrossed the imagination of an entire rural community. Presto! You have a completely functional *hacienda henequénera*.

You can arrange transportation from any of Mérida's hotels by calling **Hacienda Sotuta de Peón** at ⓒ **999/941-8639.** Call to make a reservation even if you have your own car, and be sure to bring your bathing suit; there's a cool *cenote* on the property. The best days to visit are when the giant fiber-extracting machine is in operation—Tuesday, Thursday, or Saturday. The tour starts with a visit to the henequén fields via mule-drawn carts, the same as are used to transport the leaves of the plant to the hacienda's headquar-ters. You get to see it being harvested, and later, processed at the *casa de máquinas*, and even used in the manufacturing of twine and such. Along the way you get a glimpse into the local culture surrounding henequén production. You visit a house of one of the workers, as well as the house of the *hacendado* (the owner). You can also try some of the regional cooking—there's a restaurant on the premises. Transportation and tour (in Eng-lish or Spanish) costs $45 per person, but check this because the hacienda is a newly operating business, and there might be some price adjustments. For more information see **www.haciendatour.com**.

## IZAMAL

Izamal is a sleepy town some 80km (50 miles) east of Mérida, an easy day trip by car. You can visit the famous Franciscan convent of San Antonio de Padua and the ruins of four large pyramids that overlook the center of town. One pyramid is partially reconstructed. Life in Izamal is easygoing in the extreme, as evidenced by the *victorias,* the horse-drawn buggies that serve as taxis here. Even if you come by car, you should make a point of touring the town in one of these. There is also a new sound-and-light show in the old convent. The half-hour show costs $4.50 and is held on Tuesdays, Thursdays, Fridays, and Saturdays at 8pm. It's in Spanish, but you can rent head-phones in other languages for $2.50.

## CELESTUN NATIONAL WILDLIFE REFUGE: FLAMINGOS & OTHER WATERFOWL

On the coast west of Mérida is a large wetlands area that has been declared a biopre-serve. It is a long, shallow estuary where freshwater mixes with Gulf saltwater, creating a habitat perfect for flamingos and many other species of waterfowl. This *ría* (estuary), unlike others that are fed by rivers or streams, receives fresh water through about 80 *cenotes,* most of which are underwater. It is very shallow (.3–1m/1–4 ft. deep) and thickly grown with mangrove, with an open channel .5km (¼ mile) wide and 50km (31 miles) long, sheltered from the open sea by a narrow strip of land. Along this corridor, you can take a launch to see flamingos as they dredge the bottom of the shallows for a species of small crustacean and a particular insect that make up the bulk of their diet.

You can get here by car or bus; it's an easy 90-minute drive. (For information on buses, see "Getting There & Departing: By Bus," earlier in this chapter.) To drive, leave downtown Mérida on Calle 57. Shortly after Santiago Church, Calle 57 ends and there's a dogleg onto Calle 59-A. This crosses Avenida Itzáes, and its name changes to

Jacinto Canek; continue until you see signs for Celestún Highway 178. This will take you through Hunucmá, where the road joins Highway 281, which takes you to Celestún. You'll know you have arrived when you get to the bridge.

In the last few years, the state agency CULTUR has come into Celestún and established order where once there was chaos. Immediately to your left after the bridge, you'll find modern facilities with a snack bar, clean bathrooms, and a ticket window. Prices for tours are fixed. A 75-minute tour costs about $45 and can accommodate up to six people. You can join others or hire a boat by yourself. On the tour you'll definitely see some flamingos; you'll also get to see some mangrove close up, and one of the many underwater springs. Please do not urge the boatmen to get any closer to the flamingos than they are allowed to; if pestered too much, the birds will abandon the area for other, less fitting habitat. The ride is quite pleasant—the water is calm, and CULTUR has supplied the boatmen with wide, flat-bottom skiffs that have canopies for shade.

In addition to flamingos, you will see frigate birds, pelicans, spoonbills, egrets, sandpipers, and other waterfowl feeding on shallow sandbars at any time of year. At least 15 duck species have been counted, and there are several species of birds of prey. Of the 175 bird species that are here, some 99 are permanent residents. Nonbreeding flamingos remain here year-round; the larger group of breeding flamingos takes off around April to nest on the upper Yucatán Peninsula east of Río Lagartos, returning to Celestún in October.

**Hotel Eco Paraíso Xixim** 🐾🐾 Eco Paraíso is meant to be a refuge from the modern world. It sits on a deserted 4km (2½-mile) stretch of beach that was once part of a coconut plantation. It attracts much the same clientele as the former-haciendas-turned-luxury-hotels, but in some ways it has more going for it (like the beach). Some guests come here for a week of idleness; others use this as a base of operations for visiting the biopreserve and making trips to the Maya ruins in the interior. The hotel offers its own tours to various places. Rooms are quite private; each is a separate bungalow with *palapa* roof. Each comes with two comfortable queen-size beds, a sitting area, ceiling fans, and a private porch with hammocks. On my last visit, the food was very good, and the service was great. The hotel composts waste, and treats and uses wastewater.

Antigua Carretera a Sisal Km 10, 97367 Celestún, Yuc. ☎ **988/916-2100.** Fax 988/916-2111. www.ecoparaiso.com. 15 units. High season $198 double; low season $172 double. Rates include 2 meals per person. AE, MC, V. Free parking. **Amenities:** Restaurant; bar; midsize outdoor pool; tour desk. *In room:* Coffeemaker, hair dryer, safe.

## DZIBILCHALTUN: MAYA RUINS & MUSEUM

This destination makes for a quick morning trip that will get you back to Mérida in time for a siesta, or it could be part of a longer trip to Progreso, Uaymitún, and Xcambó. It's located 14km (8⅔ miles) north of Mérida along the Progreso road and 4km (2½ miles) east of the highway. To get there, take Calle 60 all the way out of town and follow signs for Progreso and Highway 261. Look for the sign for Dzibilchaltún, which also reads UNIVERSIDAD DEL MAYAB; it will point you right. After a few miles you'll see a sign for the entrance to the ruins and the museum. If you don't want to drive, take one of the *colectivos* that line up along Parque San Juan.

Dzibilchaltún was founded about 500 B.C., flourished around A.D. 750, and was in decline long before the coming of the conquistadors. Since the ruins were discovered in 1941, more than 8,000 buildings have been mapped. The site covers an area of almost 15 sq. km (6 sq. miles) with a central core of almost 25 hectares (62 acres), but the area of prime interest is limited to the buildings surrounding two plazas next to the *cenote,* and another building, the Temple of the Seven Dolls, connected to these by a *sacbé* (causeway). Dzibilchaltún means "place of the stone writing," and at least 25 stelae have been found.

Start at the **Museo del Pueblo Maya,** which is worth seeing. It's open Tuesday to Sunday from 8am to 4pm. Admission is $6. The museum's collection includes artifacts from various sites in the Yucatán. Explanations are printed in bilingual format and are fairly thorough. Objects include a beautiful example of a plumed serpent from Chichén Itzá and a finely designed incense vessel from Palenque. From this general view of the Maya civilization, the museum moves on to exhibit specific artifacts found at the site of Dzibilchaltún, including the rather curious dolls that have given one structure its name. Then there's an exhibit on Maya culture in historical and present times, including a collection of *huipiles,* the woven blouses that Indian women wear. From here a door leads out to the site.

The first thing you come to is the *sacbé* that connects the two areas of interest. To the left is the **Temple of the Seven Dolls.** The temple's doorways and the *sacbé* line up with the rising sun at the spring and autumnal equinoxes. To the right are the buildings grouped around the Cenote Xlacah, the sacred well, and a complex of buildings around **Structure 38,** the **Central Group** of temples. The Yucatán State Department of Ecology has added nature trails and published a booklet (in Spanish) of birds and plants seen along the mapped trail.

## PROGRESO, UAYMITUN & XCAMBO: GULF COAST CITY, FLAMINGO LOOKOUT & MORE MAYA RUINS

For a beach escape, go to the port of Progreso, Mérida's weekend beach resort. This is where Meridanos have their vacation houses and where they come in large numbers in July and August. It is also the part-time home of some Americans and Canadians escaping northern winters. Except for July and August, it is a quiet place where you can enjoy the Gulf waters in peace. Along the *malecón,* the wide oceanfront drive that extends the length of a sandy beach, you can pull over and enjoy a swim anywhere you like. The water here isn't the blue of the Caribbean, but it's clean. A long pier extends several kilometers into the Gulf to load and unload large ships. Cruise ships dock here twice a week. Along or near the *malecón* are several hotels and a number of restaurants where you can get good fresh seafood.

From Mérida, buses to **Progreso** leave from the bus station at Calle 62 no. 524, between calles 65 and 67, every 15 minutes, starting at 5am. The trip takes almost an hour and costs $3.

If you have a car, you might want to drive down the coastal road east toward Telchac Puerto. After about 20 minutes, at the right side of the road you'll see a large, solid-looking wooden observation tower for viewing flamingos. A sign reads UAYMITUN. The state agency CULTUR constructed the tower, operates it, and provides binoculars free of charge. A few years ago, flamingos from Celestún migrated here and established a colony. Your chances of spotting them are good, and you don't have to pay for a boat.

Twenty minutes farther down this road, there's a turnoff for the road to Dzemul. On my last trip I didn't see any flamingos at Uaymitún but just after turning here I found a flock of 500 only 30m (98 ft.) from the highway. After a few minutes, you'll see a sign for **Xcambó** that points to the right. This Maya city is thought to have prospered as a production center for salt, a valuable commodity. Archaeologists have reconstructed the small ceremonial center, which has several platforms and temples. Admission is free.

After viewing these ruins, you can continue on the same road through the small towns of Dzemul and Baca. At Baca, take Highway 176 back to Mérida.

## EN ROUTE TO UXMAL

Two routes go to Uxmal, about 80km (50 miles) south of Mérida. The most direct is Highway 261 via Umán and Muna. On the way, you can stop to see Hacienda Yaxcopoil, which is 30km (20 miles) from Mérida. If you have the time and want a more scenic route, try the meandering State Highway 18. This is sometimes referred to as the Convent Route, but all tourism hype aside, it makes for a pleasant drive with several interesting stops. One thing you might do is make your trip to Uxmal into a loop by going one way and coming back the other with an overnight stay at Uxmal. You could plan on arriving in Uxmal in the late afternoon, attend the sound-and-light show in the evening, and see the ruins the next morning while it is cool and uncrowded.

While traveling in this area, you'll pass through a number of small villages without directional signs, so get used to poking your head out the window and saying *"Buenos días, ¿dónde está el camino para . . . ?"* which translates as "Good day, where is the road to . . . ?" This is what I do, and I ask more than one person. The streets in these villages are full of children, bicycles, and livestock, so drive carefully and, as always, keep an eye out for unmarked *topes*. The attractions on these routes all have the same hours: Churches are open daily from 10am to 1pm and 4 to 6pm; ruins are open daily from 8am to 5pm.

**HIGHWAY 261: YAXCOPOIL & MUNA**    From downtown, take Calle 65 or 69 to Avenida Itzáes and turn left; this feeds onto the highway. You can save some time by looping around the busy market town of Umán. To do so, take the exit for Highway 180, which goes to either Cancún or Campeche, and then follow signs toward Campeche. You'll be on 180 headed south; take it for a few miles and then it will intersect Highway 261; take the exit labeled UXMAL. Very shortly you'll come to the town and hacienda of **Yaxcopoil** (Yash-koh-*poyl*) (ⓒ **999/900-1193;** www.yaxcopoil.com), a ruined hacienda in plain sight on the right side of the road. In the front courtyard, now a parking lot, is a giant Indian laurel tree. You can take a half-hour tour of the place, including the manor, and the henequén factory. It's open from Monday to Saturday from 8am to 5pm and Sunday 9am to 1pm. Admission is $5. It's a little overpriced because the owners have not put much effort into making this a special attraction, but the grounds are attractive, and there are some things of interest to examine.

After Yaxcopoil comes the little market town of **Muna** (65km/40 miles from Mérida). Here you can find excellent **reproductions of Maya ceramics.** An artisan named Rodrigo Martín Morales has worked 25 years perfecting the style and methods of the ancient Maya. He and his family have two workshops in town. They do painstaking work and sell a lot of their production to archaeologists and museum stores. The first store is on the right at the junction of a bypass for Muna. Look for a typical Maya dwelling and a small store. The main store is 3km (2 miles) farther on, just as you enter Muna. Keep an eye out for two large ceiba trees growing on the right hand side of the road. Under the trees is a small plaza with stalls selling handicrafts or food. Make a right turn and go down 46m (150 ft.). On your left will be a store. It's not well marked, but it will be obvious when you get there. The name of the place is **Taller de Artesanía Los Ceibos** (ⓒ **997/971-0036**). The family will be working in the back. Only Spanish is spoken. The store is open from 9am to 6pm daily. In addition to ceramics, Rodrigo works in stone, wood, and jade. Uxmal is 15km (9⅓ miles) beyond Muna.

**HIGHWAY 18 (THE CONVENT ROUTE): KANASIN, ACANCEH, MAYA-PAN & TICUL**   From downtown take Calle 63 east to Circuito Colonias and turn right; look for a traffic circle with a small fountain and turn left. This feeds onto Highway 18 to Kanasín (Kah-nah-*seen*) and then Acanceh (Ah-kahn-*keh*). In **Kanasín,** the highway divides into two roads and a sign will tell you that you can't go straight; instead, you go to the right, which will curve around and flow into the next parallel street. Go past the market, church, and the main square on your left, then stay to the right when you get to a fork.

Shortly after Kanasín the highway has been upgraded and now bypasses a lot of villages. After a few of these turnoffs you'll see a sign pointing left to Acanceh. Across the street from and overlooking Acanceh's church is a restored pyramid. On top of this pyramid under a makeshift roof are some large stucco figures of Maya deities. The caretaker, Mario Uicab, will guide you up to see the figures and give you a little explanation (in Spanish). Admission is $2.50. There are some other ruins a couple of blocks away called **El Palacio de los Estucos.** In 1908, a stucco mural was found here in mint condition. It was left exposed and has deteriorated somewhat. Now it is sheltered, and you can still easily distinguish the painted figures in their original colors. To leave Acanceh head back to the highway on the street that passes between the church and the plaza.

The next turnoff will be for **Tecoh** on the right side. Tecoh's parish church sits on a massive pre-Columbian raised platform—the remains of a ceremonial complex that was sacrificed to build the church. With its rough stone and simple twin towers that are crumbling around the edges, the church looks ancient. Inside are three carved *retablos* (altarpieces) covered in gold leaf and unmistakably Indian in style. In 1998 they were refurbished and are well worth seeing.

Also in Tecoh are some caverns, shown by a local. The bad news is that the owner doesn't have a very good flashlight, and I found myself groping around in the dark. You'll find them as you leave town heading back to the highway. Then it's on to the ruins of Mayapán.

## MAYAPAN  ⚗

Founded, according to Maya lore, by the man-god Kukulkán (Quetzalcoatl in central Mexico) in about A.D. 1007, Mayapán quickly established itself as the most important city in northern Yucatán. For almost 2 centuries it was the capital of a Maya confederation of city-states that included Chichén Itzá and Uxmal. But before 1200, the rulers of Mayapán ended the confederation by attacking and subjugating the other two cities. Eventually, a successful revolt by the other cities brought down Mayapán, which was abandoned during the mid-1400s.

The city extended out at least 4 sq. km (1½ sq. miles), but the ceremonial center is quite compact. In the last few years, archaeologists have been busy excavating and rebuilding it, and work continues. Several buildings bordering the principal plaza have been reconstructed, including one that is similar to El Castillo in Chichén Itzá. The excavations have uncovered murals and stucco figures that provide more grist for the mill of conjecture: atlantes (columns in the form of a human figure supporting something heavy, in the way Atlas supported the sky in Greek myth), skeletal soldiers, macaws, entwined snakes, and a stucco jaguar. This place is definitely worth stopping to see.

The site is open daily from 8am to 5pm. Admission is $3.50. Use of a personal video camera is $4.

**FROM MAYAPAN TO TICUL**    About 20km (12 miles) after Mayapán, you'll see the highway for **Mama** on your right. This will put you on a narrow road that quickly enters the town. For some reason I really like this village; some parts of it are quite pretty. It's often called Mamita by the locals, using the affectionate diminutive suffix. The main attraction is the church and former convent. Inside are several fascinating *retablos* sculpted in a native form of baroque. During the restoration of these buildings, colonial-age murals and designs were uncovered and restored. Be sure to get a peek at them in the sacristy. From Mama continue on for about 20km (12 miles) to Ticul, a large (for this area) market town with a couple of simple hotels.

## TICUL

Best known for the cottage industry of *huipil* (native blouse) embroidery and for the manufacture of women's dress shoes, Ticul isn't the most exciting stop on the Puuc route, but it's a convenient place to wash up and spend the night. It's also a center for large commercially produced pottery; most of the widely sold sienna-colored pottery painted with Maya designs comes from here. If it's a cloudy, humid day, the potters may not be working (part of the process requires sun drying), but they still welcome visitors to purchase finished pieces.

Ticul is only 20km (12 miles) northeast of Uxmal, so thrifty tourists stay either here or in Santa Elena instead of the more expensive hotels at the ruins. On the main square is the **Hotel Plaza,** Calle 23 no. 202, near the intersection with Calle 26 (©997/ 972-0484). It's a modest but comfortable hotel. A double room with air-conditioning costs $30; without air-conditioning, $25. In both cases, there's a 5% charge if you want to pay with a credit card (MasterCard and Visa accepted). Get an interior room if you're looking for quiet, because Ticul has quite a lively plaza. From Ticul, you can do one of two things: head straight for Uxmal via Santa Elena, or loop around the Puuc Route, the long way to Santa Elena. For information on the Puuc route, see "The Puuc Maya Route & Village of Oxkutzcab," below.

**FROM TICUL TO UXMAL**    Follow the main street (Calle 23) west through town. Turn left on Calle 34. It's 15km (9⅓ miles) to Santa Elena; and from there another 15km (9⅓ miles) to Uxmal. In Santa Elena, by the side of Highway 261, is a clean restaurant with good food, **El Chac Mool,** and on the opposite side of the road is the **Flycatcher Inn B&B** (see listing, below).

## 2 The Ruins of Uxmal ★★★

80km (50 miles) SW of Mérida; 19km (12 miles) W of Ticul; 19km (12 miles) S of Muna

The ceremonial complex of Uxmal (pronounced "oosh-*mahl*") is one of the masterworks of Maya civilization. It is strikingly different from all other cities of the Maya for its expansive and intricate facades of carved stone. Unlike other sites in northern Yucatán, such as Chichén Itzá and Mayapán, Uxmal isn't built on a flat plane. The builders worked into the composition of the ceremonial center an interplay of elevations that adds complexity. And then, there is the strange and beautiful oval-shaped Pyramid of the Magician, which is unique among the Maya. The great building period took place between A.D. 700 and 1000, when the population probably reached 25,000. After 1000, Uxmal fell under the sway of the Xiú princes (who may have come from central Mexico). In the 1440s, the Xiú conquered Mayapán, and not long afterward the age of the Maya ended with the arrival of the Spanish conquistadors.

Close to Uxmal, four smaller sites—**Sayil, Kabah, Xlapak,** and **Labná**—can be visited in quick succession. With Uxmal, these ruins are collectively known as the **Puuc route**. See "Seeing Puuc Maya Sites," below, if you want to explore these sites.

## ESSENTIALS
**GETTING THERE & DEPARTING   By Car**   Two routes to Uxmal from Mérida, Highway 261 and State Highway 18, are described in "En Route to Uxmal," above. *Note:* There's no gasoline at Uxmal.

**By Bus**   See "Getting There & Departing" in "Mérida: Gateway to the Maya Heartland," earlier in this chapter, for information about bus service between Mérida and Uxmal. To return, wait for the bus on the highway at the entrance to the ruins. To see the sound-and-light show, don't bother with regular buses; sign up with a tour operator in Mérida.

**ORIENTATION**   Entrance to the ruins is through the visitor center where you buy your tickets (two per person, hold on to both). It has a restaurant; toilets; a first-aid station; shops selling soft drinks, ice cream, film, batteries, and books; a state-run Casa de Artesanía (crafts house); and a small museum, which isn't very informative. The site is open daily from 8am to 5pm. Admission to the archaeological site is around $10, which includes admission to the nightly sound-and-light show. Bringing in a video camera costs $3. Parking costs $1. If you're staying the night in Uxmal, it is possible (and I think preferable) to get to the site late in the day and buy a ticket that allows you to see the sound-and-light show that evening and lets you enter the ruins the next morning to explore them before it gets hot. Just make sure that the ticket vendor knows what you intend to do and keep the ticket.

Guides at the entrance of Uxmal give tours in a variety of languages and charge $40 for a single person or a group. The guides frown on unrelated individuals joining a group. They'd rather charge you as a solo visitor, but you can ask other English speakers if they'd like to join you in a tour and split the cost. As at other sites, the guides vary in quality but will point out areas and architectural details that you might otherwise miss. You should think of these guided tours as performances—the guides try to be as entertaining as possible and adjust their presentations according to the interests of the visitors.

Included in the price of admission is a 45-minute **sound-and-light show,** staged each evening at 7pm. It's in Spanish, but headsets are available for rent ($2.50) for listening to the program in several languages. The narrative is part Hollywood, part high school, but the lighting of the buildings is worth making the effort to see it. After the show, the chant *"Chaaac, Chaaac"* will echo in your mind for weeks.

## A TOUR OF THE RUINS
**THE PYRAMID OF THE MAGICIAN**   As you enter the ruins, note a *chultún,* or cistern, where Uxmal stored its water. Unlike most of the major Maya sites, Uxmal has no *cenote* to supply fresh water. The city's inhabitants were much more dependent on rainwater, and consequently venerated the rain god Chaac much more than in other places.

Rising in front of you is the Pirámide del Adivino. The name comes from a myth told to John Lloyd Stephens on his visit in the 19th century. It tells the story of a magician-dwarf who reached adulthood in a single day after being hatched from an egg, and who built this pyramid in 1 night. Beneath it are five earlier structures. The pyramid has an oval base and rounded sides. You are looking at the east side. The main face is on the west side. Walk around the left or south side to see the front. The pyramid was designed such that the east side rises less steeply than the west side so that the crowning temples are shifted to the west of the central axis of the building, causing them to loom above the plaza below. The temple doorway's heavy ornamentation, a characteristic of the Chenes style, features 12 stylized masks of what many think to be a representation of Chaac.

**THE NUNNERY QUADRANGLE**    From the plaza you're standing in, you want to go to the large Nunnery Quadrangle. Walk out the way you walked into the plaza, turn right, and follow the wall of this long stone building until you get to the building's main door—a corbeled arch that leads into the quadrangle. You'll find yourself in a plaza bordered on each side by stone buildings with elaborate facades. The 16th-century Spanish historian Fray Diego López de Cogullado gave the quadrangle its name when he decided that its layout resembled a Spanish convent.

The quadrangle does have a lot of small rooms, about the size of a nun's cell. You might poke your head into one just to see the shape and size of it, but don't bother trying to explore them all. These rooms were long ago abandoned to the swallows, which are almost always flying above the city. No interior murals or stucco work have been found here—at least, not yet. No, the richness of Uxmal lies in the stonework on its exterior walls.

The Nunnery is a great example of this. The first building your eye latches on to when you enter the plaza is the north building in front of you. It is the tallest, and the view from on top includes all the major buildings of the city, making it useful for the sound-and-light show. The central stairway is bordered by a common element in Puuc architecture, doorways supported by rounded columns. The remnants of the facade on the second level show elements used in the other three buildings and elsewhere throughout the city. There's a crosshatch pattern and a pattern of square curlicues, called a step-and-fret design, and the long-nosed god mask repeated vertically, used often to decorate the corners of buildings—what I call a Chaac stack. Though the facades of these buildings share these common elements and others, their composition varies. On the west building you'll see long feathered serpents intertwined at head and tail. A human head stares out from a serpent's open mouth. I've heard and read a number of interpretations of this motif, repeated elsewhere in Maya art, but they all leave me somewhat in doubt. And that's the trouble with symbols: They are usually the condensed expression of multiple meanings, so any one interpretation could be true, but only partially true.

**THE BALL COURT**    Leaving the Nunnery by the same way you entered, you will see straight ahead a ball court. What would a Maya city be without a ball court? And this one is a particularly good representative of the hundreds found elsewhere in the Maya world. Someone has even installed a replica of one of the stone rings that were the targets for the players, who would make use of their knees, hips, and maybe their arms to strike a solid rubber ball (yes, the Maya knew about natural rubber and extracted latex from a couple of species of rubber trees). The inclined planes on both sides of the court were in play and obviously not an area for spectators, who are thought to have observed the game from atop the two structures.

**THE GOVERNOR'S PALACE**    Continuing in the same direction (south), you come to the large raised plaza on top of which sits the Governor's Palace, running in a north-south direction. The surface area of the raised plaza measures 140 by 170m (459 by 558 ft.), and it is raised about 10m (33 ft.) above the ground—quite a bit of

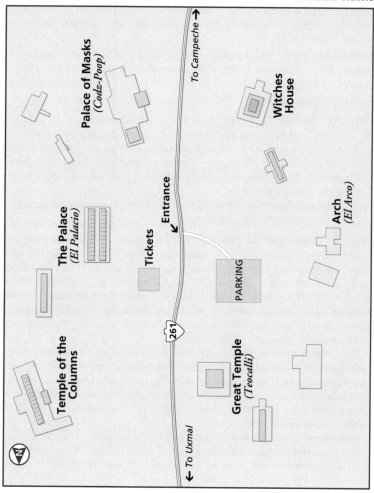

earth-moving. Most of this surface is used as a ceremonial space facing the front (east side) of the palace. In the center is a double-headed jaguar throne, which is seen elsewhere in the Maya world. From here you get the best view of the building's remarkable facade. Like the rest of the palaces here, the first level is smooth, and the second is ornate. Moving diagonally across a crosshatch pattern is a series of Chaac masks. Crowning the building is an elegant cornice projecting slightly outward from above a double border, which could be an architectural reference to the original crested thatched roofs of the Maya. Human figures adorned the main doors, though only the headdress survives of the central figure.

**THE GREAT PYRAMID**   Behind the palace, the platform descends in terraces to another plaza with a large pyramid on its south side. This is known as the Great

Pyramid. On top is the Temple of the Macaws, for the repeated representation of macaws on the face of the temple, and the ruins of three other temples. The view from the top is wonderful.

**THE DOVECOTE**  This building is remarkable in that roof combs weren't a common feature of temples in the Puuc hills, although you'll see one (of a very different style) on El Mirador at Sayil.

## WHERE TO STAY

**Flycatcher Inn B&B** *(Value)*  This pleasant little bed-and-breakfast is in the neighboring village of Santa Elena, just off Highway 261. The rooms are quiet, attractive, and spacious and come with queen-size beds and lots of decorative ironwork made by one of the owners, Santiago Domínguez. The other owner is Christine Ellingson, an American from the Northwest who has lived in Santa Elena for years and is happy to help her guests with their travels.

Carretera Uxmal–Kabah, 97840 Santa Elena, Yuc. No phone. www.flycatcherinn.com. 5 units. $40–$60 double; $70 suite. Rates include breakfast. No credit cards. Free parking.

**Hacienda Uxmal and The Lodge at Uxmal** *(★★★)*  The Hacienda is the oldest hotel in Uxmal. Located just up the road from the ruins, it was built for the archaeology staff. Rooms are large and airy, exuding a feel of days gone by, with patterned tile floors, heavy furniture, and louvered windows. Room nos. 202 through 214 and 302 through 305 are the nicest of the superiors. Corner rooms are labeled A through F and are even larger and come with Jacuzzi tubs. A handsome garden courtyard with towering royal palms, a bar, and a pool adds to the air of tranquillity. A guitar trio usually plays on the open patio in the evenings.

The Lodge is at the entrance to the ruins. It comprises several two-story thatched buildings situated around two pools and surrounded by landscaped grounds. Each building has a large, open breezeway with ceiling fans and rocking chairs. Rooms are extra large and attractively finished with details such as carved headboards. Bathrooms are large and come with stone countertops and either a bathtub or a Jacuzzi tub. Upstairs rooms have thatched roofs.

High season is from January through April except for a few days surrounding the spring equinox. For those days, the month of November, and Christmas vacation there is a higher rate than what is listed below. Low season is the first 3 weeks of December and May through October.

Carretera Mérida–Uxmal Km 80, 97844 Uxmal, Yuc. (✆) **997/976-2011.** www.mayaland.com. (Reservations: Mayaland Resorts, Robalo 30 SM3, 77500 Cancún, Q. Roo. (✆) **800/235-4079** in the U.S., or 998/887-2450. Fax 998/887-4510.) 113 units. High season $173 superior, $255 superior with Jacuzzi, $438–$556 Lodge bungalow; low season $91 superior, $145 superior with Jacuzzi, $192–$285 Lodge bungalow. AE, MC, V. Free guarded parking. **Amenities:** 2 restaurants; bar; 4 outdoor pools; tour info; laundry service; nonsmoking rooms. *In room:* A/C, TV, minibar, coffeemaker, hair dryer (upon request).

**Villas Arqueológicas Uxmal** *(★)*  This hotel is associated with Club Med, but it is just a hotel, not a self-contained vacation village. A two-story layout surrounds a garden patio and a pool. At guests' disposal are a tennis court, a library, and an audiovisual show on the ruins in English, French, and Spanish. Each of the modern, medium-size rooms has a double and a twin bed that fit into spaces that are walled on three sides. Very tall people should stay elsewhere. You can also ask for rates that include half- or full board.

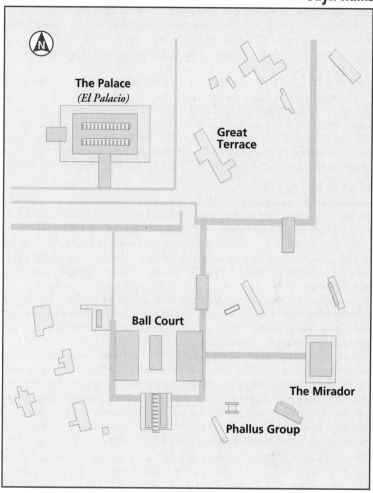

The Palace
(El Palacio)

Great
Terrace

Ball Court

The Mirador

Phallus Group

Ruinas Uxmal, 97844 Uxmal, Yuc. © **800/258-2633** in the U.S., or 997/976-2018. 48 units. $100 double. Rates include continental breakfast. Half-board (breakfast plus lunch or dinner) $18 per person; full board (3 meals) $35 per person. AE, MC, V. Free guarded parking. **Amenities:** Restaurant; bar; outdoor pool; tennis court; laundry service. *In room:* A/C, hair dryer.

## WHERE TO DINE

I've eaten well at the hotel restaurant of the Lodge at Uxmal, ordering the Yucatecan specialties, which were fresh and well prepared. I've also eaten well at the hotel restaurant at the Villas Arquelógicas, but again, keeping it simple. There are some *palapa* restaurants by the highway as you approach the ruins from Mérida. I've had good and bad experiences at these. They do a lot of business with bus tours, so the best time to try them is early afternoon.

## THE PUUC MAYA ROUTE & VILLAGE OF OXKUTZCAB

South and east of Uxmal are several other Maya cities worth visiting. Though smaller in scale than Uxmal or Chichén Itzá, each contains gems of Maya architecture. The Palace of Masks at **Kabah,** the palace at **Sayil,** and the fantastic caverns of **Loltún** are well worth viewing.

Kabah is 28km (17 miles) southeast of Uxmal via Highway 261 through Santa Elena. From there it's only a couple kilometers to Sayil. Xlapak is almost walking distance (through the jungle) from Sayil, and Labná is just a bit farther east. A short drive beyond Labná brings you to the caves of Loltún. Oxkutzcab is at the road's intersection with Highway 184, which you can follow west to Ticul or east all the way to Felipe Carrillo Puerto. If you aren't driving, a daily bus from Mérida goes to all these sites, with the exception of Loltún. (See "By Bus" in "Getting There & Departing," earlier in this chapter.)

### PUUC MAYA SITES

**KABAH** ☞   To reach Kabah from Uxmal, head southwest on Highway 261 to Santa Elena (1km/½ mile), then south to Kabah (13km/8 miles). The ancient city of Kabah lies along both sides of the highway. Turn right into the parking lot.

The most outstanding building at Kabah is the **Palace of Masks,** or Codz Poop ("rolled-up mat"), named for its decorative motif. You'll notice it to the right as you enter. Its outstanding feature is the Chenes-style facade, completely covered in a repeated pattern of 250 masks of Chaac, each one with curling remnants of Chaac's elephant-trunk-like nose. There's nothing else like this facade in all of Maya architecture. For years parts of this building lay lined up in the weeds like pieces of a puzzle awaiting the master puzzle-solver to put them into place. Sculptures from this building are in the anthropology museums in Mérida and Mexico City.

Just behind and to the left of the Codz Poop is the **Palace Group** (also called the East Group), with a fine Puuc-style colonnaded facade. Originally it had 32 rooms. On the front are seven doors, two divided by columns, a common feature of Puuc architecture. Across the highway is what was once the **Great Temple.** Past it is a **great arch,** which was much wider at one time and may have been a monumental gate into the city. A *sacbé* linked this arch to a point at Uxmal. Compare this corbeled arch to the one at Labná (see below), which is in much better shape.

**SAYIL**   About 4km (2½ miles) south of Kabah is the turnoff (left, or east) to Sayil, Xlapak, Labná, Loltún, and Oxkutzcab. The ruins of **Sayil** ("place of the ants") are 4km (2½ miles) along this road.

---

### ⟨Tips⟩   Seeing Puuc Maya Sites

All of these sites are currently undergoing excavation and reconstruction, and some buildings may be roped off when you visit. The sites are open daily from 8am to 5pm. Admission is $2 to $3 for each site, and $5 for Loltún. Loltún has specific hours for tours—9:30 and 11am, and 12:30, 2, 3, and 4pm. Even if you're the only person at the cave at one of these times, the guide must give you a tour, and he can't try to charge you more money as if you were contracting his services for an individual tour. Sometimes the guides try to do this. Use of a video camera at any time costs $4; if you're visiting Uxmal in the same day, you pay only once for video permission and present your receipt as proof at each ruin.

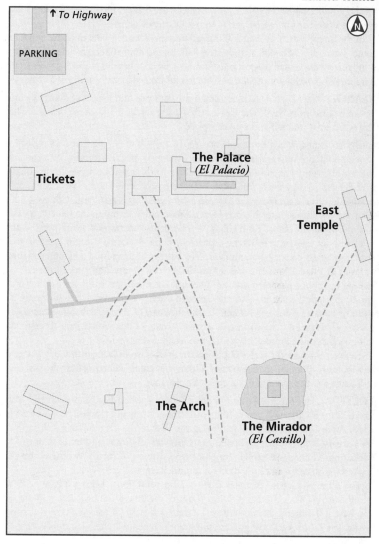

↑ To Highway

PARKING

Tickets

**The Palace**
(*El Palacio*)

**East Temple**

**The Arch**

**The Mirador**
(*El Castillo*)

Sayil is famous for **El Palacio** 🏃🏃. This palace of more than 90 rooms is impressive for its size alone. At present it is roped off because of some damage suffered in the last hurricane. Climbing is not permitted. But this is unimportant because what makes it a masterpiece of Maya architecture is the facade, which is best appreciated from the ground. It stretches across three terraced levels, and its rows of columns give it a Minoan appearance. On the second level, notice the upside-down stone figure known to archaeologists as the Diving God, or Descending God, over the doorway; the same motif was used at Tulum a couple of centuries later. The large circular basin on the ground below the palace is an artificial catch basin for a *chultún* (cistern); this region has no natural *cenotes* (wells) to use to irrigate crops.

In the jungle past El Palacio is **El Mirador,** a small temple with an oddly slotted roof comb. Beyond El Mirador, a crude stele (tall, carved stone) has a phallic idol carved on it in greatly exaggerated proportions. Another cluster of buildings, the Southern Group, is a short distance down a trail that branches off from the one heading to El Mirador.

**XLAPAK**    Xlapak (*shla*-pahk) is a small site with one building; it's 5.5km (3½ miles) down the road from Sayil. The Palace at Xlapak bears the masks of the rain god Chaac. You won't miss much if you skip this place.

**LABNA**    Labná, which dates from between A.D. 600 and 900, is 30km (19 miles) from Uxmal and only 3km (2 miles) past Xlapak. Descriptive placards fronting the main buildings are in Spanish, English, and German. The first thing you see on the left as you enter is **El Palacio,** a magnificent Puuc-style building much like the one at Sayil, but in poorer condition. Over a doorway is a large, well-conserved mask of Chaac with eyes, a huge snout nose, and jagged teeth around a small mouth that seems on the verge of speaking. Jutting out on one corner is a highly stylized serpent's mouth from which pops a human head with an unexpectedly serene expression. From the front, you can gaze out to the enormous grassy interior grounds flanked by vestiges of unrestored buildings and jungle.

From El Palacio, you can walk across the interior grounds on a reconstructed *sacbé* leading to Labná's **corbeled arch.** At one time there were probably several such arches spread through the region. This one has been extensively restored, although only remnants of the roof comb can be seen. It was once part of a more elaborate structure that is completely gone. Chaac's face is on the corners of one facade, and stylized Maya huts are fashioned in stone above the two small doorways.

You pass through the arch to **El Mirador,** or El Castillo. Towering above a large pile of rubble is a singular room crowned with a roof comb etched against the sky.

There's a snack stand with toilets at the entrance.

**LOLTUN**    The caverns of Loltún are 31km (19 miles) past Labná on the way to Oxkutzcab, on the left side of the road. These fascinating caves, home of ancient Maya, were also used as a refuge during the War of the Castes (1847–1901). Inside are statuary, wall carvings and paintings, *chultunes* (cisterns), and other signs of Maya habitation. Guides will explain much of what you see. When I was there, the guide spoke English but was a little difficult to understand.

The admission price includes a 90-minute **tour;** tours begin daily at 9:30 and 11am, and 12:30, 2, 3, and 4pm. The floor of the cavern can be slippery in places; if you have a flashlight, take it with you. Admission is $5. What you see is quite interesting. I've heard reports of guides canceling the regularly scheduled tour so that they can charge for a private tour. Don't agree to such a thing.

To return to Mérida from Loltún, drive the 7km (4½ miles) to Oxkutzcab. From there, you have a couple of options for getting back to Mérida: The slow route is through Maní and Teabo, which will allow you to see some convents and return by Highway 18, known as the "Convent Route" (see "En Route to Uxmal," earlier in this chapter). Or you can head toward Muna to hook up with Highway 261 (also described above).

## OXKUTZCAB

Oxkutzcab (ohsh-kootz-*kahb*), 11km (7 miles) from Loltún, is the center of the Yucatán's fruit-growing region. Oranges abound. The tidy village of 21,000 centers on a beautiful 16th-century church and the market. **Su Cabaña Suiza** (no phone) is a good restaurant in town. The last week of October and first week of November is the **Orange Festival,** when the village turns exuberant, with a carnival and orange displays in and around the central plaza.

## EN ROUTE TO CAMPECHE

From Oxkutzcab, head back 43km (27 miles) to Sayil, and then drive south on Highway 261 to Campeche (126km/78 miles). After crossing the state line you'll pass through the towns of Bolonchén and Hopelchén. The drive is pleasant, and there's little traffic. Both towns have gas stations. When going through the towns watch carefully for directional traffic signs so that you stay on the highway. From Hopelchén, Highway 261 heads west. After 42km (26 miles), you'll find yourself at Cayal and the well-marked turnoff for the ruins of the city of Edzná, 18km (11 miles) farther south.

**EDZNA** ⊛  This city is interesting for several reasons. The area was populated as early as 600 B.C., with urban formation by 300 B.C. From that point onward, Edzná grew impressively in a manner that suggests considerable urban-planning skills. An ambitious and elaborate canal system was dug, which must have taken decades to complete, but would have allowed for a great expansion in agricultural production and hence concentration of population. This made Edzná the preeminent city for a wide territory.

Another boom in construction began around A.D. 500, during the middle of the Classic period. This would have been when the city's most prominent feature, the **Great Acropolis,** was started.

Sitting on top of this raised platform are five main pyramids, the largest being the much-photographed **Pyramid of Five Stories.** It combines the features of temple platform and palace. In Maya architecture you have palace buildings with many vaulted chambers and you have solid pyramidal platforms with a couple of interior temples or burial passages. These are two mutually exclusive categories—but not here. Such a mix is found only in the Puuc and Río Bec areas, and only in a few examples, and none similar to this, which makes this pyramid a bold architectural statement. The four lesser pyramids on the Acropolis are each constructed in a different style, and each is a pure example of that style. It's as if the rulers of this city were flaunting their cosmopolitanism, showing that they could build in any style they chose, but preferred creating their own, superior architecture.

West of the Acropolis, across a large open plaza, is a long, raised building whose purpose isn't quite clear. But its size as well as that of the plaza make you wonder just how many people this city actually held to necessitate such a large public space.

The site takes an hour to see, and is open daily from 8am to 5pm. Admission is $4, plus around $4 to use your video camera.

## 3 Campeche ⊛⊛

251km (156 miles) SW of Mérida; 376km (233 miles) NE of Villahermosa

Campeche, the capital of the state of the same name, is a beautifully restored colonial city. The facades of all the houses in the historic center of town have been repaired and painted, all electrical and telephone cables have been routed underground, and the streets have been paved to look cobbled. Several Mexican movie companies have taken advantage of the restoration to shoot period films here.

Despite its beauty, not many tourists come to Campeche. Those who do tend to be either on their way to the ruins at Palenque (see chapter 8) or the Río Bec region (see chapter 6), or the kind of travelers who are accidental wanderers. A couple of things do need to be said: Campeche is not geared to foreign tourism the way Mérida is, so expect less in the way of English translations and such at museums and other sights. Also, expect less in the way of nightlife, except on weekend nights when they block off the main square for a street party.

If you're interested in seeing the ruins and biosphere reserve at Calakmul and the rest of the ruins along the Río Bec route, see the section "Side Trips to Maya Ruins from Chetumal," in chapter 6. **Calakmul** &&& is a large and important site, with the tallest pyramid in the Yucatán Peninsula, and if you're going that far, you should stop at Balamkú and perhaps a few other ruins in the area. From the Campeche side you can get information and contract a tour with one of several tour operators. You can also rent a car. Calakmul is too far away for a day trip. There are a few small hotels in the area. Hotel Del Mar in Campeche has two: **Chicanná Eco-village** and **Puerta Calakmul**.

From the Calakmul area it's easy to cross over the peninsula to Yucatán's southern Caribbean coast. Then you can head up the coast and complete a loop of the peninsula.

Campeche has an interesting history. The conquistadors arrived in 1517, when Francisco de Córdoba landed here while exploring the coast and stayed just long enough to celebrate Mass. Attempts to settle here were unsuccessful because of native resistance until Montejo the Younger was able to secure a settlement in 1540.

In the 17th and 18th centuries, pirates repeatedly harassed the city. The list of Campeche's attackers reads like a who's who of pirating. On one occasion, several outfits banded together under the famous Dutch pirate Peg Leg (who most likely was the inspiration for the many fictional one-legged sailors) and managed to capture the city. The Campechanos grew tired of hosting pirate parties and erected walls around the city, showing as much industry then as they now show in renovating their historic district. The walls had a number of *baluartes* (bastions) at critical locations. For added security, they constructed two forts, complete with moats and drawbridges, on the hills flanking the city. There were four gates to the city, and the two main ones are still intact: the Puerta de Mar (Sea Gate) and the Puerta de Tierra (Land Gate). The pirates never cared to return, but, in Mexico's stormy political history, the city did withstand a couple of sieges by different armies. Eventually, in the early 1900s, the wall around the city was razed, but the bastions and main gates were left intact, as were the two hilltop fortresses. Most of the bastions and both forts now house museums.

## ESSENTIALS

**GETTING THERE & DEPARTING    By Plane    Aeromexico** (© 981/816-6656; www.aeromexico.com.mx) flies once daily to and from Mexico City. The **airport** is several kilometers northeast of the town center, and you'll have to take a taxi into town (about $5).

**BY CAR**    Highway 180 goes south from Mérida, passing near the basket-making village of Halacho and near Becal, known for its Panama-hat weavers. The trip takes 2½ hours. At Tenabo, take the shortcut (right, Hwy. 24) to Campeche rather than going farther to the crossroads near Chencoyí. The longer way from Mérida is along Highway 261 past Uxmal.

When returning to Mérida via Highway 180, go north on Avenida Ruiz Cortines, bearing left to follow the water (this becomes Av. Pedro Sainz de Baranda, but there's

# Campeche

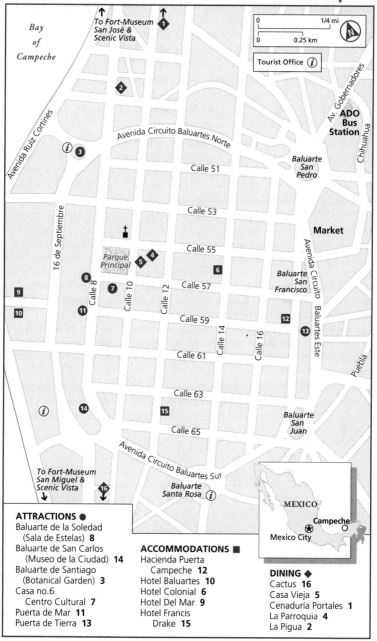

**Bay of Campeche**

To Fort-Museum San José & Scenic Vista

Tourist Office (i)

Av. Gobernadores

**ADO Bus Station**

Chihuahua

Avenida Circuito Baluartes Norte

Calle 51

Calle 53

*Baluarte San Pedro*

**Market**

Avenida Circuito Baluartes Este

16 de Septiembre

*Parque Principal*

Calle 55

Calle 57

Calle 8

Calle 10

Calle 12

Calle 14

Calle 16

Calle 59

Calle 61

*Baluarte San Francisco*

Puebla

Avenida Ruiz Cortines

Calle 63

Calle 65

*Baluarte San Juan*

Avenida Circuito Baluartes Sur

To Fort-Museum San Miguel & Scenic Vista

*Baluarte Santa Rosa* (i)

**MEXICO**

Campeche

Mexico City

## ATTRACTIONS ●
Baluarte de la Soledad
  (Sala de Estelas) **8**
Baluarte de San Carlos
  (Museo de la Ciudad) **14**
Baluarte de Santiago
  (Botanical Garden) **3**
Casa no.6
  Centro Cultural **7**
Puerta de Mar **11**
Puerta de Tierra **13**

## ACCOMMODATIONS ■
Hacienda Puerta
  Campeche **12**
Hotel Baluartes **10**
Hotel Colonial **6**
Hotel Del Mar **9**
Hotel Francis
  Drake **15**

## DINING ◆
Cactus **16**
Casa Vieja **5**
Cenaduría Portales **1**
La Parroquia **4**
La Pigua **2**

no sign). Follow the road as it turns inland to Highway 180, where you turn left (there's a gas station at the intersection).

If you're leaving Campeche for Edzná and Uxmal, go north on either Ruiz Cortines or Gobernadores and turn right on Madero, which feeds onto **Highway 281.** To go south to Villahermosa, take Ruiz Cortines south.

**BY BUS**    ADO (© 981/816-2802) offers a first-class *de paso* (passing through) bus to Palenque (6 hr.; $15) four times a day and buses to Mérida (2½ hr.; $8) every hour from 5:30am to midnight. The ADO **bus station** is on Avenida Patricio Trueba, a kilometer (½ mile) from the Puerta de Tierra.

**INFORMATION**    The **State of Campeche Office of Tourism** (©/fax 981/816-6767; www.campechetravel.com) is in Plaza Moch-Couoh, Avenida Ruiz Cortines s/n, 24000 Campeche. This is in one of the state buildings between the historic center and the shore. There are also information offices in the bastions of Santa Rosa, San Carlos, and Santiago. It's open Monday to Friday from 9am to 2pm and 4 to 7pm.

**CITY LAYOUT**    The most interesting part of the city is the restored old part, most of which once lay within the walls. Originally, the seaward wall was at the water's edge, but now land has been gained from the sea between the old walls and the coastline. This is where you'll find most of the state government buildings, which were built in a glaringly modernist style around **Plaza Moch-Couoh:** buildings such as the office tower **Edificio de los Poderes (Judicial Building)** or **Palacio de Gobierno (headquarters for the state of Campeche),** and the futuristic **Cámara de Diputados (Chamber of Deputies),** which looks like a cubist clam.

Campeche's system of street numbering is much like that of other cities in the Yucatán, except that the numbers of the north-south streets increase as you go east instead of the reverse. (See "City Layout" in "Mérida: Gateway to the Maya Heartland," earlier in this chapter.)

**GETTING AROUND**    Most of the recommended sights, restaurants, and hotels are within walking distance of the old city, except for the two fort-museums. Campeche isn't easy to negotiate by bus, so take taxis for anything beyond walking distance—they are inexpensive.

## FAST FACTS: Campeche

*American Express*  Local offices are at Calle 59 no. 4 and 5 (© 981/811-1010), in the Edificio Del Mar, a half-block toward town from the Hotel Del Mar. Open Monday to Friday from 9am to 2pm and 5 to 7pm, and Saturday from 9am to 1pm. This office does not cash traveler's checks.

*Area Code*  The telephone area code is **981**.

*ATMs*  There are more than 10 cash machines in and around the downtown area.

*Internet Access*  There are plenty of places to check e-mail, too—just look for signs with the words INTERNET or CYBERCAFE.

*Post Office*  The *correo* is in the Edificio Federal at the corner of Avenida 16 de Septiembre and Calle 53 (© 981/816-2134), near the Baluarte de Santiago; it's open Monday to Saturday from 7:30am to 8pm. The telegraph office is here as well.

# EXPLORING CAMPECHE

With beautiful surroundings, friendly people, an easy pace of life, Campeche is worthy of at least a day on your itinerary. It has some interesting museums, one outstanding restaurant, and plenty to do.

## INSIDE THE CITY WALLS

A good place to begin is the pretty *zócalo,* or **Parque Principal,** bounded by calles 55 and 57 running east and west and calles 8 and 10 running north and south. On Saturday nights and Sundays, the city closes the main square to traffic and contracts bands to play. People set up tables in the streets and the entire scene becomes a fun kind of block party. Construction of the church on the north side of the square began in 1650 and was finally completed 1½ centuries later. A pleasant way to see the city is to take the *tranvía* (trolley) tour that leaves three or four times a day from the main plaza; check with one of the tourist information offices for the schedule. The cost is $7 for a 45-minute tour.

**Baluarte de la Soledad**   This bastion next to the sea gate houses Maya stelae recovered from around the state. Many are badly worn, but the line drawings beside the stones allow you to appreciate their former design.

Calle 57 and Calle 8, opposite Plaza Principal. No phone. Admission $2.50. Tues–Sat 9am–8pm; Sun 9am–1pm.

**Baluarte de San Carlos/Museo de la Ciudad**   The city museum deals primarily with the design and construction of the fortifications. A model of the city shows how it looked in its glory days and provides a good overview for touring within the city walls. There are several excellent ship models as well. All text is in Spanish.

Circuito Baluartes and Av. Justo Sierra. No phone. Admission $2.50. Tues–Sat 9am–8pm; Sun 9am–1pm.

**Baluarte de Santiago**   The Jardín Botánico Xmuch'haltun is a jumble of exotic and common plants within the stone walls of this bastion. More than 250 species of plants and trees share a small courtyard.

Av. 16 de Septiembre and Calle 49. No phone. Free admission. Mon–Fri 9am–8pm; Sat–Sun 9am–1pm.

**Casa no. 6 Centro Cultural**   In this remodeled colonial house, you'll see some rooms decorated with period furniture and accessories. The patio of mixtilinear arches supported by simple Doric columns is striking. Exhibited in the patio are photos of the city's fine colonial architecture. Several of the photographed buildings have recently been renovated. There is also a small bookstore in back, as well as temporary exhibition space.

Calle 57 no. 6. No phone. Free admission. Daily 9am–9pm.

**Puerta de Tierra**   At the Land Gate is a small museum displaying portraits of pirates and the city founders. The 1732 French 5-ton cannon in the entryway was found in 1990. On Tuesday, Friday, and Saturday at 8pm, there's a light-and-sound show, as long as 15 or more people have bought tickets. Some shows are in English and some are in Spanish; it depends on the audience. The show is amusing.

Calle 59 at Circuito Baluartes/Av. Gobernadores. No phone. Free admission to museum; show $3 adults, $1 children under 11. Daily 9am–9pm.

## OUTSIDE THE WALLS: SCENIC VISTAS

**Fuerte–Museo San José el Alto**   This fort is higher and has a more sweeping view of Campeche and the coast than Fuerte San Miguel, but it holds only a small exhibit of 16th- and 17th-century weapons and scale miniatures of sailing vessels. This is a nice place for a picnic. Take a cab. On the way, you will pass by an impressive statue of Juárez.

Av. Morazán s/n. No phone. Admission $2.50. Tues–Sun 8am–8pm.

**Fuerte–Museo San Miguel** ₢₢    For a good view of the city and a great little museum, take a cab ($2–$3) up to Fuerte–Museo San Miguel. San Miguel is a small fort with a moat and a drawbridge. Built in 1771, it was the most important of the city's defenses. General Santa Anna captured it when he attacked the city in 1842. The museum of the Maya world was renovated in 2000 and is well worth seeing. It groups the artifacts around central issues in Maya culture. In a room devoted to Maya concepts of the afterlife, there's a great burial scene with jade masks and jewelry from Maya tombs at Calakmul. Another room explains Maya cosmology, another depicts war, and another explains the gods. There are also exhibits on the history of the fort.

Ruta Escénica s/n. No phone. Admission $2.50. Tues–Sat 9am–8pm; Sun 8am–noon.

## SHOPPING

**Casa de Artesanías Tukulná**    This store run by DIF (a government family-assistance agency) occupies a restored mansion. There is an elaborate display of regional arts and crafts in the back. The wares in the showrooms represent everything that is produced in the state. There are quality textiles, clothing, and locally made furniture. Open Monday to Saturday from 9am to 8pm. Calle 10 no. 333 (between calles 59 and 61). ₡ 981/816-9088.

## WHERE TO STAY

Rates quoted include the 17% tax.

### VERY EXPENSIVE

**Hacienda Puerta Campeche** ₢₢₢    This hotel was created from several adjoining colonial houses. It's a beautiful and original property just inside the Puerta de Tierra in Campeche's colonial center. There is a tropical garden in the center and a pool that runs through the ruined walls of one of the houses. It's quite picturesque. Rooms are colonial with flare—large with old tile floors, distinctive colors, and beamed ceilings. "Hacienda" is in the name to make it apparent that this is one of the properties connected to the four haciendas managed by Starwood hotels. (See "Of Haciendas & Hotels" in the Mérida section, earlier in this chapter).

Calle 59 71, 24000 Campeche, Camp. ₡ 800/325-3589 in the U.S. and Canada, or 981/816-7508. www.luxury collection.com. 15 units. $280 superior; $340 junior suite; $440 master suite. AE, MC, V. Free guarded parking. **Amenities:** Restaurants; 2 bars; outdoor pool; spa services; concierge; tours; car-rental desk; airport transportation; room service; babysitting; laundry service. *In room:* A/C, TV, high-speed Internet, minibar, fridge, coffeemaker, hair dryer, iron.

### EXPENSIVE

**Hotel Del Mar** ₢    Rooms in this four-story hotel are large, bright, and comfortably furnished. All have balconies that face the Gulf of Mexico. The beds (two doubles or one king-size) are comfortable. The Del Mar is on the main oceanfront boulevard, between the coast and the city walls. It offers more services than the Baluartes and is a little more expensive. You can make a reservation here to stay in the Río Bec area, or you can buy a package that includes guide and transportation. The hotel also offers a tour to Edzná.

Av. Ruiz Cortines 51, 24000 Campeche, Camp. © **981/811-9192** or -9193. Fax 981/811-1618. www.delmar
hotel.com.mx. 146 units. $135 double; $150 executive-level double. AE, MC, V. Free parking. **Amenities:** 2 restaurants; bar; large outdoor pool; gym w/sauna; travel agency; car-rental desk; business center; room service until 11pm;
babysitting; laundry service; nonsmoking rooms; executive level. *In room:* A/C, TV, dataport, safe.

## MODERATE

**Hotel Baluartes** 🌟   Between the Sea Gate and the Gulf of Mexico, this was the
city's original luxury hotel. All the rooms have been completely refurbished with new
tile floors, new furniture, and new mattresses—one king-size bed or two doubles.
They are cheerful and have good lighting, but the bathrooms are small. This year the
hotel is building an addition on its north side, scheduled to be finished in December
2006. It will add 50 rooms, all of them suites.

Av. 16 de Septiembre no. 128, 24000 Campeche, Camp. © **981/816-3911.** Fax 981/816-2410. www.baluartes.com.mx.
156 units. $95 double; $125 suite. Rates include breakfast buffet. AE, MC, V. Free guarded parking. **Amenities:** 2 restaurants; bar; large outdoor pool; travel agency; car rental; room service until 11pm; laundry service; nonsmoking rooms.
*In room:* A/C, TV, hair dryer, safe.

**Hotel Francis Drake** 🌟 *Value*   A three-story hotel in the *centro histórico* (historical
district) with comfortable, attractive rooms at good prices. Rooms are midsize and
come with tile floors and one king-size bed, two doubles, or two twins. The bathrooms are modern with large showers. Suites are larger and better furnished. The location is excellent.

Calle 12 no. 207 (between calles 63 and 65), 24000 Campeche, Camp. © **981/811-5626** or -5627. www.hotelfrancis
drake.com. 24 units. $70 double; $80 junior suite; $93 suite. AE, MC, V. Limited free parking. **Amenities:** Restaurant;
tour info; car-rental services; room service until 11pm; laundry service. *In room:* A/C, TV, minibar, hair dryer.

## INEXPENSIVE

**Hotel Colonial** *Moments*   What, you may ask, in a cheap hotel could possibly qualify for a Frommer's Mexican Moment? Well, first of all is the fact that the hotel
hasn't changed in 50 years; it exudes an air of the past long since disappeared with the
coming of globalization. The rooms have the original tiles—once made in Mérida, but
alas, no longer—beautiful things with lovely colors in swirls and geometrics; each
room has a different pattern. And then there's the plumbing, which, in my room was
so bodacious in design and execution that to hide it within the walls would have been
Philistinism. Remarkable, too, are the bathroom fixtures, the four-color paint job, and
the '40s-style furniture. Sure, you have to make sacrifices for such character—the
rooms and bathrooms are small, and the mattresses aren't the best—but even character aside, this hotel is cleaner and more cheerful than any in its class.

Calle 14 no. 122, 24000 Campeche, Camp. © **981/816-2222.** 30 units. $25 double; $35 double with A/C. No credit
cards. *In room:* No phone.

## WHERE TO EAT

Campeche is a fishing town, so seafood predominates. The outstanding restaurant is
La Pigua, where I would eat all my afternoon meals. For breakfast, you have your hotel
restaurant or one of the traditional eateries such as **La Parroquia.** For a light supper,
either get some *antojitos* (small dishes) in the old *barrio* of San Francisco, or have
supper above the main plaza at **La Casa Vieja.** If you want a steak, your best bet is
**Cactus.**

## MODERATE

**Cactus** STEAKS/MEXICAN    If seafood isn't to your taste, try this steakhouse; it's a favorite with the locals. The rib-eyes are good, as is everything but the *arrachera,* which is the same cut of meat used for fajitas and is very tough.

Av. Malecón Justo Sierra. © 981/811-1453. Main courses $9–$18. No credit cards. Daily 7am–2am.

**Casa Vieja** MEXICAN/INTERNATIONAL    I'm afraid that Casa Vieja has gotten a little old. There's been a drop in effort here, but it still has the prettiest dining space in the city—an upstairs arcade overlooking the main square. Your best option is to order something simple, and it just might be your luck that changes have been made in the kitchen.

Calle 10 no. 319. © 981/811-1311. Reservations not accepted. Main courses $6–$16. No credit cards. Tues–Sun 9am–2am; Mon 5:30pm–2am.

**La Pigua** 𝒦𝒦𝒦 SEAFOOD    The dining area is an air-conditioned version of a traditional Yucatecan cabin, but with walls of glass looking out on green vegetation. There are not many tables, so by all means, make a reservation. Spanish nautical terms pepper the large menu as the headings for different courses. Sure to be on the menu is fish stuffed with shellfish, which I wholeheartedly recommend. If you're lucky, you might find pompano in a green-herb sauce seasoned with a peppery herb known as *hierba santa.* Other dishes that are sure to please are coconut-battered shrimp with applesauce and chiles rellenos with shark. Service is excellent, and the accommodating owner can have your favorite seafood prepared in any style you want.

Av. Miguel Alemán no. 179A. © 981/811-3365. Reservations recommended. Main courses $10–$20. AE, MC, V. Daily noon–6pm. From Plaza Principal, walk north on Calle 8 for 3 blocks; cross Av. Circuito by the botanical garden where Calle 8 becomes Miguel Alemán; the restaurant is 1½ blocks farther up, on the right side of the street.

## INEXPENSIVE

**Cenaduría Portales** 𝒦 ANTOJITOS    This is the most traditional of supper places for Campechanos. It's a small restaurant under the stone arches that face the Plaza San Francisco in the *barrio* (neighborhood) of San Francisco. This is the oldest part of town, but it lies outside the walls just to the north. Don't leave without ordering the *horchata* (a sweet milky-white drink made of a variety of things, in this case coconut). For food, try the turkey soup, which is wonderful, and the *sincronizadas* (tostadas) and *panuchos.*

Calle 10 no. 86, Portales San Francisco. © 981/811-1491. Antojitos 40¢–$1.50. No credit cards. Daily 6pm–midnight.

**La Parroquia** MEXICAN    This local hangout offers good, inexpensive fare. It's best for breakfasts and the afternoon *comida corrida.* Selections on the *comida corrida* might include pot roast, meatballs, pork, or fish, with rice or squash, beans, tortillas, and fresh-fruit-flavored water.

Calle 55 no. 9. © 981/816-8086. Breakfast $3–$4; main courses $4–$12; comida corrida (served noon–3pm) $4–$5. MC, V. Daily 24 hr.

## 4  The Ruins of Chichén Itzá 𝒦𝒦𝒦

179km (111 miles) W of Cancún; 120km (74 miles) E of Mérida

The fabled ruins of Chichén Itzá (no, it doesn't rhyme with "chicken pizza"; the accents are on the last syllables: chee-*chen* eet-*zah*) are the Yucatán's best-known ancient monuments. They are plenty hyped, but Chichén is truly worth seeing. Walking among these stone platforms, pyramids, and ball courts gives you an appreciation for this ancient civilization that books cannot convey. The city is built on a scale that evokes a sense of wonder: To fill the plazas during one of the mass rituals that occurred here a millennium ago would have required an enormous number of celebrants. Even today, with the mass flow of tourists through these plazas, the ruins feel empty.

When visiting the ruins, keep in mind that much of what is said about the Maya (especially by tour guides, who speak in tones of utter certainty) is merely educated guessing. This much we do know: The area was settled by farmers as far back as the 4th century A.D. The first signs of an urban society appear in the 7th century in the construction of stone temples and palaces in the traditional Puuc Maya style. These buildings can be found in the "Old Chichén" section of the city. Construction continued for a couple hundred years. In the 10th century (the post-Classic era), the city came under the rule of the Itzáes, who arrived from central Mexico by way of the Gulf coast. They may have been a mix of highland Toltec Indians (the people who built the city of Tula in central Mexico) and lowland Putún Maya, who were a commercial people thriving on trade between the different regions of the area. In the following centuries the city saw its greatest growth. Most of the grand architecture was built during this age in a style that is clearly Toltec influenced. The new rulers may have been refugees from Tula. There is a mythological story told in pre-Columbian central Mexico about a fight that occurred between the gods Quetzalcoatl and Tezcatlipoca, which resulted in Quetzalcoatl being forced to leave his homeland and venture east. This may be a shorthand account of a civil war in Tula, different religious factions, with the losers fleeing to the Yucatán, where they were welcomed by the local Maya. Over time, the Itzáes adopted more and more the ways of the Maya. Sometime at the end of the 12th century, the city was captured by its rival, the city of Mayapán.

Though it's possible to make a day trip from Cancún or Mérida, it's preferable to overnight here or in nearby Valladolid. It makes for a more relaxing trip. You can see the light show in the evening and return to see the ruins early the next morning when it is cool and before the tour buses arrive.

## ESSENTIALS

**GETTING THERE & DEPARTING   By Plane**   Travel agents in the United States, Cancún, and Cozumel can arrange day trips from Cancún and Cozumel.

**By Car**   Chichén Itzá is on old Highway 180 between Mérida and Cancún. The fastest way to get there from either city is to take the *autopista* (or *cuota*). The toll is $7 from Mérida, $22 from Cancún. Once you have exited the *autopista,* you will turn onto the road leading to the village of Pisté. Once in the village, you'll reach a T junction at Highway 180 and turn left to get to the ruins. The entrance to the ruins is well marked. If you stay on the highway for a few kilometers more you'll come to the exit for the hotel zone at kilometer marker 121 (before you reach the turnoff, you'll pass the eastern entrance to Mayapan, which is usually closed). Chichén is 1½ hours from Mérida and 2½ hours from Cancún.

**By Bus**   From Mérida, there are three first-class ADO buses per day. There are also a couple of first-class buses to Cancún and Playa. Otherwise, you can buy a second-class bus ticket to Valladolid and a first-class from there. If you want to take a day trip from Mérida or Cancún, go with a tour company.

**AREA LAYOUT**   The village of **Pisté,** where most of the economical hotels and restaurants are located, is about 2.5km (1½ miles) from the ruins of Chichén Itzá.

Public buses from Mérida, Cancún, Valladolid, and elsewhere discharge passengers here. Fancy hotels are by the ruins, and an economical hotel lies 2.5km (1½ miles) to the east of the ruins (see "Where to Stay," below).

## EXPLORING THE RUINS

The site occupies 6.5 sq. km (2½ sq. miles), and it takes most of a day to see all the ruins, which are open daily from 8am to 5pm. Service areas are open from 8am to 10pm. Admission is $10, free for children under age 12. A video camera permit costs $4. Parking is extra. *You can use your ticket to reenter on the same day.* The cost of admission includes the **sound-and-light show,** which is worth seeing since you're being charged for it anyway. The show, held at 7 or 8pm depending on the season, is in Spanish, but headsets are available for rent in several languages. The narrative is okay, but the real reason for seeing the show is the lights, which show off the beautiful geometry of the city.

The large, modern visitor center, at the main entrance where you pay the admission charge, is beside the parking lot and consists of a museum, an auditorium, a restaurant, a bookstore, and bathrooms. You can see the site on your own or with a licensed guide who speaks English or Spanish. Guides usually wait at the entrance and charge around $45 for one to six people. Although the guides frown on it, there's nothing wrong with approaching a group of people who speak the same language and asking if they want to share a guide. These guides can point out architectural details often missed when visiting on your own. Chichén Itzá has two parts: the central (new) zone, which shows distinct Toltec influence, and the southern (old) zone, with mostly Puuc architecture.

**EL CASTILLO**   As you enter from the tourist center, the magnificent 25m (82-ft.) El Castillo pyramid (also called the Pyramid of Kukulkán) will be straight ahead across a large open area. It was built with the Maya calendar in mind. The four stairways leading up to the central platform each have 91 steps, making a total of 364, which when you add the central platform equals the 365 days of the solar year. On either side of each stairway are nine terraces, which makes 18 on each face of the pyramid, equaling the number of months in the Maya solar calendar. On the facing of these terraces are 52 panels (we don't know how they were decorated), which represent the 52-year cycle when both the solar and religious calendars would become realigned. The pyramid's alignment is such that on the **spring** or **fall equinox** (Mar 21 or Sept 21) a curious event occurs. The setting sun casts the shadow of the terraces onto the ramp of the northern stairway. A diamond pattern is formed, suggestive of the geometric designs on some snakes. Slowly it descends into the earth. The effect is more conceptual than visual, and to view it requires being with a large crowd. It's much better to see the ruins on other days when it's less crowded.

El Castillo was built over an earlier structure. A narrow stairway at the western edge of the north staircase leads inside that structure, where there is a sacrificial altar-throne—a red jaguar encrusted with jade. The stairway is open from 11am to 3pm and is cramped, usually crowded, humid, and uncomfortable. A visit early in the day is best. Photos of the jaguar figure are not allowed.

**JUEGO DE PELOTA (MAIN BALL COURT)**   Northwest of El Castillo is Chichén's main ball court, the largest and best preserved anywhere, and only one of nine ball courts built in this city. Carved on both walls of the ball court are scenes showing Maya figures dressed as ball players and decked out in heavy protective padding. The carved scene also shows a headless player kneeling with blood shooting from his neck; another player holding the head looks on.

Players on two teams tried to knock a hard rubber ball through one of the two stone rings placed high on either wall, using only their elbows, knees, and hips. According to legend, the losing players paid for defeat with their lives. However, some experts say the victors were the only appropriate sacrifices for the gods. One can only guess what the incentive for winning might be in that case. Either way, the game must have been riveting, heightened by the wonderful acoustics of the ball court.

**THE NORTH TEMPLE**    Temples are at both ends of the ball court. The North Temple has sculptured pillars and more sculptures inside, as well as badly ruined murals. The acoustics of the ball court are so good that from the North Temple, a person speaking can be heard clearly at the opposite end, about 135m (443 ft.) away.

**TEMPLE OF JAGUARS**    Near the southeastern corner of the main ball court is a small temple with serpent columns and carved panels showing warriors and jaguars. Up the steps and inside the temple, a mural was found that chronicles a battle in a Maya village.

**TZOMPANTLI (TEMPLE OF THE SKULLS)**    To the right of the ball court is the Temple of the Skulls, an obvious borrowing from the post-Classic cities of central Mexico. Notice the rows of skulls carved into the stone platform. When a sacrificial victim's head was cut off, it was impaled on a pole and displayed in a tidy row with others. Also carved into the stone are pictures of eagles tearing hearts from human victims. The word *Tzompantli* is not Mayan but comes from central Mexico. Reconstruction using scattered fragments may add a level to this platform and change the look of this structure by the time you visit.

**PLATFORM OF THE EAGLES**    Next to the Tzompantli, this small platform has reliefs showing eagles and jaguars clutching human hearts in their talons and claws, as well as a human head emerging from the mouth of a serpent.

**PLATFORM OF VENUS**    East of the Tzompantli and north of El Castillo, near the road to the Sacred Cenote, is the Platform of Venus. In Maya and Toltec lore, a feathered monster or a feathered serpent with a human head in its mouth represented Venus. This is also called the tomb of Chaac-Mool because a Chaac-Mool figure was discovered "buried" within the structure.

**SACRED CENOTE**    Follow the dirt road (actually an ancient *sacbé*, or causeway) that heads north from the Platform of Venus; after 5 minutes you'll come to the great natural well that may have given Chichén Itzá (the Well of the Itzáes) its name. This well was used for ceremonial purposes. Sacrificial victims were thrown in. Anatomical research done early in the 20th century by Ernest A. Hooten showed that bones of both children and adults were found in the well.

Edward Thompson, who was the American consul in Mérida and a Harvard professor, purchased the ruins of Chichén early in the 20th century and explored the *cenote* with dredges and divers. His explorations exposed a fortune in gold and jade. Most of the riches wound up in Harvard's Peabody Museum of Archaeology and Ethnology—a matter that continues to disconcert Mexican classicists today. Excavations in the 1960s unearthed more treasure, and studies of the recovered objects detail offerings from throughout the Yucatán and even farther away.

**TEMPLO DE LOS GUERREROS (TEMPLE OF THE WARRIORS)**   Due east of El Castillo is one of the most impressive structures at Chichén: the Temple of the Warriors, named for the carvings of warriors marching along its walls. It's also called the Group of the Thousand Columns for the rows of broken pillars that flank it. During the recent restoration, hundreds more of the columns were rescued from the rubble and put in place, setting off the temple more magnificently than ever. A figure of Chaac-Mool sits at the top of the temple, surrounded by impressive columns carved in relief to look like enormous feathered serpents. South of the temple was a square building that archaeologists call **El Mercado (The Market);** a colonnade surrounds its central court. Beyond the temple and the market in the jungle are mounds of rubble, parts of which are being reconstructed.

The main Mérida-Cancún highway once ran straight through the ruins of Chichén, and though it has been diverted, you can still see the great swath it cut. South and west of the old highway's path are more impressive ruined buildings.

**TUMBA DEL GRAN SACERDOTE (TOMB OF THE HIGH PRIEST)**   Past the refreshment stand to the right of the path is the Tomb of the High Priest, which stood atop a natural limestone cave in which skeletons and offerings were found, giving the temple its name.

**CASA DE LOS METATES (TEMPLE OF THE GRINDING STONES)**   This building, the next one on your right, is named after the concave corn-grinding stones the Maya used.

**TEMPLO DEL VENADO (TEMPLE OF THE DEER)**   Past Casa de los Metates is this fairly tall though ruined building. The relief of a stag that gave the temple its name is long gone.

**CHICHAN-CHOB (LITTLE HOLES)**   This next temple has a roof comb with little holes, three masks of the rain god Chaac, three rooms, and a good view of the surrounding structures. It's one of the oldest buildings at Chichén, built in the Puuc style during the late Classic period.

**EL CARACOL (OBSERVATORY)**   Construction of the Observatory, a complex building with a circular tower, was carried out over centuries; the additions and modifications reflected the Maya's careful observation of celestial movements and their need for increasingly exact measurements. Through slits in the tower's walls, astronomers could observe the cardinal directions and the approach of the all-important spring and autumn equinoxes, as well as the summer solstice. The temple's name, which means "snail," comes from a spiral staircase within the structure.

On the east side of El Caracol, a path leads north into the bush to the **Cenote Xtoloc,** a natural limestone well that provided the city's daily water supply. If you see any lizards sunning there, they may well be *xtoloc,* the species for which this *cenote* is named.

**TEMPLO DE LOS TABLEROS (TEMPLE OF PANELS)**   Just south of El Caracol are the ruins of a *temazcalli* (a steam bath) and the Temple of Panels, named for the carved panels on top. This temple was once covered by a much larger structure, only traces of which remain.

**EDIFICIO DE LAS MONJAS (EDIFICE OF THE NUNS)**   If you've visited the Puuc sites of Kabah, Sayil, Labná, or Xlapak, the enormous nunnery here will remind you of the palaces at those sites. Built in the late Classic period, the new edifice was constructed over an older one. Suspecting that this was so, Le Plongeon, an archaeologist working early in the 20th century, put dynamite between the two and blew away part of the exterior, revealing the older structures within. You can still see the results of Le Plongeon's indelicate exploratory methods.

On the east side of the Edifice of the Nuns is **Anexo Este (annex)** constructed in highly ornate Chenes style with Chaac masks and serpents.

**LA IGLESIA (THE CHURCH)**    Next to the annex is one of the oldest buildings at Chichén, the Church. Masks of Chaac decorate two upper stories. Look closely, and you'll see other pagan symbols among the crowd of Chaacs: an armadillo, a crab, a snail, and a tortoise. These represent the Maya gods, called *bacab,* whose job it was to hold up the sky.

**AKAB DZIB (TEMPLE OF OBSCURE WRITING)**    Beloved of travel writers, this temple lies east of the Edifice of the Nuns. Above a door in one of the rooms are some Mayan glyphs, which gave the temple its name because the writings have yet to be deciphered. In other rooms, traces of red handprints are still visible. Reconstructed and expanded over the centuries, Akab Dzib may be the oldest building at Chichén.

**CHICHEN VIEJO (OLD CHICHEN)**    For a look at more of Chichén's oldest buildings, constructed well before the time of Toltec influence, follow signs from the Edifice of the Nuns southwest into the bush to Old Chichén, about 1km (½ mile) away. Be prepared for this trek with long trousers, insect repellent, and a local guide. The attractions here are the **Templo de los Inscripciones Iniciales (Temple of the First Inscriptions),** with the oldest inscriptions discovered at Chichén, and the restored **Templo de los Dinteles (Temple of the Lintels),** a fine Puuc building. Some of these buildings have recently undergone restoration.

## WHERE TO STAY

The expensive hotels in Chichén all occupy beautiful grounds, are close to the ruins, and serve decent food. All have toll-free reservations numbers. These hotels do a lot of business with tour operators—they can be empty one day and full the next. From these hotels you can easily walk to the back entrance of the ruins, next to the Hotel Mayaland. There are several inexpensive hotels in the village of Pisté, just to the west of the ruins. There is no advantage to staying in Piste other than the proximity to Chichén Itzá. It is an unattractive village with little to recommend it. Another option is to stay in the colonial town of Valladolid, 40 minutes away.

### EXPENSIVE

**Hacienda Chichén** ☆☆    This is the smallest and most private of the hotels at the ruins. It is also the quietest. This former hacienda served as the headquarters for the Carnegie Institute's excavations in 1923. Several bungalows scattered about the property were built to house the institute's staff. Each one houses one or two units. Rooms come with a dehumidifier, a ceiling fan, and good air-conditioning. The floors are ceramic tile, the ceilings are stucco with wood beams, and the walls are decorated with carved stone trim. Trees and tropical plants fill the manicured gardens. You can enjoy these from your room's porch or from the terrace restaurant, which occupies part of the original hacienda owner's house. Standard rooms come with a queen-size, two twin, or two double beds. Suites are bigger and have sitting areas with sleeper-sofas. These come with king-size beds. The main building belonged to the hacienda; it houses the terrace restaurant.

Zona Arqueológica, 97751 Chichén Itzá, Yuc. ⓒ/fax 985/851-0045. www.haciendachichen.com. (Reservations: Casa del Balam, Calle 60 no. 488, 97000 Mérida, Yuc. ⓒ 800/624-8451 in the U.S., or 999/924-2150. Fax 999/924-5011.) 28 units. $175 double; $200 junior suite. AE, MC, V. Free guarded parking. **Amenities:** Restaurant; 2 bars; large outdoor pool. *In room:* A/C, minibar, hair dryer, no phone.

**Hotel & Bungalows Mayaland** 🦋🦋🦋    The main doorway frames El Caracol (the Observatory) in a stunning view—that's how close this hotel is to the ruins. The long main building is three stories high. The rooms are large, with comfortable beds and large tiled bathrooms. Bungalows, scattered about the rest of the grounds, are built native-style, with thatched roofs and stucco walls; they're a good deal larger than the rooms. The grounds are gorgeous, with huge trees and lush foliage—the hotel has had 75 years to get them in shape. The suites are on the top floor of the main building and come with terraces and two-person Jacuzzis. The "lodge section" consists of two groupings of larger bungalows in the back of the property surrounded by a lovely garden and pool area. Rates for November, Christmas, and the spring equinox are a little higher than posted here.

Zona Arqueológica, 97751 Chichén Itzá, Yuc. ⓒ 985/851-0100. www.mayaland.com. (Reservations: Mayaland Resorts, Robalo 30 SM3, 77500 Cancún, Q. Roo. ⓒ 800/235-4079 in the U.S., or 998/887-2495. Fax 998/887-4510.) 97 units. High season $192 double, $278 bungalow, $316 suite, $438–$520 lodge bungalows; low season $103 double, $168 bungalow, $230 suite, $192–$248 lodge bungalows. Higher rates are for units with Jacuzzi. AE, MC, V. Free guarded parking. **Amenities:** 2 restaurants; bar; 3 outdoor pools; tour desk; room service until 10pm; babysitting; laundry service. *In room:* A/C, TV, minibar, coffeemaker.

## MODERATE

**Villas Arqueológicas Chichén Itzá** 🦋    This hotel is built around a courtyard and a pool. Two massive royal poinciana trees tower above the grounds, and bougainvillea drapes the walls. This chain has similar hotels at Cobá and Uxmal, and is connected with Club Med. The rooms are modern and comfortable, unless you're 1.9m (6 ft., 2 in.) or taller—each bed is in a niche, with walls at the head and foot. Most rooms have one double bed and a twin bed. You can book a half- or full-board plan or just the room.

Zona Arqueológica, 97751 Chichén Itzá, Yuc. ⓒ 800/258-2633 in the U.S., 985/851-0034, or 985/856-2830. 40 units. $100 double. Rates include continental breakfast. Half-board (breakfast plus lunch or dinner) $18 per person; full board (3 meals) $35 per person. AE, MC, V. Free parking. **Amenities:** Restaurant; bar; large outdoor pool; tennis court; tour desk. *In room:* A/C, hair dryer.

## INEXPENSIVE

**Hotel Dolores Alba** *(Value)*    This place is of the motel variety, perfect if you come by car. It is a bargain for what you get: two pools (one really special), *palapas* and hammocks around the place, and large, comfortable rooms. The restaurant serves good meals at moderate prices. There is free transportation to the ruins and the Balankanché Cave during visiting hours, though you will have to take a taxi back. The hotel is on the highway 2.5km (1½ miles) east of the ruins (toward Valladolid). Rooms come with two double beds.

Carretera Mérida–Valladolid Km 122, Yuc. ⓒ 985/858-1555. www.doloresalba.com. (Reservations: Hotel Dolores Alba, Calle 63 no. 464, 97000 Mérida, Yuc. ⓒ 999/928-5650. Fax 999/928-3163.) 40 units. $45 double. MC, V (8% service charge). Free parking. **Amenities:** Restaurant; bar; 2 outdoor pools; room service until 10pm. *In room:* A/C, TV, no phone.

## WHERE TO DINE

Although there's no great food in this area, there is plenty of decent food. The best idea is to stick to simple choices. The restaurant at the visitor center at the ruins serves decent snack food. The hotel restaurants mostly do a fair job, and, if you're in the village of Pisté, you can try one of the restaurants along the highway there that cater to the bus tours, such as **Fiesta** (© **985/851-0111**). The best time to go is early lunch or regular supper hours, when the buses are gone.

## OTHER ATTRACTIONS IN THE AREA

**Ik-Kil** is a large *cenote* on the highway just across from the Hotel Dolores Alba, 2.5km (1½ miles) east of the main entrance to the ruins. And it's deep, with lots of steps leading down to the water's edge. Unlike Dzitnup, these steps are easy to manage. The view from both the top and the bottom is dramatic, with lots of tropical vegetation and curtains of hanging tree roots stretching all the way to the water's surface. Take your swimsuit and enjoy the cold water. The best swimming is before 11:30am, at which time bus tours start arriving from the coast. These bus tours are the main business of Ik-Kil, which also has a restaurant and souvenir shops. Ik-Kil is open from 8am to 5pm daily. Admission is $6 per adult, $3 per child 7 to 12 years old.

The **Balankanché Cave** is 5.5km (3½ miles) from Chichén Itzá on the road to Valladolid and Cancún. Taxis will make the trip and wait. The entire excursion takes about a half-hour, but the walk inside is hot and humid. Of the cave tours in the Yucatán, this is the tamest, having good footing and requiring the least amount of walking and climbing. It includes a cheesy and uninformative recorded tour. The highlight is a round chamber with a central column that gives the impression of being a large tree. You come up the same way you go down. The cave became a hideaway during the War of the Castes. You can still see traces of carving and incense burning, as well as an underground stream that served as the sanctuary's water supply. Outside, take time to meander through the botanical gardens, where most of the plants and trees are labeled with their common and botanical names.

Admission is $5, free for children 6 to 12. Children under age 6 are not admitted. Use of a video camera costs $4 (free if you've already bought a video permit in Chichén the same day). Tours in English are at 11am and 1 and 3pm, and, in Spanish, at 9am, noon, and 2 and 4pm. Double-check these hours at the main entrance to the Chichén ruins.

## 5 Valladolid

40km (25 miles) E of Chichén Itzá; 160km (100 miles) SW of Cancún

Valladolid (pronounced "bah-yah-doh-*leed*") is a small, pleasant colonial city halfway between Mérida and Cancún. The people are friendly and informal, and, except for the heat, life is easy. The city's economy is based on commerce and small-scale manufacturing. There is a large *cenote* in the center of town and a couple more 4km (2½ miles) down the road to Chichén. Not far away are the intriguing ruins of Ek Balam, the flamingo-infested waters of Rio Lagarto, and the sandy beaches of Holbox (see "Side Trips from Valladolid," below).

## ESSENTIALS

**GETTING THERE & DEPARTING   By Car**   From Mérida or Cancún, you have two choices: the *cuota* (toll road) or Highway 180. The toll from Cancún is $18, from Mérida $10. The *cuota* passes 2km (1¼ miles) north of the city; the exit is at the crossing of Highway 295 to Tizimín. **Highway 180** takes significantly longer because it passes through a number of villages (with their requisite speed bumps). Both 180 and

295 lead directly to downtown. Leaving is just as easy: from the main square, Calle 41 turns into 180 east to Cancún; Calle 39 heads to 180 west to Chichén Itzá and Mérida. To take the *cuota* to Mérida or Cancún, take Calle 40 (see "City Layout," below).

**By Bus** There are several direct buses to Mérida (13 per day) or Cancún (five per day). Each runs $11. You can also get direct buses for Playa (five per day) and Tulum (four per day). Buses to Playa take the toll road and cost $14; buses to Tulum take the shortcut via Chemax and cost $6. To get to Chichén Itzá, take a second-class bus, which leaves every hour and sometimes on the half-hour. The recently remodeled bus station is at the corner of calles 39 and 46.

There is now a daily bus to Ek Balam that departs from in front of the Palacio Municipal (see "Ek Balam: Dark Jaguar," below).

**VISITOR INFORMATION** The small **tourism office** is in the Palacio Municipal. It's open daily from 9am to 8pm, Sunday 9am to 1pm.

**CITY LAYOUT** Valladolid has the standard layout for towns in the Yucatán: Streets running north-south are even numbers; those running east-west are odd numbers. The main plaza is bordered by Calle 39 on the north, 41 on the south, 40 on the east, and 42 on the west. The plaza is named Parque Francisco Cantón Rosado, but everyone calls it **El Centro.** Taxis are easy to come by.

## EXPLORING VALLADOLID

Before it became Valladolid, the city was a Maya settlement called Zací (zah-*kee*), which means "white hawk." There is one *cenote* in town: **Cenote Zací,** at the intersection of calles 39 and 36, in a small park. A trail leads down close to the water. Caves, stalactites, and hanging vines contribute to a wild, prehistoric feel. The park has a large *palapa* restaurant. Admission is $2.

Ten blocks to the southwest of the main square is the Franciscan monastery of **San Bernardino de Siena** (1552). Most of the compound was built in the early 1600s; a large underground river is believed to pass under the convent and surrounding neighborhood, which is called Barrio Sisal. "Sisal" is, in this case, a corruption of the Mayan phrase *sis-ha,* meaning "cold water." The *barrio* has undergone extensive restoration and is a delight to behold.

Valladolid's main square is the social center of town and a thriving market for Yucatecan dresses. On its south side is the principal church, **La Parroquia de San Servacio.** Vallesoletanos, as the locals call themselves, believe that almost all cathedrals in Mexico point east, and they cherish a local legend to explain why theirs points north—but don't believe a word of it. On the east side of the plaza is the municipal building, **El Ayuntamiento.** Get a look at the highly dramatic paintings outlining the history of the peninsula. My personal favorite depicts a horrified Maya priest foreseeing the arrival of Spanish galleons. On Sunday nights, beneath the stone arches of the Ayuntamiento, the municipal band plays *jaranas* and other traditional music of the region.

## SHOPPING

The **Mercado de Artesanías de Valladolid (crafts market),** at the corner of calles 39 and 44, gives you a good idea of the local merchandise. Perhaps the main handicraft of the town is embroidered Maya dresses, which can be purchased here or from women around the main square. The area around Valladolid is cattle country; locally made leather goods such as *huaraches* (sandals) and bags are inexpensive and plentiful. On the main plaza is a small shop above the municipal bazaar. A good sandal maker

## Sweet as Honey

Valladolid also produces a highly prized honey made from the *tzi-tzi-ché* flower. You can find it and other goods at the **town market,** Calle 32 between calles 35 and 37. The best time to see the market is Sunday morning.

has a shop called **Elios,** Calle 37 no. 202, between calles 42 and 44 (no phone). An Indian named **Juan Mac** makes *alpargatas,* the traditional sandals of the Maya, in his shop on Calle 39, near the intersection with Calle 38, 1 block from the main plaza. It's almost on the corner, across from the Bar La Joya. There's no sign, but the door jamb is painted yellow. Juan Mac can be found there most mornings. Most of his output is for locals, but he's happy to knock out a pair for visitors. He also makes a dress *alpargata,* but I like the standard ones better.

## WHERE TO STAY

Aside from the hotels listed below, you can stay in town at **Hotel Zací,** Calle 44 between calles 37 and 39 (© **985/856-2167**). Another option is the **Ecotel Quinta Regia** (© **985/856-3472;** www.ecotelquintaregia.com.mx) a few blocks farther from the main square on Calle 48 between calles 27 and 29.

For something a bit different, you can stay in a small ecohotel in the nearby village of Ek Balam, close to the ruins: **Genesis Eco Oasis Ek Balam** (© **985/858-9375;** www.genesisretreat.com). It is owned and operated by a Canadian woman, Lee Christie. She takes guests on tours of the village showing what daily life is like among the contemporary Maya. There are other activities, too. She rents out some simple cabanas (either with shared or private bathrooms) that surround a lovely pool and a restaurant.

**Hotel El Mesón del Marqués** ✯   This was originally a small colonial hotel that has grown large and modern. The first courtyard surrounds a fountain and abounds with hanging plants and bougainvillea. This was the original house, now occupied mostly by the restaurant (see "Where to Dine," below). In back is the new construction and the pool. Rooms are medium to large and are attractive. Most come with two double beds. The hotel is on the north side of El Centro, opposite the church.

Calle 39 no. 203, 97780 Valladolid, Yuc. © 985/856-3042 or -2073. Fax 985/856-2280. www.mesondelmarques.com. 90 units. $55 double; $65 superior; $95 junior suite. AE. Free secure parking. **Amenities:** Restaurant; bar; outdoor pool; room service until 10pm; laundry service. *In room:* A/C, TV.

**Hotel María de la Luz**   The three-story María de la Luz is on the west side of the main square. The guest rooms have tile floors and bathrooms; three have balconies overlooking the main square. The wide interior space holds a restaurant that is comfortable and airy for most of the day.

Calle 42 no. 193, 97780 Valladolid, Yuc. ©/fax 985/856-2071 or -1181. www.mariadelaluzhotel.com. 70 units. $38 double. MC, V. Free secure parking. **Amenities:** Restaurant; bar; midsize outdoor pool; tour desk. *In room:* A/C, TV.

## WHERE TO DINE

Valladolid is not a center for haute cuisine, but you can try some of the regional specialties. Some of the best food I had was at **El Mesón del Marqués** right on the main square. There is another restaurant on the main square called **Las Campanas**, which is okay. Locals like to eat at one of the stalls in the **Bazar Municipal,** next door to the Mesón del Marqués. They also frequent the **taco stands** that set up around the square.

I did a quick sampling of *cochinita pibil, carnitas,* and *lechón asado* (all pork dishes) at the three most popular taco stands. I enjoyed it all and wasn't the worse for the wear. These stands serve customers only until around noon.

## SIDE TRIPS FROM VALLADOLID
### CENOTES DZITNUP & SAMMULA

The **Cenote Dzitnup** 𝕱 (also known as Cenote Xkekén) is 4km (2½ miles) west of Valladolid off Highway 180 in the direction of Chichén Itzá. It is worth a side trip, especially if you have time for a dip. You can take the bike trail there. Antonio Aguilar, who owns a sporting goods store at Calle 41 no. 225, between calles 48 and 50, rents bikes. Once you get there, you descend a short flight of rather perilous stone steps, and at the bottom, inside a beautiful cavern, is a natural pool of water so clear and blue that it seems plucked from a dream. If you decide to swim, be sure that you don't have creams or other chemicals on your skin—they damage the habitat of the small fish and other organisms living there. Also, no alcohol, food, or smoking is allowed in the cavern. Admission is $2. The *cenote* is open daily from 7am to 7pm. If it's crowded, about 90m (295 ft.) down the road on the opposite side is another recently discovered *cenote,* **Sammulá,** which is also worth a visit and a swim. Admission is $2.

### EK BALAM: DARK JAGUAR 𝕱𝕱𝕱

About 18km (11 miles) north of Valladolid, off the highway to Río Lagartos, are the spectacular ruins of **Ek Balam,** which, owing to a certain ambiguity in Mayan, means either "dark jaguar" or "star jaguar." Relatively unvisited by tourists, the Ek Balam ruins are about to hit it big. A new road now runs from the highway to the ruins. There is a daily air-conditioned bus from Valladolid that departs from the main square at 9am, allows a couple of hours at the ruins, and returns at 1pm. The fare is $4 round-trip.

Take Calle 40 north out of Valladolid to Highway 295; go 20km (12 miles) to a large marked turnoff. Ek Balam is 13km (8 miles) from the highway; the entrance fee is $5, plus $4 for each video camera. The site is open daily from 8am to 5pm.

In the last few years a team of archaeologists have been doing extensive excavation and renovation. What they have found has the world of Maya scholars all aquiver. Built between 100 B.C. and A.D. 1200, the smaller buildings are architecturally unique—especially the large, perfectly restored **Caracol.** Flanked by two smaller pyramids, the imposing central pyramid is about 160m (525 ft.) long and 60m (197 ft.) wide. At more than 30m (100 ft.) high, it is easily taller than the highest pyramid in Chichén Itzá. On the left side of the main stairway, archaeologists have uncovered a large ceremonial doorway of perfectly preserved stucco work. It is an astonishingly elaborate representation of the gaping mouth of the underworld god. Around it are several beautifully detailed human figures. Excavation inside revealed a long chamber filled with Mayan hieroglyphic writing. From the style, it appears that the scribes probably came from Guatemala. So far this chamber is closed to the public. From this script, an epigrapher, Alfonso Lacadena, has found the name of one of the principal kings of the city—Ukit Kan Le'k. If you climb to the top of the pyramid, in the middle distance you can see untouched ruins looming to the north. To the southeast, you can spot the tallest structures at **Cobá,** 50km (31 miles) away.

Also visible are the **raised causeways** of the Maya—the *sacbé* appear as raised lines in the forest vegetation. More than any of the better-known sites, Ek Balam inspires a sense of mystery and awe at the scale of Maya civilization and the utter ruin to which it came.

## RIO LAGARTOS NATURE RESERVE 🐾

Some 80km (50 miles) north of Valladolid (40km/25 miles north of Tizimín) on Highway 295 is Río Lagartos, a 50,000-hectare (123,500-acre) refuge established in 1979 to protect the largest nesting population of flamingos in North America. The nesting area is off-limits, but you can see plenty of flamingos as well as many other species of fowl and take an enjoyable boat ride around the estuary here.

To get to Río Lagartos, you pass through Tizimín, which is about 30 minutes away. If you need to spend the night there, try **Hotel 49,** Calle 49 373-A (© **986/863-2136**), by the main square. There is not much to do in Tizimín unless you are there during the first 2 weeks of January, when it holds the largest fair in the Yucatán. The prime fiesta day is January 6.

**SEEING THE RIO LAGARTOS REFUGE**   Río Lagartos is a small fishing village of around 3,000 people who make their living from the sea and from the occasional tourist who shows up to see the flamingos. Colorfully painted houses face the *malecón* (the oceanfront street), and brightly painted boats dock here and there.

When you drive into town, keep going straight until you get to the shore. Look for where Calle 10 intersects with the *malecón;* it's near a modern church. There, in a little kiosk, is where the guides can be found (no phone). The sign reads PARADOR TURÍS-TICO NAHOCHIN. There you can make arrangements for a 2-hour tour, which will cost $50 to $60 for two to three people. The best time to go is in the early morning, so it's best to overnight here at one of the cheap hotels along the *malecón.* I looked at a few and liked **Posada Lucy** (no phone; $25 for two).

I had a very pleasant ride the next morning, and saw several species of ducks, hawks, cranes, cormorants, an osprey, and, of course, lots of flamingos. The guide also wanted to show me how easy it was to float in some evaporation pools used by the local salt producer at Las Coloradas (a good source of employment for the locals until it was mechanized) and a place where fresh water bubbles out from below the saltwater estuary.

## ISLA HOLBOX 🐾

A sandy strip of an island off the northeastern corner of the Yucatán Peninsula, Holbox (pronounced "hohl-*bosh*") was a remote corner of the world with only a half-deserted fishing village until tourists started showing up for the beach. Now it's a semiprosperous little community that gets its livelihood from tourist services, employment at the beach hotels, and tours. It's most popular with visitors from May to September when over a hundred **whale sharks** congregate in nearby waters (why precisely they come here is not known). These gentle giants swim slowly along the surface of the water and don't seem to mind the boat tours and snorkelers that come to experience what it's like to be in the wild with these creatures. Whale sharks don't fit the common picture of a shark; they are much larger, attaining a length of up to 18m (59 ft.), and they are filter feeders for the most part, dining on plankton and other small organisms. That said, they can do some mischief if you annoy them.

The beach here is broad and sandy (with fine-textured sand). It is also shallow. Instead of the amazing blue color of the Caribbean, it's more of a dull green. There are several beach hotels just beyond town. These experienced lots of damage from Hurricane Emily in the summer of 2005. On my visit 6 months later, a couple still hadn't opened, including **Villas Flamingos** (© **800/538-6802** in the U.S. and Canada). But a personal favorite, **Villas Delfines,** which has an office in Cancún (© **998/884-8606** or 984/875-2197; www.holbox.com), was open for business and looking normal. It was charging from $90 to $150 for a large free-standing beach bungalow with a large porch, a thatched roof, mosquito netting, and plenty of cross-ventilation. This is very much an ecohotel, with composting toilets and solar water heaters. There is a pool, a good restaurant, and lovely grounds. If you want air-conditioning, try **Casa Sandra** (© **984/875-2171**).

From Valladolid, take Highway 180 east for about 90km (56 miles) toward Cancún; turn north after Nuevo Xcan at the tiny crossroads of El Ideal. Drive nearly 100km (62 miles) north on a state highway to the tiny port of Chiquilá, where you can park your car in a secure parking lot; walk 180m (590 ft.) to the pier, and catch the ferry to the island. It runs 10 times per day. When you get off in the village you can contract with one of the golf cart taxis for a ride to your hotel.

# 8

# Tabasco & Chiapas

*by David Baird*

**E**ven though these two states aren't part of the Yucatán, we've included them so that we can present Mexico's entire **Maya region.** Many travelers who go to the Yucatán to see Chichén Itzá and Uxmal also take a side trip to Chiapas to see the famous ruins of Palenque. Some go even farther, all the way to San Cristóbal, to visit the highland Maya.

However, if you have the time, you might want to make this part of Mexico the object of a separate trip. First, there's a lot to see and do; second, much of it is appreciated best when traveling leisurely; and third, transportation in and out and through the area is a bit problematic—not the kind of thing you want to do on a tight schedule.

The terrain and climate of Chiapas and Tabasco differ from the Yucatán. The lowland jungle is denser and taller than all but the most southern part of the peninsula. The central highlands of Chiapas are cool and wet, and the mountain air feels refreshing after the heat and humidity of the lowlands. The area has striking mountain vistas, deep canyons, and isolated cloud forests.

**Tabasco** is a small, oil-rich state along the Gulf coast. The capital, **Villahermosa,** has a distinct boomtown feel. It was in this coastal region that the Olmec, the mother culture of Mesoamerica, rose to prominence. At the Parque–Museo La Venta, you can see some artifacts this culture left to posterity, including its famous megalithic heads.

**Chiapas** has much that is interesting, but perhaps the areas most important to visit are the eastern lowland jungles and the central highlands. In the former lie the famous ruins of **Palenque,** a city that dates from the Classic age of Maya civilization. The ruins look unspeakably old, and the surrounding jungle seems poised to reclaim them should their caretakers ever falter in their duties. Deeper into the interior are the sites of **Yaxchilán** and **Bonampak.** The central highlands are just as dramatic but easier to enjoy. Of particular interest is the colonial city of **San Cristóbal de las Casas** and its surrounding Indian villages. The Indians here cling so tenaciously to their beliefs and traditions that at one time this area was more popular with anthropologists than tourists.

Ten years ago, Chiapas made international news when the Zapatista Liberation Army launched an armed rebellion and captured San Cristóbal. This forced the Mexican government to recognize the existence of social and economic disparities in Chiapas. Negotiations achieved minor results, then stalled. Political violence erupted again in the winter of 1997 and 1998. But no foreigners were attacked, and no restrictions were ever placed on travel to Palenque or the San Cristóbal region. Since then, especially in the last couple of years, the Zapatista movement has dropped the talk about armed insurrection in an effort to broaden its base as a political movement.

## EXPLORING TABASCO & CHIAPAS

Air service connects the Yucatán to Villahermosa, but flights are fewer now than they used to be. Traveling overland, you will likely go through Campeche, which is 5 hours from Palenque and 6 hours from Villahermosa. From Palenque, it's 4 to 5 hours to San Cristóbal depending on road conditions; from Villahermosa, it's 5 or 6 hours.

### Map Pointer

For a map of Tabasco and Chiapas, see p. 21.

You can see Palenque in a day. A couple of side trips would add a couple more days, and if you plan on going to Bonampak and Yaxchilán (the Maya ruins that border Guatemala), add another full day. San Cristóbal and the nearby villages have so much to offer that 4 days is the minimum you should spend there. And, depending on the kind of traveler you are, you might want to stop in one of smaller towns if it's convenient to your travels.

*Note:* Traveling only during the day is a good idea in this region. In any part of the world where the idea of armed rebellion has held sway, it is common to encounter sporadic banditry until things settle down. All my friends in this region say I'm wrong and swear up and down that this is not a problem. But I've heard things here and there that are at odds with what they tell me.

## 1 Villahermosa

142km (88 miles) NW of Palenque; 469km (291 miles) SW of Campeche; 160km (99 miles) N of San Cristóbal de las Casas

Villahermosa (pop. 550,000) is the capital of and the largest city in the state of Tabasco. It lies in a shallow depression about an hour's drive from the Gulf coast, at the confluence of two rivers: the Grijalva and the Carrizal. The land is marshy, with shallow lakes scattered here and there. For most of the year it's hot and humid.

Oil has brought money to this town and raised prices. Villahermosa is one of the most expensive cities in the country and contrasts sharply with inexpensive Chiapas. Though there's a lot of money, it's all being pulled to the modern western sections surrounding a development called Tabasco 2000. This area, especially the neighborhoods around the **Parque–Museo La Venta,** is the most attractive part of town, surrounded, as it is, by small lakes. The historic center has been left to decay. It's gritty, crowded, and unpleasant. The main reason to be downtown is for the cheap hotels.

Two names that you will likely see and hear are Carlos Pellicer Cámara and Tomás Garrido Canabal; both were interesting people. The first was a mid-20th-century Tabascan poet and intellectual. The best known of Mexico's *modernista* poets, he was a fiercely independent thinker. Garrido Canabal, socialist governor of Tabasco in the 1920s and 1930s, tried to turn the conservative, backwater state of Tabasco into a model of socialism. He fought for many socialist causes, but his enmity for Mexico's Catholic church is what he is most remembered for today. He went so far as to name his son Lucifer and his farm animals Jesus and the Virgin Mary.

## ESSENTIALS
### GETTING THERE & DEPARTING

**BY PLANE    Continental ExpressJet** (© **800/525-0280,** or 01-800/900-5000 in Mexico) has direct service to/from Houston on a regional jet. **Mexicana** (© **800/531-7921** or 01-800/502-2000 in Mexico; www.mexicana.com) and **Aeromexico** (© **800/237-6639** or 01-800/021-4000 in Mexico; www.aeromexico.com) both have flights

# Villahermosa Area

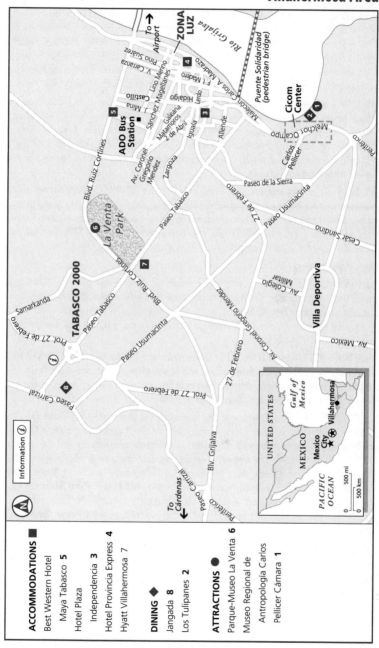

**ACCOMMODATIONS** ■
Best Western Hotel
Maya Tabasco **5**
Hotel Plaza
Independencia **3**
Hotel Provincia Express **4**
Hyatt Villahermosa **7**

**DINING** ◆
Jangada **8**
Los Tulipanes **2**

**ATTRACTIONS** ●
Parque-Museo La Venta **6**
Museo Regional de
Antropología Carlos
Pellicer Cámara **1**

To → Airport
ZONA LUZ
Río Grijalva
Cicom Center
Puente Solidaridad
(pedestrian bridge)
Malecón, Carlos A. Madrazo
Castillo
Sánchez Magallanes
Lino Merino
V. Carranza
Pino Suárez
F. T. Madero
Hidalgo
Lerdo
Allende
J. Mina
Galeana
2 de Abril
Matamoros
Iguala
Zaragoza
Av. Coronel
Gregorio Méndez
Blvd. Ruiz Cortines
ADO Bus Station
Melchor Ocampo
Carlos Pellicer
Periférico
Paseo de la Sierra
Paseo Tabasco
27 de Febrero
Paseo Usumacinta
César Sandino
La Venta Park
TABASCO 2000
Blvd. Ruiz Cortines
Paseo Tabasco
Samarkanda
Prol. 27 de Febrero
Paseo Usumacinta
Av. Coronel Gregorio Méndez
27 de Febrero
Av. Colegio Militar
Villa Deportiva
Av. México
Prol. 27 de Febrero
Blv. Grijalva
Paseo Carrizal
Periférico
To Cárdenas ↓
Information ⓘ

UNITED STATES
Gulf of Mexico
MEXICO
Mexico City ★
★ Villahermosa
PACIFIC OCEAN
500 mi
500 km

N

245

to and from Mexico City. **Aviación de Chiapas** (Aviacsa; ☎ **993/316-5700** or 01-800/006-2200 in Mexico; www.aviacsa.com) flies to and from Mexico City and Mérida. The regional airline **AeroLitoral,** a subsidiary of Aeromexico (☎ **800/237-6639** or 993/312-6991), goes through Mexico City with a connection to Veracruz, Tampico, Monterrey, and Houston. **Click** (☎ **01-800/122-5425** in Mexico; www.clickmx.com), a Mexican budget airline, provides nonstop service to and from Mexico City.

**BY CAR**   Highway 180 connects Villahermosa to Campeche (6 hr.). Highway 186, which passes by the airport, joins Highway 199 to Palenque and San Cristóbal de las Casas. The road to Palenque is a good one, and the drive takes 2 hours. Between Palenque and San Cristóbal the road enters the mountains and takes 4 to 5 hours. On any of the mountainous roads, road conditions are apt to get worse during the rainy season from May to October.

**BY BUS**   The **bus station** is at Mina and Merino (☎ **993/312-8900**; www.ticket bus.com.mx), 3 blocks off Highway 180. There are eight nonstop buses per day to/from Palenque (2½ hr.). There are seven nonstop buses per day to Mexico City (10 hr.), six deluxe service on **ADO-GL**, and two superdeluxe on **UNO.** To Campeche there are eight buses nonstop per day (7 hr.); some of these go on to Mérida.

## ORIENTATION
**ARRIVING**   Villahermosa's **airport** is 10km (6¼ miles) east of town. Driving in, you'll cross a bridge over the Río Grijalva, then turn left to reach downtown. Taxis to the downtown area cost $15.

Parking downtown can be difficult; it's best to find a parking lot. Use one that's guarded round-the-clock.

**VISITOR INFORMATION**   The **State Tourism Office** (☎ **993/316-5122,** ext. 229) has two information booths: The one at the **airport** is staffed daily from 10am to 5pm; the one at **Parque–Museo La Venta** (next to the ticket counter for the park) is staffed Tuesday to Sunday from 10am to 5pm.

**CITY LAYOUT**   The downtown area, including the pedestrian-only **Zona Luz,** is on the west bank of the Grijalva River. About 1.5km (1 mile) upstream (south) is **CICOM,** an academic organization with the large archaeology museum named for the poet Carlos Pellicer Cámara. The **airport** is on the east side of the river. Highway 180 passes the airport and crosses the river just north of downtown, becoming **Bulevar Ruiz Cortines.** To get to the downtown area, turn left onto **Madero** or **Pino Suárez.** By staying on Ruiz Cortines you can reach the city's biggest attraction, the Parque–Museo la Venta. It's well marked. Just beyond that is the intersection with **Paseo Tabasco,** the heart of the modern hotel and shopping district.

**GETTING AROUND**   **Taxis** are your best way to get around town. Villahermosa is rare for being a Mexican city without meaningful public transportation.

**FAST FACTS**   **American Express** is represented by Turismo Creativo, Av. Paseo Tabasco 1404, Col. Tabasco 2000 (☎ **993/310-9900**). The telephone **area code** is **993.** There aren't a lot of *casas de cambio,* but you can exchange money at the airport, the hotels, and downtown banks on calles Juárez and Madero. ATMs are plentiful.

## EXPLORING VILLAHERMOSA
Major sights include the **Parque–Museo La Venta** and the **Museo Regional de Antropología Carlos Pellicer Cámara.** You can hit them both in a day. There is also

an ecological park called **Yumká** (see below), which is 16km (10 miles) out of town in the direction of the airport.

Stroll about the pedestrian-only Zona Luz, and you'll see signs that investment might be returning to the old downtown area. Outside the Zona Luz, things get more unpleasant, with lots of traffic and crowds of pedestrians. But, as unpleasant as it, there are things of interest for those who like to explore current Mexican society and culture. You can walk south along the banks of the Grijalva until you come to a pedestrian bridge with an observation tower. That's the highlight. You won't miss much by keeping away.

### Museo Regional de Antropología Carlos Pellicer Cámara ☆☆ This museum
on the west bank of the river about 1.5km (1 mile) south of the town center, has a great, well-organized collection. The pre-Hispanic artifacts on display include not only Tabascan finds (Totonac, Zapotec, and Olmec), but also those of other Mexican and Central American cultures.

The first floor contains the auditorium, bookstore, and gift shop. The second floor is devoted to the Olmec. The third floor features artifacts from central Mexico, including the Tlatilco and Teotihuacán cultures; the Huasteca culture of Veracruz, San Luis Potosí, and Tampico states; and the cultures of Nayarit state, on the west coast. Photographs and diagrams provide vivid images, but the explanatory signs are mostly in Spanish. Look especially for the figurines that were found in this area and for the colorful Codex (an early book of pictographs).

CICOM Center, Av. Carlos Pellicer Cámara 511. ☎ **993/312-6344**. Admission $3. Tues–Sun 9am–5pm.

### Parque–Museo La Venta ☆☆ The Olmec created the first civilization in Mexico
and developed several cultural traits that later spread to all subsequent civilizations throughout Mesoamerica. In addition to their monumental works, they carved small exquisite figurines in jade and serpentine, which can be seen in the Museo Regional de Antropología (see above). The park and museum occupy a portion of a larger park named after Tomás Garrido Canabal, which includes a lovely lake, a zoo, a natural history museum, and a lot of green space with several walkways frequented by joggers. Once inside the park and museum, a trail leads you from one sculpture to the next. Most of the pieces are massive heads or altars. These can be as tall as 2m (6½ ft.) and weigh as much as 40 tons. The faces seem to be half adult, half infant. They have highly stylized mouths with thick fleshy lips that turn down. Known as the "jaguar mouth," this is a principal characteristic of Olmec art. At least 17 heads have been found: 4 at La Venta, 10 at San Lorenzo, and 3 at Tres Zapotes—all Olmec cities on Mexico's east coast. The pieces in this park were taken from La Venta, a major city during the pre-Classic period (2000 B.C.–A.D. 300). Most were sculpted around 1000 B.C. without the use of metal chisels. The basalt rock used for these heads and altars was transported to La Venta from more than 113km (70 miles) away. The rock is thought to have been brought most of the way by raft. Most of these pieces were first discovered in 1938. Now all that remains at La Venta are some grass-covered mounds that were once earthen pyramids. An exhibition area at the entrance to the park does a good job of illustrating how La Venta was laid out and what archaeologists think the Olmec were like.

As you stroll along, you will see labels identifying many species of local trees, including a grand ceiba tree of special significance to the Olmec and, later, the Maya. A few varieties of local critters scurry about, seemingly unconcerned with the presence of humans or with escaping from the park. Allow at least 2 hours for wandering through the junglelike sanctuary and examining the 3,000-year-old sculpture. *Note:* Don't forget the mosquito repellent.

Bulevar Ruiz Cortines s/n. (C) **993/314-1652**. Admission $4. Tues–Sun 8am–4pm.

**Yumká**    Half safari park, half ecological reserve, Yumká contains native and not-so-native wildlife. A good choice for kids, the park offers visitors a guided tour of the indigenous tropical forest, a boat tour of the wetlands ($1 extra for the ride), and a small train ride through grasslands populated with various species of African wildlife. This is a large park; allow at least 2 hours. There's a restaurant on the premises. Yumká is 16km (10 miles) from downtown in the direction of the airport. A minibus provides transportation (ask at your hotel or at a travel agency), or you can take a cab ($15).

Camino Yumká s/n, 86200 Ejido Dos Montes, Tabasco. (C) **993/356-0107**. Admission $7 adults, $5 children under 13. Daily 9am–5pm.

## WHERE TO STAY

You can expect to pay a little extra for rooms in Villahermosa. Rates here include the 17% tax. Several of the inexpensive downtown hotels have figured out that to survive they must offer nightly entertainment to their mostly businessmen clientele. It's unfortunate that they aren't really set up to do this and at the same time provide quiet guest rooms. Listed below is the only inexpensive hotel I could find that didn't have a bar.

### VERY EXPENSIVE

**Hyatt Villahermosa**  ☆☆    A simple hotel for a Hyatt, but it still has the services and amenities you'd expect. I like it better than the Camino Real (which is the other top hotel in the city) for its great location and service. A short walk away is the Parque–Museo La Venta. The rooms are large, quiet, and comfortable. A thorough remodeling all the way down to the plumbing and wiring was completed in 2004. The majority of clients are business travelers.

Av. Juárez 106, 86000 Villahermosa, Tab. (C) **800/233-1234** in the U.S., or 993/310-1234. Fax 993/315-1963. www.villa hermosa.regency.hyatt.com. 206 units. $220 double; $260 Regency Club room; $315 junior suite. AE, DC, MC, V. Free guarded parking. **Amenities:** 2 restaurants; 3 bars (1 w/live music; 1 sports bar); large pool, wading pool; 2 lighted tennis courts; small exercise room; concierge; tour desk; car rental; business center; room service until 11:30pm; laundry service; dry cleaning; nonsmoking floor; concierge level. *In room:* A/C, TV, high-speed Internet, minibar, coffeemaker, hair dryer, iron, safe.

### EXPENSIVE

**Best Western Hotel Maya Tabasco**    This hotel is centrally located between the downtown area and the modern western section. It's close to the Parque–Museo La Venta, the bus station, and the city's principal restaurant district. The rooms are large, and most are carpeted with midsize bathrooms. They don't offer any surprises, but they're scheduled to be remodeled sometime in 2006. An attractive pool area separates the hotel from the hotel's bar, which gets fairly good live talent—Latin music and comedy acts. A quiet bar inside has soft piano or guitar music.

Bulevar Ruiz Cortines 907, 86000 Villahermosa, Tab. (C) **800/528-1234** in the U.S. and Canada, or 993/358-1111, ext. 822. Fax 993/312-1097. www.bestwestern.com. 151 units. $145 double; $180 junior suite. AE, MC, V. Rates include full breakfast. Free guarded parking. **Amenities:** Restaurant; 2 bars; large pool; tour desk; free shuttle service to airport and downtown; business center, room service until 10pm; laundry service; dry cleaning; nonsmoking rooms. *In room:* A/C, TV, dataport, minibar, coffeemaker, hair dryer, safe.

## MODERATE

**Hotel Plaza Independencia** (Value) The Plaza Independencia is the only hotel in this area under $80 with a pool and enclosed parking. Get a room on one of the first three floors, which have been remodeled. End rooms, which end in 01, 02, 14, and 15, have balconies and are generally preferable. It's 2 blocks south of the Plaza de Armas.

Independencia 123, 86000 Villahermosa, Tab. (C) **993/312-1299** or -7541. Fax 993/314-4724. www.hotelesplaza. com.mx. 90 units. $68 double. AE, MC, V. Free secure parking. **Amenities:** Restaurant; bar; small pool; tour desk; business center; room service until 11pm; laundry service. *In room:* A/C, TV, minibar, dataport, hair dryer, safe.

## INEXPENSIVE

**Hotel Provincia Express** (Value) For under $50, this place is your best option. Located downtown in the Zona Luz pedestrian-only section of town, rooms here are simple, quiet, and medium-size, with good air-conditioning. Management is capable and doesn't complicate things by offering services and options that its clientele doesn't want.

Lerdo de Tejada 303, 86000 Villahermosa, Tab. (C) **993/314-5376**, or 01-800/715-3968 in Mexico. Fax 993/314-5442. willaop@prodigy.net.mx. 25 units. $49 double. MC, V. **Amenities:** Restaurant. *In room:* A/C, TV.

## WHERE TO DINE

Like other Mexican cities, Villahermosa has seen the arrival of U.S. franchise restaurants, but as these things go, I prefer the Mexican variety: **Sanborn's,** Av. Ruiz Cortines 1310, near Parque–Museo La Venta ((C) **993/316-8722**), and **VIPS,** Av. Fco. I. Madero 402, downtown ((C) **993/312-3237**). Both usually do a good job with traditional dishes such as enchiladas or *antojitos* (supper dishes).

**Jangada** ★★ SEAFOOD My new favorite restaurant in the city is an all-you-can-eat seafood buffet. Before you get to the line, you are served a small glass of delicious seafood broth and an appetizing empanada of *pejelagarto* (a freshwater fish for which Tabasco is famous—it is also, in fact, the political moniker of Andrés Manuel López Obrador, the former mayor of Mexico City and a candidate for president in 2006, who hails from Tabasco). From here, move on to the salad and cold seafood bar, which offers a seafood salad made with freshwater lobster, different kinds of ceviche, and an area where you can get a seafood cocktail made to order. There's a variety of seafood soups—don't leave without trying the shrimp-and-*yuca* chowder, a dish I remember fondly. And then, of course, there are the main dishes, including a well-made paella, charcoal-grilled pejelagarto (mild taste—light and almost nutty), and fish kebabs. Jangada is in the fancy western part of town in La Choca neighborhood. It closes early, but next door is a good Brazilian-style steakhouse (Rodizio) that stays open until 9pm.

Paseo de la Choca 126, Fracc. La Choca. (C) **993/317-6050.** Reservations not accepted. $24 per person, excluding drinks and dessert. AE, DC, MC, V. Daily 12:30–7pm.

**Los Tulipanes** SEAFOOD/STEAKS/REGIONAL Popular with the local upper-class crowd, Los Tulipanes offers good food and has excellent service. The staff tends to a full house with ease, and, on busy days, a guitar trio strolls and serenades. Because the restaurant is on the Río Grijalva near the Pellicer Museum of Anthropology, you can combine a visit to the museum with lunch here. The staff may bring you a plate of *tostones de plátano*—mashed banana chips. In addition to seafood and steaks, Los Tulipanes serves such Mexican specialties as chiles rellenos, tacos, and enchiladas. It has a wonderful buffet on Sunday.

CICOM Center, Periférico Carlos Pellicer Cámara 511. (C) **993/312-9209** or -9217. Main courses $7–$16; Sun buffet $15. AE, MC, V. Daily 1–9pm.

## A SIDE TRIP TO CHOCOLATE PLANTATIONS & THE RUINS OF COMALCALCO

Eighty kilometers (50 miles) from Villahermosa is **Comalcalco,** the only pyramid site in Mexico made of kilned brick. This site will be of interest to the hard-core Maya freaks, but it isn't as stunning as Palenque or the picturesque ruins of the Río Bec region. If you have a car, you can get there in an hour, but be prepared for a lack of good directional signs. You'll have to ask directions when you get to the town of Comalcalco. If you don't have a car, you can take a taxi, which will run $50 to $60 to get you there and back with time to see the place. Or you can take a bus to the town of Comalcalco, and a taxi from there. ADO runs first-class buses twice daily. From the town of Comalcalco; the ruins are 3km (2 miles) away. This part of Tabasco is cacao-growing country, where you can visit plantations and factories to see the cacao from the pod on the tree to the finished chocolate bars.

The fastest route from Villahermosa is Highway 180 west to a new (and, as far as I could tell, unnumbered) highway that leads to Cunduacán. The turnoff is clearly marked, but if you miss it, you can continue to Cárdenas and take Highway 187 north.

**Comalcalco** is a busy agricultural center and market town. The **ruins of Comalcalco** are about 3km (2 miles) on the same highway past the town; watch for signs to the turnoff on the right. Park in the lot and pay admission at the visitor center by the museum. The museum, with many pre-Hispanic artifacts, is small but interesting and worth the 20 minutes or so it takes to see it. Unfortunately, all the descriptions are in Spanish. It presents a history of the people who lived here, the Putún/Chongal Maya. They were traders, spoke Mayan dialect, and were believed to have founded, or at least greatly influenced, Chichén Itzá.

This city had an extension of 7 sq. km (2¾ sq. miles) but the site contains only the ceremonial center, comprising an expansive plaza bordered by pyramidal structures and an acropolis with the remains of a palace and some ceremonial structures, probably funerary temples. This city reached its height during the Classic period, A.D. 300 to 900. Of the pyramids around the plaza, one has been fully excavated. A carpet of grass grows over others, with partial excavation here and there. These pyramids were made of compacted earth with brick facing, in some places covered in stucco. To the south of the plaza and above it is the acropolis, a complex of temples and palace rooms that sits well above the plaza. There you will find a couple of structures with carvings and molded stucco with scenes of Maya royalty. There are only a few. Workers had cordoned off a couple of the structures in this complex when I was last there, and I'm not sure whether they will be open soon. Because of the fragile nature of these ruins, there are many NO SUBIR ("no climbing") signs warning visitors against scaling particular structures. But there is one path with arrows that leads you up to the **palace** where you have a good view of the whole site. You can make out the remains of a double vault and a colonnaded chamber that were the principal chambers of this palace. Seeing the ruins takes an hour or so. Admission is $3.50, and the site is open daily from 8am to 5pm.

## 2 Palenque ★★

142km (88 miles) SE of Villahermosa; 229km (142 miles) NE of San Cristóbal de las Casas

The ruins of Palenque look out over the jungle from a tall ridge that juts out from the base of steep, thickly forested mountains. It's a dramatic sight colored by the mysterious feel of the ruins themselves. The temples here are in the Classic style, with high-pitched roofs crowned with elaborate combs. Inside many are representations in stone and plaster of the rulers and their gods, which give evidence of a cosmology that is—and perhaps will remain—impenetrable to our understanding. This is one of the grand archaeological sites of Mexico.

Eight kilometers (5 miles) from the ruins is the town of Palenque. There you can find lodging and food, as well as make travel arrangements. Transportation between the town and ruins is cheap and convenient.

## ESSENTIALS
### GETTING THERE & DEPARTING
**BY PLANE**   There is no regular commercial air service to Palenque.

**BY CAR**   The 229km (142-mile) trip from San Cristóbal to Palenque takes 5 hours and passes through lush jungle and mountain scenery. Take it easy, though, and watch out for potholes and other hindrances. Highway 186 from Villahermosa should take about 2 hours. You may encounter military roadblocks that involve a cursory inspection of your travel credentials and perhaps your vehicle.

**BY BUS**   The two first-class bus stations are 2 blocks apart. Both are on Palenque's main street between the main square and the turnoff for the ruins. The smaller company, **Transportes Rodolfo Figueroa** (© 916/345-1322), offers first-class service four times a day to and from San Cristóbal (5 hr.) and Tuxtla (6½ hr.). **ADO/Cristóbal Colón** (© 916/345-1344) offers service to those destinations and to Campeche (six per day, 5 hr.), Villahermosa (nine per day, 2 hr.), and Mérida (two per day, 9 hr.).

### ORIENTATION
**VISITOR INFORMATION**   The downtown tourism office is a block from the main square at the corner of Avenida Juárez and Abasolo. It's open Monday to Saturday from 9am to 9pm, Sunday from 9am to 1pm. There's no phone in the office here. To get info over the phone before you arrive, from a different office, call © **916/345-0356.**

**CITY LAYOUT**   **Avenida Juárez** is Palenque's main street. At one end is the **main plaza;** at the other is the oversize sculpture of the famous Maya head that was discovered here. To the right of the statue is the entrance to the Cañada; to the left is the road to the ruins, and straight ahead past the statue are the airport and the highway to Villahermosa. The distance between the town's main square and the monument is about 1.5km (1 mile).

**La Cañada** is a restaurant and hotel zone tucked away in a small piece of the forest. Aside from the main plaza area, this is the best location for travelers without cars because the town is within a few blocks and the buses that run to the ruins pass right by it.

**GETTING AROUND**   The cheapest way to get back and forth from the ruins is on the white **VW buses** that run down Juárez every 10 minutes from 6am to 6pm. The buses pass La Cañada and hotels along the road to the ruins and can be flagged down at any point, but they may not stop if they're full. The cost is $1 per person.

**FAST FACTS**   The telephone area code is **916.** As for the **climate,** Palenque's high humidity is downright oppressive in the summer, especially after rain showers. During the winter, the damp air can occasionally be chilly in the evening. Rain gear is handy at any time of year. **Internet service** and **ATMs** are easily available.

# EXPLORING PALENQUE

The main reason to come here is to view the ruins, which you can tour in a morning, though some might want to take an entire day. Many people stay in the region for a few days to explore the other attractions of the area (Misol-Ha, Agua Azul, and Bonampak). But the town of Palenque has little to offer besides its convenient location, and you don't need to spend time attempting to discover its hidden charms.

## PARQUE NACIONAL PALENQUE ✸✸✸

A **museum and visitor center** sits not far from the entrance to the ruins. The complex includes a large parking lot, a refreshment stand serving snacks and drinks, and several shops. Though it's not large, the museum is worth the time it takes to see; it's open Tuesday to Sunday from 10am to 5pm and is included in the price of admission. It contains well-chosen and artistically displayed exhibits, including jade from recently excavated tombs. (The museum was robbed in 1996, but most of the jade pieces have been recovered.) Explanatory text in Spanish and English explains the life and times of this magnificent city. New pieces are often added as they are uncovered in ongoing excavations.

The **main entrance,** about 1km (½ mile) beyond the museum, is at the end of the paved highway. There you'll find a large parking lot, a refreshment stand, a ticket booth, and several shops. Among the vendors selling souvenirs are often some Lacandón Indians wearing white tunics and hawking bows and arrows.

Admission to the ruins is $5. The fee for using a video camera is $5. Parking at the main entrance and at the visitor center is free. The site and visitor center shops are open daily from 8am to 4:45pm.

**TOURING THE RUINS**    Pottery shards found during the excavations show that people lived in this area as early as 300 B.C. By the Classic period (A.D. 300–900), Palenque was an important ceremonial center. It peaked around A.D. 600 to 700.

When John Stephens visited the site in the 1840s, the ruins that you see today were buried under centuries of accumulated earth and a thick canopy of jungle. The dense jungle surrounding the cleared portion still covers unexcavated temples, which are easily discernible in the forest even to the untrained eye. But be careful not to drift too far from the main paths. There have been a few incidents where tourists venturing alone into the rainforest were assaulted.

Of all Mexico's ruins, this is the most haunting, because of its majesty; its history, recovered by epigraphers; and its mysterious setting. Scholars have identified the rulers and constructed their family histories, putting visitors on a first-name basis with these ancient people etched in stone. You can read about it in *A Forest of Kings,* by Linda Schele and David Freidel.

As you enter the ruins, the building on your right is the **Temple of the Inscriptions,** named for the great stone hieroglyphic panels found inside. (Most of the panels, which portray the family tree of King Pacal, are in the National Anthropological Museum in Mexico City.) This temple is famous for the crypt of King Pacal deep inside the pyramid, but the crypt is closed to the public. The archaeologist Alberto Ruz Lhuller discovered the tomb in the depths of the temple in 1952—an accomplishment many scholars consider one of the great discoveries of the Maya world. In exploratory excavations, Ruz Lhuller found a stairway leading from the temple floor deep into the base of the pyramid. The original builders had carefully concealed the entrance by filling the stairway with stone. After several months of excavation, Ruz Lhuller finally reached

King Pacal's crypt, which contained several fascinating objects, including a magnificent carved stone sarcophagus. Ruz Lhuller's own gravesite is opposite the Temple of the Inscriptions, on the left as you enter the park.

Just to your right as you face the Temple of the Inscriptions is **Temple 13,** which is receiving considerable attention from archaeologists. They recently discovered the burial of another richly adorned personage, accompanied in death by an adult female and an adolescent. Some of the artifacts found there are on display in the museum.

Back on the main pathway, the building directly in front of you is the **Palace,** with its unique tower. The explorer John Stephens camped in the Palace when it was completely covered in vegetation, spending sleepless nights fighting off mosquitoes. A pathway between the Palace and the Temple of the Inscriptions leads to the **Temple of the Sun,** the **Temple of the Foliated Cross,** the **Temple of the Cross,** and **Temple 14.** This group of temples, now cleared and in various stages of reconstruction, was built by Pacal's son, Chan-Bahlum, who is usually shown on inscriptions with six toes. Chan-Bahlum's plaster mask was found in Temple 14 next to the Temple of the Sun. Archaeologists have begun probing the Temple of the Sun for Chan-Bahlum's tomb. Little remains of this temple's exterior carving. Inside, however, behind a fence, a carving of Chan-Bahlum shows him ascending the throne in A.D. 690. The panels depict Chan-Bahlum's version of his historical link to the throne.

To the left of the Palace is the North Group, also undergoing restoration. Included in this area are the **ball court** and the **Temple of the Count,** where Count Waldeck camped in the 19th century. At least three tombs, complete with offerings for the underworld journey, have been found here, and the lineage of at least 12 kings has been deciphered from inscriptions left at this site.

Just past the North Group is a small building (once a museum) now used for storing the artifacts found during restorations. It is closed to the public. To the right of the building, a stone bridge crosses the river, leading to a pathway down the hillside to the new museum. The rock-lined path descends along a cascading stream on the banks of which grow giant ceiba trees. Benches are placed along the way as rest areas, and some small temples have been reconstructed near the base of the trail. In the early morning and evening, you may hear monkeys crashing through the thick foliage by the path; if you keep noise to a minimum, you may spot wild parrots as well. Walking downhill (by far the best way to go), it will take you about 20 minutes to reach the main highway. The path ends at the paved road across from the museum. The *colectivos* (minibuses) going back to the village will stop here if you wave them down.

## WHERE TO STAY

English is spoken in all the more expensive hotels and about half of the inexpensive ones. The quoted rates include the 17% tax. High season in Palenque is Easter week, July to August, and December.

### EXPENSIVE

**Chan-Kah Ruinas** 𝒢    The comfortable, roomy bungalows here offer privacy and quiet in the surroundings of a tropical forest, on the road between the ruins and the town. Because the town of Palenque isn't particularly worth exploring, you won't miss much by staying here. The grounds are beautifully tended, and there's an inviting pool that resembles a lagoon. A broad stream runs through the property. Some of the bungalows can have a musty smell. Christmas prices will be higher than those quoted here, and you may be quoted a higher price if you reserve a room in advance from outside the country. The outdoor restaurant and bar serves only passable Mexican food. Room service is pricey.

Carretera Las Ruinas Km 3, 29960 Palenque, Chi. ✆ 916/345-1100. Fax 916/345-0820. www.chan-kah.com.mx. 73 units. High season $125 double; low season $110 double. MC, V. Free guarded parking. **Amenities:** Restaurant; bar; 3 pools (1 large w/natural spring); game room; room service until 10pm; laundry service. *In room:* A/C, hair dryer.

**Misión Palenque** 🏚🏚   This hotel has returned to being the most comfortable in the city after a total remodeling of the rooms that includes new air-conditioning and other amenities. Rooms are medium-size and attractively furnished with light, modern furniture. Bathrooms are spacious with ample counters. The hotel has extensive grounds, and is very quiet. In one corner of the property, a natural spring flows through an attractive bit of jungle, where the hotel has installed the spa. Part of the spa is a *temazcal* or native American steam bath. There's also a mud bath along with the more common elements. The hotel is a few blocks east of the town's main square.

Periférico Oriente d/c, 29960 Palenque, Chi. ✆ 916/345-0241 or 01-800/900-3800 in Mexico. Fax 916/345-0300. www.hotelesmision.com.mx. 156 units. $160 double. Promotional rates sometimes available. AE, MC, V. Free guarded parking that includes vehicle check-up. **Amenities:** Restaurant; bar; 2 pools; 2 tennis courts; spa; fitness room, Jacuzzi; tour service; car rental; courtesy trips to ruins; room service until 10pm; in-room massage; babysitting; laundry service. *In room:* A/C, TV, dataport, hair dryer on request, safe.

## MODERATE

**Hotel Ciudad Real**   Though not really fancy, this hotel does the important things right—the rooms are ample, quiet, and well lit. They are comfortably, if plainly, furnished. Suites have a sitting room with sleeping sofa. Most units hold two double beds; some king-size beds are available. All rooms have a small balcony, which in the best case overlooks an attractive garden. When making a reservation, specify the hotel in Palenque. It's at the edge of town in the direction of the airport.

Carretera a Pakal-Na Km 1.5, 29960 Palenque, Chi. ✆ 916/345-1343. (Reservations: ✆ 967/678-4400.) www.ciudadreal.com.mx. 72 units. High season $115 double, $135 suite; low season $100 double, $130 suite. AE, MC, V. Free secured parking. **Amenities:** Restaurant; bar; outdoor pool; baby pool; game room; travel agency; car-rental desk; room service until 11pm; laundry service; nonsmoking rooms. *In room:* A/C, TV, hair dryer.

**Hotel Maya Tucán**   Get a room in back, and you will have a view of the hotel's natural pond. The cheerfully decorated rooms are adequate in size; they come with double beds and large bathrooms. Suites are larger and have king-size beds. The grounds are well tended and lush; scarlet macaws kept by the hotel fly about the parking lot. The Maya Tucán is on the highway to the airport. Bathrooms are larger and better lit but done with less polish than at Ciudad Real. Beds have rubber mattress covers.

Carretera-Palenque Km 0.5, 29960 Palenque, Chi. ✆ 916/345-0443. Fax 916/345-0337. mayatucan@palenque.com.mx. 56 units. High season $110 double, $130 suite; low season $80 double, $100 suite. MC, V. Free secured parking. **Amenities:** Restaurant; bar; outdoor pool; room service until 11pm; laundry service. *In room:* A/C, TV, hair dryer, no phone.

**Hotel Maya Tulipanes**   This is an attractive hotel tucked away in the Cañada. I like it for its location, and the close attention paid by the management. Service and upkeep are both good. Rooms are medium to large and come with a queen-size, a king-size, or two double beds. Tropical vegetation adorns the grounds along with some reproductions of famous Maya architecture. The Maya Tulipanes has an arrangement with a sister hotel at the ruins of Tikal, in Guatemala. The travel agency operates daily tours to Bonampak and other attractions.

# Where to Stay & Dine in Palenque

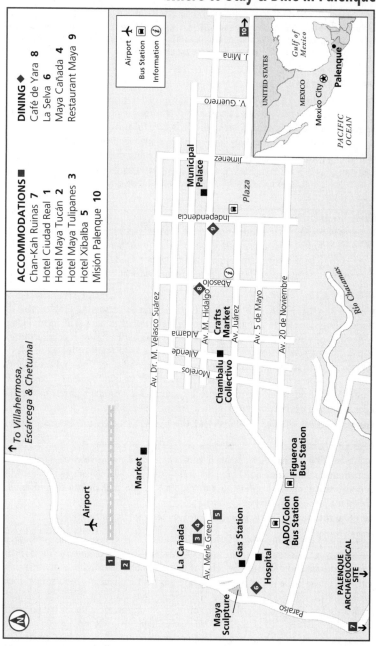

**ACCOMMODATIONS ■**

Chan-Kah Ruinas **7**
Hotel Ciudad Real **1**
Hotel Maya Tucán **2**
Hotel Maya Tulipanes **3**
Hotel Xibalba **5**
Misión Palenque **10**

**DINING ◆**

Café de Yara **8**
La Selva **6**
Maya Cañada **4**
Restaurant Maya **9**

Airport ✈
Bus Station ▣
Information ⓘ

UNITED STATES
Gulf of Mexico
MEXICO
Mexico City ⊛ Palenque ●
PACIFIC OCEAN

↑ To Villahermosa,
Escárcega & Chetumal

Airport ✈
Market ■

La Cañada
Av. Merle Green
Gas Station
Maya Sculpture
Hospital
ADO/Colon Bus Station
Figueroa Bus Station
PALENQUE ARCHAEOLOGICAL SITE →
Paraíso

Av. Dr. M. Velasco Suárez
Morelos
Allende
Aldama
Av. M. Hidalgo
Av. Juárez
Av. 5 de Mayo
Av. 20 de Noviembre
Chambalu Collectivo
Crafts Market
Abasolo
Independencia
Plaza
Municipal Palace
Jiménez
V. Guerrero
J. Mina
Río Chacamax

Calle Cañada 6, 29960 Palenque, Chi. ✆ 916/345-0201 or -0258. Fax 916/345-1004. www.mayatulipanes.com.mx. 73 units. High season $100 standard; low season $65–$75 standard. Internet packages available. AE, MC, V. Free secured parking. **Amenities:** Restaurant; bar; outdoor pool; travel agency; ground transportation to/from Villahermosa airport; room service until 11pm; laundry service; nonsmoking rooms. *In room:* A/C, TV, high-speed wireless Internet, hair dryer, no phone.

## INEXPENSIVE

**Hotel Xibalba**    This modern small two-story hotel is inspired by Maya architecture. The medium-to-small rooms are clean and cheerful. The upstairs units are a little smaller than the downstairs. Most of the beds have firm mattresses. You can arrange a trip to Bonampak or Misol-Ha with the hotel management, which owns a travel agency, Viajes Shivalva (pronounced like Xibalba: "shee-*bahl*-bah").

Calle Merle Green 9, Col. La Cañada, 29960 Palenque, Chi. ✆ 916/345-0392. Fax 916/345-0411. www.palenquemx. com/shivalva. 15 units. $45–$55 double. MC, V. **Amenities:** Restaurant; bar; laundry service; travel agency. *In room:* A/C, TV, no phone.

# WHERE TO DINE

Palenque and, for that matter, the rest of backwater Chiapas, is not for gourmets. Who'd a thunk? I had an easy time eliminating a number of restaurants that didn't even seem to be keeping up the appearance of serving food. But the situation has been improving, and you can at least get some decent Mexican food.

## MODERATE

**La Selva** ✿ MEXICAN/INTERNATIONAL    At La Selva (the jungle), you dine under a large, attractive thatched roof beside well-tended gardens. The menu includes seafood, freshwater fish, steaks, and Mexican specialties. The most expensive thing on the menu is *pigua,* freshwater lobster caught in the large rivers of southeast Mexico. These can get quite large—the size of small saltwater lobsters. This and the finer cuts of meat have been frozen, but you wouldn't want otherwise in Palenque. I liked the fish stuffed with shrimp, and the mole enchiladas. La Selva is on the highway to the ruins, near the statue of the Maya head.

Carretera Palenque Ruinas Km 0.5. ✆ 916/345-0363. Main courses $8–$17. MC, V. Daily 11:30am–11:30pm.

## INEXPENSIVE

**Café de Yara** MEXICAN    A small, modern cafe and restaurant with a comforting, not overly ambitious menu. The cafe's strong suit is healthy salads (with disinfected greens), and home-style Mexican entrees, such as the beef or chicken *milanesa* or chicken cooked in a *chile pasilla* sauce.

Av. Hidalgo 66 (at Abasolo). ✆ 916/345-0269. Main courses $4–$7. MC, V. Daily 7am–11pm.

**Restaurant Maya and Maya Cañada** ✿ MEXICAN    These two are the most consistently good restaurants in Palenque. One faces the main plaza from the corner of Independencia and Hidalgo, the other is in the Cañada. Menus are somewhat different, but much is the same. Both do a good job with the basics—good strong, locally grown coffee and soft, pliant tortillas. The menu offers a nice combination of Mexican standards and regional specialties. If you're in an exploratory mood, try one of the regional specialties such as the *mole chiapaneco* (dark red, like *mole poblano,* but less sweet) or any of the dishes based on *chaya* or *chipilin* (mild-flavored local greens), such as the soup with *chipilin* and *bolitas de masa* (corn dumplings). If you want something more comforting, go for the chicken and rice vegetable soup, or the *sopa azteca* (tortilla soup). Breast of chicken is cooked in a number of ways that are good, if not terribly original. The plantains stuffed with cheese and fried Mexican-style are wonderful. Waiters sometimes offer specials not on the menu, and these are often the thing to get. You can also try *tascalate*, a pre-Hispanic drink made of water, *masa*, chocolate, and *achiote*, and served room temperature or cold.

Av. Independencia s/n. ✆ **916/345-0042** or -0216. Breakfast $4–$5; main courses $6–$12. AE, MC, V. Daily 7am–11pm.

## ROAD TRIPS FROM PALENQUE
### BONAMPAK & YAXCHILAN: MURALS IN THE JUNGLE

Intrepid travelers may want to consider the day trip to the Maya ruins of Bonampak and Yaxchilán. The **ruins of Bonampak,** southeast of Palenque on the Guatemalan border, were discovered in 1946. The site is important for the vivid **murals** of the Maya on the interior walls of one temple. Particularly striking is an impressive battle scene, perhaps the most important painting of pre-Hispanic Mexico. Reproductions of these murals are on view in the Regional Archaeology Museum in Villahermosa.

Several tour companies offer a day trip. The drive to Bonampak is 3 hours. From there you continue by boat to the **ruins of Yaxchilán,** famous for its highly ornamented buildings. Bring rain gear, boots, a flashlight, and bug repellent. All tours include meals and cost about $50. No matter what agency you sign up with, the hours of departure and return are the same because the vans of the different agencies caravan down and back for safety. You leave at 6am and return at 7pm.

Try **Viajes Na Chan Kan** (✆ **916/345-2154**), at the corner of avenidas Hidalgo and Jiménez, across from the main square, or **Viajes Shivalva,** Calle Merle Green 1 (✆ **916/ 345-0411;** fax 916/345-0392). A branch of Viajes Shivalva (✆ **916/345-0822**) is a block from the *zócalo* (main plaza) at the corner of Juárez and Abasolo, across the hall from the State Tourism Office. It's open Monday to Saturday from 9am to 9pm.

### WATERFALLS AT MISOL-HA & AGUA AZUL

A popular excursion from Palenque is a day trip to the Misol-Ha waterfall and Agua Azul. **Misol-Ha** is 20km (12 miles) from Palenque, in the direction of Ocosingo. It takes about 30 minutes to get there, depending on the traffic. The turnoff is clearly marked; you'll turn right and drive another 1.5km (1 mile). The place is absolutely beautiful. Water falls from a rocky cliff into a broad pool of green water bordered by thick tropical vegetation with hanging vines and roots grasping the rocks. There's a small restaurant and some rustic cabins for rent for $30 to $40 per night, depending on the size of the cabin. The place is run by the *ejido* cooperative that owns the site, and it does a good job of maintaining the place. To inquire about the cabins, call ✆ **916/345-1506.** Admission for the day is $1.

Approximately 44km (27 miles) beyond Misol-Ha are the **Agua Azul waterfalls**— 270m (886 ft.) of tumbling falls with lots of water. There are cabins for rent here, too, but I would rather stay at Misol-Ha. You can swim either above or below the falls, but make sure you don't get pulled by the current. You can see both places in the same day or stop to see them on your way to Ocosingo and San Cristóbal. Agua Azul is prettiest after 3 or 4 consecutive dry days; heavy rains can make the water murky. Check with guides or other travelers about the water quality before you decide to go. The cost to enter is around $2 per vehicle and $1 per person. Trips to both of these places can be arranged through just about any hotel.

## OCOSINGO & THE RUINS OF TONINA

By the time you get to Agua Azul, you're halfway to Ocosingo, which lies halfway between Palenque and San Cristóbal. So, instead of returning for the night to Palenque, you can go on to Ocosingo. It's higher up and more comfortable than Palenque. It's a nice little town, not touristy, not a lot to do other than see the ruins of Toniná. But it is a nice place to spend the night so that you can see the ruins early before moving on to San Cristóbal. There are about a half-dozen small hotels in town; the largest is not the most desirable. I would stay at the **Hospedaje Esmeralda** (© **919/673-0014**) or the **Hotel Central** (© **919/673-0024**) on the main square. Both of these are small and simple, but welcoming.

### Ruins of Toniná ⚔

The striking ruins of Toniná (the name translates as "house of rocks") are 14km (8⅔ miles) east of Ocosingo. You can take a cab there and catch a *colectivo* to return. The city dates from the Classic period and covered a large area, but the excavated and restored part is all on one hillside that faces out toward a broad valley. This site is not really set up for lots of tourists. There's a lot of up-and-down, and some of it is a little precarious. It's not a good place to take kids. Admission is $3.50.

This complex of courtyards, rooms, and stairways is built on multiple levels that are irregular and asymmetrical. The overall effect is that of a ceremonial area with multiple foci instead of a clearly discernable center.

As early as A.D. 350, Toniná emerged as a dynastic center. In the 7th and 8th centuries it was locked in a struggle with rival Palenque and, to a lesser degree, with faraway Calakmul. This has led some scholars to see Toniná as more militaristic than its neighbors—a sort of Sparta of the Classic Maya. Toniná's greatest victory came in 711, when, under the rule of Kan B'alam, it attacked Palenque and captured its king, K'an Joy Chitam, who is depicted on a stone frieze twisted and his arms bound with rope.

But the single-most important artifact yet found at Toniná, is up around the fifth level of the acropolis—a large stucco frieze divided into panels by a feathered framework adorned with the heads of sacrificial victims (displayed upside down) and some rather horrid creatures. The largest figure is a skeletal image holding a decapitated head—very vivid and very puzzling. There is actually a stylistic parallel with some murals of the Teotihuacán culture of central Mexico. The other special thing about Toniná is that it holds the distinction of having the last ever date recorded in the long count (A.D. 909), which for all practical purposes marks the end of the Classic period.

## 3 San Cristóbal de las Casas ⭐

229km (142 miles) SW of Palenque; 80km (50 miles) E of Tuxtla Gutiérrez; 74km (46 miles) NW of Comitán; 166km (103 miles) NW of Cuauhtémoc; 451km (280 miles) E of Oaxaca

San Cristóbal is a colonial town of white stucco walls and red-tile roofs, of cobblestone streets and narrow sidewalks, of graceful arcades and open plazas. It lies in a green valley 2,120m (6,954 ft.) high. The city owes part of its name to the 16th-century cleric Fray Bartolomé de las Casas, who was the town's first bishop and spent the rest of his life waging a political campaign to protect the indigenous peoples of the Americas.

Surrounding the city are many villages of Mayan-speaking Indians who display great variety in their language, dress, and customs, making this area one of the most fascinating in Mexico. San Cristóbal is the principal market town for these Indians,

# San Cristóbal de las Casas

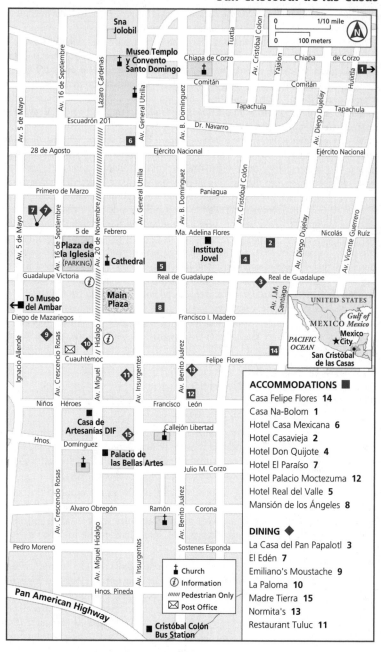

**ACCOMMODATIONS** ■

Casa Felipe Flores **14**
Casa Na-Bolom **1**
Hotel Casa Mexicana **6**
Hotel Casavieja **2**
Hotel Don Quijote **4**
Hotel El Paraíso **7**
Hotel Palacio Moctezuma **12**
Hotel Real del Valle **5**
Mansión de los Ángeles **8**

**DINING** ◆

La Casa del Pan Papalotl **3**
El Edén **7**
Emiliano's Moustache **9**
La Paloma **10**
Madre Tierra **15**
Normita's **13**
Restaurant Tuluc **11**

Map legend:
✝ Church
ⓘ Information
///// Pedestrian Only
✉ Post Office
■ Cristóbal Colón Bus Station

and their point of contact with the outside world. Most of them trek down from the surrounding mountains to sell goods and run errands.

Several Indian villages lie within reach of San Cristóbal by road: **Chamula,** with its weavers and unorthodox church; **Zinacantán,** whose residents practice their own syncretic religion; **Tenejapa, San Andrés,** and **Magdalena,** known for brocaded textiles; **Amatenango del Valle,** a town of potters; and **Aguacatenango,** known for embroidery. Most of these "villages" consist of little more than a church and the municipal government building, with homes scattered for miles around and a general gathering only for church and market days (usually Sun).

Many Indians now live on the outskirts of town because they've been expelled from their villages over religious differences. They are known as *los expulsados.* No longer involved in farming, they make their living in commerce and handicrafts. Most still wear traditional dress, but they've adopted protestant religious beliefs that prevent them from partaking in many of the civic and religious celebrations of their communities.

The influx of outsiders hasn't created in most Indians a desire to adopt mainstream customs and dress. It's interesting to note that the communities closest to San Cristóbal are the most resistant to change. The greatest threat to the cultures in this area comes not from tourism but from the action of large market forces, population pressures, environmental damage, and poverty. The Indians aren't interested in acting or looking like the foreigners they see. They may steal glances or even stare at tourists, but mainly they pay little attention to outsiders, except as potential buyers for handicrafts.

You may see or hear the word *Jovel,* San Cristóbal's Indian name, incorporated often in the names of businesses. You'll hear the word *coleto,* used in reference to someone or something from San Cristóbal. You'll see signs for *tamales coletos, pan coleto,* and *desayuno coleto.*

## ESSENTIALS
### GETTING THERE & DEPARTING

**BY PLANE**    Flights from Mexico City have been canceled. The closest airport is in Tuxtla Gutiérrez (see later in this chapter).

**BY CAR**    From Tuxtla Gutiérrez, the 1½-hour trip winds through beautiful mountain country. From Palenque, the road is just as beautiful (if longer—5 hr.), and it provides jungle scenery, but portions of it may be heavily potholed or obstructed during rainy season. Check with the local state tourism office before driving.

**BY TAXI**    Taxis from Tuxtla Gutiérrez to San Cristóbal cost around $50. Another way to travel to and from Tuxtla is by *combi.* The Volkswagen vans, which can get extremely crowded, make the run every 15 to 30 minutes and cost $3. They can be found just off the highway by the bus station. You'll have to ask someone to point them out to you because there isn't a sign.

**BY BUS**    The two bus stations in town are directly across the Pan American Highway from each other. The smaller one belongs to **Transportes Rodolfo Figueroa,** which provides first-class service to and from Tuxtla (every 40 min.) and Palenque (four buses per day, with a stop in Ocosingo—cheaper than the competition). For other destinations, go to the large station run by **ADO** and its affiliates, Altos, Cristóbal Colón, and Maya de Oro. This company offers service to and from Tuxtla (12 buses per day), Palenque (almost every hour), and several other destinations: Mérida (two buses per day), Villahermosa (two buses per day), Oaxaca (two buses per

## The Zapatista Movement & Chiapas

In January 1994, Indians from this area rebelled against the Mexican government over healthcare, education, land distribution, and representative government. Their organization, the **Zapatista Liberation Army,** known as EZLN (Ejército Zapatista de Liberación Nacional), and its leader, Subcomandante Marcos, have become emblematic of the problems Mexico has with social justice. In the last couple of years, the rhetoric of armed revolt has ended, and the Zapatistas are talking about building a broad leftist coalition—but not a political party. What this means for Mexican politics is not clear, but for travelers it means not having to worry about violent political unrest. Yes, the underlying conditions for social unrest remain, as they do all over Mexico, but no one is talking about revolution.

day), and Puerto Escondido (two buses per day). To buy a bus ticket without going down to the station, go to the **Ticket Bus** agency, Real de Guadalupe 5 (© **967/678-8503**). Hours are Monday to Saturday from 7am to 11pm, Sunday from 9am to 5pm.

## ORIENTATION

**ARRIVING**    To get to the main plaza from the highway turn on to **Avenida Insurgentes** (there's a traffic light). From the bus station, the main plaza is 9 blocks north up Avenida Insurgentes (a 10-min. walk, slightly uphill). Cabs are cheap and plentiful.

**VISITOR INFORMATION**    The **State Tourism Office** is better than the municipal office. It's just half a block south of the main plaza, at Avenida Hidalgo 1-B (© **967/678-6570**); it's open Monday to Friday from 8am to 8pm, Saturday from 9am to 8pm, and Sunday from 9am to 2pm. The **Municipal Tourism Office** (©/fax **967/678-0665**) is in the town hall, west of the main square. Hours are Monday to Saturday from 9am to 8pm. Check the bulletin board here for apartments, shared rides, cultural events, and local tours. Both offices are helpful, but the state office is open an hour later and is better staffed.

**CITY LAYOUT**    San Cristóbal is laid out on a grid; the main north-south axis is **Insurgentes/Utrilla,** and the east-west axis is **Mazariegos/Madero.** All streets change names when they cross either of these streets. The *zócalo* (main plaza) lies where they intersect. An important street to know is **Real de Guadalupe,** which runs from the plaza eastward to the church of Guadalupe; located on it are many hotels, restaurants, and the like. The market is 7 blocks north of the *zócalo* along Utrilla.

Take note that this town has at least three streets named Domínguez and two streets named Flores. There's Hermanos Domínguez, Belisario Domínguez, and Pantaleón Domínguez, and María Adelina Flores and Dr. Felipe Flores.

**GETTING AROUND**    Most of the sights and shopping in San Cristóbal are within walking distance of the plaza.

*Urbano* buses (minibuses) take passengers between town and the residential neighborhoods. All buses pass by the market and central plaza on their way through town. Utrilla and Avenida 16 de Septiembre are the two main arteries; all buses use the market area as the last stop. Any bus on Utrilla will take you to the market.

*Colectivos* to outlying villages depart from the public market at Avenida Utrilla. Buses late in the day are usually very crowded. Always check to see when the last or next-to-last bus returns from wherever you're going, and then take the one before that—those last buses sometimes don't materialize, and you might be stranded. I speak from experience!

**Rental cars** come in handy for trips to the outlying villages and may be worth the expense when shared by a group, but keep in mind that insurance is invalid on unpaved roads. Try **Optima Car Rental,** Av. Mazariegos 39 (© **967/674-5409**). Office hours are daily from 9am to 1pm and 5 to 8pm. You'll save money by arranging the rental from your home country; otherwise, a day's rental with insurance will cost around $60 for a VW Beetle with manual transmission, the cheapest car available.

**Scooters** can be rented from Darren and Natasha, a couple of easygoing Australians who tell me that they've found the best way to enjoy the city and surrounding countryside. Look for **Croozy Scooters** (© **967/631-4329**) at Belisario Domínguez 7-A.

**Bikes** are another option for getting around the city; a day's rental is about $10. **Los Pingüinos,** Av. Ecuador 4-B (© **967/678-0202;** pinguinosmex@yahoo.com), offers bike tours to a few out-of-town locations. Tours in the valley around San Cristóbal last 4 to 6 hours and cost $25 to $30. It's open daily from 10am to 2:30pm and 4 to 7pm.

---

## FAST FACTS: San Cristóbal de las Casas

*Area Code*  The telephone area code is **967.**

*Books  The People of the Bat: Mayan Tales and Dreams from Zinacantán,* by Robert M. Laughlin, is a priceless collection of beliefs from that village near San Cristóbal. Another good book with a completely different view of today's Maya is *The Heart of the Sky,* by Peter Canby, who traveled among the Maya to chronicle their struggles (and wrote his book before the Zapatista uprising).

*Bookstore*  For the best selection of new and used books and reading material in English, go to **La Pared,** Av. Hidalgo 2 (© **967/678-6367**). The owner, Dana Gay Burton, keeps a great collection of books on the Maya, and Mexico in general, both fiction and nonfiction.

*Bulletin Boards*  San Cristóbal is a cultural crossroads for travelers, and several places maintain bulletin boards with information on Spanish classes, local specialty tours, rooms or houses to rent, rides needed, and so on. These include boards at the **Tourism Office, Café El Puente, Madre Tierra,** and **Casa Na-Bolom.**

*Climate*  San Cristóbal can be chilly when the sun isn't out, especially during the winter. It's 2,160m (7,085 ft.) above sea level. Most hotels are not heated, although some have fireplaces. There is always a possibility of rain, but I would avoid going to San Cristóbal from late August to late October, during the height of the rainy season.

*Currency Exchange*  There are at least five *casas de cambio* on Real de Guadalupe near the main square, and a couple under the colonnade facing the square. Most are open until 8pm, and some are open Sunday. There are also a number of ATMs.

*Doctor* Try **Dr. Roberto Lobato,** Av. Belisario Domínguez 17, at Calle Flavio A. Paniagua (© **967/678-7777**). Don't be unsettled by the fact that his office is next door to Funerales Canober.

*Internet Access* There are Internet cafes everywhere.

*Parking* If your hotel does not have parking, use the *estacionamiento* (underground public lot) in front of the cathedral, just off the main square on 16 de Septiembre. Entry is from Calle 5 de Febrero.

*Post Office* The *correo* is at Crescencio Rosas and Cuauhtémoc, a block south and west of the main square. It's open Monday to Friday from 8am to 7pm, Saturday from 9am to 1pm.

*Spanish Classes* The **Instituto Jovel,** María Adelina Flores 21 (Apdo. Postal 62), 29250 San Cristóbal de las Casas, Chi. (©/fax **967/678-4069**), gets higher marks for its Spanish courses than the competition. It also offers classes in weaving and cooking. The **Centro Bilingüe,** at the Centro Cultural El Puente, Real de Guadalupe 55, 29250 San Cristóbal de las Casas, Chi. (© **800/303-4983** in the U.S., or ©/fax 967/678-3723), offers classes in Spanish. Both schools can arrange home stays for their students.

*Telephone* The best price for long-distance telephone calls and faxing is at **La Pared** bookstore (see "Bookstore," above) at Av. Hidalgo 2, across the street from the State Tourism Office.

## EXPLORING SAN CRISTOBAL

San Cristóbal is a lovely town in a lovely region. A lot of people come for the beauty, but the main thing that draws most visitors here is the highland Maya. They can be seen anywhere in San Cristóbal, but most travelers take at least one trip to the outlying villages to get a close-up of Maya life.

### ATTRACTIONS IN TOWN

**Casa Na-Bolom** ☆☆    If you're interested in the anthropology of the region, you'll want to visit this house museum. Stay here, if you can. The house, built as a seminary in 1891, became the headquarters of anthropologists Frans and Trudy Blom in 1951, and the gathering place of outsiders interested in studying the region. Frans Blom led many early archaeological studies in Mexico, and Trudy was noted for her photographs of the Lacandón Indians and her efforts to save them and their forest homeland. A room at Na-Bolom contains a selection of her Lacandón photographs, and postcards of the photographs are on sale in the gift shop (daily 9am–2pm and 4–7pm). A tour of the home covers the displays of pre-Hispanic artifacts collected by Frans Blom; the cozy library, with its numerous volumes about the region and the Maya (weekdays 10am–2pm); and the gardens Trudy Blom started for the ongoing reforestation of the Lacandón jungle. The tour ends with a showing of *La Reina de la Selva,* an excellent 50-minute film on the Bloms, the Lacandón, and Na-Bolom. Trudy Blom died in 1993, but Na-Bolom continues to operate as a nonprofit public trust.

The 12 guest rooms, named for surrounding villages, are decorated with local objects and textiles. All rooms have fireplaces and private bathrooms. Prices (including breakfast and admission to the museum) are $70 single, $90 double.

*Tips* **Photography Warning**

Photographers should be cautious about when, where, and at whom or what they point their cameras. In San Cristóbal, taking a photograph of even a chile pepper can be cause for alarm; locals are sensitive, especially in the San Cristóbal market. Young handicraft vendors will sometimes ask for money to be photographed.

Nearby villages have strict rules about photography. The local tour guides have good relations with the local authorities and can give you guidance.

Even if you're not a guest here, you can come for a meal, usually a delicious assortment of vegetarian and other dishes. Just be sure to make a reservation at least 2½ hours in advance, and be on time. The colorful dining room has one large table, and the eclectic mix of travelers sometimes makes for interesting conversation. Breakfast costs $5 to $7; lunch and dinner cost $11 each. Dinner is served at 7pm. Following breakfast (8–10am), a guide not affiliated with the house offers tours to San Juan Chamula and Zinacantán (see "The Nearby Maya Villages & Countryside," below).

Av. Vicente Guerrero 3, 29200 San Cristóbal de las Casas, Chi. ℂ **967/678-1418**. Fax 967/678-5586. Group tour and film $5. Tours daily 11:30am and 4:30pm. Leave the square on Real de Guadalupe, walk 4 blocks to Av. Vicente Guerrero, and turn left; Na-Bolom is 5½ blocks up Guerrero.

**Catedral**    San Cristóbal's main cathedral was built in the 1500s. It has little of interest inside besides a lovely, uncommon beam ceiling and a carved wooden pulpit.

Calle 20 de Noviembre at Guadalupe Victoria. No phone. Free admission. Daily 7am–6pm.

**El Mercado**    Once you've visited Santo Domingo (see listing below), meander through the San Cristóbal town market and the surrounding area. Every time I do, I see something different to elicit my curiosity.

By Santo Domingo church. No phone. Mon–Sat 8am–7pm.

**Museo del Ambar** ⭐    If you've been in this town any time at all, you know what a big deal amber is here. Chiapas is the third-largest producer of amber in the world, and many experts prefer its amber for its colors and clarity. A couple of stores tried calling themselves museums but they didn't fool anybody. Now a real museum moves methodically through all the issues surrounding amber—mining, shaping, and identifying it, as well as the different varieties found in other parts of the world. It's interesting, it's cheap, and you get to see the restored area of the old convent it occupies. There are a couple of beautiful pieces of worked amber that are on permanent loan—make sure you see them. In mid-August, the museum holds a contest for local artisans who work amber. Check it out.

Exconvento de la Merced, Diego de Mazariegos s/n. ℂ **967/678-9716**. Admission $2. Tues–Sun 10am–2pm and 4–7pm.

**Museo Templo y Convento Santo Domingo**    Inside the front door of the carved-stone plateresque facade, there's a beautiful gilded wooden altarpiece built in 1560, walls with saints, and gilt-framed paintings. Attached to the church is the former Convent of Santo Domingo, which houses a small museum about San Cristóbal and Chiapas. The museum has changing exhibits and often shows cultural films. It's 5 blocks north of the *zócalo*, in the market area.

Av. 20 de Noviembre. ℂ **967/678-1609.** Free admission to church; museum $2. Museum Tues–Sun 10am–5pm; church daily 10am–2pm and 5–8pm.

**Palacio de las Bellas Artes**   Be sure to check out this building if you are interested in the arts. It periodically hosts dance events, art shows, and other performances. The schedule of events is usually posted on the door if the Bellas Artes is not open. There's a public library next door. Around the corner, the Centro Cultural holds a number of concerts and other performances; check the posters on the door to see what's scheduled.

Av. Hidalgo, 4 blocks south of the plaza. No phone.

**Templo de San Cristóbal**   For the best view of San Cristóbal, climb the seemingly endless steps to this church and *mirador* (lookout point). A visit here requires stamina. By the way, there are 22 more churches in town, some of which also demand strenuous climbs.

At the very end of Calle Hermanos Domínguez.

## HORSEBACK RIDING

The **Casa de Huéspedes Margarita,** Real de Guadalupe 34, and **Hotel Real del Valle** (see "Where to Stay," below) can arrange horseback rides for around $15 for a day, including a guide. Reserve your steed at least a day in advance. A horseback-riding excursion might go to San Juan Chamula, to nearby caves, or just up into the hills.

---

### *Moments*  Special Events in & near San Cristóbal

In nearby Chamula, **Carnaval,** the big annual festival that takes place in the days before Lent, is a fascinating mingling of the Christian pre-Lenten ceremonies and the ancient Maya celebration of the 5 "lost days" at the end of the 360-day Maya agricultural cycle. Around noon on Shrove Tuesday, groups of village elders run across patches of burning grass as a purification rite. Macho residents then run through the streets with a bull. During Carnaval, roads close in town, and buses drop visitors at the outskirts.

During this time, nearby villages (except Zinacantán) also have celebrations, although perhaps not as dramatic. Visiting these villages, especially on the Sunday before Lent, will round out your impression of Carnaval in all its regional varieties. In Tenejapa, the celebration continues during the Thursday market after Ash Wednesday.

During Easter and the week after, for the annual **Feria de Primavera (Spring Festival),** San Cristóbal is ablaze with lights and excitement and gets hordes of visitors. Activities include carnival rides, food stalls, handicraft shops, parades, and band concerts. Hotel rooms are scarce and more expensive.

Another spectacle is staged from July 22 to 25, during the annual **Fiesta de San Cristóbal,** honoring the town's patron saint. The steps up to the San Cristóbal church are lit with torches at night. Pilgrimages to the church begin several days earlier, and on the 24th, there's an all-night vigil.

For the **Día de Guadalupe,** on December 12, honoring Mexico's patron saint, the streets are gaily decorated, and food stalls line the streets leading to the church on a hill where she is honored.

## THE NEARBY MAYA VILLAGES & COUNTRYSIDE

The Indian communities around San Cristóbal are fascinating worlds unto themselves. If you are unfamiliar with these indigenous cultures, you will understand and appreciate more of what you see by visiting them with a guide, at least for your first foray out into the villages. Guides are acquainted with members of the communities and are viewed with less suspicion than newcomers. These communities have their own laws and customs—and visitors' ignorance is no excuse. Entering these communities is tantamount to leaving Mexico, and if something happens, the state and federal authorities will not intervene except in case of a serious crime.

The best guided trips are the locally grown ones. Three operators go to the neighboring villages in small groups. They all charge the same price ($10 per person), use minivans for transportation, and speak English. They do, however, have their own interpretations and focus.

**Pepe** leaves from **Casa Na-Bolom** (see "Attractions in Town," above) for daily trips to San Juan Chamula and Zinacantán at 10am, returning to San Cristóbal between 2 and 3pm. Pepe looks at cultural continuities, community relationships, and, of course, religion.

**Alex and Raúl** can be found in front of the cathedral between 9:15 and 9:30am. They are quite personable and get along well with the Indians in the communities. They focus on cultural values and their expression in social behavior, which provides a glimpse of the details and the texture of life in these communities (and, of course, they talk about religion). Their tour is very good. They can be reached at ✆ **967/678-3741** or chamul@hotmail.com.

For excursions farther afield, see "Road Trips from San Cristóbal," later in this chapter. Also, Alex and Raúl can be contracted for trips to other communities besides Chamula and Zinacantán; talk to them.

**CHAMULA & ZINACANTAN**   A side trip to the village of San Juan Chamula will really get you into the spirit of life around San Cristóbal. Sunday, when the market is in full swing, is the best day to go for shopping; other days, when you'll be less impeded by eager children selling their crafts, are better for seeing the village and church.

The village, 8km (5 miles) northeast of San Cristóbal, has a large church, a plaza, and a municipal building. Each year, a new group of citizens is chosen to live in the municipal center as caretakers of the saints, settlers of disputes, and enforcers of village rules. As in other nearby villages, on Sunday local leaders wear their leadership costumes, including beautifully woven straw hats loaded with colorful ribbons befitting their high position. They solemnly sit together in a long line somewhere around the central square. Chamula is typical of other villages in that men are often away working in the "hotlands," harvesting coffee or cacao, while women stay home to tend the sheep, the children, the cornfields, and the fires. It's almost always the women's and children's work to gather firewood, and you see them along roadsides bent under the weight.

Don't leave Chamula without seeing the **church interior.** As you step from bright sunlight into the candlelit interior, you feel as if you've been transported to another country. Pine needles scattered amid a sea of lighted candles cover the tile floor. Saints line the walls, and before them people are often kneeling and praying aloud while passing around bottles of Pepsi-Cola. Shamans are often on hand, passing eggs over sick people or using live or dead chickens in a curing ritual. The statues of saints are similar to those you might see in any Mexican Catholic church, but beyond sharing the same name, they mean something completely different to the Chamulas. Visitors can walk carefully through the church to see the saints or stand quietly in the background and observe.

**Carnaval,** which takes place just before Lent, is the big annual festival. The Chamulas are not a wealthy people, but the women are the region's best wool weavers, producing finished pieces for themselves and for other villages.

In Zinacantán, a wealthier village than Chamula, you must sign a strict form promising *not to take any photographs* before you see the two side-by-side **sanctuaries.** Once permission is granted and you have paid a small fee, an escort will usually show you the church, or you may be allowed to see it on your own. Floors may be covered in pine needles here, too, and the rooms are brightly sunlit. The experience is an altogether different one from that of Chamula.

**AMATENANGO DEL VALLE**   About an hour's ride south of San Cristóbal is Amatenango, a town known mostly for its **women potters.** You'll see their work in San Cristóbal—small animals, jars, and large water jugs—but in the village, you can visit the potters in their homes. Just walk down the dirt streets. Villagers will lean over the walls of family compounds and invite you in to select from their inventory. You may even see them firing the pieces under piles of wood in the open courtyard or painting them with color derived from rusty iron water. The women wear beautiful red-and-yellow *huipiles,* but if you want to take a photograph, you'll have to pay.

To get here, take a *colectivo* from the market in San Cristóbal. Before it lets you off, be sure to ask about the return-trip schedule.

**AGUACATENANGO**   This village 16km (10 miles) south of Amatenango is known for its **embroidery.** If you've visited San Cristóbal's shops, you'll recognize the white-on-white and black-on-black floral patterns on dresses and blouses for sale. The locals' own regional blouses, however, are quite different.

**TENEJAPA**   The **weavers** of Tenejapa, 28km (17 miles) from San Cristóbal, make some of the most beautiful and expensive work you'll see in the region. The best time to visit is on market day (Sun and Thurs, though Sun is better). The weavers of Tenejapa taught the weavers of San Andrés and Magdalena—which accounts for the similarity in their designs and colors. To get to Tenejapa, try to find a *colectivo* in the very last row by the market, or hire a taxi. On Tenejapa's main street, several stores sell locally woven regional clothing, and you can bargain for the price.

**THE HUITEPEC CLOUD FOREST**   **Pronatura,** Av. Benito Juárez 11-B (© **967/ 678-5000**), a private, nonprofit, ecological organization, offers environmentally sensitive tours of the cloud forest. The forest is a haven for **migratory birds,** and more than 100 bird species and 600 plant species have been discovered here. Guided tours run from 9am to noon Tuesday to Sunday. They cost $25 per group of up to eight people. Make reservations a day in advance. To reach the reserve on your own, drive on the road to Chamula; the turnoff is at Km 3.5. The reserve is open Tuesday to Sunday from 9am to 4pm.

## SHOPPING

Many Indian villages near San Cristóbal are noted for **weaving, embroidery, brocade work, leather,** and **pottery,** making the area one of the best in the country for shopping. You'll see beautiful woolen shawls, indigo-dyed skirts, colorful native shirts, and magnificently woven *huipiles,* all of which often come in vivid geometric patterns. A good place to find textiles as well as other handicrafts, besides what's mentioned below, is in and around Santo Domingo and the market. There are a lot of stalls and small shops in that neighborhood that make for interesting shopping. Working in leather, the craftspeople are artisans of the highest caliber. Tie-dyed *jaspe* from Guatemala comes in bolts and is made into clothing. The town is also known for **amber,** sold in several shops, one of the best of which is mentioned below.

## CRAFTS

**Casa de Artesanías**    The showroom has examples of every craft practiced in the state. It is run by the government in support of Indian crafts. You should take a look, if only to survey what crafts the region practices. It's open Monday to Friday from 9am to 9pm, Saturday 10am to 9pm, and Sunday 9am to 3pm. Niños Héroes at Hidalgo. © **967/678-1180.**

**El Encuentro**    Noted for having reasonable prices, this shop carries many ritual items, such as new and used men's ceremonial hats, false saints, and iron rooftop adornments, plus many *huipiles* and other textiles. It's open Monday to Saturday from 9am to 8pm. Calle Real de Guadalupe 63-A (between Diego Dujelay and Vicente Guerrero). © **967/678-3698.**

**La Galería**    This art gallery beneath a cafe shows the work of well-known national and international painters. Also for sale are paintings and greeting cards by Kiki, the owner, a German artist who has found her niche in San Cristóbal. There are some Oaxacan rugs and pottery, plus unusual silver jewelry. It's open daily from 10am to 9pm. Hidalgo 3. © **967/678-1547.**

**Lágrimas de la Selva**    "Tears of the Jungle" deals in amber and jewelry, and no other amber shop in town that I know of has the variety, quality, or artistic flair of this one. It's not a bargain hunter's turf, but a great place for the curious to go. Often you can watch the jewelers in action. Open daily from 10am to 8pm. Hidalgo 1-C (half-block south of the main square). © **967/674-6348.**

## TEXTILES

**Plaza de Santo Domingo**    The plazas around this church and the nearby Templo de Caridad fill with women in native garb selling their wares. Here you'll find women from Chamula weaving belts or embroidering, surrounded by piles of loomed woolen textiles from their village. Their inventory includes Guatemalan shawls, belts, and bags. There are also some excellent buys on Chiapanecan-made wool vests, jackets, rugs, and shawls, similar to those at Sna Jolobil (described below), if you take the time to look and bargain. Vendors arrive between 9 and 10am and begin to leave around 3pm. Av. Utrilla. No phone.

**Sna Jolobil**    Meaning "weaver's house" in Mayan, this place is in the former convent (monastery) of Santo Domingo, next to the Templo de Santo Domingo. Groups of Tzotzil and Tzeltal craftspeople operate the cooperative store, which has about 3,000 members who contribute products, help run the store, and share in the moderate profits. Their works are simply beautiful; prices are high, as is the quality. It's open Monday to Saturday from 9am to 2pm and 4 to 6pm; credit cards are accepted. Calzada Lázaro Cárdenas 42 (Plaza Santo Domingo, between Navarro and Nicaragua). © **967/678-2646.**

**Unión Regional de Artesanías de los Altos**    Also known as J'pas Joloviletic, this cooperative of weavers is smaller than Sna Jolobil (described above) and not as sophisticated in its approach to potential shoppers. It sells blouses, textiles, pillow covers, vests, sashes, napkins, baskets, and purses. It's near the market and worth looking around. Open Monday to Saturday from 9am to 2pm and 4 to 7pm, Sunday from 9am to 1pm. Av. Utrilla 43. © **967/678-2848.**

## WHERE TO STAY

Among the most interesting places to stay in San Cristóbal is the seminary-turned-hotel-museum **Casa Na-Bolom;** see "Attractions in Town," earlier in this chapter, for details.

Hotels in San Cristóbal are inexpensive. You can do pretty well for $30 to $50 per night per double. Rates listed here include taxes. High season is Easter week, July, August, and December.

### MODERATE

**Casa Felipe Flores** 🐾🐾   This beautifully restored colonial house is the perfect setting for getting a feel for San Cristóbal. The patios and common rooms are relaxing and comfortable, and their architectural details are so very *coleto*. The guest rooms are nicely furnished and full of character. And they are warm in winter. The owners, Nancy and David Orr, are gracious people who enjoy sharing their appreciation and knowledge of Chiapas and the Maya. Their cook serves up righteous breakfasts.

Calle Dr. Felipe Flores 36, 29230 San Cristóbal de las Casas, Chi. ©/fax **967/678-3996.** www.felipeflores.com. 5 units. $85–$95 double. Rates include full breakfast. 10% service charge. No credit cards. **Amenities:** Tour info; laundry service; library. *In room:* No phone.

**Hotel Casa Mexicana** 🐾🐾   Created from a large mansion, this beautiful hotel with a colonial-style courtyard offers comfortable lodging. Rooms, courtyards, the restaurant, and the lobby are decorated in modern-traditional Mexican style, with warm tones of yellow and red. The rooms are carpeted and come with two double beds or one king-size. They have good lighting, electric heaters, and spacious bathrooms. Guests are welcome to use the sauna, and inexpensive massages can be arranged. The hotel handles a lot of large tour groups; it can be quiet and peaceful one day, full and bustling the next. There is a new addition to the hotel across the street, but I like the doubles in the original section better. This hotel is 3 blocks north of the main plaza.

28 de Agosto 1 (at Utrilla), 29200 San Cristóbal de las Casas, Chi. © **967/678-1348** or -0698. Fax 967/678-2627. www.hotelcasamexicana.com. 55 units. High season $95 double, $150 junior suite, $180 suite; low season $85 double, $140 junior suite, $170 suite. AE, MC, V. Free secure parking 1½ blocks away. **Amenities:** Restaurant; bar; sauna; tour info; room service until 10pm; massage; babysitting; laundry service. *In room:* TV, dataport, hair dryer (on request).

**Hotel Casavieja**   The Casavieja (old house) is aptly named: It has a charming old feel that is San Cristóbal to a tee. Originally built in 1740, it has undergone restoration and new construction faithful to the original design in essentials such as wood-beam ceilings. One nod toward modernity is carpeted floors, a welcome feature on cold mornings. The rooms also come with electric heaters. Bathrooms vary, depending on what section of the hotel you're in, but all are adequate. The hotel's restaurant, Doña Rita, faces the interior courtyard, with tables on the patio and inside, and offers good food at reasonable prices. The hotel is 3½ blocks northeast of the plaza.

María Adelina Flores 27 (between Cristóbal Colón and Diego Dujelay), 29200 San Cristóbal de las Casas, Chi. ©/fax **967/678-6868** or -0385. www.casavieja.com.mx. 39 units. $60–$75 double. AE, MC, V. Free parking. **Amenities:** Restaurant; bar; room service until 10:30pm; laundry service. *In room:* TV.

**Hotel El Paraíso**   For the independent traveler, this is a safe haven from the busloads of tour groups that can disrupt the atmosphere and service at other hotels.

Rooms are small but beautifully decorated. They have comfortable beds and good reading lights; some even have a ladder to a loft holding a second bed. Bathrooms are small, too, but the plumbing is good. The entire hotel is decorated in terra cotta and blue, with beautiful wooden columns and beams supporting the roof. The hotel's restaurant, El Edén (see "Where to Dine," below) may be the best in town.

Av. 5 de Febrero 19, 29200 San Cristóbal de las Casas, Chi. (C) **967/678-0085** or -5382. Fax 967/678-5168. www.hotel posadaparaiso.com. 14 units. $55–$65 double. AE, MC, V. **Amenities:** Restaurant; bar; tour info; room service until 11pm; laundry service. *In room:* TV.

**Mansión de los Angeles**   This hotel with good location offers good service and tidy rooms and public areas. Guest rooms are medium-size and come with either a single and a double bed or two double beds. The rooms are warmer and better lit than at most hotels in this town. They are also quiet. Some of the bathrooms are a little small. Most rooms have windows that open onto a pretty courtyard with a fountain. The rooftop sun deck is a great siesta spot.

Calle Francisco Madero 17, 29200 San Cristóbal de las Casas, Chi. (C) **967/678-1173** or -4371. hotelangeles@ prodigy.net.mx. 20 units. $55–$65 double. MC, V. *In room:* TV.

### INEXPENSIVE

**Hotel Don Quijote**   Rooms in this three-story hotel (no elevator) are small but quiet, carpeted, and well lit, but a little worn. All have two double beds with reading lamps over them, tiled bathrooms, and plenty of hot water. There's complimentary coffee in the mornings. It's 2½ blocks east of the plaza.

Cristóbal Colón 7 (near Real de Guadalupe), 29200 San Cristóbal de las Casas, Chi. (C) **967/678-0920**. Fax 967/678-0346. 24 units. $25–$40 double. MC, V. *In room:* TV.

**Hotel Palacio de Moctezuma**   This three-story hotel has open courtyards and more greenery than others in this price range. Fresh-cut flowers tucked around tile fountains are its hallmark. The rooms have carpeting and tiled bathrooms with showers; many are quite large but, alas, can be cold in winter. The restaurant looks out on the interior courtyard. On the third floor is a solarium with comfortable tables and chairs and great city views. The hotel is 3½ blocks southeast of the main plaza.

Juárez 16 (at León), 29200 San Cristóbal de las Casas, Chi. (C) **967/678-0352** or -1142. Fax 967/678-1536. 42 units. $35–$40 double. MC, V. Free limited parking. **Amenities:** Restaurant. *In room:* TV, no phone.

**Hotel Real del Valle** *(Value)*   This hotel has great location just off the main plaza. The rooms in the back three-story section have new bathrooms, big closets, and tile floors. The beds are comfortable, and the water is hot—all for a good price. In winter the rooms are a little cold. Amenities include a rooftop solarium.

Real de Guadalupe 14, 29200 San Cristóbal de las Casas, Chi. (C) **967/678-0680**. Fax 967/678-3955. hrvalle@ mundomaya.com.mx. 36 units. $25–$35 double. No credit cards. Free parking. **Amenities:** Laundry service. *In room:* TV, no phone.

## WHERE TO DINE

San Cristóbal is not known for its cuisine, but you can eat well at several restaurants. For baked goods, try the **Panadería La Hojaldra,** Mazariegos and 5 de Mayo ((C) **967/678-4286**). It's open daily from 8am to 9:30pm. In addition to the restaurants listed below, consider making reservations for dinner at Casa Na-Bolom (see "Attractions in Town," earlier in this chapter).

## MODERATE

**El Edén** ⋆⋆ INTERNATIONAL    This is a small, quiet restaurant where it is obvious that somebody who enjoys the taste of good food prepares the meals; just about anything except Swiss rarebit is good. The meats are especially tender, and the margaritas are especially dangerous (one is all it takes). Specialties include Swiss cheese fondue for two, Edén salad, and brochette. This is where locals go for a splurge. It's 2 blocks from the main plaza.

In the Hotel El Paraíso, Av. 5 de Febrero 19. ☎ 967/678-5382. Breakfast $5; main courses $6–$10. AE, MC, V. Daily 8am–9pm.

**La Paloma** INTERNATIONAL/MEXICAN    La Paloma I particularly like in the evening because the lighting is so well done. Both the Mexican and the other dishes are much more mainstream than what you get at Los Barrios—fewer surprises. For starters, I enjoyed the quesadillas cooked Mexico City style (small fried packets of *masa* stuffed with a variety of fillings). Don't make my mistake of trying to share them with your dinner companion; it will only lead to a quarrel over the last one. Mexican classics include *albóndigas en chipotle* (meatballs in a thick chipotle sauce, Oaxacan black mole, and a variety of chile rellenos). Avoid the profiteroles.

Hidalgo 3. ☎ 967/678-1547. Main courses $6–$13. MC, V. Daily 9am–midnight.

**Los Barrios** CONTEMPORARY MEXICAN    For Mexican food in San Cristóbal, I can't think of a better place than this. The tortilla soup was the best I've had here (called *sopa de la abuela*). For something different there's a mushroom-and–cactus paddle soup. The main courses, while kept to a manageable number, offer enough variety to please several tastes. There are a couple of novel chile relleno combinations and a chicken breast *adobado* with plantain stuffing. The restaurant is in a patio with an interesting rough-wood enclosure. It's quiet and inviting.

Guadalupe Victoria 25 (between 3 de Mayo and Matamoros). ☎ 967/678-1910. Main courses $6–$10. MC, V. Mon–Sat 1–10pm; Sun buffet 1:30–6pm.

**Pierre** ⋆ FRENCH    Who would have thought that you could get good French food in San Cristóbal? And yet, Frenchman Pierre Niviere offers an appealing selection of traditional French dishes, simplified and tweaked for the tropical surroundings. I showed up on a Sunday, enjoyed the fixed menu, and left well satisfied.

Real de Guadalupe 73. ☎ 967/678-7211. Main courses $5–$16; Sunday fixed menu $10. No credit cards. Daily 1:30–11pm.

## INEXPENSIVE

**La Casa del Pan Papalotl** VEGETARIAN    This place is best known for its vegetarian lunch buffet with salad bar. The vegetables and most of the grains are organic. Kippy, the owner, has a home garden and a field near town where she grows vegetables. She buys high-altitude, locally grown, organic red wheat with which she bakes her breads. These are all sourdough breads, which she likes because she feels they are easily digested and have good texture and taste. The pizzas are a popular item. The restaurant shares space with other activities in the cultural center El Puente. One of her friends, Julio C. Domínguez, has a textile gallery with a great collection of weavings. He is dedicated to preserving the weaver's art and goes around interviewing weavers and looking for examples of old work. The center also has gallery space, a language school, and cinema.

Real de Guadalupe 55 (between Diego Dujelay and Cristóbal Colón). ☎ 967/678-7215. Main courses $5–$10; lunch buffet $5–$6. No credit cards. Mon–Sat 9am–10pm (lunch buffet 2–4pm).

**Emiliano's Moustache** *(Finds* MEXICAN/TACOS   Like any right-thinking traveler, I initially avoided this place on account of its unpromising name and some cartoonlike figures by the door. But a conversation with some local folk overcame my prejudice and tickled my sense of irony. Sure enough, the place was crowded with *coletos* enjoying the restaurant's highly popular *comida corrida* and delicious tacos, and there wasn't a foreigner in sight. The daily menu is posted by the door; if that doesn't appeal, you can choose from a menu of taco plates (a mixture of fillings cooked together and served with tortillas and a variety of hot sauces).

Crescencio Rosas 7. ⓒ 967/678-7246. Main courses $4–$8; *comida corrida* $4. No credit cards. Daily 8am–midnight.

**Madre Tierra** INTERNATIONAL/VEGETARIAN   A lot of vegetarians live in this town, and they have many options. This one is almost an institution in San Cristóbal. The restaurant is known for its baked goods, pastas, pizza, and quiche. They also offer fresh salads and international main courses that are safe and dependable. Good for breakfast, too. Madre Tierra is 3½ blocks south of the plaza.

Av. Insurgentes 19. ⓒ 967/678-4297. Main courses $4–$8; *comida corrida* (served after noon) $6. No credit cards. Restaurant daily 8am–9:45pm; bakery Mon–Sat 9am–8pm, Sun 9am–2pm.

**Normita's** MEXICAN   Normita's is famous for its *pozole,* a hearty chicken-and-hominy soup to which you add a variety of things. It also offers cheap, dependable, short-order Mexican mainstays. Normita's is an informal "people's" restaurant; the open kitchen takes up one corner of the room, and tables sit in front of a large paper mural of a fall forest scene from some faraway place. It's 2 blocks southeast of the plaza.

Av. Juárez 6 (at Dr. José Flores). No phone. Breakfast $2–$2.50; *pozole* $3; tacos $2.50. No credit cards. Daily 7am–11pm.

**Restaurant Tuluc** *(Value* MEXICAN/INTERNATIONAL   A real bargain here is the popular *comida corrida*—it's delicious and filling. Other favorites are sandwiches and enchiladas. The house specialty is *filete Tuluc,* a beef filet wrapped around spinach and cheese served with fried potatoes and green beans; while not the best cut of meat, it's certainly priced right. The Chiapaneco breakfast is a filling quartet of juice, toast, two Chiapanecan tamales, and coffee. Tuluc also has that rarest of rarities in Mexico, a nonsmoking section. The restaurant is 1½ blocks south of the plaza.

Av. Insurgentes 5 (between Cuauhtémoc and Francisco León). ⓒ **967/678-2090.** Breakfast $2–$3; main courses $4–$5; *comida corrida* (served 2–4pm) $3.75. No credit cards. Daily 7am–10pm.

## COFFEEHOUSES

Because Chiapas-grown coffee is highly regarded, it's not surprising that coffeehouses proliferate here. Most are concealed in the nooks and crannies of San Cristóbal's side streets. Try **Café La Selva,** Crescencio Rosas 9 (ⓒ **967/678-7244**), for coffee served in all its varieties and brewed from organic beans. It's open daily from 9am to 11pm. A more traditional-style cafe, where locals meet to talk over the day's news, is **Café San Cristóbal,** Cuauhtémoc 1 (ⓒ **967/678-3861**). It's open Monday to Saturday from 9am to 10pm, Sunday from 9am to 9pm. There is also a coffee museum with a cafe inside with the confusing name **Café Museo Café.** It's at María Adelina Flores 10 (ⓒ **967/678-7876**).

## SAN CRISTOBAL AFTER DARK

San Cristóbal is blessed with a variety of nightlife, both resident and migratory. There is a lot of live music, surprisingly good and varied. The bars and restaurants are cheap.

And they are easy to get to: You can hit all the places mentioned here without setting foot in a cab. Weekends are best, but on any night you'll find something going on.

Almost of the clubs in San Cristóbal offer Latin music of one genre or another. **El Cocodrilo** (© **967/678-1140**), on the main plaza in the Hotel Santa Clara, has acoustic performers playing Latin folk music *(trova, andina)*. Relax at a table in what usually is a not-too-crowded environment. After that your choices are varied. For Latin dance music there's a place just a block away on the corner of Madero and Juárez called **Latino's** (© **967/678-9972**)—good bands playing a mix of salsa, merengue, and cumbia. On weekends it gets crowded, but it has a good-size dance floor. Another club, **Blue** (© **967/678-2000**), is in the opposite direction on the other side of the main square. It has live music on weekends playing salsa, reggae, and some electronic music. The place is dark and has just a bit of the urban edge to it. From there, you can walk down the pedestrian-only 20 de Noviembre to visit a couple of popular bars—**Revolución** and **El Circo.**

## ROAD TRIPS FROM SAN CRISTOBAL

For excursions to nearby villages, see "The Nearby Maya Villages & Countryside," earlier in this chapter; for destinations farther away, there are several local travel agencies. But first you should try Alex and Raúl (p. 266). You can also try **ATC Travel and Tours,** Calle 5 de Febrero 15, at the corner of 16 de Septiembre (© **967/678-2550;** fax 967/678-3145), across from El Fogón restaurant. The agency has bilingual guides and reliable vehicles. ATC regional tours focus on birds and orchids, textiles, hiking, and camping.

Strangely, the cost of the trips include a driver but not necessarily a bilingual guide or guided information of any kind. You pay extra for those services, so when checking prices, be sure to flesh out the details.

## PALENQUE, BONAMPAK & YAXCHILAN

For information on these destinations, see the section on Palenque, earlier in this chapter.

## CHINCULTIC RUINS, COMITAN & MONTEBELLO NATIONAL PARK

Almost 160km (100 miles) southeast of San Cristóbal, near the border with Guatemala, is the **Chincultic** archaeological site and Montebello National Park, with **16 multi-colored lakes** and exuberant pine-forest vegetation. Seventy-four kilometers (46 miles) from San Cristóbal is **Comitán,** a pretty hillside town of 40,000 inhabitants known for its flower cultivation and a sugar cane–based liquor called *comitecho*. It's also the last big town along the Pan-American Highway before the Guatemalan border.

The Chincultic ruins, a late Classic site, have barely been excavated, but the main **acropolis,** high up against a cliff, is magnificent to see from below and is worth the walk up for the view. After passing through the gate, you'll see the trail ahead; it passes ruins on both sides. More unexcavated tree-covered ruins flank steep stairs leading up the mountain to the acropolis. From there, you can gaze upon distant Montebello lakes and miles of cornfields and forest. The paved road to the lakes passes six lakes, all different colors and sizes, ringed by cool pine forests; most have parking lots and lookouts. The paved road ends at a small restaurant. The lakes are best seen on a sunny day, when their famous brilliant colors are optimal.

Most travel agencies in San Cristóbal offer a daylong trip that includes the lakes, the ruins, lunch in Comitán, and a stop in the pottery-making village of Amatenango

# Chiapas Highlands

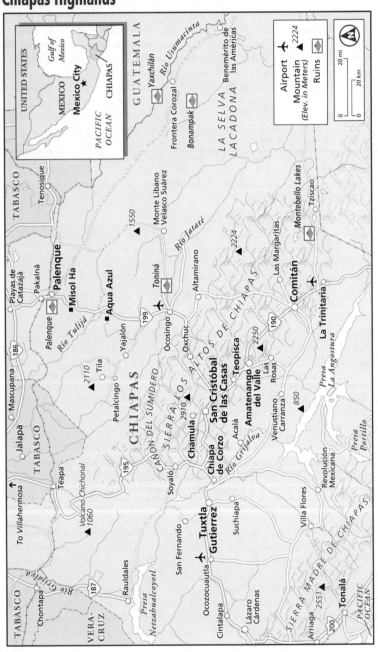

del Valle. If you're driving, follow Highway 190 south from San Cristóbal through the pretty village of Teopisca and then through Comitán; turn left at La Trinitaria, where there's a sign to the lakes. After the Trinitaria turnoff and before you reach the lakes, there's a sign pointing left down a narrow dirt road to the Chincultic ruins.

## 4 Tuxtla Gutiérrez

82km (51 miles) W of San Cristóbal; 277km (172 miles) S of Villahermosa; 242km (150 miles) NW of Ciudad Cuauhtémoc on the Guatemalan border

Tuxtla Gutiérrez (altitude 557m/1,827 ft.) is the commercial center of Chiapas. Coffee is the basis of the region's economy, along with recent oil discoveries. Tuxtla (pop. 350,000) is a business town, and not a particularly attractive one. For travelers, it's mainly a way station en route to San Cristóbal or the Sumidero Canyon.

## ESSENTIALS
### GETTING THERE & DEPARTING
**BY PLANE** **Aviacsa** (© **961/612-6880** or -8081; www.aviacsa.com) can get you to several cities in Mexico, but all flights go through Mexico City—even flights to Cancún, Chetumal, Mérida, Guatemala City, Villahermosa, and Oaxaca. **Click,** a subsidiary of Mexicana (© **01-800/122-5425** or 961/612-5402; www.clickmx.com), has nonstop flights to and from Mexico City.

Tuxtla has two airports: **Terán** and **Llano San Juan.** The airlines go back and forth with them depending on the season. Be sure to double-check which airport you're departing from, and allow enough time to get there. The Terán airport is 8km (5 miles) from town; the Llano San Juan airport is 18km (11 miles). There is taxi and minivan service from both airports.

**BY CAR** From Oaxaca, you'll enter Tuxtla by Highway 190. From Villahermosa, or Palenque and San Cristóbal, you'll enter at the opposite end of town on the same highway from the east. In both cases, you'll arrive at the large main square at the center of town, La Plaza Cívica (see "City Layout," below).

From Tuxtla to Villahermosa, take Highway 190 east past the town of Chiapa de Corzo; soon you'll see a sign for Highway 195 north to Villahermosa. To San Cristóbal and Palenque, take Highway 190 east. The road is beautiful but tortuous. It's in good repair to San Cristóbal, but there may be bad spots between San Cristóbal and Palenque. The trip from Tuxtla to Villahermosa takes 8 hours by car; the scenery is beautiful.

**BY BUS** The first-class **bus station** (© **961/612-2624**) is at the corner of calles 2 Norte and 2 Poniente (see "City Layout," below). All bus lines serving this station and the deluxe section across the street (Uno, Maya de Oro, Cristóbal Colón, Servicios Altos) belong to the same parent company, ADO. The main station sells tickets for all buses. All buses are air-conditioned and have bathrooms. There are two levels of first class; the first-class *económico* has less legroom. Then there's deluxe, which features a few extras: slightly better seats, better movies, and free coffee and soda. There are buses every half-hour to San Cristóbal, eight buses a day to Villahermosa, three or four buses a day to Oaxaca, and five to Palenque. There's usually no need to buy a ticket ahead of time, except during holidays.

## ORIENTATION

**ARRIVING**    The Llano San Juan airport is off Highway 190 west of town, about 40 minutes away; the Terán airport is off the same highway going east of town, about 15 minutes away. A *colectivo* (minivan) is much cheaper than a taxi if you can find one; they leave as soon as they are full. The ADO/Cristóbal Colón bus terminal is downtown.

**VISITOR INFORMATION**    The **Tourist Office** (© 01-800/280-3500 in Mexico, or 961/613-4499) is in the Secretaría de Fomento Económico building, formerly the Plaza de las Instituciones, on Avenida Central/Bulevar Domínguez, near the Hotel Bonampak Tuxtla. It's on the first floor of the plaza and is open Monday to Friday from 8am to 9pm. The staff at the information booth in front of the office can answer most questions. There are also information booths at the **international airport** (staffed when flights are due) and at the **zoo** (Tues–Sun 9am–3pm and 6–9pm).

**CITY LAYOUT**    Tuxtla is laid out on a grid. The main street, **Avenida Central,** is the east-west axis and is the artery through town for Highway 190. West of the central district it's called **Bulevar Belisario Domínguez,** and in the east it's **Bulevar Angel Albino Corzo. Calle Central** is the north-south axis. The rest of the streets have names that include one number and two directions. This tells you how to get to the street. For example, to find the street 5 Norte Poniente (5 North West), you walk 5 blocks north from the center of town and turn west (which is left). To find 3 Oriente Sur, you walk 3 blocks east from the main square and turn south. When people indicate intersections, they can shorten the names because it's redundant. The bus station is at the corner of 2 Norte and 2 Poniente.

**GETTING AROUND**    **Buses** to all parts of the city converge upon the Plaza Cívica along Calle Central. **Taxi** fares are higher here than in other regions.

**FAST FACTS**    The local **American Express** representative is Viajes Marabasco, Plaza Bonampak, Loc. 4, Col. Moctezuma, near the tourist office (© **961/612-6998;** fax 961/612-4053). Office hours are Monday to Friday from 9am to 1:30pm and 3:30 to 6:30pm. The **telephone area code** is **961.** If you need medical help, the best **clinic** in town is Sanatorio Rojas, Calle 2 Sur Poniente 1847 (© **961/611-2079** or 612-5414).

## EXPLORING TUXTLA

Most travelers simply pass through Tuxtla on their way to San Cristóbal or Oaxaca. The excellent zoo and the Sumidero Canyon are the top sights, and you might also visit the Parque Madero and its anthropology museum.

**Miguel Alvarez del Toro Zoo (ZOOMAT)**  ⌖    Located in the forest called El Zapotal, ZOOMAT is one of the best zoos in Mexico. The collection of animals and birds indigenous to this area gives the visitor a tangible sense of what the wilds of Chiapas are like. The zoo keeps jaguars, howler monkeys, owls, and many more exotic animals in roomy cages that replicate their home terrain; the whole zoo is so deeply buried in vegetation that you can almost pretend you're in a natural habitat. Unlike at other zoos I've visited, the animals are almost always on view; many will come to the fence if you make a kissing noise.

Bulevar Samuel León Brinois, southeast of downtown. No phone. Free admission; donations solicited. Tues–Sun 9am–5:30pm. The zoo is about 8km (5 miles) southeast of downtown; catch a bus along Av. Central and at the Calzada.

## SHOPPING

The government-operated **Instituto de las Artesanías,** Bulevar Domínguez 2035 (© 961/612-2275), is a shop and gallery. The two stories of rooms feature an extensive collection of crafts grouped by region and type from throughout the state of Chiapas. It's open Monday to Saturday from 10am to 8pm.

## WHERE TO STAY

As Tuxtla booms, the center of the hotel industry has moved out of town, west to Highway 190. As you come in from the airport, you'll notice the new motel-style hotels, such as the **Hotel Flamboyán, Palace Inn, Hotel Laganja,** and **La Hacienda.** All of these are more expensive than those listed here, which are within walking distance of all the downtown attractions.

**Hotel Bonampak Tuxtla** This hotel is almost a mile from the town's main square. It's one of those hotels in Mexico to which change comes slowly. This gives it character, and the place is well maintained. The furniture is an old heavy-style, but the mattresses are new and comfortable. The rooms could use a bit more light but they are of good size, with ample bathrooms and closet space.

Bulevar Domínguez 180, 29030 Tuxtla Gutiérrez, Chi. © **961/613-2050.** 70 units. $89 double. AE, MC, V. Free secured parking. **Amenities:** Restaurant; bar; pool; travel agency; boutique; room service until midnight; laundry service. *In room:* A/C, TV.

**Hotel María Eugenia** This five-story hotel on Avenida Central in the middle of town is well maintained. Rooms are medium-size with bathrooms to match. Most of the mattresses are firm.

Av. Central 507, 29030 Tuxtla Gutiérrez, Chi. © **961/613-3767,** or 01-800/716-0149 in Mexico. 83 units. $80 double. AE, MC, V. Free guarded parking. **Amenities:** Restaurant; bar; pool; travel agency; room service until 11pm; laundry service; dry cleaning; nonsmoking rooms. *In room:* A/C, TV, high-speed wireless Internet.

**Hotel Regional San Marcos** For a discount hotel, this was by far the best I could find in this town. It's in the downtown zone and very close to the *colectivos* that go to Chiapa de Corzo. Rooms are distributed on four floors (no elevator). They are medium in size, but cheerful. The air-conditioning window units are a bit noisy, but at this rate, it's a minor inconvenience.

1 Sur Oriente 176, 29030 Tuxtla Gutiérrez, Chi. © **961/613-1948** or -1887. hotelsanmarcos@prodigy.net.mx. 40 units. $40 double. Anyone showing a Frommer's book receives a 10% discount. MC, V. Free parking. **Amenities:** Restaurant; bar; tour info; room service until 11pm. *In room:* A/C, TV.

## WHERE TO DINE

For a full sit-down meal, you can try local Chiapan food at **Las Pichanchas,** Av. Central Oriente 837 (© **961/612-5351**). It's festively decorated and pretty to look at. The emphasis is on meat, and there are several heavy dishes on the menu. I would recommend the *filete simojovel* (a thin steak in a not-spicy chile sauce) or the *comida grande,* which is beef in a pumpkin-seed sauce. Eating here is a cultural experience, but I usually head over to the **Flamingo,** 1 Poniente 168, just off Avenida Central (© **961/612-0922**), which serves standard Mexican dishes: enchiladas, mole, roast chicken. The restaurant is owned by a Spaniard, who also owns a decent steakhouse called El Asador Castellano, which is on the west side of town. Take a taxi.

If all you want is tacos, there are several good places around the plaza called El Parque de la Marimba. This plaza has free *marimba* music nightly and is enjoyable. There you'll find a couple of local taco restaurants bordering the plaza, **Parrilla Suiza** and **El Fogón Norteño.** Both have good grilled tacos. The Parque de la Marimba is on Avenida Central Poniente, 8 blocks west of the main square.

## ROAD TRIPS FROM TUXTLA GUTIERREZ: CHIAPA DE CORZO & THE SUMIDERO CANYON

The real reason to stay in Tuxtla is to take a boat trip through the **Canyon of El Sumidero** ✹✹. The canyon is spectacular, and the boat ride is fun. Boats leave from the docks in **Chiapa de Corzo,** a colonial town of about 50,000 inhabitants that bumps up to Tuxtla. To get there take a taxi or hop on the *colectivo* operated by Transportes Chiapa-Tuxtla (2nd Oriente at 2nd Sur; ✆ **961/616-1339**). Buses leave every half-hour from 5:30am to 9:30pm. Cost is $1. The ride takes a half-hour. Ask to get off at the main square *(parada del parque).* Chiapa de Corzo has a large main square. The two main boat cooperatives have ticket booths under the archways bordering the square. But you don't have to look for these; just go straight to the boats at the embarcadero 1½ blocks below the square.

As you pass the church of Santo Domingo, you'll see a large **ceiba** tree shading the churchyard. In better circumstances these trees get even larger than this, but this one has taken up an interesting position in front of the church. The Maya felt that these trees embodied the connection between the heavens, the world of men, and the underworld because they extend into all three realms.

The **two cooperatives** (the reds and the greens identified by the color of their boats) offer the same service. They work together sharing passengers and such. Boats leave as soon as a minimum of 12 people show up. The interval can be up to an hour or as short as 10 minutes, depending on the season. The cost is $9. The ride takes 2 hours. Besides the canyon vistas, you're likely to see some crocodiles and other things of interest. The boat's pilot will explain a few things in Spanish, but much of what he says adds little to the tour. At the deepest point in the canyon, our pilot said the walls stretch up vertically 1,000m (3,280 ft.) above the water, which in turn is about 100m (328 ft.) deep at that point. I wasn't about to double-check this statement—all I know is that the view was really something. There are some interesting things happening on the walls; water seeps out in places creating little micro-environments of moss, grass, and mineral deposits. One of these places is called the Christmas Tree for its form. Our boat glided slowly by as a fine mist fell on us from the plants.

The boats operate from 8am to 4pm. They are fast, and the water is smooth. The best times to see the canyon are early or late in the day when the sun is at an angle and shines on one or the other of the canyon walls. The boats are necessarily open, so you should take an adjustable cap or a hat with a draw string or some sunscreen. A pair of earplugs would probably be nice to have, too, especially if they are connected to an iPod playing some kind of dramatic music to complement the rugged vistas. This river is the Grijalva, which flows to the Gulf of Mexico from Guatemala and is one of Mexico's largest.

If you'd rather stay in Chiapa de Corzo than Tuxtla, check out the simple but nice hotel off the main square: **Hotel Los Angeles** at Av. Julián Grajales 2 (✆ **916/616-0048**). It offers rooms with or without air-conditioning for $20 to $30 per night.

# Appendix A:
# The Yucatán in Depth

The Yucatán Peninsula is a land unlike anywhere else on earth. To begin with, it has a unique geology. The entire peninsula is a flat slab of limestone that millions of years ago absorbed the force of a giant meteor (this is the same meteor that is thought to have extinguished the dinosaurs). The impact sent shock waves through the brittle limestone, fracturing it throughout, creating an immense network of fissures that drain all rainwater away from the surface. When driving through northern and central Yucatán, you'll notice no bridges, no rivers, lakes, or watercourses. The land has this surprising uniformity on the surface. The vast subterranean basin, which stretches for miles across the peninsula, is invisible but for the area's many *cenotes*—sinkholes or natural wells that exist nowhere else. Many are perfectly round vertical shafts that look like nothing else in nature (such as the Grand Cenote at Chichén Itzá); others retain a partial roof, often perforated by tree roots—quiet, dark, and cool, they are the opposite of the warm, brightly lit outside world. To the Maya, they were passageways to the underworld.

Those curious people, the Maya, are another fascinating part of this land. The ancients left behind elegant and mysterious ruins that, despite all that we now know, seem to defy interpretation. Almost every year, archaeological excavation leads to the discovery of more ruins, adding to a growing picture of an urban civilization that thrived in an area where only scantily populated jungle now exists. What can we make of such a civilization? What value do we accord the Maya among the other lost civilizations of the ancient world? Even this is unclear, but the art and architecture they left behind are stunning expressions of a rich and complex cosmological view.

Then there was the arrival of the Spaniards, in the early 1500s—an event that in hindsight seems almost apocalyptic. Military conquest and old-world diseases decimated the native population. A new social order predicated on a starkly different religion rose in place of the old one. Through all of this, the Maya held on to their language but lost most of the living memory of their pre-Hispanic ways. What they retained they cloaked in the language of myth and legend that was worked into a rough synthesis of old and new. They selectively appropriated elements of the new religion that could help make sense of the world, and this process continues today in the many Maya communities that have native churches.

For these reasons and more, the Yucatán is a curious place; it may beckon you with its turquoise-blue waters and tropical Caribbean climate, but what will ultimately hold your attention is the unique character of the land and its people. There is no other place like it.

## 1 The Land & Its People

**SOCIAL MORES**   American and English travelers have often observed that Mexicans have a different conception of time, that life in Mexico obeys slower rhythms. This is true, and yet few observers go on to explain what the consequences of this are for the visitor to Mexico. This is a shame, because an imperfect appreciation of the difference causes a good deal of misunderstanding between tourists and locals.

Mexican acquaintances have asked me why Americans grin all the time. At first, I wasn't sure what to make of the question, and only gradually came to appreciate what was at issue. As the pace of life for Americans, Canadians, and others has quickened, they have come to skip some of the niceties of social interaction. When walking into a store, many Americans simply smile at a clerk and launch right into a question or request. The smile, in effect, replaces the greeting. In Mexico, it doesn't work that way. Mexicans misinterpret this American manner of greeting. After all, a smile when there is no context can be ambiguous; it can convey amusement, smugness, or superiority.

One of the most important pieces of advice I can offer travelers is this: Always give a proper greeting when addressing Mexicans. Don't try to abbreviate social intercourse. Mexican culture places a higher value on proper social form than on saving time. A Mexican must at least say *"¡Buenos días!"* or its equivalent, even to total strangers—a show of proper respect. When an individual meets a group of people, he or she will greet each person separately, which can take quite a while. For us, the polite thing would be to keep our interruption to a minimum and give a general greeting to all.

Mexicans, like most people, will consciously or subconsciously make quick judgments about individuals they meet. Most divide the world into the well raised and cultured *(bien educado),* and the poorly raised *(mal educado).* Unfortunately, many visitors are reluctant to try out their Spanish, preferring to keep exchanges to a minimum. Don't do this. To be categorized as a foreigner isn't a big deal. What's important in Mexico is to be categorized as one of the cultured foreigners and not one of the barbarians.

**TODAY'S MAYA CULTURE & PEOPLE**   As with lowlanders elsewhere in Mexico, Yucatecans are warm and friendly, and they show little reserve. Entering into conversation with them couldn't be easier. In the peninsula's interior, you might find people who are unexpectedly reticent, but most likely these are Maya Indians who aren't comfortable speaking Spanish. It may come as a surprise that you don't have to leave Cancún to meet the Maya; thousands come from the interior to work at hotels and restaurants in Cancún, and many can switch easily among Spanish, English, and Yukatek, the local Mayan language. More than 350,000 Maya living in the Yucatán's three states speak Yukatek, and most, especially men, speak Spanish, too.

Completely different are the estimated one million **Tabascan** and **Chiapan Maya,** who speak four different Mayan languages with dozens of dialects. The highland Maya communities around San Cristóbal de las Casas generally choose not to embrace outside cultures, preferring to

---

**Impressions**

*We both learned that the Maya are not just a people of the past. Today, they live in their millions in Mexico, Guatemala, Belize, and western Honduras, still speaking one of the 35 Mayan languages as their native tongue. They continue to cultivate their fields and commune with their living world in spite of the fact that they are encapsulated within a larger modern civilization whose vision of reality is often alien to their own.*
    —Linda Schele and David Freidel, *A Forest of Kings* (1990)

live in small mountain hamlets and meeting only for ceremonies and market days. Their cloud-forest homeland in Chiapas is cold. They, too, live much as their ancestors did, but with beliefs distinct from their peninsular relatives.

## THE YUCATAN'S GEOGRAPHY

The Yucatán is edged by the dull aquamarine Gulf of Mexico on the west and north, and the clear cerulean blue Caribbean Sea on the east. The peninsula covers almost 134,400 sq. km (51,892 sq. miles), with nearly 1,600km (1,000 miles) of shoreline. Most terrain is porous limestone, with thin soil supporting a primarily low, scrubby jungle. In most of the Yucatán there is no surface water; instead, rainwater filters through the limestone into underground rivers.

The only sense of height comes from the hills along the western shores of Campeche, rising inland to the border with Yucatán state. These are the Puuc Hills, less than 300m (984 ft.) high at their highest. The highways undulate a bit as you go inland, and south of Ticul there's a rise in the highway that provides a marvelous view of the "valley" and the misty Puuc hills lining the horizon.

## NATURAL LIFE & PROTECTED AREAS

The Yucatán state's nature preserves include the 47,200-hectare (116,584-acre) **Río Lagartos Wildlife Refuge** north of Valladolid—where you'll find North America's largest flock of nesting flamingos—and the 5,600-plus-hectare (13,832-acre) **Celestún Wildlife Refuge,** which harbors most of the flamingos during non-nesting season. The state also has incorporated nature trails into the archaeological site of **Dzibilchaltún,** north of Mérida.

In 1989, the Campeche state set aside 71,480 hectares (176,556 acres) in the **Calakmul Biosphere Reserve** that it shares with Guatemala. The area includes the ruins of Calakmul, as well as acres of thick jungle.

Quintana Roo's protected areas are some of the region's most beautiful, wild, and important. In 1986, the state ambitiously set aside the 520,000-hectare (1.3-million-acre) **Sian Ka'an Biosphere Reserve,** conserving a significant part of the coast in the face of development south of Tulum. **Isla Contoy,** also in Quintana Roo, off the coast of Isla Mujeres and Cancún, is a beautiful island refuge for hundreds of birds, turtles, plants, and other wildlife. And in 1990, the 60-hectare (148-acre) **Jardín Botánico,** south of Puerto Morelos, opened to the public. Along with the Botanical Garden at Cozumel's Chankanaab Lagoon, it gives visitors an idea of the biological importance of Yucatán's lengthy shoreline: Four of Mexico's eight marine turtle species—loggerhead, green, hawksbill, and leatherback—nest on Quintana Roo's shores, and more than 600 species of birds, reptiles, and mammals have been counted.

## 2 A Look at the Past

### PRE-HISPANIC CIVILIZATIONS

The earliest "Mexicans" were perhaps Stone Age hunter-gatherers coming from the north, descendants of a race that had crossed the Bering Strait and reached North America around 12000 B.C. This is the prevailing theory, but there is a growing body of evidence that points to an earlier crossing of peoples from Asia to the New World. What we know for certain is that Mexico was populated by 10000 B.C. Sometime between 5200 and 1500 B.C. they began practicing agriculture and domesticating animals.

### THE PRE-CLASSIC PERIOD (1500 B.C.–A.D. 300)

Eventually, agriculture improved to the point that it could provide enough food to support large communities and enough surplus to free some of the population from agricultural work. A civilization emerged that we call the **Olmec**—an enigmatic people who settled the lower Gulf Coast in what is now Tabasco and Veracruz. Anthropologists regard them as the mother culture of Mesoamerica because they established a pattern for later civilizations in a wide area stretching from northern Mexico into Central America. The Olmec developed the basic calendar used throughout the region, established principles of urban layout and architecture, and originated the cult of the jaguar and the sacredness of jade. They may also have bequeathed the sacred ritual of "the ballgame"—a universal element of Mesoamerican culture.

One intriguing feature of the Olmec was the carving of colossal stone heads. We still don't know what purposes these heads served, but they were immense projects; the basalt from which they were sculpted was mined miles inland and transported to the coast, probably by river rafts. The heads share a rounded, baby-faced look, marked by a peculiar, high-arched lip—a "jaguar mouth"—that is an identifying mark of Olmec sculpture.

The Maya civilization began developing in the pre-Classic period, around 500 B.C. Our understanding of this period is only sketchy, but Olmec influences are apparent everywhere. The Maya perfected the Olmec calendar and, somewhere along the way, developed their ornate system of hieroglyphic writing and their early architecture. Two other civilizations also began their rise to prominence around this time: the people of Teotihuacán, just north of present-day Mexico City, and the Zapotec of Monte Albán, in the valley of Oaxaca.

## THE CLASSIC PERIOD (A.D. 300–900)

The flourishing of these three civilizations marks the boundaries of this period—the heyday of pre-Columbian Mesoamerican artistic and cultural achievements. These include the pyramids and palaces in Teotihuacán; the ceremonial center of Monte Albán; and the stelae and temples of Palenque, Bonampak, and the Tikal site in Guatemala. Beyond their achievements in art and architecture, the Maya made significant discoveries in science, including the use of the zero in mathematics and a complex calendar with which the priests could predict eclipses and the movements of the stars for centuries to come.

The inhabitants of **Teotihuacán** (100 B.C.–A.D. 700—near present-day Mexico City) built a city that, at its zenith, is thought to have had 100,000 or more inhabitants covering 14 sq. km (5½ sq.

---

**Dateline**

- **10,000–1500 B.C.** Archaic period: Hunting and gathering; later, the dawn of agriculture: domestication of chiles, corn, beans, avocado, amaranth, and pumpkin. Mortars and pestles in use. Stone bowls and jars, obsidian knives, and open-weave basketry developed.
- **1500 B.C.–A.D. 300** Pre-Classic period: Olmec culture

develops large-scale settlements and irrigation methods. Cities spring up. Olmec influence spreads over other cultures in the Gulf Coast, central and southern Mexico, Central America, the lower Mexican Pacific coast, and the Yucatán. Several cities in central and southern Mexico begin the construction of large ceremonial centers and pyramids. The Maya develop

several city-states in Chiapas and Central America.

- **1000–900 B.C.** Olmec San Lorenzo center is destroyed; the Olmec begin anew at La Venta.
- **600 B.C.** La Venta Olmec cultural zenith.
- **A.D. 300–900** Classic period: Broad influence of Teotihuacán culture and the establishment there of a truly cosmopolitan urbanism.

miles). It was a well-organized city, built on a grid with streams channeled to follow the city's plan. Different social classes, such as artisans and merchants, were assigned to specific neighborhoods. Teotihuacán exerted tremendous influence as far away as Guatemala and the Yucatán Peninsula. Its feathered serpent god, later known as **Quetzalcoatl,** became part of the pantheon of many succeeding cultures, including the Toltecs, who brought the cult to the Yucatán where the god became known as Kukulkán. The ruling classes were industrious, literate, and cosmopolitan. The beautiful sculpture and ceramics of Teotihuacán display a highly stylized and refined aesthetic whose influences can be seen clearly in objects of Maya and Zapotec origin. Around the 7th century, the city was abandoned for unknown reasons. Who these people were and where they went remains a mystery.

## THE POST-CLASSIC PERIOD (A.D. 900–1521)

Warfare became more pervasive during this period. Social development was impressive but these latter civilizations were not as cosmopolitan as the Maya, Teotihuacán, and Zapotec societies. In central Mexico, a people known as the **Toltec** established their capital at Tula in the 10th century. They were originally one of the barbarous hordes of Indians that periodically migrated from the north. At some stage in their development, the Toltec were influenced by remnants of Teotihuacán culture and adopted the feathered serpent Quetzalcoatl as their god. They also revered a god known as **Tezcatlipoca,** or "smoking mirror," who later became a god of the Aztecs. The Toltec maintained a large military class divided into orders symbolized by animals. At its height, Tula may have had 40,000 people, and it spread its influence across Mesoamerica. By the 13th century, however, the Toltec had exhausted themselves, probably in civil wars and in battles with the invaders from the north.

During this period, the Maya built beautiful cities near the Yucatán's Puuc hills. The regional architecture, called **Puuc style,** is characterized by elaborate exterior stonework appearing above door frames and extending to the roofline. Examples of this architecture, such as the Codz Poop at Kabah and the palaces at Uxmal, Sayil, and Labná, are beautiful and quite impressive. Associated with the cities of the Puuc region was Chichén Itzá, ruled by the Itzaés. This metropolis evidences strong Toltec influences in its architectural style as well as the cult of the plumed-serpent god, Kukulkán.

The precise nature of this Toltec influence is a subject of debate. But there is an

---

Satellite settlements spring up across central Mexico and as far away as Guatemala. Trade and cultural interchange with the Maya and the Zapotec flourish. The Maya perfect the calendar and improve astronomical calculations. They build grandiose cities at Palenque, Calakmul, and Cobá, and in Central America.

■ **683** Maya King Pacal is buried in an elaborate tomb below the Palace of the Inscriptions at Palenque.

■ **800** Bonampak murals are painted.

■ **900** Post-Classic period begins: More emphasis is placed on warfare in central Mexico. The Toltec culture emerges at Tula and replaces Teotihuacán as the dominant city of central Mexico. Toltec influence spreads to the Yucatán, forming the culture of the Itzaés, who become the rulers of Chichén Itzá.

■ **909** This is the date on a small monument at Toniná (near San Cristóbal de las Casas), the last Long Count date yet discovered, symbolizing the end of the Classic Maya era.

■ **1156–1230** Tula, the Toltec capital, is abandoned.

*continues*

intriguing myth in central Mexico that tells how Quetzalcoatl quarrels with Tezcatlipoca and through trickery is shamed by his rival into leaving Tula, the capital of the Toltec empire. He leaves heading eastward toward the morning star, vowing someday to return. In the language of myth, this could be a shorthand telling of an actual civil war between two factions in Tula, each led by the priesthood of a particular god. Could the losing faction have migrated to the Yucatán and formed the ruling class of Chichén Itzá? Perhaps. What we do know for certain is that this myth of the eventual return of Quetzalcoatl became, in the hands of the Spanish, a powerful weapon of conquest.

## THE CONQUEST

In 1517, the first Spaniards arrived in Mexico and skirmished with Maya Indians off the coast of the Yucatán Peninsula. One of the fledgling expeditions ended in a shipwreck, leaving several Spaniards stranded as prisoners of the Maya. The Spanish sent out another expedition, under the command of **Hernán Cortez,** which landed on Cozumel in February 1519. Cortez inquired about the gold and riches of the interior, and the coastal Maya were happy to describe the wealth and splendor of the Aztec empire in central Mexico. Cortez promptly disobeyed all orders from his superior, the governor of Cuba, and sailed to the mainland.

He and his army arrived when the Aztec empire was at the height of its wealth and power. **Moctezuma II** ruled over the central and southern highlands and extracted tribute from lowland peoples. His greatest temples were literally plated with gold and encrusted with the blood of sacrificial captives. Moctezuma was a fool, a mystic, and something of a coward. Despite his wealth and military power, he dithered in his capital at Tenochtitlán, sending messengers with gifts and suggestions that Cortez leave. Meanwhile, Cortez blustered and negotiated his way into the highlands, always cloaking his real intentions. Moctezuma, terrified, convinced himself that Cortez was in fact the god Quetzalcoatl making his long-awaited return. By the time the Spaniards arrived in the Aztec capital, Cortez had gained some ascendancy over the lesser Indian states that were resentful tributaries to the Aztec. In November 1519, Cortez confronted Moctezuma and took him hostage in an effort to leverage control of the empire.

In the middle of Cortez's dangerous game of manipulation, another Spanish expedition arrived with orders to end Cortez's authority over the mission.

---

- **1325–1470** Aztec capital Tenochtitlán is founded; Aztecs begin military campaigns in the Valley of Mexico and then thrust farther out, subjugating the civilizations of the Gulf Coast and southern Mexico.
- **1516** Gold found on Cozumel during aborted Spanish expedition of Yucatán Peninsula arouses interest of Spanish governor in Cuba, who sends

Juan de Grijalva on an expedition, followed by another, led by Hernán Cortez.
- **1518** Spaniards first visit what is today Campeche.
- **1519** Conquest of Mexico begins: Hernán Cortez and troops make their way along Mexican coast to present-day Veracruz.
- **1521** Conquest is complete after Aztec defeat at Tlatelolco.

- **1521–24** Cortez organizes Spanish empire in Mexico and begins building Mexico City on the ruins of Tenochtitlán.
- **1524–35** Cortez is removed from power, and royal council governs New Spain.
- **1526** King of Spain permits Francisco Montejo to colonize the Yucatán.
- **1535–1821** Viceregal period: 61 viceroys appointed by king of Spain govern Mexico.

Cortez hastened to meet the rival's force and persuade them to join his own. In the meantime, the Aztec chased the garrison out of Tenochtitlán, and either they or the Spaniards killed Moctezuma. For the next year and a half, Cortez laid siege to Tenochtitlán, with the help of rival Indians and a decimating epidemic of smallpox, to which the Indians had no resistance. In the end, the Aztec capital fell, and, when it did, all of central Mexico lay at the feet of the conquistadors.

Having begun as a pirate expedition by Cortez and his men without the authority of the Spanish crown or its governor in Cuba, the conquest of Mexico resulted in a vast expansion of the Spanish empire. The king legitimized Cortez following his victory over the Aztec and ordered the forced conversion to Christianity of this new colony, to be called **New Spain.** Guatemala and Honduras were explored and conquered, and by 1540, the territory of New Spain included possessions from Vancouver to Panama. In the 2 centuries that followed, Franciscan and Augustinian friars converted millions of Indians to Christianity, and the Spanish lords built huge feudal estates on which the Indian farmers were little more than serfs. The silver and gold that Cortez looted made Spain the richest country in Europe.

## THE COLONIAL PERIOD

Hernán Cortez set about building a new city upon the ruins of the old Aztec capital. To do this, he collected from the Indians the tributes once paid to the Aztec emperor, many of them rendered in labor. This arrangement, in one form or another, became the basis for the construction of the new colony. But diseases brought by the Spaniards devastated the native population over the next century and drastically reduced the labor pool.

Over the 3 centuries of the colonial period, Spain became rich from New World gold and silver, chiseled out by Indian labor. The colonial elite built lavish homes in Mexico City and in the countryside. They filled their homes with ornate furniture, had many servants, and adorned themselves in imported velvets, satins, and jewels.

A new class system developed. Those born in Spain considered themselves superior to the *criollos* (Spaniards born in Mexico). Those of other races and the *castas* (mixtures of Spanish and Indian, Spanish and African, or Indian and African) occupied the bottom rungs of society. It took great cunning to stay a step ahead of the avaricious Crown, which demanded increasing taxes and contributions from its fabled foreign conquests.

Control of much of the land ends up in the hands of the Church and the politically powerful. A governor who reports to the king rather than to viceroys leads the Yucatán.

- **1542** Mérida is established as capital of Yucatán Peninsula.
- **1546** The Maya rebel and take control of the peninsula.
- **1559** French and Spanish pirates attack Campeche.

- **1562** Friar Diego de Landa destroys 5,000 Maya religious stone figures and burns 27 hieroglyphic painted manuscripts at Maní, Yucatán. Those Maya believed to be secretly practicing pre-Hispanic beliefs endure torture and death.
- **1810–21** War of Independence: Miguel Hidalgo starts movement for Mexico's independence from Spain but is executed within a year;

leadership and goals change during the war years, but Agustín de Iturbide outlines a compromise between monarchy and republic.

- **1822** First Empire: Iturbide ascends throne as emperor of Mexico, loses power after a year, and loses life in an attempt to reclaim throne.
- **1824–64** Early Republic period, characterized by almost perpetual civil war

*continues*

Still, wealthy colonists prospered enough to develop an extravagant society.

However, discontent with the mother country simmered for years. In 1808, Napoleon invaded Spain and crowned his brother Joseph king in place of Charles IV. To many in Mexico, allegiance to France was out of the question; discontent reached the level of revolt.

## INDEPENDENCE

The rebellion began in 1810, when **Father Miguel Hidalgo** gave the *grito,* a cry for independence, from his church in the town of Dolores, Guanajuato. The uprising soon became a full-fledged revolution, as Hidalgo and Ignacio Allende gathered an "army" of citizens and threatened Mexico City. Although Hidalgo ultimately failed and was executed, he is honored as "the Father of Mexican Independence." Another priest, José María Morelos, kept the revolt alive with several successful campaigns through 1815, when he, too, was captured and executed.

After the death of Morelos, prospects for independence were rather dim until the Spanish king who replaced Joseph Bonaparte decided to make social reforms in the colonies. This convinced the conservative powers in Mexico that they didn't need Spain after all. With their tacit approval, Agustín de Iturbide, then commander of royalist forces, changed sides and declared Mexico independent and himself emperor. Before long, however, internal dissension brought about the fall of the emperor, and Mexico was proclaimed a republic.

Political instability engulfed the young republic, which ran through a dizzying succession of presidents and dictators as struggles between federalists and centralists, and conservatives and liberals, divided the country. Moreover, Mexico waged a disastrous war with the United States, which resulted in the loss of half its territory. A central figure was **Antonio López de Santa Anna,** who assumed the leadership of his country no fewer than 11 times. He probably holds the record for frequency of exile; by 1855 he was finally left without a political comeback and ended his days in Venezuela.

Political instability persisted, and the conservative forces, with some encouragement from Napoleon III, hit upon the idea of inviting in a Hapsburg to regain control. They found a willing volunteer in Archduke Maximilian of Austria, who accepted the position of Mexican emperor with the support of French troops. The ragtag Mexican forces defeated the modern, well-equipped French force in a battle near Puebla (now celebrated annually as **Cinco de Mayo**). A second attempt

---

between federalists and centralists, conservatives and liberals, culminating in the victory of the liberals under Juárez.

- **1864–67** Second Empire: The French invade Mexico in the name of Maximilian of Austria, who is appointed emperor of Mexico. Juárez and liberal government retreat to the north and wage war with the French forces.

The French finally abandon Mexico and leave Maximilian to be defeated and executed.

- **1847–66** War of the Castes in the Yucatán: Poverty and hunger cause the Maya to revolt and gain control of half of the peninsula before being defeated by the Mexican National Army. But lingering warfare lasts well into the 20th century in the most remote parts of the peninsula.

- **1872–76** Juárez dies, and political struggles ensue for the presidency.
- **1877–1911** Porfiriato: Porfirio Díaz, president/dictator of Mexico for 33 years, leads country to modernization by encouraging foreign investment in mines, oil, and railroads. Mexico witnesses the development of a modern economy and a growing disparity between rich and poor.

was more successful, and Ferdinand Maximilian Joseph of Hapsburg became emperor. After 3 years of civil war, the French were finally induced to abandon the emperor's cause; Maximilian was captured and executed by a firing squad near Querétaro in 1867. His adversary and successor (as president of Mexico) was **Benito Juárez,** a Zapotec Indian lawyer and one of the great heroes of Mexican history. Juárez did his best to unify and strengthen his country before dying of a heart attack in 1872; his impact on Mexico's future was profound, and his plans and visions bore fruit for decades.

## THE PORFIRIATO & THE REVOLUTION

A few years after Juárez's death, one of his generals, **Porfirio Díaz,** assumed power in a coup. He ruled Mexico from 1877 to 1911, a period now called the "Porfiriato." He stayed in power through repressive measures and by courting the favor of powerful nations. Generous in his dealings with foreign investors, Díaz became, in the eyes of most Mexicans, the archetypal *entreguista* (one who sells out his country for private gain). With foreign investment came the concentration of great wealth in few hands, and social conditions worsened.

In 1910, Francisco Madero called for an armed rebellion that became the **Mexican Revolution** ("La Revolución" in Mexico; the revolution against Spain is the "Guerra de Independencia"). Díaz was sent into exile; while in London, he became a celebrity at the age of 81, when he jumped into the Thames to save a drowning boy. He is buried in Paris. Madero became president, but **Victoriano Huerta** promptly betrayed and executed him. Those who had answered Madero's call responded again—the great peasant hero **Emiliano Zapata** in the south, and the seemingly invincible **Pancho Villa** in the central north, flanked by Alvaro Obregón and Venustiano Carranza. They eventually put Huerta to flight and began hashing out a new constitution.

For the next few years, the revolutionaries Carranza, Obregón, and Villa fought among themselves; Zapata did not seek national power, though he fought tenaciously for land for the peasants. Carranza, who was president at the time, betrayed and assassinated Zapata. Obregón finally consolidated power and probably had Carranza assassinated. He, in turn, was assassinated when he tried to break one of the tenets of the revolution—no reelection. His successor, Plutarco Elias Calles, installed one puppet president after another, until **Lázaro Cárdenas** severed the puppeteer's strings and banished him to exile.

---

Social conditions, especially in rural areas, become desperate.

- **1911–17** Mexican Revolution: Francisco Madero drafts revolutionary plan. Díaz resigns. Leaders jockey for power during period of great violence, national upheaval, and tremendous loss of life.
- **1917–40** Reconstruction: Present constitution of Mexico is signed; land and education reforms are initiated and

labor unions strengthened; Mexico expropriates oil companies and railroads. Pancho Villa, Zapata, and presidents Obregón and Carranza are assassinated.

- **1940** Mexico enters period of political stability and makes steady economic progress. Quality of life improves, although problems of corruption, inflation, national health,

and unresolved land and agricultural issues continue.

- **1974** Quintana Roo achieves statehood and Cancún opens to tourism.
- **1994–97** Mexico, Canada, and the United States sign the North American Free Trade Agreement (NAFTA). An Indian uprising in Chiapas sparks countrywide protests over government policies

*continues*

Until Cárdenas's election in 1934, the outcome of the revolution remained in doubt. Cárdenas changed all that. He implemented massive redistribution of land and nationalized the oil industry. He instituted many reforms and gave shape to the ruling political party (now the **Partido Revolucionario Institucional,** or PRI) by bringing a broad representation of Mexican society under its banner and establishing mechanisms for consensus building. Most Mexicans practically canonize Cárdenas.

## MODERN MEXICO

The presidents who followed were noted more for graft than for leadership. The party's base narrowed as many of the reform-minded elements were marginalized. Economic progress, a lot of it in the form of large development projects, became the PRI's main basis for legitimacy. In 1968, the government violently repressed a democratic student movement. Though the PRI maintained its grip on power, it lost all semblance of being a progressive party. In 1985, a devastating **earthquake in Mexico City** brought down many of the government's new, supposedly earthquake-proof buildings, exposing shoddy construction and the widespread government corruption that had fostered it. There was heavy criticism,

too, of the government's handling of the relief efforts. In 1994, a political and military **uprising in Chiapas** focused world attention on Mexico's great social problems. A new political force, the Zapatista National Liberation Army (EZLN, for Ejército Zapatista de Liberación Nacional), has skillfully publicized the plight of the peasant in today's Mexico.

In the years that followed, opposition political parties grew in power and legitimacy. Facing pressure and scrutiny from national and international organizations, and widespread public discontent, the PRI had to concede defeat in state and congressional elections throughout the '90s. Elements of the PRI pushed for, and achieved, reforms from within and greater political openness. This led to deep divisions between party activists, rancorous campaigns for party leadership, and even political assassination. The party began choosing its candidates through primaries instead of by appointment. But in the presidential elections of 2000, Vicente Fox of the opposition party PAN won by a landslide. In hindsight, there was no way that the PRI could have won in a fair election. For most Mexicans, a government under the PRI was all that they had ever known. Many voted for Fox just to see whether the PRI would let go of power. It did, and the transition ran smoothly

concerning land distribution, bank loans, health, education, and voting and human rights.

■ **1999** The governor of Quintana Roo goes into hiding following accusations of corruption and ties to drug money. After many months in hiding, he turns himself in and is imprisoned.

■ **2000** Mexico elects Vicente Fox of the PAN party president.

■ **2002** The PAN party wins the governorship of the Yucatán.

■ **2005** Two hurricanes, Emily and Wilma, inflict great damage on Cancún, Cozumel, and the Riviera Maya.

■ **2006** Felipe Calderón, candidate for the PAN, wins an extremely close presidential

election over Andrés Manuel López Obrador, candidate for the PRD. The PRI candidate, Roberto Madrazo, comes in a distant third.

thanks in large part to the outgoing president, Ernesto Zedillo, who was one of the PRI's reformers. Since then Mexico has sailed into the uncharted waters of coalition politics, with three main parties, PRI, PAN, and PRD. To their credit, the sailing has been much smoother than many observers predicted. But the real test will be weathering the economic slowdown that accompanied the downturn in the U.S. economy, and in carrying out the presidential elections in July 2006.

## 3 Art & Architecture 101

Mexico's artistic and architectural legacy stretches back more than 3,000 years. Until the conquest of Mexico in A.D. 1521, art, architecture, politics, and religion were intertwined. Although the European conquest influenced the style and subject of Mexican art, this continuity remained throughout the colonial period.

### PRE-HISPANIC FORMS

Mexico's **pyramids** were truncated platforms crowned with a temple. Many sites have circular buildings, such as El Caracol at Chichén Itzá, usually called the observatory and dedicated to the god of the wind. El Castillo at Chichén Itzá has 365 steps—one for every day of the year. The Temple of the Magicians at Uxmal has beautifully rounded and sloping sides. Evidence of building one pyramidal structure on top of another, a widely accepted practice, has been found throughout Mesoamerica.

Architects of many Toltec, Aztec, and Teotihuacán edifices alternated sloping panels *(talud)* with vertical panels *(tablero)*. Elements of this style occasionally show up in the Yucatán. Dzibanché, a newly excavated site near Lago Bacalar, in southern Quintana Roo state, has at least one temple with this characteristic. The true arch was unknown in Mesoamerica, but the Maya made use of the corbelled arch—a method of stacking stones that allows each successive stone to be cantilevered out a little farther than the one below it, until the two sides meet at the top, forming an inverted V.

The Olmec, considered the parent culture of Mesoamerica, built pyramids of earth. Unfortunately, little remains to tell us what their buildings looked like. The Olmec, however, left an enormous sculptural legacy, from small, intricately carved pieces of jade to 40-ton carved basalt rock heads.

Throughout Mexico, carved stone and mural art on pyramids served a religious and historical function rather than an ornamental one. **Hieroglyphs,** picture symbols etched on stone or painted on walls or pottery, functioned as the written language of the ancient peoples, particularly the Maya. By deciphering the glyphs, scholars allow the ancients to speak again, providing us with specific names to attach to rulers and their families, and demystifying the great dynastic histories of the Maya. For more on this, read *A Forest of Kings* (1990), by Linda Schele and David Freidel, and *Blood of Kings* (1986), by Linda Schele and Mary Ellen Miller. Good hieroglyphic examples appear in the site museum at Palenque.

Carving important historical figures on free-standing stone slabs, or **stelae,** was a common Maya commemorative device. Several are in place at Cobá; Calakmul has the most, and good examples are on display in the Museum of Anthropology in Mexico City and the archaeology museum in Villahermosa. **Pottery** played an important role, and different indigenous groups are distinguished by their different use of color and style. The Maya painted pottery with scenes from daily and historical life.

Pre-Hispanic cultures left a number of fantastic painted **murals,** some of which are remarkably preserved, such as those at

Bonampak and Cacaxtla. Amazing stone murals or mosaics, using thousands of pieces of fitted stone to form figures of warriors, snakes, or geometric designs, decorate the pyramid facades at Uxmal and Chichén Itzá.

## SPANISH INFLUENCE

With the arrival of the Spaniards, new forms of architecture came to Mexico. Many sites that were occupied by indigenous groups at the time of the conquest were razed, and in their place appeared Catholic churches, public buildings, and palaces for conquerors and the king's bureaucrats. In the Yucatán, churches at Izamal, Tecoh, Santa Elena, and Muná rest atop former pyramidal structures. Indian artisans, who formerly worked on pyramidal structures, were recruited to build the new buildings, often guided by drawings of European buildings. Frequently left on their own, the indigenous artisans implanted traditional symbolism in the new buildings: a plaster angel swaddled in feathers, reminiscent of the god Quetzalcoatl, and the face of an ancient god surrounded by corn leaves. They used pre-Hispanic calendar counts—the 13 steps to heaven or the nine levels of the underworld—to determine how many florets to carve around the church doorway.

To convert the native populations, New World Spanish priests and architects altered their normal ways of teaching and building. Often before the church was built, an open-air atrium was constructed to accommodate large numbers of parishioners for services. *Posas* (shelters) at the four corners of churchyards were another architectural technique unique to Mexico, again to accommodate crowds. Because of the language barrier between the Spanish and the natives, church adornment became more explicit. Biblical tales came to life in frescoes splashed across church walls. Christian symbolism in stone supplanted that of pre-Hispanic ideas as the natives tried to make sense of it all. Baroque became even more baroque in Mexico and was dubbed **churrigueresque** or **ultrabaroque.** Exuberant and complicated, it combines Gothic, baroque, and plateresque elements.

Almost every village in the Yucatán Peninsula has the remains of **missions, monasteries, convents,** and **parish churches.** Many were built in the 16th century following the early arrival of Franciscan friars. Examples include the Mission of San Bernardino de Sisal in Valladolid; the fine altarpiece at Teabo; the folk-art *retablo* (altarpiece) at Tecoh; the large church and convent at Mani with its *retablos* and limestone crucifix; the facade, altar, and central *retablo* of the church at Oxkutzcab; the 16-bell belfry at Ytholin; the baroque facade and altarpiece at Maxcanu; the cathedral at Mérida; the vast atrium and church at Izamal; and the baroque *retablo* and murals at Tabi.

When Porfirio Díaz became president in the late 19th century, the nation's art and architecture experienced another infusion of European sensibility. Díaz idolized Europe, and he commissioned a number of striking European-style public buildings, including many opera houses. He provided European scholarships to promising young artists who later returned to Mexico to produce Mexican subject paintings using techniques learned abroad.

## THE ADVENT OF MEXICAN MURALISM

As the Mexican Revolution ripped the country apart between 1911 and 1917, a new social and cultural Mexico was born. In 1923, Minister of Education José Vasconcelos was charged with educating the illiterate masses. As one means of reaching people, he invited **Diego Rivera** and several other budding artists to paint Mexican history on the walls of the

Ministry of Education building and the National Preparatory School in Mexico City. Thus began the tradition of painting murals in public buildings, which you will find in towns and cities throughout Mexico and the Yucatán.

## 4 Religion, Myth & Folklore

Mexico is predominantly Roman Catholic, a religion introduced by the Spaniards during the Conquest of Mexico. Despite its preponderance, the Catholic faith in many places in Mexico (Chiapas and Oaxaca, for example) has pre-Hispanic undercurrents. You need only visit the *curandero* section of a Mexican market (where you can purchase copal, an incense agreeable to the gods; rustic beeswax candles, a traditional offering; the native species of tobacco used to ward off evil; and so on), or attend a village festivity featuring pre-Hispanic dancers, to understand that supernatural beliefs often run parallel with Christian ones.

Mexico's complicated mythological heritage from pre-Hispanic religion is full of images derived from nature—the wind, jaguars, eagles, snakes, flowers, and more—all intertwined with elaborate

### Gods & Goddesses

Each of the ancient cultures had its gods and goddesses, and while the names might not have crossed cultures, their characteristics or purposes often did. Chaac, the hook-nosed rain god of the Maya, was Tlaloc, the squat rain god of the Aztecs; Quetzalcoatl, the plumed-serpent god/man of the Toltecs, became Kukulkán of the Maya. The tales of the powers and creation of these deities make up Mexico's rich mythology. Sorting out the pre-Hispanic pantheon and beliefs in ancient Mexico can become an all-consuming study (the Maya alone had 166 deities), so here's a list of some of the most important gods:

**Chaac**  Maya rain god.

**Ehécatl**  Wind god whose temple is usually round; another aspect of Quetzalcoatl.

**Itzamná**  Maya god above all, who invented corn, cacao, and writing and reading.

**Ixchel**  Maya goddess of water, weaving, and childbirth.

**Kinich Ahau**  Maya sun god.

**Kukulkán**  Quetzalcoatl's name in the Yucatán.

**Ometeotl**  God/goddess, all-powerful creator of the universe, and ruler of heaven, earth, and the underworld.

**Quetzalcoatl**  A mortal who took on legendary characteristics as a god (or vice versa). When he left Tula in shame after a night of succumbing to temptations, he promised to return. He reappeared in the Yucatán. He is also symbolized as Venus, the moving star, and Ehécatl, the wind god. Quetzalcoatl is credited with giving the Maya cacao (chocolate) and teaching them how to grow it, harvest it, roast it, and turn it into a drink with ceremonial and magical properties.

**Tlaloc**  Aztec rain god.

mythological stories to explain the universe, climate, seasons, and geography. Most groups believed in an underworld (not a hell), usually containing nine levels, and a heaven of 13 levels—which is why the numbers 9 and 13 are so mythologically significant. The solar calendar count of 365 days and the ceremonial calendar of 260 days are significant as well.

How one died determined one's resting place after death: in the underworld (*Xibalba* to the Maya), in heaven, or at one of the four cardinal points. For example, men who died in battle or women who died in childbirth went straight to the sun. Everyone else first had to make a journey through the underworld.

# Appendix B:
# Useful Terms & Phrases

## 1 Basic Vocabulary

Most Mexicans are very patient with foreigners who try to speak their language; it helps a lot to know a few basic phrases. I've included simple phrases for expressing basic needs, followed by some common menu items.

### ENGLISH-SPANISH PHRASES

| English | Spanish | Pronunciation |
| --- | --- | --- |
| Good day | **Buen día** | Bwehn *dee*-ah |
| Good morning | **Buenos días** | *Bweh*-nohs *dee*-ahs |
| How are you? | **¿Cómo está?** | *Koh*-moh eh-*stah* |
| Very well | **Muy bien** | Mwee byehn |
| Thank you | **Gracias** | *Grah*-syahs |
| You're welcome | **De nada** | Deh *nah*-dah |
| Goodbye | **Adiós** | Ah-*dyohs* |
| Please | **Por favor** | Pohr fah-*bohr* |
| Yes | **Sí** | See |
| No | **No** | Noh |
| Excuse me | **Perdóneme** | Pehr-*doh*-neh-meh |
| Give me | **Déme** | *Deh*-meh |
| Where is . . . ? | **¿Dónde está . . . ?** | *Dohn*-deh eh-*stah* |
| the station | **la estación** | lah eh-stah-*syohn* |
| a hotel | **un hotel** | oon oh-*tehl* |
| a gas station | **una gasolinera** | *oo*-nah gah-soh-lee-*neh*-rah |
| a restaurant | **un restaurante** | oon res-tow-*rahn*-teh |
| the toilet | **el baño** | el *bah*-nyoh |
| a good doctor | **un buen médico** | oon bwehn *meh*-dee-coh |
| the road to . . . | **el camino a/hacia . . .** | el cah-*mee*-noh ah/*ah*-syah |
| To the right | **A la derecha** | Ah lah deh-*reh*-chah |
| To the left | **A la izquierda** | Ah lah ees-*kyehr*-dah |
| Straight ahead | **Derecho** | Deh-*reh*-choh |
| I would like | **Quisiera** | Key-*syeh*-rah |
| I want | **Quiero** | *Kyeh*-roh |
| to eat | **comer** | koh-*mehr* |
| a room | **una habitación** | *oo*-nah ah-bee-tah-*syohn* |

| Do you have . . . ? | ¿Tiene usted . . . ? | Tyeh-neh oo-*sted* |
| a dictionary | un diccionario | oon deek-syoh-*nah*-ryoh |
| How much is it? | ¿Cuánto cuesta? | *Kwahn*-toh *kweh*-stah |
| When? | ¿Cuándo? | *Kwahn*-doh |
| What? | ¿Qué? | Keh |
| There is<br>(Is there . . . ?) | (¿)Hay (. . . ?) | Eye |
| What is there? | ¿Qué hay? | Keh eye |
| Yesterday | Ayer | Ah-*yer* |
| Today | Hoy | Oy |
| Tomorrow | Mañana | Mah-*nyah*-nah |
| Good | Bueno | *Bweh*-noh |
| Bad | Malo | *Mah*-loh |
| Better (best) | (Lo) Mejor | (Loh) Meh-*hohr* |
| More | Más | Mahs |
| Less | Menos | *Meh*-nohs |
| No smoking | Se prohibe fumar | Seh proh-*ee*-beh foo-*mahr* |

## MORE USEFUL PHRASES

| English | Spanish | Pronunciation |
| --- | --- | --- |
| Do you speak<br>English? | ¿Habla usted<br>inglés? | *Ah*-blah oo-*sted*<br>een-*glehs* |
| Is there anyone<br>here who<br>speaks English? | ¿Hay alguien<br>aquí que<br>hable inglés? | Eye *ahl*-gyehn<br>ah-*kee* keh<br>ah-bleh een-*glehs* |
| I speak a little<br>Spanish. | Hablo un poco<br>de español. | *Ah*-bloh oon *poh*-koh<br>deh eh-spah-*nyohl* |
| I don't understand<br>Spanish very<br>well. | No (lo) entiendo<br>muy bien<br>el español. | Noh (loh) ehn-*tyehn*-doh<br>mwee byehn el<br>eh-spah-*nyohl* |
| The meal is good. | Me gusta la comida. | Meh *goo*-stah lah koh-*mee*-dah |
| What time is it? | ¿Qué hora es? | Keh *oh*-rah ehs |
| May I see<br>your menu? | ¿Puedo ver el<br>menú (la carta)? | *Pweh*-doh vehr el<br>meh-*noo* (lah *car*-tah) |
| The check, please. | La cuenta, por favor. | Lah *kwehn*-tah pohr fa-*borh* |

## 2 Menu Glossary

**Achiote**    Small red seed of the *annatto* tree.

**Achiote preparado**    A Yucatecan-prepared paste made of ground *achiote,* wheat and corn flour, cumin, cinnamon, salt, onion, garlic, and oregano.

**Agua fresca**    Fruit-flavored water, usually watermelon, cantaloupe, chia seed with lemon, hibiscus flour, rice, or ground melon-seed mixture.

**Antojito**    Typical Mexican supper foods, usually made with *masa* or tortillas and having a filling or topping such as sausage, cheese, beans, and onions; includes such things as *tacos, tostadas, sopes,* and *garnachas.*

**Atole**    A thick, lightly sweet, hot drink made with finely ground corn and usually flavored with vanilla, pecan, strawberry, pineapple, or chocolate.

**Botana**    An appetizer.

**Buñuelos**    Round, thin, deep-fried crispy fritters dipped in sugar.

**Carnitas**    Pork deep-cooked (not fried) in lard, and then simmered and served with corn tortillas for tacos.

**Ceviche**    Fresh raw seafood marinated in fresh lime juice and garnished with chopped tomatoes, onions, chiles, and sometimes cilantro.

**Chayote**    A vegetable pear or mirliton, a type of spiny squash boiled and served as an accompaniment to meat dishes.

**Chiles en nogada**    Poblano peppers stuffed with a mixture of ground pork and beef, spices, fruits, raisins, and almonds. Can be served either warm—fried in a light batter—or cold, sans the batter. Either way it is then covered in walnut-and-cream sauce.

**Chiles rellenos**    Usually poblano peppers stuffed with cheese or spicy ground meat with raisins, rolled in a batter, and fried.

**Churro**    Tube-shaped, breadlike fritter, dipped in sugar and sometimes filled with *cajeta* (milk-based caramel) or chocolate.

**Cochinita pibil**    Pork wrapped in banana leaves, pit-baked in a *pibil* sauce of *achiote,* sour orange, and spices; common in the Yucatán.

**Enchilada**    A tortilla dipped in sauce, usually filled with chicken or white cheese, and sometimes topped with mole (*enchiladas rojas* or *de mole*), or with tomato sauce and sour cream (*enchiladas suizas*—Swiss enchiladas), or covered in a green sauce *(enchiladas verdes),* or topped with onions, sour cream, and guacamole *(enchiladas potosinas).*

**Escabeche**    A lightly pickled sauce used in Yucatecan chicken stew.

**Frijoles refritos**    Pinto beans mashed and cooked with lard.

**Garnachas**    A thickish small circle of fried *masa* with pinched sides, topped with pork or chicken, onions, and avocado, or sometimes chopped potatoes and tomatoes, typical as a *botana* in Veracruz and the Yucatán.

**Gorditas**    Thick, fried corn tortillas, slit and stuffed with choice of cheese, beans, beef, chicken, with or without lettuce, tomato, and onion garnish.

**Horchata**    Refreshing drink made of ground rice or melon seeds, ground almonds, cinnamon, and lightly sweetened.

**Huevos mexicanos**    Scrambled eggs with chopped onions, hot green peppers, and tomatoes.

**Huitlacoche**    Sometimes spelled "cuitlacoche." A mushroom-flavored black fungus that appears on corn in the rainy season; considered a delicacy.

**Manchamantel**    Translated, means "tablecloth stainer." A stew of chicken or pork with chiles, tomatoes, pineapple, bananas, and jicama.

**Masa**    Ground corn soaked in lime; the basis for tamales, corn tortillas, and soups.

**Mixiote**    Rabbit, lamb, or chicken cooked in a mild chile sauce (usually chile *ancho* or *pasilla*), and then wrapped like a tamal and steamed. It is generally served with tortillas for tacos, with traditional garnishes of pickled onions, hot sauce, chopped cilantro, and lime wedges.

**Pan de muerto**    Sweet bread made around the Days of the Dead (Nov 1–2), in the form of mummies or dolls, or round with bone designs.

**Pan dulce**   Lightly sweetened bread in many configurations, usually served at breakfast or bought in any bakery.

**Papadzules**   Tortillas stuffed with hard-boiled eggs and seeds (pumpkin or sunflower) in a tomato sauce.

**Pibil**   Pit-baked pork or chicken in a sauce of tomato, onion, mild red pepper, cilantro, and vinegar.

**Pipián**   A sauce made with ground pumpkin seeds, nuts, and mild peppers.

**Poc chuc**   Slices of pork with onion marinated in a tangy sour orange sauce and charcoal-broiled; a Yucatecan specialty.

**Pozole**   A soup made with hominy in either chicken or pork broth.

**Pulque**   A drink made of fermented juice of the maguey plant; best in the state of Hidalgo and around Mexico City.

**Quesadilla**   Corn or flour tortillas stuffed with melted white cheese and lightly fried.

**Queso relleno**   "Stuffed cheese," a mild yellow cheese stuffed with minced meat and spices; a Yucatecan specialty.

**Rompope**   Delicious Mexican eggnog, invented in Puebla, made with eggs, vanilla, sugar, and rum.

**Salsa verde**   An uncooked sauce using the green tomatillo and puréed with spicy or mild hot peppers, onions, garlic, and cilantro; on tables countrywide.

**Sopa de flor de calabaza**   A soup made of chopped squash or pumpkin blossoms.

**Sopa de lima**   A tangy soup made with chicken broth and accented with fresh lime; popular in the Yucatán.

**Sopa de tortilla**   A traditional chicken broth-based soup, seasoned with chiles, tomatoes, onion, and garlic, served with crispy fried strips of corn tortillas.

**Sopa tlalpeña** (or *caldo tlalpeño*)   A hearty soup made with chunks of chicken, chopped carrots, zucchini, corn, onions, garlic, and cilantro.

**Sopa tlaxcalteca**   A hearty tomato-based soup filled with cooked *nopal* cactus, cheese, cream, and avocado, with crispy tortilla strips floating on top.

**Sope**   An *antojito* similar to a *garnacha,* except spread with refried beans and topped with crumbled cheese and onions.

**Tacos al pastor**   Thin slices of flavored pork roasted on a revolving cylinder dripping with onion slices and juice of fresh pineapple slices. Served in small corn tortillas, topped with chopped onion and cilantro.

**Tamal**   Incorrectly called a tamale (*tamal* singular, *tamales* plural). A meat or sweet filling rolled with fresh *masa,* wrapped in a corn husk or banana leaf, and steamed.

**Tikin xic**   Also seen on menus as "tik-n-xic" and "tikik chick." Charbroiled fish brushed with *achiote* sauce.

**Torta**   A sandwich, usually on *bolillo* bread, typically with sliced avocado, onions, tomatoes, with a choice of meat and often cheese.

**Xtabentun**   Pronounced "shtah-behn-*toon.*" A Yucatecan liquor made of fermented honey and flavored with anise. It comes *seco* (dry) or *crema* (sweet).

**Zacahuil**   Pork leg tamal, packed in thick *masa,* wrapped in banana leaves, and pit-baked, sometimes pot-made with tomato and *masa;* a specialty of mid- to upper Veracruz.

# Index

See also Accommodations and Restaurant indexes, below.

## ACCOMMODATIONS

## RESTAURANTS

# FROMMER'S® COMPLETE TRAVEL GUIDES

# FROMMER'S® DAY BY DAY GUIDES

# PAULINE FROMMER'S GUIDES! SEE MORE. SPEND LESS.

# FROMMER'S® PORTABLE GUIDES

## FROMMER'S® CRUISE GUIDES

Alaska Cruises & Ports of Call | Cruises & Ports of Call | European Cruises & Ports of Call

## FROMMER'S® NATIONAL PARK GUIDES

Algonquin Provincial Park | National Parks of the American West | Yosemite and Sequoia & Kings
Banff & Jasper | Rocky Mountain | Canyon
Grand Canyon | Yellowstone & Grand Teton | Zion & Bryce Canyon

## FROMMER'S® MEMORABLE WALKS

London | Paris | San Francisco
New York | Rome

## FROMMER'S® WITH KIDS GUIDES

Chicago | National Parks | Toronto
Hawaii | New York City | Walt Disney World® & Orlando
Las Vegas | San Francisco | Washington, D.C.
London

## SUZY GERSHMAN'S BORN TO SHOP GUIDES

France | London | Paris
Hong Kong, Shanghai & Beijing | New York | San Francisco
Italy

## FROMMER'S® IRREVERENT GUIDES

Amsterdam | London | Rome
Boston | Los Angeles | San Francisco
Chicago | Manhattan | Walt Disney World®
Las Vegas | Paris | Washington, D.C.

## FROMMER'S® BEST-LOVED DRIVING TOURS

Austria | Germany | Northern Italy
Britain | Ireland | Scotland
California | Italy | Spain
France | New England | Tuscany & Umbria

## THE UNOFFICIAL GUIDES®

Adventure Travel in Alaska | Hawaii | Paris
Beyond Disney | Ireland | San Francisco
California with Kids | Las Vegas | South Florida including Miami &
Central Italy | London | the Keys
Chicago | Maui | Walt Disney World®
Cruises | Mexico's Best Beach Resorts | Walt Disney World® for
Disneyland® | Mini Mickey | Grown-ups
England | New Orleans | Walt Disney World® with Kids
Florida | New York City | Washington, D.C.
Florida with Kids

## SPECIAL-INTEREST TITLES

Athens Past & Present | Frommer's Exploring America by RV
Best Places to Raise Your Family | Frommer's NYC Free & Dirt Cheap
Cities Ranked & Rated | Frommer's Road Atlas Europe
500 Places to Take Your Kids Before They Grow Up | Frommer's Road Atlas Ireland
Frommer's Best Day Trips from London | Great Escapes From NYC Without Wheels
Frommer's Best RV & Tent Campgrounds | Retirement Places Rated
in the U.S.A.

## FROMMER'S® PHRASEFINDER DICTIONARY GUIDES

French | Italian | Spanish

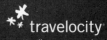